The
Palestinian
People

The Palestinian People

A HISTORY

Baruch Kimmerling

Joel S. Migdal

HARVARD UNIVERSITY PRESS

Cambridge, Massachusetts
London, England
2003

An earlier version of this book was published in 1994 as
Palestinians: The Making of a People

Cataloging-in-Publication data available from the Library of Congress
ISBN 0-674-01131-7 (cloth)
ISBN 0-674-01129-5 (paper)

*To the Palestinians and Israelis
working and hoping for a
mutually acceptable, negotiated settlement
to their century-long conflict*

CONTENTS

Part One

FROM REVOLT TO REVOLT:
THE ENCOUNTER WITH
THE EUROPEAN WORLD AND ZIONISM

Contents

MAPS

PREFACE

In 1993, our book *Palestinians: The Making of a People* came out at a critical juncture in the history of the Palestinians, the onset of the Oslo peace process. It was the first full account of Palestinian society and politics from their origins to the present and, to our delight, garnered considerable interest in both the popular press and academic journals, not least in the Middle East itself. In the ten years since the book's publication, the Palestinians (and their partners in peace—and war—the Israelis) have experienced extraordinary highs and lows. The signing of the Oslo Accord in September 1993 was accompanied by exultant hopes. Seven years later, the failure to hammer out a final peace agreement resulted in the outbreak of the bloody al-Aqsa Intifada, leading to the deepest despair. At the moment of this book's publication, in the third year of fighting after the failure of Oslo, Palestinians and Israelis are once again at a fateful juncture. The choices before them are a fight to the end for the control of all of historic Palestine or a return to negotiations that will divide the land into two mutually accepted states.

The Oslo peace process and the new Intifada have been defining events for the Palestinians. Out of the peace negotiations came the Palestine Authority, the first-ever serious self-rule of Palestinians in Palestine, as well as new social dynamics that reshaped the Palestinian people. From the turmoil of the Intifada and Israel's ferocious response have come mass poverty and near-destruction of Palestinians' fragile political and social institutions. At the end of 2002, for example, three of every five Palestinians in the West Bank and Gaza fall below the poverty line and two of three are dependent on international humanitarian organizations for their survival. Our initial thoughts were to bring the story up to date by incorporating these changes into a second edition of the 1993 book. But the events and outcomes of the last decade were so momentous and decisive that we decided to combine the basic story from the 1993 edition together with an analysis of the last decade into a newly titled volume, *The Palestinian People: A History*. This new book integrates the pre-1993 history with two new analyses. The first looks at what went right and what went wrong in the Oslo process and where Palestinians and Israelis find themselves now. The second addresses anew the complex position of the Palestinian Arab citizens of Israel, whose relationship both to Israel and to other Palestinians has been shot through with ambiguity.

Our approach in the 1993 book and in the current volume has been to reject the standard explanations for the remarkable emergence of the Palestinian people as a cohesive actor on the world scene in the 1970s and 1980s. Palestinian historiography asserted that Palestinians have always been a singular people whose solidarity and cohesion date back to the ancient Fertile Crescent; a mix of contemporary factors, including the 1967 Middle East war and the emergence of the Palestine Liberation Organization, accounted for the new high profile of Palestinians in the 1970s and 1980s. Conversely, Israeli historians claimed that no self-identified Palestinian people ever existed, at least not until the Arabs of the area were challenged by Zionism and Jewish settlement; Zionism's, and later Israel's, successes in the first two decades of existence brought about the newfound Palestinian solidarity.

We put forth a very different explanation, relying heavily on newly published but fragmented social scientific and historical material on the Palestinians. The construction of a self-identified Palestinian people in the second half of the twentieth century, we argue, was the result of two centuries in which Arabs at the grassroots level encountered, first, the powerful forces stemming from European markets and governmental administration, and later, Jewish settlement. New market forces, together with political forces pacifying Palestine and new, more efficient bureaucracies unifying it, uprooted Arab society. These forces led to new Arab settlement in the fertile plains and a society marked by the dynamic tension of coast and hill country. That tension was already evident in the mid-nineteenth century and marked the Palestinians through the entire twentieth century. The encounter with Jews and Zionism in the coastal areas, ironically, both distanced Arabs in the coastal towns from their brothers in the hill country economically and socially and yet moved them toward solidarity with those in the mountain villages.

We hoped that the innovation of *The Palestinian People*, as with the earlier book, would be its scope, its success in bringing together scattered pieces of knowledge in already published works, and, not least of all, our particular perspective and interpretation. Neither of us saw this project as one whose most important contribution would be breaking ground in generating entirely new data on Palestinian society. We have relied largely on published material in order to write an integrative, synthetic account of the conditions that spawned a distinct Palestinian society and an analysis of what possibilities lie before that society in one of the darkest moments in its history. Only in a few instances did we fill in gaps by collecting new statistics or using unpublished documents.

The particular perspective we bring to the pages that follow includes four elements. First, we focus on change at the grassroots—the movement and distribution of people, their changing life circumstances, their differing occupational structure, and the like—diminishing the weight of Palestinian central leadership while elevating the primacy of social processes at the level of everyday life. Second, we examine the dynamic interplay between various segments of the society—town and country, hill and plain, secular and religious, Christian and Muslim, diaspora and Palestine-based, and others—rather than finding some unified, essential Palestinian character. Third, though we do not discount the powerful effect of Zionism in shaping Palestinian society, we place Zionism as only one among several key world historical forces, including capitalism's insidious penetration of the Ottoman Empire, which began long before the appearance of Zionism. Finally, we recast the history of Palestine and Israel so that Jews, who had occupied center stage in most previous accounts, now have been relegated to the wings, displaced by Palestinians. All of a sudden, the former bit players and character actors have become the leading men and leading ladies.

Our perspective on the emergence of the Palestinians has continued to hold in the post-Oslo period. The analysis of the years since 1993 in Chapters 10 and 11 and parts of Chapter 6 is built on the dynamics of social change at the grassroots level and the interplay between that change and Palestinian central leadership, especially in the newly formed Palestine Authority. In particular, we argue, the emergence of two contending centers of power leading up to the 1987 Intifada—generated by young, educated secular and religious leaders with deep roots in West Bank and Gazan society—interacted with the new Palestinian government in unexpected ways, shaping the nature of social and political change. Ongoing tensions between religious and secular forces and between indigenous leaders and PLO forces coming from Tunis also defined the direction of Palestinian society and politics. The rapid changes in the West Bank and Gaza played off dynamics in other parts of Palestinian society—the more than one million Palestinian citizens of Israel and the diaspora communities. And all this occurred within the context of powerful outside forces, not least of which stemmed from the state of Israel.

Our 1993 book appeared in the tumultuous diplomatic period leading up to that indelible moment on the White House lawn on September 13, 1993, when Israeli Prime Minister Yitzhak Rabin took the outstretched hand of PLO Chairman Yasser Arafat, as President Bill Clinton nudged them together. No matter what one thought of the Oslo agreement, it certainly demanded from Jews and Palestinians alike challenging new ways of thinking about old issues and stubborn problems. The timing of the book was ideal for presenting new ideas about Palestinians and Palestinian-Israeli interaction. For Palestinians, the book affirmed their place on center stage even as it took issue with standard Palestinian accounts. The reactions to the book in reviews by Palestinian academics in the United States and elsewhere, as well as to the later Arabic editions (the book was serialized in the Israeli Arabic press and published as a separate volume in the West Bank), were quite positive. In Israel, however, the 1993 book was one of several catalysts sparking a vitriolic debate. Even the headlines and titles of the reviews and articles reflected the intensity of negative reactions to our book: "Scholarship as Fraud" or "On the Sin That We Sinned in Creating a State" (echoing Jewish penitential prayers on Yom Kippur).

At issue in Israel was the timing of the birth of the Palestinian nation, and this seemingly recondite question, critics felt, had enormous implications. For a number of our book's critics in Israel, contact between the country's Arab residents and Zionism was the determining factor in constructing a unified people. There was no self-identified Palestinian nation, the thinking went, before Zionism; its creation was a product of the local Arab residents' encounter with immigrant Jews and their dynamic political movement. We asserted then, and reaffirm in this book, that the origins of a self-conscious, relatively unified Palestinian people pre-date Zionism.

The earlier reviews took this debate very seriously indeed. Critics charged that we (along with a new generation of mostly Israeli social scientists labeled the New Historians and the Critical Sociologists) were undermining the Zionist story while supporting the construction of an alternative, Palestinian story. In fact, they went so far as to say that the new wave of scholarship, including our book, was wittingly or unwittingly challenging the validity of the historic settling of Jews in the country and the very justification for the establishment of the State of Israel. One essayist wrote of Israel's "suicide drive." Several reviews pointed specifically to our purported argument that the Palestinian people as a social entity were created as far back as 1834, thus validating Palestinians' claims that the emergence of the Palestinian people was in no way a recent event and certainly involved far more than a simple reaction to Zionism, which dates back only to around 1880. Indeed, this thinking went, if the Palestinians were already a nation, then Zionism's eventual success in securing the Jews' national rights was tainted by the fact that it came at the expense of another nation's rights.

These reviews seriously misrepresented what we had written. Our point was that the events of 1834—a territory-wide revolt against the recent Egyptian occupation—had created a structural pillar for drawing together the population of a territory, Palestine, in which the residents would much later develop into a self-identified people. Our argument posited the multivectored and long-term formation of a self-identified Palestinian people. According to the method we employed, the construction of a people or a nation is an ongoing process that lacks defining, "founding" moments in history. This method runs counter to much of established social science methodology, which tends to deal with concepts, such as nation, as hard variables that have a defining moment of incarnation.

But for all the personal attacks and the misrepresentation of the facts, the debate did indicate that the old, unquestioned assumptions about Israeli society—how it came into being, how it was shaped, and how it was now organized—were currently on the table for scrutiny and debate among Israelis themselves. Not least among these assumptions were those concerning who the Palestinians were, how they had been affected by Israel, and how they, in turn, influenced Israeli society. By 1998 and 1999, when the Hebrew edition of *Palestinians: The Making of a People* was published, however, the Oslo peace process had already had a deep impact on how Israelis thought about Palestinians. Many of the points found in our earlier book came to be incorporated into standard Israeli academic and popular assumptions about Israel's history and about the Palestinians. The new reviews were bland and mostly positive, contrasting sharply with the reviews that had appeared after the publication of the 1993 English edition.

Challenges to the notion that the Palestinians constitute a nation are rarely heard these days. Legitimate political questions continue to produce loud arguments in Israel, especially amid the carnage of 2002: Will the Palestinians be satisfied with only a portion of Palestine? Can Israel live in peace with a Palestinian state? Can the Palestinians be a viable partner in peace? Can negotiations settle the issue, or will it be resolved only through a drawn-out war? But political divisions over these questions, while sparking deep passions and sharp rhetoric in Israel, have increasingly taken place within a shared framework accepting the peoplehood of the Palestinians. In August 2002, a whopping 78 percent of Israeli Jews polled responded that they believe Palestinians have a legitimate right to a state.

For Palestinians, too, the Oslo peace process opened the door for a reconsideration of their own history and particularly their relationship to Israel. In some ways, the reconsideration of the past and of the adversary did not go as far as it did in Israel. There were no screaming debates in academic journals, newspapers, or television talk shows about how the old myths had to be reexamined. But in a quiet way, new lines of thinking did begin to emerge after Oslo. After Ehud Barak's election in Israel in 1999—a high point for hope that the Oslo process might succeed—75 percent of Palestinians on the West Bank and in the Gaza Strip expressed support for negotiations. Those responding to the survey understood that expressing support meant accepting not only Israel's legitimate existence but its permanent sovereignty over more than four-fifths of historic Palestine. Other big questions still remained almost totally immune to reconsideration among Palestinians, such as the issue of the right of return of the 1948 and 1967 Palestinian refugees, where only the faintest hints of academic rethinking could be discerned. But even the publication of the Arabic edition of our earlier book—one by Jewish Israeli and American social scientists—in Ramallah during the awful violence of the Intifada spoke volumes about Palestinians' willingness to listen to new voices and ideas that took issue with some of their old myths.

The Oslo process, for all its faults, induced Palestinians and Israelis to reconsider their shared history. That was a painful and difficult undertaking on both sides. For Palestinians, it opened the most fundamental questions, including whether, first and foremost, the basis of their peoplehood rested on a religious or secular-national basis. Beyond that, the prospect of a state and acceptance of Israel's legitimate rights raised the issue of the future relationship among dispersed Palestinian communities. And, not least, the peace process edged Palestinians into debating the ends and means of their seemingly endless struggle—a debate that involved Palestinians living in North America and Europe, as well as those in Palestine and Israel. For Israelis, Oslo meant coming to terms for the first time with elements of Israel's past that lacked the heroic glitter presented in school textbooks, starting with Israel's role in expelling Arabs in 1948.

Part of imagining a new future, it seems to us, is the ability to deal maturely and honestly with the past. For Palestinians, rethinking the meaning of the right of return would not upend the meaning of their decades of dispossession, nor would Israelis' reconsidering their historical relations with the Palestinians delegitimize the State of Israel or its founding. The peace talks did induce each side to consider how the triumphs and tragedies of the past could be shaped into a better future. For all its failures and disappointments, Oslo did begin this process of shaping the future by inducing a reconsideration of the past.

To be sure, the closing off of opportunities for a negotiated settlement through the Palestinian initiation of a new Intifada in September 2000, the harsh Israeli response, and the new political alignments that have emerged in the shadow of the ongoing violence all derailed efforts to move from a reconsidered past to a reconsidered future for Israelis and Palestinians alike. Our presumptuous hope is that this book, written amid the worst Palestinian-Israeli violence since 1948, can be one medium for Palestinians and Israelis—and Americans, who have been so deeply implicated in relations between the two—to reconceive the past and future of this troubled region. On both sides now, loud voices have proclaimed that the Oslo Accords were rotten from the outset. They have used that judgment to dismiss the desire for conciliation on the other side and, thus, the possibility of a negotiated compromise. They are urging maximalist goals on each side, meaning ultimate control of all of historic Palestine.

It is important at this moment to show the folly of these goals and the flawed thinking that lies behind them. In Part Four, we argue that the failure of the peace process did not stem from the absence of a partner ready to make the necessary compromises or from an adversary whose leaders and people were dead-set against accepting the other side's legitimate rights. Oslo's failure came, rather, from Palestinian and Israeli leaders' serious underestimation of the popular support for a negotiated two-state settlement, which exacerbated the already unstable domestic political situation on each side. Unstable politics, in turn, moved leaders away from actions that could have propelled them forward to a final accord and toward tactics aimed at day-to-day political survival, even when those undermined the peace process. Together with some flaws in the actual agreement, notably the absence of any mediation mechanisms, these patterns of state-society relations and domestic politics undercut the progress that had been made in the early 1990s.

Our message in Part Four is quite strong: the Oslo process should not be considered simply a well-meaning but wrong-headed initiative. Much actually went right and has left a crucial legacy upon which the parties may one day be able to build. Part of what went right was the beginning of the rewriting of each side's national story to incorporate the other. Coming to terms with the past in this way is an important step in moving beyond the present tempest that still rages as we write, in which violence is the default mode of relations between the two peoples. By challenging the too-easy answers inherent in their own national myths, the Palestinian and Israeli peoples can provide a way to accept each other on the piece of turf that each has claimed for itself.

ACKNOWLEDGMENTS

Albert Hourani wrote in his grand book, *A History of the Arab Peoples,* "It will be clear to specialists that, in a book with so large a scope, much of what I say is based upon the research of others. I have tried to give the essential facts and to interpret them in the light of what others have written." Of course, this book does not have the scope of Professor Hourani's, but the two centuries we do cover are far more than any pair of scholars could explore exclusively through their own primary research. Our effort was only possible because of many original works on the Palestinians appearing in recent years.

Special thanks go to a number of colleagues who read all or parts of the manuscript. They include Resat Kasaba, Joshua Teitelbaum, Zachary Lockman, Ellis Goldberg, Aaron Klieman, Shibley Telhami, Jere Bacharach, Penina Glazer, and Myron Glazer. Students and faculty in Israel, the United States, and Russia, who participated in several seminar presentations on various chapters, gave many helpful comments. Special thanks are due to Nabil al-Salah, who assisted with Arabic language materials. Also lending important support were Jolanta Lawska, Merlyn Goeschl, Ann Glazer, Jane Meyerding,

Wanli Yuan, and Shira Hochstein. We would like to acknowledge, too, the Eshkol Research Center of the Hebrew University and its director Michael Shalev for spiritual and material support, as well as the Henry M. Jackson School of International Studies at the University of Washington. The Shein Center of Social Research at the Hebrew University, then directed by Moshe Lissak, also provided a portion of the resources that made the writing of this volume possible. Joel Migdal's research and writing were also supported by the Robert F. Philip Professorship in International Studies at the University of Washington. Finally, we owe a special debt of gratitude to our families, who suffered the hogging of the family computer and other indignities so that this book could be written.

A NOTE ON TRANSLITERATION

In the transliteration of Arabic terms and names, we have decided to leave out diacritical marks; ayin and hamza are not designated. In other cases, transliteration is in keeping with scholarly convention, except in a few cases where there is a commonly accepted English spelling (thus, Gamal Abdul Nasser instead of Jamal 'Abd al-Nasir; Hussein and Husseini instead of Husayn and Husayni; *sheikh* instead of *shaykh*; *fellaheen* instead of *fallahin*). Such a system, we believe, will make the Arabic equivalent quite clear to the specialist, without burdening the general reader with the sometimes cumbersome transliteration conventions of the academy.

INTRODUCTION

Toward the end of the eighteenth century, powerful economic and political forces at work in Europe began to affect everyday life in the Middle East, eventually impelling its peoples to redefine both their communities and their visions. Such change did not come without great struggle, continuing in one form or another until the present. Social boundaries—those factors defining insiders and outsiders and what binds the insiders together—have been as much a source of the struggle as the political boundaries of the new Middle Eastern states. In the case of the Palestinians, the process of redefinition has been obscured, and even transformed, by the ongoing conflict with the Jews.

The creation of a nation involves a melding of values and myths, of people's imaginations and their identities. It demands leadership, but also a social foundation empowering the leaders and establishing the limits of what they can achieve. In this book, we are less interested in protocols and diplomacy than in the dynamics and beliefs of peasants, urban workers, merchants, and landowners, and their relationships to the leaders. For particularly with *al-Nakba*—

the catastrophic shattering of the Palestinian community in the 1948 war with the Jews—we find the content of what it means to be Palestinian shaped as much by this foundation as by the old, established leadership.[1] The Palestinian people were not mere victims, as so many accounts have presented them (although, to be sure, fate has not treated them kindly), but were active participants in the creation of their people's collective character.

We hope to write against the grain of the sort of history that has been written as part and parcel of mythmaking national projects. In different ways, Palestinians have suffered a great deal from such mythmaking. The historiographical debate has been an integral part of the conflict between Palestinians and Jews. Note the account of one national historian:

> The Palestinians' claim is predicated on the right of ownership evidenced by uninterrupted possession and occupation since the dawn of recorded history. They lived in the country when the Hebrews (of whom the Jews claim descent) came and lived there for a comparatively short period. They continued to live there during the Hebrew (and Jewish) occupation. They remained there after the last Hebrew or Jew left the country nearly two thousand years ago. . . . The people today called Palestinians or Palestinian Arabs, who have been fighting the Zionists and State of Israel which Zionism created in 1948, are largely the descendants of the Canaanites, the Edomites, and the Philistines who lived in Palestine when it was invaded by the Hebrews in ancient times. But the Hebrews finally left or were driven out two thousand years ago.[2]

The search for connection with the past has sometimes transformed history into a handmaiden of those seeking to give the nation a proper pedigree—an effort that involves denigrating the adversary's experience of the past. This exercise has been as evident on the part of Jews as Palestinian advocates. Historians sympathetic with Israel have frequently shared Golda Meir's perspective: "There was no such thing as Palestinians. When was there an independent Palestinian people with a Palestinian state? . . . It was not as though there was a Palestinian people in Palestine considering itself as a

Palestinian people and we came and threw them out and took their country from them. They did not exist."[3]

One of the best-known expressions of such a viewpoint has been Joan Peters' *From Time Immemorial: The Origins of the Arab-Jewish Conflict over Palestine,* heavily documented and, apparently, a serious work of scholarship. Its basic argument is that most of Palestine's Arab population was not indigenous. Rather it consisted of migrants, attracted by opportunities offered by Jewish settlement, who came from disparate streams and certainly did not (do not) constitute a people. "The 'Palestinians" claim," Peters explains, "is avowedly based upon 'history' and their goal is the dissolution of another state. Their alleged right of 'self-determination' is based upon the erroneous alleged '90% majority of Arabs' in 1917 on the Jewish-settled areas that became Israel in 1948."[4] But as numerous sober historians have shown, Peters' tendentiousness is not, in fact, supported by the historical record, being based on materials out of context, and on distorted evidence.[5]

Almost nothing was shared willingly between Jews and Arabs in the historiographical battle, which began in the reincarnated Palestine of the interwar years. Even the appropriation of the term "Palestinian" became a source for controversy, as seen in Golda Meir's and Joan Peters' protests. The term eventually became attached to the Arabs living in Palestine prior to British withdrawal, as well as to their descendants, while the Jews discarded it in 1948 in favor of "Israelis." For the Arabs, the term indicated not only a land of origin, but also an increasing sense of a shared past and future. In the following pages, for convenience we will refer to Palestinian Arabs as Palestinians, and to the country as Palestine, even when applied to periods in which such usage is anachronistic—when the Arabs' sense of participating in a common history had not yet evolved, and when the territory was administratively fragmented. But our use of the term for the nineteenth or early twentieth centuries should not obscure our main point, the one that has so often been missed on both sides of the historiographical divide: a Palestinian national identity, like those of other modern nations, has been created—invented and elaborated—over the course of the last two centuries.

In some ways, the Jewish national movement has shaped the Palestinian people almost as much as it did the Jews themselves. Had it not been for the pressures exerted on the Arabs of Palestine by the Zionist movement, the very concept of a Palestinian people would not have developed; and Palestinians quite accurately understand their society's essential, existential status as the direct result of Jewish political rejuvenation and settlement. They see their own lives as reflections of a catastrophe, with Zionism—as Palestinian writer Fawaz Turki has put it—"having its day and the Palestinian [movement] its eclipse," individual Palestinians ending up in "the world of the exile. The world of the occupied. The world of the refugee. The world of the ghetto. The world of the stateless."[6] Nevertheless, focusing our attention exclusively on the Palestinian Arab conflict with the Jews would obscure other important factors, particularly the extension of the world market into Palestine and the imposition of politically and administratively capable states, both beginning in the nineteenth century. Until quite recently, Palestinian writers paid scant attention to the contours of their own society, preoccupied as they were with the other, the Jews—the key to unlocking the secrets of those forces that turned their world upside down. For their part, the Zionists have been absorbed in a nationalist project rendering the Palestinians almost incidental. In the process, they have failed to grasp the extent to which their own society has been shaped by its ongoing encounter with the Palestinians. Perhaps doing so would involve too painful an encounter with Zionism's political counterpart—what we might call "Palestinism": the belief that the Arab population originating in the area of the Palestine mandate is distinct from other Arab groups, with a right to its own nation-state in that territory.[7]

As young academics, the authors of this book joined a handful of Jewish social scientists beginning, in the wake of the 1967 war, to view the Palestinians, not as anthropological curiosities, but as a social group deeply affecting the future of the Jews. In addition to its 2.4 million Jews, Israel then governed almost 1.5 million Arabs, including around 400,000 citizens of Israel, 665,000 in the West Bank and East Jerusalem, and 356,000 in the Gaza Strip. We both came to know many Palestinians, mostly in West Bank villages and on the campus of the Hebrew University. Kimmerling wrote about Jewish and Palestinian interdependence in the half century since World War I, while Migdal focused on the long-standing impact of different rulers, including the Israelis, on Palestinian society. Hovering behind all this work has been an awareness that mutual Jewish-Palestinian denial will disappear slowly, if ever. Still, recent events have made one thing quite clear: The Palestinian dream of self-determination will likely be realized only with the assent of a secure, cohesive Israel, and the Israeli dream of acceptance throughout the Middle East will likely need Palestinian approval.

As much as any people in the world, the Palestinians have suffered from media stereotypes: "terrorists" and "freedom fighters," "murderers" and "victims." At times, the Palestinian leadership has reinforced such images by insisting on a national consensus denying the rifts in their society. In the following pages, we intend to satisfy neither the demonic nor the idyllic vision of the Palestinian Arab. Rather, we will describe the contours of a people at the center of one of the most volatile conflicts of our time.

The
Palestinian
People

Part One

FROM REVOLT TO REVOLT:

THE ENCOUNTER WITH

THE EUROPEAN WORLD AND ZIONISM

1

THE REVOLT OF 1834

AND THE MAKING OF MODERN PALESTINE

PALESTINE IS THE CROSSROADS of three continents. It is a land of shifting boundaries: a political entity that vanished, only to re-emerge like a phoenix. The home of the great monotheistic religions—Judaism, Christianity, and Islam—it has been the object of countless bitter wars and struggles through nearly four millennia. It is a land of pitifully few resources and starkly beautiful terrain.

While Palestine's borders have always been vague and changing, its center has never been uncertain. Nestled in the hills of Jabal al-Quds, or the Judean Mountains, Jerusalem (in Arabic, *al-Quds*) is synonymous for most people with the Holy Land. King David and his son Solomon established the city three thousand years ago as their capital. The site of the Jewish Temple, of Jesus' last preaching and crucifixion, and of the Prophet Muhammad's ascension to heaven, it still holds the remnant of the Temple's outer courtyard wall—the Western or Wailing Wall—which is also the outer fence of the Haram al-Sharif, Islam's third holiest site. In the nineteenth and early twentieth century, it became the center for the new leadership of Arab notables.

Palestine's four natural regions surround Jerusalem. The hilly, most barren region in the eastern part of the country was the center of ancient Jewish civilization, known as Samaria and Judea and today commonly referred to as the West Bank. Its largest center remains Nablus, a town dating back to biblical times that was the heart of early nineteenth century Arabic village society. The southern Negev, starting in the town of Beersheba, long served as the home and transit route for nomadic Bedouins. For the most part, this harsh desert has remained sparsely populated through the centuries, those who did try to settle it facing the enmity of the nomads. The third region, the narrow strip forming the coastal plain, extends from Gaza in the south through Haifa's bay in the north and past the mountainous Carmel up to Lebanon. The ancient maritime civilizations—some stemming from the Phoenicians—were settled here, as well as the great cities of Palestine—Gaza, Jaffa, Haifa, Acre, and, in this century, Tel-Aviv. (By the early nineteenth century, the coastal plain was a neglected remnant of its former glory.) Finally, fertile valleys and breathtaking hills dominate the country's northern section, including the region from Acre to the hills of al-Jalil (the biblical Galilee), the Valley of Marj Ibn Amir (the Jezreel Valley), and the Baysan.

For a country of 10,500 square miles (about the size of Maryland), Palestine encompasses a remarkably varied physical environment. About half the land has been entirely uncultivable, while large portions of the other half have been rocky, sandy, or swampy, with a low and unstable amount of rainfall. But, for all the scarcity of rich soil and the inadequate irrigation, Palestine has always been a country of farmers. Archaeologists have discovered the remains of agricultural sites near Jericho, northwest of the Dead Sea, stemming from the earliest phase of human culture—approximately 8000 B.C.E.

Traditionally, these farmers have coexisted (albeit often uneasily) with the country's nomadic Bedouins. Having long laid claim, through their ties to real or fictive common ancestors, to being parts of the early Islamic nomadic communities, the Bedouins have assumed the title of the "original Arabs." According to local lore, these ancestors swept out of Arabia under the leadership of the second caliph, Umar ibn Abd al-Khattab, in the first half of the seventh century. The caliph's warriors gave an Islamic and Arab stamp lasting until now to all of Syria (including Palestine), the Fertile Crescent, and much of North Africa.

Over the centuries, Bedouin men maintained their identity as warriors while looking after grasslands, water resources, and livestock—as well as occasionally engaging in smuggling and robbery. Women reared the children, cooked and cleaned, and lent a hand in the fields or with the livestock. The strongest Bedouin loyalties were to their families and larger kinship groups, but they were quick to enter into alliances with almost any force offering material or political benefit. Their nemesis was the state, or any other central authority wishing to settle or disarm them and force acceptance of its political boundaries. Sometimes Bedouins have triumphed over such authority. At other times, the state has had its way, and at yet others, the Bedouins have assumed the leading role in the state. This took place, for example, in twentieth century Transjordan, where the Hashemite dynasty, claiming direct descent from the Prophet Muhammad, absorbed local Bedouin groups into the top echelons of the state and its army, the Arab Legion.

Starting with the dawn of Romanticism, the image of the Bedouin warriors, wild and noble, dominated both Orientalist literature and the general Western concept of Palestine.[1] But as enticing as the image was, it was only peripheral to the history of Palestinian society, which begins with the settled agriculturalists—the *fellaheen* or peasants—and their ties to the powerful landowning families that dominated rural economic and social life. It was peasants and landowners who put their indelible stamp on day-to-day life in Palestine and who were at the center of the bloody battles punctuating the last several centuries. For this reason, while the Bedouins will have their role in the story that follows, our primary focus will be on the peasants: on how the economic and administrative forces of the last two centuries have remolded them into a multilayered society, the basis for the eventual emerging of a coherent and self-conscious people.

Of all the violent struggles in Palestine, three revolts have defined the modern history of the country's Arabs. The first revolt in 1834, was a bloody attempt to stave off the momentous changes instituted by Egyptian empire builders, who ruled the country through most of the 1830s. Its suppression confirmed that the parameters of peasant society would be redrawn. While a good many Palestinians bitterly resisted the changes, the ensuing transformation laid the basis for a much more complex society. The second revolt, from 1936 to 1939, came in the context of Britain's imperial rule and was the first real effort to demonstrate decisively this fledgling nation's political will. The third is the Intifada, which began in 1987; its goal, like the rebellion in 1936, has been to lay the foundation for political independence, but now it must do so in the difficult circumstances of the powerful rule of Israel, its rival for the soil of the country.

The First Palestinian Revolt:
Origins, Progression, and Outcome

The seeds of Palestinian rebellion were planted with the country's conquest in the 1830s. The Ottomans, exhausted from trying to restore more direct rule in a number of provinces and from the draining Greek war, lost control of Syria and Palestine between 1831 and 1840. A vassal of the Ottomans, Egypt's upstart governor Muhammad Ali, overran portions of the Empire right into Anatolia and occupied them under the leadership of his son, Ibrahim Pasha.[2] In time, much of the Palestinian population, especially its Muslim majority, turned against the occupation. The total population was probably under a quarter of a million, several tens of thousands of Jews and, of the rest, about 20 percent Christian. Nothing alienated the local Arabs as much as Ibrahim's demands for conscripts. Peasants were well aware that conscription was little more than a death sentence: The term of service was frequently for life and, given the sanitary conditions and military technology of the day, there was little chance parents would ever see their sons again.

Despite his unpopularity, Ibrahim Pasha did manage to enforce security in a country that had been battered by extreme lawlessness.

The new security enabled farmers to venture in previously unculti-vated areas, merchants to forge ties to the European market from safer coastal enclaves, and pilgrims to visit the country in unprece-dented numbers. With the Egyptian administration initiating new farming techniques and helping to prepare previously uncultivated lands for farming,[3] local trade expanded, and foreign trade, while still quite small, showed some new signs of life. For the Egyptians, Syria and Palestine were to be Levantine breadbaskets, as well as a source of fresh conscripts and additional revenues for the inevitable next battle against the Ottomans. Corresponding to Muhammad Ali's push for industrial growth and cotton production in Egypt it-self, Ibrahim Pasha's attention to agriculture and trade in Syria and Palestine involved an effort to establish the basis for specialized crop production, meant eventually to supply Egypt with the raw materials it needed. To speed the process, Ibrahim allowed Chris-tians to trade in grain and livestock—activities that the Ottomans had previously banned.[4]

The tough rule and the new reforms led to the 1834 revolt's out-break in the heart of the country, uniting dispersed Bedouins, rural sheikhs, urban notables, mountain fellaheen, and Jerusalem reli-gious figures[5] against a common enemy. It was these groups who would later constitute the Palestinian people.

The revolt was centered in the key town of Nablus and, to a lesser degree, in Jerusalem, with uprisings in other towns, too; but the backbone of the fighting forces was the peasantry.[6] Nablus lay in the heart of the hilly agricultural area that, in the 1830s, was the most populated and productive part of the country. Starting as an over-sized village, it had developed into a town of 10,000 inhabitants, with a surrounding area that included some 200 villages with roughly another 100,000 people. From their bases in Nablus, nota-ble family groupings associated with the longstanding Arab cleav-age of Qays and Yaman dominated the entire region.[7] The revolt would eventually forge an alliance between these coalitions.

Jerusalem, a town of 15,000–20,000 people, was the religious seat of the region and enjoyed an unusual amount of autonomy in the Ottoman Empire. The Ottomans appointed both its religious leader, the Mufti, and its chief judge, the Grand Qadi; they exercised strong influence throughout the country, imposing levies and taxes on the city's non-Muslim inhabitants and on Jewish and Christian pilgrims, and—most importantly—controlling appointments to religious offices, schools, and the Waqf (religious endowments). Inside the city, two powerful families ruled—the Husseinis and Khalidis. In the 120 surrounding villages, the Abu Ghush clan dominated (with opposition, to be sure), partly through its control of access to Jerusalem along the strategic road from Jaffa.

The revolt's first signs came on May 19, 1834, when a number of important families and sheikhs from Nablus, Jerusalem, and Hebron informed Ibrahim's civil and military governors they could not supply the quotas of conscripts for military service demanded of them: The peasants—so went the claim—had simply fled from their villages into the difficult, mountainous terrain to the east. Since Ibrahim was already facing similar resistance in northern Syria, in the area east of the Jordan River, and in the Arabian peninsula's Hejaz (where his forces had suffered some heavy casualties), the notables' declaration would not have been totally unexpected. His response was to postpone conscription in these other areas, but to maintain strict enforcement of the policy in Palestine.

His decision turned out costly. Riots first broke out in the Hebron region. When Egyptian troops arrived, fellaheen from the village of Sair, supported by Bedouins, killed about twenty-five soldiers, and Hebronites overcame the town's small garrison, arresting Ibrahim's governor. Some local peasants began to move towards Jerusalem. In the nearby Nablus region, the Egyptians had gained the support of an important clan, the Abd al-Hadis, but that insurance policy turned out far from adequate. The Abd al-Hadis' main rivals, the Qasims, declared a general revolt against the Egyptians, refusing to supply conscripts or pay taxes. Gathering most of the country's notable families in their home village, the Qasims urged opposition to the Abd al-Hadis and Egyptian rule, at the same time mounting an unsuccessful attempt to capture Nablus.

While their storming of that city failed, their call to rid Jerusalem of the Egyptians had greater success. Hundreds of peasants from all over the hilly eastern portion of Palestine joined those marching from Hebron to lay siege to the walls of Jerusalem. When the Abu Ghush clan, with their control of the Jaffa-Jerusalem road, joined the rebel forces, the noose was drawn tight: With two thousand men carrying rifles and the support of most of the country's clans (as well as much of the Muslim population inside the besieged city), the rebellion had produced an astoundingly powerful and broad coalition of local groups.

By the end of May, Ibrahim's situation appeared desperate. The attempt by his regiment from Jaffa to relieve the Jerusalem forces ended in a disastrous ambush. The flush of rebel success broke the Abd al-Hadis' hold on Nablus which—with the Qasims now reigning—also joined the revolt, turning into the center of opposition to the Egyptians. On the last day of the month, Muslims in Jerusalem managed to open the gates, allowing the rebels to take over the city everywhere but the citadel, where the Egyptian forces took refuge. Ibrahim's foothold in Palestine had shrunk, essentially, to the four coastal towns of Gaza, Jaffa, Haifa, and Acre. In Jerusalem, the peasants set upon the local Jewish and Christian populations, looting houses and raping women. Even the local Muslim population, especially the notable families, came under the onslaught. As in the two twentieth century revolts, a deep populist strain seemed to underlie this rebellion.

Although in June Ibrahim mounted a number of counterattacks inflicting heavy artillery damage, the revolt continued to spread, his military suffering thousands of casualties at the hands of the numerically superior rebel forces. He did manage to retake Jerusalem that same month. But along with some smaller coastal towns, Haifa came under siege, and Tiberias and Safad fell in the north. In Tiberias, Muslims launched fierce attacks upon both the town's Jewish population and a number of Christian families.

Both the rebels' fury and the breadth of the revolt stemmed from Ibrahim's uncanny ability to institute change alienating almost all Muslims. Only the minorities and selected notable families had found their positions enhanced by Egyptian rule. Complementing the personal tragedy it inflicted, the dreaded conscription threatened families and whole villages with an inadequate labor supply. Notables had found the basis of their autonomy shattered. Ibrahim Pasha's centralization of tax collection had taken from the *ayan*, the notables, their most important lever of control, especially over the minority religions. The Egyptians had targeted the Bedouins, as well. Nomads no longer could impose road tolls or protection levies, and they found Ibrahim maneuvering to settle them permanently.

Ibrahim also speeded up an integration process that may have resulted, ironically, in it becoming that much easier to struggle against him. The process had already begun at the turn of the nineteenth century, when Ahmad Pasha al-Jazzar brought Palestine under single rule and administration for the first time in centuries (see chapter 2). That feat was repeated shortly before the Egyptian invasion by another Ottoman vassal, Abdallah Pasha. Based first in Sidon (now in Lebanon) and later in Acre, Abdallah established his rule in the subdistrict of Nablus and the administratively autonomous Jerusalem. While maintaining the local power of the notable families, he had brought the entire province of Sidon under his control by the eve of Muhammad Ali's conquest. These earlier efforts, as well as those fostered by local sheikhs, had resulted in some changes in peasant crop production, taking advantage of new European markets. But Ibrahim's own rule differed significantly from that of the earlier rulers in his refusal to respect the autonomy of the local notables. His radical measures of direct governance and taxation made many people, especially among the powerful ayan, feel that the social, religious, and economic fabric of the society was at risk. At the same time, those same measures, particularly ones stressing the primacy of the state over equal subjects, battered the society's previously rigid hierarchical barriers.

The Peasant Revolt in Syria, as contemporary sources and historians labeled the revolt of 1834, threatened not only the flow of conscripts and material resources to Egypt but Muhammad Ali's entire plan for its renewal. Palestine was turning into a graveyard for his dreams as well as for his soldiers. His response, not surprisingly, was rather clever. First, through deception and rumor, he convinced his foes that his reinforcements were a much bigger force than the

15,000 men and 40 cannons he actually had available (mostly in Jaffa). Next, he worked to break the coalition of notables, his most impressive achievement in this regard being to open the Jerusalem road by offering the Abu Ghush clan everything from guaranteed amnesty to positions in the Egyptian administration. Finally, he promised the harshest consequences for those who continued to defy him. Ibrahim Pasha carried out the last part of the plan. On July 4, 1834, he directed a military expedition at the heart of Qasim-led rebel forces in the Nablus region. The Egyptian soldiers reduced 16 villages to ash on their route, including those dominated by major rebel leaders. After a bloody battle, the Egyptians routed the fellaheen, publicly decapitating their leaders; they took Nablus on July 15. The final battle occurred in Hebron on August 4: The Egyptian victory there was complete and included leveling of the city, rape of the women, mass killing and conscription of the men, the furnishing of 120 adolescents to Egyptian officers to do with as they wanted.

Throughout the country, the rebels were cruelly handled. About 10,000 fellaheen were recruited and shipped to Egypt. Sections of entire towns, including the Muslim quarter of Bethlehem, were destroyed, and their inhabitants expelled or killed. And, in a measure that struck very hard, even given all the other atrocities those in Palestine faced, the Egyptians disarmed the population: For Muslim men, the rifle had become part of their identity, a symbol of honor and freedom; in the insecure conditions of the nineteenth century, it had also been seen as a necessary safeguard for one's family. Ibrahim's action was, in effect, the announcement of a new order, one in which the state would monopolize the use of violence.

That new order confronted a largely agricultural society that, while continuing to be so until well into the twentieth century, would be subject to increasingly rapid rates of change.[8] The period following the Egyptian conquest and Muhammad Ali's withdrawal at the end of the decade (with considerable European help, the Ottomans would manage to oust him) saw a change in where and how the peasants farmed, the crops they grew and the markets they were grown for, their legal relationship to the land, and their ties to the powerful social forces above them. Three forces converged to spearhead the changes, two of them increasing their impact considerably under Ibrahim Pasha's stern hand: the Europe-dominated world market, which was deepening its penetration of the Middle East and, for that matter, of peasant societies all over the world by the last part of the nineteenth century,[9] and the new, much more intense role of government in local affairs. From midcentury on, revived Ottoman control of Palestine included a spate of reforms affecting both landholding (directly) and land use (indirectly). The third and in some ways most momentous force was Zionism and Jewish settlement.

Zionism, of course, did not exist during Muhammad Ali's era. Still, the Egyptian reforms seemed to energize the Jews as they gained new rights. Accompanying the emergence of various forms of proto-Zionism, immigration to Palestine increased and the Jewish population began to grow substantially. With Zionism's much clearer impact on the country in the 1880s and after, the Jewish presence intersected with Arab agricultural life at any number of points, and a good part of Arab-Jewish frictions focused on the issues of land, water, and agricultural labor.[10]

To the naive observer, the process emerging during Ibrahim's brief tenure seemed to involve taking the agriculture of a miserably poor, technologically backward peasantry and transforming it into one increasingly marked by cash crops, technological sophistication, and higher production. John Pinkerton's *Modern Geography,* written in 1802, captures how a Westerner saw the state of the fellaheen before this wave of change. "The peasants," he wrote, "are in the most miserable situation; and although not sold with the soil, like those of Poland, are, if possible, yet more oppressed; barley, bread, onions and water constituting their constant fare."[11]

There is no denying the misery of early nineteenth century peasants, but they may have had far more autonomy and rights than Polish serfs of the time. More to the point, an oversimplified view of agricultural progress as a straight line from a set of dire conditions to the paradise of cash crops (especially citrus fruit) in the twentieth century obscures not only the dynamics of the earlier period but a much less sanguine side of rural change: the decreasing viability of agriculture as an economic bedrock for the vast majority of the Palestinian population. Palestinian peasants faced a no-win situation. When wealthier Arabs adopted new technologies they reduced overall agricultural employment and when peasants managed to hold onto their lands they found themselves uncompetitive with more modern Jewish and Arab farming. To understand the effect of this double-bind on Palestinian society, we need to look more closely at the three major forces of the world market, government intervention, and Zionism that helped transform the country's agriculture, starting with the "Peasant Revolt in Syria" and ending with al-Nakba, the Palestinian Disaster of 1948.

The World Market

The Ottoman reappearance in 1840 left some of Ibrahim's changes in place. Local Arab Christians, for example, continued playing a disproportionately large role in the country's economic life. Renewed Ottoman control also brought with it an influx of outsiders—consuls and missionaries—who spearheaded a permanent European presence in Palestine. Not far behind were European merchants, who, while mostly based in the coastal towns, carried auguries of change to rural areas.

The towns served as conduits for wheat grown in Palestine to consumers in England, Ireland, and elsewhere. Small peasants rarely had any face-to-face contact with the Europeans, but increasing numbers of Palestinian Christian merchants began to settle in the coastal towns.[12] Together with a number of Muslim landlords and tax farmers, who collected their due from the peasants in kind, they managed to establish ties with Europeans whose ships docked in the ports. A renewed wave of insecurity in the 1850s, when notable Palestinian families led a destructive round of intervillage violence, disrupted agriculture, but rural life was resuscitated with the increasing social and political order of the 1860s. The Ottoman forces, freed from participation in the Crimean War, turned their attention to establishing order in the country, especially the potentially rich coastal plain and northern valleys, and the resulting changes signaled the beginning of the end for subsistence peasant agriculture.

Palestinian farming now moved towards deep, inextricable involvement with the world market. Rising world prices in the 1860s and 1870s made ties to the European economy ever more attractive to merchants and large landowners. Much of the southern coastal land around Gaza, for example, was devoted to growing wheat, barley, and maize, which were all increasingly in demand in Europe.[13] Specialty crops also rose in popularity, with sesame, cotton, oranges, olives (for oil), and grapes (for wine) leading the way. Crops such as olives and sesame had long been Palestinian staples, but widespread cultivation of cotton, and an intensive planting of new orange orchards to take advantage of the high profits citrus fruits offered, represented a major innovation. In the 1870s, Arabs exported most of their oranges to Egypt and Turkey; by the early years of the twentieth century, Britain had become the biggest customer for high-quality oranges from Jaffa.[14]

Both overall farming output and the proportion of cash crops grew considerably. After a long stagnation, cultivation of the coastal plain and northern valleys showed a dramatic increase, many of the cash crops being concentrated in these areas. Some of the new output was a response to need, the Arab population alone expanding by about 70 percent between 1870 and World War I.[15] But a sizeable portion went to exports. Distant wars—first the Crimean and then the United States' Civil War—propelled world agricultural prices upward in the 1850s and 1860s, as did growing British and Continental affluence, which also led to greater demand.[16]

It took major changes in landholding and even local warfare around midcentury to put some groups in a position to react flexibly and quickly to new world-market opportunities.[17] Together with rising land prices—paving the way for a new Arab leadership that would stay in power until the creation of the state of Israel[18]—these changes had deep, long-term effects on the Palestinian Arabs, even before the Zionists arrived on the scene.

The New Role of Government

Once the Ottomans expelled Muhammad Ali's forces, they were none too eager to return to the type of loose rule they had previously exercised in Syria and Palestine. The Egyptian method of direct administration seemed both more secure and more lucrative; Ottoman authorities now viewed the possibility of a similar approach on their part as a way to break the rebellious independence of the notables and sheikhs once and for all. One Ottoman official told recalcitrant sheikhs, "Formerly the Turkish Government was weak in Syria and we could not compel you always to obey us, but now we are strong and if you are insubordinate I will . . . throw you into the sea."[19] Nevertheless, the Ottomans achieved only some of their aims and, indeed, unintentionally paved the way for changes that subverted some of their most important goals. Their historic use of the notables to rule the Arab provinces injected an ambivalence into policies designed to sweep away the notables' political power and adopt some form of direct rule.

First, in the Ottomans' efforts to oust the Egyptians, they armed local forces—led of course by the ayan and the sheikhs—and made tempting promises about both short-term exemption from taxes and their long-term reduction, which ended up tying the hands of Ottoman revenue collectors.[20] After the end of the Egyptian occupation in 1840, they then proceeded to neglect the country for several years, giving the notables ample opportunity to reestablish themselves; by the time the Ottomans attempted to reassert direct control in 1844–45, it was too late. Ibrahim Pasha was reported to have warned a Turkish general, "You with the assistance of the English have expelled me; you have again put arms into the hands of the mountaineers [the sheikhs]; it cost me nine years and ninety thousand men to disarm them. You will yet invite me back to govern them."[21] Ibrahim was not invited back, and the sheikhs were subjugated; but talk of tossing them into the Mediterranean notwithstanding, the Ottomans never did destroy or even bypass the town notables. (They did have some success against the rural sheikhs.) In fact, the reforms following the reconquest of Syria and Palestine expanded the reach of the ayan's power considerably beyond their own sleepy towns and subject villages,[22] their position in the country being shored up firmly by the end of the Ottoman period.[23] What did occur as the Ottomans spattered out reforms throughout the century was a change in the basis of the notables' power and control.

The larger context of this process was the Ottoman *Tanzimat*: the great push in the middle decades of the nineteenth century to salvage the decaying empire through legal and administrative changes. Ottoman authorities, attempting now to govern domains over which they had previously exercised control in name only, focused on taxation, land ownership, town government, and general administration. Their aim was to insinuate the government into the daily routine of the Empire's subjects, enhancing its ability to mobilize both people and revenues. The most important of the Ottoman reforms for Palestinian rural life involved land tenure, beginning with the land law of 1858. The land reform was one of a number of the initiatives unintentionally bolstering the ambitious ayan—and helping to create new agrarian and national relations among the Palestinians that would carry over to the middle of the next century.[24]

In this respect, a pivotal innovation was the requirement of *Tapu*: a title of ownership for all land, which, in turn demanded a centralized land register for all holdings in Palestine.[25] Previously, ownership had been demonstrated simply by cultivation; the new law allowed unoccupied land to be registered. Town notables quickly realized the tremendous potential of such land, especially as government control increased in the most fertile parts of the country. By the mid-1870s, the Ottomans had subdued Bedouin marauders, and the ayan used the new law to take possession of large estates in the valleys and plains. Here the tastes of far off Europeans began to shape a new cash-sensitive agriculture. And these estates, stretching well beyond the small towns where the notable families actually lived, became the foundation for the ayan's role as the dominant and dominating Arab class in Palestine.

At times, the notables bought lands only to turn a quick profit through resale. Later, the Zionists would become ready customers for large tracts, driving up the price of land generally. Some Arab landowners converted their estates into farms, with orchards and fields producing cash crops. The notables' ability to marshal investment capital put them in a competitively superior position to the fellaheen: Continuing to farm with traditional methods, the peasants grew in numbers in the country's far less fertile, central and eastern mountain regions and provided a pool of ready hands to undertake the work of cultivation. Many urban landowners, especially those uninvolved in the new citrus sector or who lived outside the country, showed little interest in the day-to-day working of their estates beyond collecting their due. It was the tenants on the newly reclaimed lands, drifting down from the east, who provided the muscle—and often the technical innovations—to create profit-making agricultural enterprises.

Migration westward was certainly not novel for the mountain fellaheen. Traditionally, in times of greater security some farmers would move into the frontier zone of the valleys and plains, where they built temporary extensions of their villages—the *khirba*. Now, in the latter part of the nineteenth century, the khirbas and their independent farmers reappeared, but they were dwarfed by the larger estates.[26] The movement did not come to a halt until 1948, when the flow was first reversed as refugees fled to the hills and then was choked off entirely as new boundaries came into existence.

Migrants to the coastal plain and valleys in the 1860s and 1870s were still a minority of the population, still settled mostly in 800–900 mountain villages where the rocky land afforded some insulation from both marauding bands or armies and government authorities. So did the construction of the villages themselves. Sociologist Rosemary Sayigh has noted that

> unlike many villages in the Mediterranean area, those of Palestine were not walled, but the clustering of their solid, stone-built houses in close formation, with walls almost a metre thick and flat rooftops from which lookout could be kept and stones hurled, made them a formidable obstacle to most attackers.[27]

In the hills, the central institution was *musha,* a co-ownership system that acted as an equalizing force in village life by periodically redividing land among the village clans.[28] The musha system worked to sustain the extended family (which tilled the divided parcels) as the basic social unit. It typically consisted of the father, mother, and unmarried children as well as married sons and their wives and children. Clans, too, remained important, linking extended families, often through the marriage of first cousins.[29] Given the often violent environment, the clan helped protect villagers from the ravages of war, marauding Bedouins, and *fidya* (a form of collective retribution in blood feuds).[30]

Inequalities abounded in village life. Within families, older males tended to dominate, although women exerted considerable influence through their critical role in maintaining the household.[31] With designation as an elder stemming as much from status as from chronological age, the elders' redivision of land gave them significant power within the clan, often leading to inequalities among its various family groups and sometimes to serious abuses. Inequities persisted among the clans as well, since during the land redivision process consideration was often given to those having more sons, cattle, oxen, and donkeys. Thus land division to some extent reinforced the positions of those already possessing wealth by assigning them the largest and most fertile parcels. Often, the power of a clan could be discerned by the lavishness of its *madafa*, the guest house always open to strangers or outside authorities.[32]

Although the system did not entirely equalize households and clans, it often prevented huge disparities, maintained a sense of cooperation and identity, and avoided the loss of village lands to outsiders through personal sales (which were forbidden). Later, both the British and the Zionists saw the fellaheen's inability to sell and purchase land freely as a major impediment to the progress of agriculture and of Arab villages generally.[33] They also believed that the regular redivision of the land removed incentives to improve it.[34] It is not surprising, then, that by the end of British rule, musha lands had diminished to less than a quarter of all Arab holdings.[35]

The new land law, with its official registry and proliferation of deeds, opened the way to much easier transfer of ownership, largely in the newly cultivated coastal plain and northern valleys. An unintended result of the reform was to confirm the central and eastern mountain region as a bastion of a Palestinian social and agricultural life remarkably different from that emerging in the country's western portion. The hilly region sheltered determined small freeholders who had to cope with infertile soil, overpopulation, and competition from much more advanced agriculture in the valleys and plains. With its rapid rise of population, it also served as a source of labor, first for the large agricultural estates in the latter region, and then for other enterprises starting to emerge along the coast.

Along with irreversibly altering landholding patterns and village and clan relations, the dismantlement of the musha system involved the imposition of tax after tax upon the peasantry, who found themselves—in an experience shared with peasants almost everywhere in Asia and Africa—sinking deeper and deeper into debt.[36] While urban moneylenders served as a bridge between the mountain and the plain, these moneylenders were often the same notables gobbling up land under the new reforms. In this manner they engendered a dependency upon themselves by way of cash loans, often repossessing land when peasants went deeply into arrears.[37]

The key figures in the reforms were the *mukhtars,* a new government designation for chiefs of the village.[38] Unlike the powerful village sheikhs who had preceded them and who had paid little heed to government dictates, the mukhtars were officials of the state. Once the Ottomans rid the countryside of the sheikhs and their incessant local warfare, the mukhtars emerged as important local figures—unpaid go-betweens, representing the government to the peasants and, less frequently, the peasants to the government. Their roles included recording information on births, deaths, and marriages, and local responsibility for the land registry.

But the mukhtars' most important function was to keep order: Any village watchmen or guards were under their direct supervision. The Ottoman authorities had also hoped to use them as key personnel in a more centralized tax system, but the general failure of the tax reforms meant a repeated recourse to tax-farming—an inefficient system in which the state auctioned off its revenue-collecting rights to individuals.[39]

The mukhtars were an odd mixture of powerful local figures—akin to their predecessors, the sheikhs—and mere links on the far end of the government's bureaucratic chain. Supposedly chosen by the village's male population, they often came to their positions as local strongmen or as protégés of other powerful figures. At the same time, at least in theory, they were completely subservient to the district governor, who also had a say in their selection. Unlike the sheikhs before them, they did not serve as village arbitrators and judges, instead finding themselves preoccupied with a host of petty bureaucratic tasks.

In some ways, the mukhtar lent a new unity to the village, defining its place within a more tight-knit empire. His role was intertwined with an emerging new self-definition for the local rural community: much less autonomous, more a distinct unit within a larger whole that impinged constantly on rural life. In other ways, the role simply reinforced some of the old divisions in village life, with large villages (3,000–5,000 people as opposed to the average 700–800) frequently having a number of mukhtars, each representing a major clan. Here, the tensions among these chiefs often mirrored continuing divisions in the village itself.

Village life still had a distinct pace, even in the last phase of Ottoman rule, and the mukhtars played pivotal roles in negotiating how outside pressures would be assimilated. Nevertheless, the mukhtar did not have a monopoly of control over the economic and political forces drawing Palestine's isolated villages into a widening world. Different groups in the village (or, in the plains and valleys, absentee landlords) derived considerable power from varying degrees of direct contact with outside authorities and enterprises.[40] Teachers or village preachers, for example, began reading city newspapers aloud and interpreting them to eager villagers by the start of the twentieth century.[41] A very few villages contained families that—at least by local standards—were very rich, owning a hundred or more acres of land. These families established branches in some of the urban centers and were the first to educate their sons in Western schools. Below them were a larger number of families, often farming with the help of hired seasonal hands or tenants, who would sometimes also send their sons to study in a missionary school in town. Such contacts enabled both groups to play important leadership roles inside the village and, for the most powerful, in an even wider domain.

A third group consisted of those with land supporting them but absorbing all their labor. Below them were peasant families that also owned land but whose members had to seek additional income as tenants or hired hands. Often sending sons to become tenants on the new estates in the lowlands, or even to work in the bustling coastal towns, such families—while subservient to the large landowners—did maintain an important standing in village life.

That sort of status did not exist for the poorest village groups—the tenants and hired workers with no land of their own, considered "strangers" or nonmembers of the village community. Many of them even lacked the economic leeway to send a son from the hilly region to the coastal plain. As was also true a century later, when rising oil prices created new opportunities for Palestinians in the Persian Gulf, migrants came largely from selected groups within the village. And even the positions they assumed outside would depend on their group of local origin.

Sons traveling to nearby towns or more distant ports on the coast did not always leave the village permanently—many returned not only with important resources for raising their families in the village hierarchy, but also with the new habits and ideas starting to influence the Palestinian Arabs. As time went on, more and more of these imported ideas concerned the growing Jewish presence in the country, a phenomenon that was so far affecting villagers in the mountainous region only vaguely and indirectly.

Zionism during Ottoman Rule

In the period after the 1834 revolt, even before Jews gave birth to an organized Zionist political movement in Eastern and Central Europe, there were some signs of change in the Jewish community of

Palestine. The end of Egyptian rule and the Ottoman reestablishment in 1840 served as a kind of benchmark for its increased security, the Jewish population more than doubling in the four decades between the end of the Egyptian occupation and the beginning of what is called the First Aliyah (the initial wave of Jewish immigration) in 1882.[42] But while young Jews began to establish settlements outside the existing centers of Jewish life—that is, Jerusalem and, to a lesser degree, Tiberias and Safad[43]—the community still subsisted largely through donations from other Jews abroad, and for protection they looked to the European consuls who had established themselves in Palestine after the ouster of Muhammad Ali. Only in the twenty-odd years leading up to the 1880s did some Palestinian Jews show even the remotest inclination for serious agricultural projects.

With Jews in Eastern Europe confronting increasingly hostile conditions, emigration to the West stepped up considerably in the 1880s. Palestine attracted a small fraction of that emigration, a younger and more enterprising Jewish population, sharing little with its predecessors in the Holy Land. The interest of some Jewish organizations in resettling emigrants there coincided with the Russian emergence of the *Hovevei-Zion* (Lovers of Zion), a cluster of groups dedicated to Jewish social and cultural rejuvenation.[44] Those members now making their way to Palestine argued for the flowering of the Hebrew language and for the creation of Jewish agricultural settlements, independently worked by Jewish farm laborers.

The actual agricultural enterprises of the 1880s and 1890s turned out to be tenuous ventures. If Palestine was more politically inviting than Russia, it was less than hospitable economically or in terms of public health. The arduous journey itself (not to speak of winter in the forlorn Palestinian landscape) could break the resolve of many Jews intent on reclaiming the Land of Israel. For instance, Bilu, the group often credited with ushering in the new period of immigration called *aliyah*, started in Kharkov with about 300 members in 1881; about 100 actually left to sail from Odessa and of these, about 40 reached port in Istanbul; finally, 16 stalwarts arrived in Palestine to set up an agricultural working group.[45] In one of the very first settlements, Petah Tikvah, the Jews had to abandon the enterprise temporarily because of malaria, returning only several years later. In the mid-1880s, the new agricultural settlers probably did not total more than 1,000. By the century's end, merely 21 Jewish settlements with about 4,500 inhabitants—two thirds working in agriculture—had been established.

These numbers were hardly large enough to have any serious impact on Arab agriculture. The Jews were even less likely to have an effect on Arab village life as a whole—they established their settlements on the coastal plain and in the valleys, where the peasant population was sparse, sometimes negligible, and where the Muslim town notables were then establishing their own new agricultural enterprises. In the early 1880s, the Jews could not have been perceived as very different from the Templars, a marginal group of evangelical Germans who settled in Palestine at about the same time in the belief that they were the new chosen people destined to inherit the Holy Land.[46] Most of the country's rural Arab population was simply unaware of either group's existence; those who did come into contact with them fretted over their appropriation of potentially rich land, but relations remained mostly nonviolent, if uneasy.

At times, uneasiness would give way to coexistence, even cooperation. Nevertheless, Jewish land buying, mostly of state-owned or notable-owned tracts, did affect the local peasants and resulted in numerous land disputes, especially because the fellaheen were far from reconciled to the new property rules emphasizing deed ownership rather than cultivation. Serious tension arose, for example, from 1899 to 1902, when Jews bought up considerable tracts around Tiberias.[47] The new Jewish settlements absorbed some of the local peasants as laborers (much to the distress of later, more ideological Zionists, who feared that the Jews would become an exploitative class), with most settlements using from five to ten times as many Arab workers as Jewish ones. If the Arabs were not hired, they were displaced by Jewish purchases—an issue of nearly unsurpassed importance half a century later.[48]

When the Jews, and for that matter the Templars, did have an impact on Arab agriculture, it was mostly indirect. The Templars brought a new aesthetic into the country, demonstrating to neighboring Arabs what a model settlement could be. Both Jews and Templars also introduced new farming technology. The Templars imported the scythe; along with the Jews they unsuccessfully attempted to adapt the sod-turning plough to local conditions, in order to replace the more primitive single nail plough. More success came with the "Jewish plough," an iron nail plough later elaborated into a plough with two and then three nails. Jews also developed a more sophisticated thresher and changed from human and ox to horse and donkey power, and finally to mechanical power by the end of the century.[49] Those who employed the new techniques gained a hard-edged efficiency enabling them to take advantage of both the rising world prices and the deepening penetration of the world market.[50]

A technological leapfrogging in agriculture started to take place. Arab farmers also began to adopt new methods and tools. Growing demand for oranges in England and elsewhere was stretching citrus agriculture to its limits, and existing methods of pumping water— through the use of a mule—were proving inadequate for the expanding plantations. Only the internal combustion engine's introduction would allow orchard growers to overcome the problem of pumping sufficient water from the necessary depths for a qualitative leap in citrus-devoted acreage.

Although the mountain fellaheen did not sense these innovations very strongly at first, some indirect benefits did make their way to the hill country. The clearing of long-neglected land by Jews and others, followed by the adoption of the new innovations, made the coastal plain a more attractive resource for expanding population of the hills. New jobs proliferated on the coast—not only in orchards depending on mechanically pumped water, but in flour mills and other enterprises using steam and internal combustion engines.

Rather more ominously, the mountain fellaheen were not contestants in the leapfrogging game. Their agriculture—dependent on human, not mechanical power and in many cases not even using animals—was inexorably putting them at a great disadvantage. True, they had little direct contact with the world market, but its steady nineteenth century penetration into Palestine did not bode well for those whose agriculture was coming to be viewed as backward within their own country.[51] As the economic and social links between the coast and the hills grew over time, peasants in the hinterland found themselves relegated to a dependent role in the economy, supplying cheap, unskilled labor or maintaining an increasingly uncompetitive agriculture.

The paucity of contacts between the Jews and most fellaheen was not for lack of grandiose Jewish ideas. A Zionist settlement plan of 1919 included all of the eastern portions of the country plus a good part of what was to become Transjordan, which the British did not separate from Palestine until 1922.[52] But actual settlement proved much slower and more regionally concentrated than Zionist leaders had hoped. Although the numbers of immigrant Jews did begin to swell in the final stretch of Ottoman rule (the first eight years of the new century saw a more than doubling of the number of Jewish workers, mostly farmers, to about ten thousand), concentrations in the mountainous region were negligible. Only the small number of fellaheen contiguous to the new settlements felt an unmediated Jewish presence.

But even if the scope of Jewish land purchases was limited, they did shape future Jewish-Arab relations. The Jews were establishing an economy based largely on the exclusion of Arabs from land they farmed and from the Jewish labor market. Slowly, the most fertile lands in the northern valleys and in the coastal plain passed to Jewish hands, with jobs and higher wages going to the Jewish newcomers. The logical conclusion of this process was the separate development of the Arab and Jewish economies and, eventually, the creation of two separate nationalist movements.[53]

While some Jews and Arabs managed to cooperate, relations between many, even then, were rocky.[54] As soon as one dispute between a Jewish settlement and neighboring Arab tenants or smallholders seemed settled, another would erupt. In the Tiberias district between 1899 and 1902, for example, Jewish land-buying aroused bitter opposition from a local district officer. And in Petah Tikvah, where the Jews bought peasant land that had been forfeited to Arab moneylenders and the state, the fellaheen felt the land was still rightfully theirs. In 1886, local Arab disgruntlement finally led to the settlement's ransacking and the death of a Jewish woman. Still, within a short time there, Arabs and Jews reestablished working, if mutually suspicious, relations.[55]

In the years immediately prior to World War I, Zionism acquired more ominous overtones for many Arabs. The Jews were taking everbolder steps to build a Palestinian beachhead, creating the Palestine Land Development Company in 1908 to train workers in farming and develop cooperative groups to settle newly purchased land. Jewish numbers rose to 85,000, about 10 percent of the country's population. From 1908 to 1913, the Jewish National Fund bought over 10,000 acres of farmland and stood to buy 35,000 more just as war broke out in Europe. These were still negligible amounts in terms of the country as a whole, but they did represent a major advance for the Jews. Before the war, they had even established a new city, Tel-Aviv, which threatened to overshadow Jaffa as a capital of the coastal plain. In addition, the years from 1904 to 1914 brought what the Zionists have since called the Second Aliyah, a wave of immigrants including a core of committed socialists. These Jews, mostly from Russia, became the central leadership of Palestinian Jewry, and later of Israel. The Arab community would have to confront their vision and their skills over the next half century.

Palestine on the eve of the Great War scarcely resembled the country of a century earlier. It was now a land connected to Europe by railroads, shipping lines, and a telegraph network. It joined Europe, too, through the increased number of Europeans living in Palestine, both Jews and gentiles, now appearing on the docks almost daily; by the cinema; and by the European plays that began to be staged in 1911. More and more, the notable Arab families sent their children to foreign schools in the country, or even abroad. Life in Jaffa, Haifa, and Gaza resembled that in other Mediterranean cities—Marseille, Athens, Beirut, and Alexandria—more than the towns of the Palestinian hinterland.

True, it was mainly the ayan who profited from these drastic changes, transforming their way of life and widening the social gap between them and the Arab majority. But the fellaheen by no means could avoid the effects of the European market and the Ottoman reforms, nor for that matter the Zionist presence. For one thing, they found their resources stretched to the limit as the new conditions precipitated the beginnings of a meteoric rise in the Palestinian population, tripling from the start of the nineteenth century until World War I from about a quarter to nearly three-quarters of a million,[56] Migration of some family members to the coast, and the continual shuttling of people and resources back and forth between the mountain and the plain, became as regular as the agricultural cycle itself. And, as elsewhere, the impoverished peasantry was forced to finance many of the new changes through enhanced revenue collection by the government.

The increased connections of Palestinian agriculture to the coast and to distant markets brought a change in the fellaheen's position. With the European influx and the rise of the ayan, they simultaneously gained a more central social role and became socially more marginal. They simply could not fend off the political and economic changes drawing them like a vortex—as debtors, taxpayers, titleholders, and migrants—into urban life. At the same time, they were becoming more distant from the classes above them, and were lagging technologically. Palestinian Arab society was forming two quite different branches.

After the Great War

The last seventy-five years of Ottoman rule were tumultuous for the Empire. But they passed without catastrophic changes in the daily life of Palestine—no wars in the country, no major revolts, and even internal violence fell off dramatically. The most concerted violence facing Palestinians was probably the Crimean War, which drew fellaheen conscripts far from their homes. Within the country, changes were incremental, sometimes insidious: people did not observe them from one day to the next, nor from year to year for the most part.

After 1914, things were very different. Embedded in a series of earthquakes and aftershocks, the only period approaching "normal" was that from 1922 to 1935—years also having their share of violence (the most memorable in 1929) and a rapid pace of social and economic change. Their relative tranquility was followed by the Arab Revolt, World War II, and the 1948 war.

World War I, the "war to end all wars," must have seemed nearly as apocalyptic to those in Palestine as to subjects of the European frontline states. Palestine suffered unspeakable damage; some of it, such as the denuded landscape, is still evident today.[57] Seeking fuel and fodder in their last gasp, the Ottomans cut down the country's trees and commandeered farm animals and grain. As always, the peasants took the brunt of the onslaught. After suppressing all foreign financial agencies and prohibiting the import of any capital from enemy countries at the war's inception, the Ottomans drafted thousands of fellaheen for the imperial army's lost cause, so that, as one Arab observer remarked, the country seemed to consist only of the elderly, women, and children.[58] But the peasants were not the only ones who suffered in the Great War: Links to the European world dissolved as missionaries, consuls, and others left the country, along with a large number of Jews. With the cash economy's crumbling, this emigration caused a near collapse of the way of life the ayan had fashioned in the coastal towns. By the time of British General Edmund Allenby's triumphal march into Jerusalem in 1918, the economy was in ruins.

If Jews and Arabs both suffered from the war's economic effects, the Jews fared far better on the diplomatic side of the ledger. Initially split between the two major blocs, European Jews slowly shifted support to the British. On November 2, 1917, they were granted the crucial Balfour Declaration—celebrated by Jews and condemned by Arabs to this day—which pledged Britain's support in the establishment of a Jewish national home in Palestine.[59]

For Palestine's fellaheen, the Declaration passed unnoticed, the rigors of the war being of far more immediate concern. Once the war ended, it was the new British mandate that primarily absorbed their attention, the years of British rule witnessing an economic transformation in Palestine beyond what any nineteenth century inhabitant could have imagined. Trade quickly surpassed its prewar level, restoring links to the world market. The British built a modern port at Haifa that included a refinery and facilities to export British oil pumped in Iraq. They also expanded Jaffa's port facilities and added new airports, roads, and railroads.[60]

Imports skyrocketed. The value of imported goods quadrupled in a dozen years, and with growing imports came increasing trade deficits. This negative trade balance was offset by an influx of Jewish capital, especially during the 1930s, which dwarfed the earlier Zionist efforts.

Agriculture played a central role in the new economic growth as production expanded rapidly in vegetables and other crops.[61] Even more important, citrus orchards continued expanding after the Great War, rising sevenfold in twenty years.[62] Citrus growing—most notably of the desirable Jaffa orange—so dominated the economy that Palestine was in danger of becoming a monocrop society, dependent on one dominant buyer, Great Britain.[63]

For the small Arab farmers of Palestine, much of the boom brought bitter results. Cash crops lay at its heart, farming as an exclusive source of income thus now becoming simply unviable for most smallholding subsistence peasants and their families.[64] Many Arab peasants seemed on a treadmill. Even as some devoted a portion of their acreage to truck crops, such as vegetables, they found themselves falling farther and farther behind the Jews and the most advanced Arab sector.[65] Unlike cereal production, the more profitable cultivation of citrus fruit and vegetables demanded intensive irrigation and fertilization of the soil, hence considerable investment and new skills. New orchards required about five years of investment before the fruit could be marketed. All this was beyond the capabilities and resources of most small farmers.

The peasantry also had to fight against other powerful forces. More and more, it was becoming difficult for village families, even in the mountainous regions, to hold onto land. The profitability of the newer sectors and the shortage of additional unused land in the plains and valleys made peasants' tracts increasingly desirable, which compounded the high land prices already resulting from active Jewish landbuying.[66]

If all this were not enough to batter Palestinian Arab village society, the village population grew by over 40 percent between 1922 and 1936. The Arab population as a whole expanded two to three percent yearly in this period—one of the fastest rates in the world. Although there was a significant movement from the distant hill settlements into the maritime cities, many hill villages continued to grow quite rapidly. A British survey indicated that more than half of Arab households did not have enough land for subsistence.[67] The fellaheen, for the most part, were unable to cover their expenses or keep up payments on their debts, which had reached alarming proportions—the average total debt was more than three times the average annual household income.

The boom years of the mandate, then, brought increasing desperation to Palestine's peasants. Whole families abandoned their villages for opportunities in Jewish ventures (at least until the mid-1930s), British public works projects, or new Arab enterprises. Others sent their sons to large agricultural estates or the port towns of Haifa and Jaffa, or went themselves, leaving wives and children behind. Cities swelled with peasants from the mountains. During World War II, British use of Palestine as a rearguard base created tremendous economic activity in the urban areas, particularly striking because it came in the wake of the Arab Revolt, which had temporarily driven many laborers back to their villages in the late 1930s.

Britain's Failure among the Peasantry

Through the thirty years of British rule over Palestine, mandate officials were well aware of the battering of village life. The Palestinian high commissioner received report after report decrying the effects of the restructured Palestinian economy on the Arab population. Various British commissions collected direct testimony and other evidence demonstrating the competitive squeeze on peasant agriculture and land as well as the formidable pressures working to create a landless underclass of Palestinians. For all their concern—and even their good intentions—British officials did little to ameliorate the situation. In the end their policies simply hastened the crumbling of the oldest sector of Palestinian life.[68]

The mandate turned out to be full of contradictions. Governing in a period of unsurpassed economic growth following the already momentous Ottoman transformation, the British tried to clamp a lid on social change, taking a markedly conservative stance regarding the question of Palestinian leadership. From the beginning, they aimed to win over and work through the major families of the ayan, and despite all the conflicts eventually developing between them (see chapters 3 and 4), the result would be to crown this group officially—with its Jerusalem branches at the head—as leader of the Arabs. This leadership extended beyond the Arab nationalist institutions that proliferated during the mandate; the ayan's participation in the mandatory state itself, for all their opposition to its purposes, offered a useful platform for boosting their power. The British rulers handpicked members of important Arab families, for example, to form a small corps of prestigious district officers for the government.[69] The British were frustrated at the disproportionate number of Christian Arabs ending up in such positions, despite the care they gave to such appointments. Still, those district officers who did come from important Muslim families further cemented their dominance over the rural population.

The group thus used both British support and, ironically, its opposition to the British to consolidate its position at the top of Palestinian society. At times, the notables took on the cause of villagers struggling with the mandate authorities and the Zionists; at other times, the split between peasants and the ayan led to violent clashes within Palestinian society, especially during the Arab Revolt of the late 1930s.

British rule also affected the peasantry more directly. The mandate's goals regarding village society were often the same as those of the Ottomans. In fact, the British openly adopted nineteenth century Ottoman legal precedent—specifically, the Ottoman Vilayet Law of 1913—as its benchmark for governing Palestine. Like the Turks, they sought more tax revenue, a more efficient land registration system, a breakup of co-owned musha land, enhancement of the mukhtar as the official arm of government in the village, and more productive agriculture generally.[70]

What differed was the greater British efficiency in carrying out its rule. To be sure, there were gaping holes in the administration that allowed peasants—who by necessity were experts in such matters—to circumvent rules and regulations. But compared to what the fellaheen had known previously, the British bureaucracy they encountered in the 1920s quite fully penetrated village life. In Ottoman times, the execution of law at the village level was often a haphazard affair and sometimes nearly nonexistent. Also, the Turkish hand stretched over provinces on three continents while the British mandatory state was a small, tight affair.

Reflecting their wider state policy, the British aimed for three often clashing goals within the village. First, they sought to be as nonintrusive as possible, preserving Ottoman laws where they could, respecting village custom, and working through established leadership. Second, like governments everywhere, they tried to increase their revenues. In practice, peasants faced demands for endless tithes and taxes that only accentuated their indebtedness, which had already begun to expand in the Ottoman period. Much of the growing rural debt was owed to urban moneylenders, who were usually charging 30 percent per year.

Finally, while anti-British sentiment did grow substantially during the course of the mandate, the ill feelings did not result from total disinterest by the authorities in the plight of the villagers. The British made efforts to improve their situation, and to ensure that the nearly uncontrolled economic growth did not claim them as its victims. Unfortunately, genuine British dismay failed to produce a comprehensive economic plan. Instead, British officials created programs piecemeal—cooperative societies, small loans, seed loans, and so forth—that together lacked the strength and coherence necessary to protect the fellaheen.[71]

In effect, British mandate rule pulled hard in separate directions. The mandate tried to strengthen the village leadership, but through active economic intervention reduced its importance instead. British officials worried that peasant debt would create an army of landless laborers displaced by Jews and Arab notables, but its tax policy seemed only to add to the peasants' woes. While the Department of Education created a generation of literate men in the villages (the expansion of education for rural Muslim girls was much slower),[72] government officials held to the delusion that this would have a negligible influence on day-to-day life. Mandate officials wished to keep the peasants on the land and prevent the creation of huge numbers of landless laborers; but at the same time—especially during World War II—they sank significant sums into public works in Palestine's western section, drawing thousands of peasants from their homes in the eastern, hilly regions. Given such a confusing mix of policy, it is not surprising that the peasantry became an important hub of activity and agitation during the Arab Revolt of 1936–39, which temporarily crippled the British administration in the rural areas (see chapter 4).

In addition, the ferocious pace of change had jarred even the remotest villages out of whatever autonomy they had managed to preserve during the Ottoman period. As their horizons changed from the village—and beyond that from local and even regional markets—to a larger market system and a growing national movement, the peasants looked for more government action to address their special circumstances. Instead, they found a British-run state neglecting their need to make progress in their agriculture.[73] The fellaheen did prosper momentarily from the rise in construction opportunities and agricultural prices during World War II.[74] Many were even able to pay off their onerous debts. At the same time, their farming was becoming less competitive, and those who abandoned it for the cities were relegated to the lowest-paying, unskilled jobs. Government schools had been established by the British in about half of Palestine's villages, and rural illiteracy had declined from 90 percent to 70 percent of the male population. Still, these numbers indicate that the bulk of the villagers were woefully unprepared to deal with the demands of the new life on the coast, or even the changed life in their villages, as they encountered the increasingly sophisticated agriculture of the country, except on the very lowest rungs of the social ladder.

The Gaining Momentum of Zionism

If Zionism was a mild curiosity for most Palestinian fellaheen at the end of World War I, it changed in the 1920s and 1930s into a force affecting crucial aspects of their lives. Jewish plans were more ambitious than ever. In talks with Arab political leaders, the Zionists spoke openly of their hope to bring 4–5 million Jews to Palestine.[75] The alarm these statements caused remained the motivating force behind the Arab political agenda until 1948. From World War I on, then, one of the central political issues in Palestine was whether or not the Jews would have unrestricted immigration and landbuying rights. The land issue served as an important bridge between Arab notable leaders, who were eager to build a broad constituency, and the fellaheen, who were growing fearful about the implications of huge numbers of Jews buying land in the country.

Like almost every other question concerning Jews and Arabs, there are two radically different interpretations of the Zionists' effect on the fellaheen during the mandate. It is difficult to sort out the evidence, which was mostly provided by the interested parties (including the British authorities). The Jews, who devoted much more effort to data collection than the Arabs, certainly did not deny that they were precipitating a deep transformation in Arab village society, but they tended to emphasize its beneficial character. Zionist spokesmen noted how Jewish agriculture had helped enable peasants to free themselves from debilitating "feudal" relations, which had ground them down in poverty and debt.[76] The Zionists also pointed to their introduction of new practical techniques—irrigation, growing fodder for animals, new seed varieties—for the improvement of peasant farming.[77] In contrast, Arab spokesmen (and increasingly, British authorities) dwelt on Arab displacement from land and the growing Jewish control over scarce cultivable soil. All sides tended to underplay the deleterious socioeconomic and political factors considered in this chapter. In all likelihood, the Jewish impact on the fellaheen was not nearly significant enough to cause all the beneficial results the Zionists touted; at the same time, the farmers displaced by Jewish landbuying were not a large enough group to have a great impact on the overall Arab economy.[78]

Many Arabs were attracted to the coastal areas where Jewish activity was most intense. But while between 1922 and 1944, the rural population around hill towns such as Hebron, Nablus, Ramallah, and Jenin fell significantly as a percentage of the total Arab population, the absolute numbers still rose. In fact, the rural population did not dip much below two-thirds of the total. In a bit more than two decades the number of Arabs doubled from 570,000 to 1.14 million, while the rural figures alone went from about 375,000 to nearly 734,000.[79]

The result of this stupendous increase was that farm holdings were growing smaller through continuing subdivision—this shrinkage of plot size not being offset by any great improvement in the smallholders' agricultural methods and tools. Nor had the government or any private agency materialized as a source of investment capital. The peasants still relied on moneylenders, although now more often merchants than large landowners. Some increases in production and some adoption of new crops (such as potatoes) were evident, but few smallholders could afford the risks involved in substantially changing their agricultural practices.

Jewish landbuying contributed to this malaise by shrinking the pool of cultivable Arab-owned land, about ten percent of it passing into Jewish hands by 1948. With time, an increasing share of purchases was coming from the ayan, rather than absentee owners in Lebanon or elsewhere, and from local peasants seeking to extricate themselves from debt. Already by the 1940s, few small farmers could survive without some supplementary income from the thriving nonagricultural sectors, especially construction. The combination of Jewish capital investment on the coast (producing jobs taken up by former Arab villagers) and Jewish land purchases only helped further dissolve the differences between village society and its urban counterpart.

A Century of Change in Village Life

The image of an extended peasant family eking out its living from subsistence crops, with perhaps some olive oil going to local and regional markets, was a distant memory by the mid-1940s. Cash crops and nonagricultural supplementary income were now its staples. If in the Ottoman period the Palestinian villagers seemed to be ambling toward novel habits and routines, during the mandate years they appeared to be racing into an unknown future. Since 1948 so uprooted Palestinian society, we can never really know what that future would have held. It is nonetheless clear that the village was becoming ever more marginal to that society, villagers and ex-villagers alike now constituting part of a national movement and a broader economy whose centers lay in Jerusalem, and in Haifa and Jaffa.[80]

Displacement of tenants from land bought by Jews from absentee landlords and others accentuated the new mobility. Peasants moved from the purchased land, often with monetary compensation in hand, to another village or to the city. A Zionist movement that had been resuscitated by the Balfour Declaration and the terms of the mandate added further weight to the pressures of a growing peasant population on a fixed or shrinking share of the country's cultivable land. Meanwhile, without sufficient capital and consolidated plots, small farmers found much of the new agriculture beyond their reach.

After World War I, Arab peasants faced new state officials who clucked their tongues about these trends but did little more than tighten the tax noose, so that peasants had to pay 25 to 50 percent of their income to the government.[81] While this was occurring, Jewish landbuying stepped up considerably: In the decade starting in 1933, for example, Jews bought over eighty thousand acres of Arab land. The Zionists never did have all the capital they needed for the purpose, and objectively the number of fellaheen thus alienated from the land was not very large relative to the total population (just over one thousand households between 1939 and 1945).[82] This was, nevertheless, a substantial increase over the Ottoman period, and it gains importance from the way the matter was perceived by the Palestinian community.[83]

Zionism's main impact came in different realms. The Jewish influence on the Palestinian economy as a whole left the fellaheen even farther behind the country's more privileged population. They also perceived the mandate itself as linked to Zionism, since it had legitimated the conception of a Jewish national home in Palestine. Finally, the threat from Jewish inroads cemented their ties to the town notables, who had taken the lead in opposing Zionism (as we shall see in chapters 3 and 4). That cement was crucial in the formation of a Palestinian national movement. But the future of Palestinian Arab society, and the place in it of both hill-village fellaheen and migrants to the coast, rested on more than resistance to Zionism. Notables and merchant groups, struggling among themselves to set the tone of the culture, economics, and politics that would define the Palestinian national consciousness, created institutions to which the fellaheen responded and against which they reacted. Let us now turn back to the nineteenth century in order to consider these notables and merchants more closely, and their efforts to put a firm stamp on Palestinian Arab society.

2

THE CITY:

BETWEEN NABLUS AND JAFFA

AT THE BEGINNING OF the nineteenth century, the towns up and down Palestine's coast were mere shells of their former selves, the grandeur and vibrancy of the biblical, Roman, or Arabic eras having been eroded by prolonged misery and neglect. It is true that Acre and, to a lesser extent, Haifa, had a moment of renown outside Palestine around then. In 1799, its Turkish governor, Ahmad Pasha—sometimes known as al-Jazzar—turned back the advancing, but weary and plague-weakened, French revolutionary army.[1] (Napoleon had wanted to use Palestine as a beachhead for a drive to the Euphrates.)[2] Ahmad Pasha's mix of skill, determination, and luck offered a brief respite to coastal Palestine's lethargy. After a lengthy siege, he forced Jaffa's Ottoman governor to flee the city. Like other local strongmen in the Empire, he had gained considerable advantage from the Industrial Revolution's inception on the Continent, trading Palestinian raw materials—cotton and grain—for firearms, which he used to equip the mercenaries under his command. As "master of Palestine,"[3] he succeeded in transcending the Ottoman administrative divisions of *sanjaks* and *vilayets* that had carved the

Map 1. Palestine under Ottoman Rule

Dep. of Geography, Hebrew University

country into districts including parts of today's Jordan, Lebanon, and Syria (see map 1). Ahmad Pasha now diminished the administrative role of Damascus and Sidon, enhancing that of Haifa—and exalting Acre, even over the religious influence of Jerusalem.[4] For a brief moment Palestine became as important as the key Syrian towns. Nevertheless, in making Acre the base of a personal satrap eventually reaching across the country, Jazzar had in fact turned his strength against the local population, exacting higher taxes and generally impoverishing the surrounding villages. Almost from the moment he left Acre, the town regressed to the typical sorry state of Palestine's other ports.

For most of the early decades of the nineteenth century, along the entire coast and in the maritime plain, the Ottomans could do little more than hope for some percentage of the collected taxes to find its way to the Sublime Porte.[5] Various strongmen—whether Ottoman governors or local sheikhs—enriched themselves at the expense of the population and neglected the area's infrastructure. The ships making their way to the eastern Mediterranean from Great Britain, the center of world trade, followed routes far from the run-down ports of Palestine.

British ships did not begin docking anywhere near Jaffa—little more than an overgrown village—until the late 1840s. At the century's turn, around 2,500 people lived there, mostly within the walled city. Some risked traveling outside the walls to cultivate surrounding fields, retreating at dusk to the town. A single gate in the wall looked away from the sea, and it was locked every night. Jaffa's total area—about 25 acres—was 7 percent of what it would become by the end of World War I.[6]

Visitors described Jaffa as having a ravaged look: Napoleon's armies, local sheikhs, Ottoman governors, had left their mark, drying up the traffic that had been its lifeline.[7] Jerusalem's merchants sent most of their trade (especially their locally produced soap and olive oil) through Damascus.[8] No doubt, in choosing Jerusalem as the site of their most important consuls,[9] the European powers desired to gain influence with sympathetic Christian sects tied to the Christian holy places, especially the Holy Sepulchre; but they were reflecting, as well, the reality of Palestine's political and economic center of gravity: To the degree there was urban control, Jerusalem and Nablus dominated the mountain region, where population and production were concentrated.[10]

The Inland Towns

In contrast to Jerusalem—with its chaos of religious and administrative offices, diverse ethnic makeup, and countless sects—Nablus, Hebron, and Ramallah were extensions of village society. Farmers moved out daily to work on their plots; those with a little more land rented fields to tenants or worked alongside *harraths*, hired workers.

These inland towns were cultural and economic centers for the farming villages. Each had its own character—deeply Bedouin and Islamic Hebron, relatively cosmopolitan Christian Ramallah—serving as a source of identity for village peasants. The attachment was not nearly as strong as the existential identity set by clan or religion, but still significant in defining the outer boundaries of their lives. Peasants from different villages would meet there, holding festivals and joining cults that formed around the tombs of holy men. Just as importantly, farmers with a surplus would trade there: in produce and livestock, for crops like rice or sugar, and for processed goods, including soap and fabrics.

These towns also contained workshops, the variety and amounts of their products expanding into the twentieth century. With each town surrounded by mountain villages dotted with ancient olive trees, the olive was one of the mainstays of this industry.[11] For example, by the 1920s, there were fifty soap factories in Nablus. Made from the area's aromatic olives, the soap not only met the entire country's needs, but penetrated other Middle Eastern markets (particularly Egypt) and those in Europe. This foreign trade was in any case much more the exception than the rule. The soap factories were simple affairs, with no more than five to eight workers along with the owner's family. Especially in the nineteenth century, workers were paid in kind, and in turn they became peddlers, exchanging soap for grain and other agricultural products.

All the towns likewise incorporated one or more commercial olive oil presses, and most at least one flour mill. In fact, they must have appeared startlingly alike in some ways, the economic and social life inevitably revolving around these mills. But the towns did have different economic specialties. For Nablus it was olives; Hebron produced grapes, along with blown glassware, waterbags, and candies.[12]

Nothing added more to a town's distinctiveness than its rulers—leading families continuing to dominate well into the twentieth century, even after the British established formal governing procedures and sponsored elections for mayors and municipal councils. In most instances, these were the same families of ayan and ulama—landowners and religious notables—who had directed life in the region since the early nineteenth century. Some went as far back as the seventeenth, when chiefs who had fled or were banished from other regions of the Ottoman Empire established themselves as strongmen, at the expense of the decaying central authority.

The rugged mountain landscape provided just the sort of insularity these men wanted. But this insularity was not the same as simple distance from Istanbul, many developing complex, ambiguous relations with the Ottoman authorities. At the same time that they built autonomous bailiwicks, they served as government representatives or tax-farmers. Their aim was to garner the benefits of office without the burdens of supervision and control from above, and while their stature in many ways derived from their connection to the empire, much of their energy went into subverting its efforts to rule effectively. Once the Porte instituted the Tanzimat reforms starting in 1832, official positions became all the more important to the strongmen, if for no other reason than to protect their domains from the onslaught of the new legislation.

These strongmen were responsible to a great extent for molding an assortment of villages scattered over difficult terrain into a unified distinctive region. Through their tax collection and—even more important—their protection, ruling families developed networks of lieutenants, and with them fear, influence, and occasionally even loyalty. While the coastal plain was even more dangerous than the hills, hill families did insure their positions through the ability to organize violence, their members serving as small militias and enforcers. In difficult circumstances, strongmen recruited workers, tenants, and small farmers from their villages for pitched battles. Most villagers owned an antiquated firearm.

Various coalitions among the leading families formed and re-formed, occasionally based on the two, old Fertile Crescent factions mentioned in chapter 1—Qays and Yaman—occasionally on another real or imagined division. Although protracted standoffs came to define particular towns or regions, they were never totally free of the Ottoman factor: Officials reacted when violence spread, linking dis-parate feuds into fighting alliances. While most battles were entirely local—against other families or invading Bedouin—at times they involved the Ottoman authorities themselves, supporting a gov-ernment drive or (occasionally) even opposing the designs of a gov-ernor.

As in military matters, so in politics. Even at its most tenuous, the Ottoman rule would leave its mark on local affairs. Ottoman of-ficials played on the bickering of the families, who toyed in turn with the officials by manipulating their administrative jealousies. Some families drew their strength from their Turkish ties, others from fending off the Porte's representatives. The eight or nine fami-lies dominating the Nablus region at the start of the nineteenth century struggled with one another to gain lucrative tax-farming concessions from the Ottoman authorities.

The Tuqans, emerging as leaders of one of the poles of power, were the first clan in the region to ally themselves with the Ottoman authorities, using their connections as the foundation for far-reach-ing controls.[13] Hafiz Tuqan began as a tax collector in the village of Tubas and used the capital from that position to build a lucrative soap factory in Nablus. His family came to dominate the Yaman fac-tion, while the Abd al-Hadis (who like the Tuqans transferred their power from the countryside to the town) grew in importance in the Qays coalition.[14] (The Abd al-Hadis, it may be remembered, were the notables who allied themselves with the Egyptian administration at the outbreak of the 1834 revolt.)

On a daily basis, the families were at the center of affairs in towns such as Nablus. Senior Ottoman officials did influence the struggle over which would rise to the top, but their impact generally came from behind the scene. Once a year, governors would come to the mountains to garner taxes, and to confirm a respectful, if uneasy, relationship with the central government.

To some extent, during much of the eighteenth century, a struggle for control of Nablus between the Ottoman governors in Damascus and those in Sidon offered the leading families a way to neutralize the designs of both. Even after Ahmad Pasha became the Damascus governor and began his drive for Palestinian unity, the Nablus region bent less to his will than any other part of the country. After his death in 1804, no governor of Sidon or Damascus was able to gain full control over the families despite several major military drives into the mountains. While in the 1820s Abdallah Pasha had achieved some semblance of unity, the relationship between central and local authorities changed dramatically only starting in late 1831, when Muhammad Ali began the drive through Palestine that would sweep away the Ottoman administration altogether.[15] Historian Shimon Shamir goes so far as to say that the Egyptian conquest signified "the first application to Palestine of the concept of *territorial state*. . . . This was the inception of the [country's] modern history."[16]

In the first few years of the occupation, it must have come as a surprise to the leading families of Nablus that Egyptian rule would undercut their hard-earned autonomy. At first, all but the Tuqans saw Muhammad Ali's son, Ibrahim, as a governor who would enhance their strength. They were to be disillusioned. Only the Abd al-Hadis, the Tuqans' great rivals, managed to maintain close relations with him, and even they found their status transformed from independent chiefs to links on the Egyptian administrative chain.[17]

As has been suggested in chapter 1, Muhammad Ali's conception of administration was not of a distant sovereign negotiating from weakness with powerful local lords but of a streamlined bureaucracy penetrating into the domain's remotest parts. Both the ayan and the ulama found the new bureaucracy cutting into their prerogatives and discretionary power: a rude shock to be repeated several decades later with the Ottoman introduction of the Tanzimat reforms.

The ayan's eventual response to this government penetration—adapting the tools necessary for the new conditions—was reflected both in starting to supply their sons with formal education[18] and in a move from their villages into the towns (in a number of important cases, the establishment of family branches in one or several towns). A clear sign that the old order was dead and new skills were needed came in the 1850s, when after a period of remarkably destructive interfamilial fighting, the Turks attacked. A direct assault on the Abd al-Hadis led to their complete submission.[19] The ayan learned their lesson. Even as they became more attentive to Ottoman rule, they increased the gap between themselves and the mass of the population, the peasantry.

Among the ways in which the new skills were useful was in coping with one of the Turkish pillars of the Tanzimat: their effort to transform town government. Traditionally, such government reflected power struggles among a number of forces, only one of which was the official Ottoman authority. In fact, there were cases where local forces so overwhelmed a town's Ottoman official that he was forced to leave altogether, as occurred in uprisings in Jerusalem in 1808 and 1826.

Turkish soldiers had gone to the trouble of attacking the Abd al-Hadis and other strongmen in Palestine's remote mountains precisely with the goal of preventing such chaos. The Tanzimat legislation was the logical follow-up to the expeditions, establishing the basis for permanent central control of the empire's cities. And indeed, the notables had to adapt to the bureaucracy's expansion and the establishment of town councils—the main tools of the empire's control. But as with so much of the Tanzimat, actual administration of the reforms led to a quite different effect on town and village life from what had been intended. In effect, the Ottoman tools became springboards for local forces to reassert a new sort of limited autonomy. Since the ayan and the ulama—the town's religious elite—dominated membership on the councils, they were able to shape control of municipal life.

While Ibrahim Pasha had used similar public bodies as a vehicle to appoint deputies representing various social classes and religious groups, the Ottomans found their councils overwhelmed by prominent Muslim civic and religious notables. And while Ibrahim had given the councils little more than an advisory role, the Ottomans turned over almost all areas of administration, finance, and judicial affairs, thus "reinforc[ing] their political position and . . . further[ing] their private interests."[20] They did so, as well, by taking a variety of posts in the expanded bureaucracy and using legal machinations to acquire large tracts of land.

Even with the new roles of the ayan, they could not prevent the decline of the hilly regions relative to the coastal towns. Although the rebellion against Ibrahim in 1834 had been centered in Nablus,[21] improvement in the coast's status was already evident. The population of Jaffa had nearly doubled by the 1840s (to close to five thousand people). Construction—including a protective sea wall—was evident everywhere, and exports had begun the slow climb that would gain momentum in the decades leading up to World War I.[22]

The complex relationship between Palestinian coastal city and inland town was mirrored in some other Mediterranean societies, most notably in Lebanon.[23] It involved a growing economic dependency on the port, a widening disparity in ways of life and standards of living, and, at the same time, increasing elements of social integration between town and country. In Arab Palestine, this process would be reversed only with the catastrophe of 1948.[24]

The Rise of the Coastal Towns

By the 1930s, the two most important Palestinian coastal cities, Jaffa and Haifa, had come to represent the new face of Palestinian Arab society, taking second place to Jerusalem only in the realms of politics and religion. Jaffa had the country's largest Arab concentration, with Haifa not far behind, comprising—in a country that was still largely centered on the village—more than 10 percent of the Arab population between them. Muslim and Christian merchants, bankers, displaced villagers, wage laborers, shantytown dwellers, orchard owners, all met in a cosmopolitanism distantly evoking the urban centers of classical Arab history.

Jaffa's fortunes, which began to shift in the mid-nineteenth century as trade and agriculture revived on the coast, also benefited from Jerusalem's growth and from Western fascination with the holy city. It was the port with the most direct link to Jerusalem, and in 1869 the Ottomans built a new connecting road, due at least partly to the pressure of uncomfortable Western travellers. With the pacification of the countryside by Ottoman forces in the 1850s, Jaffa also began to develop its own outer area of agricultural villages, much like Nablus and the other inland towns. The surrounding land was fertile and had plenty of water.

These villages soon developed different traits from their inland counterparts. Rising world grain prices in the 1860s and 1870s forced landowners near the port to plant cash rather than subsistence crops, or to find tenants who would. The value of exports out of Jaffa—mostly grains, and later oranges—skyrocketed, more than doubling on average between the late 1850s and the early 1880s.[25] Coastal landowners and tenants resembled the hill farmers less and less as they became tied to a network of relations with merchants, shippers, bankers, insurance agents, and others seeing to it that crops made their way to Great Britain and other countries.

Of course, changes in the coastal towns matched those of the outlying villages, as they became the basic link between Palestinian growers and European consumers. Haifa, for example, which was little more than a fishing village (less than 1,000 people; some estimates are as low as 200) in 1830, had a population of 3000 by 1850. As the century progressed so did the pace of change; by the Great War, the population was over 20,000. Not weighed down by the conservative presence of old-time notable families, Haifa became a center of regional innovation. It absorbed a new railroad and port, a growing Jewish and entrepreneurial Christian population, a Templar and Carmelite presence along with that of a considerable foreign community, and a large network of schools (many of them Catholic). Germany, in particular, singled out Haifa as a conduit for its influence in the Holy Land.[26]

In Jaffa, the original 25 walled acres grew to nearly 400, and the population of 5,000 (already double what it had been at the beginning of the nineteenth century) swelled to 50,000. Construction continued to change Jaffa's face as well. From 1880 to 1910, merchants opened 400 shops, corresponding to a heavy investment in private housing, public buildings, mosques, and commercial buildings.[27]

While there was considerable growth in the city's industry and tourism (especially Christian pilgrims from the West), the engine of change was trade. Growth rates for both exports and imports were extraordinary, surpassing even as dynamic a port as Beirut, and outperforming Tripoli and Sidon combined.[28] Wheat, sesame, and soap were all shipped through Jaffa, and oranges became the premier export. It was, in fact, oranges that made Jaffa the second largest Palestinian city by the end of the Ottoman period.[29] Imports, largely from Great Britain, fueled the growing consumption in the city and supplied both Jaffa and Jerusalem with construction material. A new train line linked the two cities in the 1890s. Surprisingly, this enormous growth in trade occurred in a hopelessly inadequate harbor. Not only was it unable to accommodate the late nineteenth century's new steamships with direct loading facilities, but it proved downright dangerous to smaller ships. When, in the mandate period, the British finally undertook port modernization, they ended up bypassing Jaffa altogether and investing in Haifa.

Such economic dynamism was not limited to these two cities. From 1880 until 1918, the population of the six leading Palestinian cities jumped by an average of 3 percent a year. Shipping dramatically expanded everywhere, once steamships took up regular routes to the eastern Mediterranean at the century's close, solidifying the value of the ports. The changes helped establish those Palestinians acting as middlemen between the European consumers and local growers, and those reorganizing agriculture to provide produce for export.

The new economic networks were making it increasingly difficult for independent peasants in the plain and in the valleys. Around Jaffa, people with sufficient resources, including bankers, were grabbing fertile land, either to invest in profitable citrus groves or in the hope that others would later pay exorbitant prices for the land. The groves did pay handsome dividends, but only after a considerable investment and waiting period—a system of credit excluding the smallholder and enhancing the position of the ayan. Wealthy land-owners used both their own capital and depended on the willingness of European merchants to offer an advance purchase of crops.

The boom in the coastal plain, along with a worrisome population rise in the inland areas, precipitated a flood of migration towards the area bounded by Jaffa and Haifa: by 1922, 200,000 people—almost a quarter of the country—lived there. The definitive eclipse of the inland towns took place under the mandate. In an outdoing of the earlier, already dramatic increases, between 1922 and 1944 (the dates of Britain's first census and last population survey), the Arab population of Jaffa and Haifa nearly tripled, at a time when the entire Arab population was nearly doubling. The figure for Haifa was 342 percent.

For the Arab migrant, the coastal cities offered a few glimpses of familiar social terrain. For instance, as in the world they came from, notable families often dominated municipal and social affairs—the Saids, Dajanis, and Bitars of Jaffa; the Shukris, Tahas, Khayats, Khalils, and Mahadis of Haifa (although the Haifa families certainly lacked the clout of those in Jaffa). But on the whole, the new urban setting—the sights and sounds, the people on the street—must have seemed much more distant than the thirty or forty miles actually involved.

For one, the typical Muslim migrant was much more likely to meet Christian Arabs, who by the end of the mandate were overwhelmingly urban (80 percent as opposed to only 27 percent of the Muslims). They also could not miss the growing numbers of Christian missionaries and travellers. Certainly, encounters between Muslims and Christians had never been unknown. In the early years of the twentieth century, the proportion of Christians among the Arab population hovered around a formidable 15 percent—a figure that was to drop gradually in subsequent years because of the higher Muslim rate of natural increase. Nevertheless, the homogeneity of many villages, and even of towns, such as Hebron, meant that until Muslims began to encounter the new social mix on the coast, many would never have come face to face with a Christian.

Both Jaffa and Haifa also had growing Jewish populations during the mandate. Even before the 1920s, Arabs in the coastal towns (and in Jerusalem, where there was actually a Jewish majority) could not avoid the Zionist project. Jaffa had already spawned a Jewish twin, Tel-Aviv, founded by Zionists on the sand dunes north of Jaffa in 1909. At the start of the nineteenth century, there had been no Jews at all in Jaffa; by the Great War, the figure was 30 percent of the city's population of fifty thousand. Trying to establish a new way of life, the Zionists concentrated their new institutions in Jaffa before the war, avoiding the more parochial setting of Jerusalem. And in Haifa, despite the Arab population's tripling between 1922 and 1944, its total in the city dropped from 74 to 48 percent as Jewish immigrants became more and more prominent.

All sorts of other Europeans could be found on the streets of Jaffa and Haifa, especially after the war—British security forces and civil servants, merchants, pilgrims, members of Christian religious orders. Migrants quickly found signs, as well, of a new Arab society: labor unions, banks, women's associations, and political parties, along with pharmacists, clinics, and a display of photographers' studios, restaurants, and shops full of Western goods. There were now private cars on the narrow roads, and British and Jewish influence—as well as Egypt's cultural impact—led to a sudden interest in scouting, camping, and sports. Jaffa, for example, fielded a well known soccer team of the Governmental Secondary Boys' School.

These institutional artifacts symbolized the lure—and decadence—of the coastal towns. First was the bicycle epitomizing a new, lower middle-class mobility and freedom. Second was the coffee house. In the inland towns, men would spend endless hours playing backgammon and smoking the nargila; here in the urban coffee houses they would both listen endlessly to oriental music (recorded or broadcast) and gain a much greater sense of contact with national and international events. Third was the cinema: a great seduction to new city dwellers, which was looked on with intense suspicion by those staying in the hills.[30]

Located in the city's central square, the modern city hall helped to furnish a sense of coherence and distinctive character to the big, open, and heterogeneous city, slicing into the old, strict controls that had governed people's daily lives. (The destruction of Jaffa's central municipal building, the Grand Sarai, by Jews early in the 1948 War thus held a special poignancy for the city's Arabs.) The new city dwellers often most intensely experienced the unsettling diversity of their social setting in the workplace. By the mandate's end half of Palestine's Arabs were already working outside agriculture, with about a third of the urban population being active in industry, craft workshops, and construction. Sizeable proportions also worked in commerce and transportation; others were bureaucrats and professionals or provided services. Coping with an utterly new milieu, they were engaged in a typical struggle to define who were the insiders, representing various levels of intimacy and trust, and the outsiders, to be feared or opposed. In the process, they collectively began to define the new social boundaries of Arab society.

In no circumstances is the reshaping of social demarcations an easy process; in the Palestine of the mandate period, it was further complicated by the fits and starts of the economy emerging along the coast. The cities plunged into depression in the late 1920s, and even more severely for a brief period beginning in 1935, forcing many recent migrants back to their home villages. In any event, throughout the mandate, a number of groups competed, none with terribly much success, in helping Arab workers cope with urban life.

At first, the Zionists tried to organize the Arabs. Undoubtedly, their motivations were mixed. Unionized Arab workers could demand higher wages, reducing some of the intense competition their Jewish counterparts faced from cheap Arab labor. On another level, some Zionists—both idealists and pragmatists—struggled to transcend the issue of wage competition, to influence the very identities of Muslim and Christian urban Arabs.

The Zionists discussed three ideas for furthering the organization effort: Jewish and Arab unions, separate unions under a central agency, parallel organizations. Only the Union of Railway, Post and Telegraph Workers, established in 1924, included both Jewish and Arab members, and that was a rather short-lived experiment. Nevertheless, despite a chorus of protests to the effect that the movement was spending too much time on the Arab question, some Zionists hoped that mixed unions would help break down divisions pitting Arabs and Jews against each other.[31]

For the most part, Zionist labor union activity was exclusive. The Histadrut—the General Federation of Jewish Workers in Palestine—remained totally Jewish for nearly four decades after its founding in 1920.[32] At the same time, its leaders preached the "liberation of the Arab working people from the bondage of its oppressors and exploiters, the ruling landowners and property holders."[33] On a practical level, this policy was largely limited to supporting Arab unions engaged in strikes, and to an Arabic-language newspaper it published for a while. Its major achievement was the creation of the Palestine Labor League: an agency encompassing both the Histadrut and Arab unions. The League did eventually manage to draw about a thousand Arab workers into its ranks.

But these were limited successes, most coming earlier rather than later in the mandate. Counteracting Jewish pressure on Arabs to leave the Union of Railway, Post and Telegraph Workers and the exclusion of Arabs from the Histadrut itself reinforced a two-tiered Palestinian labor system evident to this very day: Jewish enterprises could draw on the skills of higher paid Jewish workers and, when needed, recruit poorly paid Arab labor for low-skill tasks.[34]

Many of these enterprises also faced pressure to participate in the social transformation of the Jews into productive workers by hiring only Jewish workers. In the absence of success, and with growing Arab hostility, the Zionists paid increasingly more attention to bolstering their own defenses. And in a vicious cycle, their growing disinterest, and the miserable Arab pay and working conditions, nourished a propensity of urban Arab workers to define themselves in opposition to both Jewish workers and Jews in general.

With the Zionists thus preoccupied, in the 1930s, with forging a Jewish working class, notable Arab families took their own initiatives. For example, Rashid al-Haj Ibrahim established a workmen's organization in Haifa, but like other such efforts, it did not prove lasting. The notables' primary tool to gain leverage among the Arab population had always been the judicious distribution of patronage, particularly to peasant tenants and hired farm workers;[35] it turned out much more difficult to provide adequate rewards to migrants in the tumultuous city economy. Many of the new jobs were in Jewish enterprises and, especially after the outbreak of World War II, in British projects and agencies—both clearly outside the control of the ayan. They also faced difficulties simply because they lacked the same commitment to rising wages held by the people they wished to organize.

Communists, intellectuals, and those drawn directly from the workers' ranks also took up the challenge of labor organization.[36] The Palestine Arab Workers Society, founded in 1925, was the first such far-reaching, independent effort. Splinters of that group formed afterwards, along with similar societies, but none succeeded in meeting the wide-ranging needs of the new Arab working class, such as higher wages, job security, and protection against inflation.

There was some progress: A labor-movement congress was held in Haifa in 1930,[37] and in both the 30s and 40s unions managed to call some strikes, occasionally together with the Histadrut, whose ideology and tactics influenced Arab labor leaders even when there was no direct collaboration. In the latter decade, union leaders also negotiated a linkage of workers' wages to the cost-of-living index. A large influx of villagers into the city, taking advantage of work opportunities among the mobilized British armed forces, led to several new attempts at labor organization,[38] especially on the part of the Communist party early in World War II.

Most of these labor activities did not amount to much. Significant union-organizing progress only started to take place in the 1940s, with the flood of Arab workers entering into wage-paying, nonagricultural labor, and with the creation by the British of a responsive Labor Department.[39] In 1945, the seventeen branches of the Palestine Arab Workers Society had fifteen thousand paid members. But even the rise of union organizing during the Second World War left the Arabs with one-tenth the Jewish union membership, for a population more than twice as large. Perhaps the labor scene was still too chaotic for any organization to do better. The working class remained a jumble: wage earners with permanent jobs, itinerant laborers (often with one foot still in the village), daily laborers assigned work by labor contractors, workers in small family workshops, employees of large enterprises, the unemployed. For most, the coast's prosperity contrasted sharply with their own economic desperation and need to scratch out a living.

A Growing Palestinian Identity

The uncertainty and tenuousness of life in the city became evident—the rapid swings of the economic cycle, the consignment of Arab labor to low-skill and Jewish labor to more lucrative, high-skill positions, the precariousness of the wartime hiring rise, the predicament of workers bouncing from job to job. As one researcher describes it, it was "to a great extent . . . the continuing vitality of the village community that enabled the migrants to resist the splintering . . . and the new urban associations helped in turn to preserve the village foundations of the migrants' identity."[40] Villages became important in a practical sense, too. Resources flowed back and forth in divided clans or families. Relatives often gave emigrants a stake to establish themselves in the city, and they in turn, sent wages back to the village. Some migrants returned at every opportunity to land and houses they had managed to retain, and to their families.[41] Those who ended up moving permanently built social circles, even whole neighborhoods, around old village or regional ties. Even permanent migrants could use their home villages for security and refuge, as in the politically and economically difficult days of the late 1930s, when many Palestinians abandoned the city, at least temporarily.

Rather than engendering a comprehensive framework for ongoing urban interactions, and a viable reproduction of what had been before, the urban migrant's attachment to the village was to a mythic good life. The myth portrayed an idyllic past—centered on the primacy of family and personal ties of loyalty, rather than the impersonal relations of the marketplace or even the contrived ties created in social clubs—that continues suffusing Palestinian culture today.[42] For the most part, this ideal was a feeble lure back to the village. Facing the test of the reduced economic opportunities immediately following World War II, former villagers proved reluctant to return to their roots. They could think of the villages as home, and

use old village ties as an anchor, but in the end recreating the old social boundaries proved impossible in a labyrinth of new social experience.

What other structure might have worked is unclear. The period
of rapid urban growth may simply have been too short for Arab
workers to resolve the issues of trust and loyalty, and more research
may be needed to determine what sorts of groups did manage to coalesce. Many migrants existed on the city's margins scratching for
work and living in rundown, temporary shacks. Both official and
unofficial accounts of the time documented their experiences much
less fully than those of more educated and successful urban Arabs.
In any event, it seems that even poorer migrants had contact with
supportive institutions catering primarily to them: religious organizations, political parties, youth groups, women's associations,
sports clubs, and so forth. Although the number of such Jewish
and Zionist institutions appearing on the scene dwarfed their Arab
counterparts, to some extent hiding them from history, they were
crucially important in at least one respect: the drawing of Palestinian Arabs into a single social grouping, set off both from non-Arabs
in the country and from other Arabs outside the country.

One of the most important institutions was the set of organizations known as the Muslim-Christian Associations, first emerging
in Jerusalem and Jaffa following the Great War and then spreading
to other municipalities. The existence of the organizations was in itself remarkable, because religious tensions between Christians and
Muslims had reached new heights in the decade leading up to the
war. Religious identity was of course a cornerstone of Arab society,
and this was reinforced by British mandate policy, which, in a number of cases, treated the different religions as distinct administrative
entities. Countless incidents put one group on guard against the
other; the outnumbered Christians, in particular, viewed many of
the Islamic overtones in the growing national movement with ap-
prehension. In 1931, for example, they expressed uneasiness over an
international Muslim conference held in Jerusalem.

Despite this internal Arab division, in the 1920s the Muslim-
Christian Associations succeeded in drawing established members
of leading Muslim and Christian urban families into the struggle

against Zionism. The road to such concerted action—examined in the following chapter—was a rocky one, political factionalism plaguing the Palestinians throughout the mandate. It would be a mistake to overstate the depth of national sentiment at its start. In Jaffa, a Muslim-Christian unity emerging with the Associations in 1918 crumbled in 1923 over the issue of the city's acceptance of electrical power from a Jewish-built power plant. The rift was patched up by the decade's end, at least partly because of violent anti-Zionist outbreaks in 1929. In Haifa, where relations between Christians and Muslims had deteriorated badly towards the end of the Ottoman period, a single association did not coalesce until the 1930s; nevertheless, cooperative anti-Zionist Muslim and Christian activity began earlier.

The Muslim-Christian Associations did not initially define themselves as part of an explicitly political organization.[43] But as with other similar groups—such as the Literary Club and the Arab Club, which both catered to younger members of the leading urban families—their central principles were Palestinism and anti-Zionism. Palestinism meant the assertion of Palestine as a common homeland at a time when political boundaries were new and still quite uncertain. After a brief flirtation with the notion of their incorporation into Syria, the new organizations began to proclaim emphatically the existence of a distinct Arab people in Palestine. Even when some adopted pan-Arab programs, they took care to distinguish Palestine's Arabs from those outside the country and, of course, from the Jews and British within.

The scores of Palestinian clubs and other social groups that followed the Muslim-Christian Associations after they began to disintegrate in the 1930s reasserted this fundamental distinction. While their members most often came from the more privileged sectors of Arab urban society, the clubs hammered out social demarcations—a Palestinian profile—that also became increasingly appealing to ordinary workers facing the quandaries of urban life. Eventually, Palestinian villagers, caught between the Zionist/ayan land squeeze and their own rapidly growing numbers, would begin to adopt the same profile.

The upper classes, the workers, and the fellaheen came to the new

Palestinian demarcation through very different routes. Each group faced a unique set of challenges, humiliations, and opportunities in the rapidly changing politics and economics of the interwar years, resulting in a different sense of social boundaries regarding Jews, the British, and other Arabs. The Arab Revolt of 1936–39 brought these differences to the surface, erupting at times in mutual recriminations and even violence among the Palestinians.[44] Such factionalism, however, should not obscure the extent to which a social boundary encompassing all Palestinian Arabs began to establish itself in a few hectic decades following World War I.

One of the key elements in the emerging Palestinian profile was the growing intelligentsia. Although neither universal nor compulsory, education generally became more available during the mandate, with one-third of school-age children in schools by 1946.[45] Members of the ayan and other upper-class families were increasingly sending their sons to universities in Cairo, Beirut, and sometimes Europe.[46] They represented a remarkable increase over the handful of Arabs, mostly Greek Orthodox and Catholic, who had attended universities in the nineteenth century.

Both Jews and Arabs established institutions of higher learning in this period. The Jews founded the Hebrew University; the Arabs built the Arab College, also in Jerusalem, whose curriculum emphasized Western liberal and classical themes as well as the Islamic-Arab tradition.[47] In the late nineteenth century, a university education had served as an entrée into the newly reformed Ottoman administration. A similar mobility for men existed during the mandate, as young Palestinians became magistrates, commissioners, and other upper- and middle-level figures in the British administration. Additional avenues were opening, especially in the free professions (lawyers, teachers). This intelligentsia would play a central role in furnishing the shared aesthetic and intellectual material for a concrete expression of the new Palestinism—a cultural glue helping to keep the society together. The principal medium was the printing press, producing textbooks, fiction, history, political tracts, translations, and more. But no form seemed to capture the Palestinian imagination more than poetry.

Palestinian authors—including, for the first time, women writers—worked under the long shadow of the late nineteenth-century Arab cultural renaissance, along with that cast by contemporary Egyptian culture. Twentieth century Palestinian writers have long suffered from comparison to the creative pre–World War I generation,[48] and to Egyptian writers whose magazines, books, and newspapers inundated Palestine. Nevertheless, the mandate-period Palestinian output was considerable. In 1945, Dr. Ishaq Musa al-Husseini surveyed the publications of local authors.[49] He found fifty-four Arabic titles, published between 1919 and 1932 (several more appeared in English and French); from 1933 to 1944, the figure almost tripled.

The contemporary historian Tarif Khalidi speaks of the passionate intensity characterizing Palestinian writing of the mandate years—the intelligentsia's reaction to social violence suffered in face of the British and the Zionists: "Little wonder, then, that this frantic commitment to the cause of Palestine should produce a pervasive cultural tone of anguish and disgust, of resentment, resistance, rebellion and death."[50] Poets fused deep feelings for the soil—they must have resonated among urban migrants now holding an idealized image of the village—to the conception of a people, collectively besieged and victimized within their social boundaries. Note the words of one poet:

> This is Palestine; transformed into a sacred shrine,
> So kiss its soil, wet with dew.[51]

Another Palestinian wrote the following before his death in the Arab Revolt,

> Do not think I weep from fear,
> My tears are for my country
> and for a bunch of unfledged kids
> Hungry at home
> Without their father[52]

For many intellectuals, commitment spilled into direct political activity, some becoming prominent figures in the struggle against

Jewish settlement and British rule. As one critic puts it, "When the
. . . society arrives at historical crossroads as it gropes for a viable
definition of its identity and destination, the serious writer can ill
afford to remain uninvolved and merely watch history march by
from his aesthetic ivory tower."[53] The power of their pens, however,
may have been more considerable than that of such activity. The
British Royal Commission reported in 1937, "No less than fourteen
Arabic newspapers are published in Palestine and in almost every
village there is someone who reads from the papers to gatherings of
those villagers who are illiterate"[54] (illiteracy among peasants and
workers remained over 90 percent).

The notion of a cohesive society with a unique history, its members facing common threats and a shared future, gained ever-
broader acceptance among Palestine's Arabs in the interwar years.
The disproportionately influential urban intellectuals eventually
succeeded in drawing a broad section of the population into active
opposition to the Zionists and the British. But beyond that emerging consensus, the question of what that society should ultimately
be like produced much less agreement, with stiff resistance building
in parts of the country to the idea of the city as a model for the
future.

Opposition surfaced on the part of several groups, both from inland areas such as Nablus and from cities on the coast where many
found the new economy disorienting and alienating. Such opposition tended to focus on the port towns—seen as an insidious representation of the dislocation brought by the West—on the open
embrace of European manners and dress, and on an all-too-eager
acceptance of by-products of the Enlightenment and the Western
scientific revolution.

This amounted to a rejection of everything British, including the
technological basis for the new society; in some ways, it was unex-
ceptional. In Central and Eastern Europe and elsewhere, similar sentiments were being articulated in the 1930s. A socio-economic system based on mass production and international high finance was
in deep crisis, and those whose ways of life had been hurt at its rise
seized the opportunity to pierce the arrogance of its carriers. To be
sure, Palestinian industry paled in comparison to that of Manches-

ter—or even Prague or Warsaw.[55] Jewish factories overshadowed the Arab efforts—which in 1942-43 accounted for about 13.5 percent of total production.

Along with many other impediments—insufficient investment capital, a largely unskilled work force, the inconsistency of the world economy—the Arabs faced a British rule largely inhospitable to industrialization efforts. While European states built formidable tariff walls during the 1930s, the League of Nations required the Palestinian mandate government not to discriminate in its trading policy against any other state. At the same time, the British denied Palestine those preferences it granted to its colonies in access to markets. Such disadvantages made industrial growth all the more difficult in a period in which a formidable depression shook manufacturing worldwide.

As might be expected, Arab manufacturing in Palestine was still in an embryonic state following World War II. The dislocations of peasants stemming from the Arab Revolt of 1936-39, the huge employment increases in services and public works during the war, and Zionist purchase of land, all acted to create a labor force now pried loose from agriculture, but still largely incapable of absorption into the nascent Arab industrial sector. In 1939, the government had estimated the number of workers in this sector at less than 5,000 out of an Arab wage labor force eventually peaking at 100,000.

Nevertheless, for all its limitations, the growth in industry represented a radical departure for Arab society and a message to Palestinians about the future. Arab manufacturers were drawing increasing numbers of workers into their enterprises, adding to the pull of British and Jewish economic activity on the coast and the push of the land squeeze and rising population in the rural areas. Although most of the Arab factories were still little more than workshops, employing 5 or 6 workers including the owner and his family, there were already by the mid-1940s about 30-35 Arab industries engaging over 30 workers each.[56] And while many industries manufactured longstanding products (that is, soap and olive oil), others now manufactured cement, shoes, matches, metals, processed food, tobacco products, textiles, and so on.[57] This signaled a fundamental challenge to a society resting on the foundations of an independent smallholding peasantry and of a Muslim notable class drawing its strength from its relationship to tenant farmers.

The terms of the challenge were also established by rapidly expanding trade and commerce. From the 1930s to the 1940s, there was a 25 percent increase in the numbers of Arabs engaged in these activities, which like industry were not entirely new to Palestinian Arab society. For centuries, peasants had supplemented their incomes in hard times by peddling crafts and farm surpluses; some moved permanently to the cities to try full-time door-to-door selling or work in the bazaars. By 1900, such commerce was as indigenous as the desert sands.

Once the Great War ended, Palestinian commerce picked up its pace, thanks in no small part to a spate of improvements in roads, ports, and communications facilities in the twenty years before the war. During the mandate, Arab-owned shops proliferated much faster than the population grew. In 12 Arab towns, the number of bakeries increased sixfold from 1921 to 1939 (to nearly one thousand), and the pace was even faster in Jerusalem and Jaffa.

The mandate's new material culture was reflected in the appearance of ice cream and motorized transportation, with gas stations and garages to follow. There was a fivefold increase in cafés, and cutting hair became an established profession. Arab co-ops made their debut in the 1940s. Imports began to suffuse daily life; in a sharp reversal from what had been the norm, the Arab sector built a chronic deficit in its trade balance despite the continuing growth of citrus exports. Almost all segments of the Arab population joined the cash economy to some degree, even the peasants selling about 20 percent of their gross production.[58] By the 1940s, there were specialized marketing companies buying peasant produce directly in the villages for eventual consumption in the cities. But the impact of the capitalist economy was felt differently by various groups and regions. While some prospered in the new environment, embracing the new technology and ways of life, others suffered badly or found themselves marginalized by the changes.

Businesses demanding considerable investment also became essential parts of the Palestinian Arab economy. The large commercial enterprises tended to be in the hands of notable families or well-to-do Christians, many of them specializing in foreign trade.[59] While early in the mandate, they specialized in grains, citrus products, and food, starting in the 1930s, some began to compete with Jewish traders in merchandise such as textiles and machinery.[60]

For both poorer city dwellers and the fellaheen, the new commercial culture was problematic, offering glimpses of a life that could not be shared, bringing dislocation and distress along with ice-cream. Large farmers and exporters, for example, warmly greeted a free-trade agreement with Syria opening major markets for Palestinian watermelon and soap. But peasants found the pact opening Palestine to a flood of Syrian grain, depressing the price of their major product. There was an astounding 200 percent increase in national income from 1939 to 1943[61]—but the cash economy benefited Arab social groups very selectively.

This fact is particularly striking in regard to Palestinian Arab transactions with Jews. By the mid-1940s, Jewish buyers had acquired nearly 10 percent of the cultivable land, including nearly half of the most fertile tracts used for citrus groves. At the same time that these land purchases displaced tenant farmers and menaced smallholders by driving up land prices, Arabs who did the selling gained handsomely—a source of ongoing tension among Arabs. There were other important transactions of this nature. Repeated efforts by Zionist leaders to convince the Jews of the Yishuv to develop an autarchic economy accomplished much less than the Arab enforcement of economic separation between the two communities, starting in the general strike of 1936. Before that, 8 to 10 percent of Arab agricultural produce—vegetables, eggs, meat, and olives (between one-quarter and one-third of all cash crops)—was purchased by Jews, mostly from merchants ensconced comfortably in the country's developing commercial orbit.[62] In this manner, many considered powerful Arabs in the coastal cities as little more than collaborators with the Jews and the British injecting a hated new commercialism into the country. That unfortunate association placed great obstacles in the path of a common vision, grounded as it was in the experience of the dominant classes.

The world of finance, like that of commerce, was not new to twentieth century Palestinian society. Traditionally, Arab notables and other large landholders would tide peasants over with loans, a credit system surviving into the 1940s.[63] The new economy demanded more complex financial arrangements, seen to by a number of banks established with foreign capital, both before and after the Great War. Crédit Lyonnais set up the first bank in 1892, like others that followed, building branches in Jaffa and Jerusalem. The most prominent of the foreign banks was Barclays, already having branches in Acre, Haifa, Jaffa, Jerusalem, Nazareth, and Tel-Aviv in 1930.

In the late 1920s, Palestinian Arabs tried but failed to establish their own bank with the help of Egyptian capital. In 1930, a Palestinian returning from America, Abd al-Hamid Shuman, started up a small family-owned bank in Jerusalem. Shuman's enterprise, the Arab Bank, achieved remarkable success in a very short time—even by capturing a relatively small proportion of Arab savings, its deposits rocketed.[64] Its branches first opened in Jaffa and Haifa and extended later to Amman, Damascus, Beirut, Baghdad, and Cairo.

The Arab Bank served as a key element in the Palestinian nationalist vision, offering a basis for long-term investment and economic growth, the hope of confronting the Zionists on an equal economic footing—and even of engaging in economic warfare against them. In the rural areas, it could provide fellaheen the credit needed to avoid taking local loans at usurious rates, which had too often led to repossession of their land and, ultimately, sale of their plots to the Jews.

Seeking to cast a net far beyond the urban centers of Palestine's new economy, the new finance was thus bound to challenge existing rural patterns: the personal loan and the power relations tied up with it. In 1933, the Arab Bank spun off a subsidiary, the Arab Agricultural Bank;[65] in the 1940s—now as the independent Bank of the Arab Nation—about half its loans in fact went into agriculture. But as has been the case with so many banks established to help peasants in this century, credit found its way to the wealthiest peasants and the large landowners, rather than to their more needy compatriots. And even among people with money, new Arab-controlled financial institutions elicited as much ambivalence as the vision they symbolized: Together, the two banks attracted only 10–12 percent of total Palestinian Arab deposits, the great majority of depositors continuing to use the more familiar foreign banks. (Many others still preferred to stash their assets under the mattress.)

For those profiting from the industrial, commercial, and financial sectors of this emerging civic society, their enterprises involved an adoption of "Jewish techniques" to stave off Jewish domination.[66] But to those whose power was challenged by the reach of the new economy or who found themselves battered by it—the groups represented by Nablus rather than Jaffa—life in the coastal cities seemed less to produce weapons against Zionism than collusion with it.

In Arabic, the term *shabab* refers to young men. At times, it also refers to members of a gang. In the context of the tension between Nablus and Jaffa, it took on another meaning: those set adrift from their moorings, no longer bound by family or clan loyalties and responsibilities. For Palestinians most threatened by the new social life along the coast, the shabab represented a road not to be taken.

The condemnation of city life by those still in the hilly region, however, masked the underlying similarities between the urban shabab and the fellaheen. The shabab came mostly from families of transplanted peasants, both groups now finding themselves made marginal by changes wrought by prosperous, established Arabs. There clearly existed a potential to forge an alliance of the urban underclass with that still in the rural, eastern part of the country, and a figure who was to become a Palestinian legend, Sheikh Izz al-Din al-Qassam, managed to do so, thereby challenging the more westernized Arabs' vision of the future.

Qassam, a graduate of the Islamic al-Azhar University in Cairo, became a preacher in a Haifa mosque after he fled his native Syria in the wake of the French occupation of the country and their defeat of the Arab nationalist regime there. He began gathering supporters from nearby rural areas and the most marginal groups in the city, later using a religious court position to do the same in the northern villages. His aim was an eventual uprising of these slum-dwellers and fellaheen.

One researcher has noted that "Al-Qassam's Weltanschauung was wholly rooted in Islam, which constituted the nexus of all his ideas and deeds. [He sought to defend] Islam internally against infidelity and heresy; and politically against external enemies, namely the West—with which Islam was in political and ideological conflict—and the Zionist enterprise."[67] But, as was occurring in Egypt, Islam was now conceived in much more directly political and national terms in the face of European domination. His was not a lone voice in Palestine in building a national movement on an Islamic foundation: Along with the disintegration of the Muslim-Christian Associations, the 1930s witnessed the rise of the Young Men's Muslim Associations and other Islamic groupings.

According to contemporary memories, the sheikh would preach with a gun or sword in hand, urging "the bootblack to exchange his shoebrush for a revolver and to shoot the Englishmen rather than polish their shoes."[68]

In the early 1930s, his preaching built the foundation for a formidable underground organization with the ominous name of the Black Hand, which he used as a springboard for a call to *jihad* and attacks against Jewish settlers.[69] By 1935, he had recruited several hundred followers, in cells of no more than five men each. Other clandestine groups organized by Muslim leaders appeared on the scene, fueling Islamic-nationalist militancy in the shantytowns of Acre, the Jerusalem-Ramallah area, and elsewhere. The Green Hand—consisting of veterans of the 1929 outbreak—directed its actions mostly against the Jews and had more resemblance to bandit gangs of the past. A group led by Abd al-Qadir al-Husseini, the son of Musa Kazim al-Husseini, mostly relied on Boy Scout commanders, members of his clan, and followers from the Jerusalem area, but did not get beyond a very preliminary conspiratorial stage. (His major role came in the 1936 revolt and in 1948.) Spurned by the mainstream nationalist leadership, Qassam and a small armed band of followers (estimates run from fifteen to fifty men) set out from Haifa in the fall of 1935 only months before the outbreak of the Arab Revolt using a village near the inland town of Jenin as a base to spark and lead a peasant uprising. The British almost immediately stifled this initiative, but Qassam's death at their hands occasioned a tremendous outcry at his funeral.

Qassam's organization and revolt were too brief and surreptitious to draw definitive conclusions about what they mirrored in Palestinian society. It is in any event clear that while he struck a responsive chord among Palestine's urban underclass and the fellaheen, not only members of the secular Palestinian intelligentsia, but established Muslim leaders, found his anti-Western message extremely unsettling.[70] It conflicted with principles prevalent in Haifa and the other coastal cities, based on an appropriation of Western and Zionist techniques, if only to resist domination. These leaders, too, often had a stake in calm relations with the British—either because of British salaries to them and their relatives or because of other sorts of British patronage.

This was not the only discordant note among the Arabs. One member of a leading Nablus family, Awni Abd al-Hadi, made a strong claim before the British Royal Commission of 1937 that there was "too much [Arab] industry in the country." His cries and those of Qassam and other Muslim militants were not mere echoes from a fading past. They represented living sentiments that, while strengthening the opposition to the Zionists and the British, also signalled a tension within the Arabs' new social boundaries that would weaken the national movement and lead, in the Arab Revolt, to mutual recriminations and violence.

3

JERUSALEM:

NOTABLES AND NATIONALISM

Jerusalem of Dreams and Reality

Jerusalem . . . When I mention the name, I see the white Jerusalem of summer when the brightness is blinding and the nearly cruel light is thrown at you from every stone. I see Jerusalem in the rays of twilight—neither orange nor pink nor purple—which embrace the surrounding mountains and caress its houses of stone . . . It is hard to describe Jerusalem in words. One has got to feel it. Jerusalem is the source. It is the heart and the spirit, the soul and the oversoul.[1]

These words could have come from Christian, Muslim, or Jew, Jerusalem being, like the Holy Land itself, so deeply evocative to all three faiths. "There is no other city like it," exclaims F. E. Peters, "so solemn yet modest, so attractive and so intelligible; so earthly, even provincial, and yet somehow spiritual and universal."[2] Of course, the city's significance does not really lie in the hues of its twilight or in its solemnity and modesty, but in something much closer to the

heart of cultural myth. Note the reaction of François René Chateaubriand, catching his first glimpse of Jerusalem in 1806:

> Suddenly, at the end of this plain I saw a line of gothic walls flanked
> with square towers and behind them rose the peaks of buildings. At
> the foot of this wall appeared a camp of Turkish cavalry, in all its ori-
> ental splendor. The guide cried out: "Al-Quds! The Holy City," and
> went off at a great gallop. . . . If I were to live a thousand years, never
> would I forget this wilderness which still seems to breathe with the
> grandeur of Jehovah and the terrors of death.[3]

More than half a century later, Mark Twain echoed this shudder
of recognition: "I think there was no individual in the party whose
brain was not teeming with thoughts and images and memories in-
voked by the grand history of the venerable city that lay before
us. . . . The thoughts Jerusalem suggests are full of poetry, sublimity,
and more than all, dignity."[4]

The mythology associated with Jerusalem has not been static, the
constant struggle among Muslim, Jewish, and Christian factions for
control of the city adding layers of meaning to existing beliefs. After
the Crusaders' conquest, for example, both oblique references to al-
Quds in the Quran (it is explicitly mentioned neither there nor in
the Pentateuch) and the accounts linking Muhammad's personal
experiences to the city took on growing importance. The result was
its increased sanctification in the Islamic tradition, despite some resistance on the grounds that Mecca's special place was being diminished.

The stream of foreign Christian pilgrims and growing Jewish
presence during the nineteenth and early twentieth centuries similarly renewed the Muslim attachment to Jerusalem (as did the Israeli conquest of the walled part of the city in 1967), the struggle
with the Jews, in particular, validating and strengthening its religious importance. At the same time, the political and administrative changes after the revolt of 1834 gave Jerusalem's ruling elites an
opportunity to place their own stamp on the entire country. This
chapter recounts the rise of these elites, including their central role

in the new nationalist politics after World War I—played out, ironically, quite apart from the two most important centers of Palestinian Arab society, Jaffa and Nablus.

In the early 1800s, the real Jerusalem—as opposed to the Jerusalem of dreams—was small and rundown,[5] covering less than a square kilometer and housing fewer than ten thousand people. With a clear Arab majority, Muslims outnumbering Christians and another 20–25 percent being Jews, it was less a unified city than an accumulation of fairly autonomous sections—the Muslim, Christian, Armenian, and Jewish quarters and the Mughrabi neighborhood. Jerusalem, as a Jewish chronicler somewhat exaggeratedly put it, was "strictly confined within her high, dark wall, like a lizard in his skin," then adding that "a kind of perpetual mourning enveloped the city."[6]

Donations from abroad sustained most of Jerusalem's Jews and foreign Christians. While some people supported themselves through agriculture, farming did not hold much promise in a city more suited to being a fortress than a center for landlords and peasants. Embraced by treacherous ravines, it was largely cut off from the surrounding plains. A handful of residents worked in the usual small-scale industries (soap, textiles, leather, pottery, and Christian souvenirs),[7] but the city had always basically failed to establish a sound productive foundation for its population.

The plan of the city went back to Roman times, with its main streets modelled on the great thoroughfares of antiquity, the Cardo and the Decumanus. Much of the rest was a maze of winding alleys and courtyards. Even many of the churches, mosques, and synagogues that today seem a timeless part of the landscape were not built until the middle and end of the nineteenth century. The dominant structures, in addition to the Dome of the Rock and the nearby al-Aqsa mosque, were the Church of the Holy Sepulchre and the Armenian monastery and church.

Beyond their splendor stood dilapidated houses, muddy and unlit streets, and the filth of animal and human waste. As in antiquity, with no natural water sources of its own, the city faced chronic shortages for drinking and bathing—the Ottoman authorities paid little care to the development of water pools and aqueducts, and private cisterns often remained in disrepair. Cholera and plague descended on the city regularly through the middle of the century.

In dispirited yet melodramatic fashion, one traveller offered a typical view of Al-Quds' plight in the 1830s:

> The glory of Jerusalem has indeed departed. From her ancient high estate, as the splendid metropolis of the Jewish commonwealth and of the whole Christian world, the beloved of nations and the "joy of the whole earth," she has sunk into the neglected capital of a petty Turkish province; and where of old many hundreds of thousands thronged her streets and temple, we now find a population of scarcely as many single thousands dwelling sparsely within her walls. The cup of wrath and desolation from the Almighty has been poured out upon her to the dregs; and she sits sad and solitary in darkness and in the dust.[8]

Later, in *The Innocents Abroad,* Mark Twain would voice related sentiments: "Lepers, cripples, the blind, and the idiotic, assail you on every hand, and they know but one word of but one language apparently—the eternal 'bucksheesh'. . . . Jerusalem is mournful, and dreary, and lifeless. I would not desire to live here."[9]

Despite Twain's own gloominess, Jerusalem was in fact already in the midst of a remarkable renascence, its population growing to over seventy thousand by the Great War's outbreak. Both Arabs and Jews began to move outside the walls starting in the 1850s, with new neighborhoods forming in all directions. The city's total acreage increased nearly sixfold in the seventy-five years prior to the war, the great majority of the growth being outside the walls. Construction of churches, mosques, synagogues, and private houses was continuous, and land prices rose astronomically.[10] The number of water cisterns increased with the population, new roads connected the city to neighboring towns, and the railroad linked it to Jaffa and the sea. The nineteenth century thus saw an end to Jerusalem's three-hundred year stagnation. By the time the city was made ready for the visit of the German Kaiser in 1898, it had been transformed into the largest and politically most important urban region in Palestine—a far cry from the town Napoleon had bypassed, in favor of more strategic places such as Acre, only a century before.

The Metamorphosis of Jerusalem, 1830–1914

As elsewhere in Palestine, the fortunes of Jerusalem, and especially of its Christian and Jewish inhabitants, began to improve dramatically during the time of the Egyptian occupation. The Egyptian innovations, however, were not greeted with universal approval—for instance, by the hill-area rebels who, in the Nablus-centered revolt of 1834, poured into Jerusalem and briefly took control with the embrace of the city's Muslims. But, unlike previous Muslim uprisings (1808 and 1826), which succeeded in both driving out the city's ruler and preserving the autonomy of the powerful families, that of 1834 was a last hurrah for those who imagined they could bypass outside governing authorities.

The Egyptian ouster of the rebels signalled not only immediate, bloody retribution by Ibrahim Pasha but a long-term shift in the city's delicate social and political balance. Christians (and Jews to a lesser extent) benefited as Ibrahim opened economic activities to them, especially in commerce, as well as positions in his administration. Even with the return of Ottoman rule in 1840, the Jews and Christians kept their enhanced status, despite Muslim murmuring about revenge against them for their complicity with the Egyptians. While the number of Jerusalem's Muslims grew slowly and steadily—from about 4,000 in 1800 to approximately 12,000 prior to World War I—the Christian population exploded from less than 3,000 to almost 15,000.[11]

Even more remarkable was the rise in Jewish population, from slightly over 2,000 in 1800 to approximately half the city's 22,000 in 1870, a decade before any Zionist immigration began. By the start of the Great War, Jews constituted more than 45,000 of the 70,000 total. In the course of the century, then, Muslims slipped from being the largest of the three groups to the smallest.

Jerusalem continued to be altered after the Sublime Porte's

ouster of the Egyptians, through a slow elevation of its role as an administrative unit within the overall scheme of the empire. To be sure, other towns had not been on a truly equal footing with Jerusalem before the reforms. As a religious seat, it was furnished with a religious officer, the Hanafi Qadi, who could appoint deputies for the other towns and collect taxes for the ulama of Jerusalem.[12] Even so, its status was that of a backwater provincial center in the early nineteenth century. From this low point, it was gradually transformed into the ruling center for almost all of southern and central Palestine. In 1887, it became the capital of a sanjak, or district, no longer accountable to a provincial governor, such as the one in Damascus, but reporting directly to Istanbul.[13] About three-quarters of present-day Palestinians are descended from those who lived in the Jerusalem sanjak. Jerusalem's autonomous status, notes Abu-Manneh, "was of tremendous importance for the emergence of Palestine" later, after the end of Ottoman rule, and helped provide the grounding for a separate Palestinian identity.[14]

Towards the century's close, the new administrative links enabled the empire to increase both the absolute sum of revenues garnered from the district and the percentage of total income transferred to Istanbul. With Jerusalem as their base, the Ottomans extended their control outwards to towns such as Gaza, Hebron, Jaffa, and even Beersheba (where the Bedouin were now suppressed) and, not as successfully, to villages surrounding these towns. In the city itself, while it would have taken considerable time to be felt, by 1860 a more centralized rule modeled on Ibrahim Pasha's administration had undermined the autonomous power of Jerusalem's Muslim notable clans. Most consisted of ten to fifteen families: the most prominent names were Alami, Dajani, Husseini, and Khalidi.

Another important source of this shift in power was the rapid expansion of Jerusalem's foreign communities. As a local center, Jerusalem had few natural endowments to recommend it above other towns, and if it came to be fawned upon in the nineteenth century, it was because of a renewed international interest,[15] grounded to a considerable degree in its significance for Christians. A number of foreign powers developed a significant religious presence in the city, none greater than the Russian Orthodox Church. This followed Russia's defeat in the Crimean War and the inauguration of a regular shipping route between Odessa and Jaffa. The construction of the Russian compound, starting in 1860, at the site of a majestic viewpoint outside the walls, was an aptly symbolic gesture. In any case, from 1839 to 1854, almost every Western state, including the United States, opened a consulate there. And powerful consuls such as Britain's James Finn (his books *Byways in Palestine* and *Stirring Times* provide some of the most vivid portraits of the milieu) further cut into the influence and prerogatives of the notables. Several leading families continued to hold impressive agricultural estates in the country; some owned whole villages. But as a group Jerusalem's ayan were removed from Palestine's farming heartland and thus lacked both the strong ties to agriculture and the sorts of patron-client ties undergirding their power in towns such as Nablus.

Jerusalem's great Muslim families also lacked the commercial wealth of their counterparts in Jaffa and Haifa. They needed something else to maintain their preeminence, which turned out to be offices, both political and religious. The Ottoman creation of the municipality of Jerusalem as a corporate legal body probably occurred in 1863. The body's new institutions, such as the civil service and municipal council and those, a bit later, of the enhanced sanjak, became a haven and training ground for the families, even as the demography and character of the city changed around them. By the 1880s, the council had numerous responsibilities, from maintaining roads and water systems—along with an edict that banned tossing waste in public areas, this helped relieve the city's stench—to establishing fire and police departments, tax collection, and the like. Offices to supervise these activities proliferated. Control of key political, administrative, and religious posts both in the city proper and in the wider sanjak came to be the foundation of the notables' authority, eventually not only in Jerusalem but throughout Palestine. Younger, less established family members would often start their careers elsewhere in the Ottoman bureaucracy.

Manning such posts was not entirely new to Jerusalem's ayan and ulama. Prominent figures had long administered both the public *waqfs* (religious trusts) and private family funds. Their social prestige had put them in line to run the waqfs, which in turn, had reinforced their social and political power.[16] Some administrative positions related to the waqfs were hereditary; others could be sold, but often only to another clan member.

The ayan thus inconspicuously slipped from mostly religious offices at the beginning of the nineteenth century to largely political-administrative offices at its end, although some connection with the religious sphere continued to be important for maintaining status. The highest levels of the sanjak were occupied by Turkish Ottoman officials, but increasing numbers of Jerusalem Arabs, particularly Muslims, were making their way into the lower ranks. There were even some examples of Muslims being appointed at a level just below the governor himself, exercising authority in one part of the district or another. An Alami, for example, served as inspector of harvests for Gaza, Jaffa, and Beersheba. "These and similar cases," Haim Gerber comments, "are particularly interesting because they enabled the Jerusalem élite to lay the foundation for their later influence in other parts of the country."[17] The Ottomans at times engaged in what today would be called a privatization of government. Their method was to auction the performance of public functions, from collecting taxes to providing interurban mail service, to well placed, private contractors.

The Jerusalem ayan thus moved along a number of different routes in attempting to maintain their preeminence in the face of Ottoman power and demographic reality. As the proportion of Muslims in the city shrank, they kept a solid majority on the council. In the last council prior to the demise of Ottoman rule, six of the ten members were Muslim, two Christian, and two Jewish.[18] Part of the reason for this involved a series of Ottoman precedents resulting in Muslim overrepresentation. At the same time, the Muslims attached great importance to the new field of public service, in contrast to the Jews and Christians, whose interests rarely extended beyond their own communal groups.[19]

Prominent members of the Khalidi and Alami clans, for example, held council positions, as did those of the Nashashibis, one of the ranking clans at the end of the nineteenth century. The Ottomans guarded against any single family gaining too much power, the governor in one instance stripping the Husseinis of key posts in favor of the Khalidis, with this in mind. Nevertheless, on the whole, the notables were remarkably well-behaved subjects, especially given their proclivity to autonomy and rebellion before the 1850s. As indicated, the Jerusalem leadership's social power was grounded in neither agriculture nor commerce—thus denying it the sort of leverage available to the families of Nablus and Jaffa—but in offices created by the Ottomans, desperately attempting to shore up a dying empire.

For the notables, such a power base naturally meant severe dependency on the empire, and few Muslims opposed it until the twentieth century. The first hints of such opposition came several years after the 1908 Young Turk revolt, when anti-Ottoman feelings stirred outside Anatolia, followed by more serious resistance in World War I. Until then, the notables had shared sentiments of both Ottomanism and, in the Palestinian arena, noblesse oblige. In this regard, the very nature of Jerusalem supplied valuable experience for their later rise to the top of the Palestinian Arab nationalist struggle. It is important to recall that while in many parts of the country the Sunni Muslim majority and assorted Christian minorities had little to do with one another (towns such as Hebron barely had a Christian population), the situation in Jerusalem, as in other mixed cities, was very different. It was nearly impossible for Muslim notables holding local offices not to deal regularly with Christian Arabs, and this interaction became a cornerstone of Arab organization for confronting the British and Zionists after World War I. Similarly, the renewed foreign interest in Jerusalem and the influx of Jews offered important exposure to those who would end up ruling there for most of the next century.

At the same time, Jerusalem's new importance strengthened a sense in the ayan that they were somehow at the center of things, and this would have an important effect on their own sense of destiny in the embryonic nationalist movement. In the nineteenth century (later, as well) it also added fuel to the conflicts among the important families, wrangling for Ottoman administrative offices and for the governor's support.

Occasionally, such conflicts were intimately linked to others that were more longstanding. That between the Khalidis and the Husseinis, for example, incorporated the enduring feud between the leagues of Qays and Yaman, which had divided Arabs for centuries. The Khalidis had benefited handsomely from the Ottoman reforms at the expense of the Husseinis,[20] and in the resulting fray the Khalidis drew on the Qays as allies, while the Husseinis lined up supporters among the Yamani. As the Palestinian sociologist Salim Tamari notes, these alignments "cut across the village/city dichotomies and often united [even] Christian and Muslim families."[21] In this manner, prominent clans succeeded in fortifying wide-ranging networks as they reached out for allied families in other towns and, of course, for the non-Jerusalem branches of their own clans.

Some key notables from outside Jerusalem—the Tuqan, Abd al-Hadi, and Nimr families of Nablus, for instance—steadfastly resisted the vortex drawing them to side with one or another of the prominent Jerusalem clans. In fact, at times they sought the same sort of countrywide prominence that the Jerusalem ayan were so assiduously cultivating for themselves. But these efforts did not get very far. By the twentieth century, the clans of Nablus and other local centers could serve as little more than adjuncts, and sometimes counterpoints, to the struggles in the holy city.

British Conquest and Zionist Ambitions: The Notables' Response

The events during and immediately after the Great War confronted the Jerusalem notables with the need for many changes, none more difficult to contemplate, perhaps, than the shift from Muslim to Christian rule. Before the war, the Muslims of Palestine, like all Muslims in the Ottoman Empire, had tacitly accepted their place within an Islamic domain.[22] The war now cut them off from their political and religious center—it left them somewhat adrift in a sea of religious and ethnic groups, all vying with one another within the new British military administration.

For the notables, the administration was a mixed blessing. On the one hand, it now unified Palestine into a separate country, with Jerusalem its official center. On the other hand, the new reign brought with it, alarmingly, the Balfour Declaration of 1917:

> His Majesty's Government view with favour the establishment in Palestine of a national home for the Jewish people, and will use their best endeavours to facilitate the achievement of this object, it being clearly understood that nothing shall be done which might prejudice the civil and religious rights of existing non-Jewish communities in Palestine, or the rights and political status enjoyed by Jews in any other country.[23]

Today, roughly eighty-five years after the Declaration's issue, there is a tendency to paint Arab-Jewish relations in Palestine before World War I in idyllic colors. Palestinian author Sami Hadawi reminisces about his Jerusalem boyhood:

> I remember how we children looked forward to the yearly community festivities. In the Spring, Moslem, Christian and Jew alike took part in the Moslem Pilgrimage to the tomb of the prophet Moses and watched with delight and excitement the dance of the *dervishes* to the chanting of heroic songs and banner waving. In the summer, Moslem, Christian and Jew flocked to the Valley to take part in the Jewish celebrations at the tomb of Sadik Shameon. And in the Autumn Moslem, Christian and Jew alike picnicked in the gardens around the tomb of the Holy Virgin Mary, near Gethsemane, where the Christian community spent a day and a night rejoicing. . . . Ours was indeed a Holy City, a city of peace, love and brotherhood, where the stranger could find shelter, the pilgrim loving care and the faithful salvation.[24]

Unfortunately, in the Holy City as elsewhere, things were often much less harmonious. The Balfour Declaration was not the Jerusalem leadership's first unwelcome exposure to Zionism, which in any case had only intensified the already unsettling nineteenth century demographic changes there. In light of the city's continuing Jewish population surge in the 1880s—the period of the first wave of Zionist immigration—the Ottoman governor had made some passes at enforcing restrictions on Jewish settlement. Approximately two years after his removal in 1889, leading Jerusalem Muslims and perhaps some Christians made their first protest on June 24, 1891, by sending a telegram to the Porte asking that Russian Jews be prohibited from entering or buying land in Palestine.[25]

While at least at the political level, the ayan's anti-Zionism did not crystallize before the twentieth century, anxiety was surfacing time and again. Merchants, in particular, expressed the fear to Jerusalem officials that Jewish immigration would lead to their eventual control of Palestine's business economy. Following the century's turn, newspapers in the city increasingly covered the Zionist movement, often critically. Here as elsewhere, the Arab response was not always condemnation. Landowners appeared less troubled than merchants since they were already watching the price of land climb rapidly. And a report written in 1899 indicated that Jerusalem notables were prepared for Jewish settlement, provided that the Jews became Ottoman citizens and did not retain their foreign status. Still, after the Young Turk Revolution of 1908, which fanned local patriotism and incipient nationalism throughout the Empire, the notables came to view Zionism less through the lens of their Ottoman loyalties and more through that of the threat it posed to the Arabs of Palestine. In fact, for the first time they now began to refer to themselves as Palestinians.[26] While some worked to come to an agreement with the Zionists before the war, others called for action, including violence, against the Jews. A number of Palestinian Christians, among them several publishers, joined in the call for a new anti-Zionist consciousness that would blur the line between Christians and Muslims.

While his overall position and influence is of some question, Negib Azouri was one such intellectual, propounding "Arabism," a vague sort of Arab nationalism, as the answer to the Zionist challenge. In a pamphlet written in Paris in 1905, he prophesied darkly about the future of Jews and Arabs:

> Two important phenomena, of the same nature but opposed, are emerging at this moment in Asiatic Turkey. They are the awakening of the Arab nation and the latent effort of the Jews to reconstitute on a very large scale the ancient kingdom of Israel. These two movements are destined to confront each other continuously, until one prevails over the other. The final outcome of this struggle, between two peoples that represent two contradictory principles, may shape the destiny of the whole world.[27]

With such a political and ideological backdrop, the period after the issuing of the Balfour Declaration clearly did not find the Jerusalem notables totally unprepared for a struggle against Zionism. But they were stunned at how British intervention now became the framework for prolonged rule and for large-scale Jewish colonization of the land. They, along with other Arabs, believed that their abandonment of the Ottomans in World War I, along with Sharif Hussein's important revolt against the Ottomans during the war, should have led the British to grant them Arab independence. The revolt, in fact, had come in the wake of an agreement with the British—the McMahon-Hussein correspondence—promising independence for the Arab lands and re-establishment of an Arab Caliphate. It was ambiguous whether or not Palestine was included. Now they faced the replacement of the Ottomans by the British—and by the French in nearby Syria—and by the near-euphoria of the Jews, standing ready to govern the country along with the British. In the wake of General Allenby's conquest of Palestine in 1917 and 1918, some of the fears of the ayan began to be realized, and European rule to seem a transparent ruse to hand the country over to the Zionists. Jews argued for the official use of Hebrew either instead or alongside of Arabic, an allocation of seats on municipal councils, official recognition from the British of their special status and autonomy; and they spoke openly of creating a Jewish majority.

A chain of events served to fan these fears.[28] On the first anniversary of the Balfour Declaration, the Zionist Commission, headed by Chaim Weizmann, organized a parade. As the first public show of Jewish political power, it unsettled the Arab leaders, who petitioned Great Britain to "put a stop to the Zionists' cry." A month later, in December, 1918, a conference representing all the Jews in Palestine drew up national demands to present to the Paris Peace Conference. The result was a "Plan for the Provisional Government of Palestine," which urged largely Zionist and European control of the country, with a fairly inconsequential role for the Arabs. Zionist leaders now spoke of forming a future commonwealth—a bolder notion than that of a national home but not quite as bold as of a state, which was suggested by a number of participants, including David Ben-Gurion.

Following their conference, the Zionists met in Paris with Faysal, son of Sharif Hussein (now king of the Hejaz), and himself a key figure in the revolt against the Ottomans. Faysal, as we shall see momentarily, was to play a critical, if indirect role in the development of Palestinian nationalism; he had already met twice and established a cordial relationship with Weizmann. On January 4, 1919 in Paris, he and the Zionists signed an agreement appearing to support both the Jews' aspirations and his hopes of establishing an independent Arab regime, although the exact political disposition of Palestine was left unclear. Faysal, declaring that Palestine should have its own guaranteed status as a Jewish enclave, was unequivocal in his acceptance of unfettered Jewish immigration as long as he received his promised independent state. Shortly after the agreement was signed, the Zionists offered the Arabs a free zone at Haifa and a joint Arab-Jewish free port on the Gulf of Aqaba. The agreement, we will see, did not last long,[29] but when word of Faysal's concessions leaked out, the Palestinian notables were horrified, declaring they would "not agree to be sacrificed on the altar of independence."[30]

The dealings of European statesmen also heightened their alarm, as the Great Powers held conferences and dispatched commissions to dispose of the Great War's spoils. In July, 1920, the San Remo Conference took up the division of the territories of the Middle

East, and several months later the British replaced their military administration in Palestine with a civilian one. The first British high
commissioner was Herbert Samuel, whose origins led other Jews
(before their later disillusionment) to dub him their "king," and an
offspring of the Davidic dynasty. Within months of his appointment, leading Palestinian Arabs complained loudly about Samuel's
partiality to the Zionists.

Next in the array of international conferences was the Cairo Conference of 1921, in which Winston Churchill, the new British colonial secretary, laid out his ambitions for Britain's role in the Arab
world for the next generation.[31] In 1922, the League of Nations ratified the mandate for Palestine. Coming into effect in the fall of 1923
with the Balfour Declaration as the preamble to its principal articles, it called for the establishment of a Jewish Agency to assist in
the governance of the country.

The new, assertive Jewish nationalism, with its strong British backing and its colonization of the land, played out against this backdrop of international conferences and decisions, spurred the Jerusalem ayan to begin building an Arab national movement. This
symbiosis parallels the struggles among emerging nationalism in
the Balkans and other territories ruled by the Austro-Hungarian
and Ottoman empires during the period leading up to World War I.

Within months of the British conquest of Palestine in 1917, Palestinian notables already began organizing their response to what
they—and some British officials—called "Zionist provocations." The
response was not limited to creating new organizations such as the
Muslim-Christian Associations. The first blows in a communal war
lasting until this day occurred when Arabs attacked two northern
settlements, Tel Hai and Metullah, in February, 1920, providing the
Jews in Palestine with their first martyrs and military heroes. Less
than two months later (April 4–5, 1920), more violence was unleashed at the annual Muslim Nabi Musa pilgrimage to the traditional grave of Moses. Until then mainly a local popular religious
meeting, this now became a first, nationwide Arab-Palestinian festi-

val, and would be celebrated as such in years to come. Musa Kazim al-Husseini, the mayor of Jerusalem, invited delegates from many parts of Palestine to the celebration. Haj Amin al-Husseini, the eventual leader of the nationalist movement, returned from Damascus, where he worked in support of Faysal's short-lived kingdom. He made his first public appearance with a speech arguing that the British eventually would support Faysal's rule over Palestine. The agitated mob attacked the old Jewish quarter of Jerusalem; five Jews were killed and about 200 wounded, and when the British intervened, four Arabs killed and 32 wounded were added to the toll.[32]

More agitation followed, the source of all these outbreaks lying in political events that would have great influence both on who would emerge as the leading Arab notables and on the ultimate course of Palestinian history. At the center of the events stood Faysal—for whom the 1919 peace conference and the agreement with the Zionists were but sideshows to the establishment of an independent Arab state in Syria, with him as monarch. By "Syria," Faysal meant today's Syria and Lebanon, as well as Transjordan and Palestine (often referred to as Greater Syria). For politically aware Palestinian Arabs, the notion of such a state seemed the best route to escape both Zionism and British rule.

In January, 1919, the leading Palestinian families organized a Palestinian Arab conference under the auspices of the Jaffa and Jerusalem Muslim-Christian Associations. Despite some sentiment for Palestinian autonomy under British guidance, including that of Jerusalem's Arif al-Dajani, who presided over the proceedings, a consensus emerged to support Faysal's ambition. Zionism was strongly rejected; Palestine would remain an Arab country as part of a federated, Faysal-led Syria.[33] With Faysal's army in place in Damascus since October, 1918, and the British at first well disposed towards his desires, the prospects seemed reasonable for his emergence as a truly independent Arab ruler, capable of staving off the Zionists.

A coterie of young Arabs full of passionate intensity from towns all across the Fertile Crescent clustered around Faysal. Many—such as Iraq's Nuri al-Said—would become the outstanding Arab nationalists of their generation. Those from Jerusalem established a Damascus offshoot of their Arab Club to collaborate with Faysal's political organization, while a contingent from Nablus—a strong center of Pan-Arab and Islamic sentiments, and always a competitor to Jerusalem's dominance—both set up their own club and participated actively in Faysal's army.[34] For his part, Faysal courted the support of the Palestinians. He disowned his earlier agreement with the Zionists by supporting anti-Zionist resolutions at the Second General Syrian Congress, which elected him king in March, 1920 (the first Congress had taken place the previous July). But he had his differences with the Palestinians as well, courting the British for protection of his fragile political organization and vulnerable army. One view of the British held by politically active Palestinians was as little more than a Zionist vanguard.

Events in Damascus spilled over into agitation in Palestine. Intimations of Arab rebellion were in the air.[35] The Muslim-Christian Associations organized demonstrations supporting the Syrian scheme and lambasting Zionism (one slogan was "Palestine is our land and the Jews are our dogs"). In ways reminiscent of the great families' mobilization of peasants in the revolt of 1834, the notable-dominated Associations managed to organize events involving a broad cross-section of Arab society, but now including a much larger Arab urban sector. In the major towns, both upper and lower classes sent the strident message that the country's future was as part of a unified Arab state, with its center in Damascus; the Jews' presence would be at the sufferance of the Arabs. It was in this context that violence erupted in 1920.

Neither the stridency nor the violence ended up being of much help to Faysal or his Palestinian allies—whose support was in any case a mixed blessing. The Palestinian-dominated Arab Club turned out to be the most coherent of supporting organizations, but it also maneuvered him, unavoidably, into positions he probably would have preferred not to take, including a declaration of independence and renunciation of cooperation with the French. In response to the violent turn of events, and from fear of the French advantages in a unified Syria, the British swept in to thwart the Palestinian aspirations. They arrested some young notables and sent others—including Haj Amin al-Husseini—into flight from the country. They also removed Musa Kazim al-Husseini from the mayoralty of Jerusalem and installed a member of the family that was emerging as the major rival to the Husseinis, the Nashashibis—thus opening wider an already serious fissure among the Jerusalem notables. It was at this point that Britain confirmed its hold over Palestine at the San Remo Conference and established its civilian government under Samuel.

Faysal's fall in July—the French took military action to force him into exile—simply underscored what had already become obvious since April to many Palestinian political activists: the idea of Palestine within a Syrian Arab state was dead. The framework upon which many of the notables had pinned their hopes for building fervent loyalties and a workable political identity collapsed into rubble. At the very moment that the country's future was being decided by the British and other Europeans, the Palestinians had no workable vision of the future.

In the 1930s, George Antonius, the most famous Palestinian historian and an active nationalist, reflected on events that, with time's passage, the Palestinians have largely forgotten:

> What with the decisions of the San Remo conference, the occupation of the whole of Syria by the French, the consolidation of British control in Iraq on a basis which denied even the outward forms of self-government, and emergence of a policy of intensive Zionist development in Palestine, the year 1920 has an evil name in Arab annals.[36]

Long before 1948 came to be identified with the term, it was 1920, as Antonius noted, that was spoken of as *Am al-nakba,* the year of catastrophe or disaster. The disaster hit both individuals and the community. With Faysal's ouster from Syria, Palestinians in Damascus scattered in various directions. A number ended up in Transjordan, some being assimilated permanently into that newly formed country's politics. Others, including the founders of the Istiqlal Party, which would later play an important role in Palestine, faced eventual expulsion. Those who fled to Palestine itself, native Palestinians as well as Syrians who would settle there, found a dispirited Arab leadership in Jerusalem and Jaffa.

For the community as a whole, the new permanent boundaries in the Middle East after World War I demanded a reorientation. Some sects, such as the Druze of northern Palestine, Lebanon, and Syria, found their communities fractured. The European powers now demanded passports and visas for previously uncontrolled routes. Different currencies, customs regulations, and trade patterns forced financial and commercial restructuring in Palestine.

The new boundaries also made the Palestinians' political prospects seem bleak, particularly when compared to neighboring countries. In Iraq, the British gave Faysal a sort of booby prize, establishing him as the soon-to-be king. They did much the same for Faysal's brother, Abdallah, by setting off part of the territory planned for the Palestine mandate to be a separate country, Transjordan, under his rule. This must have been especially galling, since many of the non-Bedouin Arabs of Transjordan were practically indistinguishable from those of Palestine, branches of Palestinian families having moved east of the Jordan River in the nineteenth century to become, in effect, the country's settled population. And Syria, as well, had its political future laid out by the French, with prospects for the independent states of Syria and Lebanon.

Responding to the fiasco of Faysal's Syrian defeat, the notables began developing alternative goals and strategies. At the Third Arab Congress, held in Haifa in December, 1920, they revived the plan that Arif al-Dajani and some of the other older notables had proposed in the country-wide conference of January, 1919. That plan had stressed the autonomy of the Palestinian Arabs and their unique circumstances. The emphasis on the continuity with the congresses held in Damascus in July 1919 and March 1920 contained considerable irony, since the concept of a Greater Syria, so confidently trumpeted there, was here nowhere in evidence. Musa Kazim al-Husseini commented, "Now, after the recent events in Damascus, we have to effect a complete change in our plans here. Southern Syria no longer exists. We must defend Palestine."[37]

The new strategy focused exclusively on Palestine, and that meant addressing the threat that Zionism posed, which became a conceptual linchpin. The platform drawn up in Haifa would change little over the next few decades. It contained the following six elements: the first public recognition of Palestine, as it would be constituted by the mandate, as a distinct political entity for the people living there (although there was no legitimacy afforded to the mandate itself); a total rejection of any political or moral right of the Jews over Palestine; a declaration of unity among the Palestinian Arabs to supersede any other loyalties, such as those to religion, region, and clan; a call to the new administration to halt any transfers of Arab or state lands to Jewish control; the demand to close Palestine to further Jewish immigration; a call to recognize the Arab Executive Committee (popularly known simply as the Arab Executive) as the legitimate representative of the population before the British authorities (with a status similar to that defined for the Jewish Agency).[38] And in the fall of 1921, a Muslim-Christian delegation to London submitted an even more elaborate set of conditions, including the demand for the creation of a "national government" whose parliament would be democratically elected by the country's Muslims, Christians, and Jews, and a call for the nullification of the promise for a Jewish national home.[39]

More comprehensive Arab unity (as in the plan for a Greater Syria) was never totally done away with in the Palestinian Arabs' political agenda. In one guise or another, it reappeared throughout the 1920s and in subsequent decades, although in each of its incarnations Palestinians were often frustrated that other Arabs did not share their degree of alarm about Zionist ambitions. Still, Faysal's fall marked an important turning point. From then until 1948, Palestinian politics and loyalties were determined by the idea of an independent Palestine.

The Face of the New Palestinian Leadership

The notion of Palestinian autonomy, however vague as the basis for either a long-term vision or a concrete strategy, did signal several important trends in the social composition of the emerging politi-

cal leadership. In the first place, as Britain's administrative headquarters, emerging from the shadow of Damascus and a Greater
Syria, Jerusalem moved strongly centerstage on questions of Palestine's political future. It was not an accident that at the Haifa congress, both the head and deputy head of the Arab Executive elected
by the country-wide delegates of the Muslim-Christian Associations, Musa Kazim al-Husseini and Arif al-Dajani, were members of
prominent Jerusalem families. Husseini, who had nurtured his ca-
reer in the Ottoman bureaucracy, had been mayor of Jerusalem until he was unceremoniously removed by the British following the violence in the city that spring; Dajani was president of the Jerusalem
Muslim-Christian Association.

A marked ambivalence toward the British on the part of this Jerusalem-dominated leadership emerged at the congress. After all, Jerusalem's debt to British rule was clear enough. At the same time,
there was no escaping Britain's role in promoting Zionism through
the Balfour Declaration. The delegates trod delicately through that
problem, calling for British rule, but in a context very different from
what the Declaration implied: that of Palestinian Arab self-rule under British aegis. The immediate task was to rid Great Britain of the
ignorance, as Jamal al-Husseini put it, that had brought it to its
pro-Zionist stance and created the framework for the Jews' quicken-
ing colonization of the land.

There was one other reason for the present leadership choosing
a British connection. Husseini domination of the congress resulted
in near-total exclusion of the Nashashibi clan, which recently had
moved to become the Husseini's most significant rival for power in
Jerusalem. The Nashashibis had been closer to the French than the
British in the past few years' turmoil, and an underlying Husseini
calculation may have been that a British-leaning Arab policy would
leave them at a disadvantage. In any event, the Nashashibis soon re-
covered well enough to displace the Husseinis in British favor.

Accompanying Jerusalem's emerging dominance was a shift from
a younger to an older generation of ayan. Musa Kazim al-Husseini
was already in his seventies, and the others on the new Arab Executive were largely middle-aged or older. A number of them had estab-

lished their credentials as officials in the Ottoman Empire's Jerusalem sanjak. Their careers flourished in the context of working with an existing ruling power, whether Ottoman or British, that gave political legitimacy to a Jerusalem-based administration. In light of the Balfour Declaration, they were unequivocal in refusing to work officially for the mandate. But as members of the most representative, though never formally recognized, Arab institution, the Arab Executive, they found themselves the objects of repeated British efforts to lure them into some such cooperation.

For its part, the Executive drew increasing criticism from younger, more militant figures. Reflected in its almost ceaseless, occasionally spirited, communications with the British over nearly fifteen years was a basic stance of polite negotiation, and its role, as the contemporary Palestinian social scientist Taysir Nashif has put it, was "largely passive."[40] The country's notables continued holding congresses—the seventh and last in 1928—which in turn elected the Executive; it dissolved in 1934 upon the death of Musa Kazim al-Husseini.

While it did not displace the older leadership, a potentially far more dynamic factor in the interplay among Arabs, Jews, and the British was the emergence of Islam as a powerful political force in postwar Palestine. This was the case despite a carefully cultivated Muslim-Christian consensus, and the Muslim-Christian Associations' offering the Jerusalem notables dominance over a country-wide organizational network.

The defeat of the Ottoman Empire and the imposition of British boundaries left Palestine's Muslims without the central religious institutions that had answered to the sultan in Istanbul. A significant amount of Palestinian political action during the mandate period took place within the framework of new institutions established to fill the void. While it was the British, above all, who made them possible, they soon took on a character quite unanticipated by the mandate officials.[41]

Despite Jerusalem's exalted status as the third holiest site in Islam, under the Ottomans the status of the nonjudicial religious leaders, the muftis, was roughly equivalent to that of their colleagues in other provincial centers. The Hanafi Qadi, in contrast, was based solely in the city, selected by Istanbul and with the power to appoint deputies for other Palestinian towns. Now, finding a compliant Kamil al-Husseini as the city's Mufti and chairman of the Central Waqf Committee, the British sought to enhance his role and extend his religious authority over all Islamic Palestine. Thus, when the British appointed him as Jerusalem's first Grand Mufti (a newly established religious title) and qadi, or judge, of the main Islamic law court in Jerusalem, they succeeded in creating a new Palestinian Islamic hierarchy.

Kamil al-Husseini's untimely death in March, 1921, brought into the open the vicious squabbling among Jerusalem's Muslim notables, led by the Husseinis and Nashashibis already gnawing away at the hope of Arab unity. With a pardon from High Commissioner Herbert Samuel in hand, Haj Amin al-Husseini had returned to Palestine from his refuge among the Bedouin of Transjordan and now presented himself as the Husseini candidate to replace his brother.[42] But the opposition was intense, first from within the Husseini clan by those fearing Amin's youth and impetuousness, and later from both the Nashashibis and the Khalidis, and the struggle increasingly bitter. On one occasion, wall posters appeared in Jerusalem warning that the Jews sought to promote someone, presumably the Nashashibi candidate who would accept Zionism, squelch the Palestinian movement, sell Waqf property near the Wailing Wall (al-Buraq), and cede the Haram al-Sharif so that they could rebuild their Temple.[43]

In the midst of such political turmoil, more Arab-Jewish violence erupted in 1921, this time in Jaffa, in the wake of a May Day parade by Jewish leftists. A jittery Samuel was confronting a ticklish problem: "Here was a Christian mandatory power [with a Jewish high commissioner], committed to establishment of a Jewish National Home, controlling a Muslim majority in a country considered holy to the three main monotheistic religions."[44] Apparently hoping to diminish a growing Arab sense of alienation from his government, he took steps to strengthen the Islamic community's role as a cohesive force in Palestinian affairs. Using some questionable procedures, he appointed al-Husseini Mufti (queasiness over his past role in the Nabi Musa violence of April, 1920, led Samuel to drop the newly developed title, Grand Mufti, but Kamil's authority also accrued to his brother). Samuel also shepherded the new mufti into the position of president of another newly created body, the Supreme Muslim Council, formed in January, 1922.[45]

Samuel gave the Council far-ranging authority, affording a significant degree of self-rule for the Muslims. The Council's president (i.e., Haj Amin) would gain considerable patronage, especially through his control of the waqf and his power to appoint and dismiss almost all Islamic officials in the country. Soon after his appointment, Amin offered the highly controversial, never-settled claim that the presidency had lifelong tenure.

Using these posts of Mufti and president of the Supreme Muslim Council, Haj Amin would determine the character of the emerging Palestinian political framework. He set about placing Palestine, and the ever-simmering struggle against Zionism, at the center of universal Islamic concerns, first through an international campaign to refurbish the two revered mosques on Haram al-Sharif, al-Aqsa and the Dome of the Rock, and then through the convening of an ambitious international Muslim conference in Jerusalem in 1931. These two events propelled him into the top ranks of the Islamic world and established him as the most important leader in Palestinian history, at least until Yasser Arafat.

With a solid base for solidifying power, Amin built a countrywide network fueled by patronage and curricular control in Islamic schools. In one example of this process, he neutralized opposition in Nablus by appointing a rival nationalist leader and intellectual, Izzat Darwaza, as General Director of the Waqf endowment. Darwaza's influence would subsequently extend far beyond the Waqf, into the turbulent waters of Palestinian nationalist politics.

Although it was the British who gave Amin such wide latitude, they later were quite ambivalent about this. Often, they worried about his abuses of influence and funds and looked, as one high commissioner put it, for ways to clip his wings. At the same time, enthusiasm for doing so was dampened by what the British considered his role, in much of the 1920s and the early 1930s, in preventing what they called the religious cry from being raised—the type of violence that had broken out during the Nabi Musa celebration in 1920. The country was, in fact, relatively free of communal violence from the time Amin assumed his power until the Arab Revolt of 1936.[46]

The one, not insignificant exception to this tranquility reinforced British suspicions that without the Mufti religious mayhem would erupt in Palestine. On the holy day of Yom Kippur, 1928, Jews modified the status quo by erecting a divider between men and women praying at the Western Wall—the Jews' holiest site and an abutment to the Muslims' Haram al-Sharif. Any issue involving holy places would promptly mobilize the Supreme Muslim Council, rather than the Arab Executive, and from that point on, the Council engaged both the British and the Zionists in a running controversy over how much autonomy the Jews should have over the wall and the adjacent area. This thrust the Supreme Muslim Council into the role of Arab political spokesman to the British against the Zionists—just as the series of Arab congresses promoted by the Muslim-Christian Association were sputtering to an end. The violence took place after a decade of intermittent Zionist immigration. Barely a trickle in the early part of the decade (this had made talk of a Jewish majority seem somewhat fanciful), it had increased at a rate quite alarming to the Arabs in the few years before the riots.

The Supreme Muslim Council's refurbishing of the Haram al-Sharif with funds raised through Haj Amin's international campaign was also at issue. The Jews argued that the reconstruction was having adverse effects on the wall and their ability to pray there. In the end, the gathering storm of nationalist and communal conflict between the Zionists and the Palestinian Arabs burst over religious rites and symbols. It did so, after a summer of almost incessant wrangling, in August, 1929, as a religious melee between Jews and Muslims. Muslims called for a holy war against the Jews and eventually against the British colonial power.[47] With rallying cries of protecting the al-Aqsa Mosque, Muslims battled Jews, and then British troops, in a number of places in the country. The riots left nearly

250 Arabs and Jews dead and more than 500 wounded—the worst episode of bloodletting until that time in Jewish-Arab relations.[48]

The peak of these events occurred on Friday, August 23. Following rumors that the Jews were planning an attack on Haram al-Sharif, Arabs attacked Jewish quarters in Jerusalem, Safad, Tiberias, and Hebron, cities mainly populated by Orthodox anti-Zionist Jews. The locus of the horror was in Hebron, where 64 Jews—men, women, and children—were massacred, and the core of the old Jewish community of Hebron ceased to exist. The massacre of Hebron was a traumatic event in Arab-Jewish relations that exacerbated suspicions, mutual anxieties, and stereotypes.

Islam's rise in the emerging national movement was not lost on Palestinian Christians.[49] In part, they responded by joining in acts whose origins lay in Islam but that came to be reinterpreted as national events—the development of a kind of civil religion. The celebration of the Nabi Musa pilgrimage, into which the Supreme Muslim Council had poured considerable effort and funds, is probably the best example. Some Christians even began to speak of Islam as a national Arab culture that they, too, could embrace.

Many others harbored grave doubts. They noted the calls in the Arabic press for Christian conversion; they worried that religious slurs against Jews at demonstrations could be turned against them too; and they fretted about the Mufti's international Islamic actions, including his leading role against a Christian missionary conference in Palestine and his convening of the worldwide Muslim conference in Jerusalem. Even the pilgrimage was cause for worry, the Mufti having converted its format into a sort of teach-in, what in Arabic was called *tanwirat*. While part of it focused on the threats Zionism posed to the Arab nation—such as transfer of fellaheen land to the Jews—other parts focused on specific threats to Muslim society. The peril was to the holy mosques, through putative Zionist plans to rebuild their Temple. It was also to the moral state of Muslim society, through the corrupting practices brought to the country by the Jews, by the socialism and communism that many of the Zionists espoused, and by Western culture.

Even with the Islamic turn of Palestinian politics, some Christians, such as George Antonius, remained in the forefront of the new nationalist movement. The two leading newspapers, Haifa's *al-Karmil* and Jaffa's *Filastin*, were Christian founded, run, and written. *Filastin* was founded in 1911 by Isa al Isa, who adopted a strong anti-Zionist and nationalist editorial stance. The newspaper's reappearance after World War I and Isa's return from Damascus, along with counterparts such as *al-Karmil*, pushed the urban population towards a more nationalist perspective in the 1920s. In the 1930s, it would have a similar effect on the fellaheen. Greek Orthodox Christians, seeking support in their own struggle to Arabize the Patriarchate of Jerusalem, remained closely wedded to the Muslim nationalist leadership. Nonetheless, many Christians seemed to be resigned to the impossibility of building a secular nationalist politics among the Arabs of Palestine. Khalil al-Sakakini, a prominent Christian active in the various congresses, despaired of his role in the national movement in a letter to his son. "As long as I am not a Moslem," he wrote, "I am nought."[50]

To be sure, the expansion of Islam in Palestine did not signify the death of a national self-consciousness nurtured by the Muslim-Christian Associations.[51] Instead, what seemed to emerge was a Palestinian community, groping towards its own distinct identity, that coexisted, often uneasily, with other established, parochial identities. Tensions between clans, religious groups, city dwellers, and fellaheen remained prominent and worrisome elements of the social structure. The leadership, itself caught up deeply in these tensions, was unable to move Palestinian society beyond them—even as Zionist immigration gained increasing momentum.

Challenges to the Notables' Leadership

For the Mufti, the events of 1929 were a turning point. Just before the Western Wall upheaval, the Nashashibi-led opposition (apparently financed in part by Zionists) had made some gains against Amin al-Husseini.[52] Their success in the 1927 municipal elections was linked to intimations that the Husseinis had blown the Zionist threat out of proportion. In the upheaval's wake, they slipped to a much more marginal position. Until then, Amin had left diplomacy and the political affairs of the Palestinians to the Arab Executive. Afterwards, he moved ever more closely towards the political spotlight. The following year he was already negotiating with the British in London. As Philip Mattar has put it, he "emerged from the political violence both famous and infamous"—famous among the Arabs and infamous among the Jews.[53]

For the Palestinian community as a whole, 1929 meant a rapid political mobilization, with all sorts of new figures entering the political arena, from Jaffa professionals to Nablus peasants. Such figures, representing a new generation of 1930s activists, were for the most part based outside Jerusalem. Sheikh Izz al-Din al-Qassam, the initiator of the Palestinians' first guerrilla force, had settled in Haifa and drew his strength from the northern districts, where Jerusalem's influence had always been lowest. The leader of the Youth Congress, organized in 1932, came from the Ramleh district and looked to the surrounding coastal plain as a first source of support. In 1931, a conference of 300 young activists demanding a more anti-British position by the Arab Executive took place in Nablus.

The impact of such activity varied tremendously, but together it eroded the ayan's oligopoly of power—a process that was double-edged. While unleashing tremendous sociopolitical forces—what Ann Lesch has called "mobilization from below"—the new participants in a formerly exclusive political process also made it increasingly difficult for the Palestinians to speak in a single voice.

At least part of the problem for the notables in the 1930s arose from their leadership styles. The Jerusalem-based ayan were largely cut off from the dynamic of Jaffa, Haifa, or the villages, doing little to incorporate new urban or rural groups into political life or take account of the changing day-to-day issues confronting the entire society. The fellaheen ironically and derogatorily referred to the ayan as *effendiat al-quds,* the Masters of Jerusalem. Peasants muttered about their collaboration with the British leading to Zionist-induced displacements of tenants from the land and to high taxes.

The notables eventually did establish political parties in the

1930s, but these were closer to being social clubs for particular clans than mobilizing agents for the society at large. The Palestine Arab Party was the creation of the Husseinis, the National Defense Party of the Nashashibis, and the Reform Party of the Khalidis. Although the attitude of noblesse oblige the notables had taken with them from the Ottoman period into the mandate led them to speak for the Palestinian population, wider political involvement certainly would not have taken place within such a framework. Salim Tamari has alluded to the limited leadership role of the ayan, attributing it, at least in part, to the character of the new mandate:

> The colonial state apparatus after the First World War strengthened the role of the "leading families" of Palestine since alternative institutional mechanisms of "intermediate" power were absent. They became the mediators between the state and the rural masses and the urban poor as well as the representatives (or rather, the clemencers) of the latter towards the central authorities.[54]

From time to time, the ayan transcended this mediating role to call upon the population for popular demonstrations, but the farthest any went in social organization was the construction of patronage systems and of family networks.

Of all the leaders, Amin al-Husseini was most intent on going beyond this old way of doing things. But the very terms of his effort revealed the same weaknesses plaguing the other notables. From his position as president of the Supreme Muslim Council, Amin operated within two distinct circles. The inner circle consisted of a group holding the most powerful Islamic appointments in the country, and in order to insure loyalty as best he could, he fell back on his own clan. Husseinis held a disproportionate number of the appointments as well as of other high positions in the mandate administration, obviously furnishing good connections to British officials. The outer circle included hundreds of appointments in mosques, courts, and schools throughout the country, and his need to continuously allocate offices and honors—that is, his role at the center of a vast patronage network depending on nepotism and parochial politics—only further deepened the cleavages in Palestinian society. While his rhetoric freely incorporated a unifying imagery of an Arab, all-Palestinian community, his actions revealed a much more limited vision.

In short, the foundations of al-Husseini's power—the patronage, his call to religious sentiments, familism, and proper relations with the British administration—prevented him from leading an all-embracing national movement. In the end, the Mufti represented merely one faction, albeit the largest, to participate in that movement. To be sure, some of the new mobilization around him reinforced the predominance of the Jerusalem-led ayan. For example, in October 1929, an Arab Women's Congress drew over 200 delegates, mostly the wives of active notables.[55] Its chair was the wife of Musa Kazim al-Husseini, the head of the Arab Executive, and, predictably, its resolutions closely mirrored that group's positions. Other such activity was much less reassuring and eventually transformed British-Palestinian relations, first into acrimonious exchanges, then into full-scale violence.

Much anti-British agitation came in the aftermath of the Wailing Wall riots. A report in 1930 stemming from the riots, the Passfield White Paper, seemed to vindicate the Arab Executive's patience, promising severe restrictions on Jewish land purchases and immigration, two of the Arabs' key planks.[56] But, before the old leadership could savor its apparent victory, a letter by Prime Minister Ramsey MacDonald to Chaim Weizmann in 1931 reversed the White Paper.[57] The MacDonald letter, which the Arabs acerbically called the Black Paper, shocked the Palestinian community, with young Palestinians at a Nablus conference pressuring the Arab Executive into a much more anti-British stance. This marked the first occasion that outsiders succeeded in forcing such changes on the ayan.

Practically all the new activism had a militant, anti-imperialist tone, directed at the British, without exception viewing Zionism as a foreboding menace. But there the unanimity stopped, as different organizations pulled Palestinian society in contending directions. They divided on means. Some, including most Christians, largely stayed within the bounds of respectable diplomacy; others—among them, Istiqlal Party members and participants in the Youth Congress of 1932—participated in illegal demonstrations. Clandestine guerrilla groups such as that organized by Sheikh al-Qassam prepared for armed assault.

The activists also differed in their visions of the future. Some, such as those in the Istiqlal Party, moved towards greater pan-Arabism. "Palestine is an Arab country and natural part of Syria," read the party's *Manifesto to the Arab World* in December, 1931. Others, such as organizers of the Young Men's Muslim Association, were narrowly sectarian and markedly anti-Christian. Both stances frayed the edges of the notables' vision of a united, autonomous Palestinian nation, their answer to the failure of the Faysal-led Syria plan. Still others sought to give the old strategy an even more explicitly nationalist flavor. In 1931, Izzat Darwaza of Nablus, for instance, convinced his town's Muslim-Christian Association to change its name to the Patriotic Arab Association. Often these varying ideas were not recognized as clashing. Darwaza at the same time supported pan-Arabism, Islamicism, and an increased dedication to the Palestinian nationalist ideal.

By the mid-1930s, the Palestinians had generated the clear beginnings of a popular movement—one with significant intellectual ferment and diverse notions of its future. The ability of the Jerusalem notables to impose their will on that movement and restore its coherence had eroded badly. In a statement to the high commissioner before a demonstration in Jaffa, the members of the Arab Executive noted, "In the past, the leaders were able to appease the people, but now they have lost their influence."[58]

Among the new groups seeking to put their stamp on the movement, none stood out more prominently in the early 1930s than the Istiqlal.[59] After disappointments in Syria in 1920 (where Izzat Darwaza had been one of the party's founders) and in Transjordan a decade later, the Istiqlal reassembled in Palestine in 1932. Its rallying call consisted of two simple themes: the old, "lethargic" notable leadership had failed the Palestinian people and only British imperialism had made the Zionist threat viable, even menacing. The party coaxed Palestinians towards more defiant tactics—demonstrations and political and social boycotts. Even when, in 1935, the high commissioner convinced all five other Palestinian political parties to meet with him, at a time when Jewish-Arab relations were moving towards unbridled violence, the Istiqlal refused to join in the negotiations.

The party typified the mood of the 1930s, through both its introduction of novel political ideas and methods, and its recruitment of until then politically inactive Palestinians. It drew its leadership from the north of the country, and from Nablus and Jaffa—but not from Jerusalem. Young professionals filled its ranks. So did the ragged shabab. The zeal of both social groups deeply frightened the notable leadership, especially Amin al-Husseini.

The Istiqlal had a brief, but powerful, moment in the sun, its major impact coming in the two years after its Palestinian debut. But already by 1935, the Mufti had succeeded in discrediting its leaders and sabotaging its efforts. For the rest of the decade—the period that determined the direction of the Palestinian movement and included the bloody Arab Revolt—it was reduced to impotence. It would reemerge in the 1940s with the old leadership in disarray, as the major opposition to the Husseinis' Palestine Arab Party.

Such shifts in fortune on the part of various alternative movements should not obscure the fact that Palestinian Arab political leadership during the mandate was the province of the Jerusalem ayan. Their achievements were impressive. They grasped the political situation quickly and accurately after the demise of Ottoman rule, adapting readily to the British administration—which they understood needed them to maintain law and order in the country. Even their command of English—many had been trained in French—came quickly.

Of their accomplishments, none rivalled their ability to fashion a popular national movement out of a rapidly changing Arab population. They succeeded in establishing Jerusalem as a national center, from which they exerted their control. In today's terms, that control would be considered weak. Despite their leverage, they did not pay sufficient attention to the evolving civil society around them. Their own interests as landowners and as officeholders dependent on the

British led them to suppress or ignore other emerging groups. They did manage to prevent the rise of rival groups that might have supplanted their leadership, and they pushed competing centers, such as Nablus and Jaffa, into limited regional roles. Even with the ayan itself badly fractured, they were thus able to command broad enough—if not particularly deep—authority, across the various segments of Palestinian Arab society, to fortify it against the Zionists. Years later, after they had passed from the political scene, their program for dealing with that challenge remained deeply influential.

Heading Toward Communal Warfare

The discord manifest in the Palestinian national movement in the mid-1930s could not obscure the essence of their common struggle: Who would eventually control Palestine? The calls to pan-Arab or Islamic sentiments notwithstanding the land—as defined by the League of Nations mandate—stood at the center of the hopes and concerns of both Arabs and Jews, bestowing an increasing legitimacy on the idea of a state, even as they both became exasperated with British rule over it.

By the mid- to late 1930s, most illusions, such as reconstructing the Caliphate or establishing a pan-Arab federation linked to a Palestine with a Jewish majority, had been largely abandoned by Jews and Arabs for the harsh reality of an impending struggle.[60] In that sense, we can speak of a conflict at this point between two national movements, even if the leaders were still trying to instill a sense of national consciousness in their communities. The conflict took a variety of forms on each side, from incessant diplomatic pleadings in Jerusalem and London to organizing for future violent clashes.

A rich range of issues became arenas for battle—for instance, over how the name of the country should appear on its postage stamps. The British proposed printing the name *Palestine* in the country's three official languages, English, Arabic, and Hebrew. Quite understandably, Arab leaders strenuously argued against the inclusion of Hebrew (as they had against Hebrew programs on the Palestine broadcasting service). Equally understandably, Zionists first insisted on the term *Eretz Yisrael* in the three languages, relenting later in order to argue for at least *Palestine—The Land of Israel*. The upshot was stamps with the inscription *Palestine* in the three languages, with the addition of an almost invisible two-letter Hebrew abbreviation of *Eretz Yisrael*. The pictures on the stamps were also controversial. Interpreting the stamps of the Tomb of Rachel as part of a process of Judification of the country,[61] the Arabs insisted on representations of the Dome of the Rock—and demanded, as well, that the Arabic *Palestine* appear in larger letters. By 1938, the national movement was issuing its own stamps, to be affixed to all letters, carrying the slogan "Palestine for the Arabs."

Some private attempts were made to bridge the gap between Zionist and Arab aspirations. In the mid-1930s, Musa Alami, Awni Abd al-Hadi (one of the founders of the Istiqlal), and George Antonius held discussions with Zionist leader David Ben-Gurion, to little avail. Ben-Gurion's proposal was for an exchange of Jewish agreement to a pan-Arab federation linked to Palestine for Arab agreement to unrestricted Jewish immigration into Palestine and Transjordan, leading to an independent state with a Jewish majority. Some Arabs showed interest in the scheme, but the idea of an Arab federation linked to a Jewish state did not get far. Alarmed by every Jewish gain, most Palestinian Arab leaders saw few prospects for a settlement.

These gains appeared to be snowballing in the 1930s, with Jewish immigrants seeming to arrive in droves after the MacDonald letter. In 1932, approximately 12,500 arrived, and the number rose to 66,000 in 1935. In the decade's first half, the total Jewish population more than doubled, and the rise of Nazism precipitated a tidal wave of central European emigration, the greatest share of it ending up in Palestine.

The Arab population was itself by no means stagnant. Fewer than 500,000 Palestinian Arabs at the beginning of the century grew to close to a million by the middle of the 1930s. But this growth was not reassuring to Arab political leaders. They watched the Jewish expansion with horror. In their own backyard of Jerusalem, the numbers of Jews grew from 53,000 to 70,000 in the four years between 1931 and 1935.

Even more distressing was that this influx was taking place just as Palestinian unity seemed to unravel, the new voices and classes reducing the old leadership to ineffectual self-absorption. At the height of Zionist successes, Musa Kazim al-Husseini died, and the Jerusalem notables entered into a bout of mutual recrimination. The ayan seemed on the brink of political bankruptcy. When the need for resolute leadership appeared greatest, the Arab Executive simply passed from the scene.

4

THE ARAB REVOLT,

1936–1939

THE GREAT ARAB REVOLT in Palestine, as Arabs have called it,[1] was sparked by the murder of two Jews on April 15, 1936. Although there were some claims that the act was purely criminal, it was probably engineered for political purposes by a disciple of Sheikh Izz al-Din al-Qassam.[2] In any event, Jewish retaliation followed swiftly, leaving two Arabs dead as well. Within a few days, beatings and additional murders inaugurated a period of horrifying violence in the country. In a short time, the violence was transformed into a major Arab upheaval.

As the first sustained violent uprising of the Palestinian national movement, and the first major episode of this sort since 1834, perhaps no event has been more momentous in Palestinian history than the Great Arab Revolt. It mobilized thousands of Arabs from every stratum of society, all over the country, heralding the emergence of a national movement in ways that isolated incidents and formal delegations simply could not accomplish. It also provoked unprecedented countermobilization. Astonished by its tenacity—as were the Palestinians themselves—the British poured tens of thousands of troops into Palestine on the eve of World War II. And the Zionists embarked upon a militarization of their own national movement—nearly 15,000 Jews were under arms by the Revolt's end. Inaugurating an increasingly militarist Jewish political culture,[3] it contributed in the 1940s to a decision by Ben-Gurion and other Zionist leaders to prepare for military struggle against the Arabs rather than against the British, a change in strategy instrumental in their ultimate triumph.

Just as significant as the revolt's intercommunal and international outcomes were the social changes that followed in its wake. It highlighted Palestine's transformation from a fairly self-sufficient and homogeneous peasant society into one incorporated into world markets and politics, distinguished by division and disharmony constantly sapping the prospects of achieving common goals. Despite shared belief about the threat of Zionism and actions in pursuit of a common cause, the distance between the old leadership and the peasants became unbreachable. Much Palestinian fury came, in fact, to be directed at the most privileged Arab groups in the country. In 1937, when the ayan lost its key asset, its special ties to the British rulers, it rapidly faded. In its place came two new sorts of leadership, with characteristics marking Palestinian leaders even today: those whose influence was confined to specific regions, and those who, claiming to speak for the national movement as a whole, were based outside the country.

The social distance of the ayan from the people now became the physical distance suffered by the new national leadership. Some of its members—most prominently, Haj Amin al-Husseini—were familiar faces or came from the same families supplying Arab leaders since the Ottoman period. But on the whole it was younger, more militant, and necessarily much more inclusive, absorbing compatriots from the newly mobilized segments of society. Inversely, the Arab population found itself worn down at the revolt's end, and disarmed by British forces. When the Zionists began their own rebellion against the British following World War II, "the Palestinian Arabs," notes W. F. Abboushi, "proved too exhausted by the effort of rebellion between 1936 and 1939 to be in any condition to match it."[4]

In any event, while the Arabs' concerted opposition would not in the end bring about the demise of Zionism, they did appear, for the moment, to have the advantage. The result impelled the British to reverse their policy in support of a Jewish national home, first set out in the Balfour Declaration two decades earlier. The extensive Arab mobilization and the intensity of their activity demanded unprecedented British attention to the Palestinian position, and Palestinians somehow seemed to have developed the social and political cohesion necessary to make their point forcefully and unambiguously.

If the events between 1936 and 1939 added up to something unique in Palestinian history, some of the tactics used in the revolt and its social character grew out of the fundamental changes in Palestinian society and the growing challenge posed by the Zionists in the five preceding years. While responding to the transformation of their society in different ways, across the social spectrum, Palestinians applauded the creation of a national movement, sharing an ideology that totally negated any Jewish political right over the country. The mandate's history did not simply consist of periods of calm punctuated by unusual bursts of violence on the part of Arabs, as many accounts of the period imply. Rather, the violence was the sign of this steadily unfolding national movement and the unanimity among Palestinian Arabs about the Zionist threat.

Portents of Rebellion

Prime Minister Ramsey MacDonald's refusal to suppress the Zionists, as the Passfield Report had recommended following the violent outbreaks of 1929, caused great disappointment among the Palestinian Arabs in the early 1930s. At the same time, their leaders used the plight of the Arab victims of the 1929 riots to enhance the sense of a shared fate among the Arab population. They established aid committees for families of those arrested and killed and made the three Arabs hanged by the British into national martyrs. The deep resentment caused by both the hangings and the later MacDonald letter sent a surge of solidarity through the Arab community that had considerable impact on the Palestinian national movement— not least in a shift in hostility away from the Jews alone and towards two new targets: the British and, what at the time seemed far more remarkable, other Palestinians.

The 1936 general strike thus came only after half a decade of shifts in stance and actions vis-à-vis the British. It emerged as a shared sense that imperialism could only thwart Palestinian Arab aspirations. By the early 1930s, Palestinians were already reinterpreting the violent clashes at the Wailing Wall in 1928 and 1929 in light of this new anti-imperial stance.

> That day was a day of honor, splendour and glory in the annals of Palestinian-Arab history. We attacked Western conquest and the Mandate and the Zionists upon our land. The Jews had coveted our endowments and yearned to take over our holy places. Silence they had seen as weakness. Therefore, there was no more room in our hearts for patience and peace. . . . The Arabs stood up, checked the oppression, and sacrificed their pure and noble souls on the sacred altar of nationalism.[5]

To be sure, there had been bloody encounters with the British at the time, but almost exclusively in the context of violence directed at the Jews. Yet here Emil al-Ghawri, later the secretary of the Arab Higher Committee, refers to the riots as motivated by nationalism more than religion and directed as much against the British as the Zionists.

The new anti-mandate activism was designed not only to force the British away from their support of Zionism but also to rid the country entirely of imperial rule. Young nationalists now argued that British support of Zionism was not simply a delusion, to be corrected. Rather, Zionism was part and parcel of Western imperialism in the Middle East, and only the eradication of the latter could halt the advance of the former.

The mandate government's decision, following the 1929 turmoil, to release 587 rifles previously kept in sealed armories to isolated

Jewish settlements naturally aggravated Arab anti-British sentiment. But beyond any such direct British decisions, the strongest
force affecting Palestinian Arab opinion, transforming the British
into a prime target of Arab wrath and political action, was the appearance of new Arab militants, most prominently during the brief
flourishing of the Istiqlal Party. The Istiqlal's demand for noncooperation, like Gandhi's doctrine of disobedience, struck a highly
responsive chord among the Arab population at large.[6] A portion of
the old ayan—members of the Husseini and Nashashibi clans and
their allies, as opposed to some of the Nablus leadership, who embraced the new anti-British tone—represented a sole exception. Fearful of losing essential support for their own positions, they tempered the Istiqlal's enthusiasm for open resistance. Nevertheless,
even these notables adopted a measure in the early 1930s to boycott
official British events.

Anticipating the tone and tactics of the Arab Revolt, a group
of nationalists sympathetic to pan-Arabism—most of them young,
many Nablus based, and chafing under the Jerusalem-dominated
leadership—called a national meeting for July 13, 1931. The delegates
now thrust the British problem to center-stage, calling for a general
strike in August. The shutdown occurred peacefully in most towns,
but in Nablus itself, women and teenagers engaged in a rock-throwing melée with the British police.

That year, a series of general strikes, political demonstrations,
and violent exchanges with the police followed. While some public
protests were called by the established leadership (Musa Kazim al-
Husseini himself led an October general strike in Jerusalem), the
new activism was clearly in the hands of a younger generation. It
was expressed in the new political role of the shabab, and in the formal constitution of the Istiqlal Party in 1932. The party was forth-
right in proclaiming that the British, not the Jews, should be the
primary targets of action—in some cases, Palestinians even organized contingents of guards to protect Jews and their property during demonstrations.[7] In fact, during this period, while the British
were firing at Arab demonstrators and breaking into offices of the

Muslim-Christian Associations, not a single Jew was attacked in urban protests.

In the first half of the 1930s, internecine verbal sniping and occasional violence among the Palestinians, like the tactics being used against the British, presaged a motif of the 1936–39 revolt. Among the Jerusalem ayan, factional fighting grew to unprecedented levels, certainly slowing (without destroying) the momentum towards political unity. Late in 1929, Jerusalem's mayor Raghib al-Nashashibi commented privately that his opposition to Haj Amin al-Husseini was ten times stronger than the aversion of the Jews to the Mufti.[8] In a 1933 meeting in Jaffa, a member of the Nashashibi clan suggested that as an act of noncooperation with the British both Raghib al-Nashashibi and the Mufti resign their positions. But the tactic was little more than a ploy to remove Haj Amin from the source of his patronage and power. When it was exposed as such, it did little for either its supporters (the Nashashibi-led opposition— the *Muarada,* who declined dramatically in the following years) or for the doctrine of noncooperation.

Mudslinging and political maneuvering reached a new pitch of intensity. Defying clan loyalty, Musa Kazim al-Husseini forged an alliance with Raghib al-Nashashibi against Haj Amin. The Mufti's opponents accused him of misusing funds, and he brandished the charge that his enemies assisted the Jews in their landbuying. Substantive differences also existed. Some of the Nashashibis, at least, were much more inclined than the Mufti to grant the legitimacy of Jewish rights in Palestine and to seek some accommodation with the Zionists.

More significant than this continuing factionalism, with its intemperate charges and countercharges, was a surge of opposition to the ayan as a whole. This was initiated by the Istiqlal with others quickly joining—the radicalized urban political activists, who organized the Young Men's Muslim Association, literary groups, sports clubs, and so forth. Such organizations were of course not unique to the Arabs. Palestinians had the young, brown- and black-shirted European fascists to emulate, and even the very active local Jewish movements. In particular, the Zionist right-wing Betar and left-wing Hashomer HaZa'ir presented models of youth militancy in service of a national cause.

By the 1930s, youth groups increasingly focused their attention both on stepped up, direct political action and on the inadequacies of the national leadership. Sharp criticism was levelled both at the Arab Executive and the entire tenor of Jerusalem-dominated politics. The first national Congress of Arab Youth met in January, 1932, pointedly not in Jerusalem but in Jaffa. Establishing its main headquarters there, delegates criticized the ayan's "controlled protest" policy. The attacks escalated through the early 1930s. In part, Amin al-Husseini's collaboration furnished a platform for such denunciations. The Mufti wished to transcend the sectarian soapbox that the presidency of the Supreme Muslim Council afforded him, in favor of a more encompassing national one. At least until 1932, he was quite pleased to join in condemning the Arab Executive's old guard as "frail ghosts," unsuited for national leadership.[9]

As the decade wore on, the Istiqlal and the youth groups continued their strident criticism, but the Mufti drew back. After the signing, in 1932, of an agreement supplying the Supreme Muslim Council with new British funds, he was much less eager to criticize either the old leaders or British. Until 1936, he publicly urged the Arabs to target the Jews, not the British, although deflecting the Istiqlal's criticism had him occasionally advocating an antigovernment stance. For their part, reacting against the pretensions of the ayan, with their "feudal" titles such as pasha, bey, and effendi,[10] Istiqlal members did not hesitate to single out the Mufti, along with others, as collaborators with the imperialists. Directed against Haj Amin, this sort of criticism was enough to prompt a frenzied counterattack, which led to the rapid decline of the Istiqlal Party.

Even after it began to fade, many youth groups maintained their militancy. Boy Scouts turned out to be among the most dedicated new nationalists, "already at this stage . . . instrumental in forcing the shopkeepers and merchants to take part in nationalist strikes or as the vanguard in nationalist processions. . . ."[11] They aimed their fury at the British, the Jews—patrolling beaches in search of illegal Jewish immigrants and forming fighting groups during the revolt— and again, at other Palestinians. Like the internal bickering, such pressure tactics foreshadowed patterns that would dominate the Arab Revolt itself.

Serious religious tensions were also appearing in the Palestinian nationalist movement. These tensions were deeply grounded, merely exacerbated by both Haj Amin's base of power in the Supreme Muslim Council and the British propensity to differentiate between the Muslim and Christian communities. Muslims resented the over-representation of Christian Arabs in the bureaucracy, and the presence of foreign Christian missionaries in the country. This resentment interacted with the exclusivist Islamic component of Palestinian militancy, and the question of what role Islam would play in the emerging national identity. While most of the leadership, both the ayan and its opponents, officially set a secular independent Arab state as its goal—a concept that has since been maintained and embellished—popular feelings about the role of religion in politics were difficult to quell. There were even some scattered attacks on Arab Christians by Muslim gangs.

It is important to recall that the political evolution of Palestinian nationalism—the mass demonstrations and militant political parties, the use of mosques as bases for popular mobilization—took place against a backdrop of ever-increasing Jewish immigration, growing social dislocation, and Arab urbanization. It was in the early 1930s that the dispossessed Arab farmer became a poignant symbol of the simmering conflict between the two peoples. Perhaps no other subject had its capacity to prompt the charges and countercharges, the presentation of evidence and counterevidence to British commissions. Likewise, Arabs living in the city observed the higher wages paid Jewish workers and the call for exclusively Jewish labor in Jewish enterprises. In this context, the delegations to London, the rising Zionist tide, the periodic communal and religious violence, and the never-ending stream of British decisions were not distant echoes for ordinary Palestinians, but ever-more central daily concerns, nurturing a sharpened political consciousness. The process was furthered by the British-imposed educational system, which while surely inadequate, both drew young men, usually with strong nationalist views, back into the village as schoolteachers and fostered increasing levels of general literacy. The growing number of schools produced new consumers for the nationalism promulgated in the Arabic newspapers.

In October, 1933, thousands of Palestinians took to the streets in an anti-British demonstration in Jaffa. By the end of the day, a dozen demonstrators had been killed along with one policeman. The "Jaffa Massacre" touched off further violent demonstrations in other cities, the occupation of several towns by British troops, and an Arab general strike. One of the most respected Arab officials in the mandate government, Musa Alami, commented that "the program of the Arab youth is based only on the use of force and violence. . . . The youth prefer an open war. . . . The prevailing feeling is that if all that can be expected from the present policy is a slow death, it is better to be killed in an attempt to free ourselves of our enemies than to suffer a long and protracted demise."[12]

The rural resistance that would play such a critical role in the 1936–39 revolt was also foreshadowed by preceding events. Following the Jaffa massacre, Sheikh Izz al-Din al-Qassam, who had allegedly contemplated building a military organization from his earliest days in Haifa in the 1920s, stepped up his organizing in northern Arab villages. Combined with his Haifa sermons, he thus laid the basis for the guerrilla actions he hoped to mount against the British authorities. Although once his group was destroyed, the government labelled it a band of thieves, Qassam instantly gained a reputation among Palestinians as an important symbol of armed resistance to imperial rule, especially outside the cities. While his posthumous influence was strongest immediately following his death, that is, during the Arab Revolt, it would extend to the concerted attack by the fedayeen on the state of Israel after 1948.[13]

The Urban Revolt

Reflecting a widely shared Palestinian sentiment, the Arab Revolt was in many ways more a product of the people at the base of society, in the villages and poor urban neighborhoods, than it was of those at the top, trying to put their own stamp on the evolving national movement.[14] Indeed, recent writings have celebrated the revolutionary spirit of workers and peasants during the revolt. They have suggested that the lower classes were the true backbone of the movement and have cast doubts on the basic motives of the notable leadership.[15]

With the outbreak of violence in April, 1936, the government quickly declared a state of emergency. Jaffa became both the center for attacks by the shabab on Jews and for the initial Palestinian political responses to the attacks. Reflecting gathering anger at the British, Arab leaders called for their first general strike. Immediately, prominent notables from Nablus seconded this move by creating a National Committee, appealing to leaders of other towns to join the protest. In a matter of days, almost each one had its own National Committee.

By April 25, ten days after the first violence, the Jerusalem-based leadership created a new countrywide coordinating body, the Arab Higher Committee, to pursue the general strike and deal with the British. Led by Amin al-Husseini, it succeeded in extending the strike until October 1936.[16] Its demands did not differ substantially from those voiced before the revolt by the much tamer Arab Executive or by other Palestinians: an end to Jewish immigration, the banning of land sales to Jews, and national independence.

The first rioters, even before the calling of the local strikes, were led by the shabab. In some ways, the Arab Revolt was the shabab's debut; this product of Palestine's rapid urbanization would appear again on the national scene, most notably in the Intifada. But both the urban working class and cosmopolitan, Western-educated Palestinian Arabs played their part. The Arab Car Owners and Drivers Association, for example, imposed a shutdown of all Arab transport, and a nearly unknown Jerusalem physician named Dr. Khalil al-Budayri led intellectuals in calling for Gandhi-style, peaceful non-cooperation with the British. Inspired by the recent 45-day strike begun in February by Syrian Arabs against the French, which deeply impressed the Palestinian community, those who had been in the Istiqlal Party and others formed the National Committees and pushed for a general strike.

Quickly, the strike embraced the merchants, small shopkeepers, city workers, and Arab agricultural laborers in Jewish settlements. The shabab created local youth guard units to enforce compliance. With the paralysis of the Jaffa port and the diminished agricultural market, the strike created shortages for the Jews and British—and untold hardship for the Arabs, especially the poorer Arabs, who had difficulty gaining access to food.[17] The Arab leadership decided to raise "taxes," allowing the National Committees to create strike funds, particularly for the crucial transport workers and longshoremen. Merchants paid a levy, citrus growers 1 percent of their sales, wealthy women a portion of their jewelry. Poor families paid a one-piaster coin.

Popular revolt both offered the ayan significant new human and material resources for waging their national campaign and imposed new constraints. They found themselves saddled with the shabab, which aggressively collected the new levies but in the process began to drive wealthy Palestinians into Lebanon and Egypt. They faced demands that they and their relatives in government posts join the strike—an act threatening to erode their power bases. Their compromise was to leave government workers on the job, but to demand at least 10 percent of their wages for the strike.

A cartoon in the July 12, 1936, edition of the newspaper *Filastin* shows a startled Chaim Weizmann looking at Amin al-Husseini and Raghib al-Nashashibi, the two longstanding rivals and representatives of the two leading notable families, shaking hands beneath the spirit of Sheikh Qassam, now a symbol of the resistance. But this impressive unity was a fragile one. The varying costs that different segments of the population were paying, the hidden benefits that some were receiving, the differences in capacity to bear the pain of the strike, all served to undermine its foundations.

The sustained use of violence also frightened many notables and other wealthy Palestinians. Although mostly unorganized and poorly coordinated, it represented a repudiation of the gentlemanly diplomatic discourse they had long conducted with the British. For the time being, it was directed mostly at Jews—about eighty were killed in this initial stage—with some additional attacks on British forces and installations. Among other targets, Arabs destroyed forests planted by the Jewish National Fund, a prime symbol of Jewish settlement to both sides,[18] and repeatedly hit the railroads, a symbol of imperial rule. But the possibility existed of uncontrolled violence turning against Arabs, and this was a further source of alarm among the privileged.

A major deployment of British troops brought a respite from the urban strike and the rural violence that had accompanied it. But this lasted only until the summer of 1937 and the publication of the report by the Royal Commission (popularly known as the Peel Commission),[19] which the British had dispatched to investigate the events of 1936—and which recommended partitioning the country between Arabs and Jews.

In September, 1937, Arabs in Nazareth assassinated Lewis A. Andrews, an acting British commissioner who was sympathetic to the Zionists. The killing has been attributed both to followers of Sheikh Qassam and to the Mufti. Whatever the precise circumstances, the mandate authorities reacted strongly, proclaiming martial law within forty-eight hours and dissolving the short-lived Arab Higher Committee, as well as other Arab national agencies. Two hundred Arabs were arrested, decimating the movement's leadership. Among them were officials of the Supreme Muslim Council, the Arab Higher Committee, the local National Committees, and the activist youth organizations. The mandate authorities issued numerous arrest warrants, including those aimed at Muslim religious leaders.

Their biggest target was Amin al-Husseini, in whom they had

placed so much of their faith over the last decade. Stripped of the presidency of the Supreme Muslim Council, he was hunted in the sanctuary of the Haram al-Sharif, where he was known to have taken refuge earlier. Apparently alerted to British intentions, the Mufti succeeded in disguising himself and fleeing to Lebanon, where the French placed him under house arrest.

He never again set foot on the soil of a unified Palestine. Rather, he twice returned briefly to what formerly was part of the country. The first was for ten days to the Gaza Strip, that sliver conquered by the Egyptians in 1948. And the second was to Jerusalem, the home denied him by both his blood enemies, the Israelis and the Jordanians, until a brief visit permitted by the latter shortly before it lost any control of the city in 1967. His exile, however, would not put an end to the strong influence he exerted over events in Palestine.

Besides the arrests, the mandate officials denied reentry to leaders outside the country at the time, such as Izzat Darwaza, the former head of the Istiqlal. Some Palestinian political figures managed to flee the country; others faced deportation. In Damascus, Darwaza and a number of others established the Central Committee of the National Jihad in Palestine *(Al-Lajnah al-MarKaziyya lil-Jihad)*. Echoing Sheikh Qassam's repeated call for holy war, this is one example among many of the Palestinian nationalist movement's assimilation of Islamic religious terms into its vocabulary.[20] The Committee's official head was Darwaza, but it worked closely with the Mufti in Lebanon to garner support and supplies for the revolt and, as much as possible, to supervise the rebels still in Palestine.

But for the most part, the Palestinian elite could not continue to play an effective leadership role in the revolt. Not much of it (9 percent) participated, and only an additional 5 percent directed military operations.[21] With the demise of the urban leadership in 1937, the revolt shifted to rural Palestine, meeting with astonishing success in the hill country. Then—in a notable reversal of direction of influence that had prevailed in Palestine—it moved from the countryside to the cities. Inland towns, including Nablus, Hebron, Bethlehem, and Ramallah, were taken over by the rural rebels, who expanded their reach at the revolt's height in August and September,

1938. In Jaffa, they wrested control from the British authorities for several months, and—echoing events of the revolt of 1834—they even managed to occupy the walled portion of Jerusalem for five days. Rebel soldiers slipped into Tiberias on September 5 and killed a large number of the town's Jewish population. On September 9, they occupied Ramallah and Beersheba and in the process released prisoners from British jails.

In most towns, the breakdown of order forced the closing of banks and post offices—frequent targets of rebels seeking cash to sustain the uprising. For a period, British rule in these areas was nominal.[22] The revolt now took on a very different tenor from that of its inauguration by workers and merchants in Jaffa in April, 1936. The urban centers became as much its victims as its perpetrators. Urban agitation had already lost steam with the drastic British countermeasures of 1937. By the revolt's second and third years, much of the urban populace seemed to tire of the prolonged turmoil. The shabab, suffering from the alarming rates of Arab unemployment and thinned by migration back to villages, struggled to keep it alive but only intermittently succeeded. The focus of events had clearly shifted to rural Palestine.

The Rural Revolt

In the charged political climate of Arab Palestine, the events of April, 1936, seemed to touch the countryside directly. By May, rural national committees called for withholding taxes from the government. More dramatically, both in the Galilean hills and in the east, spurred by members of the Istiqlal, followers of Qassam and other militant Muslim preachers, peasants were organizing into guerrilla bands, taking aim at Jewish settlements and at British installations with hit-and-run tactics.

Operating from mountain caves or other hideouts, the rebels went so far as to sabotage the Iraq Petroleum Company oil pipeline to Haifa. After the Arab Higher Committee called off the general strike in October, 1936, enabling its members to ship out their prized citrus crop and peasants to attend to their harvest, agitation continued in the villages. Many peasants bought weapons and prepared for continued fighting.

By 1938, they carried the uprising on their backs. Thousands—some estimate as high as 15,000—now joined the revolt, up to 10 percent becoming permanently active fighters.[23] Most groups were purely local, operating in very circumscribed areas, with fighters continuing as best they could to farm during the day. Their diffuseness—as well as their sheer numbers—would eventually overwhelm British administrative capacity.

Alongside such bands there emerged others that were larger and more established—sometimes even clusters of allied forces fighting across broad swaths of territory. Single commanders organized as many as several hundred men into subsidiary bands, each having its own lieutenants, with authority over some thirty to sixty men, to carry the brunt of the hit-and-run fighting.[24] One commander who would later establish an indelible imprint on Palestinian history was Abd al-Qadir al-Husseini. It took some time for these complex structures to form, and the process was certainly not a smooth one. Lieutenants flouted their commanders, bands struck against one another. But, by 1938–39, they were by far the Palestinians' most effective fighting forces. In August, 1938 rebel leaders in the hills created the High Council of Command.

The biggest barrier to forming a true national fighting force—one that could be distinguished from the rural criminal gangs that had previously dotted the countryside—was the absence of a hierarchical system of command and control for the various guerrilla groups, especially the larger and more permanent ones. The effort to forge such a system began close to the revolt's onset, in the spring of 1936. It continued in the summer with the entry into Palestine of an outsider, Fawzi al-Din al-Qa'uqji, who drew the immediate attention of both local peasants and the Arab Higher Committee. He brought with him a group of two hundred experienced *mujahidin*, or holy warriors, gathered from Transjordan, Syria, and Iraq.

Like Abd al-Qadir al-Husseini, Qa'uqji's name would frequently emerge in a Palestinian context through 1948, although he lacked

Husseini's national pedigree. Born in Syria, he had been trained by the French military and, in 1925, had led a Druze revolt against French rule. After that revolt's collapse, he had served as a military adviser to King Ibn Saud, the founder of Saudi Arabia. With the support of the rebel leaders of five cooperative local bands, he now declared himself the commander of what he called the General Arab Revolt in Southern Syria—a geographic term scarcely heard since Faysal's failure at the start of the 1920s. Qa'uqji's choice for a name underscored his pan-Arab approach to the uprising, diminishing the importance of the more narrowly defined Palestinian national effort and relegating the Palestinians to one among several Arab players. Although some accounts attribute Qa'uqji's mandate to lead the rebellion to the Mufti,[25] his actions seem to have reflected a refusal to subordinate his pan-Arab vision to any local political control such as the Arab Higher Committee.

Carving out an administrative structure that could incorporate the existing rebel groups in the hills, he relegated the Palestinians to one of four main military companies. The others were Iraqi, Syrian, and Lebanese Druze.[26] He appointed Fakhri Abd al-Hadi—a man who would later play an important role in subduing the revolt—as deputy commander-in-chief. He also formed an intelligence unit to collect information (mainly from local Arab policemen and civil servants), and created a Revolutionary Court composed of local rebel leaders, who meted out severe sentences.[27] But Qa'uqji's command dissolved soon after his arrival in Palestine. In an ambush of a British military convoy and a subsequent pitched battle, the Palestinian company abandoned him, suspicious of his motives and his attempts to choke off their autonomy. Mutual recriminations and accusations followed—one even had Qa'uqji as a British agent—but the real effect was to frustrate any sense of coordination to the revolt. After the general strike, the British managed for a time to rout Qa'uqji from the country altogether, pushing him into Transjordan.

Nearly two years later, in the summer of 1938, the now exiled Haj Amin al-Husseini initiated an effort to use his followers in Damascus—the Central Committee of the National Jihad in Palestine—as a basis to gain control of the guerrilla groups. Doing so from abroad—a geographic dislocation that has come to characterize the Palestinian nationalist leadership—proved as costly and difficult then as it has since, despite Amin's increasing popularity.

The Central Committee contacted a number of people to serve as the revolt's supreme commander. After receiving several refusals, it unsuccessfully turned again to Qa'uqji. As at other times during the revolt, in the end the ayan's initiatives could do little more than confirm what already existed on the ground—in this case, a loose coordination among the largest fighting forces. For example, once Abd al-Qadir al-Husseini became commander of the Jerusalem area, he considered himself head of the entire revolt, appointing his own commander for the Hebron region and maintaining direct ties to Damascus, instead of going through the local council of rebel chiefs—actions obviously generating great resentment. Using a variety of names for the command council, including the Bureau of the Arab Revolt in Palestine and the Council of Rebellion (*Diwan al-Thawra*), the Central Committee tried to institutionalize this coordination into an official joint rebel command in 1938. But in the face of rapidly proliferating numbers of rural bands, with mutually suspicious leaders deeply distrustful of the old urban leadership, striving for individual autonomy of action, and pulling the revolt in different directions, any real central command and control remained quixotic.

Nevertheless, the rural forces succeeded in confusing the British by striking at their logistical and communications systems, as well as other targets. By the summer of 1937, there were hundreds of peasant bands undertaking near-daily acts of sabotage. With weapons pilfered or captured from the British or old surplus rifles smuggled in from neighboring countries, they wreaked havoc on the countryside. "Telephone and telegraph communications were cut, the oil pipeline from Iraq to Haifa was severed, police stations attacked, rail lines blown up, roads mined and bridges destroyed." For more than eighteen months the country's interior was controlled by the rebels.

After the harvest in June and July of 1938, the rebel units recruited thousands of peasants and opened their most effective offensive. In the face of extreme measures by British troops and the hanging of

Sheikh Farhan al-Saadi—the disciple of Sheikh Qassam who probably touched off the revolt with the murders of April, 1936—they paralyzed British and Jewish movement on the inland roads.[28] In most of the villages, the green, red, and black Arab Palestinian flag waved in the summer breeze, and rebel chiefs declared many of the rural areas liberated zones.

With the exception of the Tiberias massacre of September, 1938, and several similar episodes, the Jews managed to defend themselves fairly well during the upheaval. Their settlements remained intact, transportation between them continuing with convoys. The British were the primary Arab target, in any case. Over 40 percent of the approximately 1,800 major rebel attacks in 1938 were directly on the military or else involved sabotage to telephones, railways, roads, the pipeline, and other government property. A bit less than a quarter of the strikes were against Jews (about 1,300 cases of sniper fire) and their property.[29]

The effect of the onslaught in late 1938 was that the British lost control of most of the Arab population for months. City and countryside now came under rebel command. In the most active regions, the so-called dangerous triangle bounded by Tulkarm, Jenin, and Nablus, this had a significant effect on Arab rural life, especially in 1938 and 1939. An anthropologist depicts the transformation of the countryside:

> The various bands [in the most active regions] set up their own court system, administrative offices, and intelligence networks. While peasants and ex-peasant migrants to the towns composed the vast majority of band leaders and fighters, young urban militants played important roles as commanders, advisers, arms transporters, instructors, and judges. Qassamites were particularly well represented at the leadership level. By taxing the peasantry, levying volunteers, and acquiring arms through the agency of experienced smugglers, the bands were able to operate autonomously from the rebel headquarters-in-exile set up by the notable leadership at Damascus.[30]

This transformation entailed a muted cultural revolution, reflected in the appeal by the revolt's leaders for city Arabs to discard the fez or tarbush—the rounded hat commonly found among middle- and upper-class men in urban areas—in favor of the kafiya—the distinctive head wrap popular among the peasants. The order included urban Christians, who had never before worn the kafiya, and Arab lawyers appearing before British courts. While this innovation eased the rebels' ability to blend into the towns when they entered them, its symbolic meaning was that a head wrapping previously the mark of the underclass was now imposed, through a specific order, on the upper classes. In 1938, one educated Palestinian noted that "the fellahin do not conceal their delight at seeing their 'uppers,' the effendis, come down a peg and look like them in the matter of head dress. They feel proud having raised themselves in the social scale."[31] Once the rebellion was over, the urban population quickly discarded the kafiya and did not take it up again until the 1960s.

Both Muslim and Christian women in the cities were also ordered to veil themselves during the revolt. There is some irony at work here, since traditionally the veiling of women had been much more an urban Muslim than village custom. But now it was the rural commanders, along with the Mufti (he had always been adamant on the issue), who demanded the use of the veil, now a cultural symbol as it was in the later, Algerian struggle against the French.[32] Along with the kafiya, it became a symbolic protest against urban assimilation. Rural fighters had come to regard the urban culture that had dominated from the late Ottoman period as tainted by its proximity to the imperialists and Zionists.

The shift of influence from Jaffa and Jerusalem to the hinterland came in the wake of two extraordinary processes. The first, already described, was the rapid decimation of the ayan by the British. Possibly because the national movement's painstakingly built institutions, from the literary clubs to the Muslim-Christian Associations, had included such a narrow segment of Palestinian society, they proved extremely vulnerable in the wave of British arrests. The second process, continuing for the revolt's duration, was the new reverse migration—thousands of new and temporary city dwellers now moving, with the revolt's toll on the urban economy, back to the hills and the security of their old villages. Using Palestine as a forward outpost, the British would draw the villagers back to the coastal towns during World War II.

The shift would take on the quality of class struggle. Peasant bands demanded funding from wealthy merchants and citrus growers. They also declared a moratorium on paying debts to landowners and cancelled rents.[33] In some cases, urban landowners and creditors were barred from setting foot in villages. All of this continued the repudiation of the ayan begun in the early 1930s. The peasant bands directed the uprising against the notables as well as the British and the Jews. Increasingly, popular culture romanticized the lower classes, especially the peasantry, interpreting the revolt as a struggle against the collusion of oppressive forces, the Zionists, the British, and the ayan. It is not surprising that some upper-class Palestinians saw the rebellion's endgame as performed by thugs.

After the British finally eradicated the guerrilla groups, many peasants placed blame on the corrupt leadership. Salih Baransi, who was a boy in the village of al-Tayyiba during the revolt, remembers how "the people endured without a murmur and gave without wearying or complaining, while the leaderships showed such weakness and squandered all the fruits of the people's sacrifice." His memory is of the unselfish "role played by the peasants—their ungrudging sacrifices and generosity."[34] Another villager states that "people paid to the revolt, and they were willing to pay. Willing! As for the zu'ama' [chiefs], they never behaved properly. . . ."[35]

Writing from the heart of the turmoil, the Palestinian historian George Antonius took note of the social-revolutionary undertones to the surface anger vented on the British and the Jews:

> One of the most prevalent misconceptions is that the trouble in Palestine is the result of an engineered agitation. It is variously attributed to the intrigues of the effendi class, to the political ambitions of the Grand Mufti. . . . The rebellion to-day is, to a greater extent than ever before, a revolt of villagers. . . . The moving spirits in the revolt are not the nationalist institute leaders, most of whom are now in exile, but men of the working and agricultural classes. . . . Far from its

being engineered by the leaders, the revolt is in a very marked way a challenge to their authority and an indictment of their methods.[36]

In some very important senses, the break in the social patterns that had evolved over the last century became permanent, perhaps briefly dissolving, on occasion, in the frenzied decade between the revolt and the Zionist victory in 1948: Already battered by the effects of Palestine's incorporation into the world market, the bond between the ayan and the lower classes disintegrated, with a new leadership languishing due to its physical separation from the land and from most of the people. Jaffa and Haifa would enjoy only a brief resurgence as centers of Arab activity after 1940. And perhaps most ominously, the latter stages of the revolt seemed to revive the old lines so long dividing the Palestinians—religious tensions festered, along with those of kinship:

> This gradual killing off of the leaders was having its effect. More and more, the Rebellion was tending to degenerate from a national movement into squabbles between rival rebel bands. Beir Zeit, like many another village, was now little better than a hornet's nest of longstanding family feuds, stirred up afresh in the hope of getting some advantage through the help of this or that party of rebels.[37]

This statement is from a British school teacher in a mostly Christian village, offering her impressions of March, 1939, when the British offensive against the rural guerrillas was in full swing.

It was not simply that the breakdown of order, or of the discipline of coordinated action, opened the door to the airing of more mundane concerns. Rather, the petty feuds came to be caught up in the cycle of Arab attacks and British retribution. Even villagers attempting to stay clear of the revolt found themselves taxed by the rural bands and subject to both their collective punishment and that of the British, meted out for failing to inform on their neighbors. The British exploited religious and other factional differences, while the rebels abducted and killed a sizeable number of village chiefs—mukhtars, who were on the British payroll. They also assassinated others suspected of collaboration or against whom grudges were held, creating all sorts of new grievances on the part of their kin. Swedenburg, for example, cites the account of a former chief of a village in the Qalqilya district. A doctor had told a local band that a member of the leading al-Zaban clan was a British agent. The denounced man was killed by the rebels. In retribution the al-Zaban clan divulged the band's location to the British, which led to the death of several rebels, including the one who had carried out the execution. (The charge eventually turned out not true.) The al-Zaban clan also fired on the car of the doctor, killing his father. Similarly, we have the account of Sheikh Rabbah al-Awad—the leader of a small rebel band—concerning the assassination, in the waning days of the revolt, of a man from a notable family. He had recruited Sheikh Rabbah into the rebellion, and his father had been an old rival of the Mufti. In 1939, the sheikh assumed it was the Mufti's men who had committed the murder; at the urging of the victim's son, Rabbah and his band crossed over to the British side to help avenge the death.[38] Resentments over such issues have remained intact until this day.[39]

Such pressures and manipulations greatly exacerbated already existing village divisions. As the revolt wore on, no authority, British or rebel, was powerful enough to control the local disputes. Once the rebels were defeated, and with the victorious British discredited, the result "was the alienation of dislocated villagers from all existing forms of authority."[40]

The Revolt Turned Upside Down

Complementing the tensions of religion and kinship and the long-standing feuds between villages was a growing violence between rural and urban Palestinians. At first, demands on the latter were directed at the wealthy notables and merchants, each rebel unit, sometimes several units, determining the rate of "taxes" the wealthy would pay to sustain the revolt. When notables or merchants resisted paying, they were beaten or murdered. The violence then spread to people defined as collaborators or traitors, the problem being that the definitions were highly arbitrary. Some Arabs used "collaboration" as a way of satisfying vendettas and old grievances, thus injecting more uncertainty and lawlessness into Palestinian society.[41] The first targets were allies of the Nashashibis—the Muarada (opposition). In this way, Hassan Sidqi al-Dajani—the head of one of the most important Jerusalem families—met his death.[42]

But the civil strife went beyond the notables. As the mayor of Haifa—traditionally a city with some of the most cooperative Jewish-Arab relations—Hasan Shukri was assassinated because of alleged pro-Jewish views. Communist or labor union leaders such as Sami Taha and Michel Mitri met the same fate. A leaflet distributed by the rebels in Haifa and Jaffa warned against the use of electricity because it came from a "Jewish-British" plant. Many residents interpreted this as an effort to reduce the cities to the same level as the villages.

The Druze and Christian religious communities became targets of the rural bands, the latter being particularly singled out, in part because many wealthy merchants were Christians but also because of the uprising's strong Islamic component. In 1936, a leaflet signed by the followers of Sheikh Qassam had called for a boycott of the Christians because of the "crimes they committed against the national movement." In a march through a Christian village, one band changed its chant from "We are going to kill the British [or Jews]" to "We are going to kill the Christians." The strong intervention of Amin al-Husseini, through the preachers in the mosques, staved off any attacks on the Christian community, but many individual Christians were killed during the revolt. In the fall of 1937 and the winter of 1938, Druze villages on Mount Carmel also faced systematic attacks.

As their successes in 1938 emboldened the rebels, their decrees became more radical. They followed the moratorium on payment of fellaheen debts with death threats against loan collectors. Once they abolished rents for city tenants, they warned tenants not to rent from Jews or the British. They declared a compulsory draft for males between the ages of nineteen and twenty-three, and one commander in the Southern District, Yusuf Abu Durra, even announced the creation of a free Arab government.[43]

Many Arab city dwellers with connections and resources neither resisted the rebels nor risked their wrath, simply fleeing the country. But by the Revolt's end, nearly 500 others were dead, nearly the same as the number of Jews, creating widespread fear. After being deposed as mayor of Haifa by the British in 1938, for supporting the revolt, W. F. Abboushi's father

> went to Beirut because the revolution had deteriorated and Arabs were assassinating Arabs. Life had become insecure for the urban "aristocracy" of Palestine, and consequently, Beirut acquired a new community of political refugees made up of well-to-do Palestinians.[44]

With the dead and self-exiled added to those deported from Palestine or barred reentry by the British, the Palestinians found themselves—at a time when the course of British policies and decisions would carry as much import as at any point since the Balfour Declaration—without the groups that had reshaped their society, molded the national movement, and furnished their domestic and international spokesmen. The leadership had begun an exile continuing to this day.

Ties between the villages and the cities had existed before the revolt, through the British civil administration, Arabic language newspapers, the Arab school teachers, migration, and markets. But the revolt robbed the national movement of a symbiosis between its growing urban organization and its reservoir of rural Palestinians ready for violent action. The withdrawal and flight of large parts of the urban population, along with the weak coordination offered by an exiled leadership, resulted in bands that appeared more like traditional rural gangs. What Qa'uqji had feared and tried to prevent right at the revolt's beginning—the anarchy of fighting forces he had witnessed in the rebellion of Syrian Arabs—threatened to undo the rebel gains.

In this regard, it is important to recall that the rural Palestinians had not created the same rural sorts of organizations giving shape to life in the cities—the Boy Scouts, Young Men's Muslim Associations, the labor unions, and the like. Their uprising mirrored the structure of life in the villages, consisting of loosely organized groups, usually relatives or people who knew and trusted each other, jealously guarding their autonomy. Formal training and a hierarchical military structure barely existed. It is not surprising that the tactics and traits of traditional rural banditry often surfaced, especially when any semblance of central coordination disappeared.[45]

In the wake of the rebels' 1938 summer offensive, the situation of Palestinians in the country deteriorated badly. With the rebels stepping up their demands, many city dwellers, already exhausted by the general strike of 1936, now felt under economic and mental siege. Newly dispatched British troops offered relief: They ousted the rebel bands from the towns, relentlessly pursuing them in the villages and hills. Jewish retaliation, often coordinated with British actions, also took an increasing toll. By the end of the revolt, the Zionists' military activism differed markedly from the policy of *havlagah*, or self-restraint, the mainstream Labor Zionists (but not the Irgun), had adopted at the outset, when they had relied heavily on the British to reestablish law and order. On the Arab side, the Damascus leadership failed to supply the weapons and financial support the rebels desperately needed; as a result, the rebels made ever stiffer demands upon the foundation of their strength, the fellaheen. One peasant protested that "we . . . are falling between the devil and the deep blue sea. . . . The rebels come to our villages, take our money, food, and sometimes kill some of us. . . . [Then] the Police come to our villages following these rebels with their dogs."[46]

Like popular renegades everywhere, the rural fighters were thus assuming dual identities in the eyes of the peasants: rebels fighting foreign occupation and little more than bandits. Many peasants were thus decidedly ambivalent about the rebels. The British and Zionists naturally emphasized their criminality—many Israeli histories still use the word "gang" to describe the rebel bands and identify the revolt as the "disturbances," in this way denying its political essence. But among the Palestinian population during the mandate, even some truly criminal gangs, such as that headed by Abu Jilda, had achieved a quasi-heroic notoriety. Jilda's gang had robbed and killed English, Arabs, and Jews, but its success in embarrassing the authorities made it an object of delight and popularity.

At the revolt's apogee, its fighters were often referred to as mujahidin—a term with strong Islamic overtones. Originally it meant warriors defending the faith; in its new context, freedom fighters. One of the first national groups to define themselves in this way was the popular Green Hand, operating in the north for about four months in 1929–30 and participating in a slaughter of Jews. But by the revolt's end, such popularity had worn thin. Opposition to the bands spread by late 1938 from the cities to the countryside, ultimately leading to civil war among the Palestinians.[47]

Some villages, especially those aligned with the Nashashibi opposition rather than the Mufti, established self-defense units (at times with British encouragement and funds). A number of such units, called "peace bands," participated in the uprising or at least professed dedication to the national cause. The one organized by Sheikh Naif al-Zubi actually took part in attacks against the petroleum pipeline running from Iraq to Haifa. In reality, however, their main task was to defend their villages. Some of the Nashashibis tried to raise money for the peace bands, apparently even from the Jews and British.[48]

In certain respects, the split between the rebels and the Arabs fighting them simply reflected irreconcilable differences between those loyal to Amin al-Husseini and those siding with the Nashashibis. But by the late fall of 1938 and the winter of 1939, it was clear that what was at stake was more than a dispute among notable families.[49] Fakhri Abd al-Hadi, who had fought alongside Qa'uqji, flip-flopped several times between the rebels and their opponents before finally spearheading a large Arab force against the former. In December, 1938, notables and three thousand villagers gathered in a village near Hebron in the presence of the British regional military commander to condemn the terror of the rebels and to pledge to fight against them. The actions of these Arab anti-rebel forces helped the British quash the last stage of the revolt in 1939.

A Transformed Political Stage

In the years between the 1929 Wailing Wall riots, which had shaken the Zionist leadership's complacent faith in eventual Arab acceptance of the Zionist enterprise,[50] and the outbreak of the Arab Revolt, informal negotiations took place between Ben-Gurion and Musa Alami. But various acute differences blocked any serious progress. In particular, the rapid rise in the Jewish population prompted George Antonius and other Arabs to underscore that no agreement could come in the absence of immigration restrictions. The Arab demand flew in the face of deeply held Zionist convictions—although a number of Zionist leaders, including Ben-Gurion, refused to confront seriously the significance of Arab adamancy. In any case, until the start of the revolt, those leaders believed they could reach all their goals, whether there was agreement with the Arabs or not.

The Zionists misread the revolt from its beginning, attributing the general strike to the small class of privileged notables and failing to grasp its popular basis—at least in public. In fact, following his talks with Antonius in the midst of the Arab general strike, Ben-Gurion seemed to come to a more sober understanding of the Arab position: "There is a conflict, a great conflict. There is a fundamental conflict. We and they want the same thing: We both want Palestine. And that is the fundamental conflict."[51] And in one private meeting, he remarked that "the Arabs fight with arms, strike, terror, sabotage, murder and destruction of government property. . . . What else must they do for their acts to be worthy of the name 'revolt?'"[52]

The Zionists' essential response to the revolt was to move in two policy directions. The first was to shore up a self-sufficient Jewish economy, independent of Arab labor and markets. Although the general strike had initially caused serious dislocations in the Jewish sector, with the Jewish population now nearly 30 percent of the country's total, they were able to mobilize effectively. The second was to strengthen their illegal armed forces considerably—the policy they defined as havlagah, restraint based on defending settlements without reprisals or outside pursuit. As the revolt moved into 1937 and 1938, havlagah prevailed only intermittently. Surprise night attacks, increased military preparations, direct reprisals, all reflected a more militant, embattled outlook. By the revolt's last stages (from May, 1938 on), the Zionists collaborated closely with the British in its suppression.[53]

Some writers have claimed that before the onset of real social chaos, the British were not firm or consistent enough in securing public order.[54] In any case, from the general strike on, they showed a perfect willingness to make amends for the past failing, initiating a number of severe measures including the Palestine Defence Order-in-Council and the Emergency Regulations. Later, when unable to maintain control of Jaffa, they levelled a good portion of the walled city by creating a wide road through its center. By then they had arrested 2,600 strikers. At the end of the general strike in 1936, they had registered 145 Arabs as killed, but the actual number was probably on the order of 1,000.

With time, the British resorted to ever-heavier doses of brutal force. With the rebel occupation of the walled part of Jerusalem on October 17, 1938, they suspended civil rule and imposed military government throughout the country, using harsh and illiberal methods to break the revolt's back. Among the methods were collective fines, the demolition of houses, the use of prisoners as human minesweepers, hangings, and far-ranging military sweeps. Even while grappling with the fearful prospect of war with Germany, they committed themselves to crushing the rebellion completely. Upon signing the Munich pact, they poured new troops into Palestine, increasing their garrison to nearly twenty-five thousand men.[55] After suppressing the urban uprising at the end of 1938, they built roads into the remote hills where rebel bands were taking refuge, isolated and collectively punished collaborating villages, and built the Tegart Wall—a barbed wire barrier between Palestine and Syria—to disrupt communications and supplies.

Aside from the Gandhi-led agitation they confronted in India, the British faced no more formidable opposition to their imperial rule than that of Palestinians. This militancy induced not only a military but also a political response, with diplomatic maneuvering feverishly proceeding, and several important shifts in political policy, carrying with them a long-term impact on Palestine's Arabs. First of all, the locus of British policy-making shifted from Jerusalem to London and, within London, from the Colonial Office to the Foreign Office.[56] This freed the British from the constant, direct pressure of the Zionist and Palestinian Arab leadership and made them more responsive to the regional repercussions of Palestinian events. Next, the British ceased negotiating with Palestinian leaders, in favor of the heads of surrounding newly independent Arab states. In other words, the leadership vacuum developing among the Palestinian Arabs came to be filled by non-Palestinian Arabs. This process was actually inaugurated by the Mufti, who used the Arab heads of state to call for an end to the general strike, thus helping to extricate the Palestinian leaders from their self-inflicted dilemmas.

Finally Britain abandoned the policy line dictated by the Balfour Declaration, acceding, in good part, to the Arab demands. The revolt had begun in the wake of the failure of one British policy initiative, the scheme for a Legislative Council, and it ended on the eve of another initiative, the White Paper of 1939. The Legislative Council's purpose was to incorporate both Jews and Arabs into self-governing institutions. It foundered mostly because of Jewish insistence on communal parity, and partly because of the Arab demand for a majority rule invalidating the thrust of the Balfour Declaration.

After the general strike, the Colonial Office attempted to maintain control of the Palestinian situation by dispatching the Royal Commission headed by Lord Peel to the country. Even in its collection of evidence, the Peel Commission's presence was humiliating to the Palestinian leadership. The Arab Higher Committee's decision to boycott the commission had to be reversed in the face of stiff pressure by Arab heads of state. In the end, the commission's recommendation to partition Palestine—the last flicker of the Balfour Declaration's spirit—led to the resumption of the revolt in 1937.

For the Arabs, the 1939 White Paper had an ironic aura. Its acceptance of their demand for majoritarian national independence (in ten years' time), a strict prohibition on Jewish immigration, and a banning of land sales to Jews came just as the British finished them militarily and destroyed their national leadership. A more drastic irony was the contemptuous rejection by the exiled leadership—most notably the Mufti—of the White Paper. Perhaps nothing else was possible with the Palestinian community in a state of civil war. Perhaps an exiled leadership removed from the pressures faced by Palestine's Arab population (5,000 dead, 15,000 wounded, 5,600 detained in the revolt;[57] up to a quarter of the casualties inflicted by other Arabs) could not recognize the opportunity. Perhaps, as the Mufti's biographer suggests, Amin acted out of personal pique at the way the British had treated him.[58]

The revolt and the rejection of the White Paper thus left the Palestinian national movement in an abyss. As the fighting waned, the British killed one major rebel leader and his band dissolved; another surrendered with his band to the French in Syria; the Transjordanians extradited yet another, who was then hanged by the British. The Palestinian Arabs were exhausted and fractured, shorn of basic trust between leaders (often exiled) and followers. Paradoxically, the revolt was a distinct watershed, crystallizing the Palestinian national identity as nothing before. It offered new heroes and martyrs—most prominently, Sheikh Qassam—and a popular culture to eulogize them;[59] it constituted an unequivocal declaration that, whatever their social status, Palestinians unalterably opposed the Zionist program. To be sure, this nationalism reflected what one writer has termed the various local idioms of Palestinian nationalism.[60] But the diverse circumstances and motives should not obscure the fact that the revolt helped to create a nation—even while crippling its social and political basis.

Part Two

DISPERSAL

5

THE MEANING OF DISASTER

BETWEEN THE LAST MONTH of 1947 and the first four and a half months of 1948, the Palestinian Arab community would cease to exist as a social and political entity: a process that neither Jew nor Arab foresaw in the tumultuous years of World War II. More than 350 villages would vanish,[1] urban life would all but evaporate—war and exodus reducing Jaffa's population from 70,000-80,000 Palestinians to a remnant of 3,000-4,000—and 500,000 to 1,000,000 Palestinians would become refugees. Looking back at the situation in 1956, poet Mu'in Basisu described it in these words:

> And after the flood none was left of this people
>   This land, but a rope and a pole
> None but bare bodies floating on mires
>   Leavings of kin and a child
> None but swelled bodies
>   Their numbers unknown
> Here wreckage, here death, here drowned in deep waters
>   Scraps of a bread loaf still clasped in my hand

Here quivering dead eyes
   Here lips crying vengeance
Scraps of my people and country
   Some weeping, some crazed, some in tremor,
Scraps of my people, my father, my mother
   There's nobody left in the tents
Here Children? you ask and she'll scream
   And the torrent is jeering, she never gave birth
How to these people, black tents,
   On pale sands
     Drowned have they been forever.[2]

Accompanying this cataclysm was a drastic weakening of both axes molding the special character of the Palestinians over the previous century: (1) the tension between Nablus and Jaffa—between the more self-contained, agriculturally centered life of the inland towns and the European-facing coastal cities; and (2) the fragile structural balance achieved between the notable leadership and the society around them. With the disintegration of the country's urban backbone in 1948, the center of Palestinian life would return to the hill country in the east. At the same time, the catastrophe of 1948 and the ignominious role of the notables in it destroyed the remnants of the leadership.

In place of a familiarly constructed society, and the sense of self-worth that accompanies it, Palestinians would grasp the belief that they were the victims of an immense conspiracy and of a monumental injustice. They would see their plight as representing a breach of the cosmic order. They would seethe in anger, not only against the hated Zionists, but also against their putative allies—their Arab brothers from neighboring countries—and against a wider world that could allow such an injustice. As Fawaz Turki (born in the small town of Balad al-Sheikh, near Haifa) would note in *The Disinherited*,

The Western world, which had long tormented and abused the Jewish people, hastened to bless an event that saw an end to their victims' suffering. A debt was to be paid. Who was to pay it and where it was to be paid were not seen as of the essence, so long as it was not paid by Europeans in Europe.[3]

The experience of exile—of a tragedy perceived as both personal and national—would overshadow all else for this generation of disaster (the *jil al-Nakba*) creating both a sense of ennui and ironically, a new form of cultural ferment, largely literary in nature. (Cf. Fadwa Tuqan's explanation that "In 1948, my father died and Palestine was lost . . . These events enabled me to write the nationalist poetry my father had always wished that I would write.")[4]

A folk culture conveyed by songs and ballads, poetry and narrative would form around three motifs: the praise and memory of the lost paradise from which the Palestinians were expelled, the bitter lament of the present, and the depiction of the imagined triumphant return. In the wake of the demise of the political leadership, writers such as Tuqan and Ghassan Kanafani would use these motifs to maintain and rebuild the Palestinian national identity. This chapter recounts the factors leading to the very emergence of such a challenge, starting with the defeat of the Arab Revolt and ending with the Palestinian war against the Jews.

Between Revolt and Disaster

Emerging from the revolt's long ordeal—with its accompanying drastic economic contraction—at the onset of World War II, Palestine faced the prospect of scant respite from upheaval. The country did manage to escape the war's direct impact, but the proximity of the North African campaign reverberated. Using Palestine as an important rear base, the British invested there heavily, the ensuing economic growth being accompanied by even further erosion of peasant life and a more severe physical and psychological dislocation.[5] It took place at a time when "there were no political institutions in the country capable of carrying the banner of the nationalist movement."[6]

The revolt had not resulted in a closing of the economic gap between Jews and Arabs. While both communities suffered, the fragile Arab urban economy was ravaged, with wage-earners fleeing back to already strained villages, and Arab merchants and importers—many of whom had controlled both Jewish and Arab markets before 1936— now facing ruin. With wealthier Arabs heading for more tranquil shores, thousands of urban migrants fled back to their home villages, leaving the urban economy without its most important human resource.[7]

During World War II, the most obvious economic hardship thus came in the early years, real wages falling through 1940 and into 1941. The shipping crisis in the Mediterranean hit the ports very hard, bringing citrus exports to a halt—in 1943, they amounted to less than 10 percent of what they had been in 1938,[8] and nearly twenty thousand Arab orange-plantation workers returned to their already crowded villages.[9] These villages, accustomed to both supplemental income earned on the plantations and (prior to the revolt) on employment outside agriculture, were now forced to rely on their own land, while accommodating a sizeable proportion of an expanded Arab population.

With the British mobilization, the economic situation changed so dramatically that it threatened to destroy the old social institutions—the family, the village, even the national movement. From 1940 to 1945, the Arab economy grew by nearly 9 percent a year (compared to a 13 percent rate for the Jewish economy, which seemed to get a head start at the beginning of the war). In the two years after the war's end, the Arab sector equalled the Jewish, growing at an average rate of over 12 percent.[10] By that time, Palestine far outdistanced neighboring Arab countries on almost every economic indicator.[11]

The mobilization meant a 400 percent increase of British military investment, and vastly expanded construction.[12] The numbers of garrisoned troops increased from 90,000 (an already considerable figure) to 280,000. The mobilization required labor for everything from building barracks and roads to producing weapons and ammunition. The primary British strategy for meeting the requirement was to offer wages high enough—in the context of drastically elevated world agricultural prices—to lure fellaheen from the land. Unemployment gave way to a severe labor shortage, leading the government, as a second part of its strategy, to import thousands of workers from neighboring Arab countries. (Some of these laborers eventually returned to their home countries.)

While construction jobs in rural areas often enabled Palestinian men to stay in their villages, those in the urban work force would typically leave, for half a year at first. As the war dragged on, the stream of men, and of entire families, leaving for the coast, permanently, had become a flood. Women were left behind to manage the farms—an arrangement bringing them into a more public realm and widening their roles as household managers.

Such changes in the rural social structure interacted with others, such as the discrediting of numerous village leaders who had cooperated with the British during the revolt, and an elimination, finally, of peasant indebtedness: a problem that had haunted the fellaheen, as well as British officials concerned with the viability of village life. Rural communities managed to raise their living standard considerably, taking advantage of both a growing need for their produce in the absence of imported competition with their crops and British efforts to help them raise productivity.[13] Agricultural yields rose, in fact, by 20 percent during the war—without any significant increase in the amount of land under cultivation,[14] and while the male agricultural work force was plummeting.

For men now working in the cities, the change was even greater than for the village fellaheen. As we have seen in chapter 2, labor unions—a hapless undertaking in the years before the war—now became significant urban institutions. In part, this reflected new government policies, in part new conditions promoting an ideology of unionism—that is, the existence of a separate Arab working class supported a distinctive organization to demand its rights.[15] The new circumstances in the city often increased the individual mobility of the worker and his affinity to a larger, more impersonal Palestinian working class. In turn, both these circumstances and union encouragement of the expression of class interests ran against the grain of parochial clan, village, and religious ties—and also of the ayan's demands for national solidarity.

Radicalization of the working class through left-leaning unions proved worrisome both to the British and to the ayan, prompting conservative counter-organizing efforts by the latter.[16] Arab unionism thus became an odd amalgam, nonetheless attracting about twenty thousand workers (approximately 20 percent of all wage-earners) by the end of the war.[17] Even the British and Jews found themselves responding to the new Arab wage-laboring class. Mandate officials established arbitration boards to deal with the increasing disputes in small and large Arab factories, and the powerful Jewish labor federation, the Histadrut, once again hazarded an effort at Arab labor organizing.

Some Arab workers found themselves caught painfully between their attempts to improve the lot of workers as a class (which meant solidarity with Jewish laborers) and their deep antipathy to Zionism. Difficulties between Arab and Jewish workers stemmed both from such antipathy and from Arab resentment over being largely concentrated in the unskilled jobs. In fact, the major collaborative Arab-Jewish effort, a strike of junior civil servants against the government in April 1946, came precisely in the absence of that status gap.

With the resurgence of Palestinian nationalism in 1944, and especially with the return of Jamal al-Husseini to the country in 1946, organized labor activity among the Palestinians began to wane. But through their own experiences, and through the observation of Jewish laborers, they had glimpsed possibilities for organizing their society quite different from the ideal put forth by the notables, or even by other nationalists. A historian of Arab labor during the mandate outlines the dilemma:

> As [the unions] stressed the need for the definition and recognition of a separate working class, they began to suggest alternative principles of social integration to the thousands of workers who supported them. In their efforts to provide a positive culture to Arab workers, however, Arab unions came into real conflict with existing elites by

challenging their legitimacy. The consequences of this collision of interests were made the more complex by the deep entanglement of the labor movement with family and clan concerns and by labor's commitment to the nationalist cause. Arab workers, caught between these contrary orientations, were placed in a confusing situation. Moreover, the weakness and the eventual eclipse of the labor movement in 1947 and 1948 finally deprived them of any effective leadership.[18]

The debacle of 1947–48 thus found the Palestinians united in their opposition to Zionism, yet dislocated and disorganized. Prosperity during the war had had its costs in a complex, physical and sociocultural displacement. (Even Palestinian women—that seemingly insular segment of society—found their lives substantially changed, assimilating the changes, within the family, "in a more intensified and personal way than men.")[19]

As suggested in the above citation, the "confusing situation" of the Palestinians was exacerbated by the absence of the national leadership that had played such a prominent role in the previous two decades. Until the defeat of Rommel's army in North Africa in 1942, the British had banned political activity. Afterwards, Palestinians found that earlier arrests, deportations, and flight had done their damage. To some degree labor leaders, professionals, and Arabs working in the middle and higher echelons of the government emerged as community spokesmen during the war. But for a people who had been among the most politically violent and nettlesome in the vast British Empire, the Palestinians remained remarkably quiescent and pacified in its immediate aftermath.

In the latter half of the war, the British permitted the return of some of the old political leaders, including members of the disbanded Arab Higher Committee, but with the firm provision that these figures would not participate in any political activity. Nevertheless, there were some significant diplomatic forays: In the summer of 1940, Colonel Stewart F. Newcombe, a British representative in the service of Lord Lloyd, arrived in Baghdad and, under the auspices of the Iraqi foreign minister, Nuri al-Said, tried to reach an agreement with Jamal al-Husseini and Musa Alami. The Iraqis agreed to send troops to the western desert, and in exchange the British were to agree to the establishment of an autonomous government in Palestine and gradually to pass power and authority to local Palestinian representatives. Apparently, Winston Churchill vetoed the agreement when it came for cabinet ratification.[20] In any case, as with the mainstream Zionists, there was genuine sympathy among many Palestinians for Britain during the war, which in practice translated into a respite from harassment for the government. Leaders such as Fakhri al-Nashashibi encouraged enlistment for British army service. About nine thousand signed up directly, and another fourteen thousand joined the Transjordanian Arab Legion, a fighting force linked to the Allied deployment.[21]

Even those Palestinians who followed the lead of the exiled Mufti and pinned their hopes on a Nazi victory turned out not to pose much of a political challenge. The anti-British and anti-Jewish themes sounded by the Germans and Italians—Axis plans called for a sphere of Italian influence in the Mediterranean[22]—certainly had some appeal. Nazi propagandists attempted to present Haj Amin as a pan-Islamic figure, "der Grossmufti," and let him broadcast on Radio Berlin to the entire Middle East, North Africa, and even India, calling the faithful to jihad against the godless British-Zionist-Bolshevik forces.[23] A small Arab unit became part of the Wehrmacht, fighting on the Russian front in 1942. But the Mufti failed to rally the Arabs of Palestine to support the Germans—no organized pro-Nazi movement developed inside the country, as occurred in several other Arab lands.

In 1943, some figures banded together under the prodding of a former Istiqlal leader to renew the Fund of the Arab Nation. Its goal was to prevent the sale of Arab-owned land to Jews, who continued to acquire tracts even with the restrictions imposed on them by the 1939 White Paper. In one case, the Fund managed to raise £P100,000 for 2,500 acres of land about to be purchased by the Jewish National Fund. It also initiated a series of trials to prevent title transfers and, once again, put the issue of land on the Palestinian community's agenda.[24]

Various figures (again including some former Istiqlal heads) made efforts during the war to revive the Arab Higher Committee and to reconstitute the Istiqlal itself, along with other political parties.[25] Heads of the National Bloc party, for instance, proclaimed it the vanguard of the national movement, with Nablus as its center. That city would always tend to claim control of the national movement when Jerusalem, Jaffa, and Haifa, more closely tied to European currents, were faltering.

But such activity merely underscored the general political quiescence, resulting, perhaps, from a growing confidence after the White Paper that Britain would eventually grant Arab independence in Palestine. Many Arabs interpreted the 1944 Zionist revolt against the British authorities, spearheaded by the Irgun, as a sign of anxiety and weakness.[26] All they needed to do was bide their time.

That position, of course, turned out fraught with illusions. With the war's end and the revelations of Nazi horrors, the future of Palestine reemerged as an international issue, prompting Harry Truman, shortly after Japan's defeat, to back a proposal that the mandate accept 100,000 Jewish refugees. Within a year, the Anglo-American Committee of Inquiry made a similar proposal, and also that Britain remove the White Paper's restrictions.

Although Britain's response was rejection, the Palestinians were now alarmed—and discovered new constraints on their political activity. Since their call to end the general strike of 1936, and their participation in the Round Table Conference of 1939,[27] the independent Arab states, in fact, had begun to define the contours of Palestinian politics. In 1944, they held a conference to explore political union among themselves; when the Palestinians could not agree on the makeup of their observer delegation, the prime ministers of Iraq and Egypt did it for them. They chose the highly respected Musa Alami, perceived as generally neutral and acceptable to all Palestinians.

Between 1946 and 1948, the Husseinis had consolidated their position. Despite the war, they had succeeded in nullifying any attempts to resurrect the Istiqlal or—to the great disappointment of some Zionist leaders, who felt there still was hope for accommodation with the Palestinian opposition—to reestablish the Nashashibis: Fakhri al-Nashashibi was assassinated in late 1941, possibly as a result of orders from the Mufti. But their various efforts to gain autonomy and to reestablish an official Palestinian body on the model of the old Arab Higher Committee were thwarted by the newly formed League of Arab Nations (or Arab League). The League sent a clear message that it, not the Mufti and his associates, would be paramount. It appointed the Arab Higher Executive for Palestine, soon reverting in 1946 to the name of the Arab Higher Committee. Eventually, it included a fairly broad spectrum of Palestinian leaders, but with a decidedly Husseini stamp.[28]

Complex Arab rivalries surrounded the League's main issue—some sort of political unity versus a looser confederation or even simple cooperation among the Arab states. These states' interests in Palestine were thus in many ways inimical to the perspective of the Palestinian leaders, who in the end, were relegated to the sidelines, robbed of any possibility of autonomous action.[29] One writer has termed the process "the political and military neutering of the Palestinian Arabs."[30] Long after the Arab defeat in the 1948 war, Amin al-Husseini would suggest that the Arab states' invasion of Israel was never intended to liberate Palestine, but was a result of their own territorial ambitions.[31] The Mufti's opposition to that invasion demonstrated his feeling of powerlessness in controlling events.

In some ways, Palestinian acceptance of the reconstituted committee, with its chairmanship left open for the still exiled Husseini, made perfect sense. Back in Cairo, the Mufti was invoking the Zionist menace to build the military and financial nucleus for a government-in-exile. On the critical issue that he personified, unrelenting opposition to Zionism and to British partition of the country between Jews and Arabs, there was near unanimity. As Walid Khalidi has noted, he was still "unquestionably the paramount Palestinian leader."[32]

In other ways, the committee, full of familiar names from the old dominating families and under the long shadow of Haj Amin, left the Palestinian community in a highly vulnerable position, unwittingly confirming their powerlessness in what would be the most important few years of their history. For one, key international players harbored deep mistrust for the Mufti. The British still held him personally responsible for the Arab Revolt and refused to allow him to return to Palestine, the Iraqis had not forgiven his involvement in a coup d'état in Baghdad in 1941, and the Transjordan government saw him as an obstacle to its own territorial ambitions. At the same time, the Mufti was very distant from Palestinian events, having last been in the country a traumatic decade before.

In this respect, his situation was not much different from that of the other notables, removed more than ever before from daily Palestinian travails. By 1947, when tensions among the Jews, Arabs, and British had become extreme, thousands of wealthier Arabs fled the country, leaving little intact of the old ayan class—or even of the rudimentary leadership that had grown in the country during the war years. The workers and fellaheen who stayed behind, "leaderless and confused . . . fell easy prey to rumor and to the alarm which soon overcame all parts of the Arab population."[33]

In one or another manner, many observers have attributed the failure of the Palestinians in 1948 to their being "backward, disunited and often apathetic, a community only just entering the modern age politically and administratively."[34] The contrast with the political skill and unity of the Zionists in such accounts is always at least implicit. In fact, Jewish political prowess and unity has been vastly exaggerated—the Zionists suffered from repeated incidents of infighting and political failure. And the thesis of Palestinian political immaturity is misleading.

As we saw in chapter 4, the early 1930s witnessed a virtual explosion of new political institutions and of increased political participation, contentious though it was. But in 1948 the Palestinians were still suffering from the British military and political assaults, during the Arab Revolt, against the leadership and political institutions that had emerged in the 1930s. In the circumstances of World War II and the new constraints imposed by the Arab states, they never managed to recapture these political foundations, nor adapt politically to the vast social changes overtaking their community.

Face to Face in Communal War

The British mandate in Palestine did not so much draw to a close as collapse.[35] From 1946 on, domestic turmoil recalled the previous decade's most violent period, 1936–39—but now it was Jews who were in revolt. Attacks, kidnappings, and assassinations by the Irgun prompted one government step after another: evacuation of some British civilians from the country in January, 1947, construction of secure compounds for mandate officials, martial law in parts of the country. The fact that the Haganah briefly aided government forces against the Irgun in an action called the *Saison,* or hunting season, was of little consolation to the British, and of little interest to the Palestinians: the violence had become intolerable. By the summer of 1947, both the British administrators in Palestine and weary officials in London concluded that the cost of imposing a solution on Arabs and Jews—in terms of material resources, world public opinion, and the sentiment of Arab state leaders—was simply too high. The growing role of the United States in the Palestine affair—what London officials considered sabotage—especially the repeated personal interventions of President Truman, had corroded their resolve,[36] as had the constant, demoralizing effort of trying to curb mounting illegal Jewish immigration of Holocaust survivors. In July, key British officials in His Majesty's Government made the decision to withdraw.[37]

Some time before this (on February 18, 1947) the British had referred the Palestine problem to the United Nations, and the Special Committee on Palestine (UNSCOP) was well advanced in its own combative deliberations on the country's future; having spent five weeks in Palestine in June and July, at the end of August it issued its report. It proposed a solution that the Mufti had long dreaded, partition of the country between Jews and Palestinians,[38] along with a termination of the mandate and a prompt granting of independence.

Britain's reaction to the proposal was the hardening of its resolve to quit Palestine as fast as possible. London feared jeopardizing its position with the new Arab states if it supported partition, and it wanted no part in controlling the strife that it was certain would engulf the country if a partition plan was implemented. The effect of this hands-off policy was free play for the multiplying clashes and spreading violence that began in December, 1947.

UNSCOP's recommendations made their way to the United Nations in the form of the famous resolution advocating—along with partition—the internationalization of Jerusalem and its environs, including Bethlehem (see maps 2 and 3). Partition was the fashionable diplomatic solution of the period for a host of seemingly intractable situations, including those in Germany, India, and Korea. None of these other cases managed to forestall international war or repeated diplomatic crises, and Palestine was no exception in this regard.[39] The crazy-quilt pattern of suggested borders for the two proposed states, and the high concentration of Arabs in the proposed Jewish state (over 40 percent of the projected total population) seemed to doom the idea from the beginning.[40] Nonetheless, supported by both the Americans and Soviets, with no other solution in sight and with the mandate power having thrown up its hands in exasperation, the General Assembly passed Resolution 181 on November 29, 1947, in one of its moments of high drama. The vote was 33 to 13, with 10 abstentions.

Lobbying furiously, both Jews and Arabs had, of course, awaited the vote's outcome rather tensely. Once the UN acted, the Arab Higher Committee responded politically on February 6, 1948, declaring that it would never recognize the validity of partition, nor the UN's authority to implement it. This communique also emphasized that any attempt by the Jews to establish a state would be seen as bald aggression and would be resisted by force, as an act of Arab self-defense.[41] For its part, the World Zionist Organization responded by accepting the resolution, with some qualifications. The mainstream Zionists had decided in the summer of 1947, although not without significant internal dissent, to support a partial partition plan.[42]

The UN vote shattered two illusions shared by Jews and Arabs: that a resolution to the question of Palestine's future would not be quick and that the colonial power would pass its authority on to its successor in an orderly fashion. In the weeks that followed the vote, British administration all but disintegrated. Concerned primarily with protecting and enhancing their positions to the utmost in the face of implacable opposition, the two communities—for the first time in their history face to face without intermediaries or third-party protectors—prepared for violent confrontation.

Communal war began consuming the fabric of normalcy the day

Dep. of Geography, Hebrew University

Map 2. Two Partitions of Palestine (1921, 1949)

LEBANON

SYRIA

Haifa

Nazareth

MEDITERRANEAN SEA

Jordan River

Nablus

Tel Aviv
Jaffa

Jerusalem

Dead Sea

Beersheba

TRANSJORDAN

EGYPT

⬡ Jewish State

⬡ Arab State

⬡ Permanent Trusteeship

Aqaba

Dep. of Geography, Hebrew University

Map 3. United Nations Recommendation for Two-States Solution in Palestine (1947)

after the UN vote, with an Arab attack on a Jewish bus near the town of Lydda. The Palestinians seemed to have the upper hand, at least in numbers—their population of 1.3 million was more than double that of the 620,000 Jews. But such figures are deceptive: Jewish immigration had created a society with a disproportionate share of young men of army age—one and a half times the Arab figure.[43] And even though few Jewish women engaged in direct combat, they did have auxiliary roles closed to women in traditional Islamic societies.

The conflict's opening looked as if it had been rehearsed by the earlier Arab Revolt. Two days after the UN vote, the Arab Higher Committee called a general strike. Although key figures of the Committee assured the British that it would be peaceful, Jerusalem was wracked by violence, and the Jewish commercial sector was set ablaze. National committees, like those during the earlier revolt, coordinated Palestinian activity in various localities, and Arab leaders created a sort of home guard, modelled after efforts in Great Britain during World War II.

But two key differences marked this wave of violence: The Jews, not the British, were the primary target, and this time around the Zionists eschewed havlagah, meeting Arab attacks with a fury of their own. By the conflict's latter stages, the Jews had organized for a total war the Arabs were ill-prepared to fight.

The first week of the fighting was chaotic, setting the stage for the next four months. Skirmishes occurred around the country, Arabs expressing their anger and Jews trying to consolidate a major diplomatic triumph. Although the skirmishes stretched their forces thinly, the Jews found an advantage in the lack of coordination, sometimes even downright animosity, among the Palestinian fighting groups. Over and over again, Haganah leaders would put this to their advantage until the communal warfare's transformation into an international war in May, 1948. In any case, for the time, it was Palestinian initiative that established the pace and style of warfare.[44]

The week after the vote introduced another motif that would become familiar—the migration of Palestinians from their homes to what they hoped would be safer ground. Arabs from neighborhoods in Haifa and Jaffa spearheaded the migration. The second day of fighting, a Haganah intelligence source reported on events in Jaffa's northern suburbs: "Empty carts are seen entering and, afterwards, carts loaded with belongings are seen leaving."[45] Although Benny Morris notes that "Abandoning one's home, and thus breaking a major psychological barrier, paved the way for eventual abandonment of village or town and, ultimately, of country,"[46] such psychological barriers may in fact not have prevailed at all. As we have seen in the events of 1936–39, Palestinians had created a highly mobile society, reflecting frequent communal and economic crises. Movement to a symbolic high ground, particularly home villages away from areas of dense Jewish settlement, was an established pattern of self-defense for workers in the cities and on the citrus plantations, matching the ayan's and merchants' habit of taking refuge in more tranquil spots outside the country.[47]

In early December, 1947, the Palestinian national movement was struggling to forestall the disintegration of the Arab community and thwart the Zionists, and the Jews were still not properly prepared for combat. Haj Amin al-Husseini moved from Cairo to Lebanon to direct the combat and, as in the early stages of the Arab Revolt, many of the shabab became its backbone.

With the Jewish forces caught offguard by the early outbreak of hostilities, the Palestinians scored some impressive military triumphs. Starting on December 8, they managed to capture isolated Jewish neighborhoods and settlements. In the following weeks, their guerrilla forces attacked oil refineries in Haifa, Jewish targets in downtown Jerusalem and neighborhoods of Tel-Aviv, and transportation convoys trying to maintain communications between Jewish settlements. From their commanding positions in the hills surrounding Jerusalem, they mounted repeated attacks on Jewish traffic, almost breaking the fragile links between the coastal plain and the capital. They even managed a frontal assault in January on a concentration of Jewish settlements between Jerusalem and Hebron—the Etzion Bloc, finally destroyed by Palestinian forces, reinforced by Transjordan's Arab Legion, in the last days of the war's communal stage. That loss left a scar in Jewish memory. Confidence soared among the Palestinians, while the morale of the Jews and their backers wavered. In March, the United States withdrew its support for partition. From the Zionists' perspective, the situation in March, 1948, looked grim, with Jerusalem cut off, the Etzion Bloc and other settlements under siege and the Arab states poised for invasion upon the departure of the British.

But such Palestinian successes were camouflage for deep political and military weakness. What Antonio Gramsci has referred to as political society—organizations linking leaders and followers, ranging in Palestine from the Muslim-Christian Associations to labor unions to relatively broad political parties, such as the Istiqlal— mostly had not survived the decade of turmoil beginning in 1936. Haj Amin's handmaiden, the Arab Higher Committee, while committed to the same immediate political goals, did not create firm institutional ties to the population, nor could it count on the old leverage held by the nineteenth century notables. For all his popularity, Amin was thus in no position to impose the planning and coordination on Palestinian forces that the Zionist leadership was able to achieve for the Jewish forces. The logistics of war—assured supplies, access to weapons and ammunition, communications and planning among units, regular methods of recruitment and mobilization, the means to concentrate forces—were largely absent.

The leadership found itself hamstrung as much by its allies as by its enemies. Once the issue of the future of Palestine had been appropriated by the United Nations, King Abdallah of Transjordan, rekindling his father's Hashemite ambitions, came to the conclusion that he should acquire the Arab part of Palestine and merge it with his own country.[48] Beyond such designs, the Arab League itself constantly thwarted the Mufti's political plans: It stood in the way of his determination to create a temporary Palestinian government once the British had left; it blocked a loan to establish an Arab administration in the country; and—what was most irksome—it overlooked the Arab Higher Committee whenever critical decisions had to be made.[49]

Nowhere were such cross-purposes more evident than on the battlefield. Both the Palestinians and the Arab League fielded military forces, and throughout the communal war, rivalries and friction marked relations between them. At the outset, Palestinian forces consisted of two main groups that could mobilize fighters: a youth company of several hundred young men called *al-Futuwwa,* associated with the Husseinis, and *al-Najada,* a unit of 2,000 or 3,000 men associated with opposition notable families, mainly from Jaffa—as well as a scattering of smaller bands. With the Haganah fielding over 35,000 mostly part-time fighters, the challenge for the Palestinian leadership was immense. A number of those soldiers had benefited from British military training in World War II or cooperation with the British in counterinsurgency attacks during the latter stages of the Arab Revolt. The Arab Higher Committee tried to meet the challenge by turning to Abd al-Qadir al-Husseini—the son of Musa Kazim al-Husseini—to head these Palestinian units and mobilize an overall coordinated army. As noted in chapter 4, Abd al-Qadir had gained notoriety during the Arab Revolt by heading a major fighting band in the Jerusalem district and had considered himself the revolt's chief military leader; later, he gained additional military experience in the Wehrmacht. Now he succeeded in raising a volunteer force of 5,000 men to fight for control over the central area of Palestine.[50]

The Arab League established its own volunteer force, the Liberation Army *(Jaysh al-Inqadh),* consisting of almost 4,000 men—largely Syrian volunteers. Its leader was Fawzi al-Qa'uqji, the controversial military commander who first came to the country in the 1936 uprising, from then on constituting a thorn in the side of Amin al-Husseini. Qa'uqji represented a pan-Arab solution to the challenge of Zionism, implicitly downplaying the significance of the Palestinian national movement, its institutions and leaders, in favor of a vision reflecting his own rich experiences in Syria, Saudi Arabia, and Iraq. The Mufti protested the Arab Liberation Army's role and Qa'uqji's designation as supreme military commander for Palestinian operations. And when Qa'uqji and his army marched across the Allenby Bridge into the country in March, 1948, the Arab Higher

Committee published a communique warning that all who cooperated with "strangers" would be considered traitors and subject to expulsion from the country.

Pronouncements of that sort did little to alter the leadership's weakness. At a time of rising anxiety, Haj Amin's distance from the country once again was proving troublesome. It hindered the sort of mobilization that could have overcome factionalism, presenting a serious counterweight to Abdallah and the Arab League. In the end, the Palestinian hopes rested, not with national leaders, but with the dispersed, popular National Committees and scattered fighting units of young men, both tied closely to their specific locales. Even the minimal coordination that had existed in the Arab Revolt was now often absent.

In the context of both sides' initial military strategy, these problems were not glaring. The fighting, fought largely in intermittent and dispersed encounters, had two faces, the war of the cities and the war of the roads. The war of the cities, most intense at the very outset of the communal fighting, involved occasional sniping, mutual urban terror (mostly bomb attacks), and bloody retaliation. Among the most notorious incidents was the retaliatory raid by the Jews against the town of Balad al-Sheikh, killing sixty Arabs, in response to an attack on Haifa oil refinery workers and the Arabs' booby-trap bombing of three trucks in Jerusalem, killing fifty Jews. The war of the roads was largely initiated by Arab forces; their main success came in the almost total sealing off of Jerusalem from Jewish reinforcements and supplies by March, 1948.

Often holding the upper hand at the end of 1947 and the beginning of 1948, and with the promise of an invasion by the Arab states, the Palestinians' fortunes seemed to be rising. But as the Zionist forces began to improvise, the Arab inability to fight an all-out war became apparent. Even early on, the war of the cities had resulted in an Arab flight out of the urban areas—a process the Mufti attempted to stem by shifting to more hit-and-run attacks in the countryside. With the Haganah's increasing reliance on full-time soldiers, Palestinian forces found themselves at still greater disadvantage, and the Palestinian population came under attack through severe Jewish retaliatory acts. The Arab League's Liberation Army proved incapable of altering the situation, engaged as it was in a series of running quarrels with leaders of the Palestinian units. Despite the quarrels, efforts to field effective military forces were sabotaged most of all by a general absence of a firm political foundation. The following personal account by Qa'uqji of his lament to the inspector-general of his army could have been written, with some small differences, by Palestinian commanders:

> I strongly criticized the method of choosing officers and men, and the grave lack of military competence evinced by many of them in battle—some of the men could not even load a rifle properly. I also said that among the officers there were some elements so corrupt that I did not know how the Inspectorate-General could have agreed to their being attached to units of the Liberation Army. I told him frankly that, but for a group of loyal and energetic officers who had dedicated their lives to the great Arab cause, and but for the enthusiasm, courage and disciplined conduct of some of the companies, we should not have been able to stand up to the enemy for a single day.
>
> I told him of the scandalous lack of arms, ammunition, rations, clothing, health services and means of communication, and of the delays in giving the men their pay to send to their families.[51]

By the first months of 1948; the Zionist leadership had managed to mobilize a regular army of fifteen thousand full-time soldiers. In addition, in April Jewish units switched from reacting to Arab initiatives—a strategy termed active defense—to going on the offensive. More and more Jewish forces took advantage of divisions among Palestinian units, reflected in events such as what occurred in April in the Haifa district: a refusal by Husseini loyalists of arms, ammunition, and fighters to allies of the notable opposition.

Also in April, Abd al-Qadir al-Husseini died in battle, thus joining al-Qassam in the ranks of Palestinian national martyrs. Abd al-Qadir's death was a serious blow. With total war now being fought by regular armies, it became more and more difficult to hide the Palestinian political and military shortcomings. The British command had privately predicted in December that "in the long run the Jews would not be able to cope with the Arabs," but in February it predicted that they would, indeed, hold onto at least part of their designated state.[52] By the end of April, the turnaround was even more pronounced. Here is the appraisal of the American consul in a cable to Secretary of State George Marshall:

> Palestinian [mandate] government has generally ceased to function and central public services no longer exist. In Jewish areas Jews have taken effective control and are maintaining public services within those areas. Preparations for establishment Jewish state after termination of Mandate are well advanced. . . . In Arab areas only municipal administration continues without any central authority. . . . Morale following Jewish military successes low with thousands Arabs fleeing country. Last remaining hope is in entry Arab regular armies, spearheaded by Arab Legion.[53]

The Shattering of the Palestinian Community

The entry of the Arab regular armies after the declaration of Israel's independence on May 14, 1948, did not, of course, bring the hoped-for salvation. By the time all the fighting had ended in early 1949, the peasant communities in the north and the coastal plain had suffered severe damage, with peasant life remaining intact in areas far from Jewish settlement—particularly in the east. On the other end of the social spectrum, the notable leadership had seemed to vaporize into thin air. In its place emerged an entirely new stratum of Palestinian society, the refugees dispersed among five separate countries (see map 4). No one can say precisely how many of the 1.3 million Palestinians became refugees, the reckoning—like so much else in Palestine's legacy—becoming a constituent part of the Arab-Israeli conflict. Arab estimates varied between 750,000 and 1,000,000. The Israelis proposed 520,000, and the British between 600,000 and 760,000.[54]

Map 5 gives a sense of the new refugee society's *Ghurba*, exile. Flight of Palestinians from their homes began in December, 1947, as a fairly marginal event. As militiamen on both sides attempted to improve their positions, the fringes of neighborhoods and isolated settlements came under heavy attack. Palestinians caught in the cross fire began to seek refuge, as did Arabs living in largely Jewish neighborhoods. The result was two waves of movement. Many wealthy merchants and others with money, including leading notables, took refuge outside the country. Fleeing from the most beleaguered cities, densely populated with Jews—Jaffa-Tel-Aviv, Haifa, and Jerusalem—they landed mostly in Lebanon, Egypt, and Transjordan. This group included a disproportionate number of Christians—rekindling Muslim suspicions that they were not as committed to the national struggle. The second wave consisted of more of the upper and middle classes, as well as numerous villagers from the Jerusalem area and the coastal plain, who ended up in their home villages, or in all-Arab towns such as Nazareth and Nablus.

By February–March, 1948, the number of displaced Palestinians had reached between thirty thousand and seventy-five thousand, 2 to 6 percent of the Arab population.[55] Frightened Palestinians abandoned several entire towns and villages. Those who stayed put in cities such as Jaffa faced flying bullets, lack of food, and soaring prices; those who fled experienced the agony of displacement; and those who received them took on the burden of an exploding population.

Some villages managed to conclude "peace agreements" or non-belligerency pacts with their Jewish neighbors, and others expelled Arab fighting forces so as to avoid Jewish retaliation, but such insurance policies often failed to hold up. Palestinian flight was the reaction to the risks and insecurities of a brutal, increasingly unavoidable war between two communities, under the aegis of a power desiring nothing more, at this point, than to protect itself. A mass exodus of entire Arab families continued, despite the opposition—temporary evacuation of women, elderly men, and children excepted—of the remnants of the Palestinian leadership. It continued in the absence, at this point, of a Zionist policy to forcibly expel or evacuate Arabs—though instances of intimidation of local villages seemed to hasten the process, and isolated, ominous evictions had begun in March.[56]

In May and June of 1948, the intensity of the fighting, from scattered guerrilla-like encounters to conventional warfare, went far towards dismantling the Palestinian Arab community. As the British evacuated areas of the country, the Haganah implemented the core of its new strategic thinking, what it called Plan Dalet.

> The essence of the plan was the clearing of hostile and potentially hostile forces out of the interior of the prospective territory of the Jewish State, establishing territorial continuity between the major concentrations of Jewish population and securing the Jewish State's future borders before, and in anticipation of, the Arab invasion. As the Arab irregulars were based and quartered in the villages, and as the militias of many villages were participating in the anti-Yishuv hostilities, the Haganah regarded most of the villages as actively or potentially hostile.[57]

While Plan Dalet did not directly call for the eviction of Palestinians from their homes, it did give free reign to Haganah officers "to clear out and destroy the clusters of hostile or potentially hostile Arab villages dominating vital axes."[58] But it was not that element of the Plan that unleashed the massive exodus in April, May, and June—most Arabs had fled the chaos and insecurity rampant in areas of intense fighting before Haganah commanders had to make such decisions.[59]

At the same time that Jewish forces were pressing the Arab villages, they were winning the war of the cities. The fall of Jaffa on April 22 and of Haifa on May 13—on the eve of Israel's declaration of independence and of the invasion of the Arab armies—marked the end of urban, coastal Palestinian society. The terror of the fighting and the possibility of Jewish rule and revenge, coupled with mistreatment and intimidation by Palestinian and Liberation Army forces,[60] prompted a massive exodus. Tens of thousands left even before the two cities fell, and tens of thousands of others fled once the Jews gained total control. In all, an additional 200,000–300,000 refugees fled their villages and cities between April and June. There was a sad irony to this death-knell: Palestinian military plans had rested

Sidon

LEBANON
100,000

IRAQ
4,000

Tyre

SYRIA
75–90,000

Acre

(REMAINED
IN ISRAEL)
150,000

Haifa

MEDITERRANEAN SEA

WESTBANK
300,000

Jordan River

TRANSJORDAN
100,000

Jaffa

Jerusalem

Dead Sea

GAZA
160–190,000

Beersheba

SINAI

EGYPT
7,000

Aqaba

Dep. of Geography, Hebrew University

Map 4. The Exodus of the Palestinians (1948)

Map 5. A Refugee Camp Society (the Major Palestinian Refugee Camps, 1948–1991)

on the presumption that Jewish urban society would collapse in the hellish street-to-street fighting.

Perhaps a quarter of the entire Arab population was now displaced, but in the coastal cities the depopulation was nearly total. In Haifa, for example, the Arabs had been caught between a Jewish municipal leadership that had urged them not to flee and Haganah officers who had begun to see the opportunities presented by Arab evacuation. By the end of the communal war, only 3,000–4,000 of its 70,000 Palestinians remained.[61]

It is impossible to discuss this pivotal period without reference to Dayr Yasin, which would become the war's symbol for the Palestinians. The village was one of several attacked by Jewish forces in April in an attempt to clear the besieged roads leading to Jerusalem. That offensive was important in itself, since it marked the first time Jewish forces fought with the strategic goal of permanently ridding an area of Arab villages in order to insure the viability of their own settlements.

The sequence of events in Dayr Yasin is now scarcely disputed. The village's nonbelligerency pact with local Jewish forces did not spare it being swept into the Jewish offensive to break the Arab stranglehold on Jerusalem. Following an intense battle between Palestinian militiamen and Irgun forces with some Haganah mortar support, Palestinian forces departed and the Irgun entered the village on April 9. In brutal acts of revenge for their losses, the Jewish fighters killed many of the remaining men, women, and children and raped and mutilated others. Those not killed immediately were ignominiously paraded through Jerusalem and then sent to the city's Arab sector.

For their own purposes, both Israeli and Arab sources later inflated the number of those killed to approximately 250. A recent study by a team of researchers at Bir Zeit University found that the figure probably did not exceed 120.[62] But that does not diminish the depth of the atrocity or its short- and long-run effects. In the immediate aftermath, the massacre became the subject of intense public concern. Despite their active participation in the early stages of the battle for the village, which itself left numerous local families decimated, the Haganah commanders and central Jewish leadership distanced themselves from what had taken place and condemned it. The Arab media used Dayr Yasin as the focus of their claim that Zionism was innately wicked, and to rally Arabs behind the impending Arab invasion. Broadcasts and newspaper stories prompted popular mass demonstrations in Damascus, Baghdad, Cairo, and Tripoli, including attacks on the local Jewish communities.

The stories had the effect of catalyzing rumors and striking further fear into the Palestinians, speeding the pace with which they ran for their lives, from other villages and even from large cities such as Haifa.[63] Exaggeratedly or not, the Irgun, in fact, stressed the degree to which this one incident had turned the tide in assuring that the new Jewish state would not have a disabling proportion of Arabs. Later in the year, when Israel went on the offensive that finally defeated the invading Arab armies, the image of Dayr Yasin created an expectation of similar Jewish acts. Combined with the real determination of Israeli commanders to create Arab-free regions, this precipitated another shattering wave of exodus.[64]

In the longer term, the events at Dayr Yasin hardened the demonic images each side was developing of the other. For the Jews, the 1929 massacre in Hebron, and to a lesser extent the events in Tiberias and Safad, had fostered the idea of a murderous Arab culture.[65] And aware of this Jewish reaction, Palestinians fully expected retribution should the Jews have the opportunity—all manners of cruelty were to be expected from them. Once the fighting ended, Dayr Yasin became a key element in the Palestinian transformation of the events of 1947–49 into a cosmic injustice—the enemy was not simply a party with antithetical interests, but a pure representation of evil in a world in which the forces of fate, for the moment at least, had lined up against the Arabs.

The final decimation of Palestinian Arab society during the war involved a mass expulsion by Israelis from within the boundaries of what was to become their new state. In one ten-day period in July, 1948, Israeli commanders sometimes nudged, sometimes drove, over 100,000 Arabs into parts of Palestine held by the Transjordanians, the Egyptians, and the Liberation Army, as well as into Lebanon. At times, Muslims were expelled while Druze and Christians were allowed to remain. In the Israeli offensive in October, 1948, which routed the Liberation Army and the Egyptians, another 100,000–150,000 Arabs became refugees.

Was there, indeed, a Zionist master plan to expel the Palestinians? Walid Khalidi, among others, cites Zionist talk, even before the fighting, of population transfer, as well as other pieces of evidence that support the existence of such a plan. He derided those who view "the Palestinian exodus in an historical vacuum" or who see expulsion "only as an afterthought, an extemporized innovation, a lightning brainwave with no ideological, attitudinal, motivational, or strategic antecedents."[66]

The evidence is far more equivocal than Khalidi suggests. Plan Dalet itself was full of inner contradictions, referring to both expulsion of Arabs and their administration in secured areas. Israeli leaders were aware that mass expulsions, population exchanges, and huge movements of people had long been recognized practices during and after international wars. In fact, they cited cases such as the transfer of the Greeks from Turkey. But such abstract musing was not responsible for the shattering of the Palestinian community. The tragedy resulted from a convergence of emotions: the Jewish fear, in the aftermath of the Holocaust and with the mounting attacks in Arab countries against Jews, of what the Arabs would do if they prevailed, and of not being able to sustain a state with a vanquished and disloyal Arab population (a third or more of the state); the anxiety of Jewish commanders at having a hostile population behind their advancing lines during the fighting; the Israeli sense of what could be accomplished with abandoned Arab property; and, not least, the Palestinians' own image of what the Jews would do to them if Israel prevailed and they were left in its territory.

In general the idea of expulsion does seem to have grown along with Jewish confidence in victory. During the dark days at the end of 1947 and in the first months of 1948, the central concern was simply hanging on; later, in the wake of an Arab flight that had significantly eased their burden, the new Israeli rulers began a deliberate effort to evacuate Arabs from specific parts of their state.[67] There is no doubt that in the latter stages of the war, Israel explicitly created refugees by driving Arabs from areas it ruled. Israel attempted to create Arab-free zones in some regions, such as those around Gaza and Lydda (Lod). In other regions such as Galilee, an uneven pattern emerged in which the Israelis evicted some Arabs, others fled on their own, and others remained in their communities. One Christian village whose residents showed tenacity was Miilya, in the Upper Galilee. Historian Elias Shoufani, then a boy of 14, has recalled some of the events surrounding its final fall in October.[68] Humiliation of the villagers had begun even before the Jews broke through their lines. They had reluctantly quartered a Yemeni contingent of the Liberation Army, and Shoufani's aunt drowned herself to escape molestation by a drunken soldier.

While some residents, including Shoufani's brother, developed a sense of camaraderie with the Yemenis, who after all were fighting alongside them, many felt they had simply commandeered the village. With the breakdown of government services, particularly police protection, the fellaheen had left old feuds behind and showed a cooperative spirit in administering the village themselves. Under the threat of Jewish attack, they purchased rifles from gunrunners working both sides of the Lebanese border, thus deterring local Arab threats as well. They also used this newfound unity to forcibly prevent any family from leaving the village for Lebanon, as so many from neighboring villages were now doing.

Unable to ship their cash crop, tobacco, through the coastal ports, Miilya's fellaheen smuggled it into Lebanon in small packets to sell to local Lebanese peasants. By May, 1948, the village was facing the burden of fields captured by Jewish forces, leading to dwindling food supplies, and of a small influx of refugees from other villages. These refugees, familiar with the land near the coast, helped villagers slip behind enemy lines under the cover of night to harvest crops and slaughter cows for meat. When the Haganah entered the half-deserted village, it blew up Shoufani's house as a signal of the fate of those who kept their guns. After the village priest had arranged for a formal surrender, villagers headed back to their homes: "It was a heartbreaking sight: a pile of stones and scattered suggestions of the house's former structure."[69]

Unlike residents of Miilya, many fellaheen, such as those in the nearby village of al-Ghabisiya, moved on to Lebanon or another country once the Israelis completed their capture of the Galilee at the end of October.[70] Others, such as Najib Asad of the neighboring village of al-Birwa, were driven by Israeli soldiers to the border of the Gaza Strip and told to run as fast as they could without looking back.[71]

Partly for security reasons, partly under pressure from Jewish communities that had already taken abandoned Arab property, and partly with an eye to space for incoming Jewish refugees, Israeli leaders moved towards a decision between April and August, 1948, to bar the return of the refugees. For those accustomed to a pattern of leaving trouble through a swinging door that would soon bring them home, the Israeli ban became a disaster. The Israeli government destroyed most of the approximately 350 abandoned Arab villages and towns,[72] and arguing that the concept of land ownership was meaningless in a total war, Ben-Gurion initiated the allocation of the refugees' land to Jews. Through the middle of 1949, Israeli leaders also established about 130 new Jewish settlements where Arab villages and towns had stood, most to be populated by European victims of the Holocaust and Jews fleeing Arab countries, pouring into Israel following its declaration of independence. Both groups also occupied abandoned Arab houses in the big cities, such as Haifa and Tel-Aviv/Jaffa.

A few Israeli cities, such as Nazareth and Acre, still retained a sizeable Arab population, and about 150,000 Arabs, mostly villagers, took on Israeli citizenship. Outside the Jewish state, hundreds of thousands of refugees crowded into camps in the Gaza Strip (administered by Egypt), in Syria, and in Lebanon (see map 5). The greatest number, almost 400,000, joined the suddenly beleaguered population of the old towns, led by Nablus in Palestine's hilly eastern portion, as well as the villages—that realm of peasant society least integrated into external markets. Absorbed in 1950—in a territory that would come to be known as the West Bank—into the newly dubbed Hashemite Kingdom of Jordan, these Palestinians found their political environment changed almost as drastically as did their compatriots left in Israel.

Now, with the coastal cities practically empty of Arabs and with Jerusalem truncated and divided, the mountainous area again took on the core role in Palestinian society. This encapsulated region, the one least subject to the influences of the West over the last century, would preserve the nucleus of a dispersed Palestinian nation and foster its social and cultural reconstruction. Precious few of the institutions necessary for this task had survived, and the ayan had all but disintegrated, no group standing ready to seize its mantle.

King Abdallah of Jordan had either implicitly supported the Zionists or actively colluded in preventing the emergence of another Arab state.[73] For the next 20 years, Jordan and Israel, though apparently enemies, would often adopt policies revealing a set of shared interests: to thwart Palestinism, to dissolve the emerging separate Palestinian collective identity, and to prevent the reemergence of Palestinian nationalism.

Part Three

RECONSTITUTING

THE PALESTINIAN NATION

6

ODD MAN OUT:

ARABS IN ISRAEL

For the Palestinians as a people, Israeli modernism caused the failure of their own modernism, begun even prior to 1948. After 1948, the Palestinian minority [in Israel] was blocked off from the path to modernism, when it lost its economic, political, and cultural elite. More importantly, it lost the Palestinian city and was left [principally] as a rural society, to make its living from employment in Jewish cities that would not assimilate them. In the next phase, it lost the village by losing agriculture, thus remaining neither urban nor rural. That is the "Israeli Arab." The only modernism he knows is Jewish modernism, and he is annexed onto it as an imitator, a marginal factor, and in the best case—as carrying demands.

AZMI BISHARA, *The Arabs in Israel: An Internal Look,* 2000: 38.

ARAB CITIZENS OF ISRAEL (also known variously as Palestinian-Israelis and Israeli Arabs) emerged from *al-Nakba* as dispirited and traumatized as the refugees in the West Bank, Gaza Strip, and surrounding countries.[1] Living in the new Jewish state, though, quickly set them apart from other Palestinians. They became citizens of Israel and, until 1967, at least, were often shunned by other Arabs, even when traveling outside the country. And, within Israel, they found themselves on the lowest rung of the social and economic ladder and treated by the majority Jews as a potentially dangerous population. They became citizens of a state that celebrated its independence around the event that they considered their biggest catastrophe.

Palestinian-Israeli efforts at reconstituting Arab society and organizing themselves as a national minority in Israel ran into all sorts of obstacles. For one, they emerged from the 1948 war leaderless, dispossessed, and disorganized. Additionally, the Israeli government put tremendous barriers on association among them, at least beyond the family and village levels, from restricting travel to banning emerging national organizations. Finally, Palestinian-Israelis were remarkably heterogeneous in terms of religion, ethnicity, and ideology, making the creation of social ties all the more difficult. Disregarded in the Arab world and suppressed in Israel, they became the true odd man out in the region.

Still, taking advantage of cracks in the façade, which allowed them to organize through the Communist party and to piggyback on Israel's burgeoning economy, they overcame some of the barriers that had confined them. Groups of intellectuals, professionals, and entrepreneurs emerged to give new voice and cohesion to Arab society in Israel. While they could never escape their status as odd man out, suffering from the indifference of the state toward them and their own continuing factionalism, the Arab citizens of Israel, nonetheless, became much more formidable political actors after the mid-1970s. And they entered more fully into everyday life in Israel. Their political emergence was framed by three violent, momentous events: Land Day in 1976, the outbreak of the Intifada in the occupied territories in 1987, and the deadly clash with Israeli security forces in October 2000 after the start of the al-Aqsa Intifada in the newly constituted Palestine Authority (PA). Their place in Israel and among the Palestinian people as a whole is still uncertain, but little doubt remains that, one way or another, they will play an important role in the future of both.

The Present-Absentees

At the start of the twenty-first century, Palestinian Israelis numbered about 1.2 million of the 6.5 million citizens of the state. About 79 percent were Muslim; about 13 percent, Christian; and about 9 percent, Druze.² This population was concentrated within 120 municipal authorities. Eighty of these communities are in the north, where the approximately 920,000 residents who live in them comprise about half of the entire population of the Galilee. Another 170,000 live in the district of Haifa, and about 100,000 Bedouin live in the southern district. Half of the Bedouin have now been settled in seven permanent settlements, and the rest continue a seminomadic lifestyle in the area around the city of Beersheba. These statistics, as we will argue in this chapter, are not only quantitative but also point to essential qualitative changes in Arab life in Israel. No longer a marginal minority of the Jewish state as it was in 1948 and the years immediately after *al-Nakba,* the Arab population has become an active agent in the shaping of Israeli state and society.

In the last month of 1947 and the first four and half months of 1948, the Arab community in British Palestine ceased to exist as a coherent social and political entity. In the period leading up to British withdrawal from Palestine and its immediate aftermath, more than 350 villages and urban neighborhoods disappeared, some as if they had never existed. Urban life and institutions in the coastal cities were almost completely annihilated. War and flight shrunk the population of the lively city of Jaffa from 70,000–80,000 Arabs to only 3,000–4000.³ Of the approximately 1.3–1.4 million Arab subjects of the British mandate, almost half were displaced from their homes and communities.

The vast majority became refugees living outside the Jewish state. Others were uprooted from their original homes but remained in Israel, forbidden to return to their homes after the battles had come to an end.⁴ These internal refugees made up about 15 percent of the Palestinian Arabs remaining within the boundaries of the Jewish state (what later came to be called "the green line") after the signing of cease-fire agreements with the neighboring Arab states. All in all, about 150,000 Arabs stayed in Israel and became citizens of the state, comprising about 10 percent of all Palestinian Arabs and approximately 15 percent of the total population of the Israeli state.⁵ This last percentage dropped over the next few years as Jewish immigration from the displaced persons camps in Europe and from Arab countries skyrocketed.[6] But, by the beginning of the 1960s, the relative number of Arab citizens began to increase and today is close to 20 percent of Israel's population.

In the 1950s, three quarters of Arabs in Israel lived in the villages of the western Galilee and the "Little Triangle," the area contiguous to the coastal plane, which Israel annexed as part of its cease-fire agreement with Jordan. These villages had not witnessed mass exodus or the same type of radical thinning out that had destroyed the local populations of Haifa, Jaffa, Safed, and other cities and villages. What remained under Israeli control after the 1948 war was a remnant—a crumbling part of Palestinian Arab society, similar in many ways to the socially devastated remnants in the refugee camps surrounding Israel.

Many extended *hamulas* and even nuclear families were separated, with their members living on both sides of the armistice lines. With very few exceptions, family union was permitted by Israeli officials only in one direction—out of Israel. Israeli authorities even continued expelling concentrations of Arabs after the fighting had ended. Residents of the town of Majdal (today, Ashkelon), for instance, were deported to the Gaza Strip in September 1950. Residents of thirteen villages in Wadi Ara were deported to the other side of the armistice line in February 1951. Deportation of Bedouin tribes from within the state's borders continued until 1959.[7]

Some Palestinian Arabs tried to take advantage of their new citizen rights, turning to the Israeli courts in an effort to return to their home villages. For example, residents of the two Christian Maronite villages, Bir'm and Ikrit, have been struggling in the courts for two generations and, to date, still have not succeeded in winning their case.[8] At the end of 2001, the Supreme Court ruled that the state should financially compensate the villagers uprooted from the two villages for the lands and other possessions taken from them. The villagers rejected this proposal and are still fighting for their right to return to their original villages.

The Israeli state gave an official oxymoronic designation to its Arab citizens prohibited from returning to their lands and houses, although remaining in the territory of the state during the battles:

present-absentees. Using that new legal category, the government appropriated the present-absentees' lands through the Law of Absented Properties 1950. One estimate is that as much as 40 percent of Arab lands (about two million dunums) was confiscated through this law.

These internal refugees were resettled into existing, crowded villages and towns, in which they have been considered strangers to this day. Other villages were amalgamated into a single village. The state offered arbitrary compensation payments for Arab lands (many for less than their actual value), most of which the Arabs refused to accept. State agencies then settled Jewish immigrants on the newly appropriated lands. Thus a double aim was achieved: Jews, many of whom themselves were uprooted refugees, were settled on lands and populated the houses of abandoned neighborhoods and villages. At the same time, Arab citizens remaining within the state's borders, who were considered a fifth column, were thinned out and consolidated.[9] The new Jewish immigrants, especially in "frontier areas," helped prevent the return or infiltration of Arab refugees, among other purposes, to their places of residence from before the war.

Even when lands remained in Arab hands, Arabs had difficulty continuing to cultivate them. The state severely limited water and electricity allocations, especially in comparison to the more productive Jewish communal settlements (the kibbutzim and moshavim) in the vicinity. Arabs were also forbidden from joining cooperative bodies, such as the trade unions under the umbrella of the powerful Histadrut (the General Jewish Workers' Organization) as well as becoming members in state-sponsored marketing, credit, and purchasing co-ops.[10] Arab citrus orchards almost completely disappeared, and, by the 1950s, the peasantry (fellaheen) returned to production largely for household use, augmented by limited olive oil and vegetable production for the Jewish market. Thus, it is not surprising that many Israeli Arabs abandoned agriculture all together. At least in this regard they were similar to the Palestinians spread through neighboring Arab states. Land was at the service of those who held the political clout and resources needed to develop it and who had access to the agencies for subsidizing production and marketing—the state, the Histadrut (with its marketing and purchasing cooperatives), and the Jewish Agency, the operational arm of the World Zionist Organization in Israel that subsidized all Jewish settlements and other developmental projects.

Beginning in the 1960s and 1970s, what was left of Arab agriculture in Israel underwent substantial changes. Intensive agriculture techniques and cash crops replaced traditional peasant cultivation. The main change, however, was from peasantry to day labor. Many Palestinian citizens of Israel had been cut off from their peasant roots around 1950, as their lands were appropriated.[11] That process now picked up steam again as agriculture went from labor-intensive to capital-intensive. The drastically reduced Arab land base and the move to commercial agriculture quickened a process already begun in the British Mandate period—the transition of the fellaheen to unskilled or partially skilled, nonagricultural day labor.[12] One study revealed that about three-quarters of all urban Arab laborers had no training at all.[13] When Israel went from an excess of labor to a shortage, many Arabs finally integrated into the national economy, finding work in Jewish industry and construction companies, usually on the lower rungs of the employment ladder. During this period, the military government also loosened its hold, as one of its tasks had been to protect the labor market from an influx of cheap Arab labor that would compete with Jewish immigrant labor, primarily recent arrivals from Asia and North Africa.[14]

The change was rapid and fundamental. In 1963, the percentage of Arab agricultural laborers in Israel was slightly more than one-third of the total Arab population (in comparison to about 10 percent for Jews). After a decade, agriculture claimed only a fifth of Arab laborers. Arabs became the lower echelon of an ethno-nationally split labor market. Jews held the more skilled and high-paying jobs, whereas Arabs took lower-paying, sometimes only seasonal, jobs.[15] Even during the colonial rule of the British, the percentage of Palestinian Arabs in high-paying jobs was low relative to that of Jews.[16] The power of Jews over Israeli society's main agencies after 1948 only increased this inequality. Nonetheless, while Israel's rapid economic growth created additional discrimination and increased inequality between Jews and Arabs, it also raised Israeli Arabs' standard of living, albeit to a lesser degree than that of the Jews. Eventually, their increased standard of living, as well as their growing numbers in the overall population, translated into rising political and social strength, as well.

By opening its employment office to Arabs, the Histadrut provided fellaheen with easier access to the labor market and a degree of wage protection. At the same time, they fell under yet another means of supervision in the form of the Jewish-controlled Workers' Organization.[17] And they continued to face discrimination; the employment office still gave preference for jobs in Jewish areas to Jewish applicants. What had been touted as the universal obligation of military service became another source of discrimination against Arabs. Even without requesting it, they were granted exemption from the draft.[18] And this exemption became the basis for other sorts of institutionalized and official discrimination. Certain rights—access to certain government jobs, social security benefits, housing, even drivers' licenses—were available only to army veterans and their families. It reached the point that from 1950 to 1967, the Israeli Communist party, the principal advocate for Arab civil rights in Israel, demanded the drafting of Arabs, although this demand was not greeted with tremendous enthusiasm by the party's Arab constituency.

The essence of the *Nakba* experience for the Arabs remaining in the Jewish state was the sudden change from the status of national majority to that of a small, politically powerless minority. This traumatic transition was exacerbated by the absence of any effective national leadership with the skills and will to stand up to the institutions of the Jewish state. As one government appointee presiding over the Arab sector put it, those who remained in the state "were like a headless body . . . the social, commercial, and religious leadership had disappeared."[19] Even the Christian Arabs, who were the most educated and, in 1949, a relatively large percentage of the remaining population (21 percent, which was considerably bigger than the percentage of Christians in the worldwide Palestinian population), were left with only a few representatives from the middle and upper classes of the British colonial period.[20]

As occurred among the refugees, Palestinian citizens of Israel ended up relying heavily on local leaders. Most of these were heads of *hamulas,* and their importance grew as they took on mediation roles between their relatives and Israeli authorities and political parties. In fact, the *hamula* heads filled an even more central role than did local leaders in the refugee camps. One result was that, as these leadership positions gained in importance, inter-*hamula* rivalries intensified, becoming much sharper than they had been during the British period. Older *hamula* heads stayed in power, even while those in the refugee camps of Gaza, the West Bank of Jordan, and Lebanon slowly relinquished their place to a younger, more educated national leadership over the two decades following 1948.

The survival of the old *hamula* leaders and the intensified rivalries helped foreclose the very possibility that Arab citizens would create a general, cross-*hamula* or interregional leadership during these first two decades of the state. Even when limited urbanization and increasing levels of education led to new challenges to the veteran local *hamula* leadership in the mid-1970s, the state prevented the Arabs in Israel from creating a representative regional leadership. The Israeli state took a series of administrative and political steps to thwart the development of a new leadership, reflecting the continuing Jewish fear that the Palestinian citizens of the state could be a bridgehead to its sworn enemies. All in all, the traumatized Arab population, lacking a broad leadership, could take few steps toward constructing a national community or a renewed Palestinian identity. The two decades after the creation of Israel were very difficult ones for the Arabs in the new state. They were years marked by what sociologist Michael Hechter called internal colonialism, that is, the creation and expansion of Jewish settlements within the 1948 ceasefire borders, many on the former lands and villages of Palestinian citizens of the state.[21]

Perhaps the most painful edict was the prohibition on movement from place to place, which the military government imposed on most Arab residential areas. The journalist-poet Fawzi Al-Asmar de-

scribes the pain of confinement of the Arabs remaining in Lydda after the 1948 war:

> The Arabs were not allowed to leave their ghetto and almost all the
> Arab villages or concentrations of villages were declared [military] ar-
> eas. And the most humiliating thing for us was that our quarter and
> the other quarters in Lydda that were populated by Arabs were under
> military government, while in the rest of the city where the Jews lived
> [in abandoned Arab houses], there were no limitations on move-
> ment. Until the early 1950s we could not go out without a special per-
> mit, while the Jews, of course, were free to go anywhere except for
> into our ghetto.[22]

While somewhat loosened over time, for the most part the prohibition on movement in the 1950s and early 1960s succeeded in
greatly curtailing Arab mobility. This regulation was based on British laws issued for the emergencies of 1936 and 1945 (directed at the
Arab Revolt and the Jewish rebellion, respectively). In the fall of
1948, while the fighting was still raging, the government declared
military rule in Arab-populated areas. In 1950, the government created a military government for these areas, which remained in force
until 1966. Military government resembled emergency regulations
in other states, limiting freedom of expression, movement, and organization. Its effect was to restrict the Arab minority within a territorial enclave, excluding Arabs from the broader labor market
so they could not compete with the Jewish immigrants who were
flooding into the state and preventing them from resisting appropriation of their lands.

In the 1950s, Israel faced continuing, increasingly violent attempts at infiltration, mostly by refugee camp residents from the
other side of the cease-fire line trying to return to their homes, attempting to take back what they claimed were their belongings, or
simply seeking vengeance. Israel's retaliations led to a sort of non-
stop, low-density war, which further justified the need to maintain
harsh military governance of the Palestinian citizens of Israel (and
paved the way, too, for the 1956 war).[23]

Besides the military government, another institution controlling and reshaping the Arabs in Israel was the school—the elementary and high schools under state control. The curriculum of public schools for Arabs in Israel was written with the aim of creating a new ethnic identity for them (much as the Hashemite educational policy tried to Jordanize the Palestinians).[24] General Arab history was taught and was presented as complementary to the history of the Israeli state and Zionism. While the Koran was taught (in the 1950s and 60s, religion was thought to be a factor that could moderate ethnicity and nationalism), so too was the Hebrew Bible and Hebrew literature.

The aim was to thwart the flowering of a Palestinian Arab national identity.[25] Y. L. Benor, one of the planners of Arab education, set forth the Israeli considerations in devising the curriculum: "How can we encourage loyalty to Israel among Israeli Arabs without demanding a negation of Arab yearning on the one hand, and without permitting the development of hostile Arab nationalism on the other?"[26] In addition, the level of Arab schools remained far inferior to that of Jewish schools (even those in distant development towns). In 1997, 38 percent of all Arab twelfth graders passed their matriculation exams, in comparison to 51 percent of Jews. Among those who did pass, only 69.4 percent of Arabs met standards for university acceptance, compared to 88 percent of Jews.[27]

While portrayed by Israeli authorities as a dangerous population, tied to their brethren in hostile neighboring states, the Arabs who stayed in Israel actually were cut off from other concentrations of Palestinians.[28] After the 1967 war, when the three fragments of historical Palestine—Israel, the Gaza Strip, and the West Bank—were rejoined under Israeli control, many of the Arab citizens of Israel could again begin to define themselves as part of the larger Palestinian community. Many became supporters of the idea of Palestinian nationalism.[29] Even then, though, their contradictory experience as Israeli citizens and Arabs separated them emotionally, socially, and politically from other Palestinians. Palestinians who had experienced dispersal, exile *(ghurba),* and longing for their original home-land carried a very different set of baggage, emotions, and cultural codes coming out of the partial roots they had sunk in the far-flung places in which they had ended up.

If the experiences of the Palestinian Arabs who remained in Israel differed markedly from those who were scattered in various countries of the Middle East or migrated later to Europe, Latin America, and North America, the relationship of these Arab citizens to the Israeli state set them apart, too, from the country's Jewish citizens. In the 1950s, the Israeli regime's main concern was absorption of the waves of Jewish immigrants into the new society and culture. They were to pass through an awesome melting pot from which "the new Israeli/Jewish man" would emerge. There was, of course, no room for the Arab in this process.[30] Defined and constructed as religious or ethnic minorities (Muslims, Christians, Druze, and Circassians) in a Jewish national state, the Arab citizens were (and still are) considered as marginal, if not external, to Israeli society.[31]

The Jews, including those who had themselves just arrived in their new land, were citizens of a nation-state created by them and for them. They developed feelings of belonging, partnership, civic responsibility, pride, and emotional identification with the state and its symbols. Jews felt themselves to be sole proprietors of state resources and institutions. The army, the flag, the national anthem, and official holidays were not only Jewish but, for the Arabs, signified painful past experiences. At least some of the official holidays were actually days of collective mourning, conjuring up dark memories for its Arab citizens. Moreover, Arab citizens were forbidden from publicly expressing their collective feelings, which mostly remained hidden and suppressed. Only in 1998 did the Arabs and some Jews begin an open discussion of including the *Nakba* in the state's fiftieth Independence Day celebrations.[32]

The Palestinian citizens of Israel thus have stood inside and outside Israeli state and society. They became bilingual, bicultural citizens, raised to obey Israeli law. At the same time, much of their land was systematically taken from them. They had limited access, beyond voting, to "Israeli democracy" and to many social benefits available to Jews in the areas of welfare, jobs, housing, and other subsidized goods and services. State symbols and rituals did not conjure up the same positive emotions that they did for Jews. Their place in Israel, in short, has been shot through with ambiguity, ambivalence, and equivocalness. But their relationship to Palestinism has been no more certain. A unifying Palestinian national identity has been slow to emerge, partly due to sectarian and cultural differences among them. Arabs in Israel have tried not to emphasize their interreligious and interethnic tensions, blaming them (rightfully, to some degree) on Zionist tactics to divide and conquer. Still, these differences have affected Arabs' ability to construct a unified community and constituency in the Jewish state.

The Druze, Bedouin, and Christians

One group, the Druze, established a much closer relationship with Jews and the Jewish state than did other Arabs, but it has experienced the same sort of ambivalent status.[33] While Druze have been included in mandatory military service, they still have found it difficult to acquire full equality of rights and opportunities in the Jewish state. In terms of educational and income levels, the Druze are positioned even lower than Muslim Arabs within Israel.

Already in the 1930s, Druze leaders and the Jewish leadership in British Palestine forged important connections.[34] During the 1948 war, some Druze participated in the fighting on the Jewish side, and, after the establishment of the Israeli state in 1948, the first Druze were recruited as volunteers into the Israeli army. Since 1957, their identity card registration has been changed from "Arab" to "Druze," and they have been subject to the draft. Military service has had a major effect on the occupational structure of the community. After completing army service, as many as 40 percent have continued as army employees or served in the police force, the border police, or prisons. An additional 10 percent have been employed in petrochemical factories in jobs that also require a "security profile." Their participation in the military/security sector has offset their weakness as a small minority by bestowing them with a positive "security profile," but it also has diverted talented young Druze from other careers. It has diverted them, too, from seeking higher education, a necessary condition for social mobility in Israel. Paradoxically, in this respect, their situation has been worse than that of young Muslim and Christian Arabs.

Loyalty to the state has thus won them important benefits—security clearances, jobs in the military and other security agencies, and full-citizen obligations to serve the state. But that loyalty has not translated into full social and economic equality. Mobility has been limited. Like other Arabs, some of their lands were appropriated by the state in the wake of the 1948 war. Recently, their ambivalent status has translated into internal struggles over Druze identity. In fact, one researcher has found three identities existing simultaneously among them: exclusively Druze, Israeli-Druze, and Palestinian-Druze.[35] Beyond that, beginning in 1973, young Druze began to organize and join public protests, vote for non-Zionist parties, and renew family connections with Druze from the Golan Heights, who saw themselves as Syrians.

Christians, too, have maintained an equivocal relationship with the state and have had ongoing tensions with the much more numerous Muslims. The Christians were harmed less than the Muslims in the *Nakba*.[36] After the 1948 war, they comprised about a fifth of the total Arab population remaining in the state, but their relative numbers have decreased as a result of low birthrates and slow, constant emigration. They have been mostly an urban population, more well to do and educated than the Muslims. While the various denominations have been linked through their common Christianity, the Arab Christians have actually made up the core of secular Arab and Palestinian nationalism in Israel. Traditionally, they have been less interested in emphasizing their religion than their ethnicity, culture, and the Arab language, which are common to all.

Nonetheless, relations with the Muslim majority have not always been comfortable, as we have already seen in previous chapters. Mosque sermons, from the period of British rule until today, have aggressively targeted Christian Arabs. On the one side, Muslims have accused Christian Arabs of collaborating with colonialism and Zionism, and, on the other, Jews have considered them to be Arab nationalists and radical Palestinians.[37] The rise of the Islamic movement in Israel in the 1980s and 1990s also aggravated relations between Christians and Muslims. At the beginning of the twenty-first century, hostility has focused around control of the city of Nazareth, especially the issue of the construction of a mosque next to a Christian monastery and church.[38]

In contrast, relations between the Christians and the Druze have been much better. Their ties go back to the massacre of both communities in 1869 in Lebanon, which led to the creation of mixed Christian-Druze villages in the Galilee.[39] Druze service in the Israeli army, however, has brought about a noticeable rift between them and other Arab citizens in Israel.

Another minority within the heterogeneous Arab society in Israel is the Bedouin. At the end of the 1990s, the Bedouin population stood at 150,000. The Bedouin have been dispersed among twenty-five officially recognized villages (seven of which are towns built for them in the Negev desert) and scores of unrecognized villages. More than 100,000 Bedouin live in the northern Negev and the rest, in the Galilee. The latter have closely emulated the surrounding Arabs in terms of lifestyle, while those in the Negev have preserved many of their earlier cultural traits and sometimes even sharpened them. Since the retreat of Israeli military power from the Sinai Desert and the transfer of large military bases to the Negev at the beginning of the 1980s, relations between the state and the Bedouin concerning issues of land and government have worsened. The Bedouin demanded that 800,000 dunums of land be registered in their name, which from their perspective has been in their possession since before the Ottoman period. The government counteroffered only 30,000 dunums.[40] It seems that the disagreement has been not so much about the actual size of the territory as it has been about the differing cultural and political meanings that each side attaches to the land and its ownership.

The Bedouin, as a group, have been on the bottom rung of Israel's social and economic ladder. Their traditional occupations in agriculture and animal husbandry have declined, and most of the workforce has taken up employment in construction and services. With the downturn in the Israeli economy that began in the late 1990s, the Bedouin of the Negev (in contrast to those of the Galilee) have become the most impoverished group in Israel with the highest rate of unemployment. Their diminishing life chances have precipitated a growing alienation from Israeli society and state.

Religious, ethnic, and lifestyle differences made the creation of an Arab public—one marked by multiple ties outside kinship circles—more difficult to construct, especially in the wake of the trauma of 1948 and the subsequent actions of the Israeli state. Already suffering from being considered a dangerous population, Arabs have been hurt, too, by political and ideological differences that placed barriers to constructing Arab solidarity. Nonetheless, it was within the realm of politics that a cultural revival and the creation of groups that cut across religious and ethnic differences began.

Communism, Nationalism, and Cultural Revival

Through the mid-1960s, the Zionist parties would not accept Arabs into their ranks. Instead, they created accompanying electoral lists, which were called "Arab factions" and which included mostly *hamula* heads who had been deemed "loyal" by the security service. The only exception among Israel's parties was a small left-wing Zionist party called the United Workers party, or Mapam, which enrolled Arabs as full members. Yet, as a Zionist party, Mapam never succeeded in gaining acceptance by the Arab public as a trustworthy representative of the Arab community's collective interests. All in all, Jewish parties have not served as a welcome or productive avenue for expressing Arab political concerns.

The Arab-Jewish divide in politics dates all the way back to the British mandate. The only major political organization in which Arabs and Jews worked side by side then was the Palestinian Communist party, or PKP, which was founded in early 1923 and received official international communist recognition in Moscow one year later.[41] Underground communist organizations had been active in the area of Palestine as early as 1913, but their membership was purely Jewish. After the October Revolution in 1917, the Soviet Union demanded that expansion of the party include the "masses of laborers"—a code for its Arabization. In 1930, the Comintern disbanded the central committee of the PKP and appointed a new one with an Arab majority. But Arabization of the leadership did not help it take root in Palestinian Arab society at that time, which was at heart traditional and religious. Nevertheless, during British rule, there had been planted some seeds of Jewish-Arab cooperation around professional trade and regional unions (mostly in the Haifa area), especially the Union of Railroad Workers.[42] Still, it was clear that both communities and their leaders were not interested in encouraging Arab-Jewish cooperation and solidarity, both because of group interests and for national-ideological reasons.

In 1943, most of the Arab members left the PKP and founded the National Liberation League. The League was not incorporated into the Arab Higher Committee, and, in 1947, was the only Arab political body that openly accepted the U.N. Partition Plan.[43] This step brought about a split in the League. One faction, including Emile Habibi, Tawfiq Tubi, and Fuad Nasser, accepted the Moscow line and supported the Partition Plan, while the opposition faction of Emile Tuma, Bulus Farah, and Musa al-Dajani stuck to the Palestinian nationalist line, opposing the plan.[44] In October 1948, after establishment of the State of Israel, the vestiges of the League reintegrated, forming the Israeli Communist party (Maki). Until the establishment of the New Communist List (Rakah) in the summer of 1965, Maki continued to be the only binational Jewish-Arab political body in Israel. In elections in that summer of 1965, Rakah declared Maki its enemy, and pulled away most of Maki's Arab voters on the basis of its pan-Arab platform. By the elections of 1969, Maki had completely disappeared from both the Jewish and the Arab political maps.

Despite significant internal tensions and constant cleavages, the communist parties in Israel played a decisive role in the reconstruction and crystallization of Arab society in Israel, at least until the 1980s. They provided a home and a greenhouse for the Arab intelligentsia and served as a legitimate outlet for expression of Arab anger and protest.[45] The communists, even when expressing anti-Zionist, nationalist, pan-Arab, and, later, Palestinian nationalist positions, knew how to do so while remaining within the lines of acceptable political discourse in Israel. With the exception of marginal groups within the various incarnations of the communist party, its members never challenged Israel's right to exist outright but, rather, fought for improvement of the civil rights of Arabs in Israel and the right of all Palestinians to independently define themselves. Arabs in the communist parties also felt that, through their party affiliation, they were not completely giving themselves over to Jewish rule but could benefit, to some degree, from the protection of a powerful patron, the Soviet Union. With the collapse of the Soviet empire in 1989–1991, Arab attraction to communism weakened considerably, and remnants of the party began to look to nationalist-Palestinian partners (in the framework of the Democratic Front for Equality) in order to protect what remained of their hold on the Palestinian community in the Israeli political arena.[46]

As mentioned, throughout the first twenty years of the Israeli state, when any hint of an Arab national political organization was suppressed, only Maki succeeded, or at least partially succeeded, in giving legitimate expression to Arab distress and voices of protest. The party's universal, communist rhetoric generally managed to compensate for national demands, packaging them in a way that was acceptable in Israeli political discourse. Nevertheless, the principle in Israeli politics that no "Arab party" could participate in a ruling coalition nor could any Israeli government depend on "Arab votes" in the Knesset to remain in power was formulated during Ben-Gurion's day and still holds true even today. Half of Ben-Gurion's formulation from the early 1950s, "just not Herut and Maki" has continued to apply to Arabs, whereas the other half, "Herut" (the present-day Likud) has long since become a ruling party.[47] Only during the second term of Yitzhak Rabin in the 1990s did the votes of Arab Knesset members help sustain a government and, even then, Arabs were not formally brought into the ruling co-alition.

Maki served not only as a political party but also as a nurturing site for a new Arab, mostly Christian, cultural elite. Arab poets, writers, philosophers, journalists, and teachers created a kind of counterculture, posed against the dominant Hebrew culture. But, if this culture was out of step with the dominant intellectual climate in Israel, it was also almost completely disassociated from cultural developments in other Arab states. The party newspaper, periodicals, and Arab publishing house served as a greenhouse for the flowering of the new intelligentsia in Israel. In the Palestinian Arab context, both inside and outside Israel, almost no differentiation was made between politics and art. The only nonpolitical Arab poet of stature among Arabs in Israel in the 1950s was Mishel Hadad. Emile Habibi, the most visible Arab writer in Israel and winner of the Israel Prize for Literature, was a communist activist.[48] The most important literary magazine for Israeli Arabs in the past and still today, *Al-Jadid* (which merged later with *Al-Sharaq*, edited by Mahmud Abbas and Muhammad Ali Said), as well as more overtly political magazines, such as *Al-Itihad*, *Al-Ad*, and *Mashraf*, were all published by the Communist party. *Al-Itihad* still serves as an organ for both poets and political activists, such as Samih Al-Kasem, Mahmud Darwish, Zaki Darwish, Salim Jubran, and Tawfiq Ziad.[49] Under the auspices of these journals, a fascinating and original Arab-Israeli culture developed and, later, came to be accepted as an essential part of the larger body of general Palestinian cultural work.[50]

Aziz Haidar, an Arab social scientist in Israel, argues that, until the 1970s, very few Arabs in Israel publicly defined themselves as either Palestinian Arabs or simply as Palestinians, although signs of a new Palestinian identity could already be spotted in the work of some of the artists who flourished under the umbrella of Maki.[51] Some of them ended up leaving Israel and joining the armed resistance movements in Lebanon and elsewhere. Others stayed in Israel, making a living from teaching positions, while using codes, symbols, and allegory in order to write protest poetry and communicate with the reading public, under the watchful eye of the Israeli censor.

Many of these artists were also bitterly opposed to the *hamula* heads for their cooperation with the Israeli authorities, and some of them were even critical of the oppressive, traditionalism of broader Arab society.

Arab society in Israel had entered the 1950s as traumatized and quiescent. Much of it was displaced physically and was in the process of being further uprooted socially, as it moved from agriculture to day labor. Literally and figuratively, Israel's Arabs constituted a fenced-in community—a small minority in a now-Jewish sea. And it was riven with religious and ethnic differences. Even with all that, the odd marriage of communism and nationalism in Maki served as a platform for the first important efforts to break out of those constraints. As a vehicle to express the discontent of Israel's Arab citizens and as an intellectual hothouse, Maki began the process of restoring the voice and solidarity of Arab society in Israel—a process still incomplete.

Emergence of a Bilingual, Bicultural Society

Over time, Jewish-dominated society in Israel became more open, more sure of itself, and less Arab-phobic. Arab graduates of Israeli universities and of universities in the communist countries joined the growing Arab elite and middle class, mostly as a small core of professionals, especially teachers, lawyers, doctors, and pharmacists. Less and less were they in need of the patronage of the communist parties. Furthermore, even though most education was still funded by their *hamulas*, this new Arab class enjoyed a certain autonomy, even within its own society. The Hebrew that flowed from their mouths was frequently fluent and their accent flawless, better than that of much of the Jewish population, a population of immigrants. This new class read the same books and newspapers as the Jewish elite, went to the same plays, and spoke the same niceties as their Jewish middle-class counterparts. So much so that, after 1967, most residents of Gaza and the West Bank were amazed at how "Jewish" the "Arabs of '48," as they called them, seemed. Some of them also filled an important role for other Arabs, both in Israel and, later, in the occupied territories, by providing a crucial bridge to dominant Jewish culture. Lawyers, especially, gained skills in advancing Arab interests by successfully using the courts and other government institutions.[52]

Nonetheless, like the cultural and economic leadership that arose in the coastal region during the British period, these intellectuals, free professionals, and party activists had difficulty building a cohesive leadership and establishing political parties or other viable institutions. Political scientist Mark Tessler found that the percentage of the Arab elite in Israel in relation to the size of the Arab population was quite small compared to that in some of the developing countries in the region.[53] This elite is not only fairly marginal in numbers but suffers, too, from a contradictory status: held in high esteem in Israeli Arab society but on the margins of the dominant Jewish social, economic, and political system, which has been their reference group in the state. Only infrequently have they held positions that allow them to influence or contribute to the development of, or leave their mark on, Israeli society as a whole.[54] And, still, the Arab elites have fulfilled an important function in setting the goals, public agenda, and limits of political activity for the Arab population in Israel.

Although the mass deportations of 1948 have almost never been mentioned overtly, they have remained both a traumatic memory and a well-learned lesson that has been assimilated by the first two generations of Arabs in Israel. Arab citizens of Israel have had to walk a fine line: on the one hand, to demand their rights as citizens, to defend what remains of their lands, and to protest; on the other hand, to take caution not to give the Jewish state the opportunity to uproot them from their lands.[55]

The Family

Even in the early years of the twenty-first century, the extended family, or *hamula,* still constituted a central factor in the individual and public life of Arabs in the state; however, in the years surrounding the 1967 war, the family system failed to answer all the needs of Israel's Arab public.[56] A large portion of the extended family's power stemmed from its "political" role as a go-between for individual Arabs and rulers. As the number of Arabs working in agriculture decreased and employment opportunities outside the village limits increased, the special status of the extended family in Arab society began to erode, but never completely disappeared.[57] After 1967, its economic position also cracked, and it declined in influence. The process gained momentum when the Labor party weakened and afterward, in 1977, was ousted from power. Much of the vitality of the *hamula* and the strength of its elders lay in their relationship to this party. The new ruling party, the Likud, did not show any particular interest in politically cultivating the Arab minority, with the exception of the Druze.[58]

With the erosion of political power came corresponding declines in social power. Marriage patterns based on the extended family lost their status, as traditional first-cousin marriages and heavy dowry payments became less and less popular. The expansion of wage labor brought about decreases in family-orchestrated marriage arrangements, as well as the weakening of the old criteria that had set bride prices. For at least some families of the new educated middle class, interfamily marriage arrangements, with their strong political and economic overtones, were overshadowed by individual freedom in choice of spouse.[59]

Among educated groups in society, even the structure of the family began to change, from the extended to the nuclear family. The individualistic trends that had begun to develop within the Jewish Israeli population partially penetrated some elements of Arab society. Certainly, the old patterns did not disappear completely, even after 1967 when the market for brides and grooms grew considerably and began to cross the "green line." In his study of the town of Shefaram, sociologist Majid al-Haj discovered that traditional marriage patterns were still widespread, even though young Arabs reported that their choices were made according to personal preference and not interfamily matchmaking.[60] As bride prices and spouse selection patterns began to change, so too did other areas of family life. Growing individualism, for instance, raised the probability that young couples would establish separate households instead of becoming part of their extended families.[61] But these new patterns have had to coexist alongside the old: the extended family has continued to play important economic, political, and social roles in Arab society in Israel.

Social and Political Change in Post-1967 Israel

As part of these social changes, new organizations with political potential, not based on the *hamula,* began to appear, such as organizations constituted by internal refugees from destroyed or unrecognized villages.[62] The new, more individualistic, Arab community found, however, that, although the *local* status of the heads of big families had been damaged, the *Israeli* political system still worked through them. In the decades after the 1967 war, Israeli policy continued, as in the past, to stifle any possibility that the local educated elite would form a national leadership, capable of helping Arabs in Israel find their place in the new Israel. These buds of change had already begun to appear in the previous decade. Now, however, as the three fragments of the Palestinian people (those of the West Bank, Israel, and Gaza Strip) were reunited under Israeli rule, these changes gained momentum. One reason for these transformations stemmed from the renewed encounter of Arab citizens of Israel with Palestinians from the West Bank and Gaza, both through renewed family relations and through efforts to provide political and legal aid to their brothers who did not enjoy even the limited civil rights of the Arabs in Israel.

Two trends were central in the refashioning of Arab society in Israel and its strategies for survival after the 1967 war: the increasingly rapid decline of agrarian life and the development of a new politics. The economic boom after 1967 had a marked effect on the Arabs' standard of living and their entire socioeconomic structure. Many became independent proprietors—owners of small workshops and businesses and, in some cases, of substantial industries. From their position in the previous two decades as unskilled laborers and service providers, often the lowliest jobs in Israel, they now moved into employment that required greater occupational and entrepreneurial skills.[63] The Arabs in Israel began to enter businesses and take jobs that many Jews, mostly from Eastern Europe, were now abandoning. They acquired experience and skills in the new labor market in areas such as construction, mechanics, and semi-industrial labor as contractors and subcontractors. Road construction, public works, and a wide variety of manufacturing, often with government contracts, at least partially opened up to Arabs.[64] Just as Arab Israelis had replaced Jews from Islamic countries by moving into unskilled, low-paying, low-prestige, hard labor in the 1950s and 60s, now Israeli Arabs passed these jobs on to day labors from the occupied territories.

By the 1980s, a new Arab industrial sector was in place and employed up to 30 percent of the Arab industrial workforce and 6 percent of the total Arab workforce.[65] Arabs also initiated small businesses serving primarily local Arab, but sometimes Jewish, customers. A 1985 survey of such businesses and industries pointed to solid Arab presence in these sectors.[66] Agriculture was now just one sector among many. Wage labor outside the village and independent businesses owned by Arabs created a labor shortage in the villages, forcing farmers who remained in the villages to raise productivity and their employees' wages.[67]

All this certainly did not mean economic nirvana for Israel's Arab population. Industrialization in the Arab sector has remained fairly limited. Arab-owned businesses have tended to be small, dedicated to trade and commerce, subcontracting, craftsmanship, and transport.[68] Most factories have continued to be completely or partially dependent on Jewish industry, contracting, marketing chains, and purchase. For example, the Arab clothing industry developed in the 1980s to supply Jewish-owned large textile factories and fashion houses.

In the 1990s and at the beginning of the twenty-first century, most of these industries folded as Israel's economic transformation to high-tech proceeded and, later, a deep recession hit. Their down-fall hurt both Jewish and Arab peripheral towns. Arab-owned indus-try still tended to be concentrated in traditional sectors such as tex-tiles and food production, compared to Jewish-owned enterprises, which included more sophisticated multi- and transnational pro-duction, demanding greater technical skills and knowledge. The high-tech industries that made up Israel's so-called new economy were practically entirely Jewish. Friendly regulations and state subsi-dization, which aided politically preferred groups, applied to Jews and not Arabs. The largest concentrations of poverty, as it happens, have been among the Arab and ultra-Orthodox populations (about half of all Israeli Arabs and ultra-Orthodox were under the poverty line). Of the twenty-three official unemployment centers in the year 2000, nineteen were in Arab municipalities. In some Arab villages and towns, the unemployment rate reached 15 percent and more.[69] With the growth of a new Arab middle class has come a widening of the gap between the better off and worse off in Israeli Arab society.

Nonetheless, in the 1980s, even without substantial government investments or other advantages, Arabs in Israel often found ways around government policy (through what is called the "gray econ-omy") to make some noteworthy economic gains.[70] This sector de-veloped alongside, and separately from, the state's economy. One study pointed to approximately 300 Arab families who became large entrepreneurs and another 2000 who were among mid-range entre-preneurs and investors.[71] Together with intellectuals, free profes-sionals, national and local politicians, whose numbers reached more than 4,000 by the beginning of the year 2000, these entrepreneurs have become one of the most influential sectors in Arab society in Israel.

The overall growth in prosperity has even had an effect on less-well-off Arab citizens, including one prime example, women. A growing number of women joined the workforce in response to the increasing demand for non- and semiskilled working hands. During the 1980s, 11 percent of women of labor age were working; but, by mid-2000, about a quarter of women were officially employed (com-pared to nearly three-quarters of Jewish women), and many, many more were unofficially serving in unreported jobs, such as domestic labor and unskilled work in agriculture and small textile factories.[72] The percentage of Christian women working (about 40 percent) was about twice as high as for Muslim and Druze women.[73] Women became part of an Arab sector, significantly transformed from what it had been in the 1950s—and substantially more prosperous.

To Build a House, To Plant a Vineyard

Even with the growth of a vocal political and intellectual elite, of a new class of entrepreneurs and professionals, of a transformed occupational structure bringing increased prosperity, Arab society has remained caught between the promise of new possibilities and the containment posed by being enveloped in a Jewish state. Possibly the problem most exemplary of the reality in which the Arab community in Israel has lived is the shortage of land for residential construction. The Arab population grew from the 150,000 people who remained after the 1948 war to over a million in the year 2000. Natural growth peaked at the rate of over 4 percent a year, an almost unheard of rate worldwide. Recently however, this rate has begun to fall.[74] Over the decade of 1972–1982, the growth was 3.7 percent, meaning the doubling of the Arab population in Israel well within twenty years, although historically emigration of Arabs from Israel has partially offset the high rate of natural increase.

With the mushrooming of the population came increasingly crowded living conditions; almost two of every five Arab households included seven or more people, and, in over a fifth of all households, more than four people lived in a room.[75] Two other factors further worsened living conditions: (1) the lack of rapid urbanization and restrictions on turning agricultural lands into land for housing, which could have released pressure from the villages, and (2) the economic prosperity of the 1980s and early 1990s, which brought with it a desire and the financial wherewithal to build more and bigger houses.[76]

But authorized construction was almost impossible. Israeli law demands that all construction be carried out according to master plans for development as well as local municipality plans, themselves dependent on authorization of the district council. All new construction or additions in Israel require a license from the authorities. Arab villages, local councils, and municipalities have lacked the means and skills to develop these elaborate plans, and the state has not bothered to help them, granting priority to Jewish development towns, disadvantaged Jewish neighborhoods, and settlements in the occupied territories.[77] Thus, legal Arab construction has been frozen in place, but, at the same time, illegal construction has been booming. Much of this construction has remained untouched, but periodic house demolitions have added another layer to the reigning tension between the Israeli state and its Arab citizens.

Beyond this, state refusal of official recognition for so-called unrecognized villages has meant that they have not been provided with basic services.[78] The high rate of population growth and the restrictions on construction have come on top of severe barriers the state has placed on Arab acquisition of land. The allocation or leasing of land to Arabs involves practices and ideas at odds with Zionist ideology. To block Arab access to land, the Jewish National Fund (the JNF is an agency of the World Zionist Organization) established formal standards officially forbidding the leasing of its lands to non-Jews. Because most lands were actually owned by the JNF, it, in effect, acted as a subcontractor of the state—the Israel Land Authority—for land allocation and leasing.[79]

The result has been a rapid expansion of illegal construction, estimated at about 30 percent of all Arab residences. Some construction was authorized retrospectively; most remained in place by authorities' turning a blind eye. But the rest has become the basis of bitter conflict, which has led to the total destruction of many new houses. House demolitions remain a sword of Damocles, hovering as a constant threat over the Arab community in Israel. It is not surprising, then, that it was the tensions generated by the housing crisis that brought about the single most important event in restoring a strong voice to, and forging a new solidarity among, Israel's Arabs.

Land Day

The home and land crisis turned out to be a key catalyst for political radicalization among Arab citizens in Israel. In the decade after the 1967 war, a wave of political activism swept across the community, which reawakened some of the Jews' deepest fears. The key event occurred on March 30, 1976, when the National Committee for the Defense of Arab Lands—a political organization claiming to represent the Arab population in Israel—declared a general strike, which quickly got out of hand. As in the past, the most immediate issue was impending confiscation of Arab land by the state, which the government had announced in February of that year. Confiscation was to take place in the Galilee as part of a plan (insensitively) labeled "Judaization of the Galilee."[80] Residents of Arab villages who joined the protest demonstrations clashed with massive deployed police forces, resulting in six Arabs dead and many more wounded and arrested.

For many Arabs, the event echoed the day of bloodshed in Kfar Qassem, which had taken place twenty years before. The Kfar Qassem massacre on the eve of the 1956 Suez war had been the most traumatic event carved into the collective memory of the Arab citizens of Israel until that time. It was a painful and gaping wound, remaining a powerful symbol, even until this day. On October 29 of that year, the military administration imposed a curfew on Arab villages set to begin at five in the evening. In Kfar Qassem, notice of the curfew did not reach the fellaheen working in the fields. The village head, who himself had been informed of the curfew only half an hour before it was set to begin, warned the local army unit commander that there was no way possible to notify the farmers and shepherds in their fields on time.

Similar situations occurred in other villages, but only the local army unit in Kfar Qassem took the return of the fellaheen from the fields as a breach of curfew. Soldiers gathered those returning to the village and shot to death forty-seven men, women, and children.[81] The government made huge efforts to hide the facts of the massacre from the eyes of the Jewish public and from the international press.

In the end, though, Israeli officials were forced to admit what had occurred and put those responsible on trial. Only light, symbolic sentences were meted out to the perpetrators of the massacre, and several later even advanced to more senior positions in the army.

Land Day was very different from the Kfar Qassem massacre. Alongside the fury toward the regime and police and the mourning over the dead, Land Day brought about a new national pride. This time around, the Arab community had demonstrated a daring confidence and political awareness totally lacking in 1956; this time Arab citizens were not passive and submissive. Instead, they initiated and coordinated political activity at the national level, responding to police brutality with their own violence. What turned out to be more important is that they used the events as a permanent rallying call. In 1988, they declared Land Day a Palestinian-Israeli civil national day of commemoration and a day of identification with Palestinians of the West Bank and Gaza, to be marked by yearly demonstrations and general strikes.[82] Among Palestinians in the West Bank and Gaza Strip, these protests awakened feelings of solidarity and respect for the participants. Land Day was a key event, then, not only in forging political solidarity among Arab citizens of Israel, but in cementing the acceptance of the "1948 Arabs" back into the larger Palestinian world and into the heart of mainstream Palestinian nationalism.

Al-Ard, Abna al-Balad, and Their Successors

The internal solidarity and acceptance by other Palestinians evident after Land Day had not come easily. The first steps to form an Arab national movement in Israel date back to the end of the 1950s, when a small group of Arab intellectuals established a movement called al-Ard (the Land) with its own movement magazine.[83] This group, at first naming itself the Popular Front, formed within the Communist party in response to a police assault of demonstrators in Nazareth on May 1, 1958. Al-Ard advocated reconstruction of a Palestinian identity but also adopted Nasser's pan-Arab ideas, looking upon historical Palestine as a part of the larger land of the entire nation. Quickly, the group found itself at odds with the Communist party leadership and broke off from it.

Despite initial success in registering as a corporation (after its petition to the High Court of Justice to register was accepted), it failed in its attempts to register as a recognized nongovernmental organization and, later, in 1965, as a political party.[84] Throughout the 1960s, the group participated in an ongoing discussion of "the Arab question" both within the community and with those limited members of the Jewish public who were willing to listen. Israeli officials cautiously allowed al-Ard's criticism of the deportations of 1948, military government, and the continuation of land confiscation but became alarmed at its appeals to a variety of organizations abroad, such as the United Nations General-Secretary, the Arab League, and even the PLO, which was just then being formed. In fact, al-Ard was the first Arab group from within Israel to attract the attention of the budding Palestinian national movement outside Israel. It is not surprising, then, that the Israeli High Court of Justice declared the group illegal on the grounds that it was subversive to the very existence of the Jewish state and to Israeli democracy. Its members dispersed; some were imprisoned, and a number who had been teachers were fired from their jobs.[85]

By the 1970s, al-Ard had disappeared from the public arena—and not only because of the actions taken by the State of Israel. The Communist party leadership saw al-Ard as an ideological challenger that could endanger the party (although al-Ard's membership actually never exceeded 200 people).[86] Even outside the party, many in the Arab community, who still felt beaten down and insecure, looked on the group's actions as a danger to the community's very existence. Although al-Ard never took root in the Arab community, some of its ideas reemerged in the following decades—especially the notion of renewed Palestinism—that phoenix that reappeared each time that it seemed dead and buried.

Further steps toward forging cohesion and gaining acceptance among Palestinians outside Israel began to be taken outside the framework of the Communist party (by this time, called Rakah) in the early 1970s. In 1971, Israeli Arab university students and graduates (mostly from the "Triangle" region, with the town of Umm Al-Fahm at its center) established the Association of Arab Academics in Israel and declared Arab citizens of the state to be part of the Palestinian people and the larger Arab nation.

All these early political stirrings of Arabs in Israel had a hand in the outpouring of anger on Land Day in 1976 and in the increased social cohesion and sustained political activism that followed it. In the years after Land Day, new movements and parties, with more outspoken leaders, appeared. Especially salient was the extraparliamentary movement, Village Sons *(Abna al-Balad)*. This group gained momentum at the end of the 1970s because, among other reasons, it presented itself as a national-ideological alternative to Rakah.

Abna al-Balad was opposed to Arabs' participation in Israeli national elections and sought to narrow "cooperation" with the Zionist state as much as possible. One of its main fields of activity was the local Arab councils and municipalities.[87] Activists participating in local elections from 1978 to 1983 gradually increased their power.[88] Drawing from the ideological line of the Popular Front for Palestinian Liberation (with the exception of the idea of "armed resistance," which it did not see as suitable to conditions within Israel), the group aimed to transform Israel into a "secular and democratic" state for all its citizens. Later, Abna al-Balad's political approach changed as it joined the demand for implementation of Security Council Resolution 242 (emphasizing Israel's withdrawal from occupied territories in exchange for peace) and the establishment of a Palestinian state next to, not in place of, Israel.[89]

For all its proclamations on these bigger issues, Abna al-Balad's focus was mostly inner-directed, decrying the traditional structure of Arab society, which its leaders believed not only hindered the development of Arab society but also helped the Jews control it. They advocated "union with the Palestinian struggle," apparently under the leadership of the PLO. Most of their activities were on the university campuses, where they struggled with Rakah over control of the Arab student committees.[90] The group's power went up and down; for example, in student committee elections in 1976, Abna al-Balad won a majority of the votes at the Hebrew University; while, in the 1980s, it was almost completely erased from the political map. Again, in the 1990s, its candidates did well in elections for student committees in the universities of Haifa and Beersheba; but, by the twenty-first century, it was moribund.[91]

A number of political parties giving voice to Palestinian-Israeli interests and concerns formed, split, and consolidated in the couple of decades after Land Day. At the center of much of the activity was the party Hadash, which began as another Jewish-Arab communist party and eventually became mostly Arab (in 1996, for example, only one of its five Knesset representatives was Jewish).[92] In the 1990s, to take one instance of the consolidations and splits, Hadash joined with Abna al-Balad and others to form a group called the Front for National Action. A faction that split from Hadash, headed by Dr. Kamal al-Dahr (from Nazareth) and Muhammad Miari, was called the Progressive Movement (which participated in the 1984 elections in an electoral covenant with left-wing Jewish parties, headed by Matatiyahu Peled and Uri Avneri). Like Hadash, it created a party electoral list and demanded civil equality for Arabs of the Israeli state, recognition of and negotiation with the PLO as the legitimate representative of the Palestinian people, and establishment of a Palestinian state alongside Israel. Those on its electoral list viewed the Arabs in Israel as an inseparable part of the Palestinian people and did not believe in the possibility of acquiring true equality within the framework of the Israeli state. The faction, lacking a firm social base in Arab Israeli society, was perceived as a one-man party with a single issue (the general Palestinian issue). It disappeared after the 1992 elections.

The new parties and movements that formed and reformed after 1976 began to expose the Arab citizens of Israel to external Palestinian political streams. Most important among these were Palestinian nationalism (as represented by the PLO) and the renewed Islamic movement, especially as it gained momentum after the revolution in Iran. In the first two decades of its existence, the PLO leadership mostly disregarded Israel's Arabs. Only in 1988 did the PLO take a sharp turn in this policy, owing largely to its own painful decision to accept a state in the occupied territories and, thus, implicitly, recognize Israel. In that year, the PLO urged Arab voters to vote in the

Israeli elections for lists that would serve Palestinian national interests.

More attuned by this time to the debates inside the Palestinian
national movement, many Arabs in Israel overtly backed those factions of the PLO favoring the establishment of a Palestinian state
on part of the territory of historical Palestine, alongside Israel ("two
states for two peoples" was the formula proposed by Hadash).[93]
Even then, however, the question of whether to relate to the PLO as
the voice of all Palestinians remained an unresolved issue among Israeli Arabs. Many continued to be uncomfortable with the PLO's
combative rhetoric and its belief in "armed resistance" (which was
often seen as little more than indiscriminate terrorism). Their reservations about PLO rhetoric and practice stemmed, in part, from
their more vulnerable position as citizens of Israel as well as from
their doubts over the practicality of achieving the PLO's original objectives and the efficiency of its tactics. Their own views were often
quite pragmatic, coming from an intimate knowledge of Israeli-Jew-
ish society.

The Arabs of Israel, then, experienced growing solidarity of their
community and increasing acceptance as an integral part of the Palestinian people, especially after Land Day in 1976. Still, they were the
only part of the Palestinian world, both within and outside historic
Palestine, that did not take an active, collective role in armed struggle or in popular uprisings (the Intifadas). The very few who participated did so as individuals.[94] Thus, the Arabs in Israel were not fully
incorporated into the reconstructed national culture of the occupied territories or the diaspora (ghurba). Yet, their incorporation
into the Israeli state was also partial and conditional, creating a feeling that they would never enjoy full and equal civil rights in a Jewish
nation-state as long as it was not redefined as a state for all its citizens. Arabs in Israel have called this situation "double marginality."

From Local to National Politics

Already in the beginning of the 1950s, Israeli direct military control
over the population gave way to more indirect rule through the

hamulas. With the general liberalization of the Israeli state in the 1960s and 1970s, Arab local government began to enjoy a degree of autonomy and slowly became the main focus for Arab public life in Israel. Effectively excluded from white-collar jobs in the public sector, educated Arabs looked to the local councils and the Arab educational system for employment opportunities. Beginning in 1974, the Arab mayors organized the Council of Arab Heads of Municipalities. The immediate goal of this union was to demand the narrowing of the gap in resource allocations between Jewish and Arab local authorities. Following the trauma of the bloody Land Day events, the Council began to become involved in all issues relating to Arabs in Israel.[95]

The expanded role of the council resulted, not only from the events of Land Day, but also from the leaking, in September 1976, of the confidential *König Report*. A commission, headed by Israel König, a state official in charge of the Haifa district of the Ministry of the Interior, had represented the Arab majority in the western Galilee as a threat to state security and recommended settling more Jews in the region, repressing Arab political activity, and encouraging Arab emigration. The *König Report*'s main goal was to create a Jewish majority in the Galilee.

The hoopla it generated became a catalyst for Arab political organization. Following the Israeli invasion of Lebanon in 1982, the council, now called the Supreme Follow-up Committee, stepped up its activities.[96] The Follow-up Committee evolved into the recognized representative of the Arab community in Israel. It included representatives from most streams of Arab society in Israel—intellectuals, thinkers, religious leaders, representatives of parents' committees, Histadrut activists, politicians, and city councilmen. Its establishment was exactly the type of Arab national organization that the Israeli state had long tried to prevent. Once the Follow-up Committee became a broad forum, it succeeded in lessening the divisiveness that had plagued the Arabs for years. Israeli efforts to suppress the construction of a national identity among Arabs, emphasizing instead secondary identities and playing on the divisions within the Arab community, in the end only contributed to community solidarity.

But, just when events seemed to suggest a turning point in the relationship of Israel's Arabs to the state and society, momentum was lost. The leaking of the *König Report* in 1976, for example, created a public uproar in Israel and internationally, which at first appeared to lead to some soul-searching among Jewish officials and intellectuals about their relationship to Arab citizens. Yet, even years afterward, little changed. The state remained mostly indifferent to Israeli Arabs, while continuing the same policies of domination. Periodically, elections or some other event aroused officials or parties to pay more attention to the Arabs, usually offering some gesture of good will, but little changed fundamentally.

With the outbreak of the Intifada in 1987, the Arab citizens again received a burst of attention from the Jewish public and policymakers. Two weeks after the uprising began in the occupied territories, Arabs in Israel declared a general strike in solidarity with the Palestinian rebellion. Fears grew that the rebellion would spread into Israel proper, but those worries dissipated with the end of the strike and, again, inattention became the hallmark of official policy. Even the Follow-up Committee, which had generated so much promise in the early 1980s, sputtered. In the end, it failed to overcome fragmentation and inter-*hamula* rivalries in Israeli Arab society. Nor did it succeed in forcing the Israeli state to allocate resources more equally to its Arab citizens. By the 1990s, the Follow-up Committee's prestige and strength had ebbed considerably.

Israeli Arab citizens' failure to attract the full attention of the state and their up-and-down efforts to construct themselves as a cohesive national minority in the state did not mean that they remained static politically. From the late 1980s on, important changes did occur, especially as Palestinian Israelis connected to the unfolding events in the occupied territories. From their general strike at the beginning of the first Intifada in 1987 to the violent clash with state security forces at the beginning of the al-Aqsa Intifada in 2000, Israeli Arab society was buffeted by events in the West Bank and Gaza Strip and by the religious revival in the Muslim world generally.

The outbreak of the Intifada in the occupied territories in 1987 and Israel's attempts to put it down by sheer force spurred Member of Knesset Abdulwaheb Darawshe to resign in January 1988 from the Labor party and, in June, found the Arab Democratic Party (ADP) and its weekly "al-Diar." In the elections of that year, the party received 13 percent of the Arab vote and, in 1992, 15 percent, winning two Knesset seats. In the 1996 elections, in coalition with the Islamic party, which had previously boycotted national elections and concentrated only on local elections, it gained four seats. ADP's message was extremely sophisticated: On the one side, it demanded civil equality and full rights for Arabs in Israel, as well as the establishment of a Palestinian state in the West Bank and Gaza Strip. On the other side, it urged Arabs in Israel to participate politically, abiding by the rules of the game of the Israeli state in order to take full advantage of their political potential. It was the first Arab political body to demand joining in a government coalition, with ministers in the government itself, in order to influence "from within."[97] Politically and culturally, the ADP was the first (non-Zionist) Israeli Arab party in the Israeli political arena.

Al-Tajamo'a Al-Watani Al-Democrati (the National Democratic Assembly) was almost the antithesis of the ADP. Founded by a group of nationalist intellectuals with a pan-Arab ideology, it was headed by a lecturer in philosophy, Azmi Bishara.[98] Rejecting the ADP's "assimilationist" platform, al-Tajamo'a called for turning Israel into a state for all its citizens, instead of a Jewish state, while granting cultural autonomy to Arabs in Israel. This party criticized the Oslo Accord, which al-Tajamo'a believed was signed out of Palestinian weakness and granted legitimacy to the Jewish state without appropriate reciprocation. This position contrasted with that of all the other non-Islamic Arab parties and factions on the Israeli political map at the time. In the 1996 elections, al-Tajamo'a entered into an electoral coalition with Hadash and, through a slight tweaking of the universal-communist message of Hadash in the direction of Arab nationalism, managed to win five seats in the Knesset, including one for Bishara himself. Soon after, however, the two parties again went their separate ways.

In short, as Israeli Arabs moved from local to national politics in the late 1980s and early 1990s, their political positions became more complex and nuanced. They were no longer dealing exclusively with local issues, such as municipal budgets and building permits; they were now taking positions on weighty issues, including the Oslo Accord and possible participation in a coalition government. No doubt, the turnaround in the Tunis-based PLO policy to negotiate with Israel and accept its existence, along with the outbreak of the Intifada, impelled Israel's Arabs toward new positions and building new political organizations. But the growing relationship between Palestinian Israelis and Palestinians in the occupied territories did not always move Israel's Arab citizens to a closer identification with the Palestinian national movement. The new Palestine Authority that came out of the Oslo process led some Arabs in Israel to shy away from too strong an identification with the new Palestinian regime. In fact, the degree of their identification with the Israeli state actually appeared to grow as it became apparent that basic human rights suffered under the rule of the Palestinian Authority. When rumors surfaced toward the end of the Oslo process in 2000 about a possible land swap between Israel and a new Palestinian state, Israel's Arabs expressed overwhelming opposition to their own towns being included in the trade. In the 1990s, at least a portion of Israeli Arabs began to integrate more and more as individuals into Israeli society (which, as it liberalized, became more open to the efforts of Arabs to become true members of society).

Religious Revolution

Another dimension of the broadening field of political activity among Palestinian Israelis came as part of the larger religious transformation in the region. Like others in the Islamic world, many Muslims in Israel were caught up in the excitement of the Iranian Revolution of 1978. The religious awakening and politicization of Islam in the occupied territories also influenced many in Israel's Muslim community, either through encounters with individual residents of the territories or exposure to the colleges for religious studies (granting the degree of "sheikh") in the West Bank and Gaza. Historically, this awakening had its roots in the Arab Revolt in colonial Palestine in 1936 and the penetration of the ideas and institutions of Egypt's Muslim Brotherhood into the Fertile Crescent. Much later, in the 1970s, groups of students championing Islamic activism and revival organized on campuses in Nablus and Hebron. Once the Iranian revolution occurred, Islam gained new momentum among the Muslim population. Ideologically, it competed with secular pan-Arab nationalism offering a universal message but one tinged with a strong, local Palestinian flavor.

Already in 1979, a small underground group, Jihad Family, organized under the charismatic leadership of Sheikh Abdellah Nimr Darwish from Kfar Qassem, aiming to bring Islamic armed struggle (jihad) into Israel's borders. This organization was wiped out by the Israeli security services, and its leaders and members were sentenced to prison. Upon their release, Darwish and his colleagues established the Young Muslims movement, abandoning the idea of armed struggle and turning, instead, to social-religious and educational activities. In general, the movement began to take more moderate positions on the topics of the Jewish-Arab conflict, partition of Palestine between Arabs and Jews, and participation in the Israeli public arena.[99] Nonetheless, the movement has focused on community welfare activities as a means of political organization, much like Islamic groups in the West Bank and Gaza Strip. The group gained strength as it established community centers, self-help groups, and support for the fight against social ills such as drugs, prostitution, and consumption of alcoholic beverages. Groups of young Muslims undertook clean-up operations and renovations in Israel's Arab villages.

In some ways, these country-wide, down-to-earth actions made Rakah, the Communist party, with its struggle for national equality and civil rights, look detached and removed from people's daily problems. Its loss of popularity was most evident in the local elections of 1989 and 1993, in which Islamic candidates won a majority of the seats on a number of important local councils.[100] One of these was in the city of Umm al-Fahm, a former village that had grown sufficiently to become an official city, after the residents struggled to overcome the state's resistance to such a change in its status. By the 1990s, the Islamic movement became Rakah's and, later, Hadash's, most important political rival.

The transition of the Islamic political organizations from underground activism to provision of services was mirrored by their increasing moderation toward Israel and the Jews. In the beginning, their publication, *Al-Sirat* (which was outlawed in 1990), had been militant, preaching *jihad* against unbelievers and calling for the establishment of an Islamic Palestinian state. Over time, and at least until October 2000, radical political slogans gave way to the formula borrowed from the Israeli communists—"two states for two peoples." Their entry into the turmoil of Israeli elections seemed to moderate their positions at the very moment that Islamic groups in the West Bank and Gaza Strip were demonstrating growing militancy, especially after the signing of the Oslo agreement. As in the case of the secular Arab political organizations in Israel, a new subtlety and complexity marked the politics of Islamic organizations as they entered and navigated the waters of Israeli public life.

Arabs in a Jewish, Democratic State: The Katzir Case

Changes in Arabs' political position in the late 1980s and 1990s did not stem only from their own new political organizations or from their evolving orientation toward the state; they came too from changes in the Israeli state itself. In 1992, the Israeli Parliament adopted a series of Basic Laws, which were intended to become the basis of an eventual written constitution and important steps in shoring up democracy.[101] These Basic Laws aimed specifically to broaden civil rights in Israel, yet they simultaneously prescribed that Israel was to be a "Jewish and democratic state"—without defining the meaning of either "Jewish" or "democratic." Israel's Arabs continued to find themselves in an anomalous situation after the adoption of the Basic Laws. These foundational pieces of legislation both increased their rights and, simultaneously, excluded them from being incorporated into the basic definition of the state. These inner contradictions in the State of Israel produced a complex constitutional status for them. Some of this complexity could be seen in an important Supreme Court decision rendered in the Katzir case.

In 1995, a couple by the name of Adel and Iman Qa'adan of the Israeli Arab town of Baqa Al-Garbiya sought to purchase a plot of land in the Jewish communal settlement of Katzir in order to build a home. Refusing to sell land to them, the council clerk cited the area's official policy prohibiting the sale of plots to non-Jews. A petition was filed on the couple's behalf by the Association for Civil Rights in Israel in October 1995. The chief justice of the Supreme Court, Aharon Barak, attempted to avoid making a ruling—a characteristic response for him in sensitive cases—and suggested, instead, that the sides reach an out-of-court settlement. But the parties could not come to an agreement. On March 8, 2000, four and a half years after the petition was filed, the Supreme Court ruled definitively on the illegality of discrimination against Israeli Arab citizens in allocation of state lands by the government or any of its affiliated arms (for example, the Jewish Agency).

Immediately after the ruling was handed down, journalists, academics, and others wrote and spoke of the decision as revolutionary, even as "post-Zionist," and as a real turning point in Supreme Court history. Many even compared it enthusiastically to the well-known United States Supreme Court ruling of *Brown v. the Board of Education*—the decision that struck down the "separate but equal" doctrine of education for blacks and whites. Along with Israel's Law of Return, which privileges immigrant Jews in gaining Israeli citizenship, the denial of the right and ability to buy land has constituted the main form of legal discrimination against Arabs in Israel. The Jewish Agency, a nominally nonstate organization that allocated most of the country's land, has retained a special status in Israel and was not obliged to treat all citizens of the state equally. It was the discrimination that came out of that practice of land allocation that prompted the Supreme Court to act.

Upon closer analysis, the Court decision in favor of the Qa'adans did not furnish the petitioners with an actual remedy to their dilemma. Rather, the Court simply made a general statement about discrimination, refraining from ordering the relevant authorities to allocate the requested plot of land to the Qa'adans. Furthermore, the decision responded to the Qa'adans as individuals and did not address the larger question of discrimination against the Arab community as a whole. As social-legal scholar Alexander Kedar put it, the "Qa'adan [verdict] draws a line. The past is to be left unchallenged, untouched and unspoken. Moreover, the story of the Qa'adans is isolated from their collective identity and needs as Palestinian citizens of Israel."[102] Despite its liberal rhetoric, the verdict of the Israeli Supreme Court of Justice in the Katzir case did not improve the status of Palestinian-Israelis' civil liberties.[103] In July 2002, the Knesset tried to pass a law authorizing the agencies dealing with land allocations to lease out lands in Jewish localities only to Jewish residents for "security reasons." However, facing heavy criticism, especially from groups comparing the proposed law to ones under South Africa's apartheid regime, the government backed down and withdrew the bill.

October 2000

Arabs in Israel have been unable to escape their basic dilemma. The end of the twentieth century found them more prosperous, better organized politically, and more securely ensconced in Israeli society than at any time in the past. Still, they have failed to overcome their internal fragmentation; they have kept the new Palestine Authority and, indeed, the entire Palestinian national movement, at arm's length; in accepting Israel's existence and in working within the state, Islamic activists in the country have been at odds with those outside; and they have faced continuing political and social discrimination in Israel. The demonstrations that occurred on Land Day in 1976 demonstrated a generation ago how distrust and discrimination could quickly spill over into violence.

For all the changes that occurred in the last quarter century, October 2000 proved that the discrimination and distrust have not disappeared, even in the new circumstances of a state more actively asserting its defense of civil liberties, and they could still lead to violence. Those events of October 2000 were the closest the Arab citizens of the state ever came to civil revolt.

In that month, the residents of almost all Arab settlements took to the streets in angry protest, blocking central traffic arteries, throwing stones, and shouting slogans denouncing the state and its policies. In mixed towns (Nazareth, Acre, and even Haifa, but not Ramle and Lydda), clashes broke out between Jewish and Arab residents.[104] The police reacted with unbridled violence, replicating responses typical of those used by the occupying forces in the West Bank and Gaza Strip, including massive use of live fire. This time, however, the shooting was directed at citizens of the state. Thirteen Arabs and one Jew were killed; about 700, wounded; and hundreds more, arrested. The Barak government and the security agencies did not express any misgivings about the methods used or any sympathy for the victims. Those responsible (the Minister of Internal Security, Shlomo Ben-Ami, and the police captain of the northern district) were not dismissed, nor did they resign. Only after heavy pressure by Arab citizens, Jewish intellectuals, and the international community was a government investigation committee (the "Or Commission") appointed to look into the conditions leading to the bloodshed and to identify those responsible.

The demonstrations and ensuing violence deeply soured relations between the state and its Arab citizens. The outbreak was rooted in two sources. First was the Arab citizens' identification with fellow Palestinians over the green line, especially in light of the recent outbreak of the al-Aqsa Intifada in the previous month (see Chapter 11). Second, the violence seemed to result from Israeli Arabs' frustration with their own political and economic situation in the Israeli state. Although the Rabin administration, 1992–1995, had made significant strides in improving their condition, from 1996 on, momentum was lost in improving the situation of Arabs in Israel and in coming to terms with their position in state and society.

The bitter taste of October 2000 has lingered on. Continuing disappointment with the progress of talks between Israel and the Palestinian Authority led many Arab citizens to boycott national elections for the first time in the history of the state in February 2001. Many others cast blank ballots as a vote of protest. In the long run, the boycott and protest votes signified that the Labor party and its coalition partners on Israel's left could no longer be unconditionally certain of receiving the Arab vote. In that regard, the February 2001 elections and Labor's participation in Sharon's government continued the weakening of the ties between the Arab community's leadership and the Labor party. They demonstrated the autonomy of the new, educated generation—one more intimately involved in the Israeli experience but a generation that did not experience the intimidation of military rule and thus was more willing to take an independent course politically.

If the 2001 elections demonstrated a new political maturity by Israel's Arab citizens, they also were harbingers of a difficult new period for the Arabs. The decisive election of the right-wing Likud's Ariel Sharon dealt a severe blow to Israel's "Peace Camp." Intellectuals among Israel's Arab population expressed the fear that they were losing the political strength they had painstakingly built up in the two previous decades. Many also felt betrayed by the Jewish partners with whom they had tried to bring about a historic reconciliation between Jews and Arabs in the 1990s by working toward establishment of a Palestinian state alongside Israel.[105]

The unceasing violence that began in September 2000 in the al-Aqsa Intifada only exacerbated the Jewish-Arab divide inside Israel. Even though the participation by Israel's Arabs was miniscule, as the uprising proceeded, the number of violent incidents involving them steadily grew. Eight Palestinian-Israelis suspected of terrorism were apprehended in 2000; twenty-five, in 2001; and twenty-seven in the first half of 2002. Overt expressions of hatred against Arabs, in general, and the Arabs in Israel, in particular, increased radically among Israel's Jews. Even in the political arena, anti-Arab sentiment was used to justify legislation and policies detrimental to the Arab population and to attack Arab members of Knesset.[106] One Sharon aide spoke of the arrests of Israeli Arabs in 2002 as "an ominous development."[107] The idea of mass deportation of Arabs from within the West Bank, Gaza Strip, and even Israel proper entered Israeli discourse because of the demographic threat of undermining the "Jewish character" of the state. Others discussed stripping Israeli Arabs suspected of violence of their citizenship. Although the chances were very low that such measures would be adopted as actual policies, the open nature of the discourse was in itself worrisome.

The Arab citizens of Israel have sat in a vortex of cross-pressures, and, not surprisingly, they have responded to their dilemma with seemingly contradictory views and actions. They have continued to recognize the legitimacy of Israel in overwhelming numbers (in a 2001 survey, over 50 percent answered "yes" and another 33.7 percent answered "yes with reservations" to a question asking about their support for Israel's existence). Those numbers were only a slight decline from the 93.3 percent total in 1995.[108] They have seen their futures as being in Israel, not in a Palestinian state. Over three-quarters in the 2001 survey said they wanted to continue to be citizens of Israel. As one Israeli Palestinian researcher concluded, "They see their place, future, and organizational situation, as well as the bodies that represent them, as distinct from those of the Palestinians in the West Bank, Gaza Strip, and diaspora. This means that the Palestinians in Israel see themselves as Israeli citizens who will continue to live in the country and are not willing to move to another country, not even to a Palestinian state in the West Bank and Gaza Strip."[109]

If they have expressed support for Israel and their place in it, they have also been behind Palestinian national aspirations for the creation of a Palestinian state. Two-thirds reported that they feel closer to Arabs in the territories than they do to Jews in Israel.[110] Arabs in Israel have also felt alienated from the Israeli state and society. Ra'if Zraik, a Palestinian-Israeli lawyer from Nazareth, spoke of "an acute sense among Palestinian citizens of Israel of being alienated from public space within their homeland. . . ."[111] Most neighborhoods, even whole towns and cities, have been closed to them for living and, sometimes, even for work. Discrimination has continued to be a day-to-day problem. Palestinian-Israelis have wanted "the state to serve them on an equal footing with the Jews, provide them with equal resources, ensure that their group receives equal public services, allocate civil-service jobs fairly to members of their group, permit them full partnership in government and governing coalitions, and grant them parity in determining the nature and objectives of the state."[112] In short, Arabs in Israel have felt both a part of two contending worlds—in Israel and among the Palestinian people—and distant from the core of each. One anthropologist, calling Palestinians a "trapped minority," characterized them as "being marginal twice over, within two political entities."[113]

One way that some Palestinian Israelis have dealt with their anomalous situation has been as go-betweens. Arab intellectuals in Israel, in particular, have filled a dual role for the Arab populations in Israel and in the occupied territories. For residents of the territories, they have served as decipherers of, and interlocutors to, the reigning Jewish political culture. Among the Arab population in Israel, they introduced "authentic," local Palestinian culture and a Palestinian identity that Israel's Arabs could internalize. These intellectuals are indeed, as Dan Rabinowitz and Khawla Abu Bakr have defined them, a third generation of the Arabs in Israel—a generation neither broken and resigned to their fate as the first generation was, nor limited to acquiring more civil rights from the Jewish state.[114] Rather, they have constituted a cohort demanding full partnership in redesigning the state as multicultural and multiethnic. They have rejected Jewish exclusivity, outlining a number of routes that Israel could take in refashioning itself as a multicultural society, including cultural autonomy for the Arab minority and the establishment of a democratic, binational state in the entire area of historic Palestine.[115] But these ideas have been seen by Jews as wild-eyed, arousing deep fears and precipitating an ethnocentric backlash. Some Jews even interpreted this discourse among Arabs as a plot for bringing about the end of the Jewish state or as a recipe for large-scale interethnic civil war.[116]

Even if these radical plans do not materialize, as is most likely, the Arab community in Israel will become an integral part of the larger Israeli society. The general shift in Israel away from an all-powerful state and toward a liberal society of rights-bearing citizens has opened new possibilities for Arabs (as it has for members of some low-status Jewish communities). That change in Israel has made many Arab citizens far more comfortable with their "Israeli-ness" than in the past. Even their increased stridency in demanding rights and services has demonstrated their growing integration into the state and not necessarily their desire to separate from it. Today, the Arab citizens in the state number over one million and are about 20 percent of the total population. Within a decade, if present trends continue, their numbers could reach 25 percent of the total population. They will have an increasingly strong voice in the very public spaces in which struggles will be conducted over the character of the Israeli state as well as the fate of all Palestinians.

The unique Arab culture that formed in Israel has been different from the general Palestinian culture, but it also has been part of it. Palestinian national culture has struggled since the late 1980s with the question of Jewish rights, especially exclusive rights, over land in Palestine. To that struggle, the Palestinian citizens of Israel have brought a deep understanding of the complexity of relations between the two peoples. They have recognized the heterogeneity and variety of cultures in Israel and have shied away from the practice in many Arab countries and other Palestinian communities of demonizing the state or the Jews. As the odd man out, the Palestinian citizens of Israel hold the promise of a new bridge to the future.

7

DISPERSAL,

1948–1967

O Lost Paradise! You were never
  too small for us
But now vast countries are indeed
  too small
Torn asunder your people
Wandering under every star.

—MAHMUD AL-HUT

IN THE CENTURY LEADING to 1948, the Crimean War, the First and
Second World Wars, even the American Civil War had altered economic and social patterns in Palestine, on occasion taking the lives
of its young men. But the Palestinians were essentially peripheral to
such conflicts, and the wars themselves had not often intruded into
their fundamental routines. With the founding of Israel, the situation changed completely—the Arab-Israeli wars of 1948, 1967, 1973 (to
a lesser extent), and 1982 revolved around the question of Palestine's
future: They wove themselves into the fabric of Palestinian Arab life
and shaped the fate of the community as a whole.

As we have seen, following an extensive process of unravelling
that had already begun after the UN partition resolution, the Palestinian community dissolved under the impact of the 1948 war.
Seeming at first to represent only further displacement and defeat,
the 1967 war in fact inaugurated a period of national reintegration
and institutional renewal, along with the daily burdens of Israeli occupation. The intervening years marked a certain limbo. The Pales-

tinians were severed from the old foundations of society and politics, scarred by exile, and still stunned by the fate that had befallen them. The leaders and formal groups characterizing the post-1967 era had not yet appeared on the scene. It was the moment in Palestinian history most bereft of hope.

With 1948, in the words of Fawaz Turki, "The nation of Palestine ceased to be. Its original inhabitants, the Palestinian people, were dubbed Arab refugees, sent regular food rations by the UN, and forgotten by the world."[1] After Palestine's dust began to settle, a migration began from the hilly regions, out of the old villages and towns and out of the refugee camps, not to the coast, as in previous times, but to distant places outside Palestine. To the degree that there was any remaining Palestinian cultural center, it was Nablus, now the largest entirely Palestinian town. While Jerusalem retained its religious stature and some of its old administrative role, it was a diminished city under the Jordanians, who jealously guarded the prerogatives of their capital Amman. Never a significant economic center (apart from tourism and some commercial enterprises for the eastern part of the country), it had suffered through emigration, combat, and finally, partition between Jordan and Israel. Severed from its economic lifeline, the road to the Mediterranean coast, "it became an economic backwater."[2] With their traditional hinterlands and markets cut off, smaller towns such as Tulkarm, Jenin, and Qalqilya turned towards Nablus as the leading economic center of the West Bank.

Because of the steady erosion of peasant life, along, now, with the physical fragmentation of the Palestinian community, this preeminence was shaky at best. It contended with an increasing outward migration, motivated by economic survival and educational opportunity, to various countries, mainly in other parts of the Middle East, which became Palestinian satellite centers. (The American University in Beirut and the American University in Cairo became their most prominent institutions.) Taking on the role previously served by Jaffa, these centers reflected the influence of European, world-market values, challenging the cultural dominance of Palestine's eastern heartland, symbolized by Nablus.

As in the past, such values offered the basis of an alternative national leadership. The conditions prevailing between 1948 and 1967, even more than those during the mandate, undermined the claims of the old notable leaders. But this time, their demise was complete. In 1948, Amin al-Husseini established the All Palestine Government in Gaza. Those who stayed with him found it reduced within a few years by the Egyptians and the Arab League to window dressing. And those who threw in their lot with the Hashemites in Jordan, once it annexed the West Bank after the 1948 war, discovered that the attractive governmental positions they were offered only alienated them from the Palestinian population.[3] In ghurba, the ayan could not salvage their special status.

Ironically, when a new national leadership finally emerged in the 1960s, its experience would in some ways mirror the ayan's, as it found itself distant from those it sought to lead. After 1948, four out of every five Palestinians remained within the former mandate's territory, even if most could no longer return to their homes. But the leadership would grow disproportionately from those who had migrated, both to the Middle East and to the West.

In the period of the mandate, the idea of a Palestinian people distinct from other Arabs and Muslims had originated with members of the ayan, eventually moving down to other groups as well. After al-Nakba, this process was reversed: Former fellaheen and workers—and especially their children—many cramped in squalid refugee camps, defined a new Palestinian consciousness. To be sure, there were numerous important links between the old and new types of Palestinian nationalism, but the "bottom-up" nature of the new type had a distinctly different character.

The 20 percent of Palestinian Arabs who left Palestine went to Lebanon (over 100,000) and Syria (75,000–90,000), as well as to Iraq (4,000) and Egypt (7,000–10,000) (see map 4). In time, the steady emigration would result in exiled Palestinians outnumbering their brethren,[4] with formidable communities emerging in Kuwait (nearly 400,000 until the 1991 Gulf War), Saudi Arabia (150,000), other Gulf states (65,000), and the United States (100,000). But in the crucial, disorienting period following the 1948 war, the three communities within the old boundaries of British Palestine (the West Bank and the Gaza Strip, in particular, but also Palestinian Arabs in Israel) were instrumental in defining ghurba, not necessarily as exile from the country, but as displacement from original homes, villages, neighborhoods, and lands (see map 5). Long afterward, these refugees helped shape the national Palestinian aspiration as one for a homeland, rather than merely for a return to Palestine.[5]

First Steps Toward a New Identity: Jordan and the Palestinians

The evictions and mass flight of the 1948 war had taken place in Palestine's coastal plain, the Galilee, and the south, while the eastern region—encompassing Al-Khalil (Hebron), Ramallah, Nablus, Tulkarm, Jenin, and the Arab part of Jerusalem—which would be grafted onto Transjordan, remained largely intact. More than half of the pre-war Palestinian population of over 1.3 million was in the area now called the West Bank, the elements of its previous society still in place at the end of the war. Nevertheless, life would not be what it had been; demography and politics were the grounds of the transformation.

Only in the Gaza Strip was the pressure caused by the influx of refugees more intense than in Jordan. The population of the West Bank had grown from 400,000 to more than 700,000. While it would stabilize after 1948, this influx of desperate refugees strained all existing resources.[6] Approximately a third of the newcomers ended up in refugee camps, another third in villages, and the remainder in towns.[7] If the eastward migrations during the Arab Revolt and at the start of World War II had strained village and town institutions, the 1948 migrations simply overwhelmed them.

Demographic pressure was particularly intense along the new armistice lines with Israel.[8] Deprived of their fertile fields to the west, old villages had to turn to poorer land in the rocky hills. They also had to contend with over 130 new villages appearing between 1948 and 1967. For decades, the Palestinians had steadily moved from being part of a largely peasant society to one centered in towns and cities. And that process—Zureik's "depeasantification"—accelerated after 1948.[9] Nevertheless, Palestinians in Jordan sustained and nurtured the idea of themselves as a people of the soil, fostering symbols of lost olive trees and vineyards.

Interconnected with the impact of this population rise on both the physical and social landscape, a new set of questions emerged concerning social structure and Palestinian self-definition. Since its implanting in what became Transjordan at the beginning of the 1920s, the Hashemite dynasty under King Abdallah had tried to bind diverse peoples and tribes into a cohesive whole. After 1948, the Jordanian regime began to treat the Palestinians as but one more group or tribe that would contribute to the process of the Jordanization of the country.

For Abdallah and his regime, this would have seemed a realistic enough goal: After all, the ties between Palestinians and Jordan were not remote. In 1920, Palestinian activists had stood with the Hashemites as Abdallah's brother, Faysal, made his bid to rule Syria. In fact, part of the British compensation to the Hashemites for their loss in Syria had been a carving out, from the territory envisioned by both Zionist and Palestinian Arab leaders as part of the new Palestine mandate, of the Emirate of Transjordan for Abdallah.

With Palestinians staffing key political institutions, Abdallah had seen the territory as a beachhead for eventual rule of a larger kingdom, including Palestine, Syria, and Lebanon—and possibly other parts of the Fertile Crescent.[10] With its Islamic sites and shrines, most notably those in Jerusalem, Palestine played a large role in these ambitions, the Emir welcoming Palestinians as a reservoir of skilled and educated manpower from the time he won a degree of limited autonomy for Transjordan in 1923 (Britain granted independence only in 1946). In 1924, when Sir John Philby, the British High Commissioner for the Emirate, was replaced with Colonel P. Cox, the latter reorganized the Emirate's civil service—expelling all the Istiqlal members, who had fled from Syria in 1920 and had formed the early backbone of Abdallah's administration—with British-trained Palestinians. Roughly 10,000 took up the welcome, serving as bureaucrats, educators, businessmen, and financiers, in Amman and elsewhere.

When Abdallah's Arab Legion moved over the border into Palestine in 1948, the new Transjordanian state took on the challenge of expanding more than its territorial boundaries.[11] Longstanding relations with key Palestinian families such as the Nashashibis—the leading opposition to the Husseinis—may have encouraged Abdallah to believe that smooth absorption and integration of the Palestinians was possible. It is difficult to know whether he hoped from the start to completely replace Palestinian and other parochial identities with a tight-knit Jordanian nation.[12] In any event, after al-Nakba, he declared Jordan the only legitimate inheritor of Arab Palestine (a policy that the state more or less maintained until 1988). Abdallah's regime banned the use of the word Palestine—substituting the term West Bank in most cases. (There is thus an odd irony to the present Palestinian insistence on use of this term to confirm national identity, fighting off the Israeli effort to substitute the biblical "Judea and Samaria.") Even if Abdallah was not thinking in terms of complete assimilation—a loss of Palestinian self-definition—at the very least he believed that bringing the West Bank and its population under his control would not shake the foundations of his dynasty and his state, its social and political balance. (This offers a pronounced contrast to Lebanon, whose leaders deeply feared an upsetting by the refugees of the country's fragile equilibrium.)

In order to consolidate its control over the Palestinians, the Jordanian state executed policies on political and social levels. Following the 1948 war, it arranged two Palestinian national congresses, which provided the appearance of mastery by the Palestinians over their own political futures (although, in fact, these were largely staged events). The congresses rejected the Mufti's continuing bid for leadership through the All Palestine Government in Gaza and called upon His Majesty, King Abdallah to unify the West Bank with Jordan—"as a prelude to the unification of all the Arabs."

At both congresses, aides to Abdallah worked hard to stifle differences between the Palestinian perspective and that of the king. To a large extent, the disagreements revolved around the Palestinian insistence that the king publicly commit himself to reunifying all of Palestine and eliminating both the Jewish state and Zionist community that had settled the land—a position that ran counter to the spirit of his ongoing negotiations with the Zionist (now Israeli) leadership. Over the next two decades, first Abdallah's policies, then those of his successor King Hussein, toed a fine line between maintaining nonbelligerent relations with Israel and convincing Palestinians the regime was adequately representing them in their struggle for repatriation. In 1956, the director of UNRWA (the United Nations Relief and Works Agency) reported to the General Assembly that the Palestinian refugees "bitterly oppose anything which has even the semblance of permanent settlement elsewhere."[13] With Palestinians at the bottom of the social scale now thus defining the parameters of an emerging new Palestinism, the Jordanian government's one serious bid to resettle the refugees foundered on the rocks of their opposition.[14]

The regime also weighted representation in its own institutions to favor the minority of non-Palestinians, and it clamped down on any exclusively Palestinian political institutions. In this way, Abdallah eliminated any semblance of Palestinian political autonomy. During the 1948 war, the Arab Legion had already disbanded Palestinian political organizations and fighting groups in the areas it occupied; now it set the stage for absorption of Palestinians into Jordanian state political institutions, staffed by a combination of East Bankers and Palestinians—the ayan's remnants, along with other local Palestinian leaders, some eventually becoming prime ministers. And Jordan was the only state besides Syria that accorded the Palestinians citizenship en masse: Two-thirds of all Palestinians ended up as Jordanian citizens.

In the social sphere, the Jordanian state acted on a number of fronts. It established a comprehensive educational system for the East and West Banks to help promote a harmonious, Jordanian social whole. At the same time, it established a number of welfare and development agencies to assist refugees and others affected by the recent traumatic events. As in the period before 1948, it encouraged the gradual settlement of Palestinians on the East Bank. And, not least of all, the state used active suppression and repression to prevent any public voicing of a national Palestinian identity. Following Abdallah's 1951 assassination in Jerusalem at the hands of a Palestinian, and the abdication of Abdallah's son, Talal, because of failing mental health, his young grandson, Hussein, succeeded to the throne in 1953; his policies regarding the Palestinians did not significantly change direction.

These policies had in fact born some fruit, Abdallah succeeding for a time in building significant support among many Palestinians. For most, their loyalty rested on the hope that he could "liberate" Palestine and bring about their repatriation. They expressed a Jordanian identity passively, through simple acceptance of the new political order; had Jordanian rule continued beyond two decades, it perhaps would have eventually absorbed most West Bankers.

Some wealthier Palestinians—including those from the old notable families—feeling a stigma in being Palestinians, went further than offering such loyalty, taking on Jordanian identities.[15] While, as Brand indicates, the Jordanian effort to eliminate Palestinian nationalism played a part in the process, the effort also ran up against formidable obstacles: A tiny state, scarcely a society, was attempting to impose itself on a larger, more educated, and urbane community. From the day of annexation, Palestinians outnumbered the original Jordanians two to one. The West Bank remained exclusively Palestinian, a potential breeding ground for nationalist revival, while the East Bank was a heterogeneous mixture of Palestinians and others.[16]

Those others, the 350,000–400,000 people of the East Bank prior to the 1948 war, had much lower levels of literacy (Jordanian schools had enrolled about a quarter of school-age children; Palestinian schools, approximately half).[17] Nearly half the Transjordanians had been nomadic Bedouins; another third, small peasant farmers; most of the rest, residents of four towns whose population had ranged from 10,000 to 30,000. Amman, the capital and largest of the towns, has been described as "a hamlet with unpaved roads in the nineteen-thirties."[18] As a point of contrast, ten cities in Palestine had more than 10,000 Arabs before 1948, and three (Jaffa, Haifa, and Jerusalem), more than 60,000.[19] The more skilled Palestinians now over-whelmed the original Jordanian population in many domains—its Bedouin core only kept control of key political ministries and the army through skillful manipulation.[20]

The differences are even more striking if we take account of the distribution of Palestinians in the kingdom. The elite—the notables, merchants (particularly Christian businessmen), and profession-als—settled in West and East Bank towns. Uneducated fellaheen dis-proportionately filled the refugee camps on both sides of the Jordan River.[21] In short, when Palestinian society began to recrystallize in Jordan, it followed the old patterns of stratification from the man-date: Palestinians living in cities were even more likely to be skilled and educated, competing for key economic and political posts.

Continuing migration to the East Bank only reinforced their dominance. The flow began during the 1948 debacle, and by 1952 over 100,000 Palestinians had crossed the river, many settling in the urban areas. Today, well over 1,000,000 of the more than 2,000,000 East Bankers are Palestinians.[22] Their absorption into Jordan was further complicated by the organization of refugee society, espe-cially in the camps, and the discrimination against the West Bank (21 of the 24 camps were west of the Jordan River).[23] The camps cre-ated a new Jordanian underclass, only marginally integrated into the national economy at the end of the 1940s.

Opportunities for wage labor fell far short of available supply.[24] Agriculture was able to absorb some camp dwellers as laborers and sharecroppers, but this was limited by slow advances in farming technology and a severe shortage of cultivable land and water—only about a fifth of the refugees actually remained in farming, although many continued to think of themselves as fellaheen. The economic difficulties were reflected in abject conditions in the camps, where families lived in makeshift tents, replaced after five or six years by small shacks made from concrete blocks and covered with corru-gated metal.

Rapid economic growth, beginning in the late 1950s and gaining momentum in the half-dozen years leading up to the 1967 war, did spur greater Palestinian integration. So did a project of irrigation and electrification: the East Ghor Canal Project, opening land in the eastern Jordan Valley (the state could not complete it, nor the land distribution that went along with it, before the war).[25] But that first decade of hardship after 1948 had helped set the Palestinians apart. Cut off from the national economy, the refugee camps tended to be societies unto themselves, and the rest of the West Bank also suffered from exceedingly low investment. This was partly because of the low savings rate there, and partly because of the state's preference for East Bank investment.[26]

A key factor in reinforcing the isolation of the refugees was UNRWA. Established by the U.N. in late 1949 as a response to the refugee crisis,[27] the agency gradually became a kind of overpowering paternal force. Most camp dwellers depended on it for their sustenance, especially in the early years after the exodus,[28] marked by severe economic depression in Jordan and known as "the years of famine." Besides the rations it provided, the agency promoted many Palestinians into staff positions; its teachers, in particular, would form the basis of a new Palestinian leadership. In general, some of UNRWA's most notable achievements have involved education, improving on the desultory efforts of the British, especially for girls.

Although the agency took on an odd sort of permanence for the refugees, it also represented the impermanence of their situation: a beneficent host insuring material necessities until they could return to their homes and land. Originating, again, at the bottom of society, that sense of impermanence became a mark of the emerging Palestinian consciousness. The camps thus served as its reinforcers and rebuilders, rather than as conduits into a Jordanian social whole. (Although the Jordanian regime did try to maintain a semblance of control by demanding its headquarters be in Amman, UNRWA was largely independent.) The refugees' isolation reinforced not only family and clan ties, but those of neighborhoods and villages. Unlike Palestinians outside the camps, those in the camps, forming approximately a quarter of Jordan's population, provided almost no representatives to national political institutions—not a single one to Parliament between 1950 and 1965.[29]

At times, the refugees even managed to establish public institutions and symbols to express the reformulation of their identity. Their al-Wahda soccer team, for instance, won the Jordanian championship, as well as the avid support of Palestinians throughout Jordan. Even Arabs in Israel became fans when it beat the Ramtha team, symbolizing the East Bank and loyalty to the kingdom. Having a good understanding of the team's significance, the Jordanians reorganized and renamed it, adding non-Palestinian players to its roster.

The camp and area committees, occasionally formed by elders, village mukhtars, and notables in the immediate aftermath of the 1948 war, were less successful than the soccer team.[30] Their purpose was to represent refugee interests to the Jordanian and international authorities (the UN and various relief agencies such as the Red Cross) on questions of aid, the status of property in Israel, and so on. But they were undercut by old rivalries of clan and region and by differing interests among camp dwellers, such as the divisions between those who had owned land and those who had not. About the only division that did not reappear in the camp was that between Christians and Muslims, since the camps were 99 percent Muslim. Active interference by Jordanian officials in the committees' nomination process also kept them weak and ineffective. The government disbanded a number after receiving complaints of favoritism, jealousy, and so forth. It also kept a close and suspicious eye on any groups seeking to represent general Palestinian interests.

The most serious challenge to Jordan's claim to representation came through the General Refugee Congress, organized in Ramallah in March, 1949. The Congress empowered delegates to negotiate with Israel at forthcoming armistice talks, but they were rebuffed by the Jordanians, by other Arab delegations (which had their own advisory refugee contingent), and by Israel (which sought to deal exclusively with Arab states). It lasted as an organization into 1950 but faced opposition from all sides, including poorer refugees who felt it represented rich landowners, and other Palestinians who looked for their salvation in Arab unity.[31]

In the first decade after al-Nakba, political impotence and the failure to construct meaningful public institutions fueled the disorientation and petty bickering rife among the Palestinians. But ground-level activities (charitable, professional, and cultural) quietly continued. While they did not carry explicit Palestinian messages or symbols, organizations such as the Jaffa Muslim Sports Club and the Haifa Cultural Association (in Nablus) had an exclusively Palestinian membership; they helped both to keep alive the memory of now inaccessible places and to create new bases of association among West Bankers in their changed circumstances—often, ironically, with the support of funds from the government in Amman.

In a broader manner, the intensity of their shared experience in refugee camps and their strong sense of having suffered a common injustice helped preserve and reshape a solidarity evident even in the context of feuding and resentment. This solidarity was strengthened all the more by the West Bank's local population, which had become irritated by the refugees—they "occupied public buildings (mosques, schools, etc.), encroached on farm land, picked local crops, used scarce local water, and so on."[32] Much of that population, particularly in the border areas, expressed dismay as refugees infiltrated into Israel in desperate attempts to regain property left behind or to harvest crops, thereby prompting severe Israeli retaliation. But such divisions did not prevent the gradual development of a sense of suffering a common fate.[33]

In face of such feelings—rather than any overt political organization—the minimal political stability Abdallah had counted on when he annexed the West Bank proved highly elusive. By the mid-1950s, the Hashemite regime was confronting new factors, pan-Arab and pan-Islamic, that both further impeded Palestinian assimilation and gnawed away at this stability.

Several years after Nasser's 1952 revolution, pan-Arabism penetrated the West Bank, along with the rest of the Middle East. Perhaps no Arabs had more to gain than the Palestinians from the denigration of specific loyalties (Iraqi, Egyptian—indeed Palestinian) in favor of devotion to broader Arab unity, and they became among pan-Arabism's most fervent exponents.[34] They were, as a Palestinian who had been a member of the Communist party put it, "more

Nasserist than Nasser."[35] Pan-Arabism's emphasis on national liberation, both social and political, transformed the Palestinian dilemma from the particular to the general—it placed this dilemma in the broader historical context of the regeneration of the entire Arab people, their shedding of imperialism's shackles.

The lure of pan-Arabism was not a totally new phenomenon in Palestinian intellectual circles. Following World War I, the Palestinian alliance with Faysal, in his bid to wrest control of Syria from the French and establish a broad Hashemite kingdom, had strong pan-Arab overtones. Then too, the tension between pan-Arabism and the more exclusivist Palestinian nationalism derived from the special challenges of Zionism: Generalizing these challenges offered an attractive route towards broad mobilization against Jewish encroachment in the Middle East.

If Arab disunity was responsible for the fiasco of 1948, as Musa Alami and other Palestinian nationalists argued, then Arab unity could undo the writ of exile.[36] An Egyptian newspaper noted in 1963, "If there is any absolute and complete joy to Arabs in the establishment of a large, new and united state, it is the joy of the Palestinians. . . . The Palestinians see in the new state the beginning of their salvation from the suffering, humiliation, dispersion and despair with which they have been living for fifteen years. . . . Arab union is the only path by which they will regain their natural existence."[37] In Jordan, the combination of the voice of Arab unity emanating from Egypt and the active support of Palestinians and others from within appeared to threaten the kingdom's basis in 1956 (marked by particularly serious demonstrations and riots) and 1957: "To many Palestinians, complete Arab unity seemed just around the corner."[38]

Pan-Islam also served to generalize the Palestinian issue, tapping deep-seated loyalties among the Muslim majority, while of course once again excluding the sizeable Christian minority. It did not develop anywhere near the organization and momentum of pan-Arabism at the time, but it did evoke sentiments that many Palestinians considered far more important than those represented by fashionable contemporary ideologies. Like pan-Arabism, it rejected Western imperialism, understood as the vehicle for Zionism's success.

Many of the political parties then active in other Arab countries of the Middle East, offering their own social vision to the Palestinians, established legal and underground branches in Jordan. In the early 1950s, a number of younger Palestinians tried to create a new leadership through these parties, which—in the confusion and grinding poverty—failed to attract a significant following. (The largest had only 300–350 members, recruiting students and teachers while ignoring workers and peasants).[39] In any event, after an attempted coup—growing pan-Arabism in the Middle East and pressure by the United States to join a new anti-Communist security alliance, the Baghdad Pact, had created increasing unrest in Jordan—Hussein cracked down, banning all parties in April, 1957; although several continued to exist underground, they thus closed, as would other forms of public life, as avenues for Palestinian political expression.

Not least of the factors contributing to this dead end was the failure of unity talks among Egypt, Syria, and Iraq in 1963.[40] Arab unity held "an irresistible fascination for all political parties in the West Bank, even those parties whose self-proclaimed ideal was primarily a new social or religious, rather than national, order in the area."[41] The failure of the unity talks—like the French rout of Faysal in 1920—deepened a painful period of reassessment that began in the late 1950s, leading towards a renewed commitment to Palestinian self-reliance. But as previously, the tension between pan-Arabism and Palestinism would not entirely disappear in the 1960s; rather more recently, we have seen the former option loom large again in Palestinian support for Saddam Hussein.

A Palestinian Reservation
and the Emergence of Camp Society

Nowhere did Palestinians find more brutal conditions than in the Gaza Strip, the single, tiny part of Palestine remaining in the hands of the Egyptian army after its humiliating defeat in the 1948 war. Approximately 28 miles in length and 5 miles in width, it became one of the most densely settled regions in the world. With three-quarters of Gaza's Palestinians living in eight refugee camps, even the small comforts that Jordan could provide were absent here. Jordan's population growth came disproportionately in the rural areas, as displaced fellaheen attempted to regain some foothold in agriculture. In Gaza, where most refugees were fellaheen and agriculture continued to employ approximately a third of those able to find work, overall opportunities were so limited that, by 1967, 80 percent of the Palestinians were urban—one of the highest rates in Asia. Border villages and towns on the West Bank had lost their agricultural zones and their accustomed markets in 1948, but in Gaza the losses were much more devastating: Of the 5,000 acres of citrus plantations, barely 1,000 remained; of the 250,000 acres of grain-growing land in the Negev, less than 10 percent was still accessible.[42] In fact, only 2.5 percent of the original Gaza District remained as part of the Strip.[43] Some Palestinians, especially those who made their way to the East Bank, assimilated into the upper echelons of Jordanian society; Gazan refugees (except for a very small number of Jaffa upper-class families) failed to accomplish a similar feat.[44]

For all the upheaval Jordan's Palestinians faced, their society still retained vestiges of the past and of normalcy: farms, villages, towns and cities, citizenship, even, for a time, a lively political arena. Those in Gaza had no such vestiges. Gaza became the quintessential representation of a new culture—what we might call camp society.

The Gaza Strip's moment of political glory came with the establishment in 1948 of the Mufti-inspired All Palestine Government, with Gaza City as its provisional capital.[45] With thriving citrus exports as its lone claim to some centrality, the Gaza region had long been a fairly peripheral corner of Palestine (the poorest in the country during the mandate period). Now, it rode the back of Arab League and Egyptian power to become the nucleus of a Palestinian state. But the effort was short-lived; even the government's chosen name contained a strong dose of irony: Without control of more than a symbolic remnant of Palestinian territory, it fell upon the same hard times as other governments-in-exile in the mid-twentieth century. A number of key officials "deserted" to Jordan. Others faced the reality of an authority derived exclusively from their benefactors, Egypt and the Arab League. In September, 1952, the League dissolved the All Palestine Government and empowered the Arab states to represent the Palestinian cause.

Grim poverty and social misery became the defining characteristics of the Gaza Strip. Personal income was among the lowest in the world (one source put the figure at $80 per capita per year).[46] The Egyptian government denied Gaza's Palestinians even the limited opportunities for institution building and political participation (including citizenship) that the Jordanians granted Palestinians. After the failure of the All Palestine Government, the only attempt under Egyptian rule to carve out some political autonomy came with the establishment of an elected Council of Representatives, nominated by local committees and not destined to enjoy great success. The Egyptians reserved a meaningful political role for the already-powerful Gazan families, the mass of camp refugees finding themselves, as in Jordan, almost entirely excluded from formal public life. To the extent that the Egyptian authorities dealt with them at all, they did so through pre-1948 institutions such as the village mukhtar.[47] In 1955, the Egyptian government also selected refugees for units of fedayeen to take part in operations against Israel. This offered some important military experience, and common lore has it that the veterans of such actions became the nucleus for resistance against Israeli military occupation after 1967. But the units were always under strict Egyptian control.

Like the people crammed in there, the political status of the Gaza Strip remained in limbo from 1948 on. Egypt did not annex it, as the Jordanians had the West Bank, which reinforced a sense of temporariness—now prevailing for almost half a century—on the part of the refugees. Egypt maintained its dominion for two decades (losing control briefly between October, 1956, and January, 1957, as a result of the Sinai war), and the Israelis have held it, also without annexation, since the 1967 war. Even more than in Jordan, the "permanence of temporariness" became an emblem of Gazan society.

Egyptian government policies and the sentiments of the refugees themselves transformed the Gaza Strip into a closed reservation in the 20 years following the 1948 war. Anxious about the effects of Palestinian influx on the stability of Egyptian politics and the level of competition in the workforce, first the monarchy and then its successor, the Nasser-led regime, restricted migration from the Strip into Egypt proper. One exception was the opening of Egyptian universities to Palestinians; another, the granting of jobs as village teachers to Palestinian graduates of UNRWA vocational schools. But the border was basically sealed, and emergency law was administered by the military there until 1962. After the Sinai war, the Egyptians began to incorporate some Palestinians into the Strip's administration, along with easing some of their restrictions.

For their part, the refugees, like their counterparts in Jordan, rejected several Egyptian resettlement schemes, including one that, with UNRWA support, would have diverted Nile waters into the nearly empty Sinai Desert.[48]

As was the case in Lebanon, under these circumstances, "the only strangers who ventured into the camps were cops, invariably drunken ones at that and in groups."[49] Despite the fact that it held the second largest concentration of Palestinians, Gaza would fail to become a center of new Palestinian institution building as a result of Egyptian repression. Its contribution lay rather in the realm of consciousness and identity. The character of the society that developed there was unique, weaving memories and culture from pre-war Palestine with the poverty-stricken, harrowing life in the camps.

Deprived of its traditional agricultural lands, the Strip became an economic cripple, even the original population losing most of its previous sources of income. The refugees' income was limited principally to UNRWA aid, Egyptian administrative and military expenditures, and the smuggling of goods through the port of Gaza into Egypt. Almost no industry developed, so entrepreneurial activity was channeled into commerce, the most important means for penetrating the wall that seemed to surround the Strip. Gaza became a kind of duty-free port, which prompted the smuggling, along with shopping sprees by Egyptians wishing to circumvent the high taxes in Egypt.

Gaza's commercial life picked up when Nasser moved towards closer relations with the Soviet Union in the latter half of the 1950s. Farmers, merchants, and smugglers took advantage of the markets opening in Eastern Europe, the Gazan citrus industry expanding more than tenfold to meet the increased demand. The East Europeans exchanged construction materials and machinery for the exports.[50] In turn, many of those goods went to Lebanon for consumer items—the ones that, along with locally made goods such as wool rugs, attracted the Egyptians to shop in Gaza. Some merchants managed to prosper in this manner, but for most, economic conditions remained extraordinarily difficult—even the money sent home by those who had migrated faced stiff Egyptian currency controls.

Such migration gained momentum in the second decade of Egyptian rule, bringing badly needed income to hard-pressed families. But Gaza also paid a price for the migration, those with education, training, and some resources being the first to leave. Following the trail of petrodollars, they went to Saudi Arabia, Kuwait, Qatar, Bahrain. The result was that Gaza was left virtually without an intellectual or professional class. More than any other territory, the section of Palestinian society it harbored was homogeneous. Even before the start of the professionals' emigration, 65 percent of the refugees were classified as unskilled laborers or agricultural workers, and an estimated 90 percent were illiterate.[51]

Camp society developed distinct features from country to country and camp to camp. Those surrounding Beirut, for example, were unusual for the high proportion of their work force in industry: the camp of Tal al-Zaatar had 60 percent of its total force employed in the nearby industrial area of Mukallas, the refugees working, as usual, without government papers and thus tending to receive lower pay and fewer rights than Lebanese workers.[52] The Rashidiyya camp near Tyre developed as a reservoir for agricultural labor on the plantations of local wealthy landholders.[53]

Important similarities also developed among the camps. The Palestinian sociologist Bassem Sirhan has argued that "in fact such differences as exist consist of a descending scale of general physical conditions—space, housing, basic amenities, etc. . . . those in Lebanon and the West Bank ranking highest, Syria and Jordan next and Gaza lowest."[54]

In all camps, UNRWA was an overpowering presence—what Turki has referred to as "our contemptuous stepmother."[55] Others compared UNRWA services to "a shot of morphine," a palliative that could not cure the refugee's basic alienation.[56] Its educational and employment projects, and of course its direct relief aid, were nevertheless of obvious value in helping Palestinians reconstitute their lives after 1948. The old institutions of family, clan, and village also offered support in the face of a strange and often hostile new environment. Life in the camps thus mirrored normal Palestinian life before the war, tending to reinforce—indeed, even reinvigorate—its social institutions.

This trend was highly evident in Gaza, where the centrality of such institutions was kept alive not only by the actions of the Palestinians themselves, but also by the policies of Egyptian officials and relief workers: In the initial confusion of the refugee influx, Quaker relief workers struggled to reestablish village groupings and administer programs through the old village leadership.[57] The very process focused attention on the life that had been lost. "If a refugee in Gaza is asked where he comes from, he will answer with the name of his original village whether or not that village still stands; that is where his roots lie."[58] Fawaz Turki has commented on the recreation of Palestinian identity in exile:

> The social structure of the Palestinian family, whose atmosphere engendered a deep and constant hope for the return to Palestine, and the official discrimination against the refugee himself, created pressures that served to perpetuate the notion in the mind of the young Palestinian that he was the member of a minority, thus enhancing his Palestinian consciousness. In his home a Palestinian child, whether born in Beirut, Amman, or Damascus, would be instructed to identify himself as a Palestinian from Haifa or Lydda or any other town that had been his parents' birthplace, and his own experience would constantly remind him of this.[59]

Within the gap between remembered home and present circumstances lay deep wells of bitterness, directed at those considered the usurpers, the Israelis. Writing from the Middle East in 1951 and 1952, Stewart Alsop described the refugees as surrounding Israel "with an iron ring of hate," the refugee camps as "a reservoir of smoldering antagonism against the State of Israel and its Western backers."[60] But the alienation was not only from the despised Israelis. Perhaps no better indicator exists of the profound segregation between Egyptians, Lebanese, and Jordanians, on the one side, and the refugees they hosted, on the other, than the marriage barriers that developed. Even in the absence of religious differences, there was no common market of brides and grooms.

The social institutions of the camp created this invisible wall, drawing the refugees away from confrontation with larger Arab society,[61] into a world of memory—and, as memory itself dimmed, into their mythological Lost Garden of Palestine.[62] The Garden contrasted starkly with present conditions—poverty, humiliation, and the sense of loss of control over their personal and collective futures. At the same time, the isolation of the camps exacerbated a widespread disdain for the refugees. (Turki evokes this disdain in the form of a banal Lebanese epithet, "two-bit Palestinian.")[63] Both the isolation and disdain fed the slow formation of a new "diaspora consciousness," and an institutional infrastructure to support it.

It was not that Palestinians failed to venture outside the camps—which in Lebanon, especially, tended to be located on the edges of important cities. They did so frequently (adults and children alike, especially males), even if few city residents reciprocated. Many camps soon became strange suburbs for the cities they bordered. Surrounding land values were often quite high, and, as birth rates soared and the camps gained population, state officials took steps to make sure that the refugees' dwellings did not spread beyond the established boundaries. The result was a sort of involuted expansion, the camps becoming increasingly dense environments. Brick-built homes replaced the original tents and subsequent shacks, contrasting with the traditional Palestinian stone houses. Some poor Lebanese and Syrians, unable to find affordable housing in the cities, added to the burden by moving in.

Efforts to eke out a few square meters more for housing put intense pressure on any remaining space for mosques, schools, clinics, and the like. Sanitation and other public services, handled by UNRWA and the host municipalities, also suffered from severe neglect. Eventually water and sewage systems, indoor toilets, electricity, and even paved streets began to appear in the camps, but their escalating population kept public services at frighteningly inadequate levels. Like the hostility of nearby cities, the suffocating living conditions reinforced the distinctiveness of camp life. Studying together in segregated schools (in Lebanon, no Palestinians attended public schools), playing together in narrow alleys, sitting together in all-Palestinian cafes, the refugees developed a society—even with incessant, internecine conflict and a leadership that proved constantly inadequate.

The old village and town leadership continued to play a role in camp life until 1968—in Gaza, as we have seen, they were used as go-betweens by the Egyptians. But with the drastic decline in their power and authority before 1948, they now possessed very little real authority. In their place, economic entrepreneurs quietly began to vie for leadership, one variety being a new kind of go-between: the *rais* (boss, head). The rais would act as a contractor supplying agricultural and industrial laborers for nearby fields and companies, thus building important economic relationships outside the camp. In time, he would offer an array of other services, including permission to move within those countries where the Palestinians lacked official papers. Economically desperate refugees would pay him in both cash and loyalty.

With growing prosperity in Lebanon beginning in the 1950s and Jordan in the 1960s, many Arabs sank their savings into new homes, a traditional sign of prestige. A number of Palestinians became building contractors, accumulating significant wealth. Some of these contractors chose to escape camp life altogether, but many others became the new upper class of the camps, and another power center, surrounding themselves with entourages of relatives and friends.

Camps in the West Bank, Lebanon, and—to some degree—Syria thus began to take on a more complex social structure. Nevertheless, while exerting some influence and wielding some power, neither the old leadership nor the new entrepreneurs played a powerful role in the reshaping of a destroyed society, or managed, in fact, to rise above a purely local level. Many shied away from overt political participation altogether. They confronted a scattering of the Palestinian community, a distinct limit to the resources for developing leverage, and a grave risk in associating too closely with the host authorities. For the time being, the definition of what it meant to be a Palestinian seemed to grow spontaneously from the community's poorest, most hard-pressed members, the former fellaheen who made up the bulk of camp society.

First Steps Toward Regeneration: Education and Mobility

The ambivalent feelings that Palestinians harbored for UNRWA did not belie its importance. Although UNRWA adopted the school curricula of each host state (in Lebanon, Lebanese history; in Jordan, Jordanian history), it was solely responsible for elementary education, which became nearly universal. By the 1980s, 95 percent of all refugee children attended school at the elementary and preparatory levels,[64] one study noting that "never before in the Arab Middle East has there been as inclusive an educational system as that of the UNRWA, reaching as it does to all classes and both sexes."[65] This resulted in both the employment of many teachers and the creation of an educated generation of Palestinians, whose essential, marketable resource would be skills based on that very education. Offering the hope of "economic security in a situation where political security was virtually unachievable,"[66] and of escape from the misery of camp life, it was a strategy for survival.[67] For this reason, as one of the first teachers there has indicated, even before UNRWA established itself in the Gaza Strip, groups of Palestinians and relief workers

began recruiting teachers for a rudimentary teaching programme. They only took people who had a secondary school education—I think there were about 80 such people in the whole Strip at that time—so I began working in 1949 as a volunteer teacher. We were all volunteers then and we used to get paid two sacks of flour per month. . . . When I think back over this period, the thing that sticks clearest in my mind is just how enthusiastic we all were—teachers and pupils. I suppose for the refugees who had lost all their possessions, there was nothing else but to learn. But I also think that there was a very strong sense that we were taking things into our own hands and building our own future. Believe me, I am not the only one who thinks that things were better then with the sacks of flour than they are now with all the UNRWA dollars.[68]

A Lebanese refugee has echoed these sentiments: "In spite of all this [the pitiful conditions of the camp], we had faith that there was no road but education."[69] Sayigh has raised doubts as to whether the sacrifices involved in sending children to school were worth the payoff: The education itself was often of poor quality, there was a general fall-off in enrollment after age 14, and the opportunities for most youngsters, even with this elementary education, were severely limited.[70] What is certain is that by the 1950s, "for all but the wealthy, UNRWA schools remained virtually the only avenue to higher education."[71] From the early 1950s, the small but growing stream of secondary-school graduates found places in universities in Egypt, Syria, Lebanon, Western Europe, and North America. The establishment of a Jordanian university in 1962 was, in large part, a Palestinian undertaking, and its faculty and students were both disproportionately Palestinian.

For the Palestinians as a whole, the new generation of university graduates had two important outcomes: physical mobility and leadership. The graduates entered skilled positions in the oil economies, civil services, and schools of Arab states across the Middle East. They spearheaded the transformation of the Palestinian people into a mobile, internationally oriented society; along with events such as the 1967 war, this emigration would finally leave fewer than half of all Palestinians in Palestine. It did not occur at equal rates for all Palestinian communities—so many people poured out of the West Bank to the East Bank and beyond that its population growth was negligible; the more limited exit from Gaza allowed a growth of nearly 3 percent a year.

In Kuwait, which until the Gulf War of 1991 would house the largest Palestinian concentrations outside the original homeland, the community seemed to develop in strata. Educated male Palestinians were the first to migrate there; they became the fodder for state agencies, staffing everything from post offices to schools. Male ex-fellaheen followed, filling a wide variety of open semiskilled and unskilled positions in the developing country. Finally, wives and children followed suit and the Palestinian population of Kuwait gained a complex, fairly autonomous set of social structures.[72] In the United States, by contrast, Palestinians tended to join the cultural, academic, and scientific communities, as well as the business class. Scattered across the American expanse and absorbed into the public school system, they lacked the autonomy of their Kuwaiti counterparts.[73]

Whether autonomous or relatively assimilated, these scattered Palestinian communities, lacking their own political institutions, succeeded in forming what Ghabra has called a cross-national entity.[74] The evolution of memories of the Lost Garden, the labelling of places and institutions with names from Palestine, the emphasis on the temporariness of present life (even when people seemed well settled-in), the importance put on education as the most crucial resource, the undying hostility towards Israel, and a general insistence on maintaining a Palestinian identity were cultural vehicles that transversed great distances from the camps. The process was facilitated by regular international travel, the mobility of capital (i.e., staking a family member's emigration and receiving the remittances he would later send back), and the concentration of parts of families in different countries.

Equally important for understanding this Palestinian self-awareness was the emergence of professionals and intellectuals lacking the political reticence of the old village chiefs and new entrepreneurs. Many became outright activists, turning to a variety of ideologies centered around pan-Arabism but always focused on the Palestinian problem.[75] In the late 1950s and early 1960s, the repression they faced and the failure of Arab unity muted their social role. But after the debacle of 1967, the investments they were making would result in a new national leadership.

In the meantime, other parties staked their claims to leadership, all failing to garner much enthusiasm: most notably the Jordanian monarchy, but also Amin al-Husseini, continuing to operate his claim through the nearly moribund Arab Higher Committee, existing (albeit with very little influence) through the 1967 war.

In 1959, the government of Nasser played its own hand, leading a campaign of vilification against Amin and the Committee and forcing the Mufti to move from Egypt to Lebanon. Nasser also pushed hard for the creation of some alternative national body—what he termed a Palestinian entity—to represent the Palestinians and support his own pan-Arab ambitions.[76] King Hussein of Jordan countered with continued, severe repression of supporters of pan-Arabism; he even briefly entered a strange-bedfellow alliance with the Mufti, bringing the latter back to Jerusalem for a last visit in 1967. Another Nasser rival, President Abd al-Karim Qasim of Iraq, proposed establishing the "immortal Palestinian Republic," starting with the territory of the West Bank and Gaza.[77]

Educated Palestinians were starting to look beyond the framework of such possibilities for a national leadership. Their focus turned to self-generated organizations in the West Bank, Gaza, Lebanon, and elsewhere. Between 1959 and 1963, as many as 40 secret organizations had been formed, with anywhere from 2 to 400 members, expressing frustration with the passivity of their parents—as well as with the Arab states' propensity to use the Palestinian issue for their own purposes. After 1964, taking advantage of the renewed interest in the Palestinian problem that accompanied the formation of the PLO under Nasser's auspices, several tried to create an umbrella organization that could avoid the powerful state manipulation the early PLO experienced—a manipulation they saw as rendering it, in the words of Rashid Khalidi, "far from being an expression of autonomous Palestinian national feeling."[78]

With Arab universities bringing together talented, highly motivated Palestinians in an atmosphere of relative freedom, a scattered

Palestinian leadership thus emerged in the 1960s. Its power derived, not from its traditional place in a largely agricultural society (as was the case in Nablus), but from its manipulation of the tools and values of a modern education. To be sure, dispersal would present this leadership with grave difficulties as well as opportunities. But for the time, it served as a source of cultural cohesion.

These university graduates did not labor to regenerate Palestinian society alone. The Palestinian National Charter, embraced by the new leaders in 1968, expressed a credo much more a product of the camps in their poverty and disorientation than a slogan imposed from above: "The Palestinian personality is an innate, persistent characteristic that does not disappear, and it is transferred from fathers to sons." Unlike the three decades of British rule, when leaders defined the meaning of the word Palestinian for their followers, the two decades after 1948 saw the least privileged social groups provide the cultural content for what it meant to be Palestinian.

8

THE FEDAY:

REBIRTH AND RESISTANCE

I am against boys becoming
  heroes at ten
Against the tree flowering explosives
Against branches becoming scaffolds
Against the rose-beds turning to trenches
And yet
When fire cremates my friends
   my youth
  and country
How can I
Stop a poem from becoming a gun?

—RASHID HUSSEIN, "Opposition"

ISRAEL'S LIGHTNING VICTORY in the Six Day War followed a month of dejection and demoralization in face of Nasser's bellicose maneuvers. Immediately afterward, things of course looked very different: In addition to taking the Golan Heights from Syria and the Sinai from Egypt, Israel's forces had driven Jordan's Arab Legion from the West Bank and the Egyptian army from the Gaza Strip, uniting the territory of the old Palestine mandate and bringing the majority of Palestinians under Israeli control (see Map 6). Over 600,000 West Bankers could now resume contact with the more than 300,000 Palestinians in the Strip and with a similar number living in Israel's pre-1967 boundaries.[1] The war also precipitated another exodus of Palestinians from Palestine. Approximately 250,000 fled for the remnant of Jordan, the East Bank. The war is one of several events in the latter half of the twentieth century (others being the dissolution of the French and British empires and the Soviet Union, and the reunification of Germany) that radically transformed the world map. Its results were correspondingly momentous for both Israeli Arab citizens and Palestinians in the newly occupied territories.

To everyone's surprise, the nature of the conflict in which Jews and Arabs were embroiled was now different. After 1948, the conflict had seemed largely international—the armistice agreements, continuing border tensions, the Suez war in 1956, all involved sovereign states. From this perspective, both to its own Jewish citizens and to a larger world public, Israel seemed small and beleaguered, surrounded by much larger, hostile states that refused to accept its right to exist.

Following the 1967 war, the focus gradually drifted back to the communal problem, as in the days of the mandate: two peoples—Jews and Palestinians—claiming the same piece of soil. Israel's image thus shifted, much to the frustration of its supporters, from beleaguered to all-powerful.

With the territory of historical Palestine reassembled under a single authority for the first time since 1948, the bulk of the Palestinians once more stood face to face with the Jews, their longstanding enemies, representing an alien culture and religion. The reality of what was an almost perfect reversal of the two communities' proportions in the last years of the mandate—three million Jews now ruling slightly more than one million Palestinians—has been shrewdly and succinctly captured by poet Samih al-Qasim:

> Ladies and Gentlemen.
> We are here
> On a crossroad.[2]

The Palestine Liberation Organization, led by Yasser Arafat and his Fatah faction, would now become the institutional vehicle for

Map 6. Israel and Occupied Territories of the West Bank and Gaza Strip

attracting and directing the charged emotions of the Palestinians. It would shape their self-understanding, although stumbling when it tried to mobilize their society under the single ideological umbrella of Palestinism—and under the noses of hostile governments. But despite its centrality, it was the resources of that society that would enable the organization to play such a prominent role.

Reflecting this interplay of leaders and followers, the Palestinians developed three heroic images in the face of the difficult post-1967 conditions: The *feday* (lit.: "one who sacrifices himself") was a modern metamorphosis of the holy warrior. Sacrificing himself in the battle against Zionism, he was portrayed with head wrapped in the distinctive checkered Palestinian kafiya, gripping a Kalishnokov. The image drew on memories of those who had manned the rebel groups from 1936 to 1939 and on idealized portraits of peasants as salt of the earth—even though the membership of the PLO, which heavily promoted the image, was primarily cosmopolitan and from the cities; its early popularity bolstered the PLO claim to be the sole legitimate Palestinian representative.

The image of the survivor also evoked the fast-disappearing fellah. But this was a more passive hero, demonstrating *sumud,* or steadfastness. Enduring the humiliations imposed by the conqueror, he confirmed his sumud by staying on the land at all costs— a bitter lesson learned from 1948. Eventually, even those not tilling the land but simply staying in the occupied territories came to epitomize sumud. Finally, the survivor's counterpart was "the child of the stone," often exemplified through portraits of the *shahid,* or martyr, offering his life for the national cause by fighting against all odds. Modelled partly on the role of the shabab in the 1936–39 revolt, this was the adolescent willing to confront the enemy through rock throwing, tire burning, manning shoulder-mounted antitank rockets, and so forth.

At the end of the 1960s and in the 1970s, the feday dominated the Palestinian symbolic universe, as Palestinians groped for a response to the new conditions wrought by the June war. In the 1980s, images of the survivor and the child of the stone became more prominent, challenging what had become basic tenets of Palestinian society.

Fatah

As two of his biographers put it recently, "The ordinary facts of Arafat's life—his place of birth, his parents, his childhood, his adolescence—lay buried in the soil of his distant homeland."[3] Later, this vagueness would fuel myths among the Palestinians, hungry for a larger-than-life leader. One common story is that Arafat was born in Jerusalem, although more reliable evidence indicates he was actually born in Gaza and grew up in Egypt; another is that he was part of the Husseini clan—a connection that might have benefited him at one point, but became a liability as the ayan were discredited. He is also said to have been a member of the Muslim Brotherhood, and in fact, the Egyptians arrested him on such grounds in 1954, in connection with an attempt on Nasser's life. What is certain is that he ended up in Cairo in the early 1950s, studying to be a civil engineer and working hard as the head of the Palestinian Students' Union, which he founded with a small group of collaborators.[4]

In the 1950s, the political and cultural center of gravity in the Arab world, and an ideal site for the Union, was Cairo. Nasser swept to power, drastically altering the tenor of Egyptian and Arab politics. In the midst of Cairo's intellectual currents and crosscurrents, Arafat and his trusted colleague Salah Khalaf (who, under the name Abu Iyad, would remain Arafat's chief aide-de-camp until his assassination in 1991, probably at the hands of Iraqi agents) fashioned an agenda for the Palestinian people. Their thinking can be summed up as follows: First, the Palestinians had to take responsibility for their future—only an autonomous organization of their own could reverse their fortune. Second, their chief aim needed to be the liberation of Palestine, taking precedence over the goal of Arab unity (the key to the Nasserite revolution). Indeed, the liberation was a necessary precondition for that unity. Third, the key means to achieve liberation was armed struggle, undertaken by Palestinians themselves. And finally, Palestinians would work hand-in-hand with other Arabs and international forces on the basis of equality to help achieve the goal.[5]

Khalaf would later recall those early days at Cairo University. Approached by Arafat, who was attempting to recruit him for the Union, he found a welcome refrain in Arafat's approach: "[We] knew what was damaging to the Palestinian cause. We were convinced, for example, that the Palestinians could expect nothing from the Arab regimes. . . . We believed that the Palestinians could rely only on themselves."[6] When Arafat, in the growing fashion of educated Palestinians, moved from one exiled community to another, he transported this approach with him. But by the time of his forced move to Kuwait in 1957 to take up an engineering post, it had taken some hard knocks. Arrested earlier by Nasser, he was now harassed by him because of promises made to the Israelis to secure their withdrawal from the Gaza Strip following the 1956 Suez war. And Arafat found himself caught in the turmoil of Iraqi-Egyptian competition for Arab regional leadership.[7]

Despite the fact that the British kept their protectorate in Kuwait until 1961, Arafat and his colleagues found its Arab leaders offering them a relatively free hand to establish an organization based on the Cairo principles. They also found the growing oil wealth providing resources unimaginable in Egypt. Their underground cell, which in 1959 became *Fatah*—officially, the Palestine National Liberation Movement—began to take shape a few months after Arafat's arrival. Khalid al-Hassan, a Palestinian who had risen in Kuwaiti politics, joined the cell, giving it badly needed organizational skills. In time, Hassan became the leading ideologue of the right wing of the Palestinian movement.

The cell also began publishing a magazine, *Filastinuna* (Our Palestine: The Call to Life), which appeared every six weeks or so for the next five years.[8] Its primary purpose was to put forth Fatah's strategy of provoking the Arab states into a war that Arafat was certain would eventually end Israeli control of Palestine. In a less ambitious vein, editor Khalil al-Wazir (Abu Jihad)—Arafat's long-time aide and close companion—also saw the publication as a critical forum for diverse ideas about how to promote the Palestinian cause.[9] This worked well, and the magazine's success distinguished Arafat's small clandestine group from countless others forming in various Palestinian communities.

Both Fatah and the other groups drew their strength from the deep misery of the Palestinian situation, and from points of resistance elsewhere in the Arab world. Nasser's successful challenge to British control of the Suez Canal and the anti-French agitation of Algeria's FLN suggested it was possible to reverse the verdict of history. For all the clandestine groups, the FLN was a model of how to fashion a national liberation organization, and Arafat's own position was in fact greatly strengthened by the Algerian decision, immediately after independence in 1962, to recognize and support Fatah alone.

With Nasser beginning to use the term Palestinian entity, and Iraq's new revolutionary leader, Qasim, talking of the creation of a Palestinian republic, Palestinian militants gained confidence, despite limited resources and opportunities. In the late 1950s and early 1960s a sentiment seemed to emerge among the Arab republics to give the Palestinians an active role in the struggle against Israel—at least that is what the rhetoric suggested; actually, leaders such as Nasser and Qasim displayed extreme ambivalence towards Palestinian activists, regarding with the deepest suspicion any attempt to take the initiative or set the tone.

Along with the other groups, Fatah set out to sink roots in Palestinian society. But the task was difficult, partly because of its insistence that the sole realization of Nasser's wildly popular call for Arab unity was through Palestinian repatriation. This position did not find favor among Nasser or his avid followers—many of whom were young Palestinians. Nasser felt the Fatah militants were putting the cart before the horse. At the time, even George Habash, who subsequently became the leading Palestinian ideologue of the left, advocated working for unity of the Arab masses through revolutionary regimes as a prelude to the liberation of Palestine.

Arafat found himself moving against the current of popular feeling in the Arab world—Nasserism was pushing the entire Palestinian issue to the margins. His circumstances would eventually change, partly due to larger events—such as the failure of Egyptian-Syrian unity in 1961, and the Arab catastrophe in the 1967 war—and partly due to his own tenacity. Hassan notes how his unswerving dedication to the Palestine problem, before all else, paid off: "We reversed the slogan [of Arab unity first], and this is how we reversed the whole tide of thinking. And we managed to do that. Because when you want to talk about unity, then you have to work against the [present Arab] regimes. When we want to talk about liberation, we have to work on liberation."[10]

The 1960s catapulted Fatah and Arafat from obscurity to overall leadership of the Palestinian people. The evolution from a clandestine political cell, tucked away in a remote corner of the Arab world, to an international organization, involved several important steps. In 1963, Fatah moved towards some permanence by creating a central committee, consisting of Palestinians who eschewed the party and factional conflicts wracking the Arab world. With Arafat as chief and Wazir as second in command, the committee consolidated power and directed the organization and its membership. At the same time, in the face of objections by Khalid al-Hassan and others on the committee, Arafat pushed Fatah into a strategy calling for immediate military action against Israel.

Probably nothing but armed violence could have established the organization so quickly among the various Palestinian communities, after almost two decades of inaction and growing despair. Still, the nature of the dispersal and the disdain of Fatah's leaders for traditional party organization—cells, local committees, and the like—made it difficult for the group to educate, recruit, or consistently mobilize the larger population. The committee succeeded in coordinating the organization's own actions, less so in infusing Fatah into the everyday lives of the Palestinians. When Fatah did create some rudimentary regional subgroups, it found itself hemmed in by the governing Arab regimes.

For all these organizational liabilities, the group did capture the Palestinians' imagination, but not in ways that could have been the basis for systems of control and mass mobilization. This remained true after the 1967 war, when it built a complex central apparatus, covering areas from financial control to relations with Arab parties. Over the years, Arafat tried to make Fatah (and later the PLO, which Fatah came to dominate) into what the Jewish Agency had been for the Jews during the Palestine mandate—a state-in-the-making—but without the equivalent of the political parties and the Histadrut, which had given the Jewish Agency a firm foundation in the Jewish population.

Fatah's turn to violence came after the first Arab summit meeting, held in Cairo in January, 1964, voted to establish the Palestine Liberation Organization, the culmination of almost five years of ground-laying work by Nasser. The new PLO held its first convention in East Jerusalem's Palace Hall movie theater that spring. The motivation was Israel's completion of its National Water Carrier, diverting water from the Jordan River. Support for a Palestinian organization was a way for the Arabs to give the appearance of counteracting Israel without precipitating a direct confrontation. Nasser certainly did not intend the PLO to gain much autonomy—he wanted its semblance, while insuring that no underground groups dragged Egypt into war before it was ready.

Nasser selected a figure who had worked closely with individual Arab states and with the Arab League, Ahmad Shukayri, to build the new organization. Shukayri came from impeccable Palestinian lineage. His father had been a supporter of the Young Turks in 1908 and after being exiled by the sultan, had returned to Acre where he became a learned Muslim dignitary and an activist in the emerging Palestinian movement. Shukayri took the same route as spokesman for the Arab Higher Committee, the Arab League, and the Syrian and Saudi delegations to the United Nations. In his memoirs, he also claims a connection to al-Qassam, the Palestinian hero of the 1930s, noting that he offered his services as a lawyer to defend the surviving members of the Sheikh's group in 1935.

Shukayri had been advocating an organization to "liberate" Palestine for more than a year, but due to his bluster and self-promotion, few took him seriously. Alan Hart, Arafat's sympathetic biographer, vilifies Shukayri as the Puppet-in-Chief—a political mercenary selling himself to the highest bidder, and a demagogue who was a cross between Adolf Hitler and Ian Paisley.[11] The claim of Shukayri's opponents was that he was simply doing Nasser's bidding in creating an illusion of Palestinian autonomy while keeping the organization under tight wraps. But to the surprise of many, Shukayri was far more effective than his enemies (or their biographers) let on. To establish the PLO, he overcame the opposition of feisty old Haj Amin al-Husseini, despite the fact that his father had been an outspoken opponent of the Mufti, as well as the deep suspicions of the Jordanians and several other key regimes. His other efforts were undermined by unceasing hyperbole and demagogic statements: A "bombastic orator,"[12] perhaps best remembered for his purported threat before the 1967 war to drive the Jews into the sea, he had the temerity while in Amman to proclaim that all of Jordan, including the East Bank, was an integral part of Palestine.

The spring convention disgusted many of the Fatah activists, although several attended—Arafat, whose name was on the list of invitees, did not. They saw what they considered quiescent, hand-picked delegates ratify every proposal that Shukayri put before them. Some of those proposals, however, had long-term ramifications: the Palestinian National Covenant (revised in 1968 as the Palestine National Charter) was ratified, with its strong condemnation of Zionism and Israel—a bone in the throat of Israelis to this very day. "Zionism," the Covenant declared, "is a colonialist movement in its inception, aggressive and expansionist in its goals, racist and segregationist in its configurations and fascist in its means and aims. Israel in its capacity as the spearhead of this destructive movement and the pillar for colonialism is a permanent source of tension and turmoil . . . ."[13] The convention also emphasized the need for Palestinians to amass forces, mobilize their efforts and capabilities, and engage in holy war until complete and final victory has been attained. Toward those ends, the PLO created the Palestine Liberation Army (PLA) two years later.

For Fatah, the PLO proved a formidable competitor. A real army of their own seemed highly attractive to destitute refugees and political exiles. Droves of Fatah members abandoned ship, hoping to join the projected new PLA.[14] With almost no levers of influence and control among its own members, let alone in the wider Palestinian population, the PLO needed some audacious acts as a means of restoring its most important asset—its image. Khalid al-Hassan put it this way:

> You can say, because it is the truth, that we were pushed down a road we did not want to take by the coming into being of the P.L.O. Because of its existence, and the fact that it was not the genuine article that so many Palestinians were assuming it to be, we decided that the only way to keep the idea of real struggle alive was to struggle.[15]

The road that Hassan had not wanted to take was, of course, that of direct violence against Israel. Notions of armed struggle and popular liberation were in the air in the 1960s, leading some in Fatah to believe that they were part of a larger, inexorable world force. The success of Algeria's FLN in expelling the deeply rooted *pieds noirs* was but one of several important models. Jomo Kenyatta's triumph against British colonialism in Kenya and the efforts of the National Organization of [Greek] Cypriot Struggle (EOKA) were others. Farther away, but still extremely important in the minds of Fatah members, were the Cuban and Vietnamese revolutions. The writings of General Giap in Vietnam, Che Guevara in Cuba, and Mao Zedong, were all appearing in Palestinian refugee camps, newly translated into Arabic. Perhaps most influential of all was Franz Fanon's *The Wretched of the Earth,* which, in the Algerian context, talked of the cathartic benefits of violence against the occupier; Fanon himself was a psychiatrist who had joined the FLN.[16]

The new strategy of armed violence had roots in Palestinian society as well. Some of the key figures involved in the early raids in 1965 had had direct experience in the 1936–39 revolt. Ahmad Musah, who led Fatah's first raid, had been part of Arab fighting groups carrying out action against Jewish settlements during that revolt.[17] Another key figure in these years was Subhi Yasin, who had been a member of the Black Hand group during the mandate period, as well as a direct disciple of al-Qassam. Yasin alternately competed and cooperated with Fatah, finally merging his own group, the Organization of the Vanguard of Self-Sacrifice for the Liberation of Palestine, with Arafat's in 1968.[18]

Fatah's decision was not the first time that the Palestinians had resorted to violence since 1948. Individuals such as Ahmad Musa had periodically slipped across the border to undertake personal acts of vengeance. Also, the Suez war of 1956 stemmed in no small part from the cycle of organized guerrilla raids from the Gaza Strip on Jewish settlements and Israel's strong retaliatory actions. In fact, in later years Arafat claimed some responsibility for those Gaza-based raids through his role as student leader at the time.

But Arafat's real military role began when a Fatah team operating under the name *Assifa* (The Storm) slipped into Israel and placed an explosive charge in the Beit Netopha canal. In some ways, the action was more a comedy of errors than a serious military expedition. The Lebanese arrested the group slated to carry out the attack on the last day of 1964, but, unaware of what had occurred, Arafat and his colleagues sped through Beirut distributing a military communique reporting the purported action. Later, laden with explosives, he was arrested and held for a short time by the Syrians, even though a high-ranking Syrian officer had pledged unfailing cooperation. When a group finally did plant the explosive charge on January 3, 1965, it set the timer so late that Israelis discovered and dismantled the bomb before it went off. And on its return from the action, the Palestinian unit ran into a Jordanian patrol that killed its leader, Ahmad Musa, and arrested the others.

What made the action more than merely a series of mistakes was the reaction to it. Fatah may have learned here that it is not how much actual damage they inflict on Israel that counts as how it perceives their actions. The Israelis publicized the attack and several others that Assifa undertook in early 1965, both in their Arabic radio broadcasts and in a speech by Prime Minister Levi Eshkol. Nothing could have better demonstrated the underground group's readiness to confront the enemy directly. After a second unit infiltrated into Israel, Fatah took public responsibility. Arab regimes also helped by branding Assifa the venal creation of Western intelligence agencies seeking to push the Arabs into war before they were fully prepared (Egypt) or as "communists bent on subversion" (Jordan). Egypt's army even declared itself at war with Assifa.

Wide publicity about the execution of real acts of violence and the furor they precipitated captured the attention and respect of the frustrated Palestinians around the Arab world. From an initial act of sabotage, Palestinians thus gained a new understanding of themselves as *jil al-thawra,* the revolutionary generation. At the same time, Fatah leaders learned the difficulty of making their way through minefields—not only those laid by the Israelis but also the political minefields set out by Arab regimes. Egypt, Syria, Jordan, Lebanon—all the states bordering Israel—either hunted down the underground group's members or, when professing cooperation, constrained their every move. Nonetheless, by the outbreak of the 1967 war, Assifa, which was by now the official military arm of Fatah, had undertaken nearly 100 acts of sabotage in Israel, killing eleven Israelis and wounding sixty-two.[19] Indeed, Israeli spokesmen cited these provocations as an important catalyst of the cycle of violence leading to the war.

Recreating the PLO

As humiliating as the 1967 war had been for the Arabs, it gave Fatah new opportunities in two important areas. First, the humiliation quieted the gales of Nasserite pan-Arabism. Fatah's opposition to Nasser's philosophy—i.e., Arab unification as a prelude to the liberation of Palestine—had previously seemed a form of spitting into the wind. Now the opportunity existed for alternatives to Nasser's discredited vision, to his handpicked PLO leadership, to his insistence on control.

Second, by reuniting the Palestinian majority—this time under Israeli occupation—the war made it much easier for Fatah to penetrate Palestinian society. The combination of its universal antipathy towards the Israelis with this shift from a logistically difficult fragmentation seemed to open the way for tactics reminiscent of Mao Zedong's or Ho Chi Minh's: Fatah could provide key social services and organizations to the people and, in turn, finally develop its means of mobilization and control. And such control would be a significant innovation in Palestinian society. While before 1948, the Husseinis had insinuated themselves into people's daily lives through landholding, the Supreme Muslim Council, and clan ties, neither they nor any other claimants to Palestinian leadership had created networks of influence that were truly national in scope.

In fact, Fatah was only able to capitalize on one of the opportunities, control of the PLO turning out to be its most far-reaching political achievement. Even with Nasser's firm backing, Shukayri had never managed to establish his own control over the organization, despite his claims that the PLO he led represented the general will of the Palestinians: He ended up precipitating and dealing with one factional split after another. His crowning accomplishment was the creation of the Palestine Liberation Army—in 1959, the Arab League had resolved to put such an army in the field, but little came of the effort or of several subsequent ones.[20] Eventually, Shukayri deployed several units in Gaza. But this did not save the PLO from overall ineffectiveness, and Shukayri from political demise. The army, which did not amount to more than four or five thousand men, came under the command of each host country, rather than the PLO's appointed commander-in-chief. Shukayri simply could not achieve even the most rudimentary form of autonomy, for either the army or the PLO as a whole. Jordan, in particular, fought to erode even the slightest gains by the PLO. This problem would later plague Arafat, as well.

The 1967 war recast relations among the Arabs as no other event would until Iraq's invasion of Kuwait. Pan-Arabism, which had electrified the Arab world from North Africa to the Fertile Crescent, slowly gave way to state relations reminiscent of those in other regions, based on standard diplomacy and international negotiation. Nasser's calls for unity, directed to the peoples of neighboring Arab countries above their rulers' heads, were replaced by conciliatory steps among kings and presidents. Even the dinosaur-like monarchs became legitimate nationalist leaders in this new diplomacy.

The result was a flagging interest by Arab heads of state in the PLO. At the Khartoum summit conference in the summer of 1968— the famous meeting in which the Arab League issued its notorious three no's to Israel: no negotiations, no recognition, no peace—the final communique did not even mention the PLO. Shukayri, who had enjoyed Nasser's support before the war, now felt his bone-chilling disinterest.

With the 1967 defeat, Palestinians felt the pan-Arab foundations of their hopes disintegrated. In the war's wake, many turned to the feday—especially as represented by Fatah and its record of direct, violent action against Israel—as their only chance for salvation. Fatah in turn, nourished by the new Palestinian support, used the growing disinterest of the Arab states to create some space for itself. Sending representatives to Arab capitals, it won both financial and rhetorical support. With Fatah thus catapulting into Arab consciousness, the PLO faded. By Christmas eve, 1967, Shukayri had resigned.

Arafat moved deliberately to replace Shukayri and revive the PLO. Probably no act furthered his aims more than the battle of Karamah (a refugee camp on the East Bank) on March 21, 1968. Nettled by Fatah guerrilla attacks, the Israeli government dispatched a large military force into Jordan, in order to destroy its local headquarters. In what turned out to be the first open battle between Jews and Palestinian irregulars since 1948, the Palestinians (aided by Jordanian artillery) ambushed the Israelis, killing as many as 25 soldiers in the course of a day-long fire-fight.[21] The Israelis retreated without achieving their objective.[22] While the Palestinians lost five times as many fighters as the Israelis, the psychological effect of the battle was overwhelming: Almost immediately assuming mythic proportions (Karamah means honor in Arabic), it confirmed the primacy of the feday, propelling thousands of teenagers into Assifa and Arafat to the top of the Palestinian national movement.

Within a year of the battle, he had assumed the chairmanship of the PLO, with Fatah the dominant group in the reconstituted organization. The PLO became an umbrella organization, enveloping a number of smaller ones dedicated to armed struggle and Palestinian autonomy, of which Fatah was by far the most important. It now controlled half the seats of the Palestine National Council (PNC), the PLO's emerging parliament-in-exile. Arafat and his associates controlled the 15-member Executive Committee, while keeping rival organizations fragmented and in sight as part of the Committee and the larger Council.

For substantial periods, Arafat insisted on standing clear of Arab political in-fighting, his single-minded preoccupation with Palestine making it possible for Fatah to maintain the political, moral, and financial support of a wide variety of Arab regimes. (He paid a price for deviating from this policy—the most dramatic recent example being his support for Iraq's Saddam Hussein.) In general, Fatah also spurned questions regarding the future makeup of Palestinian society or arcane ideological debates over the need for social revolution, thus enabling it to gain a broad base of support. Such choices clearly differentiated it from other Palestinian groups now committed to striking against Israel, none of which managed to establish extensive Palestinian and Arab support.

Nonetheless, such groups did have a significant impact on the movement, setting much of the tone and tenor of the PLO, indeed of the entire Palestinian national movement. In July, 1968, Palestinians hijacked an El Al Israeli airliner to Algeria, the first of a spate of hijackings and other acts aimed at the vulnerable international air transportation system. Terrorism now became a key element of the struggle against Israel. Until 1988, Palestinian groups never admitted to it, using the term "external operations" for all armed action outside Israel and the occupied territories. In 1988, the possibility of a direct dialogue with the United States hanging in the balance, Arafat denounced—and seemed to renounce—it.[23]

Behind many such acts stood the Popular Front for the Liberation of Palestine (PFLP). Like those of Fatah, its leaders came from the student movement—but in this case from the American University in Beirut. There George Habash—its preeminent figure—and colleagues had established the clandestine Arab Nationalists' Movement; shortly after the 1967 war it merged with other groups to become the PFLP, finally joining the PLO in 1970. The Arab Nationalists' Movement's activists had originally advocated Nasserism. In the mid-1960s, it moved towards a Marxist perspective, demanding social revolution as a precondition for true Arab unity. After 1967, the Front took on a Palestine-first orientation.

Direct violent action was always at the center of its concerns. By 1964, even before Fatah, members of the Arab Nationalists' Movement's guerrilla unit had attacked Israel. But even while furnishing enough notoriety to challenge Fatah among the Palestinian population, the themes of violence and ideology divided and redivided the organization.

The first acrimonious split came when Naif Hawatma demanded a more radical approach: to break the Popular Front's relations with the inherently conservative Arab regimes and to align itself instead with popular revolutionary forces throughout the Arab world. Out of the ensuing, sometimes bloody battle came a splinter group, the Popular Democratic Front for the Liberation of Palestine, headed by Hawatma. The split with the Popular Front in 1969 was finally brokered by Fatah, which in turn got the Popular Democratic Front to join the PLO. Interestingly, the new group took the lead, after long polemical debates, in distinguishing between Israel proper (as defined by the armistice agreements following the 1948 war) and the territories it captured in 1967. By the early 1970s, these debates moved many within the PLO away from the Charter's insistence on expulsion from Palestine of post-1917 Jews and their descendants to advocacy of a secular, democratic state including Jews and a majority of Arabs. Under Hawatma's prodding, this position evolved even further; by the 1980s, the Popular Democratic Front had persuaded most of the national movement to accept the principles of (a) more flexibility regarding what had formerly been considered the absolute right of Palestinian repatriation in their original homes and (b) an Arab Palestinian state in the West Bank and Gaza, rather—at least at first—than the democratic secular state in all of Palestine.[24]

The idea of creating a Palestinian state in the occupied territories had developed slowly, one of the first to raise the possibility being Mustaffa Akhmais, imprisoned by the Israelis shortly after the 1967 war.[25] The PLO has consistently emphasized three demands—the right of return, the right to self-determination, and the right to be an independent state. The 1947 partition was seen by PLO leaders as abrogating the right to self-determination.[26] The decision to found a Palestinian state in any "liberated" part of the country (i.e., the West Bank and Gaza) was finally taken at the eleventh PNC meeting (Cairo, June 9, 1974), and marked a major tactical turning point. Many Palestinians saw it as a withdrawal in principle from the idea of liberating the entire country and a movement towards the option of a "mini-state"—the backdrop to George Habash's resignation from the PLO Executive Committee on October 26 and the establishment of a "Rejection Front."

Ahmad Jibril provoked another split. He had been a member of Fatah's Central Committee before joining the Popular Front but was dissatisfied in both cases with the insufficient commitment to direct violent action. He, too, founded a new organization, the Popular Front for the Liberation of Palestine—General Command. With an emphasis more narrowly focused on guerrilla tactics, especially across Israel's northern border, it has been implicated in scurrilous acts of violence, including the blowing up of Pan Am flight 103 over Lockerbie, Scotland, in December, 1988. Even after Jibril withdrew his group from the PLO in the early 1980s, he retained considerable influence over the worldwide image of the Palestinian national movement.

Drawing on theories of urban guerrilla warfare and cooperating with a terrorist network including Japan's Red Army, the IRA, and the Baader-Meinhof group, the Popular Front and its splinter organizations initiated a series of "external operations."[27] The most spectacular by far were the airplane hijackings. These and other acts—the mass murder of passengers by the Red Army in Israel's principal airports; the murder of Israeli athletes in the 1972 Olympics—made the Palestinian issue a media event, pushing it to the top of the world political agenda. Within Palestinian society, they offered new heroes and a sense of power.[28] In the popular imagination, the feday was someone who, like Joshua, could stop the sun in the sky. Among Palestinians everywhere, there was a renewed sense of pride and autonomy, helping to rekindle a Palestinian national consciousness, battered in the decades since the Arab Revolt.

The emphasis on terror had its costs, as well, fostering a blood-thirsty stereotype, both internationally and among those Israelis who might have sought accommodation. Israeli leaders pointed to the terrorism as proof that the Palestinian Covenant involved not only the elimination of Israel but of Jews generally. And the world's revulsion enabled these leaders to delegitimize Palestinian national claims. As indicated, Arafat and Fatah over time distanced themselves from terrorist tactics, even while apparently creating their own deadly terrorist branches, Force 17 and Black September, for a while the world's most formidable terror organization.[29] The latter was responsible for many operations, including the assassination of Jordanian Prime Minister Wasfi al-Tal in Cairo (November 28, 1971) and the attack on the Munich Olympics (September 5, 1972; death toll: eleven Israeli athletes, a German policeman, five guerrillas). It is clear, then, that while Fatah now headed the PLO, it could not control many of the organization's parts; also, the reputation and image of the PLO derived as much from acts of the smaller groups as from Arafat's and Fatah's leadership.

Arafat's new stature, and that of the reorganized PLO, were recognized implicitly at the Arab League's Rabat conference in December, 1969. To the surprise of many, the PLO—now the umbrella for a slew of guerrilla groups and much more consistent on freedom of action than Shukayri ever had been—won Nasser's enthusiastic support for engaging in direct resistance to Israeli rule. He even gave Fatah some military aid and a special broadcasting station annexed to Cairo Radio.[30]

Other states such as Syria and Iraq fell into line as well. Strains between them and the PLO did not disappear altogether: They appeared, for example, when Nasser agreed to the so-called Rogers initiative in 1970 (i.e., a cease-fire in Egypt's War of Attrition against Israeli forces dug in along the Suez Canal) or when Syria set up its own guerrilla group, Saiqa (along with Jibril's Popular Front for the Liberation of Palestine–General Command, it would quit the PLO altogether for most of the 1980s). But the overall situation was quite clear: Arafat and his Fatah colleagues had ridden the wave of Israeli success in the 1967 war, using the humiliation of the Arab states and the failure of their grand designs for Arab unity to seize leadership of the Palestinian national movement.

The PLO's Search for Roots

Modelling his effort on those of the Chinese, Vietnamese, and Cuban revolutionaries, Arafat began a push immediately after the June war to establish a permanent, popular base for resistance and revolt in the occupied territories. His dramatic failure—the Israelis forced his and his entourage's ouster at the end of the summer of 1967—was a crucial development for the guerrillas and for Palestinian society in general (see chapter 9). Ironically, Fatah's success in the battle of Karamah a year later was a result of this failure: Once driven from the occupied territories, it established its headquarters there. Nevertheless, the forced physical distance from the centers of Palestinian settlement would prove to be a persistent liability. Fatah did try to compensate for that liability with a Department of Popular Organizations, governing affiliated groups of students, doctors, peasants, and so forth, meant to mobilize the Palestinian population.[31] Compared with Shukayri's feeble efforts, Arafat's seemed quite robust.

Khalid al-Hassan has argued that the new PLO might have been all too robust: "After Karamah we were forced to make our mobilisation and ideological education [of] . . . the people in the camps by masses, by lectures, not by cells: and there is a big difference in both ways. There we deal with an individual; here we deal with the masses, with 100 at one time."[32] Within a year of Karamah, Fatah had members in eighty countries, but the cost of this growth was loss of organizational cohesion. Embraced as the symbolic representation of the national movement, the PLO found itself in a symbiotic relationship with the Palestinian people: On the one hand, it promoted—despite extreme dependence upon various host countries—a sense of their distinctiveness, autonomy, and empowerment. On the other hand, Palestinian refugees and others gave the PLO a foundation for action and a coherent audience by developing a shared culture, drawing on their memories of Palestine and the myths of the Lost Garden that they had created. But such emotional closeness notwithstanding, the Palestinians found the PLO rather distant from their practical needs and way of life.

Fatah's inattention to organization at the level of village, neighborhood, or camp made it difficult to mobilize people on a sustained basis, as well as to project a unified national will. To be sure, the proliferation of guerrilla groups complicated the task. It is impossible to account for all the organizations of "armed struggle" appearing and disappearing during this period. Some were cover names, or one-action groups, or mere paper organizations. Often, several groups would claim responsibility for a suspected or clearcut guerrilla action. Free of the limits imposed on constituencies with everyday problems, their rivalries led each to work for preservation and dominance, often against the greater national good. The result was an odd mixture of ideological purity and political irresponsibility.

Arafat thus spent much of his time trying to preside over unruly groups and overcome frictions among them. Filling the seats of the Palestine National Council, which was seen as both a functioning parliament and a state-in-the-making, came only after intense and prolonged bargaining about precisely how much representation each group would have. Another formidable diversion involved the ever-more complicated world of Arab interstate relations, ensnaring the PLO in devastating, direct confrontations with the Jordanian and Syrian armies, as well as with numerous Lebanese militias.

Two factors led to such confrontations. First, the Palestinian communities located in Arab states often turned into points of contention between these states and the PLO. Local Palestinians frequently lacked basic rights and faced discrimination in their daily dealings. Attempts by the PLO to shield them from abuses meant a collision course with Arab regimes. Second, the PLO worked under a nigh-impossible dilemma. Among its most basic goals was autonomy in pursuing Palestinian interests—its own foreign policy, the right to initiate military action and develop unmediated relations with local Palestinians, and so forth. From the Palestinians' perspective, such autonomy was important, helping to define them in the Arab world as something other than refugees and victims. More concretely, if the PLO were to succeed in building viable institutions among them, autonomy could mean acquiring services that local governments would not or could not provide.

But that potential independence rankled Arab governments, none, in the postcolonial period, being ready to give even a hint of relinquishing any part of sovereignty within its assigned borders. This sentiment notwithstanding, Arafat had some success carving out areas of autonomy in particular states, but such cases were limited. One example was in Kuwait between 1967 and 1976, when the government, after greatly restricting the admission of non-Kuwaitis into the educational system, allowed the PLO to run schools for Palestinian children. Despite difficulties in keeping the schools afloat financially and in maintaining academic standards,

> The PLO school experience contributed immeasurably to the development of national consciousness among Palestinian students. Children saluted the Palestinian flag each day, participated regularly in Palestinian cultural and social activities, and joined scouting troops as well as the Zahrat and Ashbal (associations that provided children with paramilitary and political training).[33]

This sort of success was rare. As we shall see below, the PLO managed to create broad zones of autonomy and independence for itself only in Lebanon. But there as elsewhere, its efforts led to disastrous conflict—perhaps none more so than the war with Jordan in 1970: what Palestinians came to call Black September.

After Fatah's failure to establish cells in the West Bank, Jordan became the center of its activities. Starting in the summer of 1967, first Fatah, then the PLO more generally, achieved a freedom of action calling King Hussein's control of his own territory into question. After the June war, Palestinian guerrilla suspects were released from Jordanian jails, and many fighters entered Jordan from across the

Syrian border. Palestinian military units, which had been stationed in Egypt, also relocated in the Hashemite kingdom, coming under the PLO's direct command. For the first time, the feday appeared in refugee camps wearing his uniform and proudly bearing his arms.

A short honeymoon with the regime took place after the heady battle of Karamah, King Hussein proclaiming, "We shall all be feda-yeen." But soon, rifle-toting guerrillas, unauthorized roadblocks they were manning, and related gestures prompted Jordanian officials to question whether the price for allowing the PLO free reign was worth it. Heavy Israeli artillery retaliation against Jordan's richest agricultural region, the Jordan Valley, only complicated the problem.

The smaller guerrilla groups heightened the tensions, some openly calling for the establishment of a "progressive regime" in Amman; the Popular Democratic Front for the Liberation of Palestine even tried to build local Soviets of workers and peasants among concentrations of Palestinians in the north of the country. Fatah activists spoke of converting Amman into the Palestinian Hanoi, to be used as the headquarters for an assault on the Israeli Saigon, Tel-Aviv. King Hussein and his army became increasingly anxious about all of this.

Anxiety turned into humiliation on September 6, 1970. George Habash's Popular Front for the Liberation of Palestine hijacked three international airliners and forced them to land at the stark Jordanian desert airport in Zarqa. After the Popular Front blew up the aircraft, Jordan's army, the descendant of the British-trained Arab Legion, left its barracks to disarm the guerrillas. Several of the Palestinian organizations countered by declaring the northern part of the country a "liberated Palestinian area." Full warfare ensued; using heavy armor, artillery, and air attacks, the Jordanians inflicted a shattering defeat, around three thousand Palestinians dying in the fighting. Some units preferred crossing the Jordan River and surrendering to the Israelis rather than falling into Jordanian hands. When Syrian tanks threatened to intervene, Israeli forces, acting in coordination with the United States, redeployed to deter a southern thrust into Jordan.

In the aftermath of this episode, the Hashemites closed all PLO institutions and arrested those leaders who had not managed to flee.[34] The organization's prospects seemed bleak. In the course of three years, it had failed, first, in its efforts to gain direct access to the large Palestinian population in the occupied territories, and now to that in Jordan.

In subsequent decades, relations between the PLO and Jordan fluctuated.[35] For fifteen years they were very poor; the Amman Agreement of 1985 then envisioned a confederation between Jordan and a future Palestinian state, but a year later the agreement dissolved into bitter mutual recriminations. Alternating cooperation and disputes followed regarding whether Palestinian representatives could be incorporated into a Jordanian delegation for possible talks with Israel. Relations warmed again in 1990 and 1991, when both parties supported Saddam Hussein in the Gulf War. The new Jordanian government approved by the King in June, 1991, included seven Palestinian ministers, a clear signal of readiness to return to the confederation plan. The renewed cooperation laid the basis for the joint Jordanian-Palestinian delegation to the U.S.-sponsored peace talks that began in Madrid in the fall of 1991.

Hovering behind all the vicissitudes in the relationship between Palestinians and Jordanians after 1970 was a continued presumption of complete Jordanian sovereignty within its borders—including sovereignty over Jordan's Palestinian population. When in 1988 Jordan severed the tie forged with the West Bank forty years earlier, declaring the PLO the sole representative of the Palestinian people, the move's primary purpose was to underscore this presumption by excluding Palestinians in the East Bank.[36] (The move was, in any event, hedged somewhat—West Bank civil servants, for example, continued to receive Jordanian salaries.)

In any event, the PLO's grim circumstances in September, 1970, were to undergo a remarkable metamorphosis over the following five years—the greatest period of PLO success. With the uprooting from Jordan came the development of a state-within-a-state in Lebanon, that patched-together country with a large number of Palestinians (235,000). Arafat set up his headquarters in Beirut, but the real feday presence was in the southern part of the country, close to Israel's border, where much of this population lived without the political and civic rights of refugees in Jordan, or even Syria and Egypt: "Lacking work permits and generally employed in small enterprises, most Palestinians thus labored for low wages under poor working conditions with no fringe benefits, devoid of protection under Lebanese law."[37]

For the chronically weak Lebanese regime, carved up as it was among various religious sects, the presence of the PLO brought new risks. The Israelis had already made it clear in 1968 that Lebanon was running such risks, responding to the Popular Front's El Al hijacking, with an attack on Lebanon's main airport that destroyed thirteen civilian airplanes. The I.D.F. also initiated retaliatory attacks in southern Lebanon in response to Palestinian hostilities, leading droves of Shi'ite Muslims from the south to flee north to Beirut.

Battered from all directions—Israel, the PLO, Lebanese Muslim students sympathetic to the Palestinians, camp-dwelling Palestinians who undertook their own spontaneous uprising—the Lebanese government tried to contain the guerrillas, but with only marginal success. In 1969, Nasser brokered the apparently paradoxical Cairo Agreement, offering the PLO ample autonomy and latitude in southern Lebanon while somehow promising Lebanon "sovereignty and security." For the first time, Arafat had an opportunity to carve out institutional autonomy, seemingly free of interference by jealous Arab states.

Once they entered the camps, the guerrilla groups established courts, imposed taxes, conscripted young men. They revised the curriculum in the schools, which were funded and run by UNRWA, so as to offer paramilitary training and change the tenor of social relationships in the camps. The entire spirit in them changed: The first appearance of the feday was received in mythological terms, as that of "giants [who] rose from the sea."[38] One man in the Tal al-Zaatar camp exclaimed,

> The first moment I got down from the car I saw the Palestinian flag instead of the Lebanese flag, and a group of Palestinians in fedayeen

clothes instead of the Lebanese police. As I moved through the camp I saw happiness on people's faces. . . . The *sheikh* in the mosque now spoke clearly about the homeland. . . . In the homes, mothers spoke clearly with their children about Palestine—before this was only done in whisper. There were many new projects which weren't there before: social activities, sports, meetings where people could say what they thought clearly, without censorship.[39]

Service and administrative organizations quickly followed. By the early 1980s, the Palestinian Red Crescent Society had built 10 hospitals and 30 clinics, another 47 of the latter being run by the non-Fatah guerrilla groups. Two organizations with tens of thousands of members, the General Union of Palestine Workers and the General Union of Palestinian Women, gained most of their strength in Lebanon.[40] The PLO and its allies also set up the Voice of Palestine radio network, several newspapers, a news agency (WAFA), and a research institute. The organization "had grown from a loosely organized collection of *fida'iyyin* to a vast bureaucratic network, centered in Lebanon, employing perhaps 8,000 civil servants and a budget (including that of constituent organizations) in the hundreds of millions of dollars, three-quarters of which went to support the PLO's social and administrative programs."[41] In addition, it had gained diplomatic recognition from over 50 states, established more than 100 foreign missions of its own, and won observer status in the United Nations (the platform for Arafat's well-known 1974 speech toting a partially visible, bolstered pistol). Rashid Khalidi describes the turn of fortune:

PLO Chairman Yasser Arafat was now a head of a state in all but name, more powerful than many Arab rulers. His was no longer a humble revolutionary movement, but rather a vigorous para-state, with a growing bureaucracy administering the affairs of Palestinians everywhere and with a budget bigger than that of many small sovereign states.[42]

Over time, the financial resources to sustain such a complex structure also developed, largely through aid from the Gulf states. Adam Zagorin estimates that the main financial body of the PLO, the Palestine National Fund, had yearly expenditures of approximately $233 million by the late 1980s, including over a third of that to support a standing army.[43]

While at the beginning, competition among the guerrilla organizations to control camp life was intense, by 1978 Fatah had achieved dominance. It appointed popular committees that looked after the most mundane human problems—road maintenance, the building of bomb shelters (for protection from both Israeli bombing and Arab militias) and providing proper hygiene. Fatah was especially successful in forming the youth groups mentioned above by Brand—the Zahrat (flowers) for girls and Ashbal (lion cubs) for boys—that stressed military training and the building of a revolutionary culture. This new culture emphasized the difference between the jil al-thawra—the assertive revolutionary generation—and the desolate, humiliating identities of the children's parents, the jil al-Nakba.

Some residents complained that these activities eroded the Palestinians' normally high academic motivation as well as the standing of the regular schools,[44] but there was no doubting the electrifying effect that the feday had on the Lebanese camps:

> On dark alley walls
> our comrades' deaths are announced
> posters show their smiling faces[45]

Such posters plastered the walls of the camps, and graffiti, folk songs, poetry, and stories all grew around the quasi-mystical icon of the feday, recognized as one who would gladly offer his (or in some versions, her) life to liberate Palestine.[46] These idolized recruits earned relatively high salaries, and their families gained preferred access to PLO services and jobs. Families of martyrs received special pensions.

The PLO's control went far beyond the Palestinian camps. The guerrillas had nearly free reign in a wide swathe of Lebanese territory, including the coastal cities of Tyre and Sidon. Over time, the Lebanese police all but disappeared from the streets (they simply removed their uniforms, while continuing to receive their salaries from the central government); Lebanese courts and administrative services gave way to "revolutionary" courts and to private arrangements with the guerrilla groups, especially Fatah.[47] Naturally, this power and success came with a variety of dangers, fears, and resentments, hidden and not-so-hidden. Within the camps, the old leadership felt particularly vulnerable. Sayigh quotes a camp school director:

> Most of the *wujaha* [traditional notables or leaders] collaborated with the authorities and informers, not because they were unnationalistic, but because they feared the new generation which was threatening their influence. These were the people on whom the Mufti depended—they worked together against the new current.[48]

A number of ordinary Palestinians also came to bridle under the rule of the feday. A few had established close relations with their Lebanese neighbors, even intermarrying, and opposed the wedge now dividing the two peoples. Others saw the guerrillas, many of whose families had come from the Hebron mountains and Gaza, as socially and intellectually inferior to the Haifa and Galilee Palestinians in southern Lebanon. For their part, guerrillas spoke of the Lebanese Palestinians as uncommitted to the revolution, as they called their new order, and as "embourgeoised." And to complicate matters even more, the various factions of the PLO often squabbled among themselves for control. The popular committees that they appointed were frequently underskilled, disorganized, and ineffective.

The greatest dangers, however, did not come from resentful Palestinians—most of whom gladly put up with inefficiences or even occasional indignities in return for a true Palestinian leadership—but from the Lebanese, who, like the Jordanians, feared that the guerrillas' autonomy would bring disaster. From the signing of the Cairo Agreement on, powerful elements in Lebanon were convinced that the Palestinian state-within-a-state could not coexist with Lebanese sovereignty—a conviction sharpened by Israeli retaliation for any

Palestinian armed incursions, based on a faith that Lebanese pain would translate into restrictions on the PLO. The Phalangist party of the dominant Maronite sect—the religious group most closely identified with the modern Lebanese state[49]—led the outcry. It watched Palestinian control expand from, what the Israeli media called Fatahland in the south to territorial enclaves in the north and the Biqa valley, as well as to the PLO's "capital" in the Kaka-khani district of West Beirut.

In March, 1970 (that is, before the expulsion of the PLO from Jordan) armed clashes broke out between units of the Lebanese army and guerrilla groups. A few years later (spring 1973), an Israeli raid in Beirut's rue Verdun, killing three leading PLO figures, provoked wide-scale fighting between Lebanese and Palestinian forces. The Milkart Protocols, signed in May, 1973, temporarily put an end to the warfare by precisely spelling out the boundaries for guerrilla forays and enjoining them to self-restraint. But in the end those agreements may have made the situation worse by prompting certain Lebanese factions, particularly among the Christian sects, to create their own militias. In the context of deteriorating relations among Lebanese confessional groups, the tensions helped generate one of the bloodiest communal conflicts of the twentieth century: the Lebanese civil war, lasting from 1975 until 1990 and resulting in well over 100,000 fatalities and endless human tragedy.

For the PLO and the Palestinians, this war would bring previously unimagined brutality and disasters, some of which would make Black September seem relatively benign. They would end up facing two Israeli invasions—a limited incursion in 1978 (the Litani Operation) and a full-scale attack in 1982—besides battles with numerous Lebanese militias. Encountering periodic hostility from the Syrian army, they would suffer a devastating defeat at its hands in 1976.

In the most ignominious blow of all, the PLO found its own factions mauling each other at several points during the war. In 1983, several guerrilla groups, including the Syrian-sponsored Saiqa and Jibril's Popular Front for the Liberation of Palestine–General Command, withdrew from the PLO. And a Fatah colonel, Abu Musa (Said Musa Muragha), led a mutiny against Arafat, involving pitched battles with Fatah forces. The opposition was based on a wide variety of grievances. But the key element was, as the critics saw it, the PLO's treasonous appeasement of its enemies—and its gradual abandonment of the claim to total repatriation, its acceptance in theory of an independent state limited to the West Bank and Gaza. Both Syria and Libya supported Abu Musa, and Syria went so far as to deport Arafat from Damascus (he ended up in Tunis). About 400 men were killed, and another 1,900 wounded, in this brief civil war within a civil war.[50]

Confronting such ordeals, Arafat and the PLO tottered badly. The 1982 Israeli invasion routed the 15,000-strong PLO fighting force and put its entire infrastructure under siege for nearly the entire summer. At the end of August, Palestinian military, administrative, and political forces were evacuated from Lebanon under U.S. supervision—their only shred of honor being the ability to hoist their weapons as they boarded ship in Beirut port. Arafat's personal exit on August 30 marked an end to *ayam Beirut,* the era of PLO political and military presence in Lebanon. Sixteen months later, after Israel had withdrawn from most of Lebanon and PLO fighters had infiltrated back, Abu Musa's rebellion again forced Arafat and his forces to leave.

Reestablished in Tunis, the organization moved some of its branches and training centers to Saddam Hussein's Iraq—paving the way for Arafat's support of that country in the 1991 Gulf War—after an Israeli bombing attack. By the late 1980s, the PLO was again engaging in international initiatives. Arafat engineered a short-lived dialogue with the United States, denouncing the use of terrorism and publicly recognizing the right of Israel to exist—both major concessions on his part. He also managed to reestablish his own tattered image among Palestinians and to have the Palestine National Council finally declare a state that would eventually rule in the West Bank and the Gaza Strip. Without defining its borders or establishing a government, the extraordinary 19th session of the Council, convened near Algiers from November 12 to 15, 1988, authorized a declaration of independence bearing a striking resemblance to that of Israel in 1948. Arafat proclaimed the state, with its capital in Jerusalem, on November 15, 1988.

But despite the international dazzle, the PLO had not altered the dilemma that had become evident in September, 1970: Its most basic aim, to create enough autonomy to shape Palestinian society and confront Israel, lay hostage to the whims of embattled Arab states— or of their unofficial militias or threatening or opportunistic neighbors. In 1991, for example, when the Lebanese state was taking its first steps towards reestablishing a semblance of effective rule, it turned, with the support of its powerful patron Syria, on the PLO in the south, ending its rule after several violent clashes. Arafat's desire to avoid the entanglements of Arab politics could not protect him from such fury. Indeed, writes Rashid Khalidi, "the fact that Palestinian nationalism has been in nearly constant conflict over the past few decades with both Israel and various Arab regimes is perceived as inevitable by most Palestinians."[51]

Even worse, at such times Arafat and his organization could not protect the Palestinian population. By the last half of the 1980s, this fundamental inadequacy changed the relationship of the PLO to Palestinian society in subtle but substantial ways. One of its first indications came shortly after Syria's intervention, aimed in part directly against the PLO, in the Lebanese civil war in 1976. The intervention offered the PLO's Lebanese opponents an opportunity to launch an attack on the two remaining Palestinian refugee camps in mostly Christian East Beirut. One fell quickly, but the other, Tal al-Zaatar, was besieged for almost two months, with the PLO nearly helpless to relieve the suffering and anguish. Despite substantial concessions to the Syrians, the Christian forces finally razed the camp, killing 3,000 Palestinians and evicting the others.

Another such indication was the notorious sequence of events on September 16, 1982, in the suburban Beirut camps of Sabra and Shatilla: Using Israel's protective presence around Beirut, the Phalangists entered the camps and in less than two days slaughtered anywhere between 460 and 3,000 Palestinians, including women and children—as well as Lebanese, Syrians, Algerians, Pakistanis, and Iranians who happened to be in the camps.[52] The camps thus were added to the list of places marking Palestinian martyrdom, alongside Dayr Yasin, Kafr Qasim, and Tel al-Zaatar.

The PLO's impotence did not seem to affect its popularity, or that of Arafat, among the Palestinians. Polls in 1988, for example, gave the PLO a 90 percent and Arafat a 75 percent approval rating.[53] But there were nonetheless indications of a changed relationship. On the one hand, while remaining popular through its long ordeal in Lebanon, the heroic image of the feday appeared increasingly distant from the immediate needs of the Palestinian population, and another cultural hero was beginning to challenge its dominance— the "RPG kid," named after the anti-tank shoulder rockets he toted to slow the Israeli advance. The stiff price the Israelis paid for the invasion of Lebanon (over 650 dead; 3,500 wounded) catapulted the image of the young martyr, the shahid, into the limelight. The professionally paid feday now had to share the cultural stage with the spontaneous, untrained RPG kids. Later, in the West Bank and Gaza Strip, similar adolescents throwing rocks and taunting Israeli troops would mark the rise of the children of the stones.

On the other hand, many Palestinians were now falling back on their own tenacity for self-protection, a situation reflected in the increasing evocation of the image of the survivor, whose heroism is based on sumud. Perhaps somewhat grandiloquently, Ahmad Dahbur has reflected on such poles of vulnerability and tenacity in Palestinian life:

> You hear the news about the Palestinian?
> Wherever he is they knife him
> famine strikes him and flees
> rumor hacks off an arm here, a leg there,
> the media joyfully spread the news
> the Palestinian rejects
> he accepts his days as a sword
> a hand that scatters the illusions of others
> I testify "endurance is his strength."[54]

Regardless of Lebanese fears, the PLO's power in southern Lebanon remained over an isolated enclave. Once the civil war had ended, the Lebanese state wasted little time in targeting remaining

PLO control. Arafat had succeeded in creating a popular leadership among the Palestinians for the first time in their history, and in Lebanon he had even built the semblance of a state. But his attempts to transform that leadership into one that could penetrate and shape Palestinian society beyond the Lebanese arena continued to meet impossible barriers.

PLO leaders had always understood that capturing the imagination of the Palestinians or appealing to them through an attractive ideology would in itself have been insufficient to gain the control they wanted and needed. Moreover, as the dominant faction, Fatah was often at a disadvantage compared to other groups in elaborating an effective ideology. Certainly, none of the others came close to Fatah in garnering outside material support or in sheer size (it probably had 10,000–15,000 men under arms at the end of the 1960s). But, often, their narrower bases allowed them to project more effective ideologies: Fatah seemed a catchall, sending loosely defined, often contradictory messages. It believed in "not engaging in ideological debates about the character of the regime of the liberated state at the present stage as it might split the Palestinians and divert their attention from the struggle against Israel."[55] Sometimes its voice had deep Islamic resonances; at other times, it spoke a language of secularism.[56] Sometimes it seemed to appeal to the downtrodden with the language of social revolution, at others it courted the growing Palestinian middle class. Alain Gresh has rather understated the case in noting that "Fatah is a movement with a variety of tendencies and sensitivities."[57]

Given all its difficulties, the PLO, under the control of Fatah, had managed to establish itself as the recognized leadership of the Palestinians. It had nurtured a national mythology of heroism and sacrifice, the portrait of the downtrodden refugee giving way to that of the feday—which, in turn became the catalyst for the reconstruction of the national movement. In time, armed struggle would give way to more nonviolent activity, both for the sake of international legitimacy and because of the Israeli abilities to deal with armed threats.

But even if violence had failed to reverse al-Nakba, it had succeeded in projecting the Palestinian issue into the center of international concern. The PLO's continuing frustration was that its longstanding enemy, Israel, had also consolidated its power; as it did so, its readiness to make concessions to the Palestinians decreased. Facing this formidable opponent, the PLO, at the end of the 1980s and the beginning of the 1990s, was unable to show tangible gains, despite its political evolution. Along with its other difficulties, the organization's want of definition left its leadership vulnerable to challenges from within and to the rising tide of Islamic movements.

9

STEERING A PATH

UNDER OCCUPATION

YASSER ARAFAT AND GEORGE HABASH first met in a café in Damascus shortly after the end of the 1967 war. Habash was utterly despondent; turning to Arafat he cried, "Everything is lost." Arafat's answer seemed little more than whistling in the dark. "George, you are wrong," he said. "This is not the end. It's the beginning."[1]

Arafat's brave words met not only with Habash's doubt but with the skepticism of Arafat's lieutenants. Abu Jihad recalled, "I myself was crying. Because of the way in which the Arab armies had been broken, some of our colleagues were saying that everything was finished. Some were talking about giving up the struggle and making new lives outside the Arab world."[2] But in a heated debate during the Fatah Central Committee meeting, Arafat prevailed over such skepticism, and over the opposition of his aides, gaining support for an armed popular uprising in the occupied territories.

The effort began the month after the war, when Arafat and several of his associates infiltrated into the Israeli-controlled West Bank. Hoping to establish cells there and, eventually, in the Gaza Strip, he set up his headquarters in Nablus—the city that had played such a critical role in the earlier Palestinian uprisings of the 1830s and 1930s. Several months before the Israeli occupation of the city, Arabs witnessed a revolt against the Hashemite regime. Mass demonstrations were organized and about twenty inhabitants were killed by the Jordan security forces; law and order were reestablished only after two weeks of curfew. Nablus seemed to be the ideal base for the guerrillas, with the winding alleys of its densely populated core, the Kasba, and its hinterland of remote, mountain villages. Arafat's aides established other cells in East Jerusalem and Ramallah. But for all of the optimism and the hopes promoted by these initiatives, by early fall there were practically no remnants of Fatah's presence in the West Bank. The organization had picked up stakes and relocated to Karamah, Jordan.

After the fall of the West Bank underground, few organized guerrilla activities originated there except for sporadic hit-and-run attacks. Using Palestinians previously trained by the Egyptian army, Gaza managed to sustain some limited operations, but Ariel Sharon ruthlessly crushed them, resettling about 160,000 refugees—including 70,000 in the West Bank—killing over 100 guerrillas and arresting almost 750 others in the half year beginning July, 1971.[3] Individual Palestinians or small groups maintained violent and nonviolent protest in subsequent decades, but PLO-directed attacks were almost entirely absent. The organization had become another Middle Eastern refugee.

For the nearly 1,000,000 Arabs in the West Bank and Gaza Strip, Fatah's failure had long-term consequences. After slowly emerging from the disorientation of al-Nakba, the 1967 defeat, with the annexation of East Jerusalem, had been almost as great a shock.[4] Now the Palestinians seemed all the more incapable of formulating an answer to the occupation. Anticipating what would take place in Gaza, the Israeli military had made short order of Arafat's dreams of infiltrating into the heart of Palestinian society—assisted, in part, by Fatah's own loose organizational methods. Israel's policies were summed up in the title of a book written by the first Israeli military governor of the occupied territories: *The Stick and the Carrot.*[5] The stick, in the mode of nearly all modern occupying forces, was a series of harsh, repressive measures in response to almost any demonstration of resistance; it included arrests (almost a thousand prisoners were in Israeli jails by the end of 1967), deportations, blowing up houses, and detention without trial or formal charges. Israeli military authorities also meted out collective punishments—closing schools, shops, and markets, as well as imposing strict curfews on the Arab population, in response to nearly any provocation.

The innovative aspect of Israel's occupying policies involved the carrot. Almost from the very beginning of its rule, the military rulers granted a relatively large degree of self-government to the municipalities, later allowing nearly 20 percent of the 1967 refugees to return through a family reunion program. They orchestrated two municipal elections in the 1970s, the second of which greatly expanded the roll of eligible voters and resulted in pro-PLO officials holding office. Moshe Dayan, the defense minister through 1973 and the primary architect of these policies, insisted on open bridges for the movement of people and goods between the West Bank and Jordan, as well as a permeable border between the territories and Israel. He also kept Jordan firmly at the center of all considerations of the West Bank's future. In Dayan's notion of a functional division of rule between Israel and Jordan, the area's inhabitants would continue to be subjects of the Hashemite Kingdom, while the land would be under Israel's control. Although there were qualifiers for many of his measures, the Israelis did try to foster the image of an enlightened, liberal—perhaps, even friendly—occupier. It even oversaw the establishment of the first Palestinian universities—Bir Zeit (1972), Al-Najah (1977), and Gaza Islamic (1978).

As long as both Israelis and Palestinians regarded the occupation, excluding East Jerusalem, as a temporary state of affairs, there was little motivation on either side to exacerbate tensions unduly—little cause for the Palestinians to risk their precarious situations by abetting the cells Arafat tried to establish in 1967. Still, the Israeli policies and the prowess of Israeli intelligence services were only superficial causes for Fatah's failure, interacting with a set of developments in Palestinian society that are the subjects of this chapter.

From Resistance to Institution Building

In June, 1967, the West Bank's character was shaped primarily by farming, as in the period of the mandate.[6] But what had then been a backwater now contained refugees who were more educated, less likely to have been peasants, than the rest of the West Bank population. Many had lived in the towns and cities of the coastal plain before their descent into refugee status in 1948. While the East Bank had probably changed more due to Palestinian migration than the West Bank had due to initiatives from Amman, efforts at "Jordanizing" the West Bank had made some limited headway before the June war. Nonetheless, few West Bankers considered themselves primarily Jordanians.[7] Nor did they think of themselves as "Palestinians"; indeed, use of the phrase to indicate nationality was just beginning to gain currency. Perhaps the best description of who they were in 1967—more so for the original inhabitants than for the refugees— was simply West Bankers. This did not exclude other dimensions of their identity, whether local, pan-Arab, or Islamic. Nor did it totally mask the deep rifts in the society, especially between the refugees and other residents. This said, it remains the case that the forces acting on the West Bank population had created a unique people, doggedly attached to the Palestine they now inhabited as well as the Palestine of their memories.

Gazans, also using the memory of Palestine as the basis for a new refugee identity during the nineteen years of Egyptian rule, but more cut off from the influences of other national cultures, had also developed their own distinctive subculture. The West Bank and Gazan strands of Palestinian culture only began to reconnect after the 1967 war, in the unexpected environment of a Jewish state.

Even as PLO leaders in Lebanon established their organization as an international force in the early 1970s, many seemed to realize the futility of a policy in the occupied territories resting solely on a general armed uprising. Key Palestinians on the West Bank and in Gaza were putting their energies, not into fomenting such an uprising, but into limited, local political initiatives and the creation of a variety of social organizations. An alternative strategy began to evolve at the tenth and eleventh sessions of the Palestine National Council in 1972, and 1973: aid to grassroots efforts in the West Bank and Gaza Strip—to labor unions and other sorts of organizations and institutions.

This strategy did not come easily. When Rashad al-Shawwa agreed to the Israeli entreaty to become mayor of Gaza and form a municipal council in the fall of 1971, local nationalists objected loudly. At first, the PLO refused to endorse the council. But al-Shawwa persisted, devoting himself to such issues as reviving Gaza's citrus industry. Sara Roy has observed that "with the reinstatement of a locally based municipal structure and the defeat of the resistance movement, political struggle began to challenge armed struggle as a tactical approach for dealing with the realities of the occupation."[8]

As in the early nineteenth century, Nablus was at the center of these changes. But, unlike that period, when Nablus was the heart of an agricultural hinterland, and unlike the early twentieth century, when it played the parochial foil to Jaffa's cosmopolitanism, the new Nablus was a locus of innovation: the generation of indigenous organizations that could create new social parameters.

It was imperative for the PLO, if it hoped to stay relevant, to be in the forefront of this process. Its very charisma insured that it would have an ongoing, forceful say in almost all forms of organizational life—the policies of municipal councils, the setting up and running of the new universities, the editorial policies of the Jerusalem newspapers, even the programs of the Boy Scouts.[9] But its control was limited by two important factors: its physical distance from events in the territories, and the tendency of local organizations to develop and assume autonomous capabilities as their activities expanded.

The PLO's complex relationship with the Palestine National Front, which emerged in the early 1970s to coordinate organizational activities in the territories, demonstrates the PLO's struggle to come to terms with this dilemma.[10] The shift in policy reflected in these activities raised difficult questions about precisely who was in charge. Officially, the creation of the Palestine National Front was the result of a secret decision, divulged later, by the Palestine National Council at its eleventh session, in January, 1973.[11]

In fact, the Front was the creation of a number of young Communist leaders in the West Bank. One of its initiators, the mayor of the small town of al-Birah, has noted that "following the [1973] war, we felt that we needed a collective leadership, so that our political stands and resistance to the military occupation would not be individualistic."[12] Much of this leadership was identified with the Palestine Communist party; the rest included various guerrilla groups, the Baath party, labor unions, professional associations, student groups, and women's organizations.

It gradually became apparent that the Front more closely reflected the shape of events on the West Bank and in the Gaza Strip than it did the desires of the PNC or the PLO leadership. All of its local leaders publicly accepted the authority of the PLO, while both quietly positioning themselves to influence its decision making and taking on increasing autonomy.[13] Their chief concern was reducing the West Bank's utter dependence on the Israeli economy.

As the Front's popularity grew in the West Bank and Gaza Strip, so did the suspicions within the PLO. The Palestine Communist party represented an organized force with strong roots that PLO leaders feared they could not control. In 1975 and 1976, they demanded that it refrain from propagating any messages in the territories other than those issued by the PLO. They also demanded prior review, and censorship, of any Front publications, accusing it of trying to out-maneuver the PLO.[14] Israel's own harsh response to the Front, like many related policies, ironically played into the hands of PLO members who felt excluded as a result of its activities. Through a curious coalition of the PLO, Israeli authorities (who deported numerous Front activists), and pro-Jordanian figures in the West Bank, the Front declined, finally disappearing in 1977. (It was not until 1987 that the local Communists gained a seat on the Palestine National Council.)

Rather than being exceptional, the PLO's experience with the Front was symptomatic of events to come. The Jordanians were continuing to promote the dominant leadership from the post-1948 period, naturally much more inclined to support its positions than the PLO's. Israel was scanning the horizon for leaders who would cooperate with its administration, looking either to existing local leaders or, later, to new ones through an abortive Israeli invention called the Village Leagues. With the distance from the West Bank, and in the context both of Jordan's open competition and what appeared to be Israel's policy of creeping annexation, it is not surprising that the PLO felt pressed to cement alliances with viable figures in the territories. But its sense of urgency continued to be offset by the fear of finding its authority challenged. To deal with the dilemma, it ended up granting significant latitude on local issues to its allies in the territories, while retaining for itself all "state" issues.

But the solution may have been more rhetorical than practical. Local leaders intent on creating a Western-style, democratic state, such as lawyer Aziz Shehadah of Ramallah, were as aware of the larger importance of their institution building as were the leaders of the PLO.[15] During the Jordanian period, Shehadah had already come under surveillance by the King's security forces for his views on Palestinian autonomy; by 1968, he had earned the wrath of both Fatah and Jordan. Bypassing the PLO in expressing his views to Cyrus Vance (then the U.S. secretary of state), Shehadah was subsequently assassinated.

After the demise of the Palestine National Front, other groups arose that tried to accommodate the PLO's needs and demands with those of Israel and the local population. In response to the Camp David accord, a twenty-one-member National Guidance Committee formed in 1976, serving as a meeting point for heads of the municipalities—elected in 1976—as well as for those of other nascent institutions. Both local and PLO leaders felt that the accord and subsequent Israeli-Egyptian peace treaty validated permanent Israeli control over the territories under the fig-leaf of a theoretical Palestinian autonomy. With the rush of events brought on by Sadat's visit to Jerusalem, the Committee played a key role in mobilizing local Palestinian opposition to what was occurring.

Even that consensus could not hide the conflict between those inside the territories and those outside. Despite more institutional tinkering—this time, the reconstitution of the Palestine National Front to guide the Guidance Committee—the latter organization now fell victim to the complicity of Israel, the PLO, and Jordan. First crippled, it was finally outlawed by Israel in 1984.

Fatah's leaders had somewhat more success in direct attempts at mobilizing youth than in the coordination of ongoing activities. In the early 1980s, they built "The Youth Committee for Social Work," popularly known as Shabiba (The Youth).[16] With projects designed to ingratiate itself into Palestinian society, the organization offered little challenge to the social order—it sanctified the family, separated boys and girls, encouraged the traditional village value of mutual aid, and glorified village life. Its first project was to clean and rehabilitate cemeteries, thus stressing the ties of today's youth with their ancestors.[17] And it followed by cleaning mosques, schools, and other public areas. Soon, it took on a more explicitly political role, working against land expropriations; it also aided families whose houses had been demolished by the Israeli military as a form of collective punishment, or whose members had been detained or deported. Shabiba's success became particularly evident in the early stages of the Intifada, when it was outlawed by the Israeli authorities.

But even in the case of such volunteer organizations, a tension emerged with Fatah. As we shall see below, university students rallied behind leftist political groups—the Communist party in conjunction with the Popular Front for the Liberation of Palestine and the Democratic Front—to establish a network of cells gaining far more independence than Fatah was willing to grant. Local labor unions similarly threatened Fatah's position, and were thus wrested from their democratically elected leadership, inducing a split in the General Federation of Palestinian Union Workers.

Such differences were probably inevitable. PLO leaders saw themselves as building the foundations for a Palestinian state. Local organizers, although talking of their role in this state, were in fact engaged in a very different project—erecting a civil society out of the diverse Palestinian population. In any case, the PLO faced other formidable barriers to the entrenchment in the territories its leaders sought. First, the Fatah leadership faced competition from other elements in the PLO—a rivalry not limited to youth groups—which fragmented the organization's efforts.[18] Second, the Israelis engaged in an ongoing process of deporting individuals with connections to the PLO from the territories. Their absence, coupled with difficulties the organization had with those allies who were available, reflected difficulties running much deeper than the population's unresponsiveness to the initial call to arms in the summer of 1967.

Perhaps the provisional character of the occupation made popular armed resistance seem superfluous: In the case of the 1956 Sinai war, Israel had been compelled to return the land it conquered—the Gaza Strip and most of the Sinai Peninsula—in less than half a year, without any serious public protests from the Gazan population. The image of Israeli invincibility coming out of the 1967 war may also have made such resistance seem somewhat futile. For both these reasons, the warrior was fading as a rallying point in the popular imagination—replaced, as we have suggested, with more indigenous, less remote archetypes, especially that of the survivor possessing infinite steadfastness, sumud.

Like almost any cultural concept that takes on increasing power and meaning, sumud became a subject of controversy.[19] Palestinians in the territories differed over the correct form of steadfastness in the face of an occupation turning out, in fact, to be prolonged. The more passive school argued for preserving the status quo: minimal interaction or cooperation with the enemy, and opposition, whenever possible, to any territorial or demographic change. The emphasis was on endurance and, as time went on, avoiding any pretexts for deportation.[20] Others argued for active institution building, seeing local politics as part of the process of state making.

Understood either actively or passively, the image of the steadfast survivor was endowed with an aura of glamour by West Bankers and Gazans eager to avoid the stigma attached to those who had stayed in Israel in 1948 and, many assumed, collaborated with Israel. It gave their daily lives a larger meaning and purpose—ironically, in the context of wide cooperation with the occupier: paying taxes, seeking the many permits needed for various routines, and working for Israelis, even as builders of Jewish settlements or as aides to Israeli military and police officials. Only selling land to Jews, serving Israeli intelligence, and negotiating on wider political issues without PLO permission could jeopardize that standing.

The PLO leaders understood the importance of steadfastness, of preventing a mass exodus of Palestinians from the West Bank and Gaza Strip, and subsequent land sales to Israelis. It supported a project by the Arab states—valued by them as a lever of control—to establish *Sunduq al-Sumud*, the Steadfastness Fund, to discourage migration.

But the theme of the survivor represented a threatening self-sufficiency. A newfound respect for the West Bank's indigenous forces was manifest in the incorporation of the Palestine Communist party into the Palestine National Council in 1987. While Arafat—the archetypal feday—remained the personification of Palestinian nationalism in the occupied territories, it was becoming crystal clear that the vast majority of Palestinians were not prepared to take up arms.

The Changing Structure of Society

In 1987, patterns of West Bank life ranging from marriage to migration looked very different from twenty years before—a change starting in the wake of an overheated Israeli economy in the period following the war.[21] Pent-up demand generated an extraordinarily high need for workers—especially low-skill, low-wage labor that Palestinians could readily provide—and they were gradually integrated into the Israeli labor market.[22] By the 1973 war, as much as one-third of the total work force in the occupied territories was employed in Israeli agriculture, industry, building construction, and services. This drew labor from indigenous economic activities in the West Bank and Gaza, mostly agriculture but some local industry as well.

As in the period before 1948, Palestinians now found their economy uncompetitive with, and overwhelmed by, the adjoining Jewish economy: In agriculture, Israeli gross produce per worker was four times as high as that in the West Bank.[23] Under these circumstances, the possibilities for self-sufficiency there vanished—it became a reservoir of cheap labor for Israel and its second biggest export market, after the United States.

An initial drop in production for farm produce from the occupied territories was followed by a recovery. Continued access to Jordanian markets as a result of the open-bridges policy, coupled with Israeli purchases—despite their official ban—of specialized goods, precipitated a period of recovery from a postwar slump for larger West Bank farmers. Faced with rising agricultural wages due to the lure of jobs in Israel, they began to mechanize and become more productive through use of plastic coverings for vegetables, drip irrigation, and so forth.[24] They also drew more women and children into the labor market, largely as low-paid day workers, filling the gap in the agricultural sector caused by the draw of jobs in Israel.

Overall, however, agriculture—the economic mainstay during Jordanian and Egyptian rule—played a diminishing role in the territories,[25] made even more salient by the overall rapid growth of their economy.[26] Along with the magnetic effect of the Israeli labor market, the decline was caused by a closing of large tracts of land on the West Bank as military security zones and for Jewish settlements and a severe limitation put by Israeli authorities on water use. It is ironic that even as the guerrilla groups resuscitated and glorified the cultural portrait of the heroic peasant, economic changes were making such traditional farmers historical anachronisms—a situation reminiscent of the period of the Arab Revolt in the 1930s.[27]

Throughout the West Bank and Gaza, employers were now Jewish, not Arab; banks were Israeli branches, not Arab ones. Israel had forced banks in the West Bank to break their ties to Jordanian parent companies, causing the shutdown of the local branches (it allowed the branches of the Cairo-Amman Bank to reopen in the mid-1980s). The largest local industry was still olive oil. It was followed by textiles, quarrying, and food processing.[28] Industries were increasingly coming to be subcontractors for larger Israeli manufacturers. While investment in local industry and infrastructure remained pitifully low—continuing a trend of inadequate investment begun under Jordanian and Egyptian rule[29]—consumption grew, as reflected in a remarkable boom in family-home construction. Salim

Tamari observes that "the average peasant, after saving some money, tends to put it into a separate housing unit for his own nuclear household, and converts the rest into gold jewelery."[30]

The new prosperity rested on the multiple sources of income possessed by many families, as husbands and sons worked in Israel proper. In 1987, shortly before the outbreak of the Intifada, the numbers of workers officially crossing daily into Israel peaked at 107,000—61,000 from the West Bank and 46,000 from the Gaza Strip—and the actual number was probably greater, perhaps as high as 120,000.[31] The official figure alone translated into a full 40 percent of the work force in the territories.

Indications exist that poorer families with many children were able to narrow the economic gap by sending as many as three or four workers to Israel to engage in construction, agriculture, industry, and services for Jewish employers. While their wages were low by Israel standards, in the context of the West Bank and Gaza Strip they were considerable and, when added together, allowed a rise in status and standard of living.

In the 1970s, with the migration of Palestinians to high paying jobs generated by the oil boom in the Persian Gulf, remittances from abroad—an important source of income in the West Bank and Gaza Strip since the 1950s—further supplemented wages earned in Israel. At times, the absolute number of people in the labor force on the West Bank actually decreased due to the continuing exodus. Higher skilled laborers served as engineers and teachers in the Gulf and in Jordan, which had its own economic boom in the years after 1967. The influx of capital back to the territories from all these workers probably totalled $100-200 million each year.

Other sources of capital also fueled the economic changes. Trade with Israel for industrial and agricultural goods increased considerably,[32] and there were continuing payments of salaries by the Jordanian government to civil servants on the West Bank. About $150 million came from the Steadfastness Fund, supported by the Arab states,[33] with additional aid from continuing UNRWA expenditures on education and salaries, as well as from the U.S. (about $5 million per year from 1975 to 1985) and private voluntary organizations in the West (about $20 million per year).[34] Finally, the Israelis—mainly after 1977—invested in public works, such as road building and electrification, although these were directed largely towards security and the needs of the expanding Jewish settlements.

One author has observed that "the economy of the Gaza Strip is an excellent example of how certain levels of economic prosperity can be achieved with little, if any, economic development."[35] Much the same could be said for the West Bank. For Fatah and the PLO, this combination held portentous implications; almost all the sources of vitality—the Israeli economy, the oil boom, outside capital flows, even the continuing salaries paid by the Jordanian government to civil servants—lay beyond their control. At the same time, the basis for the growth of Palestinian resentment was widening—the territories becoming mere markets for Israeli produce and suppliers of cheap labor[36]—and this generated sympathy for the PLO and feday. PLO leaders were not oblivious to this paradox. At the tenth session of the Palestine National Council in 1972, they passed resolutions calling for new trade union and welfare organizations that could mobilize the public in the territories under their auspices.

The Foundations for Uprising

The remarkable thing for both Palestinians and Israelis was that, despite all the difficulties the PLO encountered in establishing control and a capacity to mobilize, an uprising finally did materialize in the West Bank and Gaza Strip. It was not the armed rebellion Fatah advocated, but it was a massive act of resistance. It erupted in December, 1987, two decades after Arafat's call to arms, without the direction of the resistance cells he had tried to establish then. In fact, it may have surprised him as much as anyone.

The hopes that the Israeli occupation would be short-lived had proved ever-more fleeting. In October, 1967, a small group of Israelis had formed the Land of Israel movement, asserting the right of the Jewish people and the Israeli state to rule all of what had been the earlier mandated territory of Palestine. The assertion was made more and more stridently, rendering any departure from what had now become the status quo increasingly costly. The terms of the high-decibel political debate centered on the disposition of the territories—questions of defensible borders, the historical (including biblical) rights over the land, the possibilities of trading land for peace, and the settlement of Jews on the newly captured lands—while little was said about the people in them.

Almost precisely a year after the war, the Labor party-led Israeli government tabled the Allon Plan. Named after Yigal Allon, former army general and a minister with several different portfolios in the Labor government, the plan proposed a return of about two-thirds of the West Bank to Jordan, while holding onto a Jewish-settled security strip along the Jordan River. It also would have retained other areas near the old Israeli borders that would attract Jewish settlers. In the first version of the plan, the Gaza Strip was to remain a part of Israel—a preference echoed by Prime Minister Levi Eshkol and Defense Minister Moshe Dayan—although in a later one Allon conceived of Gaza as part of a Jordanian-Palestinian state.[37]

The government never adopted Allon's design, and the plan did not lead to Israel's ceding the Gaza Strip or parts of the West Bank. It did, however, legitimate the settling of Jews within the lines it advocated, adding yet another complicating factor to the difficult relations with the Palestinian Arabs. Behind the settlement, and much of the refusal to return captured territory, was a new social movement—Gush Emunim, or the Bloc of the Faithful, founded after the 1973 war.[38] By 1977, about 11,000 Jews had put down stakes in 84 mostly tiny new communities in the occupied territories, among the most important being Elon Moreh (Sebastia), Ofra, and Maale Adumim. That was the year the Israelis voted the Labor government out of office, in favor of the Likud party's nationalistic coalition, led by Menachem Begin. Under the new government and its successors, about 100,000 Jewish settlers took up residence in the occupied territories by the end of the 1980s. Most of these were concentrated in 15 settlements, largely metropolitan satellites of Tel-Aviv and Jerusalem.

The Palestinians in the West Bank and the Gaza Strip found

themselves facing a two-sided process of change. While their own society was undergoing major transformations, in good part because of a growing symbiotic relationship with the tumultuous Israeli economy, a powerful ethnic group was settling in their midst. The settlers posed an immediate problem through their exclusive and preferential rights: The Israeli government granted them a set of laws different from those of their neighbors—and, in some respects, from those of Jews inside Israel, preferred access to water and land, special security arrangements.[39] The glaring reality of second-class status now confronted the Palestinians not only during sojourns into Israel.

The settlers were also causing longer-term complications. They lobbied with considerable success for the Israeli government to include the West Bank and Gaza Strip, but not their Arab inhabitants, within the state borders, and to redefine Israeli identity to legitimate this inclusion.[40] This implied granting the Palestinians far fewer rights than the Jews or, at best, a separate set of rights altogether, within some context of local Palestinian autonomy. By the 1980s, it interacted, at times, with the ominous notion of "transferring" the Arabs—through economic inducements or deportation, depending on who was proposing the "transfer"—from the territories. While this new threat emanated from marginal political parties, once the Intifada was under way, as much as half the Jewish public subscribed to one or another of its forms.[41]

The political menace to Palestinians, then, was dynamic in nature. It did not stem from military occupation alone, but from the powerful economic forces and incrementally changing legal code that came with it, from the growing Jewish presence (increasingly after 1977 in the most heavily populated parts of the West Bank), from shifting Israeli opinions about the ultimate disposition of the territories and their inhabitants, and from the reordering of Israeli society and its politics.[42] By the early 1980s, occupation-with-a-smile had turned into hardened military rule—a stick far more than a carrot. A clear shift came as early as 1978, with the Likud's appointment of Menahem Milson to the position of administrator of the West Bank. Milson, a Hebrew University professor of Arabic literature, felt Palestinian nationalism had been allowed to grow unhindered long enough. By 1985, the term "iron fist" had entered the Israeli lexicon, introduced by the former prime minister and now defense minister of a national unity government, Labor's Yitzhak Rabin. For both Palestinians and Israelis, the occupation was having a wearing effect, exacerbating the existing proclivity to demonize one another. With pallid international initiatives failing to bring an end to Israeli rule, some Palestinians—including those born under occupation—began to advocate a move beyond steadfastness.

Along with the nature of the occupation, the character of the Palestinians was changing. West Bankers and Gazans had begun to demonstrate their solidarity with Israeli Arabs by marking Land Day. Palestinians adopted a common hymn, "Biladi, Biladi" ("My Country, My Country") from an Egyptian patriotic tune, along with composing or adopting many other songs to articulate a growing sense of common identity and protest their circumstances. A literature of resistance appeared and quickly expanded. In 1982, the military government banned the distribution of approximately one thousand books, including fiction, nonfiction, and poetry[43]—a doubtful gesture, since the items can be bought in East Jerusalem, where the military has no authority. East Jerusalem also became the base of the Palestinian press—a major tool in creating national consciousness—with newspapers distributed semi-illegally in the West Bank and Gaza, Israel, and abroad.[44] The authorities outlawed the display of the black, white, red, and green Palestinian flag, as well, but without noticeable success. In very important ways, the meetings, discussion, and political activity of the 1970s had had a cumulative effect, resulting by the 1980s in a much more tightly woven society.[45]

Probably no structures played a more important role in this regard than the new universities. Fearful of the emergence of an independent center of West Bank life, the Jordanian authorities had stood in the way of the creation of a Palestinian national university in Ramallah in 1970–71. (One of the key figures behind the effort had been Aziz Shehadah, who ran afoul of the PLO as much as he did the Jordanians; another was Sheikh Ali al-Jaabri, the traditional, pro-Jordanian leader of Hebron.) Despite this failure, local colleges did emerge on the West Bank, mostly out of well-established high schools. Besides the three major universities authorized by Dayan, there was the Islamic College of Hebron, Jerusalem University (which included three separate colleges), and Bethlehem University. The motivation for building these colleges was not so much nationalism as necessity, given the difficulty of attending outside universities and the higher incomes of Palestinian Arab families.

Once built, the colleges became centers for interpreting the occupation's common meaning. They also became the cornerstone of a quiet demand for autonomy in other spheres. With almost fourteen thousand students by 1985, their weight was considerable.[46]

In Bir Zeit, the student council put great effort into nationalistic cultural activities, including festivals, exhibits, and "Palestinian weeks." A typical one involved poetry readings, presentations of plays, and song recitals, all with strong nationalistic themes. Shinar reports that "Palestinian flags and posters with the national colors, both banned by the authorities, are usually raised and decorated with slogans such as 'Palestine, fight till the end,' 'Blessed art thou, Palestine, the ancestors' land,' 'With Allah's help we shall come back,' 'We shall return in battle with the most courageous soldiers, and 'Death to the Jews.'"[47]

University and college students were determined to carry their activities beyond the campus. Those at Bir Zeit sought to provide economic and social services to fellaheen and to the villages. Behind their participation in plowing, harvesting, road-building, and village cleaning lay the cultural theme of sumud. Its new vitality owed much to the Palestine Communist party and its strong indigenous roots. Backed by the party, the students worked to bridge the divide between rural and urban Palestinians and head off Israeli efforts to purchase land from farmers. In 1980, in the face of opposition from Fatah, Jordan, and various elements who feared activities mixing men and women, they established the Supreme Committee for Voluntary Work.[48] The committee included about 40 branches and more than 1,000 volunteers. Its credo was as follows:

> We do not only build a wall or pave a road. We are building a new human being. . . . Our purpose is to turn voluntary work into a work-

shop and a school, both able to provide our Palestinian people with pioneering individuals, bound by national ethics, firmly anchored into the land and highly dedicated to the national cause. . . .[49]

As we have seen in chapter 4, the mandate period had already witnessed the beginning of a trade union movement among Palestinian Arabs, with Communists, Zionists, and others scrambling to organize the emerging working class. Some activity had continued in the Jordanian period, especially by the Jordanian Communist party, but harsh repression had choked these grassroots efforts—in 1961, there were 16 active local trade unions in various economic sectors, compared to approximately 40 four years earlier.

After the 1967 war, union activity increased dramatically, more as a vehicle towards national unity than of class struggle. Growth was most rapid after 1975, especially in the West Bank, although the unions did not incorporate that half of the work force commuting daily to Israel, where they were not recognized. With the larger union rolls, internal battles abounded, particularly between the Communists and Fatah.[50] At stake was not only who would have his hand on the levers of power in society but also the distribution of funds provided by Arab states as a result of the 1979 Baghdad conference.

Like the student-led groups, the unions were part of an intense effort by leftist organizations to mobilize the population. Nationalism was never far from the top of their agenda. In several strikes of the important Jerusalem Union of Hotel, Restaurant, and Coffee Shop Workers—which had over one thousand dues-paying members and probably almost as many nonpaying sympathizers—demands over wages and working conditions comingled with those to expel Israeli union organizers.[51] The trade unions, with their highly democratic settings and generally fair elections—at least until Fatah's effort to control their activities[52]—were models for a common effort transcending family and other ties. They also served as excellent schools for local and regional leadership, most union leaders eventually being detained or deported by the Israelis.

There is some evidence of Palestinian women's activism as far back as 1884, protesting the establishment of the first Jewish settlements.[53] During the mandate, small groups of women, mainly from the ayan and prosperous Christian merchant families, took advantage of their relative freedom to participate in the national struggle: About 200 women participated in the Palestine Congress of October, 1929, then marching through the streets of Jerusalem chanting anti-British slogans.[54] But these efforts were very limited. It was only from the mid-1960s that broad-based women's associations became critical components in the building of a new civil society. In the West Bank—as in Israeli Palestinian society—they provided a wide array of social services for community centers, orphanages, homes for the elderly, and families facing the imprisonment of sons and husbands. The most important of these associations, Inash al-Usra (which roughly translates as "family support network"), was actually created in 1965, before Israeli occupation began. Its founder, Samiha Khalil (popularly known as Umm, mother of, Khalil), came from a middle class refugee family. She and her colleagues built branches all through the West Bank, offering women diverse training projects and employed them in a variety of ways, mainly producing traditional wares and textiles.[55] More explicitly political organizations, such as the Palestinian Women's Association and the General Union of Palestinian Women, also began to take hold on the West Bank.

Student groups, labor unions, and women's associations constituted only a small portion of the institutional network that existed at the outbreak of the Intifada in 1987. Sports clubs, a sophisticated and politicized central theater, other amateur acting groups, charities, branches of the Red Crescent Society, the Palestinian Physicians', Pharmacists' and Lawyers' Association, other professional organizations, all thrived—especially when compared to the period of Jordanian rule—helping make life under prolonged occupation viable.[56]

Occupation had also made it more likely that such voices would be heard, and that enough cohesion existed for a collective response to be effective. The occupation had substantially weakened what ordinarily would have been the most prominent and influential social class—that of the landowners and merchants.[57] While certainly not eclipsing all the differences between rich and poor, the new institutional activities, led by the university and high school graduates and

aided by the general antipathy to Israeli occupation, served as meeting grounds for diverse groups of Palestinians. The occupation thus
resulted in the first steps toward a political levelling of the society
and in bases for association across formerly unbroachable sexual
and class lines[58]—key elements in the spontaneous outbreak of the
Intifada. Equally important was the deteriorating standard of economic life in the territories during the 1980s, a major factor in the
semblance of normality during the occupation's first fifteen years
having been the burgeoning economy. As in the first half of the
1940s, fast-paced economic growth had served as a damper on collective resistance.

Three sources of prosperity had fueled this economy—Israel itself,
with its developed, labor-intensive market; Jordan, with its strong
agricultural build-up; and the Persian Gulf states, with their seemingly endless supply of petro-dollars. By the early 1980s, each had
entered a prolonged crisis, in turn choking the West Bank and Gaza.
A sense of economic hopelessness now combined with flagging
hopes that international diplomacy, the PLO, or outside Arab armies would bring an end to the occupation. (Internationally, the period had witnessed the dissolution of the alliance between Hussein
and Arafat, the disappointing Arab summit in Amman, and the
Reagan-Gorbachev meeting, all of which indicated lack of momentum towards a diplomatic solution.) A much more educated, mobile, and nonagricultural population found a world of shrinking
economic opportunities.

The contrast between the pre- and post-1980 economy in the West
Bank and the Gaza Strip is dramatic. With overall economic growth
in the period from 1967 to 1980 averaging over 5 percent annually,
the territories had witnessed an easing of the harsh material conditions the Palestinians had endured under Jordanian and Egyptian
rule. Gazans, in particular, had entered the era of occupation with
annual per capita incomes averaging $80.[59] By the beginning of the
Intifada, that figure had reached $1,700. Even in the West Bank,
which had been part of Jordan's rapidly growing economy—over 8
percent annual economic growth between 1954 and 1967—personal
consumption was far greater than at the beginning of Israeli rule,

the gross domestic product more than tripling between 1968 and 1980: an extraordinarily high rate of growth by world standards.[60] Even if those economies demonstrated little self-generating potential, they at least had made life materially palatable for most of the population.

During the late 1970s, worrisome economic signs were on the horizon. The Israeli economy, which had been a textbook case of rapid growth until the 1973 war, slipped into a long period of slow growth and stagnation.[61] Inflation, always something of a problem, became hyperinflation, with annual rates reaching 1,000 percent. In many areas of the world, inflation has been a precipitant for social unrest; its corrosive effects on wages and savings combined with the uncertainty that it fosters has often served as a mobilizing force among workers. For Palestinians, now deeply integrated into the Israeli economy, stagflation had dire consequences. By 1980, it was evident that real wages for those working in Israel were eroding, and by 1985 the slippage was quite pronounced. Workers from one West Bank village reported that their real wages were cut in half by inflation in the five-year period before 1985.[62] The resulting economic discontent, combined with the occupation, formed the basis for easy nationalist fervor.

Unemployment, first evident in Israel in the late 1970s, began to hit the territories seriously in the early 1980s. Rates of unemployment in the West Bank more than quadrupled between 1980 and 1985 to over 5 percent, hitting the young and the educated particularly hard. In the latter part of the decade, the influx of Soviet Jews exacerbated the problem of unemployment, reaching double-digit figures in Israel. The immigration had both an indirect effect on Palestinians by straining the already fragile economy they depended upon and, later, a direct impact as Soviets filled the menial jobs Arabs had formerly held. In the early 1990s, overqualified Palestinians—the products of the expanding educational system—and overqualified Soviet Jews eyed the same low-level jobs.

Just as immigration levels were rising, Israel found itself with a rapidly declining rate of new job creation, to less than 1.5 percent by 1980. The country had moved from a labor-hungry economy at the start of the occupation to one in which the work force could not be absorbed. As the politically and economically weakest part of that work force, Palestinians found the change particularly ominous.

Complicating the situation in Israel was that in outside economies. Through the 1970s, Palestinians had left the West Bank and Gaza in large numbers for opportunities elsewhere. The net outflow was as high as twenty thousand people a year—even with all the emphasis on the survivor's sumud.[63] For both migrants and family members depending on their remittances, the performance of other Middle Eastern economies was crucial.

Jordan had served both as a transit point and end point for those leaving the West Bank. For the overall period 1965–86, its economy had rapidly expanded. But high average rates of economic growth can mask sharp vacillations.[64] In the few years after the 1967 war and the loss of the West Bank, Jordan's national product had declined by one-third to two-fifths. By the time Israel assumed control of the West Bank in 1967, as many as 400,000 Palestinians had migrated in search of a better life. In the 1970s, Jordan rebounded, achieving the stupendous growth rate of 10 percent in the five years following 1977. It benefited from the good fortune of the oil states—whose petrodollars meant aid, financial investments, and remittances—and from the ill fortune of Lebanon, which lost its key financial role among the Arab states to Amman during its long civil war.

But during the 1980s, the country's absorptive capacity dried up in the wake of the larger Middle Eastern economic crisis. Remittances slipped steadily through the decade, leading to large declines in per capita income.[65] The Gulf War of 1991 simply capped an already eroding position, aid from the oil states ending and the economy contracting severely, due to Jordan's support of Saddam Hussein. Clearly, Jordan was no longer an attractive stop for West Bank workers.

The oil-producing states were also facing severe contraction. World fears of an international oil shortage at the outbreak of the Iran-Iraq war in 1980 had driven prices to unprecedented heights: A standard barrel had reached $40, compared to a figure less than one-third of that after the first series of oil price hikes following the

Arab-Israeli war of 1973. But this boom was not to last long—over-pumping in the face of such attractive rates and slackening demand due to both high cost and world recession led to a precipitous decline in prices. By the late 1980s, with a barrel selling for around $15, the real price had fallen to less than half of what it had been at the end of 1973, and less than one-third what it had been in 1980. The slump cut deeply into Palestinian economic life. Jobs disappeared, making emigration much less attractive. Remittances from workers in the Gulf countries diminished drastically.

Palestinian Arabs in the West Bank and Gaza were thrown back on the local economy and that of Israel at precisely the wrong time. Perhaps a third of those working in Israel still cultivated land and could gain some income from farming: Happily, the failure of capitalist, mechanized farming in the mountainous villages of the West Bank meant that those who could hold onto postage-stamp-sized plots had a fallback when all else failed, also serving as a source of income to share tenants who worked the land.[66] But many workers were rural dwellers without access to land; still others lived in the towns or refugee camps. The Israeli policy of carrots and economic opportunities—something for Palestinians to contemplate losing when the thought of resistance crossed their minds—meant little to a generation raised and educated under stiffening occupation, many of whose members were now unemployed and with little economic hope for the future.[67]

The bleakness of national prospects thus combined with despair over individual and family prospects. Added to this dismal brew were the personal experiences of routine harassment, occasional beatings, arrests without formal charges, and humiliating searches by security forces at roadblocks and checkpoints. Young Palestinians increasingly felt there was little to lose if they broke the rules of the game.

Intifada

On December 8, 1987, an Israeli truck hit two vans carrying Gaza laborers in Jabalya, a refugee camp packed with sixty thousand residents. The crash instantly killed four of them. Rumor—an essential ingredient in the prelude to any ethnic violence—spread quickly that the wreck was no accident, but an act of vengeance on the part of the relative of an Israeli stabbed to death several days earlier in the Gaza market. A denunciatory Palestinian leaflet—one of the uprising's major motifs—appeared in the evening.

At the funeral that same evening, thousands of mourners turned on the nearby Israeli army post, assaulting it with a barrage of stones. By the morning, the streets and alleys of the camp were filled with quickly fashioned barricades, and full-scale violence broke out, inaugurating the uprising.

Acts of violence against the occupying forces were certainly not unheard of in the territories: Between 1968 and 1975, the Israeli military counted an average of about 350 incidents a year; from 1976 to 1982, the number doubled. After that, it jumped precipitously to 3,000, which itself dramatically paled next to the outbreaks starting in December. Over the next six months, there were 42,355 recorded incidents.[68] For the first time since the occupation began, the Israeli forces lost control of the population in the occupied territories. On the uprising's first day, rioting spread to other camps in the Gaza Strip, and the next day it fanned across those in the West Bank as well. During the rest of December, the confrontations occurred largely in the camps—the sites of the most extreme misery as well as the centers of nationalism over the previous decades. Between mid-January and mid-February, villages and towns also became actively involved in the resistance.[69]

Just as important as the spontaneous extension of the rioting was the Palestinian perception of its meaning: not as expressing individual grievances, but those of all the individuals and localities together. The events soon acquired a name, *Intifada* ("shaking off"), which was consciously compared to the 1936–39 revolt.[70] The mythic qualities of the survivor now stood alongside a new cultural form— direct and sometimes violent resistance. For the third time in the last two centuries, the Arabs of Palestine had risen up in revolt.

Its fighters were not professional guerrillas, but children of the stone, faces shrouded by kafiyas or masks, standing ready to confront Israeli soldiers openly and head-on. In the popular image, they stood without feelings of inferiority—the soldier with his modern weapons, the shabab armed only with stones. Here is one among countless poems glorifying the new hero—and making the important jump from the child to the shahid, or martyr:

> Have you seen his mark in the streets
> In my bloodstream rave winds
> Flames spurt from my fingers . . .
>
> He dawned
> On people's horizon
> He woke us
> He joined us
> He bonded us all . . .
>
> Lo the moon has now risen
> He lived and was roaring
> He died and was roaring:
> Hail the stone!
> Hail the stone!
> Hail the stone![71]

Martyrdom became the means to make legendary the acts of children of the stone. The family of a martyr was accorded special honor, and posters of him were carried at demonstrations and appeared on walls. The omnipresent leaflets and folk songs acclaimed his heroic acts. Penny Johnson notes that "in the intifada, the rebellious young men, the shabab, have become the sons of all the people and their exploits legendary."[72]

The PLO financially supported the martyr's family, although canonization as a shahid occasionally led to a process of bargaining about the precise amount of support. While the popular imagination was fixed on individual, youthful heroism—indeed, often the stone throwing consisted of such spontaneous acts, and often by groups of shabab—existing organizations, such as Shabiba, and numerous new youth groups, stood behind the uprising's more institutionalized "strike forces." Within a short time, the image of the child of the stone became so powerful that Israeli soldiers were instructed to direct their fire at the "chief instigators"—those with the shrouded faces.

If the shock troops of the Intifada were represented by a young masked face, the new local leadership was represented by the anonymous leaflet, itself a way "to shroud [its] true face."[73] Territory-wide leaflets appeared by the end of December, and by January they carried the signature of the Unified National Leadership of the Uprising in the Occupied Territories, later accompanied by the signature of the PLO.[74] The Leadership consisted, at least in the first half year or so, of the second-rank representatives of the various outside guerrilla organizations—Fatah, the Popular Front for the Liberation of Palestine, and the Democratic Front for the Liberation of Palestine plus the Palestine Communist party. This mirrored the heavier influence of leftist groups inside the territories compared to outside, where Fatah's dominance was much more pronounced. (In fact, leftists claimed that the outside should be organized along the same lines.) Not naming top figures made it more difficult for the Israelis, but also for the uprising's leaders, to develop the autonomy that the Fatah-dominated PLO feared. The Leadership drew up the leaflets in the territories, based on local circumstances, and then sent them outside for modification and approval by the PLO, which broadcast them over Baghdad Radio.[75] Local shabab then distributed them in the West Bank and the Strip.

Besides containing eulogies of the shahid, the leaflets set out specific directives for the strike forces, the popular committees that had formed to implement the plans, and the general population. A primary goal articulated in the leaflets was to break the dependency of the territories on Israel, as a prelude to the establishment of a Palestinian state.[76] They called for a shunning of the Israeli civil administration, a boycott of Israeli products, a mass resignation of Palestinian police officers and tax collectors, a refusal to pay taxes, a search for alternatives to work in Israel (especially in agricultural enterprises), attacks on Jewish settlers and an end to work in the settlements, a closing of shops for part of each day, and an attempt to create alternative Palestinian institutions in industry, agriculture, education, and the like.

The results were decidedly mixed. Police officers and tax collectors did indeed resign, much to the consternation of the Israelis, who futilely used a variety of means to try to reverse the mass walkout. At great economic cost, shopkeepers heeded the call for a partial commercial strike, shuttering their stores each afternoon. But the boycott of Israeli products only partially succeeded (it did provide a boom for local workshops, benefiting from an increased demand for their own products).[77] And except for announced general strikes, which were quite effective, a substantial proportion of laborers continued to cross into Israel to work, albeit in reduced numbers; many others continued to work for the settlements.

This mirrored the mixed success of the Intifada as a whole. Its triumph in a number of areas was unprecedented. Images of the shahid electrified the population, leading to new, sustained levels of mobilization and revolutionary fervor. The poet Mahmoud Darwish captured the mood in words addressed to Israelis:

> We have that which does not please you: we have the future
> And we have things to do in our land.

Another partisan declared that "An air of popular democracy has pervaded the atmosphere."[78]

Self-reliance grew, as well. When the Israelis closed schools for prolonged periods, many Palestinians set up their own clandestine classrooms. Economically, they became increasingly self-sufficient in a number of fields, such as dairy farming—by buying cows from Israelis, they managed to satisfy 80 percent of their dairy needs—and animal husbandry. At the same time, the uprising bloodied the already faltering Israeli economy. The Bank of Israel reported that after two years of rebellion the direct cost to Israel had been 1.4 percent of its national wealth, or over $1 billion, and the indirect costs even higher.[79]

But after four years of sometimes bloody battles, the Palestinians had not managed to bring an end to the occupation or create national independence. This failure, notes one researcher, led to the redefinition of their goals, now "generally defined as the reestablishment of the Palestinian political agenda internationally, and the reaffirmation of Palestinian identity."[80] It is not surprising that after the first six months the uprising lost some of its spontaneity and autonomy. The original Unified Leadership was decimated: 69 leaders sent into exile by mid-1991, well over 600 shooting deaths,[81] and 40,000 arrests through May 1990. And the Arafat-led PLO exercised firmer control over those who replaced them.

Local leaders also found that they had to temper some of their demands on the population. Later leaflets modulated the stigma on working in Israel, imposing a ban, instead, on certain days or on specific sectors that competed with the Palestinian economy. The boycott on Israeli products was modified so that it applied to products for which a local substitute was available.[82]

Large-scale violence by a nearly permanently mobilized population gave way to small groups of resisters or even individuals who used hit-and-run tactics and sabotage—including arson in Israeli forests, torching of cars, and knifing and kidnapping of Israelis, especially soldiers and settlers in the occupied territories. By the 1990s, the Israelis were content to station their military forces safely outside most refugee camps and other communities, allowing an unanticipated degree of community autonomy. The new deployment also reduced the opportunities for head-on confrontations between mobilized groups of Palestinians and Israeli soldiers.

A sense of hopelessness had pervaded the territories in November, 1987—a feeling that all the diplomatic jet-setting by PLO Executive members and Arab statesmen would not bring an end to occupation. The Arab summit meeting that month had placed the Iran-Iraq war, not the Palestinians, at the top of the Arab agenda. That message, in fact, helped spark the uprising, as a self-reliant way of emerging from a political cul-de-sac.[83]

After more than two years of frenzied rioting and backbreaking hardship, renewed despair about the uprising's limited potential now led the Palestinians to look outside again for some way to end the occupation. By spring of 1988, the Unified Leadership's leaflets were openly calling for outside diplomatic support. Later, Palestinian support of Saddam Hussein in the Gulf War reflected a desperate hope of thus achieving what the Intifada clearly could not. After

Iraq's ignominious defeat, Roy wrote of those in the Gaza Strip, "Palestinians feel totally abandoned, increasingly helpless, and very fearful. They are harassed by the army on a daily basis and have no institutional recourse or form of appeal. Daily life is impossibly oppressive and people genuinely despair of protection."[84] And in fact, in a widely quoted statement, Defense Minister Rabin defined the measures needed to maintain security as "might, force, and beatings" and "breaking their bones." In the third year, some easing occurred, as the Israeli forces gave up on efforts to impose order on every square meter of the territories, focusing instead on central strategic areas.

Outside economic opportunities for the Palestinian Arabs had almost entirely disappeared, the support for Saddam Hussein by both the PLO and the rank-and-file having made them unwelcome in many parts of the Middle East. The once prosperous community of nearly four-hundred thousand Palestinians in Kuwait was shattered upon the Iraqi defeat—and the return of the Kuwaiti government. In late 1991, less than half of the community remained. In Jordan, the economy had suffered a dramatic slide, affecting both Palestinians there and those on the West Bank whose salaries were in Jordanian dinars: The value of the dinar in January, 1989, was less than half of what it had been only six months before. Once the Gulf crisis began in August, 1990, the decline intensified.

In the occupied territories themselves, the dismal economic performance in the period leading up to the uprising turned drastically worse: Communities were reporting unemployment rates of 30 to 40 percent. Conditions deteriorated further with the UN coalition's bombing of Iraq and the Iraqi Scud missile attacks on Israel starting in January, 1991. The standstill of the Israeli economy and the Palestinians' exclusion from it once the war ended were combined with the cut-off of Arab aid to the PLO, some of which had been funnelled to the territories. With a drastic cut in their cash flow, retailers in the territories complained of a falloff in business of almost 80 percent.

Although accurate figures are hard to come by, some collected for Gaza indicate, at the very least, the magnitude of the problem. In the first three years of the Intifada, Palestinians in Gaza saw a 30 percent decline in their gross national product; a drop in per capita income from $1,700 to $1,200, with some families losing as much as three-quarters of their income; a 75 percent decline in remittances from outside; and a sharp drop in income from work in Israel. Once the Gulf War began, work in Israel stopped altogether and after the war did not even come close to the depressed prewar level. Soviet immigrants, who themselves were desperate over the lack of economic opportunities, now stepped into the open jobs. In the month after the end of the war, ten thousand West Bank and Gazan Palestinians worked in Israel—less than 10 percent of the pre-Intifada numbers. Large increases in child labor, requests for UNRWA supplementary feeding programs (up 200 percent), and sharp rises in the numbers requiring emergency food aid are a few indicators of the desperate economic straits in Gaza.[85]

Some early, sketchy figures for the West Bank indicate similarly dire conditions. Four months after the start of the Intifada, West Bank gross domestic product had declined by 29 percent, individual consumption by 28 percent, and employment by 36 percent.[86] The $200 million share of both Gazan and West Bank subcontractors in Israel's construction industry evaporated. Exports to Israel dropped by 50 percent in the first year of the uprising, and then continued to decline.

Despite all these difficulties, the Intifada still stands as the preeminent event in the Palestinians' recent history, galvanizing a sense of community and nationhood; it has fostered what Laurie Brand has termed their reempowerment.[87] But, like its predecessor, the Arab Revolt of 1936–39, it has exposed rifts corresponding to this greatly heightened sense of unified purpose.[88] Any communal uprising brings conflicts over what the new society will be into much starker relief—who will lead it, what the relationship of leaders to followers will be, which beliefs and symbols will prevail. This occurs despite efforts to paper over tensions and project an air of unity.

With hindsight, we can see how the 1936 revolt allowed a surfacing of important questions about the Palestinians' future. Conflicts between merchants and shabab, coastal city dwellers and inland villagers, Christians and Muslims, all revolved around that future. The closeness of the Intifada makes us somewhat myopic on this score, but we can still form an idea of the important questions regarding Palestinian leadership and the role of religion in the definition of their society. The fact that nearly half as many Palestinians in the occupied territories have been charged and killed as collaborators by other Palestinians as have died at the hands of the Israeli military hints at some very strong clashing currents beneath a unified oppositional front.

The 1987 outbreak of sustained revolt by a mobilized population took the established national leadership by surprise just as had that of the Mufti and his colleagues at the general strikes rocking Palestine in April, 1936. Like Amin al-Husseini, Yasser Arafat was quick to associate himself with the new revolt, speaking on the second day of "the children of the stones in our beloved, holy country" as the contemporary achievements of the Fatah–PLO revolution—a connection that proved very important for the PLO's effort to reestablish its international position after the Lebanese fiasco.

Even with the association between the PLO and the Intifada, some strain between the organization's top echelons and the Unified Leadership seems to have emerged during the first half year or so. There is considerable disagreement about the level of overt conflict afterward. Some argue there was complete harmony between the outside and inside leadership—that the Unified Leadership simply "sees itself as the local political and activist arm of the PLO."[89] Others see a continuation of the battle for local autonomy at work between them.[90]

But open conflict is less the issue than the more subtle tensions determining the place of the local leadership in the overall national movement. In the period leading up to the uprising, Gazan and West Bank leaders had been afforded short shrift by the PLO leadership. The Intifada now enabled residents in the territories to influence the PLO's political positions more strongly and directly, to play a major role in determining the national political agenda, and to transform the accepted national tactics. In particular, the local leadership pushed the PLO towards acceptance of Israel, a two-state solution to the conflict, and participation in U.S.-sponsored peace talks with Israel despite the formal exclusion of the PLO.[91] In fact, according to a Helena Cobban interview with Arafat, it pushed the PLO Executive to abandon armed struggle within the context of the Intifada.[92] Communications from West Bank and Gaza leaders, notes Cobban, "could no longer be downgraded by the PLO leaders as had sometimes been the case before December 1987."[93] Teitelbaum and Kostiner echo this point: "Not only had the Palestinian movement become a mass movement, but its political center of gravity had shifted."[94]

The relatively smooth process by which the PLO incorporated the Unified Leadership into a more prominent national role was attributable, in part, to a single individual. He was Arafat's aide Abu Jihad, the editor of *Filastinuna*, who also served as the PLO's overall coordinator in the occupied territories, and who worked endlessly to avoid open rifts with the young leaders there. It is simply too soon, at the time of this writing, to assess whether his assassination in April, 1988, in Tunis—almost certainly by the Israelis—may have led to a long-term erosion of that link.

For Arafat's PLO, the ability to gain the public deference of the Unified Leadership and to have other Arabs identify the organization with the dramatic and popular Intifada was critical. It enhanced the PLO's own position in face of others still trying to shape the future of the Palestinians—King Hussein of Jordan and President Hafiz al-Asad of Syria, in particular. Abandoning his long struggle with the PLO for influence on the West Bank, the Jordanian king formally disclaimed his sovereignty on July 31, 1988. (This was something of a shock. Even after the 1976 municipal elections in the West Bank resulted in the rise of pro-PLO officials, the Jordanians had continued to press their influence.)[95] This step allowed the final triumph of an educated, internal leadership with few attachments to the Hashemites. (It should be added that King Hussein did not shut the door altogether—West Bankers, for instance, still held Jordanian citizenship and passports.)

At the same time, the dogged Syrian opposition to Arafat began to lessen, although no reconciliation took place until 1991. With such pressure behind it, the PLO recognized Israel's right to exist, renounced terrorism, initiated diplomatic contacts with the United States, and had the Palestine National Council declare the creation of a Palestinian state at its November, 1988, meeting in Algiers. Unfortunately for the PLO, it could not sustain its new international position. After its refusal to condemn a terrorist attack, the U.S. broke off the contacts; later, its ties to Saddam Hussein eroded much of the goodwill it had accumulated. But it still served notice that, by deftly incorporating the Unified Leadership, it had gained power in the struggle to control Palestinian society. The remaining question was whether Palestinians from the West Bank and Gaza Strip—the so-called inside leadership—could wrest meaningful influence and control from the Tunis-based, outside leadership. Once again Nablus, now termed "the city of martyrs" in the Arab press for its sacrifices during the Intifada, faced off against a contending center of power—but in this instance the contender lay far from the shores of Palestine.

No struggle for the future of Palestinian society became more clear in the course of the Intifada than that over the future role of Islam. Even the most secular and national figures appropriated cultural symbols that had strong Islamic resonances. But the conflict went deeper than such appropriation. Just as in the 1936–39 revolt, the uncertainty associated with rebellion thrust the question of religion back into popular concerns. In the 1930s, the Mufti had used his religious office and the institution of the Supreme Muslim Council as a springboard for national leadership. Sheikh Qassam had employed his position as a Haifa preacher to touch off the general strike and the peasant uprising. And the Arab Revolt itself had revealed intense anti-Christian sentiments by some of those agitating against the British and Jews. The last two decades of the twentieth century have been a period in which Islam has played a much more overt role in Middle East politics, from Algeria to Iran. While to some of the educated, urban population of the 1930s it may have appeared a living anachronism, by the time of the Intifada it had emerged as a self-assured and active alternative to European-style nationalism. In the Gaza Strip, especially, Islamic organizations challenged the entire worldview of the various elements comprising the PLO and the Unified Leadership.

The major Islamic group, Hamas (or the Islamic Resistance Movement, which was the Palestinian branch of the Muslim Brethren), and a smaller faction, Islamic Jihad, aimed to establish an Islamic state in Palestine and, perhaps later, throughout the Arab Middle East. They rejected the nationalists' aim of a secular, religiously pluralistic state.[96] Their target was not so much individual Christians or Druze, as in the 1930s, but the very foundation of the inclusive nationalist conception of who the Palestinians are. The sorts of bridges between nationalist and religious activism that had dominated the 1930s, including the view of the Mufti himself, were now much less in evidence. Hamas thus posed not just an ideological challenge but—like the Communist party and other indigenous groups—an internal social challenge to the movement based in Tunis and Baghdad.

As in the rest of the Middle East, the prime mover of the Islamic revival in the occupied territories was the Iranian Revolution of 1978. But even that event came in the midst of a dramatic rise in prayer attendance and the building of mosques, especially in the Gaza Strip. By the 1980s, there was clear evidence of Islamic entry into the Palestinian political realm. In 1979, student elections at Bir Zeit University—the most important and the most secular of the Palestinian universities—had led to important victories for avowedly Islamic candidates. They came away with 43 percent of the vote, and in subsequent years regularly garnered 30–35 percent in universities throughout the West Bank. This success was the result of determined, grassroots organizing, stressing the importance of individual and moral change.

Standing behind Hamas was the imposing figure of Sheikh Ahmad Ismail Yasin of Gaza. The military court had sentenced him to thirteen years in prison in 1984, after Israeli authorities had discovered sixty rifles in his home, but he won early release as part of a larger prisoner exchange. His influence was evident in Islam's growing activism in the Gaza Strip—in his success at gaining control of the Islamic University and ridding it of pro-PLO forces. Once the uprising began, Sheikh Yasin moved to forestall a complete PLO appropriation of the Intifada. He broadened his base in the West Bank and, breaking with his long-time practice, began to allow his movement's use of some nationalist symbols and language.

The desire of both Yasin and Arafat to keep the fires of the uprising burning, and to direct Palestinian fury against the Israelis, not each other, helped minimize the number of open clashes between their followers. Both the Islamic and nationalist forces encouraged resistance to the Israelis, with the Muslims usually calling for more violent action and the Unified Leadership shunning arms and direct violence. But sniping between them still occurred. Differences had already been evident after the founding of the precursor to Hamas in the Gaza Strip in the mid-1980s. Yasin's group—deeply influenced by the Egyptian Muslim Brethren—undertook both verbal and physical assaults on the PLO and its allies, particularly on the pro-PLO Red Crescent Society.

During the course of the Intifada, Hamas began to disregard directives set out in the Unified Leadership's leaflets, issuing its own instructions to the population. The two sets of leaflets called for different strike days, offered different instructions, and used different language. Nearly a year into the Intifada, Hamas issued a convenant that implicitly challenged the near-sacrosanct National Covenant adopted by the PLO in 1968. It emphasized that the land of Palestine is an Islamic trust (or waqf), to be guarded by Muslims until Judgment Day.[97]

Like their Jewish fundamentalist counterparts, Hamas activists stressed the holiness of the land itself and the consequent impossibility of considering any trades of land for peace. It was this notion that made Hamas so critical of the PLO's diplomacy in 1988, and its sanctioning in 1991 of the peace talks starting in Madrid: "Such conferences are nothing but a form of judgement passed by infidels on the land of the Muslims."[98]

Given the twin tragedies of 1948 and 1967, both the PLO and the Unified Leadership saw this sort of rhetoric as threatening the reconstruction of the nation, and they began to respond in kind. In one leaflet they demanded that fundamentalist elements cease playing on factional interests, "displaying negative stands and manifestations. For, they are serving the enemy, whether they wish it or not."[99] Hamas insisted on continuing unity, dismissing the leaflet as an Israeli forgery. Whether it was one, the growing divergence was becoming a worrisome factor for the national forces—as was the deepening Islamic orientation of lower-level PLO members themselves.[100] The Israelis, who at first thought they might employ the Islamic groups as a tool to weaken the PLO and undermine the uprising, had also begun to grasp the implications of their success. They moved against the Islamic leadership in 1989, eventually arresting Sheikh Yasin.

The conflicts among Palestinians about the shape and character of their society are far from over. As indicated, in the context of the ongoing struggle with Israel, there were strong pressures to downplay them.[101] But when tactics and strategy are matters of life and death, it is difficult to keep differences under wraps. It is thus not surprising that the Intifada sparked both debate about and changes in the role of women in society. Women seemed pulled in two directions: Especially in the West Bank, many participated publicly in the rebellion,[102] some believing it would be the road to their own liberation.[103] At the same time, within a year of its outbreak, all but a few determinedly leftist women had donned the hijab (headscarf) in the Gaza Strip, at least in part because of pressure from the militant Islamic organizations. Early in that campaign, the male leadership of the nationalist groups offered little support for those not wanting to do so.[104]

Given previous experience of Palestinian Arab women activists in Lebanon, the disregard for women was not so surprising. While taking a stand for more equality, in the end, the organization had "declined to be an arena for a radical restructuring of the gender order"; its first priority was in building national unity, not in dealing with the specifics of women's circumstances.[105]

In leaflet 43, the Unified Leadership finally took a firm stand against harassment of women, and the split in this respect at least was now open. A few years before the Intifada, Rosemary Sayigh addressed a predicament that became acute in its course: "With Palestinians increasingly polarized between progressive [nationalist] and reactionary [religious] currents, women are likely to pay a heavy price for over-visibility."[106] Novelist Sahar Khalifa would echo this theme. Because she wrote on the plight of women, her critics were "astounded and shocked. They feel that I exaggerate, that I focus on peripheral matters and not on what is germinal. In their opinion what is most important is to write about our conflict with Israel, with imperialism, with the Arab world." Her goal was to show "how our society stifles women, puts them in cages, blocks up their vast reserves of energy." But critics claimed that she "was imitating American feminist views by ignoring the real solution for women which is to be found within the framework of the national struggle. . . ."[107]

Social upheaval can catalyze and confirm changes incipient for years or decades. The Intifada validated the replacement of the old landed elite with a new leadership bred in the schools and universities of the West Bank and Gaza. When the rioting broke out, Israeli civil administrators turned to the village mukhtars and the old notable leadership,[108] who, to the astonishment of the Israelis—and perhaps the old leaders themselves—could do little to stem the tide of resistance. It had become uncertain precisely where authority within Palestinian society lay.

The question had been complicated over the years by the Israeli, Jordanian, and PLO discouragement of any visible, independent new leadership. Those personalities who did emerge in the occupied territories to offer political or social initiatives, including the elected mayors, faced arrest, deportation, detention, assassination. Nonetheless, university teachers, journalists, and other professionals gained enough respectability and political support to be seen as "inside" representatives of the West Bank and Gaza. In the early 1990s, their claim was reinforced by the international discrediting of the "outside" PLO leadership for siding with Saddam Hussein, by the insiders' active role at the Palestine National Council meeting in Algiers in 1991, and—most importantly—by their role as the Palestinian delegation to the new peace talks. Among the most prominent of these figures is Faysal al-Husseini, the son of the canonized shahid, Abd al-Qadir al-Husseini, who led Palestinian fighting forces in the Arab Revolt and the 1948 war. (He is also the grandson of Musa, the first leader of the national movement in the 1920s and early 1930s, and nephew of Jamal.) Probably the most public figure has been Hanan Ashrawi, a Christian Palestinian and professor of English literature at Bir Zeit University, who has articulated the Palestinian case in an international arena better than ever before. Another Bir Zeit professor, Sari Nusayba, also comes from a prominent Palestinian family—his father was Jordan's minister of defense and director of the most prestigious "national" Palestinian economic institution, the Eastern Jerusalem Electric Company.

The ultimate influence of these and other insiders[109] or of younger less visible members of the Unified Leadership is still unclear; what is quite apparent is that social changes would no longer be dictated by a Palestinian leadership from on high—and certainly not by a leadership based in Amman or Damascus. Nor should the conflicts among Palestinian groups be understood as simple leadership struggles, although they certainly constitute an important element of the larger conflicts. The symbols and practices evolving among the entire population of the West Bank and Gaza Strip from 1948 to 1967, and then again after the onset of Israeli rule, created the possibility of Palestinian action. Whether they now offer the hope for an end to occupation, for national independence, and for reconciliation with Jews and Israel, is too soon to tell.

Part Four

ABORTIVE RECONCILIATION

10

THE OSLO PROCESS:

WHAT WENT RIGHT?

They closed up the campaign
And won their victory
Crossed over us from end to end
Forgave
The victim for his errors when he apologized
For things that will come across his mind,
They switched the bell of time
And won victory.

MAHMUD DARWISH (From "A Nonlinguistic
Quarrel, with Umar al-Quais")

IN THE HALF CENTURY since World War II, three series of events, all involving the Israelis, have stood above all else in the making of the Palestinian people. They are the catastrophe of 1948, with its loss of possible autonomy and the creation of the refugees; Israeli occupation of the West Bank and Gaza Strip since 1967; and the Oslo peace process, with the soaring hopes it generated for undoing that occupation and winning autonomy, at long last, and, then, the deep despair it engendered less than a decade after it began. The effects of the last of these, the Oslo process, on the Palestinian nation are just now becoming evident. From the beginning of 1993, when a handful of Israeli and Palestinian negotiators assembled in Norway, to early 2001, when the two headstrong leaders of Israel and the Palestinians, Ehud Barak and Yasser Arafat, aborted their last-ditch efforts to reach a final-status agreement, Palestinian society underwent momentous changes.

Oslo began with bright optimism on both sides for conciliation—65–75 percent of West Bank/Gaza Palestinians and Israeli Jews expressed support for the initial accord—and ended in dejection, recriminations, and violence. The hopelessness that followed the breakdown of the talks at Camp David in July 2000, where American President Bill Clinton had assembled Barak and Arafat and their high-powered teams, and of several subsequent sets of talks in the months after Camp David stemmed from the inability to secure their signatures on the dotted line of a final status agreement. Still, despite the failure to rise over that final hurdle, the unfolding Oslo process had some remarkable achievements. Above all else, it had initiated the first-ever Palestinian self-governance, which, even if somewhat limited, reshaped society and politics in new and unexpected ways. Some of these were quite encouraging and others, very discouraging to those hoping for a vibrant, open society and for coexistence between Palestinians and Israelis in the country.

This chapter and the next investigate what went right and what went wrong in the Oslo process within a broad social, political, and cultural context. To answer the first of those questions, this chapter begins by analyzing the factors that induced Israelis and Palestinians to abandon their almost exclusive means of dealing with one another since the 1920s, armed conflict, in favor of negotiations aimed at ending the standoff. It then elaborates precisely what did go right as the two sides signed their historic agreement and then followed that with seven more years of negotiations. Chapter 11 will then analyze the failure of the process, which brought the two nations full-circle to all-out violence, just as Barak and Arafat engaged in endgame negotiations. Together, this chapter and the next explore the critical changes that occurred in Palestinian society throughout the period of the peace process and into the years of violence, the al-Aqsa Intifada.

The Path to Oslo

A number of prior factors helped ready the sides for official face-to-face contacts. Several dated all the way back to the immediate aftermath of the 1967 war, and others appeared in the 1970s and 1980s, almost two decades before Palestinians and Israelis actually negotiated officially. Changes were brewing back then among both the Palestinians and Israelis. On the Palestinian side, already in 1968, Salah Khalaf (Abu Iyad), the man considered the head ideologue of the progressive stream of Fatah, suggested far-reaching changes in Palestinian goals that implied the need for a dialogue with the Israelis. Instead of simply calling for the creation of a Palestinian state in all of Palestine, he devised the formulation of "a democratic and secular state." His idea was rejected by the Fatah mainstream and the PLO at the time because of its implied equality for Jews and because of sensitivity to its "secular" dimension, which could provoke confrontation with conservative Islamic elements.

By the 1970s, another position taking note of the existence of Israel and the formidable Jewish settlement in the land was expressed by Iz al-Din Klak (the PLO's representative in Paris), Said Khamami,[1] and, most prominently, Dr. Issam Sartawi, one of Fatah's most visible intellectuals and diplomats. The plan became public in 1977, when Sartawi proposed coexistence with Israel on the basis of a peace agreement between a Palestinian state in the occupied territories according to the June 4, 1967, cease-fire lines, known in Israel as the green line. The implicit acceptance of Israel's existence in the plan led to the assassination of all three of these Palestinian leaders by emissaries of radical PLO groups. Posthumous vindication came for them a decade later, on November 15, 1988, when Arafat declared a Palestinian state in precisely this territory, 22 percent of the area that the British had controlled, at the nineteenth session of the Palestine National Council in Algiers. This declaration put aside Palestinians' claims to all of Palestine and, implicitly at least, recognized Israel.

Some of the new thinking about the conflict within the PLO

leadership in the 1970s was echoed at the grassroots level in the West Bank and Gaza Strip. The renewed encounter between Israeli society (both Jews and Arabs) and the Palestinians in the occupied territories after 1967 began to break down many of the stereotypes held of the Jewish state and its society. They appeared to some Palestinians as more varied and multifaceted, as well as less western and imperialist, than what they had imagined from afar from 1948–1967. Some residents of the territories began to see Israel as more than an "artificial and temporary creation," a state, perhaps, with which, under certain conditions, one could come to an accommodation. The illusory and self-defeating image of Israel as an artificial political and social entity on the brink of collapse became much less popular, although some held onto that canard into the twenty-first century.[2]

New approaches to the conflict were aired inside Israel, too, in the 1970s. And then after 1982, the debacle in its war in Lebanon uncovered a deep war-weariness and spawned the development of large social movements pushing for a change in the state's basic strategic vision. Beyond Lebanon, such a change pointed to the possibility of reconciliation with the Palestinians.

These early glimmers of change in each camp were complemented by some tentative contacts between the two sides. A handful of courageous ordinary citizens and politicians, such as Arye (Lova) Eliav and Sartawi, engaged in nonsanctioned negotiations in the 1970s, paving the way for the unthinkable to become thinkable. In addition to these Palestinian-Israeli direct contacts, the peace treaty between Egypt and Israel in 1980 set important parameters for later Palestinian-Israeli engagement. For the Arab world, the treaty brought an end to the general consensus that had held since World War I: the impermanence and immorality of a non-Arab political entity in its midst. In this earlier consensus, the Zionist entity was equated with the Crusader state of 1099–1187, which, by force, had planted an alien presence in *Daar al-Islam,* the world of Islam. But, in 1187, the Glorious Salah al-Din (commonly known as Saladin) al-Ayubi overcame the foreigners in the Battle of Khittin, liberating Jerusalem, and later his successors chased the intruders from the land entirely in the Battle of Ayn Jalut in 1260. The Arab consensus saw the crusader experience as a harbinger of the fate of the temporarily high-flying Zionist settlement and Israeli state.

By no means did a new consensus emerge in the Arab world after Egypt and Israel signed their treaty. Palestinians, in particular, saw the peace as a treacherous stab in the back. Still, the peace accords hammered out in 1978 at what is now known as Camp David I created three key precedents. First, the successful negotiations established the very possibility of conciliation and political agreement between Arabs and Jews—and, specifically, between Arab states and the Jewish one. Ironically, the Egyptian-Israeli agreement confirmed the position against pan-Arabism that Fatah itself had championed after Palestinian disappointment with Nasser's pan-Arabism in the 1967 war. Even though Egyptian leaders presented the treaty as benefiting the Arab world generally, it was widely understood in the Arab world as Egypt's pursuing its own national interests (those of its particular *watan*, or homeland) over those of the larger Arab nation.

Second, the agreement established the practice of exchanging territories for peace as the key to success. More than that, it implicitly promoted the idea of all territories conquered in 1967 in exchange for total peace as the mode for any future agreements. Both sides found it extremely difficult to accept the territories-for-peace formulation. For Israel, diffuse aspirations for peace were intricately woven into its culture. As David Ben-Gurion had put it, Israel "always had an arm outstretched towards peace." It was the Arabs, Jewish Israelis felt, who were the impediments to achieving peace. As Yehoshafat Harkabi, Israel's military and later academic guru on the Arabs, put it in the 1960s, Israel had only unidirectional control over the conflict: It could escalate but not move toward resolution. Now, Israeli society and its leaders had to face all the difficulties of turning a Utopian ideal into concrete reality.[3] They needed to give up actual territory and settlements for an abstract concept, peace. Additionally, they had to face the existential anxiety of Zionism's reversibility after decades of following the principle of incremental accumulation ("another dunum and another goat").[4] For the Egyptians, the practice not only shattered the Arab consensus but also transgressed the concrete resolution of the Arab League adopted in Khartoum in 1968, barring member states from recognition of Israel and negotiations and peace with it—the famous three no's.

The third precedent involved the Palestinians themselves. In a letter accompanying the agreements (dated March 26, 1979), Israel and Egypt agreed to open discussions immediately on founding an elected administrative council in the West Bank and Gaza Strip for Palestinians there. The new self-governing authority would be the basis for granting full autonomy to their residents and would exist for a transition period of five years. In that time, the final status of the occupied territories and its residents would be settled. Israel even consented to the notion of withdrawing its forces from the territories and redeploying them within secure areas agreed on by all sides. While nothing came of this codicil, it became, along with the 1974 and 1988 decisions of the Palestinian National Council, a kind of legal basis for the Declaration of Principles (DOP), signed on the White House lawn on September 13, 1993, and for the founding of the Palestine Authority, the centerpieces of the Oslo process.[5]

Following the Egyptian-Israeli peace treaty, other factors in the early 1980s nudged the two sides toward a reconsideration of their basic policies. For the PLO, the destruction of its enclaves in Lebanon continued a process physically separating the organization from the people it purported to represent. Once the PLO was reestablished in far-off Tunis, both its leaders and followers found the notions of armed struggle and building a "state in the making" increasingly hollow. Beyond that, Israel's creation of facts on the ground lent a sense of urgency to Palestinian leaders that time was running out for them to reverse the occupation of the territories that Israel conquered in 1967. The numbers of Jewish settlers kept growing throughout the 1970s and 1980s in an expanded Jerusalem and in the rest of the West Bank and in the Gaza Strip.[6] The number of settlements grew to well over 100 and settlers, to over 100,000. Also, the Israeli government requisitioned more than half of untitled lands in the West Bank.[7] These events, according to Meron Benvenisti, led some Palestinians to fear the gradual gathering of forces for a second *Nakba*.[8]

As much as events and processes from 1967 to the early 1980s prepared the ground for shifts in strategy on both sides, the key catalysts bringing about the Oslo agreement emerged in the latter part of the 1980s, after Mikhail Gorbachev had begun instituting his fateful reforms in the Soviet Union. Four factors stand out.

1. Soviet reform and then collapse and the end of the Cold War raised fears among Israeli and Palestinian leaders that led to reconsiderations of basic strategy. Certainly, Palestinian and Israeli leaders were not the only ones who thought that the implosion of the Soviet Union made violent strategies used in a variety of existing civil conflicts untenable now. Suddenly, old strategies seemed shop-worn. It is not happenstance that the early 1990s saw serious new bids for negotiated peace in many festering disputes in such scattered places as Northern Ireland, South Africa, Angola, El Salvador, Guatemala, Cambodia, and Korea. In each of these cases, different sorts of doubts arose among the combatants about the ability to sustain the struggle and achieve ultimate success. In Central America, to take one example, the demise of Soviet-brand socialism sparked a rethinking of ideology within the revolutionary left. "The socialist paradigm, the 'guiding light' of revolutionary movements in the developing world, was suddenly perceived to have lost its legitimacy."[9]

Reconsideration of strategy by Israelis and Palestinians did not come from this sort of delegitimation of their ideologies. Their worry was that the emerging new structure of international relations would leave them without the crucial outside support from which they had benefited during the Cold War. But change is never easy. For leaders on both sides, what they saw to be the imperatives of the new world power structure often ran head-on into the demands of their domestic constituencies, not to speak of their comfort with old habits. Change did not come automatically, by any means, but it did come.

For the PLO, the quick and unimaginable descent of the USSR precipitated an immediate and obvious crisis. In a world that had been defined by the standoff of the two superpowers, the Palestinians had relied heavily on Soviet underpinning. Support ranged from backing in world forums, such as the United Nations, to actual military training and aid. For all Soviet clients in the Cold War, its collapse unleashed unbridled panic and internal soul-searching about how to proceed without a patron in a dangerous and uncertain world. The PLO was no exception. The end of the Cold War and the Soviet slide and disintegration forced a basic reconsideration of how to proceed with its nationalist struggle in the absence of its protector.

The reaction in Israel to the petering out of the Cold War was more complex. Its leaders at first felt a giddy sense of triumph; after all, *its* superpower had won. What could be more reassuring? But that sense of satisfaction evaporated all too quickly. Israeli policymakers began to examine the basis of their gains in the Cold War.

During the years of superpower confrontation, Israeli officials had argued to U.S. leaders, quite convincingly in fact, that Israel was America's best bargain. Israel, they pointed out, provided a potent bulwark against possible Soviet expansion in the Middle East at far less than the cost that the United States incurred in other hotspots. In fact, U.S. outlays for Israel were less than 2 percent of those associated with conventional deterrence of the Soviet Union in central Europe and northeast Asia, which ran together annually to nearly a quarter of a trillion dollars. At no time was Israel's deterrent role clearer than during Black September, 1970, when its threatening statements and military deployment resulted in the tanks of pro-Soviet Syria turning tail and abandoning the pro-Soviet PLO in its losing battle against pro-U.S. Jordan.

With no Soviet client states, such as Syria, to deter in the aftermath of the Cold War, Israeli officials wondered, what motivation was there for the sole remaining superpower to support them so enthusiastically? Did U.S. support hinge on its Cold War needs? Actually, that question has not disappeared to this day and has led in Israel to unceasing efforts to uncover new ways to nurture the American-Israel friendship, find new rationales for it (as in their joint commitment against rogue states or to the war on terrorism), and forge new alliances in U.S. society (as with the Christian right, which, for example, developed a political theology speaking of *two,* complementary chosen peoples, the people of Israel and the Christian people of the United States).

In short, for both the PLO and Israel, the disappearance of the Soviet Union and, with it, the existing structure of an American-dominated world order created new uncertainties over whether their old strategies would find the same kind of international support as in the past. Both were forced into intense domestic debates as to what strategic changes the new world structure called for, if they were to achieve their primary goals (or if those goals needed to be modified). If negotiations seemed to be the new international strat-egy-of-choice in the 1990s, both the PLO and Israel faced difficult impediments to actually sitting down with each other. Not least of these were muscular domestic groups opposed to conciliation, as well as religion's changing role on each side.

For instance, the 1980s and the Intifada had spawned powerful new Islamic groups rejecting even a hint of territorial compromise, which would have to be the basis for any possible negotiations. Sim-ilarly, in Israel, the expanded power of the national religious bloc, with its new Messianic orientation, and the emergence of a new, strange amalgam, the *haredi-leumi* (nationalist ultra-Orthodox), among other groups, made the path to the peace table anything but smooth. The new single-superpower world afforded Palestinians and Israelis plenty of motivation to think about sitting down with each other for the first time. But it did not create any clear path on how to do that, nor did it make those resisting negotiations simply disappear.

2. The reconfiguration of the global economy led to anxieties on both sides as to where they would fit in the new world economic order. Changes in the structure of international relations also further opened the door for a transformation in the world economy. The political tri-umph of the United States meant, too, the victory of a special brand of economic neo-liberalism—what came to be called the Washington Consensus—especially as a recipe for others to adopt. New neo-liberal norms in the world economy demanded that officials in states with troubled economies remove their administrations from active participation in global markets; at the same time, these new standards held these leaders evermore accountable for the perfor-mance of those economies. The heads of Israel and the PLO were no exception in facing increasing pressure based on larger economic changes way beyond their control, although not always in precisely the same way as other state leaders. The difficulties for Palestinians and Israelis centered on the relationship of their societies' economic fortunes to their military and political postures.

Three key factors—all related—signaled a change in the structure of the world economy in the late 1980s, albeit in uncertain directions. First was the havoc of booms and busts in the oil market. Wild price fluctuations had begun in the wake of the oil boycott in the 1973 war. That first spike in oil prices had spawned uncountable petro-dollars, ending up in the hands of leaders of oil exporting states. Most of these petro-dollars wended their way to large Western banks, where they were turned around into loans to states in Latin America, Asia, the Middle East, and Africa. These loans went to both oil importers, which faced steep new energy costs, and oil exporters themselves, which looked to create economic sustainability beyond the life of their oil reserves. That lending quickly enough caused crushing debt for most of the borrowers. The debt burden for the importers became a problem almost immediately. For oil exporters, the problems became obvious once oil prices plummeted at the beginning of the 1980s and made it impossible to make the debt payments, which had been calculated on incomes premised on continuing high oil prices and income. The vaunted debt crisis that marked the last two decades of the twentieth century began with oil-exporting Mexico and gripped the world economy in the mid- to late-1980s, just as the Soviet Union was disintegrating (in fact, its disintegration was spurred by the collapse in government revenues as its oil-export earnings shriveled).

Israel was among those debtor oil-importing countries, facing interest payments alone that ate up half or more of the government's total budget. And the PLO found itself financially dependent on oil-exporting countries experiencing the ups-and-downs of oil prices—not a situation that bred financial security or consistency for Arafat and his organization. Promised payments to the PLO from oil producers, especially among the Gulf states, came in late or never arrived at all. Ordinary Palestinians, meanwhile, filled key positions in booming Middle East oil economies but were highly vulnerable when prices dropped in the 1980s.

Second, the new chic word of the late 1980s, globalization, signaled a process of world economic restructuring that threatened to widen the gap between haves and have-nots even more, determined by access to the new information technology and direct foreign investment associated with it. For both Israelis and Palestinians, it was still an open question in the 1980s whether they would end up in the haves or have-nots category. Israel faced a difficult period, coming out of years of hyperinflation and declining manufacturing and agricultural sectors. Increasing rates of productivity had lagged far behind growing consumption—a recipe for economic disaster. The government had seemed incapable of instilling discipline on the economy, until a unity government reined in public spending in the mid-1980s under the leadership of Shimon Peres. Now, as Israel entered the last decade of the twentieth century, economists pinned their hopes on a transition to the new information age, spurred by foreign investment. But this was an iffy process and depended heavily on being able to instill confidence in the West that Israel was a prime (peaceful) site for foreign investment.

Palestinian leaders also understood that any political autonomy that they might eventually achieve would succeed only with a river of foreign investment, especially direct foreign investment, with all its know-how. But it was not at all clear from where such capital would come, especially now that the Soviet Union was out of the picture. The PLO's image was associated in much of the West with terror and violence, not the kind of characteristics that instilled confidence in investors. If a Palestinian state did emerge, it would have to compete for scarce funds with other former Soviet clients—and the 15 countries that came out of the former Soviet Union—not to speak of other needy countries in the third world.

Third, the world at the end of the 1980s seemed to be dividing into three economic blocs marked by a dominant currency for each—the dollar, deutsche mark, and yen. Like other non-European state leaders in the Mediterranean region, Israeli and Palestinian officials wondered whether they would be excluded from these emerging clubs, especially the one based on the deutsche mark. Competition among Mediterranean countries, both those inside the European Community (EC) and those in the Middle East and North Africa, was intense. Often hawking the same agricultural products, they jockeyed for preferential agreements with the EC. For Israelis and Palestinians, both already peripheral to the economic integration based on the deutsche mark, their image as players involved in unending conflict hurt their possibilities of hooking into that bloc.

Israeli policymakers and, to a lesser degree, Palestinian officials, dreaded that all three of these new economic circumstances might permanently leave their people on the outside of a newly-restructured world economy. Israelis worried, for example, that the impending economic integration of Europe, dubbed Europe 1992, could spell economic isolation for a country, such as Israel, on the periphery of the continent. European impatience with Israel's policies toward the Palestinians and the continued occupation of the West Bank and Gaza, Israelis fretted, could create new hurdles for deepening ties with the EC. Palestinians agonized that their devastated economy might never be able to compete for direct foreign investment or integrate into the new globalized economy. And fluctuating oil prices only increased the burden that any future Palestinian government would have to take on. Thinkers on both sides suggested that the never-ending conflict between them scared off potential investors and threatened the stability needed to gain access to restructured markets. Coming out of the early- and mid-1980s when the economy of Israel and the occupied territories was in considerable turmoil, both sides worried about the effect of their constant state of war on their chances of becoming part of the new economy.[10] Both feared being tossed onto the economic dustbin of history.

3. *The Intifada threatened leaders on both sides.* In the last chapter, we analyzed the complex effects of the Palestinian uprising that began in late 1987. Here it is worth emphasizing that, for both sides, the Intifada combined with the other factors listed here, raising serious

questions about their existing strategies. For Israeli leaders, the concerns extended from issues such as the morale of their own citizenry to ones focusing on the uprising's added detrimental effects on the flow of international capital and preferred access to European markets. Israelis saw the danger signs of an internationally deteriorating image for the state, as television pictures of soldiers confronting Palestinian children played across Europe. They wondered if that might raise the possibility of diminished U.S. support or result in Israel's being ostracized, as had happened with South Africa and apartheid, now that the Cold War had ended. Not least of all, the Intifada called into question whether the centerpiece of Israeli strategy, the deterrent effect of the Israel Defense Forces, could remain strong in a struggle defined largely by the policing of an unarmed insurgency rather than conflict between conventional armies.

PLO officials in distant Tunis were already alarmed about the development of a new, independent Palestinian leadership in the process of creating and sustaining the Intifada. That leadership presented challenges of place (the Intifada's leaders were inside Palestine, not abroad), generation (the new leaders were often twenty to thirty years younger than PLO officials), and orientation (many of the uprising's leaders were religious rather than secular and almost none was taken with the old-style socialism of some of the older generation).

Added to the PLO's concern over an alternative leadership was the clear international repositioning of its key state backers in the Arab world in response to the demise of the Soviet Union and to economic globalization. A common refrain among elites in Arab states, especially on the far edges of the Arab world (Migdal interviewed in Yemen and Morocco, among other Arab countries in the early 1990s), was that the Palestinian-Israeli conflict was a continuing impediment to their own integration into the emerging new world order. Referring to a period a decade later, Edward Said, the noted Palestinian-American intellectual and cultural critic, spoke of "the sheer exasperation of most of the Arab regimes with the whole Palestinian problem." The situation was quite similar in the early 1990s, when Arab leaders also wished that "Arafat and his people would simply either behave or quietly go away."[11] PLO leaders could not help but worry that the rise of new, young Palestinian leaders in the Intifada, both secular and religious, could prove to be tempting alternatives to the PLO for Arab state leaders eager to wash their hands of the Palestinian issue. They fretted, too, about the long-term commitment of Arab leaders and the larger Arab public to the Palestinian cause.

4. The Gulf War turned nightmares into reality. Nothing confirmed all the anxieties of Israeli and PLO leaders about the changing state of the world as much as the Gulf War. Iraq's conquest of Kuwait on August 2, 1990, set in motion a series of events that confirmed for key Israeli and PLO politicians and thinkers the need to search for new strategic policies, especially in respect to one another. The Gulf War galvanized the two sides to undertake a new approach to their own conflict.

In Israel, once again, the initial reaction was that Saddam Hussein's gambit and President George Bush's strong reaction to it would play into Israel's hands. After all, in any impending war it could offer the United States the best army, hospitals, base facilities, and servicing of the U.S. war machine found anywhere in the Middle East. Some Israeli leaders felt, in the first flush of excitement and horror after Saddam's annexation of Kuwait, that a functional replacement for the Cold War had finally appeared, cementing the importance of Israel to the United States.

But that optimism quickly faded, as U.S. officials made it crystal clear to the Israelis that they were a liability to the war effort against Iraq on several counts. First, even a whiff of Israeli participation in the multilateral coalition the United States was cobbling together to oppose Iraq would lead to Arab and other Muslim states' defection. Any role at all for Israel threatened the success of U.S. policymakers in delicately incorporating countries such as Syria into the coalition. Second, Saddam Hussein worked hard to win broad Arab and Muslim support against the United States by linking the Kuwaiti incursion to the Palestinian issue, at least rhetorically. "Today Kuwait, tomorrow Jerusalem." For its part, the Bush administration quickly distanced itself from Israel (and from Israel's position on the Palestinian issue) precisely in order to thwart the development of such an Arab-Muslim coalition. American pressure, in the end, induced the Israeli government to sit on its hands as Iraq rained missiles on Israeli cities during the war. Many Israeli leaders felt that the Gulf War's damage to the effectiveness of the state's vaunted deterrence and retaliation policies, as well as to domestic morale, was far greater than any destruction of Israeli property caused by Saddam's missiles. Bush's new world order seemed to exclude Israel, even threaten it, rather than offer it glittering new opportunities.

Iraq's invasion turned out to be even more disastrous for the PLO and Palestinians generally. Saddam Hussein's statements about Jerusalem and the Palestinian issue, not surprisingly, made a deep, positive impression on the Palestinian rank-and-file, inside and outside historic Palestine. But any open identification of Palestinian leaders with Iraq held great peril. The PLO's major state supporters in the Arab world joined the U.S.-led alliance against Iraq. Caught between the sentiment in the street and the admonitions of his backers, Arafat tried to steer a middle course, but to no avail. Leaders of the United States and the oil-rich Arab countries that bankrolled the PLO interpreted his stance as pro-Iraqi, leading to the cut-off of funds. In effect, the organization was bankrupt, forcing it to close many of its missions around the globe. Much of the anger of key Arab officials at the Palestinians and the PLO came to a head after Iraq's defeat. Kuwaitis identified the 300,000–400,000 Palestinians in Kuwait as allies of Iraq—as traitors—and drove the overwhelming majority of Palestinians living there out of the country.

By the time the dust settled in the Gulf War, neither Israelis nor Palestinians had felt so isolated internationally for at least a generation. That war had struck Palestinian and Israeli leaders like a bolt of lightening. All the nettlesome doubts that had insinuated themselves into thinking about their basic goals and strategies, especially concerning each other, had suddenly snowballed during the Gulf War into full-blown crises. Drained by the Intifada that had dragged on for years, Israeli and Palestinian leaders now had to come to terms with a new and frightening international isolation, as well. It was in that environment that the Bush administration sold the idea for a multilateral conference in Madrid designed as a bridge from violence to substantive negotiations, first through an international conference and then breaking down into bilateral negotiating sessions.

Oslo Accord

By the end of 1991, the Soviet Union had disappeared, the United States was edging into unprecedented world military- and economic-policy dominance, the U.S.-led coalition had pulverized the Iraqis, and Microsoft had begun to drive the world economy. In the midst of these radical changes on the world scene, Palestinians and Israelis started meeting about their futures. What began fitfully in Madrid in December 1991 suddenly generated a fevered pitch of excitement in August 1993. Israel and the PLO made the startling announcement that their representatives had secretly completed a framework for future negotiations that could end their conflict. It was a breathtaking moment—one of heightened anticipation, even extraordinary optimism.

While no one had predicted an Oslo-type accord, a number of important domestic happenings for Palestinians and Israelis alike indicated that the pot was simmering with new ideas and approaches to the conflict. These included the PLO's 1988 decision to declare a state in Gaza and the West Bank, thereby accepting a two-state solution; the endorsement in Israel, by select policymakers from both the left and right, of the idea of unilaterally withdrawing from the densely populated Gaza Strip; the election of a Labor government in Israel in 1992 replacing the hard-line government of Yitzhak Shamir; and the frustration on both sides with the ongoing negotiations in Washington under the framework of the international conference initiated in Madrid.

Informal talks in Oslo began early in 1993 between several Israeli academics and mid-level PLO officials, including Ahmad Khuri (Abu Alaa) and Mahmud Abbas (Abu Mazen), under the auspices of the Norwegian government and its Foreign Minister, Johan Jurgen Holst.[12] As the negotiators gained confidence in one another at their secluded hideaway, a number of key points became the foundation for a full-blown agreement, including the willingness of the Palestinians to accept an interim settlement without determining, at the moment, the final arrangements for a permanent settlement; PLO readiness to govern the Gaza Strip (as long as at least a symbolic part of the West Bank also came under its control); and Israel's concurrence to the establishment of a Palestinian National Authority (PNA, or often simply referred to as the Palestine Authority, PA) as the governing structure.

In August 1993, the PLO and the Israeli government announced that they had come to an agreement. Officially, the Declaration of Principles (DOP) was signed in Washington on September 13. The preamble of the declaration set out core principles, affirming Palestinians' and Israelis'

determination to put an end to decades of confrontation and to live in peaceful coexistence, mutual dignity and security, while recognizing their mutual legitimate and political rights.

REAFFIRMING their desire to achieve a just, lasting and comprehensive peace settlement and historic reconciliation through the agreed political process.

RECOGNIZING that the peace process and the new era that it has created, as well as the new relationship established between the two Parties as described above, are irreversible, and the determination of the two Parties to maintain, sustain and continue the peace process.

RECOGNIZING that the aim of the Israeli-Palestinian negotiations within the current Middle East peace process is, among other things, to establish a Palestinian Interim Self-Government Authority, i.e. the elected Council . . . , and the elected Ra'ees [Chairman] of the Executive Authority, for the Palestinian people in the West Bank and the Gaza Strip, for a transitional period not exceeding five years from the date of signing the Agreement on the Gaza Strip and the Jericho Area, leading to a permanent settlement based on Security Council Resolutions 242 and 338.[13]

REAFFIRMING their understanding that the interim self-government arrangements contained in this Agreement are an integral part of the whole peace process, that the negotiations on the permanent status, that will start as soon as possible but not later than May 4, 1996, will lead to the implementation of Security Council Resolutions 242 and 338, and that the Interim Agreement shall settle all the issues of the interim period and that no such issues will be deferred to the agenda of the permanent status negotiations.[14]

The first stage outlined in the DOP obligated Israel to turn over most of the territories of the Gaza Strip (with the exception of the Jewish settlements in the Katif bloc) and the Jericho area (according to the Cairo Agreement of May 4, 1994) to the PLO. The accord stated that "authority will be transferred to the Palestinians in the following spheres: education and culture, health, social welfare, direct taxation, and tourism. The Palestinian side will commence in building the Palestinian police force. . . ."

In the following stage, the Interim Agreement (sometimes referred to as Oslo II), effected mostly in late 1995, the PLO gained sole control over all Palestinian cities and the highly populated refugee camps in the West Bank and Gaza Strip (with the exception of settled Jewish areas in the city of Hebron). The total territory transferred to sole Palestinian control (Area A) in these two stages was about 3–4 percent of the West Bank and Gaza Strip. Also agreed upon was an intermediate division of the rest of the territory of the West Bank and Gaza Strip into two areas of governance: an area of about 70 percent of the territory consisting of sole Israeli control— the Jordan valley, all the Jewish settlements in the West Bank, and their venues of access (Area C)—and an area of about 27 percent of the land in which there was joint control—most of the rural areas of the West Bank including about 440 villages and their surrounding lands (Area B). In Area B, the Palestinian Authority was to have control over civil-administrative issues and Israel, over military and security issues; joint armed patrols were also arranged for Area B.

All in all, these initial stages constituted what the preamble referred to as "the interim self-government arrangements." Working under the assumption that taking small steps builds trust, the interim arrangements were intended to incrementally transfer the entire Palestinian population of the West Bank and Gaza Strip (with the exception of East Jerusalem and the surrounding metropolitan area) to Palestinian governance. The Jewish settlements in the territories (including access roads) and their populations would remain intact under Israeli control for the time being.[15] This agreement was supposed to last five years, during which time a final agreement would be reached determining the status of the Palestine Authority, the fate of the Jewish settlements, the disposition of East Jerusalem, the possible return or repatriation of the refugees (including how many, from where, and to where), the division of water in the joint aquifer, and so on.[16] The Israelis also were to ensure free and secure land movement between the two parts of the PA-governed territory (the West Bank and the Gaza Strip), release political prisoners, and grant aid (together with the United States and the European states) for developing an economic and social infrastructure in the areas ruled by the Palestine Authority, including an international airport and a deep-water port in Gaza. In exchange, the Palestinians would give recognition to Israel; end guerrilla warfare; and commit to preventing acts of terror against Israel, Israelis, and even residents of the Jewish settlements in the occupied territories.

An astounding proportion of these plans and promises were actually put into effect between 1993 and the end of 1995. Israeli forces did redeploy, the Palestine Authority assumed control of increasing portions of the Palestinian population, the parties crafted the Interim Agreement (almost on time), and the PA took control of West Bank cities. Israel's first redeployment out of most of the Gaza Strip and Jericho ended in May 1994, paving the way for assumption of control in those areas by the Palestine Authority. On July 1 of that year, Arafat moved from Tunis to Gaza, with great fanfare and ceremony. With the signing of the Interim Agreement on September 28, 1995 (about a third of a year beyond the self-imposed deadline), the way was open to the Palestine Authority's governing more than 90 percent of the West Bank and Gazan Palestinian population (but less than 5 percent of these territories). About two-thirds in Area A were completely under the Palestine Authority's jurisdiction, and the other one-third were in Area B, where Israel maintained control over security.

Once Israel's redeployment for 1995 began, a series of catastrophic events slowed the peace process considerably. An Israeli assassin killed Prime Minister Yitzhak Rabin, Islamic groups undertook a series of bombings in Israeli cities in early 1996, and Binyamin Netanyahu, who had opposed Oslo from the outset, defeated Rabin's successor, Peres, in elections for prime minister. Still, even in this period of slowing momentum, the process continued to mark up some important accomplishments. On January 20, 1996, Palestinians participated in their first elections for their own government, electing the Palestinian Legislative Council. That election set the stage for Israel's dissolution of its civil administration and military government. And, in January 1997, Israel redeployed within Hebron, after an agreement had been secured between Arafat and the new Israeli prime minister, Netanyahu, which put virtually all the Palestinian population in the territories under the control of the Palestine Authority.

What Went Right?

Despite these successes, the Oslo process noticeably slowed after Rabin's assassination and, particularly, after Netanyahu's election. Indeed, with the hindsight of a decade after the signing of the Declaration of Principles, the peace process and all its accomplishments in those early years of 1993–1995 looked like a brief, unsuccessful interlude in the near-century of Palestinian-Israeli violence. The rosy excitement of the summer of 1993, which reached new heights by late 1995, flagged as final status negotiations stalled; and, by the end of the decade, hope had turned into full-fledged cynicism among Palestinians and Israelis alike. By 2001, when all-out violence resumed, the obvious question became: what went wrong?

Before addressing that question, however, it is worth asking a prior question: what went right, at least initially? It is very important to ask this question, if for no other reason than if all Israelis and Palestinians gained for their efforts was a new Intifada, efforts at future peace seem pointless. All the two sides can do in that case, to paraphrase Israeli commentator Gershom Gorenberg, is oil their guns and dig their graves.[17]

We need to ask what sorts of building blocks, if any, did the first-ever official negotiations between the PLO and Israel leave for the two sides, even when relations later turned terribly sour? Additionally, for both, the new relationships, decisions, and institutions coming out of their contacts with each other shaped social and political life throughout the 1990s and beyond. The Palestinians, especially, found the fallout from the Oslo process decisive in fashioning the contours of their emerging self-identified people and the developing relations between their (incipient) state and society. While what follows is not an exhaustive list, we single out six results of the peace process, each of which shaped not only the relations between Palestinians and Israelis but also Palestinian society itself and the values and practices that were at its foundation.

1. The Israeli-Palestinian agreement unmasked a large majority on each side for a negotiated settlement. If partition would ever work, it would need to be accepted broadly by the two societies, not just by a handful of leaders holed away in a castle in Norway. Even though the Oslo agreement was negotiated in complete secrecy, without any forewarnings to the Israeli and Palestinian people, it was greeted with enthusiasm by a large majority of both populations. Sara Roy, a long-time student of Palestinian society, wrote of how

> joy and hope returned . . . with the signing of the Oslo agreement. I was in Gaza City when the Israeli army redeployed from the urban areas of the Strip in May 1994. The freedom to walk their streets without fear or harassment left Palestinians ecstatic. That night, Gaza City's main commercial street throbbed with thousands of people, many in their finest clothes. . . . There were dancers and singers. The stores were open, food was free, and children had all the chocolate they wanted. The city was a swirl of light and color.[18]

On both sides, it was clear that the initial document represented extraordinary compromises, departing from positions that had repeatedly been presented by leaders as nonnegotiable. And it was understood widely, too, that the planned five years of negotiations until a final settlement would bring even more painful compromises. Still, the polls on both sides uncovered a large majority supporting the accord and its principles of territorial concessions and mutual acceptance.

Palestinian pollster Khalil Shikaki tracked attitudes of West Bank and Gaza Palestinians from the initiation of the Oslo process.[19] In the month that the Declaration of Principles was signed, September 1993, two-thirds backed the peace process. Palestinians' enthusiasm ebbed and flowed during the next few years; but, by 1996, in the wake of Israeli troop withdrawals after the interim agreement was signed, support for the peace process ballooned to a whopping four-fifths of the population. That turned out to be the high point. But even during the administration of Binyamin Netanyahu, 1996–1999, support never fell below 60 percent and, after Ehud Barak's election in 1999, it rose again to 75 percent.

In short, what had been unthinkable for decades—Palestinians' accepting far less than what they felt was their birthright—now became a topic, not only among intellectuals and policymakers, but a supported idea in the population of the territories generally. The "street" in the Middle East often connotes something ominous—a dark, vengeful, undifferentiated public keeping leaders from adopting "reasonable" policies. But the Palestinian street, like that in Israel, was empowering leaders to proceed with the negotiations begun in Oslo, with all the compromises they entailed. Public sentiment clearly backed the idea of partition into two states—even if the specifics remained murky. What turned out to be tragic was that the leaders on both sides tuned in much more to the naysayers, that hardcore minority rejecting partition—a two-state solution—altogether, than to the majority supporting the peace process.

At the same time that the public expressed widespread support for the Oslo process, this hardcore minority voiced vitriolic opposition to it. Even among the founding fathers of Fatah itself—not to mention members of the Democratic Front, the Popular Front, and the Islamic Movement—important figures, such as Hani al-Hassan and Farouk Khaddumi, completely rejected the agreement.[20] They saw the construction of the Palestine Authority, and perhaps afterward also of a nominal Palestinian state, in such a small part of historic Palestine, in a torn and divided territory, as a disaster.[21] The new state, if it ever emerged, would be a vassal of Israel. Major opposition to the agreement also came from Palestinians in the *ghurba*, diaspora, who felt that the PLO leadership had abandoned them by implying a surrender of their right of return *(al-awda)*.[22] They saw the right of return as the central tenet of the Palestinian diaspora experience—the basic right of every person and collectivity that had been ripped from the Palestinian homeland by force.[23]

A prime example of another sort of opposition from abroad came from the most renowned Palestinian intellectual, Edward Said, whose critique of Orientalism in Western writing and thinking had swept through intellectual circles across the world. Said, a moderate within Palestinian circles who had always supported the PLO and Arafat, immediately came out against the DOP and viewed the arrangements between the PLO and Israel as a total surrender to Zionism and the West. According to this critique, shared by other important Palestinian diaspora intellectuals, such as Rashid Khalidi, a professor at Columbia University who was then at the University of Chicago and was also a former supporter of Arafat, Israel had applied the classical colonial strategy of converting direct military control into indirect control by taking advantage of Palestinian collaborators (the dupes of the Palestine Authority) and utilizing economic, technological, and military superiority.

Khalidi and others felt that the secret Oslo negotiations had sabotaged the talks in Washington, DC, coming out of the Madrid Conference, in which the Palestinians could have won much better conditions. Other Palestinian critics of the agreement, mostly "internal" people (such as Haidar Abd al-Shafi and Mahmud Darwish), were willing to accept the principles of the agreement with Israel, including recognition of the Israeli state, but criticized the concessions that Arafat and the mainstream made. Israel's conditions for signing, they felt, raised doubts as to its true intentions. This opposition, for example, protested leaving Jewish settlements in the Palestinian territories (especially in the heart of Hebron and the Gaza Strip), postponement of the final status talks over Jerusalem, delayed release of Palestinian prisoners, and the small amount of territory to be transferred initially to the Palestine Authority.

For all the unhappiness with the Oslo Accord inside the PLO, among exiled intellectuals, and within the growing Islamic movement, the popular foundation for proceeding with negotiations was quite strong. The high-profile signing had managed to pull the veil from the myth that Palestinians would accept nothing less than the destruction of Israel and throwing the Jews into the sea. More than that, when a concrete agreement was proposed and signed, most Palestinians lined up behind it, even if they quibbled with some of its provisions. A majority of Palestinians were eager for a truly independent state, even if it was one covering only a fifth of historic Palestine.

2. *For the first time, each side accepted the legitimacy of the other's existence.* All sorts of images of what the relations between the Israeli and Palestinian states would eventually be were floated in the years after the signing of the Oslo Accord. Even at the height of the renewed and sustained violence after September 2000, these ideas continued to circulate (but with much less assuredness than before). Arafat, for example, wistfully spoke in 2002, in an interview with an Israeli newspaper, of "a Benelux-like relationship between Israel and the Palestinian state with open borders."[24] Shimon Peres, Israel's one-time prime minister, was most vocal about future relations, talking of an economically integrated New Middle East. Whatever the precise form that coexistence would take, it depended on more than an acceptance of one's own state in only a portion of historic Palestine. It was conditioned on accepting the legitimate right of the *other* also to establish a state in part of Palestine. Unlike the Palestinians' declaration of a state in 1988, this time Israel's legitimacy was explicitly, not implicitly, stated. The mutual recogni-

tion that was enshrined in the Declaration of Principles formally conferred the assent of each nation to the national aspirations of the other.

This point was made forcefully in the very first paragraph of the DOP. Israelis and Palestinians agreed to "recognize their mutual legitimate and political rights."[25] The accord attempted to make the idea of mutual legitimacy concrete by specifying numerous areas of proposed cooperation that would link Palestinians and Israelis in such mundane areas as electricity, transportation, and water.

Beyond the language of the accord, both Arafat and Israeli Prime Minister Rabin acknowledged in the months and years after the signing that the tactical basis of the conflict had changed once each recognized the mutual legitimate and political rights of the other. The transformation was from what social scientists call a zero-sum game to a non-zero-sum game. Zero-sum refers to a situation in which any gains by one side are seen as coming only through a corresponding loss by the other side—you win, I lose, and vice versa. Non-zero-sum suggests a condition in which gains by one side can also mean corresponding benefits for the other—a win-win situation. Rabin understood that the building of strong political institutions in the Palestine Authority would redound to Israel's benefit, as well. And Arafat knew that an increased sense of security among Israelis would make the public more disposed to move toward a final status agreement acceptable to Palestinians.

Of course, the recognition of the legitimacy of the other could not come simply by fiat. Still, the signatures did imply a commitment by the leaders to work toward the reconstruction of their own national narratives so as to make room for the narrative of the other, that is, recognizing the other as a nation with a collective understanding of its own right to a state in the territory the British had mapped out as Palestine. For Israelis, that modification would mean incorporating Palestinians into a rendering of national history from which they had been almost entirely absent. Palestinians, in contrast, had always had Israelis as part of their people's story—but as a bogeyman. Now, each nation was on the road to reconsidering the role of the other in its own history. Mutual recognition meant moving from national myths that were black and white to much more difficult ones that were replete with shades of gray.

3. Each side renounced the dominant tactic it had used for three-quarters of a century in dealing with the other: violence—and committed itself to the principle that only negotiations would resolve the conflict. In the Oslo Accord, violence was the hinge on which all else turned. Every speaker on the podium at the signing of the Declaration of Principles knew that and addressed it and its flip side, peaceful cooperation, in one way or another. PLO official Mahmoud Abbas put it in the most straightforward way: "We have come to this point because we believe that peaceful coexistence and cooperation are the only means for reaching understanding and for realizing the hopes of the Palestinians and the Israelis." Metaphors abounded. Guns were to turn into shovels; it was the eve of opportunity, a farewell to arms, the end of violence and war. The DOP pledged the two parties to "strive to live in peaceful coexistence and mutual dignity and security and achieve a just, lasting and comprehensive peace settlement and historic reconciliation through the agreed political process."

As it turned out, violence never left the equation of Palestinian-Israeli relations. Because Israel continued to rule Palestinians, violence on the part of its security forces was almost a foregone conclusion. And extra-legal violence, such as the terror attack by a settler, Baruch Goldstein, in Hebron in 1994, killing twenty-nine Muslim worshippers and wounding many others, added fuel to smoldering fires. From the Palestinian side, the PA leadership was left with very little leverage in its negotiations with Israel without the threat or use of violence. And a major stumbling block in moving toward a final status agreement was violence by groups and individuals not controlled by the Palestine Authority (as well as the festering question of whether the Palestine Authority could and should control them).

Even though the peace process foundered through the use of violence, the acceptance by both sides of a principle of nonviolence created an important precedent. It set the parameters for both the practices each side needed to adopt in moving toward a settlement and an ideal for future relations. The principle forced both sides to confront the question of its day-to-day tactics of dealing with the other, as well as the issue of what eventual relations would be (separation? avoidance? integration? federation? or?).

4. The Oslo Accord acknowledged and addressed the primal fear of both Palestinians and Israelis, inducing an acceptance of the concept of partition and the incipient rewriting of each nation's national narrative. Any move toward stability in the region would require a mutually acceptable partition plan. There is, quite simply, no other route to peace. Proposals to divide the country between Jews and Arabs had been circulating since the 1937 Peel Commission Report without much success. Neither side liked the idea of splitting the small piece of land, and certainly nothing even close to a mutually acceptable plan had been tabled before the 1990s. Still, it is unimaginable to think about a war-free region without the acceptance by Palestinians and Israelis of a division of the territory that had been British-ruled Palestine. The challenge in 1937 was to find or generate such acceptance, and the challenge is no different today. All the years of fighting had not changed the conflict from its essence as a turf war.

It was the mutual acceptance of the idea of partition, if not the specifics, which lay at the heart of the Oslo agreement. But acceptance would have to mean much more than acquiescence by some, or even all, policymakers to the notion of splitting the land, based on one formula or another. For both Israelis and Palestinians, partition implied, too, the incorporation of the boundaries of what would be their truncated state into a widely accepted national narrative. That is no mean feat. The new boundaries of a state in a portion of what was British Palestine would have to take on a value as the rightful, even sacrosanct, encapsulation of the nation's heartland. Irredentism would have to fall away.

To give some idea of what it means to have boundaries reshape a national narrative, Israel's experience after the 1948 war is very instructive. After that war, Israelis had moved toward the modification of their national story to accept—indeed, embrace—the intrinsic value of a state in only a portion of the land. Shlomo Avineri, Israel's most esteemed political scientist and a former director of the Foreign Ministry, put it this way:

> One issue which was central to the political debate within the Jewish Yishuv (community) in the late 1930s and the 1940s—the debate about partition—was over. The armistice lines of 1949 were considered by practically all Israelis as the realistic definite borders of Israel. If, prior to 5 June 1967, the Arab countries had been ready to sign a peace agreement with Israel on the basis of the existing frontiers, there would have been an overwhelming Israeli consensus in favour of accepting this, perceiving this Arab readiness as a major concession and a tremendous achievement for Israel. With very few exceptions on the lunatic fringe of Israeli politics, there was no irredentist call in Israel during the period of 1949–1967, advocating an Israeli initiative to recapture Judea and Samaria, or even the Old City of Jerusalem. This post-1948 consensus was visible across the spectrum of Israeli politics.[26]

The messy Israeli boundaries after the 1949 armistice, then, assumed a sanctity of their own for Israelis. "They imparted a stability to state and society," Migdal wrote in *Through the Lens of Israel*. "The state molded its reach to them and people simply assumed that those arbitrary lines would permanently define the extent of Israeli society."[27] The borders started to become an integral part of the national narrative by providing the frame for a sense of we-ness, or common identity—what it meant to be an Israeli. Israel's conquering of all of Palestine in the 1967 war undid those borders and also the special place the truncated state with those crazy-quilt boundaries had begun to assume in public culture. The uncertainty over Israel's ultimate borders after 1967 opened new, acrimonious disputes about the national narrative, even about what it meant to be an Israeli. These bitter struggles were an unforeseen consequence of Israel's amazing military victory, and they have lasted into the twenty-first century.

Palestinians never had Israel's post-1948 luxury of what seemed at the time to be permanent borders. The uncertainty over what boundaries would finally prevail—or if there would be a Palestinian state with boundaries at all—thwarted the full development of a national narrative. All sorts of questions hung unanswered: What would the ultimate boundaries be? Would there be a separate identity for those inside the boundaries of the Palestinian state? Would there be diasporas? What would be the relationship of the diasporas to the state and the nation? Part of the difficulties that Palestinian officials had in making concrete proposals on the issue of the "right of return" during the Oslo process, for example, stemmed from this unfinished narrative as to what the Palestinian state and, even more, the Palestinian people would be. Who would be at their center and who at their periphery? Would refugees in Lebanon and elsewhere be absorbed into a truncated Palestinian state, repatriated to their original homes in Israel, or monetarily compensated and settled permanently in their host countries? The difficulty in coming to policy decisions on these questions stemmed, in great part, from the absence of a reigning national narrative among Palestinians generally, and those in the occupied territories specifically.

Without a resolution of the boundary question, Israelis and Palestinians each found it difficult to construct a broadly accepted identity and sense of we-ness, especially after the 1967 war. Implicitly, at least, the Oslo Accord addressed that problem on several levels. One factor was its setting out an agenda for determining a final status agreement. The assurance that there *would be* a final agreement after five years of negotiations, even if the boundaries coming out of the talks were only roughly apprehended by the public in the mid-1990s, already had an effect in molding the emerging understanding of what the nation would be.

Beyond the power of the agenda, Oslo's Declaration of Principles addressed the primal fear on each side in moving toward territorial compromise. For Israelis, that basic fear was that "*they* will never be happy until Israel is destroyed." No matter how much Israel would compromise, most Jewish Israelis' gut feeling prior to Oslo was that the Palestinians would not be satisfied until Israel would be wiped off the map and Israelis, thrown into the sea. For Palestinians, the fear was that "what you see is all you will ever get." They felt that Israel was intent on permanent occupation of the West Bank and Gaza Strip (or some facsimile of occupation through indirect control) and committed to thwarting the emergence of any sort of truly autonomous Palestinian state.

The Declaration of Principles began the process of addressing Israeli apprehensions by committing the accepted representative of the Palestinian people, the PLO, to a partition of the land and acceptance of Israel's existence in whatever would be the agreed-upon borders. Arafat explicitly addressed the Israeli fear at the Oslo signing ceremony: "Our people do not consider that exercising the right to self-determination could violate the rights of their neighbors or infringe on their security."[28] For the Palestinians, the declaration set a path for Israeli withdrawal and the assumption by Palestinians of their own governance, implying that what you see today is *not* what you will get at the end of the process. Israeli Foreign Minister Peres spoke to the Palestinian fear at the same ceremony: "I want to tell the Palestinian delegation that we are sincere, that we mean business. We do not seek to shape your life or determine your destiny." Arafat explicitly assured his people that the accord committed Israel to the creation of an independent, truly autonomous Palestinian state in the West Bank and Gaza Strip.

While the primal fears did not disappear immediately for either people, the Oslo agreement did initiate a process of mutual assurance designed to mitigate each side's dread. These reassurances opened the door for Israelis and Palestinians to imagining their own nations' existing within set borders. It was within this new imagined reality that the first steps for constructing and repairing their national narratives could take place. The Oslo Accord did move Israelis to begin to incorporate Palestinians into their understanding of themselves. That painful process certainly was not completed in the decade after Oslo, but it did result in important debates over the meaning of past events, the content of school textbooks, and the makeup of university curricula.

For Palestinians, the reconstruction of the national narrative began, too, although more slowly and fitfully. For example, in 1993 polls, a majority of the Palestinian population in the occupied territories indicated support for amending the Palestinian National Charter to remove the sections that were anathema to Israel (although support waned to just over one-third of those polled by 1999, when the peace process had stalled). Also, the post-Oslo reality allowed for the creation of autonomous Palestinian institutions, both social and political—and, with them, the beginnings of a renewed national narrative—with an actual and imagined territorial reach. Finally, some key Palestinian leaders placed the concept of partition into the context of Palestinian national aspirations. Here is Mohammed Dahlan, a key figure in the Palestine Authority, in 2002: "There is no reason each side can't hold on to its dreams. But there is only one solution: two states living side by side—a Palestinian state along the June 67 borders, with its capital in Arab east Jerusalem, where Palestinians can live in freedom, dignity and independence, with a fair resolution of the refugee problem—and an Israeli state in peace and security."[29]

5. The process spawned dozens of sets of negotiations between Israelis and Palestinians—beyond the official talks. The peace process became a kind of cottage industry among Palestinians and Israelis. Already in the aftermath of the Madrid Conference, especially the multilateral negotiations in Washington, scores of Palestinian and Israeli academics, technical experts, and others participated—some as official members of the negotiating teams, others as advisers. What began as talks between a few Israeli academics and second-rung PLO officials in early 1993 blossomed into multiple volunteer (and paid) teams of advisers, who continued to draw up position papers, policy statements, scenarios, and the like until the very end of the Oslo process in January 2001. And, even after that, low-level meetings continued to occur—so much so that one magazine referred in 2002, at the height of violence, to the "privatization of peacemaking."[30]

In any case, for the eight years of the Oslo process, cadres of educated Israelis and Palestinians spent countless hours with each other—and preparing for their sessions with each other—figuring out the nitty-gritty details of how the two peoples could coexist. Beyond their role as direct advisers, many of these Palestinians and Israelis engaged in back-channel negotiations, or what is sometimes called Track 2 negotiations, on issues broad and narrow. But these advisers were not the only ones engaged in the back channels. Religious leaders, business people, labor activists, academics, and others took part in all sorts of semi-official and unofficial talks. Some negotiations, such as those in Stockholm in 2000, carried the weight of the Israeli government and the Palestine Authority. Others were conferences, publicly and privately held at such places as the Palestinian universities or the Harry S. Truman Institute for Peace of the Hebrew University of Jerusalem, with no direct links to policymakers. Still others were simple talk sessions on issues ranging from the status of Jerusalem to the disbursement of tax receipts.[31]

These sessions varied tremendously in their direct utility. Some hammered out common positions on difficult, if narrow, issues of conflict. Others ended in acrimony. Some yielded lasting friendships across national lines; others reinforced caricatures and stereotypes. No one monitored the tens of sessions that were held, but we can venture to say that these conferences and talks produced some important direct and indirect results. Most directly, they produced actual documents on important issues indicating areas of agreement (and disagreement). These documents will almost certainly serve as a sort of template in future negotiations; that is, it will be very hard for either side to demand a totally new starting place for negotiation on these issues. The points of agreement, in particular, will serve as points of departure in future efforts at forging peace. Indirectly, key elites, many of them among the best and the brightest of a young, educated generation, committed a sizeable part of their lives for these eight years to finding a path toward coexistence. That commitment among an important part of each population can serve as a foundation for future attempts at reaching a final status agreement. In addition, they forged important relations with each other, learning styles, points of sensitivity, redlines, and more.

6. *The Oslo process created the first-ever Palestinian government.* No matter what kinds of constraints it faced, no matter how limited its scope of action, no matter how torturous its efforts to build effec-

tive governing institutions, the Palestine Authority gave Palestinians their own government for the first time in their history. As
Rashid Khalidi put it, for all the limitations surrounding it, "the
new Palestinian Authority has more power over more of its people
in more of Palestine than any Palestinian agency has had in the
twentieth century."[32] Negotiations after the signing of the DOP produced the Transfer Agreement (officially, the Agreement on Preparatory Transfer of Powers and Responsibilities) in August 1994. West
Bank and Gaza residents, after centuries of rule by Ottomans, British, Jordanians, Egyptians, and, of course, Israelis, now experienced
indigenous leaders' ruling in much of their day-to-day lives. Sometimes that governance was surprisingly effective; most times, it was
frustratingly inefficient, even corrupt. Still, it consisted of Palestinians ruling Palestinians.

When the mainstream Palestinian leadership signed the Oslo
agreement, it apparently saw that agreement as both the minimal
and optimal program for the short term.[33] In any case, for the first
time ever, the Palestinians came close to having an actual state of
their own, that is, the existence of a political entity with authority
and independent central control within a part of historic Palestine.
And they harbored, too, the hope to expand control and authority
over these and additional areas of the country.

The Palestine Authority adopted state mannerisms and rituals.
The PLO chairman became the "President"; those responsible for
various portfolios (the number of which grew to 35 by 2002) were
termed ministers; and the various departments turned into ministries. The Palestine Authority adopted the flag and national anthem
of the PLO, as well as its diplomatic representatives abroad. A government radio station and several regional television stations were
established, which aired many government-approved programs. A
fragile judiciary system was also founded, which attempted to present itself, without great success, as independent of the executive. On
January 25, 1996, a short time after the signing of the interim agreement and the redeployment of Israeli troops out of the main population centers, the Palestine Authority organized general elections in
the West Bank and Gaza Strip under foreign surveillance. Palestin-

ians saw the newly elected 88-seat Legislative Council as a parliament for all intents and purposes.[34] Fatah-supported candidates received an overwhelming majority of the votes.[35] The Legislative Council, whose purpose turned out to be more to signify representation of the Palestinian people through the elections than actually to play a weighty legislative role or serve as a check to the authority of the President, even had its sessions broadcast through the new PA-established media outlets.

The greatest challenge for the Palestine Authority was to build a sense of acceptance, or legitimacy, among the people of the territories, while establishing security, control, and authority. Questions of security, in particular, preoccupied the leadership. To maintain security in Area A, the parties agreed that the Palestine Authority could construct a contingent of police and various other security forces (such as the Preventive Security Force, the General Intelligence Service, the Special Security Force, and the Presidential Guard/Force 17). PLO negotiators pushed for the creation of these security forces for several reasons. The construction of a Palestinian police force made possible the return to Palestine of a large share of the *fedayeen* units (and their families), who had been deported from Lebanon to Tunis, as well as other units of the Palestine Liberation Army that had been dispersed to other countries. Returning units from Tunis and elsewhere were integrated, side by side, with local forces (also made up mostly of Fatah veterans).

Together, all these units became the main institutional underpinning of the Palestine Authority's regime. In fact, "the ratio of policemen to citizens is one of the highest in the world."[36] The men who originally staffed these security units came to be referred to as the Old Guard (as opposed to the Young Guard of the Tanzim, which emerged as a powerhouse in the second Intifada).[37] Many of the complaints by the Young Guard revolved around the security forces' heavy-handed, authoritarian methods, often abusing people's basic rights.

The police forces became the essential cog of the Palestine Authority's burgeoning organizational machine, which quickly began to look more and more like the overgrown bureaucracies of other countries in Africa and the Middle East. In the absence of productive economies in many countries of the third world, or at least ones not productive enough to keep up with high birth rates and high school graduation rates, these unwieldy government structures have served as a source of jobs for the population and a magnet for direct foreign aid. Much the same happened in the West Bank and Gaza. Already in 1995, as many as 60,000 people were employed by the Palestine Authority. In Gaza, about a quarter of the residents were dependent on PA salaries. Indeed, acceptance of the Palestine Authority by the population depended in no small part on the patronage doled out through jobs in the new bureaucracy. The 5,000-strong Gazan civil administration under the Israelis ballooned to 40,000 in the Palestine Authority.[38] In fact, in Gaza as much as 40 percent of the work force was on the public payroll. A year after the establishment of the Palestine Authority, its budget was a whopping one-third of the total GNP of the territory it governed. The huge operating deficit that all this public employment created turned out to have some very detrimental economic effects on the territories.

The police forces, in particular, became pump primers for jobs. About half the jobs in the Palestine Authority were in these security forces. Also, the Palestinian security forces, both in their uniforms and armaments (ranging from light to mid-range), became a central part of the symbolic accoutrements of state-building. According to the Oslo Accord, the branches of the security forces could total 9,000 men (later expanded to 18,000); but, in reality, they quickly grew to as many as 45,000 and, at the same time, fragmented into nine (or possibly as many as twelve or more) all-too-autonomous local commands. Among those that eventually became part of the security network were Fatah's Tanzim (the "Organization") and al-Aqsa Brigades, both of which became notorious in the Intifada that broke out in 2000. They were composed of young locals (as opposed to those brought from Tunis), who saw themselves both as responsible for internal security (citing the hapless, formal "blue police") and as a force to be turned against Israel, if need be.[39] The heads of the main security forces, including Muhammad Dahlan and Jibril Rajub, of the Preventive Security Forces in Gaza and the West Bank, respectively, succeeded in acquiring considerable power in the 1990s but basically remained dependent on Arafat and identified with the regime.

Later, beginning in October 2000, when the Oslo agreement broke down and violence erupted, the lines blurred considerably between the official forces of the Palestine Authority and various other armed militias in the occupied territories with varying degrees of support and control.

Beyond security, the need to create legitimacy and authority demanded that the Palestine Authority build both a sense of we-ness among Palestinians and a feeling among the population that the Palestine Authority was the true representation of the people. But the achievement of both these goals was no easy task. For many Palestinians, the Palestine Authority itself was a mixed blessing, bringing some self-government to Palestinians, at long last, but not the hoped-for state. Even among the leaders of the PLO who stood with Arafat, the focus was not so much on this interim institution, the Palestine Authority, as on the final arrangement, through which they would supposedly win an independent and sovereign state for the first time in Palestinian history.

They foresaw this state as located on the West Bank and Gaza Strip, with East Jerusalem as its capital. It would include, they imagined, either no Jews at all or, perhaps, only a small minority of Jewish settlements and settlers. Scattered Palestinians in the diaspora would be addressed by the new state's own "law of return," with the government probably encouraging their selective immigration at a pace it saw fit, based largely on the state's absorption ability economically.[40] But the image of the state and its actual practices did not coincide.[41] The actual government they had in the Palestine Authority, as opposed to the one in their mind's eye, had clipped wings, without the ability to control its airspace, ports, immigration (including return of diaspora Palestinians), foreign relations, and more. The challenge of establishing its authority and legitimacy in such conditions was monumental.

Similar challenges existed in creating a sense of we-ness among the population. One central question was how to build a shared imagined community for all its residents, extending, as well, to the

Palestinians in the *ghurba*. That is, how could the national narrative move beyond a shared sense of victimization and the Lost Garden, the themes that came out of the catastrophe of dispersal and of the life in the camps? While these themes had served Palestinians well as a kind of national cement in the past, they now threatened to strangle the national movement with a debilitating nostalgia.

A number of PA officials focused on the establishment of an educational system, the construction of a new curriculum, and the writing of relevant textbooks that would sketch out the social and cultural borders and characteristics of the new Palestinian identity. Schooling would be a central means of building their imagined community. Up until this time, the educational system in the West Bank had been mainly based on the Jordanian curriculum, in order to prepare students for the Jordanian matriculation examinations *(tawjihi)*. In the Gaza Strip, the Egyptian curriculum had held sway. The rest of the curriculum developed in the schools run by the United Nations Relief and Works Agency for Palestine Refugees in the Near East (UNRWA).

An independent Palestinian curriculum—including the creation of a national history and myths, a true national narrative—had already begun to be formulated in the 1960s in Kuwait and Lebanon. Now, in building on these efforts, the Palestine Authority recruited the best of the local intelligentsia in order to formulate a curriculum and write textbooks. It established a new Ministry of Education in 1994 and invested it with the power to take charge of teacher training and to revamp the curriculum (in the Center for Curriculum Development, set up in 1994 in Ramallah, funded by Italy and assisted by UNESCO).[42] The inadequate supply of teachers and their poor training were addressed through a program to train 1,000 teachers at a time.[43] The development of a national curriculum was at the center of the new ministry's activities. By 1996, the Center for Curriculum Development produced "The Comprehensive Plan for the Development of the First Palestinian Curriculum for General Education," a 600-page, two-volume work. This was followed by the "First Palestinian Curriculum Plan," in 1998, which was approved by both the PA executive and the Legislative Council.[44]

But all these reforms proved to be much harder to effect than anyone had imagined, involving a long and complicated process—one demanding many more resources than the Palestine Authority could marshal. Rote teaching by unqualified teachers continued to be the norm. Indeed, ministry officials said that poorly trained teachers blocked serious organizational and curricular reform.[45] Extremely low salaries and oversized classes made it very difficult to recruit top-grade teachers. Tensions between teachers and the Palestine Authority, especially over salaries, resulted in a number of teacher strikes and the detention and holding incommunicado of a leader of the teacher's movement by the PA security forces. Political favoritism in appointments, both in the ministry and individual schools, also undermined planned changes. These difficulties in the Palestine Authority's establishing an educational system on sound footing simply compounded the effects of the repeated school closures during the al-Aqsa Intifada, further compounding the alarming growth of functional illiteracy in Palestinian society that had already begun in the first Intifada. Educational reform would be slow and could not be counted on to produce the kind of national cohesion for which PA officials hoped.

For all the hurdles that it encountered in establishing its authority and shaping the people in such a way that it, the Palestine Authority, would universally be seen as the institutional representation of that society, the organization of a Palestinian government was a tremendous achievement. If the Palestine Authority was not a state, it came close to being one. It was an internationally recognized political entity with centralized control within a given territory—itself a part of historic Palestine—with the promise inhering in it of expanding that control over more territory, more people, and more functions. Its constituents had the image of it as a state—both for better and for worse—and its practices resembled those of states around the world.

For the first time since 1948, the Palestinian leadership returned to Palestine and settled in among the people (a process that was not always easy or comfortable for the leaders or the residents, due to the years of separation between them during the leadership's exile and differences in culture, generation, and interests). Once the Palestine Authority was up and running, it became hard to imagine a reversal—a move back from centralized Palestinian leadership in Palestine. Even at the height of the violence between Israel and the Palestinians in 2001 and 2002, Israeli leaders—including right-wing leaders who had vigorously condemned the Oslo Accord—spoke of the inevitability of a Palestinian state and the impossibility of reestablishing direct Israeli governance of the West Bank and Gaza.

The gravest threat to the continued life of the Palestine Authority came in late March 2002, in the wake of a major Passover-holiday suicide bombing in the Israeli town of Netanya. Israel drafted a portion of its reserve soldiers and declared the beginning of Operation Defense Shield. The assault's explicit goal was "to wipe out the Palestinian infrastructure of terror." One after another, tank and other land forces under the cover of Apache helicopters entered PA-controlled West Bank territories, cities, refugee camps, and even villages. Of the major towns, only Hebron and Jericho escaped the assault. Israeli forces captured and imprisoned thousands of suspects in detention camps. According to a report of Amnesty International, between February 27 and May 20, 2002, which included the period of the operation, Israeli forces arrested, imprisoned, and interrogated 8,500 Palestinians. Most were gradually released.[46] But the Israeli forces did not stop there. They systematically destroyed national and public Palestinian institutions, including buildings, radio and television stations, information banks, and documents (some were taken as spoils to Israel)—all of which the Palestinian Authority, in the guise of a state-in-the-making, had taken great care to build.[47] Water, electricity, and road infrastructure were also badly damaged.

But even at these darkest moments of violence and escalating retaliation in 2002, when Israeli tanks occupied practically all the West Bank cities and the military set around-the-clock curfews, the idea of Palestinian self-government remained intact. Even if the Palestine Authority no longer could undertake most of the practices of what states do—from building archives to collecting taxes—its image by the Palestinians as the appropriate governing authority for the Palestinians remained intact. While Israeli reoccupation and its subsequent practice of short-term incursions into the cities destroyed much that the Palestinians had built and while Israeli rhetoric (picked up, too, by the United States) included the need for a new Palestinian leadership, there was no retreat from the idea of Palestinian self-government. That, in itself, was a great achievement of the Oslo process.

The accomplishments of the Oslo process were formidable and have had a lasting effect on the political and social terrain of the Palestinians. But, as is already clear, every one of those achievements—a majority accepting a two-state solution, the forswearing of violence, mutual acceptance of legitimacy and recognition of the other's primal fear, and the creation of a Palestinian government—suffered badly through the peace process and into the period of the al-Aqsa Intifada. Each of the successes of the Oslo process has had—and will continue to have—long-term effects on Palestinians and their relations with Israel. In the best of worlds, they will be the building blocks for a future go at peace, for two independent states coexisting peacefully. But at the moment of this writing, it is hard to see beyond the veil of violence. All we can ask is, what went wrong?

11

THE OSLO PROCESS:

WHAT WENT WRONG?

With every passing day, [Palestinians'] ability to keep a sense of
stability becomes more difficult.

(DAOUD KUTTAB, journalist and director of the Institute
of Modern Media at al-Quds University in Ramallah,
August 16, 2002)[1]

DESPITE THE CORNERSTONES laid by the Oslo process for eventual Palestinian-Israeli coexistence and the normalization of Palestinian society—the unveiling of the pro-compromise majorities
on each side, mutual acceptance, the renunciation of violence as a
permanent strategy, recognition by each side of the other's primal
fear, the creation of multiple channels working toward coexistence,
and the establishment of Palestinians' first-ever self-government—
the twenty-first century opened with a reversion to brutal violence,
unmitigated hatred, and mutual demonization. The scenes of public space in Israel and Palestine were no longer those of people se-
renely sipping their Turkish coffee in chic cafes but of mobs chanting "Death to the Arabs" and dancing in the streets at the news of
suicide bombs ripping innocent civilians to shreds.

Israel's flirtation with a normal, secure everyday life came to an
abrupt end. And, for Palestinians, the return of the hopelessness of
1948 and 1967, the erosion of the significant economic gains that
they had made in the 1980s, the unceasing violence, all made the
heady days of late 1993 seem like a mirage. At the end of the man-

dated period set out in the DOP's agenda, there still was no Palestinian state, no return of refugees, no sovereignty over Jerusalem, and no respite from Israel's dominion over their lives. By mid-2002, the brutal violence of the al-Aqsa Intifada had crippled Palestine's fledgling political institutions and threatened the fragile social cohesion Palestinians had painstakingly constructed in the decades after 1948 and 1967.

What went wrong? Why did the Oslo Accord fail to deliver? Five key elements doomed the Oslo peace process. These factors point to the accord's grounding in the power imbalance of the two sides and its inattention to mechanisms that could arbitrate differences between the Israelis and Palestinians and enable the parties to deal with naysayers, particularly those willing to use terror. The absence of such rules, in effect, gave these groups a veto power over the course of the peace process.

Most of all, the following factors demonstrate that peace cannot simply emerge from secret negotiations among leaders closeted away in a magical castle. The central argument throughout this book, from the first rumblings of change in the early 1800s to creation of a self-identified people in the shambles of dispossession in the last half of the twentieth century, is that the creation of the Palestinian nation has been as much the product of events, acts, and institutions at the grassroots level as it has been of the doings of top leaders. In fact, the developments at the lowest levels of society have shaped and constrained those at the top. This argument held through the peace process, as well. The Palestinian public's response to, and participation in, the Oslo peace process determined whether it would succeed.

Frontloading and Backloading of Benefits

Each side came to the negotiating table in Oslo with a shopping list of goals. Israel's principal aims could be summarized in two words, security and acceptance. Since 1948, Israeli leaders had fought to have Israel accepted as a legitimate state internationally. And their day-to-day preoccupation was security—the violent threats posed by Arab states, largely through conventional warfare, and by nonstate groups (such as Fatah), through guerrilla warfare and terrorism. Israeli strategy for most of its existence gave primacy to surrounding Arab states in terms of goals, security, and acceptance. Its leaders' thinking was that if Israel persevered and finally gained acceptance from its neighbors, neutralizing their threat to Israel's well-being by making conventional warfare too costly or undesirable, then hostile guerrilla groups and other nonstate actors, indeed the entire Palestinian problem, would simply melt away. Israel's peace treaty with Egypt was the crowning achievement in this strategy.

Oslo was a complete reversal of that strategy for Israel, because it gave first priority to the Palestinian issue and assumed that resolving *that* issue would make resistance to Israel disappear in the region at large. Israeli leaders were by no means fully agreed on this sudden 180-degree turn in strategy, nor were individual leaders, such as Rabin and Barak, unambivalent about the change in course—in fact, every Israeli prime minister in the 1990s thought, at one time or another, that Syria was a better bet as the primary peace partner than the PLO. All this equivocation led to zigzags in Israeli policy, which badly damaged the Oslo process.

In any case, when the Israelis did commit to the Palestinians-first track in 1993, they maintained the same overall aims that they had harbored since 1948, gaining acceptance as a legitimate state and solving the security problem, only now tactically using the Palestinians as the lever to the rest of the Arab world rather than the opposite.[2] The Oslo Accord seemingly accomplished those goals, *frontloading* precisely those benefits to Israel. By frontloading, we mean that the agreement gave Israel what it desired most of all at the signing, without any delay. The Declaration of Principles incorporated recognition of Israel by the PLO and an immediate halt to violence into its terms at the very signing of the agreement and its accompanying protocols. Palestinians were supposed to prevent attacks against Israelis wherever they were—inside Israel or in settlements located on Palestinian territories.

PLO leaders, too, came to the Oslo negotiations with their own shopping list, but the inequality of power between Israel and the PLO enabled Israel to postpone the achievement of most Palestinian goals. Israel's hold on all the land of historic Palestine, its overwhelming firepower, its many advantages as an actual state, its financial resources, all put it in a much stronger bargaining position at Oslo. Indeed, it was the imbalance of power that was inscribed into the Declaration of Principles through its unequal timing of concessions that so soured Palestinian intellectuals, such as Edward Said, on the entire Oslo process.

While the PLO did receive some benefits up front, including recognition as the legitimate representative of the Palestinian people (in a letter sent by Israel four days before the signing of the DOP) and a toehold in Palestine (after about a year), its most cherished ends were *backloaded;* that is, they were implicitly promised, PLO officials believed, as benefits that would come in the course of the five years of negotiations or, most likely, as elements in the final status agreement. These included, of course, the creation of a sovereign state but also the elimination of Jewish settlements in the West Bank and Gaza Strip, a just resolution of the refugee problem through some formula recognizing Palestinians' right of return, free movement between the West Bank and Gaza Strip, a capital city in Jerusalem including Palestinian sovereignty over *haram al-sharif* and the Arab neighborhoods of the city, and the creation of a sustainable Palestinian economy including control over sufficient water resources.

The continuing effects of the initial power imbalance, leading to the frontloading of benefits for Israelis and the backloading of benefits for Palestinians, were momentous. Because Israel had already received most of what its leaders wanted, the incentives to make further painful concessions were low, especially ones that involved huge domestic costs. And most of what they had to give up—settlements, parts of Jerusalem, access to water, territory—had powerful, vocal domestic Jewish constituencies committed to maintaining them for Israel. Even more, the fact that Israel had most of its gains in hand when follow-up negotiations began on an interim agreement and, later, on a final-status agreement meant that the Palestinians had very few levers with which they could influence Israeli negotiators.

Compounding Palestinian weakness was the fact that, while Israel's benefits were clearly spelled out, the Palestinians' backloaded benefits were not specified in the Declaration of Principles. The agreements were created according to Henry Kissinger's doctrine of "constructive opaqueness," that is, agreeing to general principles and leaving the details hazy, thus allowing each side to present the agreement to its own public as if it had achieved its central goals. While this method may have worked well for agreements between the United States and China or Vietnam, nations separated by thousands of miles, it was not suitable here. Not only were the details unspecified for only one of the two parties—the Palestinians—this was a case of populations living side by side with continuous interaction among broad segments of the two populations. In such a situation, any small incident or source of friction could cause immense tension and events that could threaten the peace process.

Palestinians and Israelis apprehended the course of the long negotiations that were to follow and the details that would be hammered out quite differently. Palestinians felt that their tremendous concessions at the outset—giving up 78 percent of historic Palestine and recognizing the Jewish state's right to exist—were so far-reaching and painful, that the backloaded benefits would not require many further compromises. They imagined an agreement like the Israeli-Egyptian formula: "Peace in exchange for all of the territory captured during the war of 1967." For the Israelis, however, the agreement was perceived as just the beginning of negotiations. The backloaded benefits for the Palestinians would demand further bargaining over the scope of the territories ceded, the fate of the settlements, and patterns for military control over the whole space.

In sum, the Palestinians found it very difficult to extract Israeli concessions as the negotiations wore on. It was not lost on Palestinian leaders that the one element that could be meted out to exert continuing pressure on the Israeli government and induce it to sweeten the pot in the negotiations—violence—had been relinquished at the outset. The temptation to reclaim violence as a lever, either indirectly by turning a blind eye toward actions by "unauthorized" groups, such as Hamas, or directly through Fatah-backed perpetrators, was enormous.

Backloading of benefits for the Palestinians meant the incentive structure for them was entirely different from that of the Israelis. They were induced to make more and more concessions now in order to receive those hoped-for final benefits later. Israelis knew that, as did Palestinian critics of Oslo. Indeed, the drumbeat of the Palestinian intellectual critics, especially in the United States, was that the readiness to make concessions in order to have a state would lead to one that was nothing more than an impotent South African Bantustan. Israel would maintain true control over Palestinians' lives, even if it no longer ruled directly through a civil and military administration. Beyond that, the Israelis kept in their pocket all the as-yet-undelivered benefits, thus maintaining tremendous leverage over the Palestinian leadership.

Of all the points of contention between the sides, none more strongly reflected the frontloading/backloading asymmetry than Israeli settlements in the West Bank and Gaza Strip. Palestinians inside and outside the territories saw Israel's unwillingness to dismantle settlements and, even worse, its continuous thickening of settlements through the entire Oslo process as an ominous sign. From the signing of the Oslo agreements to the year 2000, the number of settlers in the West Bank doubled, reaching nearly 380,000, including those in the captured parts of Jerusalem.[3] Now that Israel had what it wanted from the frontloaded benefits it gained in the Oslo Accord, Palestinians believed, it would fail to deliver on its promises; the settlements would be a form of permanent occupation and emasculation of any Palestinian "state" that might be created. The extraordinary public investment in the territories by Israel, particularly intensive building of expensive bypass roads, was a further indication to both the Palestinian leaders and public that backloading actually translated into a tease that would never be realized.

For Israeli leaders, especially those from the Labor party, the settlements were irritants that threatened the party's hold on government. Their motivation was to postpone any move on the settlement issue, which would inevitably test their fragile coalitions, until the last possible moment, that is, the final status agreement. Palestinians would have to take on faith that Israel's intentions were honorable. During the entire Oslo process, not a single Israeli prime minister reassured the Palestinians by indicating that all, or even most, settlements would be dismantled. On the contrary, in the year 2000 alone, the number of Jews in the Palestinian territories (not including the annexed areas of Jerusalem) grew by more than 8 percent. Only in 2002 did a serious candidate for the prime minister post, Amram Mitzna, emerge who was willing to make the evacuation of settlements part of his platform.

To conclude, the Oslo Accord created an agenda that would take years to work through. But it saddled the ensuing process with a structure marked by an imbalance of power between the negotiating partners. It frontloaded benefits for Israel and backloaded them for Palestinians. Yet Oslo included an incentive structure that did not provide much sense of urgency to Israelis to take the steps necessary for Palestinians to achieve those backloaded benefits, or even reassure Palestinians that they would actually materialize. In addition, it contained few levers for Palestinians to induce Israel to move forward expeditiously.

Both sides soon grew weary of the extended process and its complicated agenda, especially its interim features, but both sides also were apprehensive about moving directly to final status negotiations and the extensive concessions that a final agreement would undoubtedly demand. The peace-making process was based on a gradual, step-by-step process of arrangement-making. The basic idea was to create trust and confidence between the two peoples. But the leaders of both peoples were hesitant to make hard and fateful decisions on real issues, which undermined the process. Issues such as the final borders, the status of holy shrines in Jerusalem, the future of the Jewish settlements, the refugee problem, or how to share common aquifers remained open and were not tackled until the marathon sessions at the very end, in Camp David and at Taba in 2000 and 2001.

Unstable Politics on Both Sides

For more than 20 years, no government in Israel succeeded in winning reelection. Menachem Begin, in 1981, was the last Israeli prime minister to form a government on his own for a second term, and even he did not serve that full term. Despite the Knesset's attempts to stabilize electoral politics through a series of legislative reforms, support for the two main parties continued to erode. Small, special-interest parties mushroomed and exercised extraordinary leverage. Coalitions became thin, weak, and unstable. As a result, highly mobilized interest groups could successfully threaten the life of governments. Prime ministers were preoccupied with keeping their fragile coalitions intact, cobbling together odd unions of parties with opposing interests. Their attention focused on placating particular groups that threatened to bolt and then, immediately after, in dealing with another coalition faction offended by the concessions to the first group. Indeed, every Israeli government after the signing of the Oslo Accord—those headed by Yitzhak Rabin, Shimon Peres, Binyamin Netanyahu, Ehud Barak, and Ariel Sharon—faced similar challenges in terms of constructing and then maintaining a coalition. Nurturing the coalition—even just keeping it intact—increasingly preoccupied each successive government's leaders, especially after a honeymoon period of about a year in office. Balancing domestic concerns with the painful concessions that the Oslo process necessarily demanded became more and more difficult as each government's term wore on.

For Rabin and his foreign minister, Peres, that balancing act was especially complicated. Their belief that the Palestinian-Israeli conflict had changed from a zero-sum to a non-zero-sum game tempered their temptation to triumph in every round of negotiations. They indicated their understanding that Arafat had to appear to his population to be winning real concessions from Israel if Palestinians were going to remain behind the Oslo process. Even so, the fragility of their governing coalition and their constant looking over their shoulders at domestic constituencies limited their willingness to forego victories in the negotiations. They were well aware, for example, that Palestinians saw Israeli settlement activity as a barometer of Israel's commitment to eventually deliver Oslo's backloaded benefits; yet not a single Israeli settlement was dismantled during their watch, and the overall number of settlers continued to increase at an alarming rate.

Once Netanyahu was elected in early 1996, he made it clear that the zero-sum mentality had returned: he construed every Palestinian gain as an Israeli setback. Netanyahu did not openly and officially discard Oslo and continued talks with the Palestinians under American auspices. He even came to additional interim agreements, including the withdrawal from the West Bank city of Hebron (with the exception of a Jewish enclave) and the Wye Agreement (November 16, 1996). In the framework of the Wye Agreement, Israel agreed to transfer control over additional portions of the West Bank to the Palestine Authority, and thus *de facto* the entire urban population (with the exception of that in Jerusalem) and most of the population of the refugee camps came under PA governance. Nevertheless, as a result of the Wye Agreement, the radical right abandoned Netanyahu's Likud party, a move that eventually helped topple his government.[4]

The Oslo process survived under Netanyahu, but a change could be felt in the atmosphere and in relations between Israel and the Palestinians. Mutual trust was shaken. In addition to the hostile tone of the new government toward the Palestinians, the controversy surrounding the Western Wall Tunnel contributed to this change in the political climate. On September 25, 1996, the Israeli government opened the tunnel, which extended underneath *haram al-sharif*—an act considered by Muslims as a threat to the status quo of the mosques above. The opening of the tunnel incited demonstrations and riots during which about 40 Palestinians were killed and 100 injured. Tensions also rose as construction plans were expanded into areas of Arab Jerusalem and in the settlements. The beginning of a new Jewish neighborhood of Har Homa in greater Jerusalem touched a particularly raw nerve among Palestinians. A radical, nationalist rhetoric and scorn for Palestinians began to mark official Israeli discourse. That change made it all the more difficult for the PA leadership to sell the idea to its constituency that patience would bring the Palestinians their cherished goals. On the settlement issue, particularly, Palestinians could expect very little at all, since the settlers were one of Netanyahu's biggest and most enthusiastic constituencies. Netanyahu's tenure also made Palestinians fear that Israel's political instability, its oscillations between right and left, sabotaged the long-term commitment and steadfastness that the Oslo process demanded.

On May 17, 1999, Ehud Barak was elected to Prime Minister on the Labor party ticket under the slogan, "Continuation of the Rabin Legacy." His election raised big hopes for the rehabilitation of relations of trust between Israel and the Palestinians, in particular, and the Arab world, in general. Barak's brief and rocky tenure, which lasted until early 2001, a bit over a year and a half, epitomized a government with a tin ear toward both the domestic constituencies it needed in order to keep its narrow coalition afloat and Oslo's requirements of measured, continuing confidence-building measures that would reassure Palestinians that the process was headed in the right direction.

Israel's move back to the right, yet again, in 2001 with the landslide election of Sharon finally and fully reversed the logic of Oslo from mutual reassurance to a vicious cycle of violence. Indeed, Sharon's tenure marked the end of the Oslo process. All in all, Israel's volatile politics during the entire Oslo period induced the country's leaders to place immediate domestic concerns ahead of the long-term policies, concessions, and commitments that the peace process required. Managing domestic coalition politics in Israel overwhelmed foreign policy and subverted the possibility of fashioning long-range policies for the entire decade following the signing of the Declaration of Principles. In particular, none of the left-wing prime ministers succeeded in translating the overwhelming majority of the electorate expressing support for the peace process into a workable electoral majority.

Instability in Palestinian politics also took a steep toll on the Oslo peace process, although it assumed a very different hue from Israel's electoral ping-pong and its coalitional gyrations. Unlike Israel, the Palestine Authority had only one head, Yasser Arafat, for the entire eight years in which negotiations took place. Instability in Palestinian internal politics came through veiled, ongoing struggles for authority among the Palestine Authority, two other societal centers of power, and Israel's administration in the West Bank and Gaza Strip. These struggles drained Palestinian leaders' energy and, as in Israel, focused them on short-term, internal power-jockeying. In addition, Arafat's leadership, it turns out, both masked and encouraged instability and weak governmental institutions at the next levels down of the Palestine Authority. And weak governmental institutions only increased preoccupation with domestic, everyday issues instead of the big-picture issues associated with the Oslo process.

Two societal centers of power posed serious challenges to Arafat as he and his aides organized the new Palestine Authority. Both of these centers—the educated, secular local leaders and the Islamic groups—matured in the course of the Intifada that began in 1987. These two centers came out of the burgeoning Palestinian universities in the territories, many of whose graduates later fortified their ties to each other in Israeli prisons. Many became professionals. Often, they were recruited on campus to serve as candidates or political cadres in the highly competitive and politicized student elections.

Through a variety of civic institutions, from the Boy Scouts to the Voluntary Works Program (which started as a literacy campaign and mushroomed into a multifaceted series of volunteer experiences), secular students and professionals cut their teeth as local leaders in the 1970s and 1980s, even before the Intifada began. They came not from the notable class, for the most part, but from common Palestinian families in refugee camps, villages, and towns.[5] While often focused locally, their efforts mobilized Palestinians from all over the West Bank and Gaza Strip into cross-cutting civic organizations and volunteer efforts. As much as anyone, they were responsible for the emerging civil society in territories. Indeed, their construction of the organizational basis for ongoing relations beyond one's kinship group, in the absence of a Palestinian state protecting them and in the face of an Israeli state hounding them, proved to be one of the most remarkable feats in the making of the Palestinian people.

By the end of the 1980s, these organizations of civil society employed 20,000–30,000 workers. In the absence of a state, the new Palestinian elite had cultivated alternate mechanisms in civil society. Without tax revenues, their organizations depended, in large part, on foreign sources. During the period of the first Intifada, these organizations gained momentum, and, by the early 1990s, provided about 60 percent of services associated with medical clinics and first aid, about half of those in hospital services, about 30 percent of those associated with education, and almost all aid and rehabilitation services for the disabled. They also provided agricultural extension services, counseling and support for those in need, aid for former prisoners, and more.

Already facing opposition from the old notable leadership (with which the Israelis worked in governing the area), the students and professionals encountered an additional, unexpected foe, the PLO, as they began to build civic institutions. Tensions between the outside PLO and the local leadership date back, in fact, to the mid-1970s. An article in the PLO's academic journal in 1976, for example, commented, "It would be a big mistake if we push the establishment of a leadership framework within the occupied land. . . ."[6] During the Intifada, these tensions grew even worse. Tunis-based officials worried that the success of self-appointed leaders in the territories, sustaining the uprising through local popular committees, would undermine the central authority of the PLO. Already, the characteristic pattern that would occur in the post-Oslo period was evident during the Intifada: "The PLO increasingly fragmented the institutions created within civil society. . . ." The PLO's maxim was: "The stronger territorial [local] movements become, the weaker and smaller scale the public institutions in the territory must be."[7] Because of its own fear of competitors for leadership, the PLO thwarted the construction of a civil society that broadly linked the towns and villages of the West Bank and Gaza Strip in favor of continued fragmentation.

With the construction of the Palestine Authority, it began to take upon itself large portions of the functions that these associations of civil society had previously fulfilled. Indeed, within the framework of the Palestine Authority, different ministries were established precisely for this purpose (Health, Welfare, Education, Higher Education, Media, and so on). But the new government offices did not always garner the same sort of respect that the organizations of civil society did. Often, particular agencies became identified with the people who headed them—loyalists to the President. The "state" was much less efficient and actually provided fewer services than did the voluntary organizations.

In these circumstances, the old PLO opposition to the emerging civil leadership intensified under the rule of the Palestine Authority, as it "tried to impose its centralized power hierarchy on a population in which day-to-day authority was located at the grass roots. . . ." Arafat and his aides set out to undercut the autonomous authority of the new university-produced secular leadership through "co-optation, coercion, and forced marginalization."[8] Leaders of civic organizations, for example, were all-too-often hauled off to explain their actions to Force 17 security officials. In 1995, the General Security Forces *(al-mukharbat al-umma)* circulated a questionnaire to all the voluntary organizations, in an attempt to learn about their members, the internal structure of the organizations, their goals, means of operation, and funding sources. The questionnaire had a chilling effect on institutions of civil society. It did not bode well for the development of democracy among the Palestinians.

Much of the energy and attention of Arafat and his staff, then, was channeled into their attempt to curb the local leadership. Their success in neutering the new local leaders came, ironically, through allying with the old notable leadership and starving the new leadership's organizational base—the relief organizations (many of them medical), neighborhood associations, and, especially, the popular committees that had been the backbone of the Intifada—by keeping firm control of revenues, especially foreign aid. Fear of competitors for leadership from the impressive group that had emerged from Palestine's universities and Israel's prisons, in effect, led Arafat and his aides in the Palestine Authority to dismantle, rather than build, Palestine's emerging civil society.

The attitude of the PA leadership toward the educated secular leaders was part and parcel of its general orientation, which was to treat any domestic opposition "as an enemy to be put down with force."[9] It is not surprising, then, that PA officials doled out similar treatment to the second center of power in society, which had also matured during the Intifada, the Islamic groups. Spurred on by the revolution in Iran and the continuing oppressiveness of Israeli occupation, Hamas, in particular, took big strides in the 1980s in linking different elements of Palestinian Muslim society in the territories. It succeeded in appealing to a couple of key social elements, which had previously not been politically mobilized. First were those Palestinians in the West Bank and Gaza Strip who, like Arab citizens of Israel in the 1950s and 1960s, faced the disorienting process of change from peasant life to that of the day laborer.

Second were Muslims, especially those in refugee camps who, during the 1980s, showed a marked increase in religious practice, such as modest dress, daily prayer, fasting, Koranic recitation, and more. The growth in the importance of Islam in the refugee camps was even faster than for the Palestinian population as a whole, which also showed marked increases in religiosity, and the new religious groups paid special attention to the camps.

As had been the case for the secular local leaders, the universities also provided a nurturing environment for the new Islamic movement. Indeed, it was the support garnered by the Muslim Brethren and then Hamas among intellectuals, especially in the universities, that so alarmed secular PLO leaders. Once the Intifada began, the struggle between the PLO and Islamic groups intensified. One Hamas leader, Mahmoud al-Zahhar, for example, lambasted the PLO publicly in 1991, citing the "corruption in the PLO, and [its] misuse of funds."[10] The Palestine National Council's declaration of a Palestinian state in the West Bank and Gaza in 1988, implicitly accepting Israel's acceptance, was perhaps the pivotal event in driving a deep wedge between the PLO and the Islamic groups. Hamas condemned this shift, as it later did the Madrid Conference in 1991 and the Oslo Accord in 1993. The idea of territorial concessions to Israel, of two states coexisting in Palestine, was anathema to the entire Islamic movement.[11] Division on this basic principle—in effect, whether to accept partition of the territory that had once been British-controlled Palestine—continued into the twenty-first century and the al-Aqsa Intifada, a term that itself had deep religious significance.

Once the Declaration of Principles was signed in 1993, Hamas became the foremost opposition in the West Bank and Gaza Strip to accommodation with Israel. It made unequivocal disparaging statements about the agreement and Arafat's role in signing it: "We consider this to be a great historic act of treason and a dangerous one which will begin the dissolution of this leadership which has sold the struggle, sold the blood and sold the rights of the Palestinian people."[12] But its relationship both to Oslo and the Palestine Authority was more complex than this statement lets on. Hamas came to be divided between two camps. First were those who favored, at least during the initial stage of euphoria and great hopes, integration with Arafat's popularly supported regime, piggybacking, they hoped, onto the emerging widespread image of the Palestine Authority as the appropriate government for Palestinians. Second were those who advocated sticking with the traditional goals of holy war against the Jews, liberation of the holy land, and, only then, establishment of a theocratic Islamic state.[13]

At times, Hamas officials accepted the reality of the new framework created by the Oslo Accord and made concessions to it and the Palestine Authority. Some in the Islamic movement sought integration into the *Sulta* (the regime), which would force Fatah to take them into consideration and grant them an appropriate position and influence within the new Palestine Authority. That meant recognition, appropriate representation in national institutions, conservation of the traditional nature of Palestinian society, and, mostly, positions and budget allocations. For those opposing the agreements, renewal of guerrilla warfare was intended to bring about the breakdown of the agreements with Israel and prove that the Palestine Authority did not rule the territories, nor could it provide Israel with its most cherished goal—security. While neither camp among the Islamic groups ever wavered in the rejection of a two-state permanent solution, in the belief that Israel must ultimately be destroyed, some members did accept the notion of liberating Palestine in steps, which meant approval of a Palestinian state in a portion of Palestine (and thus, implicitly, the acceptance of Israel, at least temporarily). "We accept that there is government in Palestine and beside it the government of Israel for now. But in the future, we don't accept that."[14] Their acknowledgment of the institutions coming out of the Oslo Accord as at least partially legitimate can be seen in the fact that some Hamas-affiliated candidates, running as individuals, even won election to the Palestine Authority's Legislative Council in 1996.

Further complicating the Palestine Authority's relationship to this opposition was the transformation of Hamas and the Islamic Jihad into the primary threat in Israeli officials' minds (a turnaround from the early years of the Intifada, when these officials often courted Hamas in order to weaken the uprising's internal and external secular leadership). For PA leaders, Israel's new perception that Hamas was the biggest threat portended that any action PA security forces might take against the Islamic organizations would be construed by Palestinians as doing Israel's bidding.

Not only did the Islamic movement draw PA officials' energy and attention away from the Oslo process, then, it also heightened the specter that the Palestine Authority was nothing but a shill for Israel and could never be the basis of a truly autonomous state. Beyond that, Hamas and Islamic Jihad's success in perpetrating acts of terror against Israel through the entire Oslo process and beyond made the Israeli public and its leaders feel that the Palestine Authority was not doing nearly enough to curb these groups and thus was not a trustworthy partner for peace. Many began to suspect that the Palestine Authority leaders, especially Arafat, were playing a double game through a complicit "division of labor" between the PA and the Islamic groups.

Early in the peace process, between April 6, 1994, and August 21, 1996, Hamas and the Islamic Jihad organizations succeeded in carrying out a series of terrorist attacks in Israel's major cities, the most serious of these coming in early 1996, only months after the assassination of Rabin. Tens of people were killed and hundreds wounded. These attacks fueled what had been a relatively dormant internal opposition in Israel and eroded the legitimacy of the nascent Palestine Authority and of Arafat himself in Israeli eyes. The "coordinated security" between Israeli and Palestinian security forces, which was anchored in the agreements between the two sides and was, from the standpoint of the Israeli government and public opinion, a necessary condition for continuation of the process, began to seem purposeless. In Israeli eyes, the Palestine Authority was either unable or unwilling to act against fellow Palestinians, because it feared the start of a Palestinian civil war. At the very best, as far as Israelis were concerned, the Islamic movement held a veto power over the reconciliation process between the Israelis and the Palestinians because of the Palestine Authority's inability to curb the militants. At the very worst, the Palestine Authority was explicitly or implicitly sanctioning this violence, in direct violation of its pledge in the Oslo Accord, in order to bring pressure on Israel to make greater concessions.

Whatever the exact relationship of the PA top brass to Hamas, the loss of life among Israeli citizens and the massive damage in the central areas of the big cities undercut the positive public opinion, favoring the Oslo and Cairo agreements, which led to Israel's redeployment in Gaza and Jericho, in the first year of the peace process. The attacks also helped revive the opposition in Israel, which had been stunned into relative silence when Oslo was first announced, in part because of the relief and hope with which so much of the public greeted the accord. Now the attacks seemed to validate the opposition's claims that "this is not a peace." The public support so desperately needed for the Israelis to continue on with the Oslo process eroded quickly, further magnifying the difficulties of keeping a coalition together. Indeed, the bombings were a major factor leading to the electoral defeat of Peres, the most pro-Oslo of all Israeli politicians, to Netanyahu, an outspoken foe of the peace process.

Israel's harsh retaliation to the terror, in turn, chipped away at the Palestinian public's backing for Oslo. Each attack brought an Israeli riposte, including closures and enclosures that barred the movement of Palestinian labor into Israel as well as much of the movement within the West Bank and Gaza Strip. Nothing else Israel did in the West Bank and Gaza Strip caused as much hardship to Palestinians and ensuing political instability in Palestinian politics as did its policy of repeated closures.

Hamas bombings in the mid-1990s led to a new addition to the Israeli lexicon, the concept of "separation," which created yet another threat to the peace process. It involved an intentional reduction in the minimum of contact between the Israeli and Palestinian population, without giving up Israeli military control over the Palestinians. Physical barriers included wire fences, mined areas, and reserved areas patrolled by military and police forces. In its first stage, the program was put into effect around the Gaza Strip, although Jewish settlements and large military forces meant to protect them remained within the strip. The psychological rationale of the program was that, after so many years of deep-seated ethnic conflict, "wounds could not be healed" by any means other than total separation of the two peoples. From the Palestinian point of view, the construction of these segmenting barriers, cutting so many Palestinian workers off from access to their jobs, just reinforced what they began to see as the apartheid character of the Israeli state.

The vicious cycle of Palestinian terrorist acts and Israeli retaliation worsened the economic situation for the residents of the occupied territories (in the Gaza Strip, there were reports of malnutrition, even of starvation), making Palestinian politics more volatile and the Palestinian public more skeptical about the worth of the Oslo process.[15] The brazen attacks brought about a rise in the prestige of the Islamic resistance movement and the development of the image of a new Palestinian hero and *shahid*. The most famous was Yahya Ayyash, also known as the "engineer," who reputedly was responsible for the preparation and direction of most of the attacks. His eventual assassination by Israeli intelligence placed him first among a pantheon of martyrs, mostly youngsters who began a series of suicide bombings in 1994. It also reopened the door to deadly bombings in Israel in early 1996, which apparently had been suspended by Hamas for a good part of 1995.

In terms of the attractiveness of cultural symbols, electoral appeal, and threats to the peace process, the Islamic center of power posed a formidable challenge to the Palestine Authority. But Arafat's options for dealing with this challenge were limited. In the first couple of years of the Palestine Authority, at least, it simply did not have efficient enough intelligence agencies to eliminate the attacks on Israel, which, in addition to all else, threatened the PA's authority and very existence. Also, arresting cultural heroes and going after those considered near-saints by portions of the population held their own dangers for Arafat. Using his security men, such as those in Force 17, which he had brought to Palestine with him, against the Islamic groups also had pitfalls. These security forces faced an uphill battle in gaining public trust; many local Palestinians saw the new security men, many of them born abroad, almost as foreigners. Their status as outsiders was exacerbated by a cultural and generational gap as well; Arafat's security men tended to be ten or twenty years older than the key secular and religious leaders who were proving to be so popular.

The danger of confronting the Islamic groups directly became obvious to Arafat when violence quickly erupted between the Palestine Authority and the Islamic movement once the PLO's leadership relocated to Palestine. When the Palestine Authority announced a wholesale collection of firearms, ammunition, and other instruments of war from the population, the Islamic groups objected outright. On November 22, 1994, shortly after the PLO's assumption of power, a bloody clash broke out in Gaza between the PA militia and local residents, who were demonstrating for Hamas and against the Oslo process. PA forces fired on the crowd and killed a number of people (accounts run from 13-16 dead) and injured many others (the estimates run as high as 200 wounded). Arafat took a public relations beating and, as a result, attempted thereafter to avoid overt, violent conflict with Hamas and Islamic Jihad, which, of course, led Israelis, in turn, to question his commitment to Oslo. As with the secular opposition, his emerging tactic was to divide and control the Islamic groups through political and economic cooptation, particularly by doling out posts and favors. Despite his efforts, though, other violent clashes did occur over the years. Whatever the means PA officials used to cope with the Islamic challenge from 1994 on, they found that dealing with the formidable Islamic opposition constantly constrained, diverted, and undermined them during the years of difficult negotiations with Israel.

If the internecine struggle, in which Arafat attempted to wrest authority from the local educated leadership and their civil institutions as well as divide and coopt the powerful Islamic movement, were not enough, PA leaders had to deal with a third center of power, Israel, not only as a negotiating partner, but as a continuing governing presence in the territories as well. Israel's forces still maintained control of key elements of governance throughout the West Bank and Gaza Strip—full control in Area C, security in Area B, control of key roads, access through ports and the new airport, travel between the West Bank and Gaza Strip, and more. From the early years of the occupation, Israeli officials, wittingly and unwittingly, became players in struggles of power within Palestinian society. Israel, as we noted, had encouraged the Islamic movement at the expense of the PLO early in the Intifada. Similarly, while most of Israel's attention was directed toward neutralizing outside threats from Fatah and other violent groups during the 1970s and 1980s, the Israeli civil and military leadership also tried, without much success, thwarting the development of centers of authority headed by the new, secular local leaders in the West Bank and Gaza Strip. Glenn Robinson, who studied the first Intifada, wrote that, rather than stymie the new secular elite, the Israelis unwittingly abetted the creation of this new group of leaders.

Israel, by grudgingly allowing Palestinian universities to open and expand, ironically assisted in the formation of a new political elite drawn from a far broader stratum of Palestinians than the narrowly based notable elite of earlier generations. Because of the very size of this new elite, Israeli attempts to vanquish it—through deportations, encouraged emigration, imprisonment, extended closures of universities, and the like—proved futile.[16]

Now, with the creation of the Palestine Authority, Israel continued to have a major impact on how power in Palestinian society and politics was parsed. It controlled everything from the revenue flow going to the Palestine Authority through remittance of collected taxes to travel of Palestinians to jobs in Israel and within PA-governed territory. The result of its continued hulking presence was to focus the Palestinian leadership on daily irritants in its relations with Israel as well as its need to demonstrate domestic control in the face of its emasculation by Israel, instead of the bigger picture of a final status agreement. Israel's continuing role in day-to-day governance also meant that Arafat could never satisfactorily respond to his critics' question of whether the new Palestinian government really governed.

The Palestine Authority's preoccupation with delegitimizing other centers of authority and countering Israel in day-to-day governance led it to employ all sorts of tactics that were anathema to institution building. One scholar summarized its techniques as falling into three categories: "concentration of power, surveillance (intimidation), and largesse that purchases quiet and supporters (bribery)."[17] Another researcher referred to its engaging in "deinstitutionalization instead of state building."[18] Any institutions that it did build were undermined by yet other institutions that it fashioned: civil courts by security courts, police forces by official and semiofficial militias, nongovernmental service organizations by so-called shadow ministries, the semiofficial development agency PECDAR (Palestinian Economic Council for Development and Reconstruction) with presidential control of development funds, a separation of the legislature and executive by an incorporation (read: cooptation) of legislators into executive functions, and much, much more. Human rights abuses intimidated the opposition.[19] One pattern seemed to be the transfer of everyday control to local strongmen from among the old notables, who, although in name represent-ing the Palestine Authority and the President, in fact acted on their own.

Deinstitutionalization went hand in hand with Arafat's personal style of rule. His regime, notes one writer, "could be labelled semi-authoritarian, with personalisation circling around Yasir Arafat al-lowing patronage relations and weakened institutions."[20] Another researcher comments on Arafat's style by writing *"l'état c'est Arafat."* He added, "The personalization of politics directly undermined the core political strength of the new [secular] elite, which was col-lective action through institution-building."[21] Beyond undermining his own institutions, Arafat had a penchant for playing musical chairs with his aides, which prevented anyone below him from con-centrating enough loyalty and strength through an extended stint in a key agency to challenge him—and, as a result, from concentrat-ing enough power to build effective institutions. Many key figures, such as Bassam Abu Sharif, Hani al-Hasan, and Mahmud Abbas, simply disappeared from politics or were shifted to less powerful posts. In many ways, Arafat resembled a New York professional dog-walker, who constantly reined in some and let the leash out for oth-ers, all in an effort not to be dragged into the gutter himself. The ef-fect on Palestinian politics was to preempt transparent procedures, shuffle talent around in a way that undermined institutional stabil-ity and strength, and keep Arafat's attention on day-to-day political machinations—the street curb in front of him—instead of on the broader horizon, the long-term, delicate Oslo process.

Repeated Interruptions and Absence of Arbiters

The shift from the Madrid- to the Oslo-framework was momentous. It removed the negotiations from Washington's harsh glare and the penchant of the negotiators on both sides to posture for the press instead of addressing those sitting across the table. The switch put Fatah and the PLO, the key Palestinian organizations, directly into the bargaining process, rather than having their officials' whispering into the ears of quasi-autonomous Palestinian negotiators from the West Bank and Gaza Strip. In addition, the Oslo talks gave the Palestinian side independent standing for the first time, rather than as an adjunct of the Jordanian delegation. In short, the sessions in Oslo put Israeli and Palestinian negotiators together on the same level for person-to-person talks in a way that had not happened before. While, for some time later, a number of Palestinian-American intellectuals maintained the illusion that success had been just around the corner in the Washington talks in 1992–1993, in fact the Norwegians had rightly seen that the Madrid framework was a dead end.

But the Norwegians' success in bringing the parties into frank, direct talks on an equal footing, without the intervention of the United States, created a different series of obstacles, too. A key problem was the absence of an official, credible intermediary with sufficient clout to change the behavior of both sides. Almost immediately after the signing of the Declaration of Principles, the two sides began a litany of complaints that the other side was not living up to the terms of the signed agreement. Periodically, through the next seven years, the Israeli government and the Palestine Authority released statements specifying the other side's transgressions of the Oslo Accord and, later, of the Interim Agreement and subsequent pacts. Many of Israel's charges involved the ballooning of the number of officers in the PA security forces. The Oslo agreements originally permitted 9,000 police officers and later expanded that to 18,000, but the actual number by the beginning of the al-Aqsa Intifada in the various PA security forces probably reached 45,000. The Palestine Authority, in turn, accused the Israeli government of failing to meet one deadline after another for redeployment and withdrawal from specified territory. Even when the Oslo process was considered dead by most, after the breakdown of the Taba talks in January 2001 and the escalation of horrible violence, the two sides continued to charge that each side was breaking this or that provision of their agreements.

The strength of the process—the unmediated talks between Palestinian and Israeli officials—also turned out to be its weakness. No mechanism was built into the Declaration of Principles for arbitration when charges flew back and forth that the agreement's provisions were being breeched. While the United States played an informal role for most of the 1990s, it did not have the official status that it had had in the Madrid framework and was often reluctant to intervene in spiffs. Without an arbitrator or mediator, each side resorted to threats of suspending, and actually suspending, negotiations when it felt the other side had egregiously disregarded Oslo's terms.

Interruptions in negotiations became more common than actual talks. Already, by December 1993, a mere three months after the historic signing, the process was deadlocked. The first deadline of that month, for the beginning of the Israeli pullout from Gaza and Jericho, was missed. In February 1994, Israeli settler Baruch Goldstein's rampage in Hebron killing Muslim worshippers led PA officials to withdraw from the negotiations temporarily. Islamic groups began their own series of attacks in Israel two months later as a response to the massacre. And so it went.

Anti-Oslo militants on both sides discovered a dirty little secret: they had virtual veto power over the negotiations, because every outrageous act that they perpetrated brought yet another interruption, another setback to the peace process. With each new Palestinian terrorist act, Israel not only engaged in a new wave of arrests; it imposed closures, enclosures, house demolitions, and other collective punishments over the areas of PA control as well as on those areas that remained under Israeli control. Israel delayed carrying out further stages of the agreements (transfer of additional areas to the Palestine Authority, release of prisoners, authorization of movement between the West Bank and Gaza for students, transfer of tax funds to the PA, and right of passage for Palestinian workers employed in Israel), which also frequently brought the peace process to a halt. In particular, the failure of both Netanyahu and Barak to hand over additional land after the Wye Agreement of 1998 was signed made Palestinians extremely skeptical that any final status accord would actually be implemented.

The collective punishments Israel administered led to economic stagnation and contraction in the territories, further eroding public support for the peace process. By the year 2000, Israeli officials had lost confidence in the Palestine Authority's willingness and ability to rein in Islamic groups and began systematically assassinating individuals it considered to be behind attacks on Israel, following the precedent it had set with the murder of Yahya Ayyash four years earlier. This policy further fanned Palestinians' hatred and distrust, making it more and more difficult for the two parties to move ahead in negotiations. As it became clear that the 1999 deadline for a final status agreement would not be met, Arafat announced that he would unilaterally and officially declare a state in the lands controlled by the Palestine Authority, fanning similar sentiments on the Israeli side. With no mechanism for arbitration, each side acted on its own to punish the other's perceived transgression of the agreements and, in so doing, hurt its own standing with the other side as a trustworthy partner.

These interruptions stemming from accusations that the adversary was not living up to the terms of agreements were compounded on the Israeli side by recurring flirtations with Syria. As mentioned, every Israeli prime minister from the signing of the talks in 1993 through their breakdown in early 2001 stepped back from negotiations with the Palestine Authority in order to pursue an agreement with the Syrians. Probably, none of these initiatives involving Syria was more damaging to the Palestinian-Israeli peace process than the one undertaken by Barak after he was elected in 1999. It was a moment in which the stars were lined up for a possible breakthrough in the negotiations. Barak, coming from Israel's Labor party, replaced Netanyahu, who had repeatedly expressed his dislike of the Oslo process. While Barak had expressed his own strong reservations about Oslo as Rabin's chief of staff, he entered office on a platform of pursuing a final status agreement with the Palestinians.

Beyond that, the United States had a second-term president. The likelihood of a first-term U.S. president pushing hard for each side to make the necessary concessions was small, especially after the two first-term presidents who did lean hard on the negotiating parties to secure Middle East progress, Jimmy Carter and the first George Bush, had not been reelected. It became a maxim in American politics that American Jewish voters and other voters backing Israel did not respond positively to Israel's being leaned on, even if the result was as positive as the Egyptian-Israeli peace treaty. Bill Clinton, as a second-term president, did not have these concerns about reelection. Moreover, from 1993 on, he developed a deep personal commitment to achieving Middle East peace.

These factors indicated that the moment for serious negotiations on a peace agreement between Palestinians and Jews, after more than three-quarters of a century of clashes, might be at hand. But it was at that very moment that Barak, with Clinton's apparent support, backed away from negotiations with the Palestinians in order to enter into a prolonged dance with Hafez al-Assad, the Syrian president. In the end, with Clinton meeting directly with Assad in Geneva and pressuring him mightily, the Syrians rejected the Israeli overture. But valuable time had been lost. By the time Barak turned back to the Palestinian issue in spring 2000, Clinton was near the end of his term. He no longer had the clout he had had a year before. The hastily convened last-ditch effort at Camp David in July 2000, in the summer of the Democratic and Republican nominating conventions for the next president, left almost no margin for error.

The Declaration of Principles had set out a clear timetable and agenda for talks that would lead to a final status agreement. The timetable was intended to keep the negotiations on track. One of the most positive achievements of the Oslo process was how close the parties came to living up to the timetable for the interim agreement—it was adopted in later September 1995, only two months beyond the official deadline. But already then storm clouds hung over the entire process. Without an officially designated third party to deal with charges from one side or the other, Israel and the Palestine Authority themselves applied sanctions directly to one another, often in the form of temporarily withdrawing from the talks. Quickly enough, those who wanted the talks to fail, the hard-line opposition on each side, learned that they could sabotage the process through acts that made the parties themselves suspend negotiations. These interruptions, along with those caused by Israel's recurring flirtation with Syria, subverted the Oslo process, putting tremendous pressure on both sides as the final deadline was approached and then extended.

Misreading of the Public on Each Side

Underlying all the reasons for the failure of the peace process was the nature of state-society relations on each side. The best place to start looking for answers as to what went wrong is at the grassroots level. Leaders on both sides frequently misjudged the amount of popular support that they would need in order to proceed with agreements and misread how much support actually existed in the public for a two-state solution. They underestimated how much the process could affect the public and how much, in turn, the affected public could shape leadership and the state of the negotiations. And, for much of the eight-year period of negotiations, they were insensitive to the delicate public-private balance that any negotiations demand.

Negotiations generally have a double two-faced component. The first two-faced element involves conveying one set of messages to the adversary, in private, and the opposite to one's constituency, publicly. To the opponent sitting across the conference table, negotiators whine that it is they who are making all the meaningful concessions while the adversary is not negotiating in good faith, not offering anything of value. At the same time, these negotiators publicly trumpet their gains to their constituents, "Don't worry. We are making only the most minor concessions to our adversaries; in no way are we retreating from our core aims." The second two-faced component comes in regards to these same constituents. As negotiators are reassuring the public about how little of true value they are giving up, they also need to be preparing constituents for the actual, difficult concessions that will be made. One political science theory speaks of the difficult process of making taboo subjects and red lines (for example, "not giving up an inch of our birthright") into questions of public debate (such as "should we give up land? should we swap land? how much?").[22]

Both Israeli and Palestinian leaders failed to address their public sufficiently in the course of negotiations and, when they did, they did very little to prepare their constituencies for the painful upcoming concessions. Barak, for example, repeatedly promised the indivisibility of Jerusalem, keeping from the public any hint of the sorts of compromises that his government was eventually willing to make, including ceding Arab-populated portions of the city and control over what Israelis call the Temple Mount *(Har Ha'bayit)* to the Palestine Authority. Jewish public opinion in Israel and in the Diaspora was simply not sufficiently prepared for the far-reaching historical compromises that the Barak government proposed in 2000. The failure to lay the groundwork among Jews was particularly evident in the issues of full, or nearly-full, withdrawal from the West Bank (Israeli leaders repeatedly spoke in terms of unrealistic percentages of the territories that would go to the Palestinians, ranging from 40 to 80 percent), Palestinian control over the Islamic holy shrines in Jerusalem, and the need to take moral and political responsibility for the *Nakba*.

The Palestinian leaders were even worse in managing information to the public than Israeli ones. They did not purposely leak or discuss, in a way that would generate public debate, key concessions that they would have to make—a changed meaning of "the right of return" from physical return to compensation for most refugees, the possibility of acceptance of a limited number of Jewish settlements, the possibility of land swaps, compromises on Jerusalem, security concessions to Israel that would cut into the new state's sovereign power, and more. Of particular sensitivity was the full right of return for refugees and their offspring (today numbering 3.5 million) to the localities from which they had been uprooted during the 1948 war and full compensation for their suffering and lost property.[23] Many of the villages that the refugees yearned for have long since disappeared or are now inhabited by Jews who have transformed them totally. Israeli Jews have seen massive return as tantamount to the destruction of their state. The Palestinian leadership knew all this very well, but the issue was never debated in Palestinian society and it was not once raised during all the talks held between 1992 and Camp David.

When the time came to make those concessions in late 2000 and early 2001, Arafat felt that Palestinians were not ready for such far-reaching compromises. In fact, even before he went to Camp David, he cautioned that the Palestinians were not prepared for what the talks would bring. Perhaps he was right; but if he was, it was because of his own earlier lack of leadership in preparing the ground properly, either in terms of the private negotiations with the Israelis or in terms of the Palestinian public. To his constituents, he showed only one face—the triumphant hero who would win for the Palestinians everything for which they had longed. Similar to Rabin and Barak, he did not expose the second face—the leader preparing his people for difficult losses in addition to the gains.

Arafat's weakness at the end of the long path of negotiations resulted in part because of his own shortsighted style of leadership—the dog-walker style he employed. But structural factors, ones built into the Oslo process and the creation of the Palestine Authority, led him to fear putting trust in his constituents, in their capacity to handle the bad news as well as the good. What were these factors? For leaders to accept an agreement in which concessions are backloaded, as they were in the Oslo agreement, requires sustaining people's confidence in the interim that the nation's true aims will be realized in the end. Leaders have to convince their followers to keep the faith. But each new concession to Israel by Arafat and his lieutenants from 1993 on brought an erosion in Palestinians' beliefs that they would ever reach their goals. Arafat, personally, and the Palestine Authority, generally, faced deteriorating approval ratings, especially after 1995, as the Palestinian population increasingly lost confidence in their ability to induce the Israelis to make the necessary concessions.

With violence as the only lever that Palestinians could see to extract concessions from Israel, they ironically supported the peace process in high numbers and, at the same time, the use of violence against Israel. For example, in late 2001, a survey indicated that 71 percent of Palestinians in the West Bank and Gaza supported a return to Israel-Palestine negotiations, while 61 percent stated that armed confrontations helped achieve Palestinian rights in ways that negotiations could not.[24] The growing belief in the efficacy of violence, which showed up in polls from late 1995 on, demonstrated a faltering faith that negotiations alone could accomplish what the Palestinian people wanted. By the summer of 2002, the Palestinian public may have been losing faith in violence as a mechanism to achieve their national goals. A poll in August of that year indicated that nearly two-thirds felt that a new approach was needed, and 72–92 percent supported the use of various sorts of nonviolent action.[25]

Arafat also continually gave mixed messages because of his conflicting aims of building a sense of Palestinism, which would be linked in the public's mind to his new government, the Palestine Authority, and making the Oslo process work. In trying to construct a national identity around the Palestine Authority, Arafat and his aides dragooned the print, radio, and television media into his efforts, building the collective identity on the basis of its opposition to the "other," the Israelis.[26] But it became very difficult to sustain a portrayal of Israel as both the dispossessing enemy and the partner who would deliver the key backloaded benefits of Oslo: a sovereign state, Jerusalem, and the right of return. This dilemma intensified when the peace process slowed noticeably after the assassination of Rabin.

A harsh lesson learned by the leaders of both Israel and the Palestine Authority in the endgame talks in summer and fall of 2000 and January 2001 was that negotiations could not succeed without popular support. The structure of the Oslo agreement with its imbalance of power between the negotiating partners, the frontloading of benefits for Israel and backloading for Palestinians, inadvertently cut the legs out from beneath the continuing Oslo process. It eroded the backing of the public that the process needed in order to succeed, and it opened the door for the relegitimization of violence as a tool for Palestinians to achieve their goals. The resumption of violence, of course, only further undercut the public's belief that the process would succeed. And, for Israelis, the violence eroded faith

that Arafat and the Palestine Authority could be a trustworthy negotiating partner.

Finally, negotiations demand that officials from each side indirectly and directly address the public from the other side. As we have
seen, at the celebration of the signing of the Declaration of Principles, spokespeople for both sides explicitly reassured their counterparts about their long-term intentions. At least in part, those statements were aimed over the heads of the people sitting at the dinner
to the larger public on the other side. Those toasts by Palestinian
and Israeli officials addressed the primal fear of the other. But once
the festivities were over, the leaders paid far too little attention to
sustaining public support across the divide. To be sure, there were
moments, such as Arafat's visit to Rabin's widow after the assassination, but these were few and far between. Israeli leaders' insensitivity
to the issue of Jewish settlements in the West Bank and Gaza Strip
and their penchant for collective punishment—closures, general economic sanctions, mass deportation, hassles at border crossings, retribution against relatives and towns from which terrorists came—all
led to the resurfacing of Palestinians' primal fear, that the Israelis
were bent on permanent control over them and the territories. It
was of little wonder, then, when Barak made an offer at Camp David in 2000 that he and most Israelis saw as historic and far-reaching, Palestinians assimilated it as just another recipe for permanent
neocolonial rule over the Palestinians by Israel.

Arafat, too, misjudged the importance of taking account of Israeli public sentiments. His reluctance to clamp down on those intent on torpedoing the peace process, his willingness even to allow
violence by Islamic groups as a means of stepping up the pressure
on Israel, raised the Israeli primal fear. More and more, Israelis
felt denied the major public goods that the peace process was supposed to bring them, acceptance as a legitimate state and personal
and collective security. And they began to feel that the Palestinians
would never be satisfied, Oslo or no Oslo, until Israel were wiped
off the map. Later, the al-Aqsa Intifada was seen by many Israelis as confirmation of Palestinians' determination not to accept a
compromise because of the deep-seated commitment to destroy
Israel.

Failure to Achieve Economic Well-Being
for Palestinians

Both sides recognized that the ability of the Palestine Authority to take root in the West Bank and Gaza Strip and, indeed, the ultimate success of the Oslo process rested on an improvement in the quality and standard of living of Palestinians in the territories.[27] A decade prior to Oslo had seen a marked upswing in Palestinians' economic fortunes. Oil prices had been high, which meant plenty of money flowing from Palestinians in the Gulf States back to their families in the territories. Others profited from work in Israel, with often multiple jobs in a single family; by 1987, these jobs accounted for a whopping 28 percent of the GNP of the territories. New cars, television antennas, and houses appeared all over the West Bank.

But the mid-1980s turned out to be the economic heyday for Palestinians in the territories. Their standard of living had already deteriorated badly by the time of the signing on the White House lawn in 1993. The fall in oil prices, the Intifada, and an end of remittances from Palestinians in Kuwait, who were expelled at the end of the Gulf War, were the chief culprits in precipitating a sharp downturn in the economy. Still, hopes were high at the time of the signing of the Declaration of Principles, largely due to promises of an influx in capital from outside contributions and loans for the development of economic infrastructure and social institutions. Just weeks after the Oslo signing, forty-three states gathered in Washington to pledge billions in aid.

The entire peace process was premised on the assumption that both sides had an economic interest in making peace work, and, if mutual economic interests did not yet exist, then they could and should be created. More than anyone, Peres, with his vision of "a new Middle East," personified this assumption.[28] Some sociologists even saw the process through the wider perspective of globalization, with peace linking the region to the wider global economy, which would be in the interests of Israeli, Arab, and international industry.[29] There was an economic euphoria that overlooked the obstacles caused by long-term hatred and ethnic divisions. In addition, elements of the Palestinian leadership and social elite, like others in neighboring Arab countries, feared such an approach and viewed it as a sort of economic colonization, which would replace direct Israeli military rule in the region with indirect technological and economic control.

In any case, these lofty ideas for economic integration were followed by equally lofty promises of new inflows of capital to the fledgling Palestine Authority. By October 1993, various donor states and agencies—including the World Bank and forty countries, including the United States, European states, Arab states, and Japan—had promised inflows of $6.5 billion, with an actual transfer of $4.4 billion to be effected by 2001. Within a year, $195 dollars per head, computed on an annual basis, had been transferred to the West Bank and Gaza Strip economy—the highest amount of per capita international aid ever awarded.

The money was channeled almost entirely through the new Palestine Authority, and the lion's share was kept to pay for the creation of new PA institutions: 44 percent for the salaries of PA employees of all kinds, 12.6 percent for the police, 11 percent for other governmental agencies.[30] There were also the beginnings of three-way Palestinian-Jordanian-Israeli economic initiatives (such as industrial parks), which took advantage of Israeli capital and knowledge together with Palestinian and Jordanian cheap labor.[31] Another source of new funds also came out of the Oslo process. According to the economic protocol of the agreement between the PLO and Israel signed in Paris in April 1994, 75 percent of taxes withheld from Palestinians working in Israel was to be transferred to the PA.[32] Within a few years, the influx of capital and the beginnings of new economic projects began to bear some fruit throughout the West Bank and Gaza Strip.

But, even with some successes to point to, the Palestinian economy from 1995–2000 lagged far behind expectations, causing disappointment among the population. Several factors accounted for the economy's relatively poor performance, despite the great expectations generated, especially by the promise of huge new international investments. The gap between promised dollars from abroad and actual transfers was substantial. Continuing low oil prices curtailed the flow of cash from Arab oil exporters, as well as remittances from Palestinians working in oil-exporting countries. International agencies held back money because of the absence of standard accounting procedures by the Arafat government.[33] In fact, rumors of rampant corruption associated with the names of PA leaders discouraged both international aid and direct foreign investment. The whispering about corruption also lent strength to the Islamic opposition, contributed to demoralization of the population, and raised the level of crime. Additionally, tensions between the negotiating partners, Israel and the Palestine Authority, slowed the flow of capital into the territories. In February 1997, Arafat estimated that Israel owed $1.3 billion dollars to the Palestine Authority (mostly from taxes withheld on goods produced in the territories and social security withheld from workers' salaries).[34] Continuing tensions also led Israel to turn down the PLO's request to open a central bank and print Palestinian money.[35]

The redirection of international aid from Palestinian civic organizations to the Palestine Authority resulted in a rapid decrease in monetary support for the agencies in civil society providing social services. According to various estimates, annual support for the voluntary organizations fell from $170–$240 million to $100–$120 million. Precisely the people most in need of services suffered from these cutbacks, but the PA leadership feared building up these civil organizations and continued to keep those foreign funds channeled through the Palestine Authority from them.[36] The establishment of the Palestine Authority seemed to worsen living conditions for the Palestinian population in the West Bank and Gaza Strip, rather than improve them.[37]

Wealthy Palestinians in the *ghurba* had been expected to invest in development of the homeland.[38] But most of their private investment was in private construction, especially of expensive houses, and service businesses (such as hotels); only a small amount went into industry. As security began to deteriorate, especially with the beginning of the cycle of Islamist attacks and Israeli retaliations and, later, with the reoccupation of the territories, so too did private investments and the activity of international organizations, until their funds dried up almost entirely after the beginning of the al-Aqsa Intifada.

For most of the population of the West Bank and Gaza Strip, the beginning of political autonomy had raised hopes for improvement in the quality of life. These hopes, however, went largely unrealized, with the possible exception of a thin stratum, which began to blossom as a result of the transfer of authority from Israeli military rule to the Palestine Authority.[39] In fact, the opposite occurred. The standard of living for most of the Palestinian population (especially in the Gaza Strip) fell after the beginning of the extended closures.[40] Beginning in the mid-1990s, as a result of continuing terrorist activities and retaliatory closures, about 95,000–150,000 Palestinian laborers lost their jobs in Israel, and, with the implementation of the concept of separation, their places were filled by Asians and Eastern European laborers.[41] "Palestinian per capita incomes actually *declined* in each year following the Oslo Agreement, dropping by almost one-quarter before stabilizing in 1998. . . . By mid-1997, and despite the disbursement of some $1.5 billion in international aid, more than two-thirds of Palestinians expressed the view that the peace process had harmed the economy."[42] The closures, Roy reported, led to a separation of the West Bank and Gaza economies and, even within each of them, patterns of economic autarky, in addition to weakening links with the Israeli economy.[43]

Compared to the economic situation after the outbreak of the al-Aqsa Intifada in September 2000, the latter part of the 1990s now seem like halcyon days. The uprising inflicted a black-hole recession on the territories (and a serious, but less severe, one on Israel, as well). In 2000 alone, there was a 12 percent drop in actual per person income and another 19 percent in 2001. The World Bank estimated that about three-fifths of the PA's population was living below the poverty line in the midst of the al-Aqsa Intifada, and in Gaza, the fraction was as high as four-fifths. The physical destruction and the destruction of PA institutions prevented collection of taxes, and the Israeli refusal to transfer the taxes it collected brought about a loss of $305 million by December 2001. Only in mid-2002 did Israel begin to transfer small portions of this sum back to the Palestine Authority. But even more meaningful was the loss of $2.4 billion in gross national income. The economy simply ground to a halt at the beginning of the twenty-first century. In the summer of 2002, unemployment crept up incredibly to nearly 50 percent of the workforce.

In short, the Oslo peace process was premised on a new economic dawn. Perhaps unrealistically, the new economy of the Palestine Authority was to emerge as integrated with, but not subservient to, the Israeli economy. It was to receive a shot in the arm from new inflows of capital from international organizations, Western donor countries, Israel itself, Arab state donors, private expatriate Palestinian and other foreign Arab investors, and direct foreign investment by Western corporations. Its own new institutions would collect taxes, and Israel would transfer revenues, as well. But, in the last half of the 1990s—a period when the world economy was in high gear, when globalization was creating unprecedented cross-border flows of capital, when Israel was experiencing a high-tech economic renaissance, and when Oslo temporarily transformed the Palestinians into the darlings of the international community—the Palestinian economy foundered and the quality of people's everyday life deteriorated. One researcher summed up the state of the economy in 2000, even before the flare-up of violence:

> External assistance has not established a viable economic system for Palestine, which remains geographically fragmented and heavily dependent on Israel for trade, labor export, and many other things. The Palestinian economy has yet to develop clear areas of comparative advantage and remains highly vulnerable to external shocks. There have been serious problems of institutional development. The PA's large public-sector payroll, irregularities in the fiscal regime, and problems of corruption and off-the-books financing (through the monopolies) have all risen, in part, for political reasons. But whatever their short-term political utility to the regime, they all represent legacies that will weaken future economic development efforts.[44]

The assumptions that promised a new economic dawn simply did not hold as the Oslo process stumbled forward. And when the peace talks finally came to a halt, replaced by the violence of the al-Aqsa Intifada, the Palestinian economy plummeted.

The Road Back to Violence

The Palestinian popular revolt quickly developed into a full-scale, inter-communal war blurring the distinction between front and rear, between civilians and fighters. During two years of escalating violence (between October 2000 and October 2002) more than 625 Israelis were killed in a total of 14,280 attacks. Some 1,380 Palestinians were killed by Israeli military forces and settlers. A total of 4,500 Israelis were injured in terrorist attacks, and the Palestinian Red Crescent organization reported a total of 19,684 Palestinians wounded (although other groups have much higher estimates for the injured). All the dreams and agreements to change the currency of relationships between Palestinians and Israelis from violence to negotiations, to transform the essence of the relationship from enemy to partner, all went up in flames. While immediate precipitants to the violence certainly existed—not least of which was Sharon's ill-advised visit to *haram al-sharif* at the end of September 2000, backed by over 100 Barak-supplied security forces—the flaws in the Oslo process, particularly those that excluded the public or took it for granted, laid the groundwork.

Even as frantic final status talks took place in Camp David and then in Sharm al-Sheikh and Taba, both in Egypt, and even as President Clinton generated his own proposals to break the deadlock, Oslo was doomed. The skewed incentive structure with its front-loaded benefits for Israelis and backloaded promises for Palestinians; the unstable and, consequently, shortsighted politics on both sides; the absence of a third party to whom each side could take its complaints; the loss of faith by Palestinians as their economic fortunes went down; and, probably what was most important of all, the failure to incorporate the public into the process, all prepared the ground for a new dance of death.

It is ironic that the violence escalated at the end of a half-year of the most intensive—and seemingly productive—negotiations on final peace that Israelis and Palestinians had ever had. The course of these talks have been covered extensively elsewhere; suffice it to say here that, despite many subsequent recriminations, the two sides settled most of the outstanding issues between them.[45] The Clinton proposals in December 2000 set out in writing what the parties had actually agreed to and narrowed the choices of the still outstanding issues. Eventually, both sides accepted those proposals and, at Taba, in early 2001, developed a comprehensive "non-document," officially disowned by both sides, that will nonetheless be the template for any future settlement. By the end of January 2001, both sides were closer to agreement than ever before, as the Israeli and Palestinian negotiators themselves later acknowledged; but, at this point, the Palestinians were well into their new uprising and the fed-up Israeli electorate, a short time later, replaced Ehud Barak with Ariel Sharon. Negotiations ended for the foreseeable future. Israelis claimed there was no negotiating partner, and some Palestinians again trumpeted the aim of a Palestinian state in all of Palestine. Each side revived the other's primal fear and existential anxiety.

Ariel Sharon's provocative visit to *haram al-sharif* during the talks on the status of Jerusalem was fuel for the fire, and, ironically, it served as a powerful recruitment tool for a renewed Palestinian rebellion. From the time of the massacre at Sabra and Shatilla during the Lebanon war in the 1980s, Sharon had become a symbol of Israeli oppression of Palestinians.[46] The youth took to the streets again now, threw stones, and burned Israeli and American flags. In Gaza, they tried to "occupy" settlements in the Netzarim enclave and, in the West Bank, storm Jewish settlements. Israeli soldiers and settlers opened fire, and armed Palestinian militia men returned their own live fire, a marked departure from the earlier Intifada.

Palestinians defined the new outbreak as a second Intifada, this time in defense of the holy al-Aqsa mosque, as national motives now mixed with religious symbols (as they did, increasingly, on the Israeli side, as well). The violence grew into a full-fledged rebellion and thus became the fourth in the series of uprisings in Palestine—joining the rebellion of 1834, the Great Arab Revolt in 1936, and the first Intifada in 1987—that framed the making of the Palestinian people. The al-Aqsa Intifada directed discontent not only at the Israeli occupation but also toward the inefficiency, corruption, and authoritarian rule of the Palestine Authority and its inability to bring about the expected economic development, rise in the standard of living, and true liberation from Israeli occupation. The uprising also brought growing dissatisfaction with Arafat's leadership into the open. Aiming the people's wrath both outward and inward, the al-Aqsa Intifada was reminiscent of the Great Arab Revolt of 1936–1939.

If it resembled the uprising against the British, it differed from the first rebellion against Israeli occupation. During that first Intifada, the Palestinians had strictly refrained from the use of firearms in order not to give the Israelis an excuse to use their overpowering military advantage and to preserve, as well, the popular color of the uprising. This time peaceful demonstrations and rock-throwing were rare, because, among other reasons, the Israelis were no longer located among the major concentrations of the Palestinian population, having redeployed in the course of the Oslo process. Instead, in the first stage, the Palestinians took up firearms against military personnel and settlers.

The violence subsequently took an even more deadly turn as, again and again, Palestinian suicide bombers indiscriminately hit the civilian population within Israel's borders, with the Islamic movement, at first, usually taking responsibility. The growing use of human bombs was a huge step up in the interethnic warfare. Palestinians, for the first time, found a strategic answer to Israel's overwhelming military superiority and succeeded in causing heavy losses on the Israeli side, paralyzing Israeli routines and economic and social life. Although the Islamic organizations initiated the use of this method, the underground military arms of Fatah (for example, "Fighters of the Al-Aqsa Brigades") began to sponsor the suicide bombings, as well, if only to compete for popular support. The suicide attacks gained momentum and, in March 2002, became an almost daily event.

Arab-Jewish relations once again took on the familiar trappings of an interethnic war, in which not only armies and militias fought but a growing number of civilians found themselves both as perpetrators and victims. The chain of violence and counterviolence was further exacerbated by the Israeli army, which responded with precise (and sometimes, tragically, not-so-precise) fire from helicopters, airplanes, and tanks. Afterwards, the army moved on to assassinations of those marked as the grassroots leaders of the Palestinian violence and then, of Palestinian officials, as well.[47]

The goals of both sides in the renewed fighting were murky. Sometimes, each acted as if the violence was positioning it for a more advantageous position in upcoming bargaining; at other times, the violence seemed cathartic; in some instances, it seemed to be used only to mollify the public; and, in still other cases, each acted as if it could wear down and, ultimately, defeat the other, obviating the need to partition the land. The last of these goals was the most ominous, bringing the primal fear of the other to the surface. Indeed, the new discourse in Israel on so-called transfer, forcibly removing Palestinians from the country, increased Palestinian fear. Now Palestinians began to raise the specter not only of continued occupation but also of the possibility of ethnic cleansing.[48]

Sharon, who was elected on the platform of the right-wing Likud party (called "the national camp" in Israeli political parlance), seemed to want a total nullification of the agreements and their political implications. Although he never declared this outright,[49] the policy of the Sharon government appeared to be intended to gradually and systematically destroy the agreements and the PA institutional infrastructure and leadership, especially rejecting the leadership of Arafat, while carefully and gradually preparing Israeli and world opinion for these moves.[50] Especially after the events of September 11, 2001, Sharon pushed the conception of Palestinian terror as part of the global terror against which the United States was fighting, undoing the legitimacy that the Oslo Accord had conferred upon the Palestinian national movement. In any case, with the beginning of Operation Defense Shield in March 2001, Israel's military posture indicated that Israeli leaders believed that the uprising—indeed, any serious resistance to the occupation—could be defeated militarily.

For his part, Arafat, ominously, more than once expressed his ambivalent relationship to the agreements with Israel. Several times, he cited to his Arabic-speaking listeners the Hudaibiyya Agreement between the Prophet Muhammad and the Jewish tribes in the Arabian Peninsula. Muhammad signed this covenant during a period of weakness and out of exigency; but later, when his power increased, he broke the agreement and uprooted the tribes from their lands. Others, both in the Islamic groups and in Fatah militias, spoke openly of their belief that Palestinians could ultimately triumph completely, destroying Israel and setting up a Palestinian state in all of Palestine. Besides its brutal violence, the horror of the warfare lay in the retreat from an acceptance by each side of the inevitability and necessity of partitioning Palestine, of a two-state solution.

One goal that emerged for the Palestinians in the process of the uprising was seeing it as a war of independence. The struggle in which the Palestinians were engaged was not unlike the wars and rebellions at the inception of other nation-states, including of course Israel. These wars have created a set of heroic myths in the forging of new states. For Palestinians, the Intifada did certainly bring the kinds of internal struggles over the content of the national narrative and the revolt's ultimate aims that have marked the process in which new myths have been created in other new states. Here, a new martyrology—the *shahid* who is willing to lay down his life through suicide bombing—was incorporated into the emerging narrative of the Palestinian people and a possible future state. The violence was seen as the antidote to continuing and creeping Israeli domination, especially through the Jewish settlements in the West Bank and Gaza Strip. At least in the earlier stages of the revolt, public opinion rallied strongly behind the suicide bombers. All sorts of new rituals, including mass funerals, wall posters, and the playing of presuicide videos, developed as part of the martyrology.

But wars of liberation can as easily create victims among those who make them as among those at whom they are directed. In the course of the Intifada, Arafat himself seemed to become one of the Intifada's victims. Besieged in his presidential compound in Ramallah during Israel's Operation Defense Shield in spring 2002, Arafat eventually bought his own freedom of movement by handing over others holed up in the compound with him. Among those in the compound with him were figures wanted by the Israelis, especially several who had allegedly participated in the assassination of an Israeli cabinet minister. Arafat's deal severely damaged his already diminishing prestige among Palestinians. Even before Arafat regained his freedom of movement, the siege itself had emphasized his weakness and his dependence on Israel, the Americans, and the Europeans.

After the siege, for the first time, demands began to come from within the Palestine Authority for far-reaching governmental and legal reforms.[51] Quickly, those reforms were internationalized with the creation in July 2002 of the Task Force on Palestinian Reform, which included representatives from the United Nations, the United States, the Russian Federation, the European Union, Norway, Japan, the World Bank, the International Monetary Fund, and Israel, in addition to those from the Palestine Authority. The Task Force established seven groups examining reform in civil society, financial accountability, local government, market economy, elections, the judiciary, and the PA's administration. The furor over reform, of course, was a not-so-subtle swipe at the existing PA leadership, especially Arafat. It emphasized, too, the lack of autonomy for the Palestine Authority.

Beyond the Intifada's biting Arafat's hand were more serious problems stemming from the continuing violence. With injuries to Palestinians numbering in the tens of thousands, permanent disability for a significant share of the population loomed on the horizon. One study at Bir Zeit University estimated that 13 percent of those wounded in the fighting would be permanently disabled.[52] Initial indications were that about a quarter of these people were school age and as many 85 percent, below 35 years of age.

Institutions, too, were a major casualty of the war. Israel's "Operation Defense Shield" and, even more so, "Operation Determined Path," begun in June 2002, inflicted the most devastating blow to the Palestine Authority's fledgling institutions. As one official put it, "They sought to destroy anything that was a sign that we are a

civilized people."[53] During and after the fighting, Israeli forces lev-
eled buildings, confiscated documents, destroyed equipment, van-
dalized offices, and seized monies. In several ministries, for example,
sledgehammers seem to have been used to destroy equipment and
furniture, even toilets.[54] The painstaking efforts that Palestinians
had made from 1994 on in establishing a public sector were wiped
away in a matter of weeks.

The damage to the Palestinians was not only physical, and it
was not confined to their fragile political institutions. Palestinian
culture, too, came in for a battering. As in the decade after 1948,
the trauma seemed to produce a lost generation. The closures of
schools and universities (on top of all the missed time during the
first Intifada), not only increased functional illiteracy, it produced a
generation without many of the skills that would be needed for rebuilding. As several Palestinian intellectuals lamented, it also produced youngsters whose greatest aspirations were inflicting death
on themselves and others, whose hopes were not for this world but
the world to come.

The Oslo process was one in which, haltingly, Palestinians had
begun moving their national story from victimhood and nostalgia
for the Lost Garden and from resistance and armed struggle, to
building institutions and gaining autonomy and to economic renaissance and social reconstruction. It is difficult to say at this moment how difficult it will be to recapture the sense of purpose and
the attentiveness to the challenges of internal reformation with
which the Oslo period had instilled the Palestinian people within
Palestine. At this writing, it is unclear whether the Intifada can truly
be a war of liberation—liberating Palestinians not only from Israeli
rule but from illusions about what the future holds for them. If the
war of liberation can be a step toward internal reconstruction and
acceptance of two states in historic Palestine, it will have succeeded.
But if it leads only to the glorification of death and to the illusion
that Israel, like the earlier Crusader state, will simply melt away,
then it will do nothing but prolong the Palestinians' bondage.

CONCLUSION

What I mean is that no people—for bad or for good—is so freighted with multiple, and yet unreachable or indigestible, significance as the Palestinians. Their relationship to Zionism, and ultimately with political and even spiritual Judaism, gives them a formidable burden as interlocutors of the Jews. Then their relationships to Islam, to Arab nationalism, to Third World anticolonialist and anti-imperialist struggle, to the Christian world (with its unique historical and cultural attachment to Palestine), to Marxists, to the socialist world—all these put upon the Palestinian a burden of interpretation and a multiplication of selves that are virtually unparalleled in modern political or cultural history.

EDWARD SAID, *The Question of Palestine,* 1979

THE MAKING OF A PEOPLE is not a volcanic experience, coming out of a singular, critical moment in which forces converge to create a gigantic eruption. It is, rather, a long process, with all sorts of reversals and changes of direction, marked by continuing struggle against others, particularly powerful others, and internal struggles among contending groups. From all those struggles emerge a set of dominant myths, practices, institutions, goals, and even social divisions that enable otherwise disparate individuals and groups to think of themselves as a whole, set off from other peoples. Subsequently, that self-awareness can wax and wane; it can take on new boundaries, excluding some who had been included and including previously shunned groups; and it can even disappear altogether.

In the middle decades of the twentieth century, Palestinians developed a self-identity as a people set apart. This self-awareness came in the wake of the first encounters of the Arab residents of the territory with British colonialism and the Jewish society of immigrant settlers. But its roots date to the external and internal struggles that began two centuries ago and, even farther back, to earlier origins and layers, including local Arabism (counterposed to Ottomanism), Islamism, the holiness and administrative centrality of Jerusalem, and regional and clan identities.[1]

This process of constructing a self-identified whole did not end once most Palestinians saw themselves as a people set apart. The story that Palestinians have fashioned about themselves has been an evolving one, shaped and reshaped by continuing struggles with those outside, and among those inside, the collectivity. Sometimes, those struggles weakened the sense of peoplehood. Immediately after the disaster of 1948, especially, Palestinian identity faded in the wake of dispersal and the collapse of the modern, urban portion of society. But in the wake of that trauma, a number of "bubbles," particularly in the refugee camps and among tiny groups of students and intellectuals, breathed new life into a renewed collective self-consciousness, centered now around the notion of the Lost Garden. Ironically enough, it was the new "disaster" of the 1967 war that truly reinvigorated the notion of a Palestinian people, as the majority of Palestinians were reunited under Israeli rule.

Even then, Palestinians faced extraordinary hurdles in fashioning their national story—the narrative that would connect individual Palestinians to one another in their minds. Many of these hurdles, of course, were associated with the lack of a state framework, the statelessness that became their distinctive mark. Difficulties in creating a clear sense of "who we are" resulted from the absence not only of central institutions, such as courts and a single school system, which establish basic rules of the game for interaction with one another and inscribe and convey the national story. Palestinians also lacked clear boundaries, which enable people to fashion answers to questions of "what are we," "what are our origins," and "what do we want to be?" Israeli rule and the continued dispersal of many Palestinians outside Palestine also made it difficult to construct a Palestinian elite and leadership, which could figuratively bring together all the Palestinian peripheries.

While statelessness has created undeniable barriers for Palestinians in shaping their national story, the historian Rashid Khalidi showed how the very absence of a formal political Palestinian identity, with a state's standard paraphernalia of identity cards and passports, paradoxically, strengthened Palestinians' self-awareness, in some ways, by emphasizing their common fate and dependence on travel documents of other states.[2] Arriving at border crossings, or even the (hated) checkpoints between Israel and the occupied territories, Palestinians have been dealt with differently, often in a humiliating fashion, from others who hold passports of sovereign states. Absence of a state may have played into the hands of the making of the Palestinian people in another way as well. Because they lacked a central authority, they developed a vibrant civil society, particularly in the 1970s and 1980s in the occupied territories. This civil society consisted of new, voluntary and service organizations, which breathed life into a sense of Palestinism. In an odd twist of fate, it was only during the rule of the Palestine Authority itself that this civil society, weaned in the difficult conditions of occupation, crumbled.

After the Oslo Accord was signed, the Palestine Authority did provide a new focus for Palestinian identity. Palestinian self-government brought tremendous pride to Palestinian communities throughout the Middle East and beyond, although that pride was tinged with trepidation. The PA defined the boundaries in which it ruled and, probably what was even more important, gave a clear idea that Palestine's future boundaries would encompass the West Bank and Gaza Strip. But, as its treatment of civil society demonstrated, the PA's effectiveness in creating a vibrant nation out of disparate Palestinians was mixed. The reaction of Israeli-Palestinians to the Palestine Authority—strong support of it coupled with very serious misgivings about its operations—may have typified the responses of other communities as well. They recoiled from its repressive policies, including ones that attempted to stifle almost any sort of public debate about the people's future direction and about the reconciliation of different Palestinian communities. The efforts of the Palestine Authority to preempt or authoritatively direct this debate notwithstanding, in almost every site where a Palestinian community could be found, people began public discussion of central questions about the Palestinians' future. Even with the establishment of the Palestine Authority, every Palestinian community has managed to maintain its own internal discourse and, especially with the increased use of the Internet, a transnational Palestinian discourse has flourished, as well.

Some of the subjects of public debate reflect Palestinians' special circumstances of dispersal, occupation, and statelessness. Some are new, such as the challenges of self-government and the fallout from the al-Aqsa Intifada. And still others are longstanding questions that echo the problems, issues, and struggles of other peoples around the globe. The social rift between Jaffa's metropolis and the eastern hills around Nablus, for example, mirrors a pattern found around the entire Mediterranean coast. Throughout the region, the impact of the European market and closer administrative and political control widened the gap between coast and hinterland. As elsewhere, the Palestinian fault line underscored two very different responses to the challenges that increasingly made the old village life and beliefs unviable. The first was to embrace many of the new ways—Western education, values, dress, technology—as the basis for molding a new nation. The second highlighted the Godlessness, emptiness, and alienation accompanying the penetration of Palestine by Europe. This response called for reaffirmation of the old pillars of society—religion, village, kinship—now within the context of a heightened sense of peoplehood. Here, the cultural artifacts of the West were not seen as weapons to secure a rightful place on the world stage but as elements confirming Palestine's relegation to the wings. That tension, recast today in the secular-religious contestation, has continued to mark Palestinian society.

The internal struggles in Palestinian society, such as the one across the Jaffa-Nablus divide, changed over time, shaped most conspicuously in social upheavals suddenly mobilizing the society and pitting the contending worldviews against one another. These eruptions—the Revolt of 1834, the Arab Revolt of 1936–1939, and the Intifada starting in 1987—functioned as exclamation points in a meandering narrative of change marking the response of society as a whole to other forces (Egyptian, British, and Zionist) imposing themselves on Palestine. In the twenty-first century, the al-Aqsa Intifada, as much as any of the earlier uprisings, was an event in which Palestinians took matters into their own hands against those who ruled them. And, like those earlier rebellions, it also brought into stark relief the contending forces in Palestinian society itself, especially between Islamic and national-secular forces.

The future making of the Palestinian people will involve continued public debate and struggle over how to respond to the basic challenges they will encounter. What are the questions that Palestinians face in the difficult circumstances of the dawn of the new century? We have identified six issues with which they will have to grapple—diversity within unity, territory versus authority, the right of return, the character of the regime, full independence versus federation, and the relationship of Palestinian-Israelis to Israel. The decisions before which the Palestinians stand on all these issues will undoubtedly have far-reaching implications, too, for Israeli society and the fate of both the Palestinian and Jewish people, who, whether or not they like it, are highly interdependent. Indeed, the questions challenging one people have often mirrored the dilemmas faced on the other side.

Diversity within Unity

Palestinians were cast to the wind in 1948, a dispersal that created distinct communities, not only widely separated physically but also divided by a host of other factors as well. Each community developed its own history, goals, relationship to Palestinism, and survival tactics. The fact that refugees from distinct areas of Palestine ended up in different countries and were treated differently in each place strengthened prior regional differences among them. And, of course, almost half the Palestinians were not uprooted from Palestine at all but remained in Israel, the West Bank, and Gaza.

The so-called 1948 Arabs who remained within Israel's borders exemplify the distinctiveness of each of the Palestinian communities. They constructed their community on the basis of a seemingly inconceivable identity, Israeli-Palestinian-Arabs—a sort of contradiction in terms. But, for them, this identity was taken for granted. The Israeliness of these Palestinians was looked on suspiciously by other Palestinians and smelled of "betrayal." They could not understand how an Arab and, moreover, a Palestinian, could cooperate with and participate in an Israeli state based on Zionist ideology. Only after the 1967 war did the 1948 Arabs come to be understood and accepted in the larger Palestinian universe. Indeed, it was members of the Israeli-Arab community who first suggested the formula of "two states for two peoples," which became an important contribution to Palestinian (and Israeli) political thought.

The Oslo agreements and the founding of the Palestine Authority emphasized and sharpened the differences between Palestinians remaining in exile *(ghurba)* and those in various parts of the homeland, between refugees and permanent residents, and even between the small minority of exiles who enjoyed the privilege of returning to their homeland together with Arafat in 1994 and those who remained outside Palestine. On top of all that were distinctions among Palestinians of the West Bank, Gaza Strip, and Israel—whether or not they were refugees. The creation of a self-governing authority only exacerbated these differences, as Palestinians in historic Palestine were again divided between different centers of rule after a generation of being united under Israeli governance. Paradoxically, both the differences and the unity within the Palestinian people were simultaneously deepened.

Will the Palestine Authority or a successor state become the sole, or at least dominant, center, even for Palestinians living outside it, in the way that Israel has become a focal point for Jews worldwide in such issues as the safety of diaspora communities, Jewish scholarship and music, and study abroad programs? Will the Palestinian diaspora be drawn culturally to the new Palestinian center or will its parts drift in different directions? Part of the answers to these questions will depend on how the Palestine Authority itself develops, especially in the wake of its near destruction in Israel Operation Defense Shield and follow-up military incursions in the spring and summer of 2002. Indeed, by September 2002, Muhammad Dahlan, the former PA head of security in Gaza and now Arafat's security chief, could say that there is no more Palestine Authority. "The only thing that remains is Arafat and the salaries."[3] If the dark days of violence lead to peace talks, as occurred after the first Intifada, especially important questions for Palestinians as they contemplate a future state will be the nature of the PA's authority and its relationship to those longing for return.

Size of the Territory Versus Self-Determination and Authority

The Oslo agreements contained only vague promises for the establishment of such a state. What sort of authority a state would have and what compromises in sovereignty would be built into a final agreement remained purposely undefined. Even in the best of circumstances, the state will remain dependent on at least two regional powers—Israel and Jordan. Within those parameters, its future scope, both in territory and power, is still a matter of dispute among Palestinians. For one, the historic compromise of accepting a state in only 22 percent of Palestine remains an open issue. While the public demonstrated strong support for such a ministate after the signing of the Declaration of Principles, a hardcore opposition did remain. The al-Aqsa Intifada revived irredentist dreams beyond this hardcore, and the strong majority supporting a two-state solution seemed to evaporate. Only in the latter stages of the uprising did the illusion of creating Greater Palestine seem to lose force. But clashes between Islamic and PA forces could portend civil unrest, even civil war, over the question of final boundaries. Ultimately, acceptance of Israel and a two-state solution will require a fundamental rewriting of the Palestinians' story about themselves, not an easy task under any circumstances.

Beyond the question of territorial scope is that of the sort of authority and power a new Palestinian state should have. In the midst of revolt, some Palestinians called for reform in, and democratization of, the regime.[4] Palestinian statesmen and intellectuals spoke up, in large part because of the failure of the Palestine Authority to manage the confrontation with Israel and to establish an efficient, noncorrupt regime.[5] Perhaps the most telling of these critiques was in an open letter published in a number of Arabic newspapers by Nabil Amr, a former minister in Arafat's government and a member of the Legislative Council. He argued that the Palestine Authority had failed the test of building credible institutions or a rule of law and pinned the failure on the uprising against Israel. "Today, after two years of bloodshed," he wrote in September 2002, "we call for exactly what we refused [at Camp David], only after we became sure it was impossible to achieve."[6]

But the question for Palestinians is more far-reaching than the issue of reform of PA institutions: What sort of state should be established? Should it be the definitive center of Palestinian life or should it be one center among many? What authority would it or should it delegate to civil society? These questions are tied to the fate of the al-Aqsa Intifada. Failure to see the uprising through to where it could be interpreted by many Palestinians as a successful war of liberation would threaten the Palestine Authority's centrality and legitimacy. But success—or what could be interpreted as success—might create an overly centralized state, choking civil society—just what those calling for reform feared. On the other hand, a dramatic enough success might afford the PA leadership the luxury of selling the idea that a deal involving "territory in exchange for self-determination," that is, a two-state solution, would be worthwhile. It might, too, give it the leeway to accept restrictions on the new state's sovereignty, such as the size of its armed forces or the alliances it could make, while still maintaining its legitimacy.

Return and the Right of Return

Among Palestinians, no question has been more vexing than the issue of return *(al-awda)* and the right of return. It has been the fundamental building block of Palestinism. Personal and collective "return" of those uprooted (in the 1948 war as well as the 1967 war) from their villages, neighborhoods, homes, gardens, and fields, most of which no longer even exist, has served as the common denominator for Palestinian collective memory and myth. Even at the height of the Oslo process, Palestinian political leaders refrained from any statement that could be interpreted as even hinting at surrender of the right of return. They continued to use Security Council Resolution 194 as a mantra indicating their steadfastness in not giving up the fundamental Palestinian goal of return of the refugees.[7]

The Palestinian narrative that originated in the refugee camps of Jordan, Gaza, and Lebanon in the 1950s consisted of one simple version—the return of the uprooted to their original homes and land. Over the years, however, a second version of the narrative began to emerge in circles of intellectuals, one that was compatible with the wording of Resolution 194; and, after the Oslo signing, this version challenged the first, at least among Palestinian intellectuals. It conceded that full return was impossible and argued that material compensation should substitute for actual return for the majority of refugees.

No doubt among most Palestinians, the original variant has continued to be accepted as the basic tenet of Palestinism. In mid-2001, the Israel/Palestine Center of Research and Information surveyed a random sample of 1,600 people who had been uprooted in the 1948 and 1967 wars, now living in refugee camps, villages, and cities of the West Bank and Gaza Strip.[8] The principal findings of this survey were as follows:

- Almost all refugees indicated that they were not willing to accept compensation instead of return (98.7 percent of the general refugee population selected "strongly agree" or "agree"

to the statement that compensation cannot replace return).
Among the general population, almost as high a percentage
(93.1 percent) similarly rejected compensation in place of
return.
- The limited option of using the criterion of "family
  reunification" as the basis for selecting those who will return
  was universally rejected as a possible solution to the refugee
  problem.
- On the question of compensation, 68.9 percent suggested that
  they would accept return even if it meant no material
  compensation.

In sum, those who fled or were expelled from their homes in 1948
and 1967 have continued to see "return" as a basic right that should
not be relinquished under any political circumstances. They have
been adamant that their right should be understood literally and
not be traded for compensation or rehabilitation in another region
or state. Despite all the changes since 1948, the refugees, interestingly, have continued to respond as if basic political, social, and spa-
tial conditions had not changed, as if it were possible to travel back
through time to some idyllic point in the past. Jewish Israelis in
overwhelming numbers have indicated that they would interpret
such a literal reading of the right of return as nothing less than a
blueprint for the destruction of their state.

The second version of return has been accepted only by some intellectuals and was strongly hinted at by Arafat in an op-ed piece
in the *New York Times* in 2002, in the midst of the al-Aqsa Intifada.
In that article, he acknowledged and addressed Israel's demographic
concerns. This version entails realization of the right of return
within the framework of the borders of a new Palestinian state in
the West Bank and Gaza Strip. Only a limited number would return
to the territory Israel controlled and, even then, not to their original
lands and homes. Others, including those rejecting repatriation to
the new Palestinian state, would be incorporated as full citizens into
the countries to which they had fled.

Those who have cautiously suggested this variant have argued that its execution must be accompanied by a declaration asserting the validity, at least on an ideological level, of refugees' full and original right of return, and by Israel's accepting responsibility for creating the refugee problem in the first place. But on a practical level, these thinkers have indicated that "return" will be carried out only gradually, based on the economic and social ability of the sovereign Palestinian state to absorb and assimilate the returning refugees. Those in the most dire straits, both economically and politically, such as the refugees in Lebanon, would be given first preference. The refugees would be compensated for their destroyed and abandoned property. Finally, the Palestinian state would legislate a general "Law of Return" similar to that of Israel.

This approach represents an attempt at compromise between the powerful myth of return and the practical possibility of realizing it. But the tension between the mythic and the practical may very well grow as a Palestinian state develops. Conflicts among different groups of Palestinians could deepen, especially as settled groups vie for scarce resources with returning refugees. Certainly, this version of return, with its proviso for the incorporation of some refugees into their host societies, will stamp Palestinians as a "people of diasporas," legitimating what before had been seen only as a temporary condition dictated by necessity. The official sanctioning of this configuration of Palestinians will further demand a refashioning of their narrative. And it will require an institutionalization of the relations between the new center in a Palestinian state and the satellites in *ghurba*. A central question will be the degree to which the new state will serve as an arbitrator and gatekeeper of relations even among those in the diaspora.

Manner of Regime and Social Arrangement

The state's role in governing those in the West Bank and Gaza Strip, as well as in the Palestinian diaspora, will depend heavily on what sort of state it becomes. At the center of debates about the character of the governing authority has been the question of democracy versus the autocratic-paternalistic style developed in the guerrilla-type leadership of Fatah. Of course, even Fatah had to operate in the federated structure of the PLO and to pay heed to other voices. From the very establishment of the Palestine Authority, intense conflicts broke out between the PA leadership, on the one side, and the media and intellectuals, on the other, around the subjects of freedom of speech and association. Both the experience in forging a vibrant civil society under the difficult conditions of Israeli occupation and the development of a freewheeling Palestinian intelligentsia in the United States, Europe, Lebanon, and elsewhere primed Palestinians for an open society. New human and civil rights organizations sprung up almost immediately after the PA's establishment, but most had disappeared by November 2000. The wide-ranging civil powers that the Oslo agreements had afforded the Palestine Authority coupled with its multiple security forces, staffed by Palestinian guerrillas brought in from abroad, immediately set up an adversarial situation with the population as well as with veterans of the first Intifada and former graduates of Israeli prisons.

Another question about the emerging character of the regime has come in the realm that could be called state-mosque relations. As in other countries in the Middle East and beyond, Islam has loomed large in struggles over the character of politics and society. While the resurgence of Islam and its politicization has been a transnational phenomenon, with groups and events in different countries feeding off each other, the growth of Islam as a political-religious force in Palestine has been largely a home-grown phenomenon. Rooted in local community aid and service institutions, it has developed a distinctive understanding of *jihad* in the context of Israeli rule. And, through that, the Islamic movement has made itself the largest and most important opposition force in the territories.[9] Rooting itself first in the 1980s Intifada and later in its opposition to the Oslo Accord, it undercut the power of the PLO and then the Palestine Authority. The movement's greatest success was in ambushing the peace process in the years after the signing of the Declaration of Principles.

The movement succeeded, too, in forcing the PLO and Palestine

Authority themselves to change. Increasingly, they co-opted both the symbols and, when possible, the personnel of the Islamicists. At the same time, Hamas, the most prominent of the Islamic groups, underwent changes as it faced the reality of Palestinian self-government. Within Hamas, some elements, centered largely in the political arm of the organization, advocated working with the secular forces in achieving an end to the occupation through diplomacy, while others, especially in fighting units, pressured for the continuation of *jihad*. The breakdown in talks between the Palestine Authority and Israel, escalation of the armed struggle, and the return of the right wing to power in Israel, all in 2001, helped to blur the differences between Fatah and the Islamic movement, while at the same time sharpening divisions within each. In short, the debate on state-mosque relations has not been a simple opposition between two opposing forces. The common struggle against Israeli occupation and limits imposed by their shared sense of Palestinian unity have resulted in an odd synergy, which has led fighting and political factions of each, respectively, to adopt some of the characteristics and positions of the other. It is within this context that public debate has taken place.

Differences between secularists and religious forces, however, are likely to spring up again. A new Palestinian state will inevitably be forced to deal with the place of Islam within it, while also taking into consideration the status of its prominent Christian minority. This challenge has already begun to manifest itself in Palestinian society with regard to the status of women and the place of the family in Palestinian society.

After emerging as a force in the 1980s, women's groups pushed hard under the Palestine Authority for representation in state institutions and equality under the law and for improved social conditions for women.[10] The PA leadership tried to walk a tightrope, making minimal changes and deferring most issues to the indeterminate future, as it kept a close eye on the position on gender in Hamas and in the Islamic movement in general. In certain realms, women's organizations grew impressively and pushed for ongoing change; but in many ways, women remained bound within a highly patriarchal society.[11] The structure of the family, and especially the rights of women within the family, are both a microcosm and a representation of the people as a whole. Struggle over the status of women—as subjected to their fathers and brothers or as free-acting individuals—will be at the center of the struggle in a new Palestinian state over the nature of Palestinian society as liberal-individualistic or religious-hierarchical.

Full Independence Versus Federation

From the inception of the Palestinian national movement in the wake of World War I and the Balfour Declaration, it has been caught between the poles of full independence and integration into a larger national framework. Faisal's brief reign in Damascus after World War I attracted Arabs from Palestine as an escape from the dual stranglehold of British rule and the threatening Zionist settlement. Again, after *al-Nakba*, pan-Arabism became a lifeline for a traumatized and leaderless people. The failures of both Faisal after World War I and Nasser in the 1967 war sent the Palestinians, almost dialectically, back to ideas of self-sufficiency and nationalism in a much narrower framework, that of Palestine only. But the difficulty of displacing the Zionists created a sense of helplessness among Palestinian leaders, sending them back, yet again, to alliances and ideas of federation that could change the status quo.

Perhaps the most popular recurring idea was of some sort of federation between Jordan and Palestine. This notion dates back to the 1930s when some expressed the need to reunify Palestine and the Hashemite Kingdom of Trans-Jordan, following the first proposal to partition Palestine, the Peel Commission Report. Jordanian annexation of the West Bank after the 1948 debacle effected that federation, at least for a portion of Palestine; and, after Jordan lost the West Bank to Israel in the 1967 war, the idea of a federation resurfaced on several occasions.[12] Nonetheless, there are two problems with seeing "Jordan as Palestine and Palestine as Jordan." First, the Hashemite Bedouin regime has been foreign, repressive, and illegitimate in the eyes of many non-Jordanian Palestinians.[13] And, while there have been moments of cooperation between Fatah and the Jordanian regime, the dark cloud of Black September, the Jordanians' routing and expulsion of PLO forces in 1970, still hangs heavily over the PA leadership.

A second reason that the Palestinian political elite has hesitated in pursuing the so-called Jordanian option is the danger of implicitly renouncing its claims on all of Palestine. The transformation of Jordan into a Palestinian state could serve to undermine the validity of the Palestinians' basic moral and political claims to the other parts of Palestine, that is, either to the territories under Israeli control or to the entire territory. Nonetheless, the idea of some sort of federation with Jordan, which could counter a future Palestinian state's clear weaknesses—small territory, lack of territorial contiguity, paucity of natural resources, and more—periodically resurfaces and promises to be a recurring theme in Palestinian public debate. In a future Palestinian state, it is possible, too, that ideas for forcible expansion will be directed not at a seemingly immovable Israel but toward the eastern bank of the Jordan where an anachronistic monarchy rules a largely Palestinian population.

Other sorts of possible federation have come up from time to time, some involving a loose federation with Israel. Today, these ideas are not part of the public debate among Palestinians (or Israelis, for that matter). Especially after the al-Aqsa Intifada, the possibility of this idea reappearing seems remote. Not only has the atmosphere been clouded, but Palestinians justifiably fear that any sort of union with Israel will be yet another façade for continued Israeli control—domination without occupation. Still, with the inevitable weakness that will plague a new Palestinian state, various ideas for integration into a larger political union of some sort will inevitably be voiced. In the past, Palestinians leaned toward more closely identifying with other Arabs in various pan-Arabist schemes or with other Muslims through Islam, and at other times, toward a more particularistic self-definition as Palestinians. We can expect the same pendulum to swing back and forth in the future as well. But, just as before, these alternatives will never be mutually exclusive;

one or the other will become prominent, depending on the internal balance of power and the nature of external forces pressuring society.

Palestinian-Israelis:
Integration, Autonomy, or Separation?

Israel's Palestinian citizens have a complex relationship with both Israel and the Palestinian people—what has been called their double marginality. The last generation has brought a marked increase in feelings among Israeli Arabs that they are an integral part of the Palestinian people. At the same time, they have become much more vocal about discrimination against them as citizens in Israel. Still, over and over, they have expressed their commitment not only to the land but also to maintaining their status as citizens of the Israeli state. They have emphatically rejected separation from Israel—through emigration to the Palestine Authority or through a land swap that would transfer their homes to a Palestinian state. That being said, they have continued to debate their relationship to the Israeli state and society.

One option presented has been for the Arab citizens to resign themselves to their limited and partial rights and to demand improvement in their economic and social situation, including broader integration into Israel's public life and new job opportunities, especially in the civil service. If their proportion of the population increases from its present 20 percent, their political weight will also grow, increasing their opportunities to extract more resources and services from the state. Smart political tactics as a community can lead to substantial improvement in life chances for individuals, even if, as a group, Palestinian-Israelis remain a circumscribed minority. They would still most likely be in a better position in terms of standard of living and personal rights compared to Arabs in neighboring countries or even in a new Palestinian state.

A second option is for them to pursue growing cultural autonomy and self-administration of villages and Arab municipalities.

This tactic could partially satisfy their aspirations to express their separate identity and, perhaps, mitigate feelings of collective deprivation. But this option threatens to exacerbate their double marginality—making them an even more remote presence in both Israeli and Palestinian society. It also places their personal mobility, the increasing life chances for them as individuals, in jeopardy, distancing them from Israel's central institutions. It also threatens to bring back open discussion of possible separation from Israel, which itself could further alienate them from the Jewish population. Such a debate could undermine the majority position among them to remain active and full citizens of Israel. In all likelihood, the first option will dominate, as Israel's Arab citizens become a more visible part of the workforce, including in the civil service, and a more vocal part of Israel's political arena.

A Dance of Death or a Dance of Life

The public debates and internal struggles, already evident in Palestinian discourse and actions, will only grow in intensity as the possibility of a state of Palestine becomes real. As for all peoples-in-the-making and new states, the primary challenge will be to channel these debates and struggles into the shaping of a binding national narrative. Conversely, the biggest threat is fracturing of this narrative into fragments that either are at war or simply ignore one another. The very first question we posed—can the Palestinians simultaneously maintain both the many voices of their diversity and their national unity—is the one that underlies all others. To the extent that a Palestinian state provides space for alternative voices from civil society and from the diaspora, it improves the chances for creatively moving the story of the Palestinians ahead and for creating a renewed basis for national unity.

Despite the fractures among the Palestinians threatening to undermine the meaning of Palestinism, one element has united them and distinguished them. That special element, of course, has been Zionism and, later, Israel. The prominent Palestinian place on the agenda of international politics and world opinion resulted from a territorial struggle with the Jews. The ancient conflict between two great civilizations, the Arab and the Israelite, and two great religions, Islam and Judaism, only amplified the political conflict of the last century.

Jewish-Arab antagonism simmered in the last decades of Ottoman rule and then erupted into full-scale conflict in the years of the British mandate. The importance of these thirty years of British government cannot be overestimated.[14] Not only did the British define the physical boundaries of the state, which by the logic of colonial rule would eventually be given to the country's majority—the Arabs—but they also created the conditions that carved out what would be the social boundaries of the Palestinian Arab people. Yet the formation of such a people in this case did not ensure that the logic of colonialism would be played out, as the mandate also fostered the formation of a Jewish society in Palestine, a society able to establish its own state-in-the-making that frustrated the Arabs' aspirations. When the colonial state collapsed, the Palestinian Arabs lacked the organization to challenge Jewish society effectively, in good part because the British had decimated Palestinian institutions during the Arab Revolt (much as the Israelis decimated Palestinian institutions sixty-five years later, during the al-Aqsa Intifada).

We have argued that telling the story of Zionism or Palestinism is impossible without understanding the impact they had on one another. For the Palestinians, the story centers on *al-Nakba*, a catastrophe that produced, ironically, a strong collective consciousness transcending all the fractures. In the misery of the camps—in the permanence of temporariness—refugees developed a powerful new nationalism. Its fuel was longing and injustice, humiliation and degradation—bitterness and hatred toward Jews, the West, other Arabs, and the cosmic order itself. At its heart was a vision of returning to a Lost Garden. The right to do so was perceived as self-evident and a condition for rebuilding the cosmic order destroyed in *al-Nakba*.

While the communities of exiles, scattered through the countries of the Middle East, formed the foundation of the new Palestinism, the 1967 war returned the focus to the reunited territory of the old Palestine mandate. Israel's overwhelming victory produced not only another wave of refugees but also the rise of a new outside leadership and the creation of a civil society within the occupied territories. The PLO outsiders and insiders in the West Bank and Gaza Strip cooperated and contended, struggling over the image of the Palestinians' future, all within the context of the Palestinian consciousness created in the refugee camps in the decades following *al-Nakba*. They pushed and pulled at the edges of the meaning of Palestinism, so that now the images of the Lost Garden and the inalienable right to return to their original homes contend with the pragmatic possibility of independence in only a part of Palestine for only part of the Palestinian people. Even the establishment of the Palestine Authority and its attempt to monopolize the writing of the Palestinians' story could not suppress the discourse and struggles in Palestinian communities over what the Palestinian future will be.

At this point, the struggles taking place within Palestinian society have no more clear an outcome than those between Jews and Arabs. What is unmistakable is that both Israelis and Jews worldwide will have a significant role in determining the Palestinian future, as will Palestinians in determining that of the Israelis, and thus the Jews. The Palestinian poet Mahmud Darwish saw a powerful symbiosis linking Palestinian and Israeli, Arab and Jew. There will be a time, he wrote, when

> the Jew will not be ashamed to find the Arab part inside of himself, and the Arab will not be ashamed to declare that he is constituted also by Jewish elements. Especially when talking about Eretz Yisrael in Hebrew and Falestin in Arabic. I am a product of all the cultures that have passed through this land—Greek, Roman, Persian, Jewish, and Ottoman. A presence that exists even in my language. Each culture fortified itself, passed on, and left something. I am a son to all those fathers, but I belong to one mother. Does that mean my mother is a whore? My mother is this land that absorbed us all, was a witness and was a victim. I am also born of the Jewish culture that was in Palestine. . . .

History has linked the two peoples and national movements. Neither can make the other disappear, as the al-Aqsa uprising once again has proved, and neither can achieve peace without fulfilling some of the most deeply held aspirations of the other.

It was this sense of being locked in an embrace in which neither side could make the other disappear that finally drove Israel and the PLO to the bargaining table in the 1990s. The Declaration of Principles, signed on September 13, 1993, laid out a blueprint for their intertwined future. That act changed Israel's and the PLO's relationship to each other. The last ten years were bracketed by the signing of the Oslo Accord and al-Aqsa Intifada. This period has constituted yet another stormy decade in the history of the Palestinian people and their relationship to the Jews. They have been hurled from high hopes to abysmal despair, from nearing their dream of their own sovereign state (even if in only a small part of historic Palestine) to renewed attempts to wipe out their political autonomy—what we might call politicide.

What the failure of Oslo showed is that for the two sides to succeed they must incorporate their larger publics into the process. The story is not that of the making of the Palestinian leadership but the making of the Palestinian people. And the same goes for the Jews. The accord unveiled a large majority on each side ready to make historic compromises, to accept two states in what had been British Palestine; but the ensuing process moved each public toward deep alienation, ready to start a new uprising and to elect Ariel Sharon. The brutal violence since the beginning of the new century has now left both sides deeply fatigued and even further alienated. To move back from the edge of this abyss, leaders and their societies alike must now begin to acknowledge that the writing of their own unfinished story depends, in great part, on the ability of the other society to continue writing its story.

CHRONOLOGICAL LIST OF MAJOR EVENTS

Date	Palestinian history	Events related to Palestinian history
635–37	The Arab tribes capture Jerusalem from the Byzantines and make the province of Palestina Prima into a military district (*jund*) of Filastin; Arabization and Islamization of the region	
641		Arab conquest of Byzantine Egypt
661		Muawiya, the founder of Umayyad dynasty, proclaims himself caliph in Jerusalem, having Damascus as his capital
685–705	Caliph Abd al-Malik builds the Dome of the Rock mosque to emphasize the holiness of the city, in opposition to his rival who controls Mecca and Medina	
705–715	His son Walid builds al-Aqsa mosque in Jerusalem	
715–717	Suleiman, the seventh Umayyad caliph, builds Ramleh as his residence	
1095		The famous scholar Abu Hamid al-Ghazali from Nizamiyya Academy of Baghdad resides in Jerusalem, where he begins work on his volume *The Revivification of the Science of Religion*, one of the major efforts of Islamic theology

Date	Palestinian history	Events related to Palestinian history
1099–1187	Crusaders invade Palestine and establish the Latin Kingdom of Jerusalem; major massacre of Arab and Jewish population of the territory	
1187	Salah al-Din (Saladin) reconquers Jerusalem and creates a new Islamic dynasty; the Ayubidis rule over a part of the region	
1260		In the battle of Ayn Jalut (Nazareth) the Egyptian-based Mamluks defeat the Mongol hordes of Hulagu (grandson of Genghis Khan) and overcome the remaining Crusader fortifications
1260–1515		The region is under the rule of the Mamluk military caste and its sultans, after it deposes the Ayubid dynasty
1515–1917	During the rule of Suleiman the Magnificent (1520–66), the old city of Jerusalem is walled	With some interruptions, the country is incorporated into Turkish Ottoman rule
1798		Napoleonic campaign in Egypt; battle of the Nile
1799	Ahmad al-Jazzar, the governor of Acre, turns back the French army, gaining control over most of Palestine	
1808	Muslim revolt in Jerusalem against Ottoman governor; more power for local families	
1826	Second rebellion of the Jerusalem Muslims; Christians and Jews attacked	
1830	Ibrahim Pasha, the Ottoman governor, gains considerable control and autonomy over the country	
1831–40	Egyptian conquest of the region, including Palestine, and its incorporation into the Egyptian state	
1834	Major revolt of the region against the Egyptians, focused mainly in Palestine	
1839		Proclamation of a program of reorganization in the Ottoman Empire

Date	Palestinian history	Events related to Palestinian history
854–56		Crimean War
856		Reform in the Ottoman Empire with a more detailed statement than in 1839, followed by land tenure changes
860–61		Intercommunal rifts in Lebanon and Syria
1861–65		Civil War in the U.S.
1863	Creation of the municipality of Jerusalem under Ottoman law, first nucleus of modern local government	
1868–75		Ottoman civil code
1876		Ottoman Constitution
1881–82		Pogroms in Eastern Europe against the Jews; Arab revolt in Egypt; British occupation of Egypt
1882–1904		First wave of Jewish settlers immigrate to Palestine (First Aliyah)
1878	Establishment of Petah Tikvah, the first Jewish colony in Palestine	
1891		Ahad Ha'am (Asher Ginzberg] publishes his article "Truth from Eretz Israel [Palestine]" warning his fellow Jews of the danger of ignoring Arabs' feelings in Palestine
1892	Establishment of Palestinian branches of Crédit Lyonnais in Jaffa and Jerusalem	
1897		First Zionist Congress launches the Basel Program with the aim of resettling the Jewish people in Palestine and establishing the World Zionist Organization
1899–1902	Arab-Jewish tension following large Jewish land purchases in the Tiberias region	
1904–14	Second wave of Jewish immigration; demand by Jews for exclusive use of Jewish labor in Jewish colonies and in Zionist-funded enterprises	

Date	Palestinian history	Events related to Palestinian history
1905		Nagib Azouri publishes his *Le reveil de la nation arabe,* envisioning the conflict between major national movements in the Middle East—those of the Arabs and Jews
1907		Yitzhak Epstein, a Hebrew teacher from Galilee, publishes in *Shiloach* an essay warning the Zionist settlers that uprooting Arab tenants from the land will cause hatred against the colonization and the crystallization of a common Arab consciousness that will turn against the Jewish settlement
1908	Appearance of the first Palestinian newspaper in Haifa, *al-Karmil,* with the major aim of fighting against land transfers from Arab to Jewish ownership	Young Turks revolution in Istanbul
	Palestinian delegates, elected to the Ottoman parliament, warn against "Judification" of the country, frequent tension between Arabs and Jews	
1911	*Filastin,* a large Arabic newspaper, is launched in Jaffa	
1914		World War I breaks out
1915–16		Correspondence between the British high commissioner in Egypt (Henry McMahon) and Sharif Hussein of Mecca leads to agreement between British and Arabs on establishment of an Arab kingdom in the Middle East in exchange for an Arab military revolt against the Ottomans; Arabs believe Arab kingdom includes Palestine
1916		Secret Anglo-French agreement to divide Ottoman Middle East provinces (Sykes-Picot agreement)
June 1916		Hussein proclaims Arab independence and revolts against the Ottomans

Date	Palestinian history	Events related to Palestinian history
917	Ottoman forces in Jerusalem surrender to British forces	The Balfour Declaration: British support for establishment of a Jewish national home in Palestine
1918	All of Palestine occupied by British forces	End of World War I; Treaty of Versailles and League of Nations Covenant approved; General Arab (Syrian) Congress, including prominent Palestinians, held in Damascus rejects Balfour Declaration and considers Palestine part of southern Syria
1919	Arab Literary Club and Arab Club founded to propagate Arab nationalism; Kamil al-Husseini appointed by the British as grand mufti of Jerusalem, emergence of a new Muslim hierarchy in place of the center in Istanbul	
1919–20	Muslim-Christian Associations formed countrywide, protesting against Balfour Declaration and claiming Palestine as part of Syria	
1920	As part of Arab unrest in Syria against the French, Arab rebels attack two Jewish settlements in the north of Palestine	
	Faysal's proclamation excites the Arab population of Palestine; riots in Jerusalem and Jaffa (following the Nabi Musa festival); some notables arrested by the British; Amin al-Husseini's flight; Musa Kazim al-Husseini, the mayor of Jerusalem, replaced by Raghib al-Nashashibi	Faysal proclaims the independence of Syria and himself as king; the revolt is suppressed by French troops
	First Palestinian National ("Third Syrian Arab") Congress meets in Haifa, constituted from delegates from Muslim-Christian Associations and other notables; the Congress nominates the Arab Executive Committee, which is perceived (and recognized de facto) by the British as the political leadership and representative of the Arab community in Palestine (until 1935); the Congress demands British recognition as representatives of the Arab Palestinian population, as well as independence, an	San Remo Peace Conference assigns Britain the mandate over Palestine

Date	Palestinian history	Events related to Palestinian history
	immediate halt to Jewish immigration and land acquisitions	
1921	Kamil al-Husseini dies	
	Riots in Jaffa; Arabs kill 46 Jews; a British commission of inquiry attributes the disturbances to Arabs' anxiety about increasing Jewish immigration; Amin al-Husseini is appointed Mufti of Jerusalem, and pardoned by High Commissioner Herbert Samuel	
1922	Creation of the Supreme Muslim Council to fill the vacuum left by the removal of Islamic Ottoman rule; Amin al-Husseini elected president of the Council	
	Britain issues a "White Paper" emphasizing that only a part of Palestine is considered the Jewish national home and excluding East Palestine (Transjordan) from the mandate	
1925	Establishment of Palestinian Workers' Society (PAWS) as a moderate trade union movement led by Sami Taha	
1927	Municipal elections end in a resounding Nashashibi-led opposition victory	
1929	Countrywide riots against Jews, including the massacre of many members of the old non-Zionist community of Hebron, following fears and rumors of Jewish intentions to gain control over the Wailing Wall; Arab Women's Congress in Jerusalem adopts strong nationalist positions	
1930	The Arab Bank established by the Abd al-Hamid Shuman family, competing with Barclays	
1931	Pan-Islamic Congress held in Jerusalem, attended by 145 delegates from the Muslim world, reinforces Amin al-Husseini's position as an Islamic leader	
1932	National Congress of Arab Youth convened in Jaffa	

Date	Palestinian history	Events related to Palestinian history
	Formation of the first modern Palestinian political party, the Istiqlal ("Independence"); strong pan-Islamic ideology and revival of the idea of Palestine as a natural part of southern Syria; creation of additional quasi-parties: Palestine Arab party (Husseinis), National Defense party (the opposition, or the Nashashibis), and Reform party (Khalidis)	
1933	Establishment of the Arab Agricultural Bank to grant loans to fellaheen (from the 1940s, it is called the Bank of the Arab Nation)	
	Meetings of some Palestinian leaders (Musa Alami, Awni Abd al-Hadi, and George Antonius) with the just-appointed chair of the Jewish Agency, David Ben-Gurion, in an attempt to find some accommodation between the contrasting demands of the two national movements; no understanding achieved	
	Arab Executive Committee declares a general strike and mass demonstrations are held in the major cities; the protest is directed solely against British rule, demanding independence, immediate halt of Jewish immigration and land acquisition, and establishment of a local government based on proportional representation; British police and troops suppress the protest movement	
1935	Sheikh Izz al-Din al-Qassam, leader of a small guerrilla group, killed by British forces	
1936	Following minor clashes with Jews, National Committees are established in all towns and some villages; the Jerusalem committee adopts the slogan "No taxation without representation." Some local leaders call for a general strike, forcefully implemented by the shabab. All Arab political parties and organizations merged into the Arab Higher Committee, led by Amin al-Husseini; waves of violence; the	A 45-day general strike in Syria against French rule; French promise to consider granting independence

Date	Palestinian history	Events related to Palestinian history
	British lose control over the country despite reinforcements; the Great Arab Revolt breaks out	
	A Syrian officer, Fawzi al-Qa'uqji, enters Palestine, leading volunteers from Arab countries to conduct guerrilla warfare against the British	
	The Arab Higher Committee accepts the call of the Arab states to end the 175-day general strike that exhausts the Arab economy	
1937	The Peel Commission publishes its report recommending partition of Palestine into a Jewish state, an Arab state incorporated into Transjordan, and British enclaves; both parties reject the proposal; the Arab revolt is renewed	
	Nazareth district commissioner assassinated by Palestinians; the British outlaw the Arab Higher Committee and other Arab political organizations; five leaders deported to the Seychelles; two hundred arrested; Amin al-Husseini escapes to Lebanon	
1938	Insurgence and counterinsurgence escalate; thousands of fellaheen join guerrilla rebel forces; Amin al-Husseini establishes the Central Committee of the National Jihad and the Council of Rebellion in Damascus	Close cooperation between mainstream Jewish paramilitary organization (Haganah) and British forces; Col. Charles Wingate trains and leads joint counterinsurgence units
	Rural rebels control most of the inland towns, such as Nablus, Hebron, Ramallah, Tiberias, Beersheba, and even parts of Jaffa and the walled portion of Jerusalem; well-to-do families leave Palestine; Palestinian counterinsurgence groups fight the rebels; civil war among the Arabs	
	British military rule over the country; reinforcements from Britain; military pressure on the hilly regions; recapture of the Arab Old City of Jerusalem by British troops; guerrilla groups disbanded and leadership killed or captured	

Date	Palestinian history	Events related to Palestinian history
	Opposition leaders organize and fund "peace bands," fighting against rebel groups and defending villages and neighborhoods	
	Partition (Woodhead) Commission declares Peel Commission partition proposal "impractical"; proposes an Arab-Jewish-British conference for solving the problem of Palestine; deported Palestinian leaders released	
1939	London Conference convened; talks end without agreement; Malcolm MacDonald, colonial secretary of state, launches a new British policy for Palestine (1939 White Paper): after ten years of a transitional period, an independent, unitary (i.e., Arab-ruled) Palestinian state, annual Jewish immigration of 15,000, and heavy restrictions on Jewish land purchases; de facto withdrawal from Balfour Declaration; House of Commons approves the new policy	George Antonius publishes *The Arab Awakening*, the first comprehensive history of the Arab nationalist movement
		World War II breaks out
1940	Publication of Land Transfer Regulations, restricting official Jewish purchases; de facto sales continue	
1941	Economic prosperity; establishment of the Congress of Workers and Union of Section of Arab Workers, both unions under communist influence	Formation of Jewish shock units (Palmach)
		German invasion of Soviet Union; British troops sent to overthrow pro-German regime in Iraq, with assistance of Jewish units
		The U.S. enters World War II
1942	Following a Nablus conference, PAWS splits; formation of communist-led Federation of Arab Trade Unions	Ben-Gurion declares the policy of prompt creation of a "Jewish Commonwealth" in Palestine; awareness of the scope of the Holocaust
1944	Revival of Arab National Fund; new board of directors, replacing Amin al-Husseini's supporters	Etzel (the Irgun) declares an anticolonial revolt against Britain

Date	Palestinian history	Events related to Palestinian history
1945		End of World War II; millions of uprooted people, among them hundreds of thousands of Jewish survivors of the Nazi Holocaust; formation of the Arab League; the Jewish leadership begins a policy of sending ships to Palestine with unauthorized immigrants
	Najjada, a paramilitary organization, founded by Nimr al-Hawari in Jaffa	Declaration of the "Jewish Revolt" against British by the mainstream paramilitary Haganah; negotiations with other Jewish underground organizations on coordination among them
	New statement of policy (White Paper of 1945) launched by British Foreign Secretary E. Bevin; more restrictions on Jewish immigration; proposal to set up Anglo-American Committee of Inquiry	
	Reconstitution of the Arab Higher Committee	
1946	Jamal al-Husseini allowed to return to Palestine; takes control of a reorganized Arab Higher Committee	
	The Anglo-American Committee of Inquiry recommends the immediate entry of 150,000 Jewish immigrants and abolition of the 1940 Land Transfer Regulations	
	Amin al-Husseini arrives in Egypt to try to regain control over Palestinians; new attempt of unity by creation of an Arab Higher Executive; full-scale Jewish underground operations, mainly against British targets and infrastructure (railroads and bridges); Etzel blows up the British administration headquarters (a wing of Jerusalem King David Hotel)	Transjordan gains independence from Britain
1946–47		Another London Conference; Britain submits an autonomy plan based on division of the country into provinces; first round attended only by Arab states; second round

Date	Palestinian history	Events related to Palestinian history
		includes participation of Palestinian and Jewish delegations; Arabs demand a unitary state; conference ends without results
1947	Bevin submits the problem of Palestine to the UN; UN special commission (UNSCOP) appointed and sent to Palestine; organization of a second paramilitary organization, the Futuwwa, under the control of Jamal al-Husseini	
	Publication of UNSCOP report: majority recommend partition; minority, a federative solution	Arab League meeting in Aley (Lebanon) reaffirms Bludan resolution to use oil as a weapon in the struggle over Palestine
November 29, 1947	The Palestinians and the Arab states reject partition; the Zionists accept	UN General Assembly adopts Resolution 181, recommending the establishment of Jewish and Arab states in Palestine and the internationalization of the Jerusalem area
1948	Arab Higher Committee declares a general strike; full-scale intercommunal war breaks out in Palestine	
	Abd al-Qadir al-Husseini returns to the country and proclaims himself the chief commander of Palestinian forces	
	Arab League calls for volunteers for an Arab Liberation Army (ALA) under the command of Fawzi al-Qa'uqji	
	Brigades of ALA irregulars arrive in North Palestine in January; selective abandonment by middle- and upper-class members from the big cities, and flight from the villages captured by Jewish forces in the coastal plain	Political Committee of Arab League rejects all demands of Amin al-Husseini and declares that the Arab Higher Committee does not represent the Palestinian people; all funds allocated to the League's Palestinian Council
	Fawzi al-Qa'uqji establishes his headquarters in central Palestine; ALA irregulars arrive in Jaffa; significant successes for the Arab irregulars; the main roads of the country are blocked; Yehiam, Gush Etzion, Hulda, and Neve Daniel convoys destroyed; Jewish Jerusalem under siege	

Date	Palestinian history	Events related to Palestinian history
	Successes for Jewish forces facing ALA in the north; in March, they capture and demolish Arab villages on the coastal plain, including Abu Kabir and Jabalya; Plan D adopted, allowing for securing Jewish settlements and the roads to them even beyond the territories allocated for the Jewish state and for destroying Arab localities and expelling their inhabitants if necessary for security reasons	
	In April, Abd al-Qadir al-Husseini is killed in a counterattack by Jewish forces on the strategic village of Castel, dominating the way to Jerusalem; major demoralization among Palestinian irregulars; massacre in the village of Dayr Yasin, about 120 villagers killed; Palestinian leadership tries to halt the flight; Arab Higher Committee calls on Palestinian Arabs not to leave	Mass demonstrations in Damascus, Baghdad, Cairo, and Tripoli calling to "save the Palestinian brethren"; pogroms in local Jewish communities; Arab League committee meets to discuss the ALA failures and the Dayr Yasin events
	Qa'uqji withdraws from Mishmar Haemek; Jewish forces take over Tiberias, Haifa, and additional villages; Arab population flees or is expelled; Jaffa under siege; a Jewish convoy to the Mt. Scopus campus of Hebrew University massacred	Lebanon and Syria announce the intention of sending troops to Palestine in April; Iraq concentrates troops in Transjordan
1948	In April, battle over Jaffa continues; an ALA unit reinforces its defenders; all Arab neighborhoods of West Jerusalem are captured by Jewish forces and their inhabitants driven out	
	In May, Jewish forces capture Safed and its rural hinterland; Jaffa surrenders and the majority of its Muslim population leaves; the remaining Jewish settlements of Etzion bloc (in the mountain region) surrender to the Arab Legion	
	The end of the British mandate in May; the State of Israel is proclaimed; Egyptian regular forces cross the border into Palestine, Arab Legion (Transjordanian) forces cross the Jordan River westward; Syrian troops move to cross the border; the 1948 war breaks out on May 15	The Soviet Union and the United States recognize Israel; creation of the Israel Defense Forces (IDF)

Date	Palestinian history	Events related to Palestinian history
	Major battles between advancing Arab armed forces and Israeli forces; most Arab villages are evacuated following the force movements; Israeli decision prevents Arabs from returning to evacuated villages; formation of refugee camps in May and June in Gaza, territories controlled by the Arab Legion and Lebanon	
	The All Palestine Government, with a temporary site in Gaza, is established by Amin al-Husseini	
	End of first truce in July; major Israeli offensive on three fronts, mainly to clear the Tel Aviv-Jerusalem road including the Lydda-Ramleh region; this action leads to a new wave of about 100,000 Palestinians fleeing to territories held by Arab Legion, ALA, and Egypt; a portion of the Palestinians evacuated by force	
		Lausanne peace talks fail in September, mainly due to Israel's refusal to "repatriate" the Palestinian refugees
	The Jericho Conference in November calls on Abdallah to annex the West Bank to TransJordan	
	Continuing battles and expulsion of Arabs from the conquered territories by Israeli armed forces; remaining Arab population is moved from one place to another according to perceived security requirements	
	In December, the UN General Assembly Resolution 194 (III) recognizes the right of the Palestinian refugees to return "and live at peace with their neighbors"	
1949		Armistice agreements between Israel and Lebanon, Transjordan, and Syria are signed; Israel holds about 80 percent of the total territories of Western Palestine; the eastern mountain area ("West Bank") is under Transjordanian rule; the "Gaza Strip" is under Egyptian occupation

Date	Palestinian history	Events related to Palestinian history
1949–56	Constant infiltration of Palestinians across the armistice lines causes casualties and unrest in Israel, which adopts a policy of retaliation against the Arab states and the "sources of infiltration"; military clashes along the armistice lines	
1950	Military government imposed on most Israeli Arabs; in April, the West Bank is formally annexed to Jordan; the United Nations Relief and Works Agency (UNRWA) begins operations	
1951	Yasser Arafat reorganizes the Palestinian Students' Union in Cairo	Nationalization of oil in Iran
	George Habash organizes the Arab Nationalists' Movement, with a leftist pan-Arabist ideology; its Palestinian branch will develop into the Popular Front for the Liberation of Palestine (PFLP); it initiates some sabotage activities against Arab and "imperialist" targets	King Abdallah of Jordan killed at prayer in al-Aqsa mosque
1952	The Arab League dissolves the All Palestine Government and empowers the Arab states to represent the Palestinian cause	Free Officers coup in Cairo; the end of the monarchy
1955		Alliance among Iraq, Pakistan, and Turkey ("Baghdad Pact") links them to Britain and the Western bloc
1956	47 Israeli Arabs killed in Kafr Qasim village after violation of curfew	Nationalization of Suez Canal; Israel conquers Gaza Strip and most of Sinai Desert; Anglo-French intervention
1957	Most of the Arab members of the Israeli Communist party (MAKI) split away, forming the almost purely Arab Communist list (RAKAH)	Israeli withdrawal from the Sinai Desert and Gaza Strip
1958		Formation of Egyptian-Syrian federation, creating the United Arab Republic, arouses pan-Arab sentiment

Date	Palestinian history	Events related to Palestinian history
1959	Fatah is created by Arafat and associates; al-Ard group starts to publish an Arab nationalist periodical in Israel; Khalil al-Wazir (Abu Jihad) issues in Lebanon the clandestine Fatah magazine *Filastinuna;* the Arab Higher Committee and Amin al-Husseini forced to move from Egypt to Lebanon	Muamar Qaddafi overthrows the monarchy in Libya
1962		Civil war in Yemen, removing the monarchy; Egypt backs the republicans, sending a military expedition
1964	Al-Ard outlawed by Israeli authorities after an attempt to establish it as an Arab nationalist party in Israel	In January, the first Arab summit in Cairo concludes with a statement about the need to "organize the Palestinian people enabling them to play their role in the liberation of their country and to achieve self-determination"
	In May, the First Palestinian National Council (PNC) convenes in Jerusalem, chaired by Ahmad Shukayri; it adopts the Palestine National Charter as the Basic Constitution of the Palestine Liberation Organization; a Palestine Liberation Army is also planned	
1965	Fatah launches its armed struggle for the liberation of Palestine; Communique No. 1 of al-Assifa, its military branch, is issued	
1966	Abolition of the Military Government that had ruled Israeli Arabs	Syrian Baath party conference decides to establish a Palestinian paramilitary organization, Saiqa
1967	Following Israel's victory in the June war, the entire territory of the former Palestine mandate comes under Israeli control, including about 650,000 Palestinians of the West Bank and East Jerusalem and 356,000 in the Gaza Strip; East Jerusalem is annexed to Israel and the rest of the captured territories, including the Golan Heights and the Sinai Desert, are put under military administration	In August, an Arab leaders' summit in Khartoum rejects any negotiations with Israel

Date	Palestinian history	Events related to Palestinian history
	Arafat attempts to establish his headquarters inside the occupied territories, trying to provoke and lead a popular uprising; by the end of December, all of his network is destroyed by Israeli intelligence and Arafat has left the territories	
	In September (through November), teachers and students strike against Israeli occupation in the West Bank; first general strike in Nablus	
	George Habash's group joins other small guerrilla organizations to form the Popular Front for the Liberation of Palestine (PFLP)	
1968	In March, Fatah fighters, aided by Jordanian artillery, repel an Israeli attack on Fatah's headquarters at Kara-mah (in the Jordan Valley). At the fourth session of PNC in July, the guerrilla groups led by Fatah take over the PLO, which becomes an umbrella organization of different streams, with Fatah predominance; the National Convenant is revised; an Israeli civilian airliner is hijacked by the PFLP and lands in Algiers	
	A Syrian-backed guerrilla group headed by Ahmad Jibril splits from the PFLP and forms its own PFLP—General Command	
1969	Naif Hawatma splits from the PFLP and founds the pro-Maoist Democratic Front for the Liberation of Palestine (DFLP). At the fifth session of the PNC in February, Arafat nominated as chair of the ruling Executive Committee (EC). The "Cairo Agreement" between Arafat and the Lebanese Army commander, Emile Bustani, permits "regulated guerrilla activities" in Lebanon; this agreement will be the basis of the state-in-a-state infrastructure built by the PLO in Lebanon	
1969–71	Demonstrations against Israeli rule in all major cities of the West Bank; sporadic Palestinian uprisings and guerrilla activities in the Gaza Strip	

Date	Palestinian history	Events related to Palestinian history
1970	A multiple hijacking is initiated by the PFLP; planes land in the desert area of Zarqa in Jordan and are blown up	
	Jordan armed forces begin to destroy the infrastructure of the guerrilla forces around Amman and the refugee camps; civil war between Palestinians and Jordanian troops; the guerrilla forces are defeated in what comes to be known as "Black September," and their headquarters are moved to Lebanon	
1971	Israeli security forces "pacify" the Gaza Strip	Assassination of Wasfi Tal, Jordanian premier and minister of defense, the first operation of "Black September," a Fatah-led organization under the command of Ali Hasan Salamah and Salah Khalaf (Abu Iyad)
	Foundation in Israel of the Arab Academic Union	
1972	PLO's Executive Committee establishes a central council as an intermediate level between the EC and the PNC, making the decision-making process more flexible	
	The Japanese Red Army guerrilla group, in coordination with Wadi Haddad, PFLP's chief of operations, hits Ben-Gurion Airport ("Operation Dayr Yasin"); Black September takes Israeli Olympic team as hostages in Munich; most of the hostages and guerrillas are killed during an abortive German police attempt to rescue the athletes	
1973	In April, Israelis launch a commando action against Fatah headquarters in Beirut, killing several Fatah commanders	The October War begins with a surprise Egyptian-Syrian attack on Israel; Henry Kissinger brokers separation of forces agreements in preparation for a Geneva peace conference
	Formation in the West Bank of the Palestine National Front (controlled by the Communist party) challenging the "outside" PLO leadership	

Date	Palestinian history	Events related to Palestinian history
1974	Arab Summit recognizes the PLO as the sole legitimate representative of the Palestinian people; Arafat speaks to the UN General Assembly in New York	
	In July, the 12th PNC adopts the idea of establishing "a Palestinian national authority in any area liberated from Israeli control," the so-called mini-state option; George Habash (PFLP) resigns from the PLO Executive Committee, establishing with the pro-Syrian guerrilla organization the Rejectionist Front; faced with the possibility of Palestinian participation in the Geneva Peace Conference, the Rejectionist Front is enlarged to include the PFLP-GC, the Arab Liberation Front (Iraqi backed), and other small guerrilla groups	
	Creation of the Committee of the Heads of Arab Local Councils, which becomes the Supreme Follow-Up Committee and acts as the leadership and representatives of the Israeli Arabs	
1975–91		Civil war in Lebanon with PLO participation; Syrian intervention in the civil war leads to gradual Syrian control over Lebanon, except for a small "security zone" in southern Lebanon that is dominated by Israel
1976	Municipal elections in the West Bank lead to PLO supporters being swept into office (Bassam al-Shaka in Nablus, Fahd Qawasma in Hebron, Karim Khalaf in Ramallah, Ibrahim Tawil in al-Bira); the elected mayors and other prominent figures form a nucleus of an internal leadership, the National Guidance Committee	
	The first Land Day (March 30) includes a general strike and protests of Israeli Arabs against land expropriations; six Arabs are killed; in 1992 it is declared a national holiday	

Date	Palestinian history	Events related to Palestinian history
	Christian right-wing militias in Lebanon, supported by Syria, enforce a siege on Tal al-Zaatar, a Palestinian refugee camp; the siege ends with a massacre of the camp inhabitants	
1977	Abu Abbas splits from PFLP-GC and forms Palestine Liberation Front (PLF)	The nationalist right-wing party Likud comes to power in Israel; the settlement of the occupied territories by Jews accelerates
	Appearance of the radical nationalist group "Sons of the Village" among Israeli Arabs	President Sadat of Egypt visits Jerusalem and speaks at the Knesset
1978	Seaborne Fatah guerrillas hijack a bus on the main coastal highway of Israel; thirty-seven people are killed, including six guerrillas	Israel undertakes a limited invasion of Lebanon (Operation Litani) and occupies a strip in southern Lebanon, constructing a buffer zone held by a local Israeli-supported militia
	Israeli-Fatah ("Habib") agreement on a cease-fire along the Lebanon-Israel border	Camp David accords signed; Israel recognizes the "legitimate rights of the Palestinians" and commits to granting them "full autonomy" after a transitional period of five years; Israel also commits to withdrawal from the Sinai Desert in exchange for peace with Egypt
	Menahem Milson appointed as civilian administrator of the West Bank; tries to establish a local counterbalance to the PLO by forming the Village Leagues, armed groups headed by Mustafa Doudeen	Revolution in Iran; a radical Muslim regime is established, promoting a militant Islam throughout the Arab world
1982	The National Guidance Committee is outlawed; general strike and mass demonstrations in the West Bank and Gaza Strip	
	In June, Israeli troops invade Lebanon in collaboration with the Maronite-Christian forces; Israel's major aim is to destroy the PLO's quasi-state infrastructure; the first large-scale Israeli-Palestinian war since 1948; heavy battles and casualties on all sides; West Beirut comes under siege and bombardment	

Date	Palestinian history	Events related to Palestinian history
	In August, the PLO evacuates its forces and headquarters from Beirut to Tripoli, with its fighters carrying only their personal arms; a new headquarters is established in Tunis	Bashir Gemayel elected president of Lebanon in August; 22 days later, he is killed by an explosive probably planted by Syrian agents
	In September, Christian-Maronite militias, under Israeli protection, massacre Palestinians in the Sabra and Shatilla refugee camps	
1984		Jewish settlements in the West Bank and Gaza Strip increase and now have about 80,000 settlers
1985	The Amman Agreement on a confederation between a future Palestinian state in the West Bank and Gaza Strip and Jordan is signed by King Hussein and Arafat; after a year the agreement is voided by King Hussein	
1987	On December 9, a general popular uprising, the Intifada, breaks out in the Gaza Strip and spreads to the West Bank; popular committees are formed; a unified leadership of the revolt is formed inside the territories; its directives are ratified by the "outside" PLO and are spread mainly by leaflets; power shifts toward "inside" leadership	
1988	In March, the Unified Leadership calls for Palestinian policemen to quit	
	In April, Khalil al-Wazir (Abu Jihad) is assassinated, most probably by Israeli agents	
	In November, the 19th session of the PNC convenes in Algiers and declares an independent Palestinian state; following heavy pressure by the U.S., which holds out recognition of and a dialogue with the PLO, Arafat declares in Geneva that the PLO recognizes the rights of all parties concerned in the Middle East conflict to exist in peace and security, including the State of Palestine, Israel, and other neighbors; Arafat denounces terrorism, and U.S. opens dialogue	

Date	Palestinian history	Events related to Palestinian history
1988	The Islamic Movement wins the municipal election in the Israeli Arab town of Umm al-Fahm	
1989	When Arafat refuses to condemn a terrorist attack by a PLO constituent organization, the U.S. suspends the dialogue with the PLO	
1990	In December, 17 Palestinians are killed and nearly 200 wounded after jittery Israeli security forces open fire near al-Aqsa mosque	Iraq invades Kuwait; a multinational force is created by the U.S.
1991	In January, Salah Khalaf (Abu Iyad) is assassinated, probably by the Abu Nidal organization, perhaps at the behest of Iraq	Massive Jewish immigration from the Soviet Union to Israel
	The Intifada turns inward as collaborators and other "suspects" are killed by Palestinian "shock troops" or individuals; vigilante activities on the part of Jewish settlers	The U.S.-led force defeats Iraq in the Gulf War; the PLO is hurt diplomatically by its support of Iraq; the Palestinian community in Kuwait of over 300,000 is reduced to several thousand and is badly persecuted
	In November, peace talks begin in Madrid (continue later in Washington) between Israel and Arab delegations (including Palestinians from the occupied territories as part of a joint Jordanian-Palestinian delegation); the peace talks are the product of U.S. diplomatic efforts and are held under the auspices of the U.S. and USSR	
1992	December 22: In response to the killing of border policeman Nissim Toledano, Israel carried out an executive order for the expulsion of 415 suspected Hamas activists to Lebanon. The deportees remained near the Israeli border in difficult winter conditions after the government of Lebanon refused to accept them. Both the deportation itself and the condition of those expelled caused an international uproar.	The Labor party returns to power in Israel, promising to implement Palestinian autonomy within a year

Date	Palestinian history	Events related to Palestinian history
	Deportations lead to a rise in Palestinian support for the Islamic groups in the occupied territories, with a corresponding drop in support for the PLO	
1993	Secret negotiations between Palestinian and Israeli officials in Norway	
	January 20: Informal talks under Norwegian sponsorship begin between Israeli academics and mid-level PLO representatives, with the aim of exploring possibilities for reconciliation between the Palestinians and Israelis	
	Israeli Foreign Ministry officials join the talks in Norway. As the possibility of interim arrangements grows, the Israeli Foreign Minister and Prime Minister, along with top Fatah leaders, become involved indirectly by supervising the talks	
	A Declaration of Principles (DOP) is drafted; the DOP includes Israel's recognition of the PLO as the legitimate representative of the Palestinian people and the agreement to grant full autonomy to the Palestinians under PLO leadership for five years, starting in the Gaza Strip and Jericho; the final status of the autonomous entity will be negotiated later; Palestinians interpret the agreement as an interim stage toward the establishment of an independent state	
	September 13: Formal signing of the Declaration of Principles in Washington ("Oslo I") by the PLO and Israel. The DOP grants the Palestinian National Authority (PNA, or, simply, Palestine Authority, PA) autonomous status in a small portion of the West Bank (Jericho) and most of the Gaza Strip	

)ate	Palestinian history	Events related to Palestinian history
	September 13: The Declaration of Principles is signed by Yasser Arafat and Yitzhak Rabin, including an understanding that by December 13 an agreement would be reached on the withdrawal of Israeli troops from the Gaza Strip and Jericho, and that by April 13, 1994, Israeli troop redeployment would be completed; the PLO would assume civil authority in those regions and deploy its own police forces	
		Jordan and Israel conclude a framework for a peace agreement
		Intensification of terror acts by Jewish settlers against Palestinians as part of their political protest movement against the PLO-Israel agreement; with similar motives, Hamas members and other figures step up the murder of Jews in Israel and the Occupied Territories
	Most of the non-Fatah elements within the PLO and the Islamic movements reject the DOP; some Fatah leaders express objections to Arafat's concessions to Israel	
		Some progress in the Israeli-Arab multinational negotiations in Washington and other locations; Syria takes a hard line by supporting the groups rejecting the PLO-Israeli agreement
	In December, difficulties occur in PLO-Israeli talks; the December 13 deadline for the "Gaza-Jericho plan" is missed and high-level negotiations continue; most of the members of the Islamic movements who were expelled are returned to the occupied territories	
1994		Presidents Bill Clinton of the U.S. and Hafez al-Assad of Syria meet in Geneva; Syria indicates its readiness to negotiate a full peace with Israel in exchange for full Israeli withdrawal from the Golan Heights

Date	Palestinian history	Events related to Palestinian histor[y]
	Several months after missing the December 13, 1993 deadline, Israel and the PLO sign an agreement opening the way for Israeli troop withdrawal from the Gaza Strip and Jericho and the beginning of limited PLO self-rule there	
	February 25: A radical religious Jew (Baruch Goldstein) carries out a suicide massacre in the Patriarchs' Cave, a holy place for the Jewish and Islamic religions; his aim seems to have been to create a chain of responses that would bring about a stop to reconciliation between Palestinians and Jews; twenty-nine praying Muslims are killed and tens of others wounded	Rising fear in Israel in response to growing Islamic terror; demonstrations against the "peace process" organized mostly by groups of settlers in the territories, religious radicals, and secular right-wing activists gain momentum in Israel
		The number of Jewish settlers in the Occupied Territories reaches over 150,000
		October 26: Signing of the Israeli-Jordanian Peace Agreement; Israel acknowledges Jordanian sovereignty over several border areas in which Israeli presence continues (as a formal lease); Israel grants Jordan "special status" over the Islamic holy places in Jerusalem
	Early April (to mid-March 1996): A series of about 10 terrorist attacks in Israeli urban centers by radical Islamic suicide bombers kill 100 and wound hundreds of others; expanded closures are imposed on the Occupied Territories; the PA and its machinery begin to take root and spread over the area; dozens of Hamas and Islamic Jihad leaders and fieldworkers are arrested	
	In an economic protocol, the PLO and Israel agree that 75 percent of taxes withheld from Palestinian workers in Israel will be transferred to the PA	

Date	Palestinian history	Events related to Palestinian history
	In May, the first Palestinian self-government begins with PLO self-rule in Jericho and the Gaza Strip	
	May: An agreement allowing initial entry of the PA and its militia forces into most of the area of the Gaza Strip and the Jericho region	
1995		November 4: Israeli Prime Minister Yitzhak Rabin is assassinated by a national religious youth in the hope of bringing a stop to the process of transferring territories to PA control; Rabin is blamed for "betrayal" of the idea of "the Greater Land of Israel"
	September: Interim agreement (sometimes referred to as "Oslo II") grants rule over all Palestinian cities (except Hebron) to the PA (Area A, about 4 percent of the West Bank) and joint Israeli-Palestinian rule over village areas (Area B); expansive areas in the Jordan Valley, Jewish settlements, and their access roads remain under sole Israeli control (Area C)	
	Israel redeploys its military forces in compliance with Oslo II	
1996	April 24: The 21st conference of the PNC is held in Gaza; an 88 percent majority of the 504 representatives decides to revoke all articles of the Palestinian National Charter that conflict with the Oslo agreements; the PNC Legislative Council is given the responsibility for formulating a new charter within six months	April: In light of attacks by the Lebanese Islamic Hezbollah organization and under public pressure, especially in light of the upcoming elections, Shimon Peres announces Operation Grapes of Wrath; this series of air strikes on southern Lebanon causes massive flight of 200,000 citizens; damage in Kafr Kana causes the death of about 100 Lebanese citizens
		May 29: Early general elections in Israel and the razor-thin victory of Binyamin Netanyahu, presiding over a bloc consisting of right-

Date	Palestinian history	Events related to Palestinian history
		wing-national-religious, secular right-wing, and Ultra-Orthodox factions; the new government declares it necessary to implement the Oslo agreements, granting autonomy to the Palestinians, but it toughens its position and demands discussion of "final status arrangements" concerning the Occupied Territories (including East Jerusalem, over which the Israelis demand sole sovereignty, with allocation of special status over the Islamic holy sites to Jordan)
	September 25–27: Following the opening of a tunnel dug by archaeologists under the area of al-Aqsa (the Temple Mount), large-scale rioting sweeps the West Bank and Gaza Strip; about 40 Palestinians and 11 Israelis are killed, and 100 wounded from each side; the Palestinians attack a site being used as a Yeshiva near Nablus; Israelis try to rescue soldiers stationed there, using (for the first time since the PA's creation in the territories) tanks and helicopters	
1997	January 16–17: The Israeli government authorizes the Hebron Agreement; the Israeli army transfers control over the city, with the exception of the Jewish enclave, to the PA	
	January 22: Yasser Arafat declares that at the end of the interim agreement period, the Palestinians will unilaterally declare the establishment of a Palestinian state	
	February 27: About 1,000 Palestinians protest in Bet Sahour against the Israeli plan to build in the Jerusalem neighborhood of Homa (Ras al-Amud)	February 4: Two army helicopters bringing soldiers to Lebanon crash by accident, killing seventy-three soldiers; the accident becomes a turning point in Israeli public opinion on the subject of continued control of southern Lebanon

ate	Palestinian history	Events related to Palestinian history

March 12: A suicide bomber sets off an explosion in central Tel Aviv, killing three and wounding forty-seven; total closure is imposed over the West Bank and Gaza Strip

March 19: Netanyahu proposes canceling incremental withdrawal and establishing Camp David style talks for a final status agreement; Arafat rejects the proposal

July 30: Two suicide bombers set off explosions in a Jerusalem marketplace; 13 Israelis are killed and 170 wounded; the Iz al-Din Brigades takes responsibility; the Hamas political leader, Abdellaziz Rantisi, denies responsibility; the Israelis respond with expanded closures and many arrests

August 12: Large demonstrations in Nablus call for Arafat to stand up to Israeli pressure aiming to break the resistance movement

September 4: Three suicide bombs detonate in Jerusalem killing 5 Israelis and wounding 192; the Al-Qassem Companies take responsibility

98   January 21: The World Bank decides to fund an industrial area for export products in al-Muntar (Gaza Strip)

September 27–29: Demonstrations in the Arab-Israeli city of Umm al-Fahm against government intentions to use 62 dunums of olive orchards as a firing range; the police use live fire, and about 100 Arabs and 15 policemen are injured; a general strike among Palestinian-Israelis is called in protest of police violence

October 17–23: Wye Plantation talks

The Wye Plantation Agreements: Israel agrees to initiate the third stage of Oslo II—freeing Palestinian prisoners and detainees; the PA pledges to reduce the scope of armed militias, to collect arms from residents, and to increase coordination of security forces

Date	Palestinian history	Events related to Palestinian history
	October 19: A hand grenade is thrown at a bus stop in Beersheba, wounding sixty-four	
	October 30: The PA working council authorizes the Wye Agreement	
	November 16: The Knesset authorizes the Wye Agreement, contingent on the PA's implementation of the agreement to collect illegal arms	
	November 20: Israel transfers 1.1 percent of Area C to total Palestinian control and frees 250 prisoners; virtually all Palestinian population concentrations in the West Bank and Gaza Strip have now been transferred to PA control	
	November 24: An international airport is opened in Gaza	
	December 10: The central council of the PLO meets in Gaza, authorizing Arafat's letter to Clinton canceling articles of the National Charter that deal with the extermination of Israel	
	December 12: Eight opposition groups from within the PLO, Hamas, and Islamic Jihad meet in Damascus to reaffirm their opposition to the Oslo process and to the changes in the National Charter	
	December 14: In the presence of the U.S. President, the PNC cancels articles of the National Charter that deal with the extermination of Israel and appoints a committee for reformulating the charter	
	December 20: The Israeli government halts continued implementation of the Wye Agreement, claiming that the Palestinians are not fulfilling their part of the agreement	
		December 28: New elections are set in Israel; Benjamin Begin resigns from the Likud in order to form a right-wing opposition bloc to Netanyahu

ate	Palestinian history	Events related to Palestinian history
ᴐ9		January 20: King Hussein's eldest son, Abdullah, is appointed heir to the throne in place of the crown prince, Hasan
	February 6: Large demonstration in Hebron at the PA offices demanding both an end to cooperation with Israel and the CIA as well as the freeing of prisoners by Israel	February 7: King Hussein dies and his son Abdullah assumes the throne in Jordan
		February 14: About 200,000 ultra-Orthodox Jews demonstrate in Jerusalem against the Supreme Court decision to draft yeshiva students; counter-demonstration of 50,000 secular citizens
	February 15: Naif Hawatma is expelled from the Rejectionist Front after shaking hands with the President of Israel at Jordan King Hussein's funeral	
		May 17: Ehud Barak, the Labor party candidate, is elected Prime Minister; the big parties, Labor and Likud, continue losing power; Shas, a religious-ethnic party of Mizrahi Jews, gains strength; a secular party ("Shinui") wins six seats; Barak declares efforts toward a final agreement with the Palestinians and his intention to bring it to a popular referendum but then bypasses Palestinians in favor of efforts to gain settlement with Syria
	May 23: Israeli army withdraws from the security zone in southern Lebanon	May 18: A Jewish construction project in the Ras al-Amud (Har Homa) neighborhood of Jerusalem begins
	May 27: Clashes between the Israeli police, on the one side, and Palestinians and Israeli peace activists, on the other, over construction in the Ras al-Amud neighborhood	May 27: Binyamin Netanyahu retires from political life

Date	Palestinian history	Events related to Palestinian histor
	June 22: Demolition of an Arab house in Lydda sparks protest; the police open fire using rubber bullets; MK Azmi Bishara and sixteen other demonstrators are injured; clashes in the Ein al-Hilwa refugee camp (Lebanon) between supporters of Fatah and the Islamic movement over control of the camp	
	July 3: The PA declares a day of wrath in protest of settlement expansion; response is minimal	
		July 5: The International Covenant for Arab-Jewish Peace based in Ramallah organizes a conference in Cairo on the subject of normalization with Israel; about 700 Egyptian intellectuals and public figures organize a counterconference
		July 6: An expanded government is formed in Israel
		July 15: Clinton-Barak meeting in Washington; Barak promises implementation of the Wye Agreement, announces that most settlements will remain in place after a final status agreement
		The signers of the Fourth Geneva Convention condemn Israel for violation of human rights and actions in the Occupied Territories and declare the settlements illegal
		Australia, Canada, the U.S., and Israel boycott the conference
	July 27: Israel and the PA open negotiations on the construction of a joint industrial area in the Karni region (Jenin)	
	August 2: At reconciliation talks in Cairo between Fatah and the Popular Front, the possibility of coordinating over the final status issue is discussed; George Habash refuses to meet with Arafat	

ate	Palestinian history	Events related to Palestinian history
	November 16: Israeli armed forces enter several cave villages in the area of southern Mount Hebron and expel more than 700 Palestinian residents	
000	March 4: About 100 Palestinians from the diaspora put forth a call to emphasize the refugee issue and the right of return in talks with Israel	
	March 8: The Israeli Supreme Court decides against discrimination in allocating land to an Arab family in a Jewish communal settlement	
	March 21: Israel implements the second stage of the Interim agreement, transferring 6.1 percent of Area B to Area A; the PA now fully controls 18 percent and partially controls 22 percent of the West Bank	March 22–26: The Pope visits the Holy Land; among other places, he visits Bethlehem and the Dehaisha Refugee Camp
	March 27: The Minister of Interior returns 250 dunums of land appropriated for public use to the Palestinian-Israeli village of Kafr Qasim	
	April 27: At a party convention George Habash, the head of the Popular Front, announces his desire to retire and appoints Abu Ali Mustafa (killed later by the Israelis) as his successor	
	May 20: Stormy demonstrations in West Bank cities of Hebron, Nablus, Jenin, Ramallah, and Tulkarm; 5 Palestinians dead and about 500 wounded	May 23: Total withdrawal of Israeli troops from southern Lebanon; the Southern Lebanese Army is disbanded; some of its members take refuge in Israel
		June 10: Syrian President Hafez al-Asad dies; his son Bashir is appointed his successor; both Netanyahu and Barak were seemingly close to an arrangement with Syria and only Asad's demand for access to the Sea of Galilee prevented agreement

Date	Palestinian history	Events related to Palestinian histor
		July 9: The Barak government becomes a minority government whe Shas, the National Religious Party, and Israel B'Aliya leave in protest to Barak's agreement to final status talks; Meretz, which had left earlier in protest against Shas's remaining in the coalition, supports the government from the outside
	July 11–25: An attempt to arrive at a final status agreement between the Palestinians and Israel fails (Camp David II); each side blames the other for the conference's failure	
	July 27: The Israeli Ministry of Interior announces that the Jewish population of the West Bank and Gaza Strip has grown by 13,000 in the past year and now approaches 200,000 people	
		August 2: Israeli Foreign Minister David Levy resigns from the government, blaming Barak for deceiving his supporters by his promise not to divide Jerusalem
	August 8: Suicide bomb explodes in the Jerusalem pizzeria, Sbarros: fifteen killed and tens wounded	
	August 10: Salim Zaanun of the PNC announces that Arafat will unilaterally declare the establishment of a Palestinian state (the declaration is not made)	
	August 15: Construction of Gaza Port begins	
	September 29: Sharon's visit to *haram al-sharif* is considered a provocation by the Palestinians and insensitively timed during negotiations over arrangements for Jerusalem; demonstrations and riots break out throughout the West Bank, with violence directed mostly toward settlers and the Israeli army; Palestinian militia men join as individuals and groups, using live fire against the Israelis; the escalating vio-	September 28: Israeli opposition head, Ariel Sharon, known as indirectly responsible for the Sabra and Shattila Massacre and other murderous acts against Palestinians, visits the areas of the mosques and *haram al-sharif* (the Temple Mount); his visit awakens a fierce emotional storm, leading to mass demonstrations against continuing Israeli

Date	Palestinian history	Events related to Palestinian history
	lence, which turns into ethnic warfare between Israel and the PA by early 2002, is termed the "Al-Aqsa (or Second) Intifada" and is later seen by some as the beginning of a war of independence	presence in the Palestinian territories
	September 30: Twelve-year-old Muhammad al-Durrah is killed during exchange of fire between Israeli soldiers and Palestinian armed forces; the event is captured by TV cameras, and the young martyr becomes a symbol of the renewed Palestinian struggle	
	October 1–8: Palestinian-Israelis hold protests identifying with Palestinians in the West Bank and Gaza; they use roadblocks and throw stones; the police react with massive live fire; twelve Arab citizens (and one resident of the territories) are killed, hundreds are injured	
	October 9: Riots between Jews and Arabs in Jaffa; Jews try to burn down the Hassan Beck Mosque	October 12: Two Israeli reserve officers mistakenly find themselves in a Palestinian controlled area and are taken to the police station in Ramallah; an angry mob beats them to death; the event, broadcast on TV, has a strong impact on Israeli public opinion
	November 15: The Israeli government establishes the Orr Commission to investigate the October events in which thirteen Arabs were killed in Israel	
	December 17: Israel initiates a policy of extrajudicial executions or assassinations (called "focused elimination") of those found responsible for terrorist acts and armed resistance; Tanzim activist Samih al-Malabi is among the first murdered	
	December 30: Fatah Secretary General in the West Bank, Dr. Thabat Thabat, is assassinated by Israeli agents	

Date	Palestinian history	Events related to Palestinian histor
2001	January 5: A boat full of armaments destined for Palestinians in the territories, Karine A, which was bought in Iran, is intercepted and captured by Israel, causing great embarrassment to the PA but also great pride among the Palestinians	January: George W. Bush, Jr., assumes the U.S. presidency; he takes a much more hands-off orientation to Israeli-Palestinian issues than did his predecessor, Bill Clinton; his statements through the year are more unequivocally pro-Israel
	January 14: Assassination of Raad al-Karmi, the head of the Tanzim in Tulkaram	
	February 1: Two suicide bombers blow themselves up in central Jerusalem: eleven killed and about ninety wounded	February 6: Special elections for Prime Minister in Israel; Ariel Sharon, the Likud candidate, is elected by a large majority, but with the lowest turnout ever, mostly because of the boycott by Palestinian-Arab citizens
	April 4: Assassination of Iyad Khadran, leader of the Islamic Jihad in Jenin	
	May 15: In a speech to the Legislative Council, Arafat proposes regime reforms, democratization, and new elections	March 27–28: Supporting a Saudi initiative, the Convention of Arab States in Beirut proposes a full peace agreement with Israel, including normalization of relations, in exchange for withdrawal to 1967 borders and the establishment of a sovereign Palestinian state with Jerusalem as its capital; Israel does not respond to the proposal
	June 1: A suicide bomber blows himself up at the Dolphinarium discotheque in Tel Aviv: eighteen are killed and tens wounded	
	August 25: Assassination of Abu Ali Mustafa, secretary of the Popular Front	
		September 11: Terror attack of the Al-Qaida organization against U.S. targets (destruction of the Twin Towers in New York and damage to the Pentagon) causes anti-Islamic and anti-Arab sentiment throughout the world; President Bush declares a fierce global war on terror

Date	Palestinian history	Events related to Palestinian history
	September 17: Sharon calls Arafat a "Bin Laden" and Israel's responses in fighting Palestinian terror to be a part of the global war against terrorism	
	October 17: Rachvam Zeevi, head of the Moledet movement, supporting "transfer" (the forcible resettlement of Palestinians outside the country) and Israel's Minister of Tourism, is assassinated by a Palestinian hit team	October: Anglo-American air and, later, land attacks against Afghanistan (the host regime supporting Al Qaida and its head Osama Bin Laden) with the aim of destroying the organization's infrastructure, killing its leader, and replacing the theocratic regime in Afghanistan
	December 2: Two suicide bombers and a car bomb explode in central Jerusalem: about 10 killed and 150 wounded	
2002	March 2: A suicide bomber blows himself up in an ultra-Orthodox neighborhood in Jerusalem: nine killed and fifty wounded	
	March 7: A suicide bomber blows himself up in the West Bank settlement of Ariel: fourteen wounded	
	March 10: A suicide bomb is detonated in the Jerusalem cafe Moment: about eleven killed and tens wounded	
	March 27: Passover eve a suicide bomber killed 29 and wounded about 150 persons in a hotel in Netanya celebrating the holiday	
	March 29: Beginning of Operation Defense Shield; the Israel army reoccupies parts of Area A in the West Bank under PA control (with the exception of Jericho), claiming to be "destroying the infrastructure of terror"; one after another, the major cities, refugee camps, and some villages are occupied; in most cases, Israeli forces do not face strong resistance; about 8,500 suspects are taken to Israeli prisons for investigation	
	Arafat's headquarters in the city of Ramallah (the Muqata) is placed under siege	

Date	Palestinian history	Events related to Palestinian history
	March 30: The first female suicide bomber blows herself up in a commercial center in a Jerusalem neighborhood: about three killed and twenty-six wounded	
	A suicide bomber blows himself up in a Tel Aviv cafe: thirty-seven wounded, five seriously	
	March 31: A suicide bomber blows himself up in an Arab-owned Haifa restaurant: fourteen killed and thirty-one wounded	
	April 2–19: Israeli forces enter the Jenin Refugee Camp and face strong resistance; 23 Israeli soldiers are killed and more than 100 wounded in the fighting; 50 Palestinians are killed; entire quarters of the camp, including 500 houses, are destroyed as a result of Israeli fighting methods; the Palestinians accuse Israel of carrying out a massacre; the international community is summoned; UN Secretary General appoints an investigation committee; Israel refuses the committee entry	April–June: Israeli military actions in areas of the PA stir waves of protest throughout the world (mostly in Europe), accompanied by anti-Semitic statements and incidents
	April 2–May 2: A group of Palestinians on Israel's most-wanted list takes refuge in the Church of the Nativity in Bethlehem; fighting in the surrounding area stirs international interest; after extensive negotiations, some of the refugees are deported to Gaza and some to the European states	
	April 3–21: The Battle of Nablus takes place mostly in the old city (Casbah) and the Balata and Askar refugee camps; the Palestinians report about 80 dead and 300 wounded	
	April 10: A suicide bomber blows up a bus on the way from Haifa to Jerusalem: eight killed, twenty wounded	
	April 13: Suicide bomber in the Jerusalem marketplace: 6 killed and 80 wounded; Marwan Barghouti, Fatah General Secretary, considered one of the most visible and dominant figures in the PA, is ar-	

rested by Israel on the suspicion of involvement with the Al-Aqsa Martyrs' Bat-
talion, the terrorist arm of Fatah

April 21–May 20: Israel retreats from
Ramallah, yet continues siege on Arafat's
headquarters in the city; Israel demands
extradition of those inside (especially
Zeevi's assassins and Ahmed Saadat, secretary of the Popular Front); after negotiations, the most wanted persons are
transferred to a prison in Jericho under
Anglo-American supervision; the extradition wounds Arafat's prestige in the eyes
of the Palestinians

　　　　　　　　　　　　　　　　　May 5: In light of the wave of hos-
　　　　　　　　　　　　　　　　　tility sweeping the world in the
　　　　　　　　　　　　　　　　　wake of the September 11 events,
　　　　　　　　　　　　　　　　　leaders of forty-two Muslim states
　　　　　　　　　　　　　　　　　gather in Malaysia to crystallize an
　　　　　　　　　　　　　　　　　interpretation of the concepts of
　　　　　　　　　　　　　　　　　"jihad" and suicide combat; differ-
　　　　　　　　　　　　　　　　　ences of opinion are not reconciled

May 7: Suicide bomber blows up a pool
hall in Rishon L'Tzion: fifteen killed and
fifty wounded

May 15: Arafat promises the Legislative
Council that there will be regime reforms,
immediate elections, consolidation of the
various security mechanisms, increased efficiency, and democratization

May 17: The Legislative Council proposes
reforms, including abolition of the State
Security Courts

May 19: A suicide bomber blows himself
up in the Netanya marketplace: three
killed and about fifty wounded

May 23: A suicide bomber blows himself
up in Rishon L'Tzion: two killed and
about forty wounded

June: Israel declared Operation Determined Path—actually reoccupying all
area A for indefinite period

Date	Palestinian history	Events related to Palestinian history
		June 24: President George W. Bush conditioned the establishment in an unspecified future of a Palestinian state with ending any terror or resistance activities, the change of present Palestinian leadership (by free election), and "democratization" of the PNA
	July 18: Tanzim, the Palestinian militia connected to Yasir Arafat's Fatah faction, was preparing to announce a unilateral cease-fire with Israel; European Union officials led an effort for a cease-fire, which intensified over the previous two weeks and was supported by Jordanian and Saudi diplomats, people familiar with the process said; Bush administration officials had been informed of the effort, they said	
	July 22: The spiritual leader of Hamas, Sheikh Ahmed Yassin, announced that Hamas would be willing to agree to a cease-fire, including a halt to suicide bombings, in exchange for Israeli withdrawal from the areas that had previously been under Palestinian administration under the Oslo agreements	
	July 23: Israeli warplane dropped a one-ton bomb, killing Sheikh Salah Shehada, a leader of Hamas' military wing; thirteen other people were killed, nine were children; suspicions that the attack was intended to produce massive rage among Palestinians and to impede or scuttle this cease-fire initiative	

NOTES

Introduction

1. The term *al-Nakba* (catastrophe, disaster) was coined by Syrian scholar Constantine Zurayk in the event's immediate aftermath: "The defeat of the Arabs in Palestine is no simple setback or light, passing evil. It is a disaster in every sense of the word and one of the harshest trials and tribulations with which the Arabs have been afflicted throughout their long history—a history marked by numerous trials and tribulations." See *The Meaning of Disaster* (Beirut: Khayat's College Book Cooperative, 1956), p. 2. The Arabic title of the book is *Ma'na al-Nakbah*.

2. Frank C. Sakran, *Palestine, Still a Dilemma* (Washington, D.C.: American Council on the Middle East, 1976), pp. 104–5. There are numerous other works making similar points. See, for example, Samir S. Saleeby, *The Palestine Problem* (London: The Institute of International Studies, 1970), ch. 2.

3. Cited in *The Sunday Times*, London, June 15, 1969.

4. From *Time Immemorial: The Origins of the Arab-Jewish Conflict over Palestine* (New York: Harper & Row, 1984), pp. 402–3.

5. Her numbers were characterized by Norman Finkelstein (*In These*

Times, September, 1984) as "the most spectacular fraud ever published on the Arab-Israeli conflict . . . a field littered with crass propaganda, forgeries and fakes. . . ." Similar evaluations were expressed by notable historians: Albert Hourani, *The Observer,* March 5, 1985; Yehoshua Porath, "Mrs. Peters' Palestine," *The New York Review of Books,* January 16, 1986. In *Trends in the Demographic Development of Palestinians, 1870–1987* (Tel-Aviv: Shiloach Institute, Tel-Aviv University, 1989) [Hebrew, mimeo], Gad Gilbar shows that, contrary to what Peters contends, the migration factor was far less significant than natural increase. See also Justin McCarthy, *The Population of Palestine: Population History and Statistics of the Late Ottoman Period and the Mandate* (New York: Columbia University Press, 1990), who writes "These and myriad other methodological and factual errors make Peters' work demographically worthless" (p. 41). Besides the manipulative use of facts, the book suffers from a failure to take account of Palestinian social structure and its inner dynamics and development. (More interesting, perhaps, is the acceptance the book gained in intellectual circles.) In any case, our position is in line with this statement from Porath's review: "But even if we put together all the cases [Peters] cites, one cannot escape the conclusion that most of the growth of the Palestinian Arab community resulted from a process of natural increase" (p. 37).

6. Turki, a refugee who grew up in Lebanon, has written some of the most poignant and biting material about the condition of exile, most notably in his book, *The Disinherited: Journal of a Palestinian Exile* (New York: Monthly Review Press, 1972).

7. See Muhammad Y. Muslih, *The Origins of Palestinian Nationalism* (New York: Columbia University Press, 1988), passim. For the best overall account of the history of Palestinian nationalism, see the three-volume history by Y. Porath, *The Emergence of the Palestinian-Arab National Movement: 1918–1929* (London: Frank Cass, 1974); *The Palestinian Arab National Movement: 1929–1939* (London: Frank Cass, 1977); and *In Search of Arab Unity* (London: Frank Cass, 1986).

1. The Revolt of 1834 and the Making of Modern Palestine

1. The image—cultivated, among others, by Lawrence of Arabia, the British soldier, intelligence agent, and diplomat who assisted the Hashemite revolt against the Ottoman Empire during World War I—was a relatively late one in Western culture. It was preceded by a depic-

tion of Arabs, Bedouins, and the Orient in general as evil. See Maxime Rodinson, *Europe and the Mystique of Islam* (Seattle: Near Eastern Studies Dept., University of Washington, 1987), p. 66. The move towards a more favorable view began with the Renaissance and Enlightenment. The image was created by poets, novelists, playwrights, and painters, as well as by travelers and diplomats: Delacroix, Chateaubriand, Mark Twain. As Albert Hourani describes it, some of its elements were "The Arab horseman as savage hero, the seductiveness of beauties in the *harim*, the charm of the bazaar, the pathos of life continuing among the ruins of ancient grandeur" (*A History of the Arab Peoples*, Cambridge, Mass: Harvard University Press, 1991, p. 300). Among the important works conveying the image were Antoine Galland's translation of *The Arabian Nights*, Walter Scott's *The Talisman*, Disraeli's *Tancred*, and Goethe's *Westostlicher Diwan*. This process has been well described in Edward Said, *Orientalism* (New York: Vintage Books, 1978), esp. ch. 1.

Even earlier Jewish proto-Zionist and Zionist writers and painters depicted the original "healthy" Jews of the area, back to biblical times, as typical Bedouin. The message was that Jews had to return to that sort of virtuous life. The first Jewish paramilitary organization in Palestine, Hashomer (the Guard) dressed its men as Bedouins and explicitly socialized them to behave as noble Bedouins. Along with Lawrence's *Seven Pillars of Wisdom: A Triumph* (London: Jonathan Cape, 1935), pp. 2-11, see Tovia Ashkenazi, *Tribus semi-nomades de la Palestine du Nord* (Paris: Libraire orientaliste Paul Geuthner, 1938), pp. 7-19.

2. On Egyptian occupation and rule and the revolt against the Egyptians, see Assad Jibrail Rustum, *The Royal Archives of Egypt and the Disturbances in Palestine, 1834* (Beirut: American University of Beirut, Oriental Series, No. 11, 1938). For engrossing descriptions of this affair, see Rustum, *A Corpus of Arabic Documents Relating to the History of Syria under Mehemet Ali Rasha*, vols. 1-5 (Beirut: American University of Beirut, 1929-34); idem, *The Royal Archives of Egypt and the Causes of Egyptian Expeditions to Syria, 1831-1841* (Beirut: American University of Beirut, 1936). See also Moshe Ma'oz, *Ottoman Reform in Syria and Palestine, 1840-1861: The Impact of the Tanzimat on Politics and Society* (Oxford: The Clarendon Press, 1969), pp. 12-16; and Shimon Shamir, "Egyptian Rule (1832-1840) and the Beginning of the Modern Period in the History of Palestine" in Amnon Cohen and Gabriel Baer, eds., *Egypt and Palestine—A Millennium of Association (868-1948)* (New York: St. Martin's Press, 1984), pp. 214-31.

3. Ma'oz, *Ottoman Reform in Syria and Palestine*, 16.

4. Faruk Tabak, "Local Merchants in Peripheral Areas of the Empire: The Fertile Crescent during the Long Nineteenth Century," *Review 11* (1988): 179–214.

5. For pioneering discussion of this episode see Mordechai Abir, "The Revolt of the Year 1834 against Egyptian Rule and Its Background" (unpublished M.A. thesis, Hebrew University, 1961) [Hebrew]. The account that follows is mostly taken from Abir's excellent study. See also Rustum, *The Royal Archives of Egypt*, p. 411; Neophytos of Cyprus, *Extracts from Annals of Palestine, 1821–1841*, trans. S. N. Spyridon. (Jerusalem: Ariel, 1979), pp. 78–80, 106–8.

6. Gabriel Baer, "Fellah Rebellion in Egypt and the Fertile Crescent" in Baer, *Fellah and Townsmen in the Middle East* (London: Frank Cass, 1982), pp. 253–323.

7. The division between Qays and Yaman goes back to rivalries between the two main tribes in the Arabian peninsula during the initial period of Muslim conquest of the Middle East and the establishment of the Ummayad dynasty (661–750). See Hourani, *A History of the Arab Peoples*, 30. This division continues to have some meaning for Syrian, Lebanese, and Palestinian Muslim society, as an organizational principle of local factionalism. See Miriam Hoexter, "The Role of the Qays and Yaman Factions in Local Political Divisions: Jabal Nablus Compared with the Judean Hills in the First Half of the Nineteenth Century," *Asian and African Studies* 9 (1973): 249–311. However, the continuing factionalism did not necessarily reflect the original lineages that divided the two leagues, but was used in contemporary times as a principle of legitimacy for any coalition formation—what Salim Tamari calls fictive alignments. See "Factionalism and Class Formation in Recent Palestinian History," in Roger Owen, ed., *Studies in the Economic and Social History of Palestine in the Nineteenth and Twentieth Centuries* (Carbondale: Southern Illinois University Press, 1982), pp. 181–86. See also R. A. Stewart MacAlister and E. W. G. Masterman, "A History of the Doings of the Fellahin during the First Half of the Nineteenth Century, from Native Sources: Part III," *Palestine Exploration Fund Quarterly* (January, 1906): 33–50.

8. More than three-quarters of the Arab population still farmed for a living in the 1920s. See Eric Mills, *Census of Palestine—1931* (Jerusalem: Government Printer, 1933), pp. 17, 23. The 1931 November census updated and corrected the first British census of October 1922.

9. See Alexander Scholch, "European Penetration and Economic Devel-

opment of Palestine, 1856–82" in Owen, ed., *Studies in the Economic and Social History of Palestine*, 10–87; Haim Gerber, *The Social Origins of the Modern Middle East* (Boulder: Lynne Rienner Publishers, 1987); Charles Issawi, *An Economic History of the Middle East and North Africa* (New York: Columbia University Press, 1982), pp. 62–76. Iris Agmon argues that the impact of foreign capital on the building of the Palestinian economy was highly fragmentary and unbalanced: The roads and ports were developed, the land tracks enlarged, new crops and types of cultivation introduced, and banking, postal, and transportation services were founded, but basically cultivation techniques remained very primitive. See "Foreign Trade as a Catalyst of Change in the Arab Economy in Palestine, 1879–1914," *Cathedra* (October 1986): 107–32 [Hebrew]. See also Sa'id B. Himadeh, ed., *Economic Organization of Palestine* (Beirut: American University Press, 1938); Joel S. Migdal, *Palestinian Society and Politics* (Princeton: Princeton University Press, 1980), pp. 19–32 (on socio-political aspects of the problem); I. M. Smilianskaya, "The Disintegration of the Feudal Relations in Syria and Lebanon in the Middle of the Nineteenth Century" in Charles Issawi, ed., *The Economic History of the Middle East* (Chicago: University of Chicago Press, 1966), pp. 227–47. For the attempts to intensify Ottoman rule over Palestine, see Ma'oz, *Ottoman Reform in Syria and Palestine*, part II; Carter V. Findley, "The Evolution of the System of Provincial Administration as Viewed from the Center" in David Kushner, ed., *Palestine in the Late Ottoman Period: Political, Social and Economic Transformation* (Jerusalem: Yad Ben Zvi, and Leiden, Netherlands: E. J. Brill, 1986), pp. 3–29.

10. Neville Mandel, *The Arabs and Zionism Before World War One* (Berkeley: University of California Press, 1976), pp. 13–25 and 76–79; Baruch Kimmerling, *Zionism and Territory: The Socioterritorial Dimensions of Zionist Politics* (Berkeley: Institute of International Studies, University of California, 1983), pp. 8–21; Kenneth Stein, *The Land Question in Palestine, 1917–1937* (Chapel Hill: University of North Carolina Press, 1984), pp. 4–7 and 36–39; Abd al-Wahab Kayyali, *The Modern History of Palestine* (London: Croom Helm, n.d.), pp. 13–21 and 171–74.

11. John Pinkerton, *Modern Geography* (1802), p. 27. While Europeans viewed Palestine as poor and marginal, many Arabs saw it as the heart of the Arab world. See Muhammed al-Nahhal, *Palestine: Land and History* (Amman: Dar al-Galeel, 1984); pp. 7–24 [Arabic].

12. Ruth Kark, *Jaffa—A City in Evolution, 1799–1917* (Jerusalem: Yad Ben Zvi, 1984), pp. 116–79, 204–13 [Hebrew]; Resat Kasaba, Caglar Keyder, and Faruk Tabak, "Eastern Mediterranean Port Cities and Their

Bourgeoisies: Merchants, Political Projects, and Nation States," *Review I* (1986): 121–35; Ruth Kark, "The Rise and Decline of Coastal Towns in Palestine" in Gad G. Gilbar, *Ottoman Palestine, 1800–1914: Studies in Economic and Social History* (Leiden: E. J. Brill, 1990), pp. 69–89.

13. Other parts of the country responded to the new opportunities. By 1872, for example, 90 percent of the fertile Marj Beni Amer, or Esdaelon plain, in the north, was under cultivation, half with wheat and barley. See C. R. Conder, *Tent Work in Palestine* (London: Palestine Exploration Society, 1878), pp. 112–13.

14. The intense labor the orchards required meant that wealthier farmers, who could afford the substantial investment in irrigation and young seedlings, had to recruit numerous share tenants or wage laborers from the hills. From 1880 until the outbreak of World War I, the acreage for citrus orchards more than quadrupled. The number of cases of fruit shipped through Jaffa's port increased more than thirtyfold in the half century before the war, partially due to the increased acreage and partly as a result of new, more efficient agricultural techniques. See for example, A. Aaronsohn und S. Soskin, "Die Orangengarten von Jaffa," *Trupenpflanzer: Organ des kolonial wirtschaftlichen Komitees 6* (1902): 341–61. Usually the most reliable sources for trade data are the Great Powers Consuls' reports. For a general survey see Roger Owen, *The Middle East in the World Economy 1800–1914* (London: Methuen, 1981).

15. It is estimated at 350,000 for 1870, at 600,000 for 1914, and at 1,290,000 for 1947. This followed a long period of stagnation and even population losses (in part due to the cholera epidemic of 1865–66). The portion of immigrants (mostly from Egypt, Syria, and Lebanon) was about 10 percent, and the annual natural growth seems to have been one of the highest in the Middle East, above 20:1,000. Our demographic proximations on the Ottoman period are mainly based on Gad Gilbar, "Trends in Demographic Developments of the Palestinian Arabs, 1870–1948," *Cathedra 45* (1987): 42–56 [Hebrew] and Alexander Scholch, "The Demographic Development of Palestine, 1850–1882," *International Journal of Middle East Studies 17* (1985): 485–505.

16. Scholch, "European Penetration"; Issa Mustafa Alami, "Some Aspects of the Development of Palestinian Peasant Economy and Society, 1920–1939" (unpublished Ph.D. dissertation, University of Edinburgh, 1984), pp. 117–247.

17. The source of capital was not always that market. Since Muslim reli-

gious law prohibits moneylending for interest, the need for capital created a new socioeconomic arrangement, the *sharika* contract, considered valid by the Sharia courts. This was a small-scale but well-established form of economic entrepreneurship: a contract of partnership between a worker or peasant and a person of resources (land and/or money) to share in the profit from growing any cash crop (mainly grains), olive trees, cattle husbandry, and camel or motor transportation. See Ya'akov Firestone, "Production and Trade in an Islamic Context: Sharika Contracts in the Transitional Economy of Northern Samaria," *International Journal of Middle East Studies* 1 (1975): 183–209; 2 (1975): 308–25; Gabriel Baer, "The Impact of Economic Change on Traditional Society in Nineteenth-Century Palestine" in Moshe Ma'oz, ed., *Studies on Palestine During the Ottoman Period* (Jerusalem: The Magnes Press, 1975), pp. 495–98.

18. This argument is confirmed by later developments in the economic, social, and political spheres around Nablus. See Sarah Graham-Brown, "The Political Economy of the Jabel Nablus" in Owen, ed., *Studies in the Economic and Social History*, pp. 88–177.

19. Ma'oz, *Ottoman Reform in Syria and Palestine*, 78.

20. Ibid., 77.

21. Ibid., 85.

22. The *Nizam-i Cedid*—the remodeled Ottoman army—helped impose the rule of the Abd al-Hadi clan and the Tuqans in the area surrounding Nablus, the Abd al-Rahem Amir family (rooted around the large village of Durah) in the Hebron region, and two rival peasant-based clans, Abu-Ghush and Samhan, in the mountainous countryside around Jerusalem.

23. Ma'oz, *Ottoman Reform in Syria and Palestine*, 196; Yehosua Porath, "The Social Aspects of the Emergence of the Palestinian Arab National Movement" in M. Milson, ed., *Society and Political Structure in the Arab World* (New York: Humanities Press, 1973), pp. 93–144.

24. Kemal Karpat, "The Land Regime, Social Structure and Modernization in the Ottoman Empire" in W. Polk and R. Chambers, eds., *Beginnings of Modernization in the East* (Chicago: University of Chicago Press, 1968), pp. 68–89.

25. Stein, *The Land Question in Palestine*, 3–28. The legislation's original purpose was to grant the peasants land directly in exchange for the payment of an entry fee, Tapu (pronounced "Tabu" in Arabic), and a tithe. But the state was unable to collect the farm taxes (determined mostly by the *Mejlis*, the local councils) on its own, and needed the

service of local notables. They "became patrons of villages and this was one of the ways in which they came to establish their claims to ownership over them" (Albert Hourani, "Ottoman Reforms and the Politics of Notables" in Polk and Chambers, *Beginnings of Modernization*, 49). See also S. J. Shaw, "The 19th Century Ottoman Tax Reforms and Revenue System," *International Journal of Middle East Studies* 6 (1975); Doreen Warriner, "The Real Meaning of the Land Code" in Charles Issawi, ed., *The Economic History of the Middle East*, 72–78; Frederic M. Goadby and Moses Doukhan, *The Land Law of Palestine* (Tel-Aviv, 1935); Samuel Bergheim, "Land Tenure in Palestine," *Palestine Exploration Fund Quarterly Statement* 26 (1894): 191–99.

26. David Grosman, "Rural Settlement in the Southern Coastal Plain and the Shefelah, 1833–1943," *Cathedra* 45 (1987): 57–86 [Hebrew]. Much has been written on share tenancy from the mandate period on, but little has focused on the formative period at the end of the nineteenth century. See Ya'akov Firestone, "Crop-sharing Economics in Mandatory Palestine," *Middle East Studies* 11 (1975): 3–23, 173–94; Salim Tamari, "From the Fruits of their Labour: the Persistence of Sharetenancy in the Palestinian Agrarian Economy" in Kathy and Pandeli Glavanis, eds., *The Rural Middle East: Peasant Lives and Modes of Production* (New Jersey: Zed Books, 1990), pp. 70–94.

27. *Palestinians: From Peasants to Revolutionaries* (London: Zed Books, 1979), pp. 15–16.

28. See Ya'akov Firestone, "The Land-equalizing Musha Village: A Reassessment" in Gilbar, ed., *Ottoman Palestine*, 91–129; Stein, *The Land Question in Palestine*, 10–15; Alami, *Some Aspects of the Development of Palestinian Peasant Economy*, ch. 2.

29. Hilma Granquist, *Marriage Conditions in a Palestinian Village* (Helsingfors: Societas Scientrarium Fennica, 1935). Some of these patterns are vividly described in Yusuf Haddad, *Society and Folklore in Palestine: A Case Study of al-Bassa Village* (Nicosia: Research Center, Palestine Liberation Organization, 1983), pp. 67–110 [Arabic]. For an excellent analysis of the changes that occurred in the Palestinian family before and after the mandatory period, see Majid Al-Haj, *Social Change and Family Processes: Arab Communities in Shefar-A'm* (Boulder: Westview Press, 1987).

30. See E. A. Finn, "The Fellaheen of Palestine—Notes on Their Clans, Warfare, Religion and Law," *Palestine Exploration Fund Quarterly Statement* (1897): 31–45. (Finn, whose sharp observations are an important record of the period, was the spouse of the British Consul in Jerusa-

lem between 1845 and 1863); P. J. Baldensperger, "Morals of the Fella-hin," ibid, 123–34. For a comparison with similar patterns, see Richard Antoun, *Arab Village: A Social Structural Study of Trans-Jordanian Peasant Community* (Bloomington: Indiana University Press, 1972), pp. 88–91. Also see C. T. Wilson, *Peasant Life in the Holy Land* (London: J. Murray, 1906); Sayigh, *Palestinians,* 10–24. Compare with the contemporary structure of Palestinian village and fellaheen subculture as described by Shukri Araaf, *The Palestinian Arab Village: Structure and Land Usage* (Jerusalem: Arab Studies Society, 1986) [2nd ed., Arabic]. *Fidya* was later used as a mobilizing mechanism against the Zionists and the British.

31. The woman's inferior status was reinforced by jokes, folktales, and the tradition of machismo in village life. See Haddad, *Society and Folklore in Palestine,* 189–230, for a detailed account of this subculture. Much later, the rise of Palestinian nationalism and the resistance movement considerably changed the social position of Palestinian women. See Matiel Mogannam, *The Arab Woman and the Palestinian Problem* (London: Herbert Joseph, 1937), pp. 57–84; Yvonne Haddad, "Palestinian Women: Patterns of Legitimation and Domination" in K. Nakhleh and E. Zureik, eds., *The Sociology of the Palestinians* (London: Croom Helm, 1980), pp. 147–99; Mariam Mar'i, "The One Good Thing That Has Resulted From the Intifada," *Israeli Democracy* (Summer 1989): 15–17.

32. For a vivid recollection of this aspect of village life, see Sayigh, *Palestinians,* 18.

33. See, for example, Eliezer Volcani, *The Fellah's Farm* (Tel-Aviv: Agricultural Experimental Station, The Jewish Agency for Palestine, Bulletin No. 10, 1930); John Hope Simpson, *Report on Immigration, Land Settlement and Development* (London: HMSO, 1930, Cmd. 3686); Government of Palestine, *Report by Mr. C. F. Strickland of the Indian Civil Service on the Possibility of Introducing a System of Agricultural Cooperation in Palestine* (Jerusalem: Government Printer, 1930), p. 11; Stein, *The Land Question in Palestine,* 14–15.

34. Kimmerling, *Zionism and Territory,* 32–33; Abraham Granott, *The Land System in Palestine: History and Structure* (London: Eyre and Spottiswood, 1952), p. 218.

35. There is debate among historians about how entrenched the institution was in the late Ottoman period. Some claim that virtually all the land in the central mountain region was co-owned prior to the Ottoman land law of 1858. According to this view, the steady erosion of

musha that continued into the second quarter of the twentieth century resulted from increased government intervention: first the Ottoman reforms and later British policies. Others read the fragmentary evidence to say that it was already in decline by 1858, the Ottoman legislation simply nudging the process along. Whatever the precise situation, the element of musha that became a casualty of the 1858 (and subsequent) reforms was its freezing of land ownership. See, for example, Granott, *The Land System in Palestine*, 218.

36. The authorities also reassessed taxes on the gross value of the harvest rather than the net value and finally tried to collect their revenue in hard cash, which was extremely difficult for smallholders to lay their hands on, rather than as a portion of the harvest. See Migdal, *Palestinian Society and Politics*, 14–17.

37. Salim Tamari describes this patronage system as follows: "A single peasant or a whole village crushed relentlessly under despotic taxes and debts placed themselves, together with their lands, under the protection of the town notable, who then interposed himself between his dependents and the tax collectors or creditors, and he looked after their taxes and court cases." For the entire process see Tamari, "Fractionalism and Class Formation in Recent Palestinian History" in Owen, ed., *Studies in the Economic and Social History*, 188–200. Another pattern was sharetenancy, by which the tiller was remunerated for his labor by a share of his yield; see Tamari, "From the Fruits of their Labour" in Glavanis and Glavanis, eds., *The Rural Middle East*, 53–94.

38. For the role of the mukhtar, see Gabriel Baer, "The Office and Functions of the Village Mukhtar" in Migdal, *Palestinian Society and Politics*, 103–23.

39. In fact, the office of the mukhtar was established by the Ottoman Law of 1864 as a *muhazam*, or tax farmer, but the office's authority was actually much larger: Mukhtars possessed police power in all spheres of life. See Gabriel Baer, "The Economic and Social Position of the Village Mukhtar in Palestine" in Gabriel Ben-Dor, ed., *The Palestinians and the Middle East Conflict: Studies in Their History, Sociology and Politics* (Ramat Gan: Turtledove, 1978), pp. 101–18.

40. Sharif Kana'ni and Bassam Al-Kaabi, *Ein Houd*—Monographs on Palestinian Destroyed Villages Series, No. 1 (Bir Zeit: University of Bir Zeit, Center of Documentation and Research, 1987), pp. 22–29 [Arabic]; for a later variation of this phenomenon, see Dov Shinar, *Palestinian Voices: Communication and Nation Building in the West Bank* (Boulder: Lynn Rienner, 1987), pp. 86–87.

41. Kana'ni and Al-Kaabi, *Ein Houd,* p. 44. The University of Bir Zeit in the West Bank developed a project of documentation and oral history of Palestinian villages destroyed in 1948 and immediately after (see chapter 5). A number of our descriptions in the following pages are based on this documentation program.

42. Neville Mandel, "Turks, Arabs and Jewish Immigration into Palestine: 1882-1914," St. Anthony's College Papers Series, No. 17 (Middle Eastern Affairs Department, Oxford, 1965), pp. 77-108. The majority of the Jewish immigrants were subjects of foreign great powers and under the protection of consuls (of Russia, Austro-Hungary, Germany, France, and the U.S.) in the framework of the capitulations system.

43. For an excellent account of this period, see David Vital, *The Origins of Zionism* (Oxford: Oxford University Press, 1975). For the Jewish settlement process, see Alex Bein, *The Return to the Soil* (Jerusalem: Am Oved, 1952).

44. Walter Laqueur, *A History of Zionism* (New York: Schocken, 1972), pp. 75-83; Mandel, *The Arabs and Zionism Before World War One.*

45. Laqueur, *A History of Zionism,* 75. The immigrants generally did not see themselves as a part of the European colonization movement of the "non-white territories," but as a national movement. See Shlomo Avineri, *The Making of Modern Zionism* (New York: Basic Books, 1981).

46. On the Templars, who founded their first colonies in 1875-76, see Alex Carmel, "The German Settlers in Palestine and their Relations with the Local Arab Population and the Jewish Community, 1868-1918" in Ma'oz, ed., *Studies on Palestine,* 443-65. On September 22, 1866, American Christian colonists from "The Church of the Messiah," moved by similar religious feelings, tried to settle in Palestine but gave up after one year in face of the harsh conditions of the country.

47. Kimmerling, *Zionism and Territory,* 15.

48. Mandel, *The Arabs and Zionism,* 77-79, 102-7, 166-69.

49. The Abd al-Hadi clan, for example, used land to practice horticulture following the examples of the Templars. Scholch, "European Penetration," 23; D. Giladi, "The Agronomic Development of Old Colonies in Palestine, 1882-1914" in Ma'oz, ed., *Studies on Palestine,* 175-89; Shmuel Avitsur, "The Influence of Western Technology on the Economy of Palestine During the Nineteenth Century" in Ma'oz, ed., *Studies on Palestine,* 485-94. Later the interactions between Jews and Arabs became more complex. See Baruch Kimmerling, "A Model for Analysis of Reciprocal Relations between the Jewish and Arab Communities in Mandatory Palestine," *Plural Societies* (Autumn, 1983): 45-68.

50. It must be noted that not all the crops and agricultural technologies imported by Europeans fit local conditions, and the Templars as well as the Jewish settlers adopted many of the fellaheen technologies after the failure of the imported techniques. See Shaul Katz, "Ideology, Settlement and Agriculture during the First Decade of Petach-Tikvah," *Cathedra* 22 (1982): 74–81 [Hebrew].

51. Graham-Brown, "The Political Economy of Jabel Nablus," 90–92.

52. Stein, *The Land Question in Palestine*, 39.

53. *Land, Labor, and the Origins of the Israeli-Palestinian Conflict—1882–1914* (New York: Cambridge University Press, 1989), pp. 91–122; Baruch Kimmerling, *Zionism and Economy* (Cambridge, Mass: Schenckman, 1983), pp. 19–39.

54. Ahad Ha'am (pseud. for Asher Ginzberg), the famous Zionist writer and analyst, warned in 1893 that Jewish land purchases and employment policies would turn the local Arab population into an eternal enemy. A similar statement was made by the Galilean teacher Yitzhak Epstein in the seventh Zionist Congress (1905), reproduced under the title "The Hidden [Arab] Question" in the Hebrew Zionist organ *Ha'Shiloach* 17 (1908). Both figures forecasted the creation of a *local* Arab national movement as a reaction to Zionism. See also Yosef Gorny, *Zionism and the Arabs, 1882–1948* (Oxford: Clarendon Press, 1987), pp. 57–65. Later the policy toward tenants was changed, and in addition to the money paid for land, the Zionists also paid compensation to the displaced tenants, or preferred to buy lands already free of tenants. See Stein, *The Land Question in Palestine*, 38–48; also, Leah Doukham-Landau, *The Zionist Companies for Land Purchase in Palestine, 1897–1914* (Jerusalem: Yad Ben-Zvi, 1979) [Hebrew].

55. Mandel, *The Arabs and Zionism*, 38.

56. See Gilbar, "Trends in Demographic Developments," 47–49.

57. See Samir M. Seikaly, "Unequal Fortunes: The Arabs of Palestine and the Jews during World War I" in Wadad al-Qadi, ed., Studio *Arabica et Islamica: Festschrift for Ihsan ᶜAbbas on his Sixtieth Birthday* (Beirut: American University of Beirut, 1981), pp. 399–406.

58. I. al-Nimr, *Tarikh jabal Nablus wa-l-Balqa* (Nablus, n.d.), vol. 3, p. 132. The isolation of the territory from the outside world primarily hurt the Jewish settlement, but the war hurt the Arab community, too: Thousands of Jews and Arabs died from epidemics and famine; 11,000 Jews (up to 35 percent of their prewar population) emigrated or were expelled. The export of oranges and other items halted completely, and the abrupt devaluation of the Turkish currency made it com-

pletely non-negotiable. See Stein, *The Land Question in Palestine,* 3, 4, 16, 19, 24, and 41.

59. The Declaration was a statement of intent, issued in the form of a private letter from the British foreign secretary Arthur Balfour to Lord Rothschild. Arab historiography has argued that the Balfour Declaration has no value in light of the commitments of Sir Henry McMahon, the British ambassador in Cairo, to Sharif Hussein of Mecca, promising "freedom of the Arab peoples." See George Antonius, *The Arab Awakening: The Story of the Arab National Movement* (New York: Capricorn Books, 1946), pp. 413–427. Even though Palestine was not mentioned in McMahon's letter, the Arab claims were that the western boundary of the Arab independent area, as proposed to Sharif Hussein, was the Mediterranean Sea. For the text of the declaration, see Chapter 3, p. 73.

60. Shalom Reichman, *The Development of Transportation in Palestine, 1920–1947* (Jerusalem: Ministry of Transportation, 1969) [Hebrew].

61. The three-year average yield of vegetables, for example, soared from 11,000 tons to 205,000 tons in just 20 years.

62. From roughly 5,000 to 35,000 acres. Most of the data and analysis on the economy of the Mandatory Palestinian state is based on Himadeh, *Economic Organization of Palestine;* David Horowitz, *The Development of the Palestinian Economy* (Tel-Aviv: Bialik Institute and Dvir, 1948) [Hebrew, second and enlarged edition], pp. 169–79, Jacob Metzer, *Technology, Labor and Growth in a Dual Economy's Traditional Sector: Mandatory Palestine, 1921–1936* (Jerusalem: Falk Institute, 1982); idem, "Growth and Structure of the Arab Economy in Mandatory Palestine—A Historical Overview," *Economic Quarterly* 137 (1988): 129–45 [Hebrew]; idem, *Growth and the Structure of the Palestinian Arab Economy* (Jerusalem: Falk Institute for Economic Research, Research Paper no. 200, 1988) [Hebrew]; Raja Khalidi, *The Arab Economy in Israel: The Dynamics of a Region's Development* (New York: Croom Helm, 1988), pp. 7–34; Jacob Metzer and Oded Kaplan, "Jointly but Severally: Arab-Jewish Dualism and Economic Growth in Mandatory Palestine," *Journal of Economic History* 45 (1985): 327–45; Z. Abramowitz and Y. Gelfat, *The Arab Economy in Palestine and Middle Eastern Countries* (Tel-Aviv: HaKibbutz HaMeuchad Press, 1944) [Hebrew]. For an analysis of the Palestinian state economic policy, see Nachum T. Gross, *The Economic Policy of the Mandatory Government in Palestine* (Jerusalem: Falk Institute, 1982) [Hebrew].

63. Oranges, lemons, and grapefruits—mostly shipped to the British

Isles—accounted for 80 percent of the country's export revenue and over 90 percent of its agricultural exports. Abramowitz and Gelfat, *The Arab Economy in Palestine,* 44.

64. Vegetable fields and citrus groves expanded rapidly in the country as a whole, while the production of cereals was much flatter. Large tracts owned by town notables and Jews produced oranges; the small fragmented plots of the fellaheen, for the most part, produced the cereals. In the two decades following the war, Jewish investment in citriculture reached $75 million. See Hurewitz, *The Struggle for Palestine* (New York: Schocken Books, 1976), p. 30. Intensively cultivated field crops also gained, with up to a quarter of them sold to the growing Jewish market by 1935. The same pattern could be seen in raising animals: the number of fowl (more and more the commercial product of Jewish communal settlements) increased fourfold from 1930 to 1943, while sheepherding (still mostly the domain of poorer Arabs) inched up only slightly.

65. See Metzer and Kaplan, "Jointly But Severally," 339–41.

66. A British report noted that in one village in the hilly region 30 percent of the land titles passed from smallholders to largeholders in the 1920s. The report was popularly known as the French Report, after its author, Lewis French. Government of Palestine, *Report on Agricultural Development and Land Settlement in Palestine* (Jerusalem: Government Printer, 1931], pp. 23–25.

67. Government of Palestine, *Report on the Economic Conditions of Agriculturalists in Palestine and Fiscal Measures of Government in Relation Thereto* (Jerusalem: Government Printer, 1930). Popularly known as the Johnson-Crosbie Report, this survey was one of nine undertaken during the mandate, eight by the British and one Anglo-American. The commission that wrote it surveyed 104 villages.

68. Gross, *The Economic Policy of the Mandatory Government,* 4, pinpoints the following major goals of the British mandatory state economic policy: to avoid any burden on the British taxpayer as a consequence of holding Palestine, to promote British exports and help British firms to operate in the country, to maintain a stable and efficient government accepted by a satisfied population, to support the country's economic and cultural development in the frame of reference of European capitalism, and all this with minimal interference in local traditions and the existing social fabric.

69. Ylana N. Miller, *Government and Society in Rural Palestine, 1920–1948* (Austin: University of Texas Press, 1985), pp. 49–54.

70. Migdal, *Palestinian Society and Politics*, 24–31.

71. Miller, *Government and Policy in Rural Palestine*, 84.

72. See Nabil Ayyub Badran, *Education and Modernization in the Palestinian Arab Society, 1: The Mandatory Period* (Beirut: Palestine Liberation Organization Research Center, 1968) [Arabic].

73. Even after the revolt was broken by the British in 1939, earlier events "left villagers with little reason to see the law as protective rather than intrusive or, at best, irrelevant." Miller, *Government and Policy in Rural Palestine*, 128. See also Muhammed al-Nahhal, *The British Policy toward the Arab Palestinian Land Question* (Beirut: Filastin al-Muhtallah, 1981), pp. 53–68 [Arabic].

74. Nachum Gross and Jacob Metzer, *Palestine in World War Two: Some Economic Aspects* (Jerusalem: Falk Institute, Discussion Paper No. 87, 1987 [mimeo]), p. 6; Metzer, "Growth and Structure of the Arab Economy in Mandatory Palestine," pp. 129–45.

75. David Ben Gurion, *My Talks with Arab Leaders* (New York: The Third Press, 1972).

76. Ben Gurion stated in 1928 that "according to my beliefs, we do not have the right to deprive even a single Arab child, even if by means of that deprivation we will achieve our [national] goals." David Ben-Gurion, *We and Our Neighbors* (Tel-Aviv: Davar, 1931), p. 150, and Ben-Gurion, *My Talks*, 23–24.

77. See Volcani, *The Fellah's Farm*, 74–77.

78. Stein, *The Land Question in Palestine*, passim; Kimmerling, *Zionism and Territory*, passim.

79. See Gilbar, "Trends in Demographic Developments," 45.

80. See Kark, *Jaffa;* Mahmud Yazbak, "Arab Migration to Haifa: A Quantitative Analysis Following Arab Sources, 1933–1948," *Cathedra* 45 (1987): 131–46 [Hebrew]; Yosef Washitz, "Villagers' Migration to Haifa in the Mandatory Period: Was It an Urbanization Process?" *Cathedra* 45 (1987): 113–29 [Hebrew].

81. Pamela Ann Smith, *Palestine and the Palestinians, 1876–1983* (New York: St. Martin's Press, 1984), pp. 52–53.

82. Between 1931 and 1939, the mandatory government's definition of an alienated *fellah* was narrowed. The landless were defined as "such Arabs as can be shown to have been displaced from the lands which they occupied in consequence of the land passing into Jewish hands, and who have not obtained other holdings on which they can establish themselves, or other equally satisfactory occupation" (Stein, *The Land Question in Palestine*, 128–29). Perhaps the major land transfers,

which left many fellaheen families without lands, were the purchase of Marj Beni Amer (Jezreel Valley) and Wadi Hawarith (Hefer Valley). Following an inquiry in 1931–32, 2,663 claims were submitted by landowners and tenants who claimed to have been hurt by the Jewish land purchases; only 899 of these claims were accepted.

83. Kimmerling, *Zionism and Territory*, pp. 111–112.

2. The City: Between Nablus and Jaffa

1. Ihsan al-Nimr, *Tarikh fabal Nablus wa al Balq'a*, vol. 1 (2nd ed.) (Nablus: Matba'at 'ummal al-Matabi' al-Ta'awiniyya, 1973), pp. 223n and 205–7 [Arabic].

2. See the colorful description of Amnon Cohen, *Palestine in the 18th Century: Patterns of Government and Administration* (Jerusalem: Magnes Press, 1973), pp. 27–29.

3. Ibid., pp. 69, 313. Ottoman rule tried to unify southern Palestine, combining the Jerusalem, Jaffa, and Gaza districts under the leadership of Muhammad Abu-Maraq, as a counterbalance to Acre's governor. However, in 1802 Jazzar forced Abu-Maraq to surrender. The second time the *sanjaq* (district) of Jerusalem was separated from the center and unified with the sanjaq of Nablus was during the preparation for the Egyptian Muhammad Ali's invasion of Palestine in 1830. See Adel Manna, "The Sanjaq of Jerusalem: Between Two Invasions (1798–1831)—Administration and Society" (unpublished Ph.D. dissertation, Hebrew University, 1986), p. ii [Hebrew].

4. Cohen, *Palestine in the 18th Century*, passim.

5. Bernard Lewis, *The Emergence of Modem Turkey* (New York: Oxford University Press, 1976), pp. 34–37. The "Sublime Porte" refers to the center of the Ottoman authorities, the palace from which the Sultan ruled. The term comes from the manifold gates, or doors, leading up to the palace, which in Turkish are referred to as "the big gate."

6. Based on figures of Ruth Kark, "The Contribution of the Ottoman Regime to the Development of Jerusalem and Jaffa, 1840–1917" in David Kushner, ed., *Palestine in the Late Ottoman Period*, 46.

7. Among the visitors writing on Jaffa and the rest of Palestine were Laurence Oliphant, *The Land of Gilead* (Edinburgh: W. Blackwood, 1880) and (as noted above) Mark Twain, in *The Innocents Abroad, or The New Pilgrim's Progress: Being Some Account of the Steamship "Quaker City's" Pleasure Excursion to Europe and the Holy Land* (New York:

Harper, 1905). For an anthology of other travelers' descriptions, see Thomas Wright, ed., *Early Travels in Palestine* (London: H. G. Bohn, 1848).

8. They also exported to Jericho, Nablus—and even to the Galilee and Gaza. See Amnon Cohen, *Economic Life in Ottoman Jerusalem* (Cambridge: Cambridge University Press, 1989), pp. 86–87.

9. As the eminent Palestinian historian A. L. Tibawi put it, the great powers' rivalry in Palestine "was often manifested during the nineteenth century in one power upholding the claims of one Christian sect against those of another Christian sect, upheld in turn by another power, or against the Turkish authorities." *Arab Education in Mandatory Palestine: A Study of Three Decades of British Administration* (London: Luzac, 1956), p. 6.

10. According to an Egyptian census, of 466 villages in central and southern Palestine in 1833 (including the districts of Gaza, Jaffa, Lydda, Ramallah, and Hebron), the Nablus and Jerusalem districts claimed 323 or nearly 70 percent. In fact, the Nablus district accounted for over 200 villages. See Mordechai Abir, "Local Leadership and Early Reforms in Palestine, 1800–1834" in Ma'oz (ed.), *Studies on Palestine*, 285.

11. Like much else in these towns, for years the olive industry resisted changes that, by the turn of the twentieth century, entrepreneurs along the coast openly welcomed. As late as 1928; mechanical engines had been introduced into a mere 6 percent of the approximately 500 oil presses in the country. In the 1930s, change began to overtake the industry: By 1941, one-quarter of the presses were engine-driven.

   The data for this section were compiled from Yaacov Shimoni, *The Arabs of Palestine* (Tel-Aviv: Am Oved, 1947), pp. 186–89 [Hebrew]; Abramowitz and Gelfat, *The Arab Economy in Palestine*, 212–23 [Hebrew]; Yosef Waschitz, *The Arabs in Palestine* (Merhavia: HaKibbutz HaArtzi, 1947) [Hebrew] pp. 87–94; Baruch Kimmerling, *The Economic Interrelationships between the Arab and Jewish Communities in Mandatory Palestine* (Cambridge: Center for International Studies, Massachusetts Institute of Technology, 1979), pp. 47–58; Nachum Gross, *The Economic Policy of the Mandatory Government in Palestine* (Jerusalem: Falk Institute, Discussion Paper No. 816, 1982 [mimeo]), pp. 1–66.

12. Another common specialty was woven fabrics. The largely Christian town of Bethlehem, exploiting the increasing numbers of European pilgrims from the 1830s on, manufactured holy items and souvenirs sculpted from local olive wood.

13. al-Nimr, *Tarikh Jabal Nablus,* 152.

14. Abir, "Local Leadership and Early Reforms in Palestine," 286–89.

15. Abir argues that by the time of the Egyptian invasion, the autonomy of the Nablus chiefs was about to be undone by the Ottoman authorities, in any case: that the possibilities for maneuvering between Sidon and Damascus were largely gone, and the drive for centralization in the Empire was very strong. Ibid., pp. 301–2.

16. Shimon Shamir, "Egyptian Rule (1832–1840) and the Beginning of the Modern Period in the History of Palestine," in Cohen and Baer, eds., *Egypt and Palestine,* 220–21.

17. al-Nimr, *Tarikh Jabal Nablus,* 319–34.

18. The inland families sent them to Ottoman or Muslim academies, while those on the coast were more likely to provide a Western education.

19. Owen, *The Middle East in the World Economy,* 174.

20. Ma'oz, *Ottoman Reform in Syria and Palestine,* 93.

21. al-Nimr, *Tarikh Jabal Nablus,* 325–28.

22. Charles Issawi, "The Trade of Jaffa, 1825–1914" in Hisham Nashabe, ed., *Studia Palaestina: Studies in Honour of Constantine K. Zurayk* (Beirut: Institute for Palestine Studies, 1988), pp. 42; 50–51. The rise of Jaffa and Haifa coincided with the incorporation into a world trade network of towns such as Beirut, Alexandria, and Port Said. See Kark, "The Rise and Decline of Coastal Towns in Palestine" in Gilbar, ed., *Ottoman Palestine,* 69–89. See also Kark, "Transportation in Nineteenth Century Palestine: Reintroduction of the Wheel" in *The Land that Became Israel: Studies in Historical Geography* (New Haven: Yale University Press, 1989), pp. 67–70.

23. Through the eighteenth century, Beirut "remained a curiously small and insignificant agglomeration." In the nineteenth, it assumed cultural, social, and economic dominance in Lebanon. See Samir Khalaf, *Lebanon's Predicament* (New York: Columbia University Press, 1987), p. 219. Also, see Yasar Eyup Ozveren, "The Making and Unmaking of an Ottoman Port-City: Nineteenth-Century Beirut, Its Hinterland, and the World-Economy" (unpublished Ph.D. dissertation, State University of New York at Binghamton, 1990). For the classic analysis of the distinction between Mediterranean coast and hinterland, see Fernand Braudel, *The Mediterranean and the Mediterranean World in the Age of Phillip II,* vol. 1 (New York: Harper & Row, 1972).

24. This trend was diametrically reversed during the years of the Arab Revolt. See Rachelle Leah Taqqu, "Arab Labor in Mandatory Palestine,

1920–1948" (unpublished Ph.D. dissertation, Columbia University, 1977), p. 64.

25. See, for example, Alexander Scholch, "The Economic Development of Palestine, 1856–1882," *Journal of Palestine Studies* 10 (1981): 48.

26. Alex Carmel, *The History of Haifa Under Turkish Rule* (Jerusalem: Yad Ben-Zvi, 1977), p. 161 [Hebrew].

27. Kark, "The Contribution of the Ottoman Regime" in Kushner, ed. *Palestine in the Late Ottoman Period,* 46–47. Construction continued as a major activity after the First World War. Not surprisingly, building along with work in quarries and cement factories constituted the largest sector absorbing migrants to the coastal cities between the wars.

28. Issawi, "The Trade of Jaffa, 1825–1914," in Nashabe, ed. *Studia Palaestina,* 43–45.

29. Jaffa became the orange capital of Palestine, and citrus the country's major export: by 1910, it accounted for about one-third of the total income from exports shipped through the city, with the number exported quintupling in the three decades leading up to the Great War. Gad G. Gilbar, "The Growing Economic Involvement of Palestine with the West, 1865–1914" in Kushner, ed., *Palestine in the Late Ottoman Period,* 191; Owen, *The Middle East in the World Economy,* 265.

30. To this day, movies are prohibited in the town of Hebron.

31. Neil Caplan, *Palestine Jewry and the Arab Question, 1917–1925* (London: Frank Cass, 1978), p. 133.

32. In 1966 the Histadrut officially removed the word "Jewish" from that title.

33. David Ben-Gurion, quoted in Neil Caplan, "Arab-Jewish Contacts in Palestine After the First World War," *Journal of Contemporary History* 12 (1977): 647.

34. See Gershon Shafk, *Land, Labor and the Origins of the Israeli-Palestinian Conflict* (New York: Cambridge University Press, 1989), pp. 55–60 and 69–78; Michael Shalev, *Labour and the Political Economy of Israel* (Oxford: Oxford University Press, 1991), pp. 1–18.

35. Rachelle Taqqu, "Peasants into Workmen: Internal Labor Migration and the Arab Village Community under the Mandate" in Migdal, *Palestinian Society and Politics,* 271.

36. On the Communist effort, see Musa K. Budeiri, *The Palestinian Communist Party, 1919–1948: Arabs and Jews in Struggle* (London: Ithaca Press, 1979). The author himself was a leading figure in the mandate period Communist party.

37. Maher al-Charif, "Le premier congres ouvrier arabe: Emergence du mouvement ouvrier arabe en Palestine" in René Gallissot, ed., *Mouvement ouvrier, communisme et nationalismes dans le monde arabe,* Cahiers du Mouvement Social 3 (Paris: Les Éditions Ouvrières, 1978), pp. 147–56.

38. For an idea of how World War II affected labor patterns, note the statistics for Haifa: Out of a total of 15,000 workers in 1943, almost 10,000 worked for the government and the British army (7,000 just for the army). Another 2,000 worked for international oil companies. See Itzhak Klein, "The Arabs in Haifa under the British Mandate: A Political Economic and Social Survey," Occasional Papers on the Middle East (New Series), No. 5 (University of Haifa, The Jewish-Arab Center, Institute of Middle Eastern Studies, 1987), p. 59 [Hebrew].

39. This is discussed in chapter 5.

40. Taqqu, "Peasants into Workmen," 271.

41. Shulamit Carmi and Henry Rosenfeld, "The Origins of the Process of Proletarianization and Urbanization of Arab Peasants in Palestine," *Annals of the New York Academy of Sciences* 220 (1974): 470–85.

42. This distinction was so meaningful in Palestinian society that it continued to be used in the refugee camps even 30 years after it had lost any practical meaning. See Sayigh, *Palestinians: From Peasants to Revolutionaries,* 25–40; and Danny Rubinstein, *The Fig Tree Embrace—The Palestinian "Right of Return"* (Jerusalem: Keter, 1990), pp. 23–32 [Hebrew].

43. Muslih, *The Origins of Palestinian Nationalism,* 162.

44. This is discussed in chapter 4.

45. Adnan abu-Ghazaleh, "Arab Cultural Nationalism in Palestine during the British Mandate," *Journal of Palestine Studies* 1 (1972): 39. In the cities, these figures reached 85 percent, while in the villages they remained around 20 percent. More boys were in schools than girls: in the villages, more than 10 times as many; in the towns, more than 50 percent. From 1914 under the Turks to 1944 under the British, the number of public schools for Arabs went from 98 to 480 and the number of pupils from 8,248 to 71,662. See Tibawi, *Arab Education in Mandatory Palestine,* 20, 49. Still, chronic underfunding and the lack of sufficient places for children prompted Arab protest in the 1930s and a subsequent British inquiry by the Department of Education. Public schools began to accommodate Christians as well as Muslims, although disproportionately large numbers of Christians continued attending private foreign schools.

46. One estimate placed the number of Palestinians studying at the

American University of Beirut in 1945 at approximately five hundred, with an additional three hundred at Egypt's universities and colleges. See Shimoni, *The Arabs of Palestine*, p. 387.

47. In the 1940s, the Arab College evolved into a university-level college, qualifying its graduates for a London University certificate.

48. Tarif Khalidi, "Palestinian Historiography: 1900–1948," *Journal of Palestine Studies* 10 (1981): 59.

49. *Awdat al-Safina* (Returning of the Ship), pp. 37–39 [Arabic].

50. Khalidi, "Palestinian Historiography," 60.

51. Abd al-Karim al Karmi (Abu Salma), cited in A. M. Elmessiri, ed., *The Palestinian Wedding: A Bilingual Anthology of Contemporary Palestinian Resistance Poetry* (Washington, D.C.: Three Continents Press, 1982), p. 26.

52. Cited in *Poetry of Resistance in Occupied Palestine*, translated by Sulafa Hijjawi (Baghdad: Al-Jumhuriya, 1968), p. 12.

53. Muhammad Siddiq, *Man Is a Cause: Political Consciousness and the Fiction of Ghassan Kanafani* (Seattle: University of Washington Press, 1984), p. xi.

54. Cited in Richard J. Ward, Don Pertez and Evan M. Willson, *The Palestinian State: A Rational Approach* (Port Washington, NY: Kennikat Press, 1977), pp. 6–7.

55. In 1928, 1939, and 1942, the mandate government surveyed the industry, and additional data are available from the general population survey of 1931 and other sources. Unfortunately, the figures are not comparable as definitions of industry and handicrafts varied. In 1942–43, the survey reported a total of 1,558 small plants and workshops for all of Palestine. See Government of Palestine, *A Survey of Palestine*, 3 vols. (Jerusalem: Government Printer, 1946); Supplement (Jerusalem, 1947); see also P. J. Loftus, *National Income of Palestine* (Jerusalem: Government Printer, 1946); E. Mills, *Census of Palestine* (Jerusalem: Government Printer, 1933).

56. Shimoni, *The Arabs of Palestine*, 189.

57. The largest share was food processing (43 percent). The other figures: shoe production—16 percent; tobacco products including cigarettes—9 percent; metallurgy and textiles—5 percent each. The increasing availability of hydroelectric power from the Jordan River and power plants in Tel-Aviv and Haifa made this expansion and diversification feasible. From 1921 to 1939, the number of Arab enterprises using mechanical power went from 7 to 541.

58. Government of Palestine, *Report of Committee on the Economic Condition of Agriculturists and the Fiscal Measures of Government in Relation Thereto*

[Johnson-Crosbie report] (Jerusalem: Government Printer, 1943), pp. 60–61. One report in the 1930s estimated that the fellaheen bought £P700,000 to £P800,000 worth of goods from the towns, including clothing, matches, oil, rice, and sugar. "Under the Ottoman Empire, Palestine, like other parts of the Empire, used the Turkish pound as the legal money in circulation. This continued until the occupation of Palestine by the Allies, when the Egyptian pound was made legal tender along with the British gold sovereign in 1917. In 1926 the Palestine Currency Board was established and the Palestinian currency was legally defined in 1927. The Egyptian pound and the British gold sovereign were withdrawn from circulation as the Palestinian pound [£P] took their place. The monetary standard for Palestinian currency was the sterling exchange standard." Ahmad K. Katanani, "Economic performance of Palestine before 1948," *Dirasat* 13 (1986): 52.

59. In 1927, the government listed 259 Arab importers and 133 exporters; those numbers expanded to 317 and 160 respectively in 1933.

60. The total volume of Arab foreign trade in this period appears impressive. Imports expanded by more than 50 and exports by 67 percent in the 15 years after 1922. On a per capita basis, however, the results are less striking, less than 4 percent growth for imports and 22 percent for exports.

61. Katanani, "Economic Performance of Palestine," 35.

62. In fact, Jews purchased approximately a quarter of the net Arab national product in 1935, Arabs in turn consuming about 8 percent of that of the Jews. In that year, the Arabs shipped about £P2 million worth of products abroad and sold another £P1 million to the Jews, and about 12,000 Arabs worked for Jewish enterprises. See Metzer and Kaplan, "Jointly but Severally," 328; Abramowitz and Gelfat, *The Arab Economy in Palestine*, 104; Zvi Sussman, *Wage Differentials and Equality within the Histadrut* (Ramat Gan: Massada, 1974), p. 40 [Hebrew].

63. One survey found a cumulative peasant debt of about £P1 million in 1930, on which the fellaheen paid an average annual interest of 30 percent. (In the 1940s, peasants retired much of that debt as a result of the good economic conditions brought on by the war.)

64. From £P55,000 in 1931 to £P376,000 two years later, £P775,000 by 1942, and £P7 million at the end of the Second World War.

65. A similar attempt to found the Arab Industrial Bank failed. Shimoni, *The Arabs of Palestine*, 232.

66. Khalil al-Sakanini, *Palestine after the Great War* (Jerusalem: Beit al-

Maqdas Printer, 1925), ch. 3 [Arabic]. Sakanini, an Arab patriot, was an educator who wrote scores of textbooks for the modern Palestinian Arabic schools. While his general views were humanist and liberal, he took a hard line against Jewish settlement. His selected diaries were published in Hebrew under the title *Such Am I, O World* (Jerusalem: Keter, 1990) and provide the Hebrew reader a unique window into the world of a Palestinian intellectual between 1914 and 1950.

67. Shai Lachman, "Arab Rebellion and Terrorism in Palestine 1929–39: The Case of Sheikh Izz al-Din al-Qassam and his Movement" in Elie Kedourie and Sylvia G. Haim, eds., *Zionism and Arabism in Palestine and Israel* (London: Frank Cass, 1982), p. 61. For more on Qassam's influence, see chapter 4. See also S. Abdullah Schleifer, "The Life and Thought of Izz-id-Din al-Qassam," *Islamic Quarterly* 23 (1979): 78.

68. This was not the first time that the name Black Hand was used by Arab nationalists. An attack in 1920 by more than 2,000 Bedouin fighters on a British military installation was suspected of being the signal for a general uprising against the British, which never materialized. The aim was unification with Syria under Faysal. One of the key forces in planning the uprising and stockpiling weapons was the Black Hand, an underground organization that spread from Jaffa to other towns, possibly under the direction of the Arab Literary Club. It existed from about 1919–23.

69. Ted Swedenburg, "Al-Qässam Remembered," *Alif: Journal of Comparative Poetics* 7 (1987): 17.

70. Members of the Nashashibi and Khalidi families dissociated themselves from the violence of Qassam's group. Only after Qassam's death did most of the leadership identify itself with him. See Yuval Amon-Ohanna, *The Internal Struggle within the Palestinian Movement—1929–1939* (Tel-Aviv: Hadar, 1981), pp. 270–71 [Hebrew]. Also see Ghassan Kanafani, *The 1936–39 Revolt in Palestine* (Beirut: Committee for Democratic Palestine, Popular Front from the Liberation of Palestine, n.d.). Even the eventual leader of the Palestinian nationalist movement, Amin al-Husseini, seemed to oppose the violence of November 1935 at a time when he was involved in intensive diplomatic discussions with Britain and hoped to achieve an agreement for autonomy in stages. See Yehoshua Porath, *The Palestinian National Movement: From Riots to Rebellion, 1929–1939* (London: Frank Cass, 1977), p. 139. Subhi Yassin argues that Amin was always hostile to Qassam, but this seems to be a distortion of Amin's attitudes. See *The Great Arab Revolution in Palestine, 1936–1939* (Cairo, 1959), p. 22 [Arabic].

3. Jerusalem: Notables and Nationalism

1. Aliza Auerbach quoted in Cornell Capa, ed., *Jerusalem: City of Mankind* (New York: Grossman, 1974), p. 118.

2. *Jerusalem: The Holy City in the Eyes of Chroniclers, Visitors, Pilgrims, and Prophets from the Days of Abraham to the Beginnings of Modern Times* (Princeton: Princeton University Press, 1985), p. ix.

3. Cited in Peters, *Jerusalem*, p. 562.

4. *The Innocents Abroad* 2: 326.

5. An excellent account of conditions can be found in Yehoshua Ben-Arieh, *Jerusalem in the Nineteenth Century: The Old City* (New York: St. Martin's Press, 1984), pp. 2–4 and 82–83.

6. Cited in Ruth Kark and Shimon Landman, "The Establishment of Muslim Neighborhoods in Jerusalem, Outside the Old City, During the Late Ottoman Period," *Palestine Exploration Quarterly* 112 (1980), 113–114. Kark and Landman show that in the early part of the century there were scattered Muslim buildings (religious structures, seasonal residences) outside the walls, but that serious Muslim construction there did not begin until the 1860s. It mostly involved the upper classes, and was limited compared to that of the Christians—the first to undertake large-scale construction—and that of the Jews.

7. See Amnon Cohen, *Economic Life in Ottoman Jerusalem* (New York: Cambridge University Press, 1989), pp. 6–10.

8. Edward Robinson, *Biblical Researches in Palestine, Mount Sinai and Arabia Petra. A Journal of Travels in the Year 1838*, vol. 2 (Boston: Crocker & Brewster, 1841), p. 81.

9. Twain, *The Innocents Abroad*, p. 329.

10. Kark, "The Contribution of the Ottoman Regime" in Kushner, ed., *Palestine in the Late Ottoman Period*, 46–49.

11. Gilbar, *Trends in the Demographic Development of the Palestinians*, 12; Butrus Abu-Manneh, "The Population of Palestine in the 1870s According to Ottoman Censuses," paper delivered for a conference on "Palestine 1840–1948: Population and Migration," Haifa University, June, 1986.

12. Manna, *The Sanjaq of Jerusalem*, vi-vii. The position of deputy to the Mullah in Jerusalem was for generations the monopoly of the al-Khalidi family, and, by virtue of this position, this family managed to accumulate great influence over public affairs in Jerusalem and beyond. Khalidis were appointed as deputies in Nablus, Jaffa, Gaza, and other cities.

13. In judicial and military matters there was some subordination to gov-

ernors in Beirut and Damascus, but in most matters, the chief administrator of the Jerusalem sanjak was equivalent to a provincial governor. See Haim Gerber, "The Ottoman Administration of the Sanjaq of Jerusalem, 1890–1908," *Asian and African Studies* 12 (1978): 37.

14. Butrus Abu-Manneh, "The Rise of the Sanjak of Jerusalem in the Late 19th Century," in Ben-Dor, ed., *The Palestinians and the Middle East Conflict*, 25.

15. See Kushner, ed., *Palestine in the Late Ottoman Period*, 247–330.

16. Gabriel Baer, "Jerusalem's Families of Notables and the Wakf in the Early 19th Century," in Kushner, ed., *Palestine in the Late Ottoman Period*, 109–22.

17. "The Ottoman Administration of the Sanjaq of Jerusalem," 44.

18. In most instances, the Ottomans simply appointed the members of the council, but in 1908 an election for the council took place. The voters consisted of 700 Muslims, 300 Christians, and 200 Jews. See Ruth Kark, "The Jerusalem Municipality at the End of Ottoman Rule," *Asian and African Studies* 14 (1980): 124.

19. See Daniel Rubinstein, "The Jerusalem Municipality under the Ottomans, British, and Jordanians" in Joel L. Kramer, ed., *Jerusalem: Problems and Prospects* (New York: Praeger, 1980), pp. 62, 74.

20. Abu-Manneh, "The Rise of the Sanjak of Jerusalem," 26–28.

21. "Factionalism and Class Formation" in Owen, ed., *Studies in the Economic and Social History of Palestine*, 181.

22. See Yehoshua Porath, *The Emergence of the Palestinian-Arab National Movement, 1918–1929* (London: Frank Cass, 1974), pp. 160–62.

23. For a full account of all drafts of the text—including this, the final one—and for a full history of it, see Ronald Sanders, *The High Walls of Jerusalem: A History of the Balfour Declaration and the Birth of the British Mandate in Palestine* (New York: Holt, Rinehart, Winston, 1983).

24. *Bitter Harvest: Palestine between 1914–1979* (Delmar, NY: Caravan Books, 1979), pp. 299–300.

25. Mandel, *The Arabs and Zionism*, 39–40.

26. Ibid., 174.

27. *Le Réveil de la nation arabe dans l'Asie Turque* (Paris, 1905), p. v.

28. See Porath, *The Emergence of the Palestinian-Arab National Movement*, 39–69, 307–9.

29. For a brief account of it and other post-war arrangements, see Charles D. Smith, *Palestine and the Arab-Israeli Conflict* (New York: St. Martin's Press, 1988), pp. 55–66.

30. Porath, *The Emergence of the Palestinian-Arab National Movement*, 89. See also Porath, *The Palestinian National Movement*, 7–10; 14–24. The move-

ment is also analyzed in Ann Mosley Lesch, *Arab Politics in Palestine, 1917–1939: The Frustration of a Nationalist Movement* (Ithaca: Cornell University Press, 1979), and Ann Mosely Lesch, "The Palestinian Arab Nationalist Movement Under the Mandate" in William B. Quandt, Fuad Jabber, and Ann M. Lesch, eds., *The Politics of Palestinian Nationalism* (Berkeley: University of California Press, 1973), pp. 7–42.

31. See Aaron S. Klieman, *Foundations of British Policy in the Arab World: The Cairo Conference of 1921* (Baltimore: Johns Hopkins University Press, 1970), pp. 117–22 and 129–31.

32. For details, see Porath, *The Emergence of the Palestinian-Arab National Movement,* 69–105.

33. Ibid., 84. Porath writes of the divisions at the congress: "It is hardly coincidental that it was the heads of two important families of Jerusalem, ᶜArif Pasha al-Dajani and Ismaiᶜil al-Husayni, who led the movement for 'Palestine for the Palestinians,' just as it was no coincidence that they were supported by the class of notables and community elders, in contrast to the opposition of the youth. The establishment of a separate government for Palestine would turn the notables of Jerusalem and the heads of the influential families into office-holders, ministers, and future heads of state. On the other hand, the youthful partisans of unity could only gain from unity with Damascus. Around Faysal converged their contemporaries and ideological comrades from Syria and Iraq, who had been the decisive element in his regime, pre-empting the veteran Damascene elite." On the contribution of the Emir Faysal to Palestinian nationalism, see Muslih, *The Origins of Palestinian Nationalism,* 115–30.

34. Porath, *The Emergence of the Palestinian-Arab National Movement,* 86–87. See also Abu-Manneh, "The Rise of Jerusalem in the Late 19th Century," 28: "Even after the establishment of mandatory Palestine through the joining of the sanjaks of Jerusalem, Nablus and Acre, Jerusalem held its primacy; yet, for a long time, there existed another two centers, Nablus and Acre (Haifa), the notables of which were not always ready to take the lead of those in Jerusalem."

35. Kayyali, *Palestine, A Modern History* (London: Groom Helm, n.d.), pp. 70ff.

36. *The Arab Awakening,* 312.

37. Cited in Porath, *The Emergence of the Palestinian-Arab National Movement,* 107.

38. Ibid., 117–18; 175–81.

39. The only demand that the British completely—and promptly—accepted was giving the Arab Executive the same official status as the

Jewish Agency. In exchange, they demanded official Arab recognition of the mandate, which the Palestinian politicians never gave. The idea of establishing an elected representative body of the entire population met with strong Zionist resistance; they proposed parity—a body half of Arab representatives and half of Jews, with veto power for the British. The Palestinians boycotted an election held in February-March, 1923 for secondary electors to an advisory council. In the late 1920s the Arabs accepted the establishment of such a council, but now the Zionists opposed it. See Porath, *The Palestinian National Movement*, chs. 1 and 3; Kayyali, *Palestine*, 84–129.

40. "The Bases of Arab and Jewish Leadership During the Mandate Period," *Journal of Palestine Studies* 6 (1977): 113.

41. For a detailed description and analysis of the British motives and the developments leading to the rise of the new religious establishment, see Porath, *The Emergence of the Palestinian-Arab National Movement*, chs. 2–3. For a general discussion, see Uri Kupferschmidt, "Islam on the Defensive: The Supreme Muslim Council's Role in Mandatory Palestine," *Asian and African Studies* 17 (1983): 204–5.

42. For more on al-Husseini, see Philip Mattar, *The Mufti of Jerusalem: Al-Hajj Amin al-Husayni and the Palestinian National Movement* (New York: Columbia University Press, 1988); Zvi Elpeleg, *Grand Mufti* (Tel-Aviv: Ministry of Defence Publishing House, 1989) [Hebrew]; Taysir Jbara, *Palestinian Leader Hajj Amin al-Husayni: Mufti of Jerusalem* (Princeton: The Kingston Press, 1985). See also Muhammed Amin al-Husseini, Truths *Regarding the Palestinian Problem*, 2nd ed. (Cairo: Dar al-Kitab al-Arabi bi-Masr, 1957) [Arabic].

43. Mattar, *The Mufti of Jerusalem*, 25.

44. Uri Kupferschmidt, "Attempts to Reform the Supreme Muslim Council" in Ben-Dor, ed., *The Palestinians and the Middle East Conflict*, 35.

45. See Porath, *The Emergence of the Palestinian-Arab National Movement*, ch. 4.

46. For an excellent description of Palestinian notable politics between 1929 and 1936, see Porath, *The Palestinian National Movement*, 234–40; 184–206.

47. On the use of religious symbols in cases where Muslims faced Western powers, see Rudolph Peters, *Islam and Colonialism: The Doctrine of Jihad in Modern History* (New York: Mouton, 1979), pp. 3–5. For special reference to the Palestinian case, see pp. 94–104.

48. What role Amin played in these events, especially in their early stages, remains controversial. Arab writers have stressed his moderation—a view shared by many British officials of the time—Jewish writers the

incendiary nature of his speeches. It is a fact that he and other Jerusalem-led notables signed a proclamation dissociating themselves from
Arab mob action, once it was well under way.

49. See Daphne Tsimhoni, "The Arab Christians and the Palestinian Arab
National Movement During the Formative Stage," in Ben-Dor, ed.,
The Palestinians and the Middle East Conflict, 73–98.

50. Cited in ibid, 76.

51. See Nels Johnson, *Islam and the Politics of Meaning in Palestinian Nationalism* (London: Kegan Paul International, 1982), pp. 9–30; Donna Robinson Divine, "Islamic Culture and Political Practice in British Mandate Palestine," *Review of Politics* 45 (1983): 71–93.

52. Porath, *The Emergence of the Palestinian-Arab National Movement,* 276.

53. *The Mufti of Jerusalem,* 33.

54. "Factionalism and Class Formation," in Owen, ed., *Studies in the Economic and Social History of Palestine,* 192.

55. Kayyali, *Palestine,* 150.

56. *Palestine: Statement of Policy by His Majesty's Government in the United
Kingdom* (London: HMSO, 1930, Cmd. 3692).

57. For the text of MacDonald's letter see Walter Laqueur, ed., *Israel Arab
Reader: A Documentary History of the Middle East Conflict* (Middlesex:
Penguin Books, 1970), pp. 50–55. For a good analysis of British-Zion-
ist relations at that time, see Norman Rose, *The Gentile Zionists: A Study
in Anglo-Zionist Diplomacy, 1929–1939* (London: Frank Cass, 1973), esp.
pp. 1–40.

58. Cited in Kayyali, *Palestine,* 172.

59. See Joseph Nevo, "The Palestine Arab Party, 1944–1946," *Asian and African Studies* 14 (1980): 99–115.

60. See for example, Jaber Shibli, *Conflict and Cooperation in Palestine* (Jerusalem [Jordan]: al-Umma Press, 1950) [Arabic]; Naji Allush, *The Arab
Resistance in Palestine: 1917–1948* (Beirut: Dar al-Talia, 1970) [Arabic]; Isa
al-Sifri, *Arab Palestine Under the Mandate and Zionism* (Jaffa: New Palestinian Bookstore, 1973) [Arabic].

61. See Nabil All Shaath and Hasna Reda Mekdashi, *Palestine Stamps
(1865–1981)* (Beirut: Dar al-Fata al-Arabi, 1981), pp. 7–8.

4. The Arab Revolt, 1936–1939

1. *Al-Thawrah al-Arabiyyah al-Kubra fi Filastin.* For detailed descriptions
and analysis of the revolt, see John Marlowe, *Rebellion in Palestine* (Lon-

don: Crescent Press, 1946) esp. chs. 10 and 12; Porath, *The Palestinian National Movement*, chs. 6–9, esp. pp. 233–73; Abd al-Wahab Kayyali, *Palestine: A Modern History* (London: Croom Helm, n.d.), pp. 155–227; Tom Bowden, "The Politics of Arab Rebellion in Palestine, 1936–1939," *Middle Eastern Studies* 11 (1975): 147–74.

2. The strongest argument to this effect is made by Shai Lachman, "Arab Rebellion and Terrorism in Palestine 1929–39: The Case of Sheikh Izz al-Din al-Qassam and his Movement" in Kedourie and Haim, eds., *Zionism and Arabism in Palestine and Israel*, 78. In *Arab Politics in Palestine*, 217, Lesch notes that the attack on the Jews was carried out by a group led by Sheikh Farhan al-Saadi, who had been a follower of Sheikh Qassam.

3. See Uri Ben-Eliezer, "Militarism, Status and Politics: The First Israeli Generation and Political Leadership during the Forties" (unpublished Ph.D. dissertation, Tel-Aviv University, 1988), pp. 1–31 [Hebrew].

4. "The Road to Rebellion: Arab Palestine in the 1930's," *Journal of Palestine Studies* 6 (1977): 46.

5. Emile al-Ghawri, *Palestine Through Sixty Years* 2 (Beirut: Dar al-Taliya, 1973), pp. 132–34 [Arabic].

6. Kayyali, *Palestine*, 169–71.

7. Yehuda Slutsky, *The History of the Haganah: From Defense to Struggle* 2 (Tel-Aviv: Am Oved, 1964), p. 459 [Hebrew].

8. See Manuel S. Hassassian, *Palestine: Factionalism in the National Movement* (Jerusalem: Palestinian Academic Society for the Study of International Affairs, 1990), pp. 107–32.

9. September 17, 1931, edition of *al-Jami'ah al-Arabiyah,* quoted in Porath, *The Palestinian National Movement*, p. 111.

10. Ted Swedenburg, "The Role of the Palestinian Peasantry in the Great Revolt (1936–1939)" in Edmund Burke III and Ira M. Lapidus, eds., *Islam, Politics, and Social Movements* (Berkeley: University of California Press, 1988), p. 186.

11. Porath, *The Palestinian National Movement*, 123.

12. Cited in Yehuda Taggar, "The Arab Revolt of 1936 in the Perspective of the Jewish-Arab Conflict" in Shmuel Almog, ed., *Zionism and the Arabs* (Jerusalem: The Historical Society of Israel and the Zalman Shazar Center, 1983), p. 169. For more on the colorful figure of Alami as a British civil servant, Palestinian nationalist, and educator, see Geofrey Furlonge, *Palestine Is My Country: The Story of Musa Alami* (London: John Murray, 1969).

13. A group in the 1980s claiming credit for placing a bomb on a TWA

flight even named itself after Qassam. In the summer of 1992, Israeli forces uncovered a clandestine group in Ramallah which was part of the Islamic Hamas faction (see Chapter 9), also named after Qassam. In fact, one Palestinian intellectual who himself became a revered martyr, Ghassan Kanafani, likens Izz al-Din to Che Guevara, Cuba's legendary revolutionary leader. See *The 1936–39 Revolt in Palestine* (Beirut: Committee for Democratic Palestine, Popular Front for the Liberation of Palestine, n.d.), pp. 3-5, 11–14. Perhaps a more apt analogy would be to Franz Fanon, the noted writer who in the Algerian context extolled the cathartic effect of violence by the colonized against the colonizer. Kanafani (1936–72) was not only a writer but a member of the Popular Front for the Liberation of Palestine. He was killed by a car bomb, probably by Israeli agents, in Beirut, on July 8, 1972. Among his most important literary works, which expressed the traumatic experiences of being uprooted and of refugee life, are the collections *Death of Bed No. 12* (1961), *Land of Sand Oranges* (1963), and *A World Not Our Own* (1965). See his *Men in the Sun and Other Palestinian Stories*, translated by Hilary Kilpatrick (Washington, DC: Three Continents Press, 1978). On his literary works and ideology see Stepan Wild, *Gossan Kanafani: The Life of a Palestinian* (Wiesbaden: Otto Harrasowitz, 1975), and Muhammad Siddiq, *Man Is a Cause: Political Consciousness and the Fiction of Gossan Kanafani* (Seattle: University of Washington Press, 1984).

14. Bowden, "The Politics of the Arab Rebellion."
15. Ghassan Kanafani accuses what he calls "the feudal clerical leadership" of being reactionary elements, colluding with the imperialists. See *The 1936–39 Revolt in Palestine*, 3-7.
16. Bowden, "The Politics of Arab Rebellion," 152.
17. Porath, *The Palestinian National Movement*, 173–74.
18. Baruch Kimmerling, *Zionism and Territory*, ch. 7. Over 35,000 acres of citrus and fruit trees were destroyed.
19. *Palestine Royal Commission Report* (London: HMSO, 1937, Cmd. 5479, Peel Commission).
20. Kupferschmidt, "Islam on the Defensive," 206; Porath, *The Palestinian National Movement*, 133–37.
21. See, Bayan Nuweihid al-Hout, "The Palestinian Elite during the Mandate Period," *Journal of Palestine Studies* 9 (1979): 109.
22. James P. Jankowski, "The Palestinian Arab Revolt of 1936-1939," *The Muslim World* 63 (1973): 227.
23. Yuval Arnon-Ohanna, "The Bands in the Palestinian Arab Revolt,

1936–1939: Structure and Organization" *Asian and African Studies* 15 (1981): 229–47. Among the most prominent band leaders were Abd al-Qadir al-Husseini (see below) and Abd al-Rahem al-Haj Muhammad, both self-styled commanders in chief; Arif Abd al-Razzaq, a loyal follower of the Mufti with a history of criminal activity in a rural gang; and Yusuf Abu Durra, who coordinated with Muhammad. Some bands and their leaders are discussed in Tom Bowden, *The Breakdown of Public Security: The Case of Ireland 1916–1921 and Palestine 1936–1939* (Beverly Hills: Sage, 1977), pp. 208–10. Also, see Bowden, "The Politics of Arab Rebellion," 156.

24. Arnon-Ohanna, "The Bands in the Palestinian Arab Revolt," 251.

25. See, for example, Jbara, *Palestinian Leader Hajj Amin al-Husayni,* 151. Haj Amin's relationship to Qa'uqji wavered through the years. As we shall see, in a later stage of the revolt, the Mufti's Damascus group asked Qa'uqji to lead the rural rebellion once again. In 1947, the Arab League appointed him leader of the newly formed Arab Liberation Army over Husseini's objections.

26. Ibid., 235.

27. Porath, *The Palestinian National Movement,* 190.

28. On the rebels' control see Smith, *Palestine and the Palestinians,* 64; on the actions of the British troops see Porath, *The Palestinian National Movement,* 299ff.

29. Bowden, "The Politics of Arab Rebellion," 153.

30. Swedenburg, "The Role of the Palestinian Peasantry in the Great Revolt," in Burke and Lapidus, eds., *Islam, Politics and Social Movements,* 192.

31. Dr. Khalil Totah, cited in Theodore Remain Swedenburg, "Memories of Revolt: The 1936–39 Rebellion and the Struggle for a Palestinian National Past" (unpublished Ph.D. dissertation, University of Texas at Austin, 1988), p. 25.

32. Kupferschmidt, "Islam on the Defensive," 204–5.

33. Smith, *Palestine and the Palestinians,* 64.

34. "The Story of a Palestinian under Occupation," *Journal of Palestine Studies* 11 (1981): 5.

35. Swedenburg, "Memories of Revolt," 213.

36. Antonius, *The Arab Awakening,* 405–6.

37. Cited in Miller, *Government and Society in Rural Palestine,* 124.

38. Swedenburg, "Memories of Revolt," 157–65.

39. Ibid., 153–54.

40. Miller, *Government and Society in Rural Palestine,* 138.

41. This is evident in the archive of one Palestinian group, captured by the Haganah, the Jewish underground paramilitary organization. The material includes reports from the field, correspondence between different local and district leaders, and decisions of military courts. See Ezra Danin and Ya'acov Shimoni, *Documents and Portraits from the Arab Gangs Archives in the Arab Revolt in Palestine, 1936–1939* (Jerusalem: Magnes Press, 1981) [Hebrew].

42. Dajani had broken with the Nashashibis, and some figures associated with the Husseinis have suggested it was the British, not the Mufti's men, who murdered him. See Swedenburg, "Memories of Revolt," 201.

43. Arnon-Ohanna, "The Bands in the Palestinian Arab Revolt," 284–85.

44. Abboushi, "The Road to Rebellion," 27.

45. Bowden tends to romanticize the rural nature of the bands, but correctly points to the organizational difficulties of basing a rebellion on rural groups with only attenuated connections to the major urban changes affecting the society: "It was in this remnant feudal society that the coterie of landed aristocrats, their class symbolized by the Mufti, attempted to politicize a rebellion which was for most of its combatants an affair of the heart, the seasons, and above all the soil." *The Breakdown of Public Security,* 189.

46. Cited in Miller, *Government and Society in Rural Palestine,* 127.

47. See Abboushi, "The Road to Rebellion," 42.

48. Porath, *The Palestinian-Arab National Movement,* 251–54.

49. A division of the population into Husseini and Nashashibi camps is possible for some districts but not others. The northern portion of the country, for example, was largely removed from that conflict.

50. Elyakim Rubinstein, "Zionist Attitudes on the Jewish-Arab Conflict Until 1936," in Almog, ed., *Zionism and the Arabs,* 35–72, argues that the pre-1929 Zionist orientation to the Arab question was not one of complacency and reflected no comprehensive policy, consisting rather of ad hoc responses.

51. Cited in Shabtai Teveth, *Ben-Gurion and the Palestinian Arabs: From Peace to War* (New York: Oxford University Press, 1985), p. 166.

52. Cited in Yehoyada Haim, *Abandonment of Illusions: Zionist Political Attitudes Toward Palestinian Arab Nationalism, 1936–1939* (Boulder: Westview Press, 1983), p. 36. In *Collusion across the Jordan: King Abdullah, the Zionist Movement, and the Partition of Palestine* (Oxford: Clarendon Press, 1988), p. 14, Avi Shlaim states that "A wide gulf separated Ben-Gurion's public utterances on the Arab question from his real convictions."

53. Haganah forces, in the framework of the "Special Night Squads,"

were highly trained by the British Officer Charles Wingate. See Yehuda Bauer, *From Diplomacy to Resistance: A History of Jewish Palestine, 1939–1945* (Philadelphia: The Jewish Publication Society of America, 1970), pp. 12–13.

54. Bowden, *The Breakdown of Public Security,* 227, writes: "Palestine had in effect by 1936 become something of a haven for brigands, revolutionaries and escaped criminals seeking to avoid the comparative severity of justice in the neighbouring French territories."

55. Bowden, "The Politics of Arab Rebellion," 166–69.

56. See Aaron S. Klieman, "The Divisiveness of Palestine: Foreign Office Versus Colonial Office on the Issue of Partition, 1937," *The Historical Journal* 22 (1979): 423–41.

57. See Walid Khalidi, ed., *From Haven to Conquest: The Origins and the Development of the Palestine Problem* (Beirut: Institute for Palestine Studies, 1971), appendix 4, pp. 848–49.

58. Mattar, *The Mufti of Jerusalem,* 84.

59. Schleifer, "The Life and Thought of 'Izz-id-Din al-Qassam," 78, suggests that Qassam was "particularly vulnerable to the same process of political appropriation that to a lesser degree threatens all heroes."

60. Swedenburg, "Memories of Revolt," 175–77.

5. The Meaning of Disaster

1. See Kimmerling, *Zionism and Territory,* 123.

2. Translated by Rivka Yadlin from an anthology edited by Abd al-Kahman al-Kayyali, *Palestinian Poetry and the Nakbah* (Beirut: Institute for Arab Studies, 1975), p. 235 [Arabic].

3. Turki, *The Disinherited,* 11.

4. Cited in Donna Robinson Divine, "Palestinian Arab Women and Their Reveries of Emancipation" in Susan C. Bourque and Divine, eds., *Women Living Change* (Philadelphia: Temple University Press, 1985), p. 57.

5. In the 1920s and the first half of the 1930s, the Arab sector grew 7.5 percent a year, the Jewish average being 22.5 percent. The Jewish economy had about one-fifth of its workers in agriculture and an equal fraction in industry; in 1922 two-thirds of the Arab population were in agriculture, the figure still being over 50 percent in 1935. Manufacturing absorbed less than 10 percent of Arab workers throughout the period.

6. Al-Hout, "The Palestinian Political Elite during the Mandate Period," 89.

7. The rural economy also deteriorated: Weather was bad throughout the revolt, cutting into overall production, and with a frequent lack of urban markets, crops simply rotted.

8. A drop from almost three-quarters to only 2.5 percent of total exports. Government of Palestine, *Statistical Abstract* (Jerusalem: Government Printer, 1941, 1943, 1944–45). An excellent source of data on the wartime economy is found in Z. Abramowitz, "Wartime Development of Arab Economy in Palestine" in Sophie A. Udin, ed., *The Palestine Year Book,* vol. 1 (Washington, D.C.: Zionist Organization of America, 1945), pp. 130–44. See also Robert R. Nathan, Oscar Gass, and Daniel Creamer, *Palestine: Problem and Promise—An Economic Study* (Washington, D.C.: Public Affairs Press, 1946), pp. 155–62, and Nachum T. Gross and Jacob Metzer, "Palestine in World War II: Some Economic Aspects" (Jerusalem: Falk Institute, Discussion Paper No. 87, 1987 [mimeo]).

9. The effect on the Jewish economy was even more severe, since on the eve of the war citriculture composed 63 percent of its total agricultural product, compared to 21 percent for the Arabs. David Horowitz, *The Development of the Palestinian Economy,* 215.

10. Gross and Metzer, "Palestine in World War II," 4.

11. See G. H. Sealous, *Economic Conditions in Egypt* (London: Department of Overseas Trade, HMSO, 1936); A. Konikoff, *Transjordan: An Economic Survey* (Jerusalem: Economic Research Institute, The Jewish Agency, 1946). Konikoff described Transjordan as a poor, exclusively agricultural country, with all its economic survival based on the linkage with the Palestinian economy and British aid and support. In Syria and Lebanon, traditional industry was almost completely destroyed following the First World War; a new more developed and modern industry began to arise but not at the same rate as in Palestine. See George Hakim, "Industry," in Sa'id B. Himadeh, ed., *Economic Organization of Palestine* (Beirut: American University Press, 1938), pp. 119–76.

12. Taqqu, "Arab Labor in Mandatory Palestine," pp. 165–66. Taqqu notes that "the extensive recruitment of Arab villagers into wage labor had been the hasty byproduct of war, accomplished over a brief span. It was a necessarily incomplete and inconsistent process, whose immediate effect was to fragment rural Arab society" (p. 187).

13. Miller, *Government and Society in Rural Palestine,* 141.

14. Abramowitz, "Wartime Development of Arab Economy in Palestine," pp. 130–35.

15. On the creation of the working class, see Haydar Rashid, "The Formation of the Arab Labor Movement in Palestine," *Shu'un Filistiniyya* (April 1981): 134 [Arabic].

16. Taqqu's comment: "The Arab labor movement suffered from an inherent structural weakness: its justification lay in the separate consciousness and claims of workers, while its attachments to a corporate image of Arab society continued on many levels. The movement thus reflected the growing disparity in the Arab community between the dominance of old elites on one hand and the emerging recognition of a new social reality which was no longer well served by those elites on the other." See "Arab Labor in Mandatory Palestine," 212.

17. Ibid., 287.

18. Ibid., 322.

19. Divine, "Palestinian Arab Women and Their Reveries of Emancipation" in Bourque and Divine, eds., *Women Living Change,* 76. Since 1948, the role of women seems to have changed much more dramatically. See Ghazi al-Khalili, "Palestinian Women and Revolution, 1948–1967," *Shu'un Filistiniyya* (December, 1967), pp. 12–19; and Jamil Hilal, "Preliminary Notes on the Contribution of Palestinian Women in Production," *Shu'un Filistiniyya* (June, 1981), pp. 145–51 [both in Arabic].

20. All such intensive diplomatic efforts made by various factions of the British government during the war were to achieve an agreement that would satisfy the Palestinian Arabs. See Y. Porath, *In Search of Arab Unity* (London: Frank Cass, 1986), pp. 78ff.

21. Slutsky, *The History of the Haganah* 3: 112 [Hebrew].

22. Francis R. Nicosia, *The Third Reich and the Palestine Question* (Austin: University of Texas Press, 1985), p. 177.

23. Among the Axis forces, Amin al-Husseini's group was not the only one: An Iraqi group headed by Rashid All al-Kailani vied with it to represent the Arabs in Berlin and Rome. Al-Husseini never succeeded in receiving a public commitment from Hitler supporting independence for Palestine and the other Arab countries. Instead, in April, 1942, Count Ciano, the Italian foreign minister, declared that Italy would be ready to grant "every possible aid to the Arab countries in their fight for liberation, to recognize their sovereignty and independence, to agree to their federation if this is desired by the interested parties, as well as to the abolition of the national Jewish Homeland in Palestine." See Jbara, *Palestinian Leader Hajj Amin Al-Husayni,* 184–85.

See also Elpeleg, *Grand Mufti,* 68. Postwar Zionist propaganda used the activities of al-Husseini as a powerful argument in favor of Jewish claims, depicting the entire Arab community as collaborators. In his own writings after the war, al-Husseini admitted his alliance with Germany and Italy against the common Jewish-British enemy, but emphasized his complete rejection of racist Nazi ideology. See *Truths Regarding the Palestinian Problem,* 115–17.

24. Shimoni, *The Arabs of Palestine,* 355–57.

25. Joseph Nevo, "The Renewal of Palestinian Political Activity 1943–1945," in Ben-Dor, ed., *The Palestinians and the Middle East Conflict,* 59–72; and Nevo, "The Palestinian Arab Party, 1944–1946," 99–101. See also Jamal Qadurah, "The Emergence of Political Parties in Palestine: The National Defense Party," *Shu'un Filistiniyya* (January–February, 1985).

26. The three main Jewish underground groups began their revolt against the British at different times and at some points worked against each other. The Lehi, or Stern Gang, fought the British in the early years of World War II. Members of the right-wing Irgun Zvai Leumi (commonly known as Etzel or just the Irgun) and the mainline Haganah worked with the British to eliminate Lehi's activities and jail its members. After the Irgun began to fight in February, 1944, the Haganah moved (at times, with the mandate authorities) to extinguish the revolt. Finally, for a short time starting in October, 1945, the Haganah joined the United Hebrew Rebellion. See Slutsky, *History of the Haganah* 3: 205–8; and David Niv, *Battle for Freedom: The Irgun Zvai Leumi* (Tel-Aviv: Klausner Institute, 1967, 1970), vols. 2–4 [Hebrew]. For the difficulties of the British authorities in dealing with the Jewish revolt, see David A. Charters, *The British Army and Jewish Insurgency in Palestine, 1945–1947* (London: Macmillan, 1989), p. 80. In the end, it was not Jewish revolt that drove the British from Palestine but fear of a renewal of the 1936–39 Arab Revolt. See Michael J. Cohen, *Palestine and the Great Powers, 1945–1948* (Princeton: Princeton University Press, 1982), pp. 223–27.

27. With Britain facing increasing pressure from Germany and stubborn resistance from the Arabs in their revolt, Malcolm MacDonald, the new colonial secretary, assembled a conference (known variously as the London Conference or St. James's Conference on Palestine or Round Table Conference) of Palestinian Arabs, Zionists, and representatives of Arab governments, opening on February 7. The conference's wider Arab framework was intended to pressure the Palestin-

ians into accommodating a solution to the problem of Palestine on British terms. See Porath, *In Search of Arab Unity*, chs. 1–2; Nicholas Bethell, *The Palestinian Triangle: The Struggle between the British, the Jews, and the Arabs, 1935–48* (London: Steimatzky, 1979), pp. 47–66.

28. Arif al-Arif, *The Disaster* (Sidon: Al-Maktaba al-Arabiyya, 1956), pp. 42–45 [Arabic]. The League, founded on March 23, 1945, was a political union of the independent Arab states meant to affirm their common historical, linguistic, and cultural heritage. When in March, 1943, the Egyptian prime minister called for a conference to establish the union, the composition of a Palestinian delegation immediately became an issue. See Robert W. Macdonald, *The League of Arab States* (Princeton: Princeton University Press, 1965), pp. 35–37. One of Alami's tasks for the League was to establish Arab information offices abroad. Following the emergence of the United States as a decisive influence on the future of Palestine and its growing involvement in the region, Alami established the Arab Office in Washington, D.C., in 1947. The Office was closed in May, 1948, at the start of the Arab states' military intervention in Palestine. See *Middle East Journal* 2 (1948): 321.

29. Meir Pa'il, "The Problem of Arab Sovereignty in Palestine, 1947–1949: Arab Governments versus the Arabs of Palestine" in D. Carpi, ed., *Zionism*, vol. 3 (Tel-Aviv: Hakibutz Hameuchad for Tel-Aviv University, 1973), pp. 439–89 [Hebrew].

30. Benny Morris, *The Birth of the Palestinian Refugee Problem, 1947–1949* (New York: Cambridge University Press, 1987), p. 14.

31. *The Truth about the Palestinian Affair* (Cairo: Salafiya Press, 1954) pp. 43–47 [Arabic].

32. "The Arab Perspective" in Wm. Roger Louis and Robert W. Stookey, eds., *The End of the Palestine Mandate* (Austin: University of Texas Press, 1986), pp. 112–13.

33. Taqqu, "Arab Labor in Mandatory Palestine," 323.

34. Morris, *The Birth of the Palestinian Refugee Problem*, 17.

35. The phrase is used by J. C. Hurewitz, "Historical Overview" in Louis and Stookey, eds., *The End of the Palestine Mandate*, 145.

36. See Michael J. Cohen, *Palestine to Israel: From Mandate to Independence* (London: Frank Cass, 1988), ch. 12.

37. The formal decision was taken on September 20, 1947.

38. Three of UNSCOP's 11 members (India, Iran, and Yugoslavia) proposed an independent federal state following a three-year preparatory stage under a UN designated authority. There is some evidence that the Mufti would have accepted partition had he been the chief au-

thority in the Arab sector (ironically, King Abdallah of Transjordan made the same stipulation). See Michael J. Cohen, *Palestine and the Great Powers, 1945–1948* (Princeton: Princeton University Press, 1982), pp. 267–68.

39. Robert Schaeffer, *Warpaths: The Politics of Partition* (New York: Hill and Wang, 1990); pp. 153–65.

40. The Jewish state was meant to include about 600,000 Jews and 500,000 Arabs, and the Arab state 20 Jewish settlements. See Baruch Kimmerling, *Zionism and Territory*, 121. For another view, see Walid Khalidi, "Plan Dalet: The Zionist Master Plan for Conquest of Palestine," *Middle East Forum* (November 1961): 22–28.

41. United Nations Palestine Commission, First Special Report to the Security Council, S/676, February, 1948, p. 6.

42. Again with deep reservations, they had also supported a British partition plan put forth in the Peel Commission report in 1937. The British and American Morrison-Grady Plan of 1946 contained a similiar idea—that for provincial or cantonal autonomy.

43. Government of Palestine, *A Survey of Palestine*, pp. 59–61. See also Cohen, *Palestine and the Great Powers*, 307.

44. Cohen, *Palestine and the Great Powers*, 304.

45. Cited in Morris, *The Birth of the Palestinian Refugee Problem*, 45–46.

46. Ibid., 41.

47. One source's estimate of 40,000 emigrants during the Arab Revolt, while a mere 5 percent of the same author's figure for refugees created in 1948–49, is formidable enough to suggest that psychological barriers were long gone. See Rony E. Gabbay, *A Political Study of the Arab-Jewish Conflict: The Arab Refugee Problem* (Geneva: Droz, 1959), p. 66.

48. Shlaim, *Collusion Across the Jordan*, 89ff.

49. Cohen, *Palestine and the Great Powers*, p. 306.

50. Sayigh, *Palestinians: From Peasants to Revolutionaries*, 77; al-Arif, *The Disaster*, 42.

51. Fauzi al-Qawuqji, "Memoirs, 1948: Part I," *Journal of Palestine Studies* 1 (1972): 48.

52. Cited in Cohen, *Palestine and the Great Powers*, 311.

53. Ibid., 344.

54. See Morris, *The Birth of the Palestinian Refugee Problem*, 297–98; Gabbay, *A Political Study of the Arab-Jewish Conflict*, 167, 175; Janet L. Abu-Lughod, "Demographic Transformation of Palestine" in Ibrahim Abu-Lughod, ed. *The Transformation of Palestine* (Evanston: Northwestern University Press, 1971), pp. 139–64; Gilbar, *Trends in the Demographic Development of the Palestinians*, 3–12.

55. The lower figure is for the period through mid-March and was culled from the sources by Steven Glazer, "The Palestinian Exodus in 1948," *Journal of Palestine Studies* 9 (Summer 1980): 104. The higher figure comes from Morris, *The Birth of the Palestinian Refugee Problem*, 30. Morris, for all his oversimplifications of Palestinian life prior to the war, has done a masterful job of collecting the scattered evidence about the exodus. Unless otherwise noted, the numbers and composition of refugees presented here will come from his book.

56. Nur-eldeen Masalha, "On Recent Hebrew and Israeli Sources for the Palestinian Exodus, 1947–49," *Journal of Palestine Studies* 18 (1988): 124, argues that "the objective [of the Jewish forces] was to shock, frighten, and throw the [Arab] communities off balance, forcing Arab neighborhoods and villages to evacuate."

57. Morris, *The Birth of the Palestinian Refugee Problem*, 62.

58. Ibid., 64. See also *The Conquest of the Arab and the Mixed Cities During the War of Independence* (Ramat Efal: Israel Galilee Center for the Study of the Jewish Defence Power—the Hagana, 1989 [mimeo]), pp. 9–12 [Hebrew].

59. Ibid., 63.

60. Many members of the Liberation Army were drawn from the margins of their own societies and included not only soldiers of fortune, but criminals and other deviant elements. See Muhammad Nimr al-Khatib, *As a Result of the Catastrophe* (Damascus, 1949) [Arabic].

61. Morris, *The Birth of the Palestinian Refugee Problem*, 73–95.

62. Sharif Kanani and Nihad Zitawi, *Dayr Yasin*, Monograph No. 4, Palestinian Destroyed Villages series, second edition (Bir Zeit: Center of Documentation and Research, Bir Zeit University, 1987), p. 6 [Arabic].

63. Israel's official Israel Defense Forces *History of the Independence War* (Tel-Aviv: Maarachot, IDF Publishing House, 1959), p. 117 [Hebrew], with a preface by David Ben-Gurion, makes this point.

64. Menachem Begin, *The Revolt* (New York: Henry Schuman, 1951), p. 155, argues that "what was invented about Deir Yassin helped in fact carve the way of Jewish victories on the battlefield."

65. Yehoshafat Harkabi, *Arab Attitudes Toward Israel* (New York: Hart, 1972), pp. 113–70, for an account of hostility and the concept of the enemy.

66. Khalidi, "Plan Dalet: Master Plan for the Conquest of Palestine," 6.

67. See Masalha, "On Recent Hebrew and Israeli Sources for the Palestinian Exodus," 129. Morris, *The Birth of the Palestinian Refugee Problem*, 113, here offers a somewhat different perspective:

If at the start of the war the Yishuv had been reluctantly willing to countenance a Jewish State with a large, peaceful Arab minority, by April the military commanders' thinking had radically changed: the toll on Jewish life and security in the battle of the roads and the dire prospect of the invasion of Palestine by Arab armies had left the Haganah with very narrow margins of safety. The Yishuv could not leave pockets of actively or potentially hostile Arabs or ready-made bases for them behind its geographically unnatural front lines.

68. "The Fall of a Village," *Journal of Palestine Studies* 1 (1972): 108–21.
69. Ibid., 113.
70. Nafez Abdallah Nazzal, "The Zionist Occupation of Western Galilee, 1948," *Journal of Palestine Studies* 3 (1974): 72.
71. Ibid., 76.
72. Morris, *The Birth of the Palestinian Refugee Problem,* 155.
73. The leading proponent of the thesis that Israel and Jordan actively conspired is Shlaim, *Collusion across the Jordan.* See also Dan Schueftan, *A Jordanian Option: The "Yishuv" and the State of Israel vis-a-vis the Hashemite Regime and the Palestinian National Movement* (Tel-Aviv: Yad Tabenkin and Hakibbutz Hameuchad, 1986) [Hebrew], pp. 75–99, which argues that there was de facto cooperation. For a Palestinian critique of the Jordanian role, see Anis Sayigh, *The Hashemites and the Palestinian Question* (Beirut: al-Muharir adn Asriya Library, 1966) [Arabic].

6. Odd Man Out: Arabs in Israel

1. While we prefer the term "Arab citizens," because it is more inclusive than other terms used in the literature, we do employ other terms, including Israeli-Arabs and Palestinian-Israelis. Any term is likely to be problematic in one context or another. Our intention in using the term "Arab citizens of Israel" is in no way to remove them from the general Palestinian people. Rather our intention in using the phrase—and in the overall argument of this chapter—is to emphasize dialectically the complexity of their identity and their special position in the Jewish state. We also have no intention of removing and setting apart ethnic groups within the Palestinian collectivity such as the Druze or the Circassians, who define themselves as Palestinians, but do not necessarily see themselves as Arabs. Most Palestinian and radical Jewish researchers and writers prefer to call this population "Palestinian citizens of Israel," most likely for ideological reasons. See for example,

Dan Rabinowitz and Khawla Abu Bakr, *The Stand Tall Generation: The Palestinian Citizens of Israel Today* (Jerusalem: Keter, 2000), p. 4 [Hebrew].

2. To the Christian group can be added about 300,000 non-Arab Christians—most from among the latest arrivals from the former Soviet Union.

3. All descriptions, analyses, and statistics are still in dispute. The lower estimate is given by C. Kamen, "After the Disaster: The Arabs in the State of Israel, 1948–1950," *Notebooks on Research and Critique* 10 (1984): 18–20 [Hebrew]. The higher estimate is based on UNRWA data and has been adopted by Ian Lustick, *Arabs in the Jewish State: Israel's Control of a National Minority* (Austin: University of Texas Press, 1980), p. 51. The same figures are used by Sammy Smooha, *The Orientation and the Politicization of the Arab Minority in Israel* (Haifa: The Jewish-Arab Center, Institute of Middle East Studies, 1984), p. 79.

4. Hillel Cohen, *Present Absents: Palestinian Refugees of 1948 in Israel* (Jerusalem: The Research Center of Arab Society in Israel and Van Leer Institute, 2000), pp. 3–4 [Hebrew].

5. At the end of the fighting of the 1948 war, fewer than 100,000 Arabs remained in the territories under Israeli control. Their numbers grew to 150,000 as a result of the cease-fire with Jordan and the success of a few to reinfiltrate. See George Kossaifi, "Demographic Characteristics of the Arab Palestinian People," in Khalil Nakleh and Elia Zureik, eds., *The Sociology of the Palestinians,* (London: Croom Helm, 1980), p. 25. On refugee numbers, see United Nations, *Report of the Economic Survey Mission of the Middle East* (New York: United Nations, 1949), p. 22. Laurie A. Brand, *Palestinians in the Arab World: Institution Building and the Search for a State* (New York: Columbia University Press, 1988), p. 150. Brand estimates that there were 900,000 Palestinians in Jordan in 1949, including 70,000 who had already settled on the East Bank. Gad G. Gilbar, *Trends in the Demographic Development of the Palestinians,* mimeo [Hebrew]. Gilbar puts the number on the West Bank at 670,000. An estimate based on the 1950 Jordanian census cites 742,000 Palestinians on the West Bank and 184,700 on the East Bank, demonstrating an already apparent tendency of West Bank Palestinians to migrate east.

6. In the area that came under supervision of the Israeli state, there had been about 900,000 Arabs and 600,000 Jews. The number of Jews doubled within three years. Baruch Kimmerling, *Zionism and Territory: The Socioterritorial Dimension of Zionist Politics* (Berkeley: University of California, Institute of International Studies, 1983).

7. Documentation is cited in Charles S. Kamen, "After the Catastrophe I: The Arabs in Israel, 1948–51," *Middle East Studies* 23 (1987): 453–95.

8. Baruch Kimmerling, "Sovereignty, Ownership and Presence in the Jewish-Arab Territorial Conflict: The Case of Bir'm and Ikrit," *Comparative Political Studies* 10 (1977): 155–76.

9. Academic books in Israel were also written in this manner. For example, Jacob M. Landau, *Arabs in Israel: A Political Study* (London: Oxford University Press, 1969).

10. The Histadrut was one of the most powerful political and economic organizations in the pre-state Jewish community as well in the state period till the 1980s. The Histadrut was one of the major ruling institutions of the Zionist-Socialist camp. See Michael Shalev, "Jewish Organized Labor and the Palestinians: A Study of State/Society Relations in Israel," in B. Kimmerling, ed., *The Israeli State and Society: Boundaries and Frontiers* (Albany: State University of New York Press, 1989), 93–133.

11. Henry Rosenfeld, "Men and Women in Arab Peasant to Proletariat Transformation," in Stanley Diamond, ed., *Theory and Practice: Essays Presented to Gene Weltfish* (New York: Mouton, 1989), p. 196.

12. I. Arnon Raviv, *From Fellah to Farmer: A Study on Change in Arab Villages* (Rehovot: Settlement Study Center, Agricultural Research Organization, and Bet-Dagan: The Volcani Center, Publication on Problems of Regional Development, 31. 1980).

13. Sami F. Geraisy, *Arab Village Youth in Jewish Urban Centers* (Ann Arbor: University Microfilms, 1971), p. 82.

14. By 1963, there were more Arabs working in construction than in agriculture. See State of Israel, *Workforce Survey, 1963* (Jerusalem: Central Bureau of Statistics, 1964), 52–53 [Hebrew], the state gave high priority to these patterns, which were part of the nation-building process. It heavily subsidized rural settlements of new immigrants and protected them from competition by cheap Arab labor and agriculture. Baruch Kimmerling, *Zionism and Economy* (Cambridge: Schenkman, 1983). For the structure of Arab labor and its development in the first decade of Israel's existence, see Yoram Ben-Porath, *The Arab Labor Force in Israel* (Jerusalem: Falk Institute for Economic Research, 1966) [Hebrew].

15. See Edna Bonacich, "The Past, Present, and Future of Split Labor Market Theory," *Research in Race and Ethnic Relations* 1 (1979): 17–64. See also Shlomo Swirski and Deborah Bernstein, "The Rapid Economic Development of Israel and the Emergence of the Ethnic Division of Labor," *British Journal of Sociology* 33 (1982): 64–85.

16. Shalev, "Jewish Organized Labor and the Palestinians: A Study of State/Society Relations in Israel," pp. 93–134. Similar phenomena can be detected during the British colonial period. See Deborah Bernstein, *Constructing Boundaries: Jewish and Arab Workers in Mandatory Palestine* (Albany: State University of New York Press, 2000). Also Zachary Lockman, *Comrades and Enemies: Arab and Jewish Workers in Palestine, 1906–1948* (Berkeley: University of California Press, 1996).

17. Shalev, "Jewish Organized Labor."

18. Druze and Circassians are legally obligated to participate in the draft. Bedouin and Christians may volunteer for military service. A law exempting or excluding Muslims from military service has never been legislated, but because draft notices are individual and the army service of every individual is contingent upon agreement of the Minister of Defense, draft notices are customarily not sent to Muslim Arabs. See D. Horowitz and B. Kimmerling, "Some Social Implications of Military Service and Reserves System in Israel," *Archieves Europeenes de Sociologies* 15 (1974): 262–76.

19. Yehoshua Palmon, the first Advisor on Arab Affairs to the Israeli Prime Minister, cited in Lustick, *Arabs in the Jewish State*, p. 48.

20. Abner Cohen, *Arab Border Villages: A Study of Continuity and Change in Social Organization* (Manchester: Manchester University Press, 1965), p. 118; Subhi Abu Ghosh, *The Politics of an Arab Village in Israel* (Princeton: Unpublished Ph.D. dissertation, 1965), p. 33.

21. On the concept of internal colonization, see Michael Hechter, *Internal Development, British National Colonialism: The Celtic Fringe in 1536–1966* (Berkeley: University of California Press, 1975).

22. Fouzi El-Asmar, *To Be an Arab in Israel* (London: Frances Pinter, 1975), p. 23.

23. Benny Morris, *Israel's Border Wars, 1949–1956: Arab Infiltration, Israeli Retaliation and the Countdown of the Suez War* (Oxford: Clarendon Press, 1993).

24. Sami Khalil Mar'i, *Arab Education in Israel* (Syracuse: Syracuse University Press, 1978), p. xii. Majid Al-Haj, *Education, Empowerment and Control: The Case of the Arabs in Israel* (Albany: State University of New York Press, 1995).

25. Ibrahim Makkawi, "Role Conflict and the Dilemma of Palestinian Teachers in Israel," *Comparative Education*, 38 (2002): pp. 39–52.

26. Quoted in Makkawi, "Role Conflict and the Dilemma of Palestinian Teachers in Israel," p. 44.

27. Shlomo Swirski and Alon Etkin, *Eligibility for Baccalaureate Certificates*

by Localities, 1999–2000 (Tel Aviv: Adva Center for Information on Equality and Social Justice, 2001) [Hebrew].

28. Adriana Kemp, "'Dangerous Populations:' State Territoriality and the Constitution of National Minorities," in Joel S. Migdal, ed., *Boundaries and Belonging: State, Society, and the Formation of Identity* (New York: Cambridge University Press, forthcoming).

29. Aziz Haidar, "The Different Levels of Palestinian Ethnicity," in M. S. Esman and I. Rabinovich, eds., *Ethnicity, Pluralism and the State in the Middle East* (Ithaca: Cornell University Press, 1988), p. 108.

30. Baruch Kimmerling, *The Invention and Decline of Israeliness: State, Society and the Military* (Los Angeles: University of California Press, 2001).

31. See Baruch Kimmerling, "Ideology, Sociology and Nation Building: The Palestinians and Their Meaning in Israeli Sociology," *American Sociological Review* 57 (1992): 446–60. Today Arab researchers speak about "double marginality": their marginalization in Israeli society and within the general Palestinian collectivity.

32. Baruch Kimmerling, "Between Celebration of Independence and Commemoration of al-Nakba: The Controversy over the Roots of the Israeli State," *MESA Bulletin,* 32 (Summer 1998): 3–7.

33. The Druze can be seen as Arabs even though their ethnic origin is unclear; they can also be seen as a separate unit that infused into the margins of Arabness. See Kais M. Firro, *A History of the Druzes* (Leiden: E. J. Brill, 1992).

34. Kais M. Firro, *The Druzes in the Jewish State: A Brief History* (Leiden: E. J. Brill, 1999).

35. Firro, *The Druzes in the Jewish State.*

36. A recently disclosed document indicates that David Ben-Gurion avoided the deportation of the population of largely Christian-Arab Nazareth after its conquest in 1948, because of the city's meaning to the Christian world. Ben-Gurion's command went contrary to the intention of Northern Front Commander Moshe Carmel.

37. Indeed many of the most evident leaders of the Palestinian national movement have been Christians, beginning with George Antonius and Khalil Sakhakani (the Jerusalemite intellectual and pedagogue who wrote tens of textbooks used throughout the Arab states) and ending with George Habash, the leader of the Popular Front for the Liberation of Palestine. In the 1950s, the Greek Catholic archbishop Maximus Khakim was recognized by all Arabs in Israel for his charismatic speeches in the struggle against land confiscation and injustices of the military government. Today, another Christian, the doctor of philosophy Azmi Bishara—founder of the Al-Tajamo'a movement

and a member of Knesset—is known for his expressions of unmistakably nationalist and pan-Arab sentiments. To these should be added the cultural critic Edward Said.

38. Dan Rabinowitz, *Overlooking Nazareth: The Ethnography of Exclusion in a Mixed Town in Galilee* (New York: Cambridge University Press, 1996).

39. Daphna Zimhoni, "The Christians in Israel: Between Religion and Politics," in Elie Rechkes, ed., *Arabs in Israeli Politics: Identity Dilemmas* (Tel Aviv: Dayan Center, 1998), pp. 63–72 [Hebrew].

40. As'ad Ghanem, "Margins of a Marginal Society: The Bedouin Uniqueness," in Elie Rekhes, ed., *Arabs in Israeli Politics: Identity Dilemmas* (Tel Aviv: Dayan Center, 1998), pp. 85–90.

41. The international center for guidance and coordination of all communist parties in the world, located in Moscow.

42. See Bernstein, *Constructing Boundaries* and Lockman, *Comrads and Enemies*.

43. Communists in Iraq were even hanged for both their open support of the Partition Plan and their opposition to Iraqi entry into war with Israel.

44. Called Maki until 1965, the Communist party ended up entirely Jewish. It denied the legitimacy of both Zionism and Arab nationalism. After 1965, it was termed Rakah, and began to draw both its rank-and-file and its voters largely from among the Arab community. See Elie Rekhes, "Jews and Arabs in the Israeli Communist Party," in M. S. Esman and I. Rabinovich, eds., *Ethnicity, Pluralism, and the State*, 121–39. Also see Elie Rekhes, *The Arab Minority in Israel: Between Communism and Nationalism* (Tel Aviv: Hakkibutz Hameuchad, 1999) [Hebrew]. On Jews and Arabs in Mapam, see Yael Yishai, "Integration of Arabs in an Israeli Party: The Case of Mapam, 1948–54," in Elie Kedourie and Sylvia G. Haim, eds., *Zionism and Arabism in Palestine and Israel* (London: Frank Cass, 1982), pp. 240–55.

45. Only later in the early 1990s did this end. Arab intellectuals began to perceive this "home" as too stifling, dogmatic, and monolithic. They began to escape from it and go in search of alternate frameworks or of a lack of frameworks at all. This, for example, is how the poet Samih Al-Kassem attacked the Communist party and explained his repudiation of it after thirty years of membership (*Al-Arabi*, December 8 and 12, 1989).

46. As'ad Ghanem, "The Rise and Decline of the Communist Party (Maki): Discussion of Causes," *Studies in Israel's Revival* (Beersheba: Center of Research of Ben Gurion's Legacy), 4 (1994): 549–55.

47. Herut was the right-wing "Revisionist" party, led at the time by

Menachem Begin. Thus, Ben-Gurion's exclusion was not ethnocentric but political.

48. Habibi's most well-known book, in Hebrew translation called *The Pessoptimist*—a mixture of "optimist" and "pessimist"—includes an ironic, well-honed description of Jewish-Arab reality in Israel.

49. The writer and essayist Anton Shammas describes the poetry of Arabs in Israel as "bad," because thematically it has never left the village nor attempted to meet the real and much more complex "new Arab experience" in Israel. See *The Arab Literature in Israel* (Tel Aviv: Shiloach Center for Research of Middle East, 1976), p. 42 [Hebrew].

50. Arab newspapers in Israel today have increased their readerships immensely, but have become more nonpolitical and tabloid, much like the Hebrew press. They still include national and ethnic remarks, but any clear ideological emphasis has disappeared. *Al-Sinara* and *Kul Al-Arab* appear twice weekly, reaching a wide market and competing between themselves. The latter organizes an annual Israeli Arab beauty pageant—a revolutionary act that has come under dispute. *Sawt Al-Haq Al-Hurriyah,* the Islamic movement's weekly paper (of the stream led by Kamal Khatib and Raad Salah) conducts an active campaign against the entire enterprise of *Kul Al-Arab,* particularly its more "superficial" columns such as the family and sexual advice columns, matchmaking and personal ads, personal problems columns, and the like. Another weekly, *Fasal al-Maqal,* owned and operated by al-Tajamo'a under the leadership of Azmi Bishara, tries to integrate a commercial and Arab national ideological approach. In addition, there are many local papers, the most visible of which is *Panorama* (Taibe and the "Triangle" region). In the beginning, this weekly focused on local issues and sports, but slowly became a general and political weekly with a liberal-individualist emphasis. Today *Panorama* competes with *al-Sinara* and *Kul Al-Arab.* In 1997, 20 local unauthorized radio stations sprang up in the Arab community (out of the more than 115 non-licensed such stations broadcasting in Israel).

51. Aziz Haidar, "The Different Levels of Palestinian Ethnicity," in M. S. Esman and I. Rabinovich, eds., *Ethnicity, Pluralism and the State,* 108. A decade later in 1989, using a sample of Palestinian university students in Israel and a multiple-choice questionnaire, Nadim Rouhana found that the question, "How would you define yourself?" was answered by the following selections: 43.5 percent chose Palestinian in Israel, 25.7 percent Palestinian Arab, 10.6 percent Israeli Palestinian, 5.5 percent Palestinian Arab in Israel, 4.5 percent Palestinian, 4.1 percent Arab, 2.7

percent Israeli, 2.1 percent Other, and 1.4 percent Israeli Arab. Nadim N. Rouhana, *Palestinian Citizens in an Ethnic Jewish State* (New Haven: Yale University Press, 1997), p. 122.

52. A cadre of these lawyers later became central figures in the military courts, defending those arrested in the Occupied Territories. See George Emile Bisharat, *Palestinian Lawyers and Israeli Rule: Law and Disorder in the West Bank* (Austin: University of Texas Press, 1989), pp. 92–95. Some of them also created human rights organizations. See Hassan Jabareen, "On the Oppression of Identities in the Name of Civil Equality," *Addallah's Review: Politics, Identity and Law* 1 (1999): 27.

53. Mark Teller, "Arabs in Israel," in Ann Mosely Lesch and Mark Tessler, eds., *Israel, Egypt, and the Palestinians: From Camp David to Intifada* (Bloomington: Indiana University Press, 1989), p. 101.

54. Al-Haj, *Education, Empowerment and Control;* Nadim Rouhana and As'ad Ghanem, "The Democratization of a Traditional Minority in an Ethnic Democracy: The Palestinians in Israel," in E. Kaufman, S. Abed, and R. Rothstein, eds., *Democracy, Peace and the Israeli Palestinian Conflict* (Boulder: Lynne Reinner, 1993), pp. 163–88.

55. The *sumed*, the Palestinians who remained under Israeli rule, later took a similar approach when the Israeli state took control of the West Bank and Gaza Strip in the 1967 war.

56. Al-Haj, *Social Change and Family Processes,* pp. 66–72.

57. Some of the largest sources of employment in Israel, with the exception of government service, are the local authorities and various types of local services. In a report submitted in November 2000, following the October Events, O. Yiftachel, R. Khamaisi, and A. Kedar emphasized that "there are few Arab settlements in which local employment (aside from those employed by the local authorities) surpasses 10 percent, whereas most Arab laborers find employment in the Jewish sector. This is due to the low level of commercial and industrial development, stemming partially from the low level of economic initiative and attraction of external capital, and also from the position of Arab settlements as the lowest priorities on the national agenda, from discrimination in distribution of incentives for development, and from the lack of regional cooperation." See Dan Rabinowitz, As'ad Ghanem, and Oren Yiftachel, eds., *After the Rift: New Directions for Government Policy towards the Arabs in Israel,* An Emergency Report by the Inter-University Research Team, submitted to Mr. Ehud Barak, Prime Minister of Israel, November 2000 [Hebrew].

58. Likud had success with only a few Druze villages and families.

59. Rosenfeld, "Men and Women," 205.

60. One survey showed that by the 1980s as many as 85 percent of Arab households consisted of nuclear families. See Al-Haj, *Social Change and Family Processes,* p. 93. In the 1970s, surveys showed the figure to have been about 55 percent. See Smooha, *Arabs and Jews in Israel I,* 37.

61. This phenomenon would have been more rapid had legal Arab construction been made possible by, for example, the release of agricultural land for construction or allocation of state land for this purpose, not to mention provision of government subsidized housing for Arabs, as was done throughout several decades for Jews.

62. Cohen, *The Present Absents.*

63. Aziz Haidar, *On the Margins: The Arab Population in the Israeli Economy* (London: Hurst, 1995).

64. Henry Rosenfeld, "The Class Situation of the Arab National Minority in Israel," *Comparative Studies in Society and History* 20 (1978): 395.

65. On the nascent shift to wage labor during the earliest years of the state, see Amihoud Israeli, "The Employment Revolution among Non-Jewish Minorities of Israel," *Hamizrah Hehadash* 26 (1976): 232–39 [Hebrew].

66. Raja Khalidi, *The Arab Economy in Israel: The Dynamics of a Region's Development* (New York: Croom Helm, 1988), p. 172.

67. Arnon and Raviv, *From Fellah to Farmer,* pp. 23–25.

68. Haidar, *On the Margins;* Ruth Klinov, "Arabs and Jews in the Israeli Labor Force," *Working Paper No. 214* (Jerusalem: Department of Economics, Hebrew University, 1989).

69. Poverty and alienation are factors in the high rate of violence and crime among the Arab population: 30.7 percent of offenders brought to trial in 1999 were Arabs. The rate of convicted offenders to every 1,000 people is much higher among Arabs (16.9 percent) than among Jews (7.7 percent).

70. Haidar, *On the Margins,* p. 131.

71. Aziz Haidar, *The Emergence of the Arab Bourgeoisie in Israel* (Jerusalem: Arab Thought Forum, 1986), Chapter 1 [Arabic].

72. Nabil Khattab, "Ethnicity and Female Labour Market Participation: A New Look at the Palestinian Enclave in Israel," *Work, Employment and Society,* 16 (March 2002): 93, 98.

73. Khattab, "Ethnicity and Female Labour Market Participation," p. 99.

74. Between the 1980s and 90s, the predicted number of children per Arab woman fell considerably. Among Muslim and Christian woman respectively, the decrease was from 4.5 and 2.3 to 3.4 and 1.9.

75. The rates for Jews were five and one, respectively.

76. Construction on agricultural lands, almost the only lands left in Arab villages, requires authorization to change status of the lands—authorization that is almost never granted for Arabs. Rabinowitz et al., *After the Rift*.

77. The state did not help with the exception of the short period of Rabin's government from 1992 to 1995.

78. In 1995, eight of the eighty unrecognized villages were recognized and began to receive some of the services and infrastructure (water, electricity, telephone, access to road construction, and mother-child clinics) allocated to state citizens. Most residents of these villages are internal refugees who were uprooted from their homes in the 1948 war or Bedouins whom the state wants to install in permanent settlements.

79. Kimmerling, *Zionism and Territory*.

80. See Kimmerling, "Sovereignty, Ownership and Presence."

81. The Arabs counted 49 martyrs as a result of the massacre and its aftermath. A legal suit was filed on forty-three counts of murder. Of the remaining six, four were Kfar Qassem residents for whom the cause of death remained unclear, one died from a stroke the day following the massacre and had been counted among the martyrs by the villagers, and another was an eight-month-old fetus who died in its mother's womb when she was murdered. Ruvik Rosenthal, ed., *Kfar Qassem: Myth and History* (Tel Aviv: Hakibbutz Hameuchad, 2000) [Hebrew].

82. In June 1987, the holiday was renamed Equality Day; in December 1995, it began to be called Peace Day; since 1999 the name has once again returned to its original Land Day. These changes reflect the hopes that Arab citizens put on the possibility of appeasement between the Palestinians and Israelis. They also reflect their changing moods with each political turn.

83. Because the authorities did not permit the group to publish a weekly (or any other periodical), in October 1959, the group published thirteen singular publications (for which they did not need a permit), each under a different title including the word "Al-Ard." The thirteenth time an error was made and the magazine was distributed under the title of a previous issue. The authorities took advantage of the error and forbade publication of the magazine in any form.

84. Even the appeal itself to participate in elections was a fundamental change and served as a sort of recognition of the Israeli state. Previously, the party had preached nonparticipation in the Israeli political game. Later, the Islamic movement would do the same.

85. See Sabri Jiryis, *The Arabs in Israel* (New York: Monthly Review Press,

1976). Jiryis was himself a graduate of the Faculty of Law at the Hebrew University and a visible member of Al-Ard. In 1976, he published this book in Hebrew and became the first Arab to write such an account of discrimination and persecution of Arabs in Israel. He described military government threats and the different means for confiscating land and property from internal and external refugees. The authorities tried to prevent the books' distribution, especially outside of Israel. In addition to Jiryis, other visible personalities in Al-Ard were the ideologue Mansur Qardosh, the Haifa teacher Habib Nawfal Qahwaji, the Acre wholesaler Mahmud Suruji, and the charismatic teacher from Taibe Salah Baransi.

86. It was mostly due to Al-Ard's position that some Arabs boycotted Israeli elections. Participation in elections was assumed to be a sort of collaboration with the oppressive regime.

87. Control over local municipalities was the only autonomous source of power for Israeli Arabs and the communist party. Yet the party failed to manage the municipalities efficiently. Thus not only did the municipalities suffer discrimination from the Israeli authorities, but also had to neglect local problems (such as unpopular tax collection) in order to deal with "high politics." See Majid Al-Haj and Henry Rosenfeld, *Arab Local Government in Israel* (Boulder: Westview, 1990), pp. 66–68.

88. Abna al-Balad appeared under different names in the various municipalities. Thus, for example, they were called Al-Nahada in Taibe and Al-Fajar in Arara. In the universities, they adopted the name the Progressive National Movement.

89. Jacob Landau, *The Arab Minority in Israel, 1960–1991: Political Aspects* (Oxford: Clarendon Press, 1993).

90. This body, unlike the general Student Union, is not recognized by the universities. The Arab student committees served more as a source of mutual support and a public Arab arena for struggles among the various political streams.

91. In the 1990s, Abna al-Balad joined other groups to form the Front for National Action.

92. Azmi Bishara, the founder of Al-Tajamo'a, the Democratic National Assembly and a Hadash member of Knesset, has stressed a very nationalistic rhetoric. He has gone so far as to abandon claims for equality, in favor of claims for "cultural autonomy" for Arabs in Israel—a claim perceived as a separatist call.

93. Adoption of the formula was virtual recognition by at least some of

the Arabs in Israel of the Israeli state as "the state of the Jewish people." It would have been difficult to claim the existence of an "Israeli people" while claiming minority status within it and would have meant at least temporary discarding the binational approach.

94. Majid Al-Haj, "The Impact of the Intifada on the Arabs in Israel: The Case of Double Periphery," in A. Cohen and G. Wolsfeld, eds., *Framing the Intifada: Media and People* (New Jersey: Albex Publishing Corporation, 1993), pp. 67–79. According to Israeli officials, sabotage committed by Arabs in Israel increased from 69 incidents in 1987 to 238 in 1988, but then decreased to 187 the following year. Of these 187 incidents, 91 were acts of arson; 28, Molotov cocktails; 17, explosives; 8, stabbings; 8, violent assaults; 6, shootings; and 3, hand grenade attacks. More frequent were "subversive nationalistic incidents." In 1989, these included 119 stone throwings, 104 anti-Israeli or pro-PLO graffiti, 92 hoisting of Palestinian flags, 15 road blocks, 14 defamations of state emblems, 4 layings of false explosive, and more (Al-Haj, "The Impact of the Intifada on the Arabs in Israel," pp. 19–20). Since October 2000 the number of Israeli Arabs who have collaborated with Palestinian guerrilla groups to different degrees and in different manners has increased considerably, but reliable data are not available. As'ad Ghanem and Sara Osetzki-Lasar, *Green Line, Red Lines and the Israeli Arabs Facing the Intifada* (Givat Haviva: Institute of Arab Studies, 1990) [Hebrew].

95. The committee sent a reminder to Prime Minister Yitzhak Rabin demanding recognition for Israeli Arabs as a national minority and part of the Palestinian people, and not merely a collection of religious and ethnic groups. The demand for the return of confiscated land was also raised (Al-Haj, 1988).

96. At this point, the committee was under the charismatic leadership of the mayor of Shefaram, Ibrahim Nimir Hussein (Abu Hatem). Abu Hatem was dislodged from his position as mayor in the local elections of 1998 and, ever since, the power of the committee has constantly declined.

97. In 1992 and 1993, Darawshe demanded full participation in the government coalition and not just a part in the blocking vote that made the Labor-Meretz government possible (*Kul Al-Arab*, October 22, 1993). The demand was not answered, because the government was already stigmatized enough in the eyes of many Jewish citizens for its dependency on "Arab votes." In any case, ADP did not have the realistic option of not supporting a government that had begun talks with the

PLO and initiated the "peace process." In addition, during this period, the Arab municipal sector and educational system were enjoying an unprecedented influx of resources. Nonetheless, this influx in no way brought about equality in resource allocation.

98. Al-Tajamo'a is itself actually a federation of different groups, including remnants of Muhammad Miiari's Progressives and various local groups such as Al-Nasser from Umm Al-Fahm, Al-Nahadha from Taibe, the Socialist party from Magar, the Sons of Tira, and others.

99. A more radical stream of the Islamic movement exists under the leadership of Sheikh Raad Salah, past mayor of Umm Al-Fahm, and Sheikh Kamal Khatib (from Kfar Kana). The members of this stream object to overintegration in the Jewish state (which they believe goes against the "spirit of Islam") and to participation in elections. Even this stream, however, does not preach the use of violent methods.

100. The Islamic movement won victories in five other local councils (Kfar Qassem, Kabul, Juljuliyah, Kfar Bara, and the Negev Bedouin town of Rahat). Its total representation in local councils hovers around 50 seats.

101. For historical reasons, Israel does not have a constitution. In 1948, however, it was decided that the constitution would be put together piece by piece over time through the legislation of Basic Laws.

102. Alexander Kedar, "The Time of Majority, Time of Minority: Land, Nationality and Statutes of Limitations in Israel," *Iyunei Mishpat* [Legal Studies] 21 (1998): 665–745 [Hebrew]. Baruch Kimmerling, "Jurisdiction in an Immigrant-Settler Society: The Jewish and Democratic State," *Comparative Political Studies* 2002, 35, 10:72–84.

103. At the time the final version of this chapter was written in July 2002, the plot of land requested was still not in the Qa'adans' possession nor had the Court's ruling been implemented.

104. On October 9–10: Riots between Jews and Arabs in Jaffa. Jews tried to burn down the Hassan Beck Mosque.

105. Meretz remained outside the coalition and continued to support a two-state solution for peace. Yet it took a moderate oppositional stance for fear of falling outside what was considered the national "consensus." Thus, for example, Meretz refused to support conscientious objectors, when the state adopted a policy of reoccupation of territories under PA control and methodical destruction of PA institutions and symbols.

106. Recently, attempts similar to those made in the past have sought to revoke social security allocations for multiple-child families whose household heads are not "army veterans." Efforts have also been made to limit parliamentary immunity of Arab Knesset members, especially of Azmi Bishara and Ahmed Tibi, the sole representative of the Arab Revival Movement. Bishara has close and open ties with the Syrian elite, and Tibi is thought to be close to the PA elite. The Knesset has retracted Tibi's parliamentary immunity and forbidden him from visiting the Palestinian territories.

107. Quoted in *The New York Times*, August 27, 2002, p. A9.

108. As'ad Ghanem, "The Palestinians in Israel: Political Orientation and Aspirations," *International Journal of Intercultural Relations* 26 (2002): 137.

109. Ghanem, "The Palestinians in Israel," p. 140.

110. Ghanem, "The Palestinians in Israel," p. 139.

111. Quoted in Dan Rabinowitz, "The Palestinian Citizens of Israel, the Concept of Trapped Minority and the Discourse of Transnationalism in Anthropology," *Ethnic and Racial Studies* 24 (January 2001): 66.

112. Ghanem, "The Palestinians in Israel," p. 147.

113. Rabinowitz, "The Palestinian Citizens of Israel," p. 73.

114. Rabinowitz and Abu Bakr, *The Stand Tall Generation*.

115. Nadim Rouhana, "The Bi-National Option," pp. 201–42; As'ad Ghanem, "A Palestinian-Israeli Bi-national State within the Territory of Historical Palestine," 271–99, both in Ozacky-Lazar, A. Ghanem, and I. Pappe, eds., *Seven Roads: Theoretical Options for the Status of the Arabs in Israel* (Givat Haviva: The Peace Research Institute, 1999) [Hebrew].

116. Sammy Smooha, "The Status Quo Option: Israel as an Ethnic Democracy," in Ozacky-Lazar et al., *Seven Roads*, 23–77.

7. Dispersal, 1948–1967

1. Turki, *The Disinherited*, 29.

2. See Elisha Efrat, "Changes in the Settlement Pattern of Judea and Samaria during Jordanian Rule," in Kedourie and Haim, eds., *Palestine and Israel in the 19th and 20th Centuries*, 207; Avi Plascov, "The Palestinians of Jordan's Border" in Owen, ed., *Studies in the Economic and Social History of Palestine*, 209. Palestinians did fruitlessly demand that the Jordanians revive and restore Jerusalem and make it the country's sec-

ond capital. The Jordanians systematically moved its administrative functions to Amman. Arab Jerusalem faced some economic revival in the 1960s, connected mostly with the tourist trade.

3. See Pamela Ann Smith, "The Palestinian Diaspora, 1948–1985," *Journal of Palestine Studies* 15 (1986): 96–98.

4. The *Palestinian Statistical Abstract, 1980* (Damascus: PLO Central Bureau of Statistics, 1981), puts the figure at nearly 4.5 million Palestinians (up from 1.3 million in 1947), of whom 58.8 percent lived outside Palestine.

5. See Smith, "The Palestinian Diaspora," 90–108; Tibawi, "Visions of the Return," 507–26; Rubinstein, *The Fig Tree Embrace*, 23–26.

6. Antoine Mansour, "The West Bank Economy: 1948–1984" in T. Abed, ed., *The Palestinian Economy*, p. 71, estimates the increase in population of the West Bank in 1948–49 at 59.4 percent, or a gain of 276,500. He also estimates the yearly rate of population growth from 1952 to 1967 at 0.54 percent.

7. A smaller percentage actually started out in the camps, but some drifted there when they found no other means of sustenance.

8. The rural population growth was over 100 percent for the two-decade period (more than twice the rate for the urban areas). See Efrat, "Changes in the Settlement Pattern of Judea and Samaria," in Kedourie and Haim, eds., *Palestine and Israel in the 19th and 20th Centuries*, 197ff.

9. See Elia T. Zureik, "Reflections on Twentieth-Century Palestinian Class Structure," in Nakleh and Zureik, eds., *The Sociology of the Palestinians*, 47–63. In a study of Lebanese refugees published in 1977, it was found that 68 percent of the respondents' grandfathers had worked in agriculture while only 17 percent of the sample did so now, about three-quarters working in the service sector. The study was conducted by Samir Ayoub and is quoted in Sayigh, *Palestinians: From Peasants to Revolutionaries*, 121.

10. For the general historical, sociopolitical, and economic development of Transjordan, see Manib al-Madi and Saliman Musa, *The History of Jordan in the Twentieth Century* (Amman: 1959) [Arabic]; Aqil Abidi Hyder Hasan, *Jordan: A Political Study, 1948–1957* (London: Asia Publishing House, 1965); A. Konikoff, *Transjordan: An Economic Survey* (Jerusalem: Economic Research Institute, the Jewish Agency for Palestine, 1946); George Harris, *Jordan—Its People, Its Society, Its Culture* (New Haven: Human Relations Area Files, 1958); Frederick Gerard Peak, *A History of Jordan and Its Tribes* (Coral Gables: University of Miami Press, 1958); Benjamin Swadran, *Jordan: A State of Tension* (New York: Council

for Middle Eastern Affairs Press, 1959); Paul A. Jureidini and R. D. McLaurin, *Jordan: The Impact of Social Change on the Role of the Tribes* (New York: Praeger, 1984). Also see Anis Saigh, *The Hashemites and the Palestine Question)* (Beirut, 1966) [Arabic]; Yosef Nevo, *Abdullah and the Palestinian Arabs* (Tel-Aviv: Shiloach Institute, Tel-Aviv University, 1975), pp. 37–119 [Hebrew]. For Abdallah's own account, see *Mudhakkirat al-Malik Bin al-Husayn* (Jerusalem, 1946) [Arabic]; *My Memoirs Completed* (Washington: American Council of Learned Societies, 1954) [English].

11. See Shaul Mishal, *West Bank/East Bank: The Palestinians in Jordan, 1949–1967* (New Haven: Yale University Press, 1978), pp. 1–12; Avi Plascov, *The Palestinian Refugees in Jordan, 1948–1957* (London: Frank Cass, 1981), pp. 16–19; Brand, *Palestinians in the Arab World,* 161–62.

12. For this view, see Naseer H. Aruri, *Jordan: A Study in Political Development* (The Hague: Martinus Nijhoff, 1972). An opposing view is of Jordan as a polity dominated by its Bedouin minority, seeking control over (but not cultural integration with) other groups. See, for example, Clinton Bailey, *Jordan's Palestinian Challenge, 1948–1983: A Political History* (Boulder: Westview Press, 1984), pp. 3–4; and Arthur R. Day, *East Bank/West Bank: Jordan and Prospects for Peace* (New York: Council on Foreign Relations, 1986), pp. 62–67.

13. Cited in Roger N. Baldwin, "The Palestine Refugees," *Current History* (November 1957): 296.

14. There was no shortage of resettlement schemes tabled by various parties. See, for example, S. G. Thicknesse, *Arab Refugees: A Survey of Resettlement Possibilities* (London: Royal Institue of International Affairs, 1949), pp. 17–19, 41–44.

15. Brand, *Palestinians in the Arab World,* 165.

16. Mishal, *West Bank/East Bank,* 9.

17. Aruri, *Jordan,* 35–36.

18. A. K. Abu-Hilal and I. Othman, "Jordan" in C. A. O. Van Nieuwenhuijze, ed., *Commoners, Climbers and Notables: A Sampler of Studies on Social Ranking in the Middle East,* in *Social, Economic and Political Studies of the Middle East,* vol. 12 (Leiden: E. J. Brill, 1977), p. 140.

19. The urban Palestinian population was around 37 percent vs. 23 percent for Transjordanians. See Amnon Kartin, *Changes in Settlement Patterns in Transjordan on the Background of the Palestinian Migration, 1948–1967* (unpublished M.A. thesis, Tel-Aviv University, 1987), pp. 58–59 [Hebrew].

20. Mishal, *West Bank/East Bank,* 40–46. Kartin indicates that 34 percent of Palestinian youngsters through age 15 were students in different

schools, against 18 percent in Transjordan. In Arab Palestine there had been a physician for each 3,333 persons, in Transjordan, for each 10,000. One daily newspaper was published in the kingdom in 1944, against 3 dailies, 10 weeklies and 5 quarterlies in Arab Palestine. The employment structure of the kingdom was fairly homogeneous, as the vast majority were fellaheen or nomads. As noted in chapters 2 and 3, the Palestinian economic structure was changing rapidly.

21. For a description of the biggest refugee camp on the West Bank, Jelazun camp (near Ramallah), see Shimon Shamir, "West Bank Refugees—Between Camp and Society," in Migdal, ed., *Palestinian Society and Politics,* 146–68; see also Yoram Ben-Porath, Emmanuel Marx, and Shimon Shamir, *A Refugee Camp in the West Bank: An Interim Report,* Jerusalem, April 1968 [Hebrew, mimeo].

22. For some basic statistical data and socio-economic indicators see Hashemite Kingdom of Jordan, First *Census of Population and Housing,* vol. 3 (Amman: Department of Statistics, 1961); International Bank for Reconstruction and Development, Economic Mission to Jordan, *The Economic Development of Jordan* (Baltimore: The Johns Hopkins University Press, 1957); A. Thavirajah, S. Akel and H. M. Abugarah, "Mid-Decade Demographic Parameters of Jordan and Population Growth," in *Demographic Measures and Population Growth in Arab Countries* (Cairo: Cairo Demographic Center, 1970). See also R. Patai, ed., *The Hashemite Kingdom of Jordan* (New Haven: Yale University Press, 1957), pp. 45–77; Kartin, *Changes in Settlement Patterns in Transjordan,* 56–57. For political reasons, Jordan's official statistics do not use Palestinian nationality in its census and demographic surveys. Aruri, *Jordan,* 45–48, estimates that the Palestinians constitute about two-thirds of East-Jordan. See also A. Sinai and Alien Pollack, eds., *The Hashemite Kingdom of Jordan and the West Bank—A Handbook* (New York: American Academic Association for Peace in Middle East, 1977), p. 121. The same estimate is made in "Divorce First, Then Cohabitation," *The Economist,* June 1, 1974.

23. There were 53 camps total in Lebanon, Gaza, Syria, and Jordan.

24. Sarah Graham-Brown, "Agriculture and Labour Transformation in Palestine" in Glavanis and Glavanis, eds., *The Rural Middle East,* 57.

25. This project diverted water by gravity flow from the Yarmouk River into a 44-mile canal in the Jordan Valley running parallel to the east side of the Jordan River. It added about 30,000 acres of irrigated land, as well as labor-intensive fruit and vegetable cultivation, mostly by the much more skilled Palestinian fellaheen. Michael P. Mazur, *Economic*

Growth and Development in Jordan (Boulder: Westview Press, 1979), pp. 145–47.

26. Mansour, "The West Bank Economy," 74.

27. The Clapp Commission (formally, the United Nations Economic Survey Mission) recommended the establishment of a UN organization to handle refugee assistance after it calculated that over 650,000 were in need of help. Resolution 302 of the General Assembly on December 8, 1949, created the United Nations Relief and Works Agency for Palestine Refugees in the Near East. UNRWA began operations on May 1, 1950. It was preceded briefly by the United Nations Relief for Palestine Refugees (UNRPR).

28. UNRWA became one of the major sources of indirect income and capital influx for all Jordan—approximately half of total external transfers in the early 1950s. See Issa Naman Fakhoury, *An Analytical Study of Jordan's Balance of Payments, 1950–1968* (Amman: Central Bank of Jordan, 1974), p. 75. In 1951, UNRWA helped the Jordanian government establish the Jordanian Development Bank. The Jordanian economy was also eventually bolstered by the private capital of wealthy Palestinians—Arab banks had released about £2.5 million of it at the end of 1955, with about 60 percent going to Jordan. See Palestine Arab Delegation, *Report of the United Nations Conciliation Commission for Palestine, 1948–1961* (New York, n.d.), p. 64. These deposits improved the situation of the old wealthy Palestinian families and reinforced class differences.

29. Aruri, *Jordan*, 48.

30. Plascov, *The Palestinian Refugees in Jordan*, 16–26.

31. Ibid., 23.

32. Plascov, "The Palestinians of Jordan's Border," 212.

33. Rosemary Sayigh, "The Palestinian Identity Among Camp Residents," *Journal of Palestine Studies* 6 (1977): 3–22.

34. The Mufti saw pan-Arabism as a threat to his own waning leadership. He broke with Nasser and moved from Cairo to Beirut in 1959, living there until his death 15 years later. See Mattar, *The Mufti of Jerusalem*, 113–14.

35. A Palestinian identified as Yasser, cited in Paul Cossali and Clive Robson, *Stateless in Gaza* (New Jersey: Zed Books, 1986), pp. 21–22.

36. Musa Alami, "The Lesson of Palestine," *The Middle East Journal* 3 (1949): 373–405.

37. *Gumhuriyyah*, April 14, 1963. Cited in Bailey, *Jordan's Palestinian Challenge*, 16.

38. Ibid., 13. Other crises were the assassination of the king in 1951 and of the prime minister in 1960.

39. See Amnon Cohen, *Political Parties in the West Bank Under the Jordanian Regime, 1949–1967* (Ithaca: Cornell University Press, 1982), pp. 15–26, 239–51.

40. Malcolm Kerr, *The Arab Cold War—1958–1964: A Study of Ideology in Politics* (New York: Oxford University Press, 1965), pp. 59–101.

41. Cohen, *Political Parties in the West Bank*, 26.

42. Muhammad Ali Khulusi, *Economic Growth in the Palestinian Gaza Strip, 1948–1961* (Cairo: United Commercial Press, 1967), pp. 42–43 [Arabic].

43. Ziad Abu-Amr, "The Gaza Economy: 1948–1984" in Abed, ed., *The Palestinian Economy*, 101.

44. Gaza's original population was in the city of Gaza itself, the town of Khan Yunis, and 15 villages.

45. The formal head of the government was Ahmad Hilmi Pasha, and Jamal al-Husseini was foreign minister. The Mufti, in fact, spent only a bit more than a week in Gaza before the British pressured the Egyptian government to have him return to Cairo.

46. Abu-Amr, "The Gaza Economy," in Abed, ed., *The Palestinian Economy*, 103.

47. See Eric Cohen, "Report on a Comparative Research of Two Towns: Chan Yunes in Gaza Strip and Nablus in the West Bank" (Department of Sociology, Hebrew University, April 1968 [Hebrew, mimeographed]).

48. Similar sentiments against resettlement were found in Syria. See Fred C. Bruhns, "A Study of Arab Refugee Attitudes," *Middle East Journal* 9 (1955): 130–38.

49. Turki, *The Disinherited*, 49.

50. Cossali and Robson, *Stateless in Gaza*, 20.

51. Beryl I. Cheal, "Refugees in the Gaza Strip, December 1948–May 1950" (unpublished M.A. thesis, University of Washington, 1985), p. 8.

52. See H. Mundus, *The Labor and the Laborers in Camp Palestine* (Beirut: Palestine Research Center, 1974), pp. 34–51 [Arabic]. Fewer than 3 percent of the refugees held work papers in 1969.

53. For a vivid description of the Rashidiyah camp over four decades, see Zvi Lanir and Elles Dobronsky, *Appointments in Rashidiya* (Tel-Aviv: Dvir, 1983) [Hebrew].

54. "Palestinian Refugee Camp Life in Lebanon," *Journal of Palestine Studies* 4 (1975): 91. A complete analysis of the camps in Lebanon in the 1960s and early 1970s, arguing for a basic similarity between them, may be

found in Bassem Sirhan, "The Refugee Camps—A Sociological View," *Shu'un Filastiniyya* (1974): 47–72 [Arabic].

55. Turki, *The Disinherited*, 58.

56. Quoted in Bruhns, "A Study of Arab Refugee Attitudes," 134.

57. Cheal, "Refugees in the Gaza Strip," 48. For some of the same conclusions, see Sirhan, "Palestinian Refugee Camp Life in Lebanon," 102.

58. Cheal, "Refugees in the Gaza Strip," 39.

59. Turki, *The Disinherited*, 39.

60. *New York Herald Tribune*, November 25, 1951; March 15, 1952.

61. Bruhns, "A Study of Arab Refugee Attitudes," 130–38.

62. Sayigh, *Palestinians: From Peasants to Revolutionaries*, 10, quotes the common Palestinian refrain, "We lived in Paradise."

63. Turki, *The Disinherited*, 47, 56.

64. Cheal, "Refugees in the Gaza Strip," 54.

65. Heinz R. Hink and Kent L. Pillsbury, *The UNRWA School System and the Palestine Arab Refugee Problem* (Tempe: Bureau of Government Research, University of Arizona, 1962), p. 10.

66. Brand, *Palestinians in the Arab World*, 13.

67. Badran, *Education and Modernization in Arab Palestinian Society*, 1–14; see also Ibrahim Abu-Lughod, "Educating a Community in Exile: The Palestinian Experience," *Journal of Palestine Studies* 2 (1973): 94–111.

68. Cited in Cossali and Robson, *Stateless in Gaza*, 11.

69. Quoted in Sayigh, *Palestinians*, 118.

70. Ibid., 120.

71. Brand, *Palestinians in the Arab World*, 13.

72. Shafeeq N. Ghabra, *Palestinians in Kuwait: The Family and the Politics of Survival* (Boulder: Westview Press, 1987), pp. 33–35, 63–77.

73. See Riyad Mansur, "The Palestinian Immigrant Community in the United States and its Demographic Condition," *Shu'un Filistiniyya* (February 1980): 84–106 [Arabic]. Mansur argues that the American authorities have recently encouraged the migration of Palestinians to the U.S. as part of an Israeli-American conspiracy to defeat the Palestinian struggle.

74. Ghabra, *Palestinians in Kuwait*, 81ff.

75. I. Stockman, "Changing Social Values of the Palestinians—The New Outlook of the Arab Peasant," *New Middle East* (June, 1969): 18–31.

76. See Moshe Shemesh, *The Palestinian Entity, 1959–1974: Arab Politics and the PLO* (London: Frank Cass, 1988], chs. 1 and 2.

77. Ibid., 8ff.

78. Khalidi, "The PLO as Representative of the Palestinian People" in

Augustus Richard Norton and Martin H. Greenberg, eds., *The International Relations of the Palestine Liberation Organization* (Carbondale: Southern Illinois University Press, 1989), p. 59.

8. The Feday: Rebirth and Resistance

1. See State of Israel, *Census of Population 1967: West Bank of Jordan, Gaza Strip, Northern Sinai and the Golan Heights* (Jerusalem: Central Bureau of Statistics and Israel Defense Forces, 1967).

2. Samih al-Qasim, "Resignation from the Death Insurance Company (About those who started thinking after June 5, 1967)" in Issa J. Boullata, ed., *Modern Arab Poets, 1950–1975* (Washington, D.C.: Three Continents Press, 1976), p. 117.

3. Janet Wallach and John Wallach, *Arafat: In the Eyes of the Beholder* (New York: Lyle Stuart, 1990), p. 11. See also Alan Hart, *Arafat: Terrorist or Peacemaker?* (London: Sidgwick and Jackson, 1984), p. 30.

4. Arafat's organization eventually united with one in Syria in 1959 to form the General Union of Palestinian Students (GUPS), which would become a potent source of Palestinian activism in the following decades. It formed branches in Europe and the United States.

5. See Helena Cobban, *The Palestinian Liberation Organisation: People, Power and Politics* (New York: Cambridge University Press, 1984), p. 24; and Rashid Hamid, "What Is the PLO?" *Journal of Palestine Studies* (Summer 1975): 90–109.

6. Cited in Cobban, *The Palestinian Liberation Organisation*, 21–22.

7. Hart, *Arafat: Terrorist or Peacemaker?*, 120.

8. Wallach and Wallach, *Arafat*, 106, claim that the Mufti was an early and substantial supporter of Arafat and his magazine. Their claim is based on the report of the Mufti's son-in-law, Muheideen al-Husseini.

9. For more on Abu Jihad see chapter 9. A survey of the publication's contents can be found in Naji Alush, *The March to Palestine* (Beirut: Dar al-Talia, 1964), pp. 37–42. Alush was one of the first rebels against Arafat's leadership in the late 1970s. Al-Wazir, the editor of the magazine, was born in Ramleh. In the early 1950s, he initiated raids of vengeance against Israel from Egyptian territory. Finally, he was arrested by the authorities and expelled from Egypt. Before moving to Kuwait, he was a teacher in Saudi Arabia for a short time. Later, he was the deputy commander-in-chief of the Palestinian military forces, responsible for guerrilla actions. In the late 1980s, he was killed

in a special Israeli commando operation. Another central figure of this circle was Farouk Khaddumi, later in charge of external and political affairs. Other members of the inner circle, who were also members of GUPS were Salim al-Zaaun and Zuhair al-Alami. In one issue, the magazine published excerpts from the "The Protocols of the Elders of Zion."

10. Quoted in Cobban, *The Palestinian Liberation Organisation*, 24.

11. Hart, *Arafat: Terrorist or Peacemaker?*, 164–65.

12. Wallach and Wallach, *Arafat*, 110

13. Both the Covenant and the later Charter can be found in Yehoshafat Harkabi, *The Palestinian Covenant and its Meaning* (London: Vallentine Mitchell, 1979). The section cited here is on page 110.

14. Hart, *Arafat: Terrorist or Peacemaker?*, 168, estimates that Fatah lost between 80 and 90 percent of its membership.

15. Ibid., 171.

16. Fanon (1925–61), born in Martinique, was a psychiatrist in a public hospital in Algiers when, in 1956, he joined the FLN and became one of its main ideologues.

17. Ehud Yaari, *Strike Terror: The Story of Fatah* (New York: Sabra, 1970), p. 60.

18. Ibid., 40–43

19. *Middle East Record—1969–1970* (London, 1971), p. 789. See also, Arie Yodfat and Yuval Arnon-Ohana, *PLO Strategy and Tactics* (London: Croom Helm, 1981), p. 118; and Yehoshafat Harkabi, *Fedayeen Action and Arab Strategy*, Adelphi Papers, No. 53 (London: Institute of Strategic Studies, 1968). According to Harkabi's account, 14 Israelis were killed, but the impact on Israeli society was considerable. When the author conducted a survey among military officers, politicians, students, and kibbutz members, the estimated number of those killed was between 40 and 300.

20. Hamid, "What is the PLO?," 93.

21. According to several sources, the CIA warned the Jordanians about the planned attack. The Jordanian chief-of-staff passed the information to Fatah, advising it to evacuate the camp. Fatah refused and prepared the local resistance. See Cobban, *The Palestinian Liberation Organisation*, 41–42.

22. Shlomo Aronson and Dan Horowitz, "The Strategy of Controlled Retaliation—The Israeli Case," *Medina U'Mimshal* (Summer 1971): 92–93 [Hebrew].

23. "As for terrorism, I announced it yesterday in no uncertain terms, and

yet, I repeat it for the record that we totally and absolutely renounce all forms of terrorism, including individual, group, and state terrorism" (Arafat in his December 14, 1988, press conference in Geneva). Joshua Teitelbaum has noted that "the official Arabic translation of Arafat's press conference statement quoted him as saying that the PLO 'rejects' terrorism *(narfuduhu)* not 'renounces.' A few days after the press conference, he told Vienna Television: 'I did not mean to renounce.'" See "The Palestine Liberation Organization" in Ami Ayalon and Haim Shaked, eds., *Middle East Contemporary Survey,* vol. 12 (Boulder: Westview Press, 1988), pp. 256–57.

24. Alain Gresh, *The PLO, The Struggle Within: Towards an Independent Palestinian State* (Atlantic Highlands, N.J.: Zed Books, 1988), pp. 124–26.

25. See Yaari, *Strike Terror,* 163ff.

26. See Teitelbaum, "The Palestine Liberation Organization," 252–53.

27. Jillian Decker, *The PLO: The Rise and Fall of the Palestine Liberation Organization* (London: Weidenfeld and Nicolson, 1984), ch. 33.

28. One of these heroes was a woman, Leila Khaled, who participated in two hijackings and wrote the book *My People Shall Live: An Autobiography of a Revolutionary* (London: Hodder and Stoughton, 1973).

29. The Israelis claimed that Black September was a secret wing of Fatah. Eliezer Ben-Rafael has argued that Black September was directly under the command of Salah Khalaf (p. 38), in *Israel Palestine: A Guerrilla Conflict in International Politics* (Westport: Greenwood Press, 1987)—a book based mainly on Israeli intelligence and military sources. Fatah has consistently denied this charge. No doubt the organization's roots were in Fatah, but its direct control of Black September is not clear. Salah Khalaf (Abu Iyad) claimed that the group was formed spontaneously by guerrilla fighters from several organizations, including Fatah, following the frustration of a clash between the Jordanians and the Palestinians in 1970. See Eric Rouleau, *My Home, My Land* (New York: Times Books, 1981), pp. 131–32. According to Cobban, *The Palestinian Liberation Organisation,* 55, Fatah decided to cut its relations with Black September and then lost all control over it, especially after the defection of the Iraqi-supported Sabra al-Banna ("Abu Nidal"), who formed the "Black June" guerrilla group.

30. See Shemesh, *The Palestinian Entity, 1959–1974,* 106–8.

31. Don Peretz, "Palestinian Social Stratification—The Political Implications" in Ben-Dor, ed., *The Palestinians and the Middle East Conflict,* 423.

32. Cited in Cobban, *The Palestinian Liberation Organisation,* 49.

33. Brand, *Palestinians in the Arab World,* 120.

34. Cobban, *The Palestinian Liberation Organisation*, 48–53; Brand, *Palestinians in the Arab World*, 166–72.

35. See Emile F. Sahliyeh, *The PLO After the Lebanon War* (Boulder: Westview Press, 1986), pp. 115–38, 205–44.

36. The "Jordanization" of the East Bank's Palestinian population continues to be substantial. See Harkabi, *The Palestinian Covenant*, 35.

37. Rex Brynen, *Sanctuary and Survival: The PLO in Lebanon* (Boulder: Westview Press, 1990), pp. 27–28.

38. Lanir and Dobronsky, *Appointments in Rashidiya*, 59.

39. Sayigh, *Palestinians: From Peasants to Revolutionaries*, 164–65.

40. Brynen, *Sanctuary and Survival*, 140.

41. Ibid.

42. Khalidi, *Under Siege: PLO Decisionmaking during the 1982 War* (New York: Columbia University Press, 1985), p. 59. Khalidi's claim of effective rule over Palestinians "everywhere" is greatly exaggerated.

43. "Auditing the PLO," in Norton and Greenberg, eds., *The International Relations of the Palestine Liberation Organization*, 197–98. It is almost impossible to estimate the scope of the PLO's economic activities, its sources, kinds of investments, and criteria for use and distribution of funds. From the late 1960s until its annexation by Iraq in August, 1990, Kuwait collected 5 percent of its Palestinian employees' income as a "liberation tax," which was given annually to the Palestine National Fund under Fatah control. In December, 1977, Kuwait established the "Sunduk al-Sumud," a fund to support the resistance and Palestinian culture in the occupied territories. See Brand, *Palestinians in the Arab World*, 122–25. In the late 1960s, Saudi Arabia also introduced the liberation tax (see Cobban, *The Palestinian Liberation Organisation*, 45), and similar arrangements were made by other traditional Arab regimes. Khalid al-Hassan has lauded Kuwait, Saudi Arabia, Qatar, Morocco, the Sudan, Tunisia, and others in this respect: "We never had to remind them to send what they have promised." See Cobban, 199. The PLO, according to Neil C. Livingstone and David Halevy, *Inside the PLO: Covert Units, Secret Funds and the War against Israel and the United States* (New York: William Morrow, 1989), has controlled a $2 billion budget, as well as large investments. Some have claimed this fortune has led to institutional and personal corruption in the organization's rank and file. Arafat remains one of the few figures in the movement around whom no rumors of corruption circulate.

44. Bishra Sirhan, *Palestinian Children: The Generation of Liberation* (Beirut: Palestinian Research Center, 1970], pp. 76–78.

45. Mai Sayigh, "Lament" in Salma Khadra Jayyusi, ed., *Modern Arabic Poetry: An Anthology* (New York: Columbia University Press, 1987), p. 416.

46. See Matti Steinberg, *Trends in Palestinian National Thought* (Jerusalem: Leonard Davis Institute, The Hebrew University, 1988), pp. 30–31 [Hebrew].

47. For different perspectives on the "territorialization" of the Palestinian guerrilla movement, see Brynen, *Sanctuary and Survival,* 161–80; Khalidi, *Under Siege,* 17–42; Sayigh, *Palestinians: From Peasants to Revolutionaries,* 156–87; Yaari, *Strike Terror,* 328–49; Lanir and Dobronsky, Appointments in *Rashidiya,* 55–102. For the decomposition of the Lebanese state in general, see D. C. Gordon, *The Republic of Lebanon: Nation in Jeopardy* (Boulder: Westview, 1983); Edward P. Haley and Lewis Snider (eds.), *Lebanon in Crisis* (Syracuse: Syracuse University Press, 1979).

48. Sayigh, *Palestinians: Prom Peasants to Revolutionaries,* 168.

49. See Meir Zamir, *The Formation of Modern Lebanon* (Ithaca: Cornell University Press, 1985), esp. ch. 2, pp. 38–96.

50. On the revolt inside the PLO see Yezid Sayigh, "Struggle Within, Struggle Without: The Transformation of the PLO Since 1982," *International Affairs* 65 (1985): 243–71. For the description of the ideological dimension of the struggle, see Muhammed al-Shuquair, "The History of the Split inside Fatah," *al-Safir* (Beirut), June 26 and 27, 1983 [Arabic]. For English excerpts, see *Journal of Palestine Studies* 13 (1983): 167–83; Eric Rouleau, "The Mutiny Against Arafat," *MERIP Reports* No. 119 (November–December 1983); Sahliyeh, *The PLO After the Lebanon War,* 139–204.

51. "The PLO as Representative of the Palestinian People" in Norton and Greenberg, eds., *The International Relations of the Palestine Liberation Organization,* 60.

52. The data given by Israeli intelligence to the Kahan Commission of Inquiry were 700–800 dead. The Lebanese Commission estimated 460 victims, and the Palestinian Red Crescent 2,000–3,000. Lebanese death certificates were issued for 1,200 people. See Zeev Schiff and Ehud Yaari, *Israel's Lebanon War* (New York: Simon and Schuster, 1984), p. 282. As is well known, the events caused a political storm in Israel, as people tried to deal with the army's—and Ariel Sharon's—complicity.

53. Cited in Khalidi, "The PLO as Representative of the Palestinian People" in Norton and Greenberg, eds., *The International Relations of the Palestine Liberation Organization,* 64–67.

54. Dahbur, "In Memory of 'Izziddin al-Qalaq" in Jayyusi, ed., *Modern Arabic Poetry*, 196.

55. Harkabi, *The Palestinian Covenant*, 39.

56. John W. Amos, *Palestinian Resistance: Organization of a Nationalist Movement* (New York: Pergamon Press, 1980), p. 45. Amos notes the ideological and personal ties between Fatah's founders and the Muslim Brotherhood. See also Emile F. Sahliyeh, "The West Bank and the Gaza Strip" in Shireen T. Hunter, ed., *The Politics of Islamic Revivalism: Diversity and Unity* (Bloomington: Indiana University Press, 1988), pp. 94–99.

57. Cresh, *The PLO*, 42.

9. Steering a Path under Occupation

1. Cited in Alan Hart, *Arafat: A Political Biography* (Bloomington: Indiana University Press, 1984), p. 235.

2. Ibid.

3. See Ariel Sharon (with David Chanoff), *Warrior—An Autobiography of Ariel Sharon* (New York: Simon and Schuster, 1989), pp. 248–60.

4. For a vivid description of the first period of Israeli occupation see Rafiq Halabi, *The West Bank Story* (New York: Harcourt Brace Jovanovich, 1982).

5. Shlomo Gazit, *The Stick and the Carrot: The Israeli Administration in Judea and Samaria* (Tel-Aviv: Zmora, Bitan, 1985), pp. 21–35 [Hebrew].

6. This amounted to two-fifths of the work force. See Fawzi A. Gharaibeh, *The Economies of the West Bank and Gaza Strip* (Boulder: Westview Press, 1985), pp. 21–23, 59. See also *Statistical Abstract of Israel—1978*, no. 29 (Jerusalem: Central Bureau of Statistics, 1979). The data in this chapter, unless otherwise noted, are from *Judea, Samaria and Gaza Area Statistics*, vol. 17 (Jerusalem: Central Bureau of Statistics, 1987), p. 412, as well as previous publications of the CBS, and various publications of the Bank of Israel, e.g., A. Bergman, *The Economic Growth of the Administered Areas, 1968–1973* (Jerusalem: Bank of Israel, 1974) [Hebrew]; and Raphael Meron, *Economic Development in Judea-Samaria and Gaza District* (Jerusalem: Bank of Israel, Research Department, 1988), pp. 7–19 [Hebrew]. (Note the shift of the terms in which the occupied territories are officially defined.) Other sources for data are Meron Benvenisti, *The West Bank Project: A Survey of Israel's Policies* (Washington, D.C.: American Enterprise Institute for Public Policy Research,

1984); and Sara Roy, *The Gaza Strip Survey* (Jerusalem: The West Bank Data Base Project, The Jerusalem Post, 1986). For an early analysis of the political implications of the absorption of these territories into Israel see B. Van Arkadie, *Benefits and Burdens: A Report on the West Bank and Gaza Strip Economies Since 1967* (Washington, D.C.: Carnegie Endowment for Peace, 1977).

7. Shaul Mishal begins his *West Bank/East Bank: The Palestinians in Jordan, 1949–1967* (New Haven: Yale University Press, 1978) with the following incident: "In February 1971, Qadri Tuqan, a Palestinian Arab from Nablus . . . who served as a minister in Jordan's government during the 1960s, died while on a visit to Beirut. His body was returned to Nablus through the East Bank of Jordan. There, his coffin was wrapped with a Jordanian flag. But when it crossed the river into the West Bank, a Palestinian flag replaced the Jordanian one" (p. 1). Several local designs competed to be the official Palestinian national flag. Finally, in 1964, the PLO decided on the ancient flag of the Sharif of Mecca, a white, green, and black striped design with a red triangle. This flag was one of several carried by Palestinians in the 1936–39 Arab Revolt. See Mahdi Abd al-Hadi, *The Development of the Arab Banner* (Jerusalem: Author's Publication, 1986) [Arabic].

8. "The Gaza Strip: Critical Effects of the Occupation" in Naseer Aruri, ed., Occupation: *Israel Over Palestine* (Belmont, Mass.: Association of Arab-American University Graduates, 1989), p. 259.

9. Shmuel Sandier and Hillel Frisch, *Israel, the Palestinians, and the West Bank: A Study in Intercommunal Conflict* (Lexington, Mass.: Lexington Books, 1984), p. 97. They speak of the PLO as a charismatic ideological center.

10. An earlier attempt at establishing such a coordinating body was made by reconstituting the Supreme Muslim Council. It advocated returning the West Bank to Jordan. After Israel deported Council members, the first effort at creating a National Guidance Committee followed. See Halabi, *The West Bank Story*, 37–40.

11. Helena Cobban, *The Palestinian Liberation Organisation*, 173.

12. Cited in Emile Sahliyeh, *In Search of Leadership* (Washington, D.C.: Brookings Institution, 1988), p. 52. The same picture emerges from a colloquium held by the Front at the Institute of Palestine Studies on July 3, 1981, and partially published in *Shu'un Filistiniyya* (1981): 45–77 [Arabic].

13. Ibrahim Dakkak, "Back to Square One: A Study in the Re-Emergence of the Palestinian Identity in the West Bank, 1967–1980" in Alexander Scholch, ed., *Palestinians over the Green Line: Studies in the Relations be-*

tween Palestinians on Both Sides of the 1949 Armistice Line Since 1967 (London: Ithaca Press, 1983), p. 90. Dakkak was himself one of the leading figures in the Front.

14. See Joshua Teitelbaum and Joseph Kostiner, "The West Bank and Gaza: The PLO and the *Intifada*" in Jack A. Goldstone, Ted Robert Gurr, and Farrokh Moshiri, eds., *Revolutions of the Late Twentieth Century* (Boulder: Westview Press, 1991), pp. 298–323.

15. Hillel Frisch, "The Building of Palestinian Institutions in the Occupied Territories, 1967–1985" (unpublished Ph.D. dissertation, Hebrew University, 1989), p. 97 [Hebrew].

16. One source puts Shabiba membership at 40,000. See Yezid Sayigh, "The Intifada Continues: Legacy, Dynamics and Challenges," *Third World Quarterly* 11 (1989): 36.

17. Ibid., 230–31.

18. The new National Front included members of the Popular Front for the Liberation of Palestine, which joined the PLO in 1980. The left-wingers used the Front as a means to limit Fatah control. See Frisch, "The Building of Palestinian Institutions," 70–78.

19. For some echoes of this controversy, see Ibrahim Dakkak, "Development from Within: A Strategy for Survival," in Abed, ed., *The Palestinian Economy*, 287–310. For a literary expression of the ideology of sumud see Raja Shehadeh, *The Third Way: A Journal of Life in the West Bank* (Jerusalem: Adam, 1982), pp. 4–7.

20. Lesch and Tessler, "The West Bank and Gaza: Political and Ideological Responses to Occupation," *Israel, Egypt and the Palestinians*, 269.

21. For an intensive study of such changes see Marisa Escribano and Nazmi El-Joubeh, "Migration and Change in a West Bank Village: The Case of Deir Dibwan," *Journal of Palestine Studies* 11 (1981): 150–60.

22. Salim Tamari, "The Palestinians in the West Bank and Gaza: The Sociology of Dependence" in Nakhleh and Zureik, eds., *The Sociology of The Palestinians*, 84–111.

23. Sandier and Frisch, *Israel, the Palestinians, and the West Bank*, 50.

24. Fertilizer use per acre more than quadrupled from 1968 to the early 1980s, with the use of six times as many tractors. In the years after 1968, agricultural productivity doubled.

25. It went from producing more than a third of the wealth on the West Bank immediately after the war to producing only a quarter by the mid-1980s.

26. Growth averaged 6 percent annually in the West Bank and 5 percent in Gaza into the late 1970s.

27. The agricultural labor force fell from 39 percent of the total work

force in 1968 to nearly half that figure, 22 percent, in 1985. By 1986, more than 50 percent of West Bank land and 30 percent of Gaza land were under Israeli control. See Meron Benvenisti, Ziad Abu-Zayed, and Danny Rubinstein, *The West Bank Handbook: A Political Lexicon* (Jerusalem: Jerusalem Post, 1986). On Israeli land-use policies, see Kami S. Abdulhadi, "Land Use Planning in the Occupied Territories," *Journal of Palestine Studies* 19 (1990): 46–63. See also Sabri Jiryis, "Domination by the Law," *Journal of Palestine Studies* 11 (1981): 83ff, and other articles in that issue. On Israel's water crisis and its implications for water use in the occupied territories, see Uri Davis, Antonia E. L. Maks, and John Richardson, "Israel's Water Policies," *Journal of Palestine Studies* 9 (1980): 3–31. On the preferential access to water for Israeli settlers and the crisis for West Bank agriculture and cities, see Sarah Graham-Brown, "The Economic Consequences of the Occupation" in Aruri, ed., *Occupation*, 300–25.

28. Bakr Abu-Kishk, *Arab Industry in the Occupied Territories* (Jerusalem: al-Multaqa al-Fikri al-Arabi, 1981), p. 8 [Arabic]. Less than 10 percent of the wealth and less than 15 percent of the labor force of the territories were accounted for by the 4,000 or so workshops, most with fewer than 10 workers, that constituted the industrial sector. See Simcha Bahiri, *Industrialization in the West Bank and Gaza* (Boulder: Westview Press [the West Bank Data Base Project], 1987); Van Arkadie, *Benefits and Burdens*, 123–25; Graham-Brown, "The Economic Consequences of the Occupation" in Aruri, ed., *Occupation*, 326–32.

29. On the territories' integration into the Israeli economy, see Tamari, "The Palestinians in the West Bank and Gaza" in Nakleh and Zureik, eds., *The Sociology of the Palestinians*, 85.

30. "Building Other People's Homes: The Palestinian Peasant's Household and Work in Israel," *Journal of Palestine Studies* 11 (1981): 31–66.

31. These data were collected about two to three months before the beginning of the uprising, which considerably decreased the number of laborers from the territories employed in Israel. See *Judea, Samaria and Gaza Area Statistics* (Jerusalem: Central Bureau of Statistics, November 1987), pp. 34–35. The real number seems to be higher, because the statistics referred mainly to "authorized" employment. To this, we have to add persons (mainly young women and girls) working in their homes or neighborhood centers, producing semifinished products for Israeli manufacturers from pieces distributed by local subcontractors. Tamari (ibid, 97) estimates that about *half* of all wage earners of the occupied region were dependent on employment in Israel. To this, we

may add the local employees of the various Israeli military and civilian authorities and, later, those employed by the Jewish settlers. The Palestinians constituted about 8 percent of the total Israeli labor force during the late 1970s and 1980s. For the implications for Israeli society see Moshe Semyonov and Noah Levin-Epstein, *Hewers of Wood and Drawers of Water: Noncitizen Arabs in the Israeli Labor Market* (New York School of Industrial and Labor Relations, Cornell University, Ithaca, 1987), pp. 9–12, 48–51, 62–64.

32. It totaled 70–80 percent of the territories' total exports and imports, far ahead of commerce with Jordan, which was the next largest trading partner. Unofficially, some Palestinians served as go-betweens for the Jordanian and Israeli economies.

33. Israeli attempts after 1982 to control distribution of those proceeds seem to have failed. At first the capital that came in through the Fund was used to finance municipal governments, education, and housing, but after the outbreak of the Intifada it poured into welfare relief for those who lost family members or homes in the fighting.

34. Meron Benvenisti, *US Government Funded Projects in the West Bank and Gaza Strip* (Jerusalem: The West Bank Data Base Project, 1984). See also Mansour, "The West Bank Economy" in Abed, ed., *The Palestinian Economy*, 77; Gideon M. Kressel, "Consumption Patterns in the Administered Territories after a Decade of Israeli Rule" in Raphael Israeli, ed., *Ten Years of Israeli Rule in Judea and Samaria* (Jerusalem: Truman Institute and Magnes Press, 1980), pp. 84–106 [Hebrew]; D. Zakai, *Economic Developments in Judea-Samaria and the Gaza District, 1985–86* (Jerusalem: Bank of Israel, 1988), 35.

35. Sara Roy, "The Gaza Strip: A Case of Economic De-Development," *Journal of Palestine Studies* 17 (1987): 56. Roy continues: "De-development is defined as a process which undermines or weakens the ability of an economy to grow and expand by preventing it from accessing and utilizing critical inputs needed to promote internal growth beyond a specific structural level. In Gaza, the de-development of the economic sector has, over two decades of Israeli rule, transformed that economy into an auxiliary of the state of Israel."

36. Ziad Abu-Amr, "The Gaza Economy: 1948–1984" in Abed, *The Palestinian Economy*, 117.

37. Yerucham Cohen, *The Allon Plan* (Tel Aviv: Hakibbutz Hameuchad, 1969), pp. 171–89 [Hebrew]. See also, Yishai, *Land of Peace*, pp. 67–70.

38. For the development of the political and theological positions of Gush Emunim, see Gideon Aran, *From Religious Zionism to a Zionist Re-*

ligion: The Origins of Gush Emunim as a Messianic Movement in Contemporary Israel (unpublished Ph.D. dissertation, Hebrew University, 1987) [Hebrew]; Myron J. Aronoff, "The Institutionalization and Cooptation of a Charismatic-Messianic Religious-Political Movement" in David Newman, ed., *The Impact of Gush Emunim: Politics and Settlement in the West Bank* (London: Croom Helm, 1985), pp. 45–69; Ian Lustick, *For the Land of the Lord: Jewish Fundamentalism in Israel* (New York: Council on Foreign Relations, 1988); David Weisburd, *Jewish Settlers Violence: Deviance as Social Reaction* (University Park: The Pennsylvania State University Press, 1989). See also Gush Emunim, *Master Plan for Settlement of Judea/Samaria* (Jerusalem, March 1978), p. 23 [Hebrew]. The plan (known as the Drobless Plan) was redrafted and adopted by the Settlement Division of the World Zionist Organization in October, 1978 and again in 1981. See World Zionist Organization, *The One-Hundred-Thousand Plan for Year 1985 for Settlement Development in Samaria and Judea* (Jerusalem: Settlement Division, 1981) [Hebrew].

39. The Israeli legal system equalizes "the status of Jews in the territories with that of other Israelis, without changing the legal status of the territories or that of the indigenous Arab population, and without shattering the myth of a military government that complies with international law." Eyal Benvenisti, *Legal Dualism: The Absorption of the Occupied Territories into Israel* (Boulder: Westview Press [the West Bank Data Base Project], 1990), p. 3; see also Moshe Drori, "The Israeli Settlements in Judea and Samaria: Legal Aspects" in Daniel J. Elazar, ed., *Judea, Samaria, and Gaza: Views on the Present and Future* (Washington, D.C.: American Enterprise Institute, 1982), pp. 44–80.

40. See Ehud Sprinzak, "The Iceberg Model of Political Extremism" in Newman, ed., *The Impact of Gush Emunim*, 27–45; Ian Lustick, "Israeli State Building in the West Bank and the Gaza Strip: Theory and Practice," *International Organization* 4 (1987): 151–71; Kimmerling, "Between the Primordial and the Civil Definitions of the Collective Identity" in Cohen, Lissak and Almagor, eds., *Comparative Social Dynamics*, 262–83.

41. See *The Jerusalem Post*, August 19, 1988 (based on data of the Guttman Institute of Applied Social Research) and *Davar*, August 3, 1984. The first political group that openly demanded mass expulsion by force was Rabbi Meir Kahane's party, Kach. The party won one of the 120 seats of the Israeli parliament. In the 1988 elections, the party was not allowed to run, because the Israeli Supreme Court ruled that it had a racist platform. Another party, Moledet, headed by retired General R. Zeevi, ran under the slogan of "transfer." The platform called for vol-

untary transfer, that is, persuading the Palestinians to leave by giving them some material incentives. Moledet won two seats in 1988 and no seats in 1992. See Asher Arian, *Politics in Israel: The Second Generation*, revised ed. (Chatham, N.J.: Chatham House, 1989), p. 92.

42. For the internal struggle and changing policy of Israel towards the 1967 occupied territories, see Yael Yishai, *Land or Peace: Whither Israel?* (Stanford: Hoover Institution Press, 1987). For analysis of the changes in the Israeli socio-political system see Dan Horowitz and Moshe Lissak, *Trouble in Utopia: The Overburdened Polity of Israel* (Albany: State University of New York Press, 1989).

43. See Hanan Mikhail Ashrawi, "The Contemporary Palestinian Poetry of Occupation," *Journal of Palestinian Studies* 7 (1978): 77–111; A. M. Elmessiri, "The Palestinian Wedding: Major Themes in Contemporary Palestinian Poetry," *Journal of Palestine Studies* 10 (1981): 77–99; Ann Mosely Lesch, "Closed Borders, Divided Lives: Palestinian Writings," UFSI Reports, No. 28, 1985; Shinar, *Palestinian Voices*, pp. 14–17, 61–66.

44. The two pro-Jordanian newspapers are *al-Quds* and *An-Nahar*. The two pro-PLO newspapers are *al-Fajr* and *Shaab*. For more on the Palestinian press under occupation see Dov Shinar and Danny Rubinstein, *Palestinian Press in the West Bank: The Political Dimension* (Jerusalem: The West Bank Data Base Project and Jerusalem Post, 1987).

45. See Aryeh Shalev, *The Intifada: Causes and Effects* (Tel-Aviv: Papyrus, 1990), pp. 28ff [Hebrew]. Israeli Arabs were part of this process of Palestinization. See Sammy Smooha, "The Divergent Fate of the Palestinians on Both Sides of the Green Line: The Intifada as a Test" (paper presented at the session on State, Nation and Ethnic Violence, International Sociological Association, XII World Congress of Sociology, Madrid, July 12, 1990).

46. The figure is from the Palestinian Academic Educational Council in Jerusalem. The Council, which was founded in September 1977, was one of the major meeting points for the local elite. Frisch, "The Building of Palestinian Institutions," 124–49, argues that professionally it failed, not having enough power to impose any real coordination among the institutions. Concerning the number of students, see Hamada Faraana, "The Aims of Higher Education in the West Bank and the Gaza Strip," *Samid al-Iqtisadi* 7 (1985) [Arabic]. The number increased until December, 1987, when all the institutions were closed as one of the Israeli responses to the uprising.

47. *Palestinian Voices*, 105; see also *Al-Bilad al-Arab*, 13 May, 1984. The "nationalistic character" of Bir Zeit was also reflected in its student

union's struggle to change the teaching language from English to Arabic—and in the deportation of its head, Hanna Nasser.

48. Frisch, "The Building of Palestinian Institutions", 207–12.

49. From an address to the Sixth Voluntary Work Camp in Nazareth, 1980. See Dakkak, "Development from Within" in Abed, *The Arab Economy*, 305.

50. For a detailed description of the internal struggles within the Palestinian labor movement, see Joost R. Hiltermann, "Before the Uprising: The Organization and Mobilization of Palestinian Workers and Women in the Israeli-Occupied West Bank" (unpublished Ph.D. dissertation, University of California at Santa Cruz, 1988), ch. 3.

51. The cited data are from the Arab Thought Forum (1981), an intellectual, semi-academic research and cultural institution founded in 1977 in Jerusalem.

52. Frisch, *The Building of Palestinian Institutions*, 197–215.

53. See Hamida Kazi, "Palestinian Women and the National Liberation Movement: A Social Perspective" in Khamsin Collective, *Women in the Middle East* (London: Zed Books, 1987), p. 27. Women also protested the Balfour Declaration. See Soraya Antonius, "Fighting on Two Fronts: Conversations with Palestinian Women" in Miranda Davis, ed., *Thud World—Second Sex* (London: Zed Books, 1983), p. 63.

54. See Julie Peteet, "Women and the Palestinian Movement: No Going Back?" *MERIP Report* No. 138 (January–February, 1986): 20.

55. "When a girl begins to earn money," the founder is quoted as saying, "she may begin to impose conditions on her family. We don't encourage such a spirit in our girls." Quoted in Rosemary Sayigh, "Encounters with Palestinian Women under Occupation," *Journal of Palestine Studies* 10 (1981): 12.

56. See for example Mustafa Barghouthi and Rita Giacaman, "The Emergence of an Infrastructure of Resistance: The Case of Health" in Jamal R. Nassar and Roger Heacock, eds., *Intifada: Palestine at the Crossroads* (New York: Praeger, 1990), pp. 73–87.

57. Ziad Abu-Amr, "Class Structure and the Political Elite in the Gaza Strip: 1948–1988" in Aruri, ed., *Occupation*, 94.

58. The progress of women has actually been uneven: Certainly education and new forms of wage labor have been emancipatory, but in at least one rural West Bank village there are signs of increased domestication. See Analiese Moors, "Gender Hierarchy in Palestinian Village: The Case of Al-Balad" in Glavanis and Glavanis, eds., *The Rural Middle East*, 195–207.

59. Ann M. Lesch, "Gaza: Forgotten Corner of Palestine," *Journal of Palestine Studies* 15 (1985): 45.

60. *Statistical Abstract of Israel—1985,* no. 36 (Jerusalem, Central Bureau of Statistics, 1985).

61. In fact, the story of the Israeli economy is made up of two separate histories. From 1948 to 1973, Israel averaged 10 percent growth annually in its national product, a figure among the highest in the world; from 1974 to 1988, the pace slowed to just over 3 percent with wealth per capita rising less than 2 percent annually.

62. Graham-Brown, "The Economic Consequences of the Occupation" in Aruri, ed., *Occupation,* 341, 347–49.

63. Ibid., 349–50. About three-quarters of that figure was from the West Bank, where Palestinians benefited from the ease with which they could obtain a Jordanian passport for fairly easy travel.

64. The average was 5.5 percent a year, according to the World Bank, although numbers on the Jordanian economy for that period should be seen more as orders of magnitude than exact representations.

65. They slipped 8 percent, in the first half of 1987 alone, and grant aid fell by 30 percent between 1982 and 1988. Jordanian economic growth showed some residual strength in the first half of the 1980s (about 4.1 percent), but declined rapidly in the last half of the decade. Figures are from The World Bank, *World Development Report, 1989* (New York: Oxford University Press, 1989); *The World Bank Atlas, 1989* (Washington, D.C.: The World Bank, 1989); *Trends in Developing Economies, 1989* (Washington, D.C.: The World Bank, 1989); United Nations Industrial Development Organization, Industrial Development Review Series, *Jordan: Stimulating Manufacturing Employment and Exports,* prepared by Regional and Country Studies' Branch, December 24, 1987.

66. See Tamari, "From the Fruits of Their Labour" in Glavanis and Glavanis, eds., *The Rural Middle East,* 70–94.

67. Israeli policymakers took some belated cognizance of this, instituting a series of policies in late 1991, designed to spur the growth of West Bank and Gaza Strip businesses. *The New York Times,* December 1, 1991, p. 8.

68. See Meron Benvenisti, *1987 Report: Demographic, Economic, Legal, Social and Political Developments in the West Bank* (Boulder: Westview Press, 1987), p. 47; Shalev, *The Intifada,* 209–10.

69. Penny Johnson and Lee O'Brien with Joost Hiltermann, "The West Bank Rises Up," *MERIP Report* No. 155 (1988): 6. This essay and others from the *MERIP Report* have been reprinted in Zachary Lockman and Joel Beinin, eds., *Intifada: The Palestinian Uprising Against Israeli Occupa-*

tion (Boston: South End Press, 1989); see also Adil Yahya, "The Role of the Refugee Camps" in Nassar and Heacock, eds., *Intifada*, 95.

70. The term was not new. Yasser Arafat used it in a 1973 speech celebrating the "8th year of the Palestinian Revolution" (the first Fatah attack in January 1965), to designate the internal resistance against the occupation. See *The Yearbook of the Palestinian Problem—1973*, n. 10 (Beirut: Institute of Palestinian Studies, 1976), p. 3. The term also appeared many times in Palestinian periodicals. In 1987, it was probably coined by Mohammed Milhem, former mayor of the West Bank town of Halhoul.

71. Excerpts from Mansur's poem "The Shrouded Face," translated by Dr. Rivka Yadlin of the Truman Institute of the Hebrew University.

72. "Stories of Daughters," *MERIP Report* No. 165 (1990): 29.

73. Ze'ev Schiff and Ehud Ya'ari, *Intifada: The Palestinian Uprising—Israel's Third Front* (New York: Simon and Schuster, 1990), p. 190.

74. A study of the leaflets was done by Shaul Mishal with Reuben Aharoni, *Speaking Stones: The Words Behind the Palestinian Intifada* (Tel Aviv: Hakibbutz Hameuchad, 1989) [Hebrew].

75. Radio Al-Quds, controlled by Syria, was used by Jibril's Popular Front for the Liberation of Palestine-General Command.

76. See Salim Tamari, "The Uprising's Dilemma: Limited Rebellion in Civil Society," *Middle East Report* 20 (1990): 7. See also the semi-clandestine publication in English, FACTS Information Committee, *Towards a State of Independence: The Palestinian Uprising, December 1987–August 1988* (Jerusalem: September, 1988), and the highly biased paper by Samiah K. Farsoun and Jean M. Landis, "Structure of Resistance and the 'War of Positions': A Case Study of the Palestinian Uprising," *Arab Studies Quarterly* 11 (1989): 59–86.

77. On the "Intifada Profiters" and the familial workshops in the West Bank, see Danny Rubinstein in *Haaretz*, October 9, 1990. Unfortunately, at the time of this book's writing, no reliable economic data on the West Bank and Gaza Strip were available. Some reporting is available in Richard Toshiyuki Drury and Robert C. Winn, *Plowshares and Swords: The Economics of Occupation in the West Bank* (Boston: Beacon Press, 1992), ch. 2.

78. The poem is "Those Who Pass Between Fleeting Words," in Lockman and Beinin, eds., *Intifada*, 26. The second citation is found in Adel Samara, "The Political Economy of the West Bank 1967–1987: From Peripheralization to Development" in *Palestine: Profile of an Occupation* (Totowa, N.J.: Zed Books, 1989), p. 23.

79. Bank of Israel, *Annual Report, 1989* (Jerusalem: Government Printer, 1990), p. 83.

80. Sara Roy, "The Political Economy of Despair: Changing Political and Economic Realities in the Gaza Strip," *Journal of Palestine Studies* 20 (1991): 67.

81. B'TSELEM, *Information Sheet: June–July 1990 Update* (Jerusalem: The Israeli Information Center for Human Rights in the Occupied Territories, 1990): 34. B'TSELEM was founded in February, 1989, by Israeli intellectuals, lawyers, journalists, and parliament members in order to collect data on human rights violations, based on independent fieldwork as well as Israeli and Palestinian sources. Its findings are usually about 20 to 30 percent higher than those of Israeli official sources and 30 to 35 percent lower than those of its Palestinian counterpart, *al-Haq*, a Ramallah-based organization.

82. Shaul Mishal, "'Paper War'—Words Behind Stones: The Intifada Leaflets," *The Jerusalem Quarterly* 51 (1989): 89.

83. Samih K. Farsoun and Jean M. Landis, "The Sociology of an Uprising: The Roots of the Intifada" in Nassar and Heacock, eds., *Intifada*, 31.

84. Roy, "The Political Economy of Despair," 68.

85. Ibid., 61–62.

86. Reported on Israeli television, August 29, 1988, and in *an-Nahar*, August 30, 1988.

87. "The Intifadah and the Arab World: Old Players, New Roles," *International Journal* 45 (1990): 501.

88. Many comparisons of the two revolts have been made. See, for example, Kenneth W. Stein, "The Intifadah and the 1936–1939 Uprising: A Comparison of the Palestinian Arab Communities," The Carter Center of Emory University, Occasional Paper Series, Vol. 1, no. 1 (December 1989); and Muhammad Khalid Al-Azhari, "1936 Revolt and 1987 Intifada (A Comparative View)," *Shu'un Filistiniyya* (1989): 3–26 [Arabic].

89. See Helga Baumgarten, "'Discontented People' and 'Outside Agitators': The PLO in the Palestinian Uprising" in Nassar and Heacock, eds., *Intifada*, 207–26, and Ali Jarbawi, "Palestinian Elites in the Occupied Territories: Stability and Change through the Intifada," ibid., 288.

90. For example, Emile Saliyeh, cited in ibid., 287.

91. Teitelbaum and Kostiner, "The West Bank and Gaza," 317–21; and Hillel Frisch, "From Armed Struggle Over State Borders to Political Mobilization and Intifada Within It: The Transformation of PLO

Strategy in the Territories," *Plural Societies* 19 (1991): 92–115, esp. 114–15. Frisch argues that the leadership in the West Bank and Gaza Strip used the many organizations that had developed in the territories as a basis for the Intifada but failed to create territory-wide organizations. Territorial consolidation failed because the PLO feared potential national competitors. See Frisch, "Between Diffusion and Territorial Consolidation in Rebellion: Striking at the Hard-Core of the Intifada," *Terrorism and Political Violence* 3 (1991): 39–62.

92. Helena Cobban, "The Palestinians: From the Hussein-Arafat Agreement to the Intifada" in Robert O. Freedman, ed., *The Middle East from the Iran-Contra Affair to the Intifada* (Syracuse: Syracuse University Press, 1991), p. 262.

93. Ibid.

94. Teitelbaum and Kostiner, "The West Bank and Gaza," 316.

95. See, for example, David McDowall, *Palestine and Israel: The Uprising and Beyond* (London: I. B. Tauris, 1989), p. 100: "The PLO's victory removed neither Jordan nor the traditional elite from the scene. The new mayors were summoned to Amman and reminded of the value of good relations for marketing agricultural produce to Jordan. Each was helped to assess the balance of loyalty by the offer of financial assistance to his municipality."

96. On the Islamic groups among Palestinians, see Jean-François Legrain, "Islamistes et lutte nationale palestinienne dans les territoires occupés par Israel," *Revue française de science politique* 36 (1986): 227–47.

97. Lisa Taraki, "The Islamic Resistance Movement in the Palestinian Uprising," *MERIP Report* No. 156 (1989): 31.

98. Ibid.

99. Mishal, "'Paper War,'" 82.

100. This was reported even before the Intifada in *The Manchester Guardian*, May 18, 1986.

101. See, for example, Dale Bishop, "Mosque and Church in the Uprising," *MERIP Report* No. 152 (1988): 41–42.

102. See Rita Giacaman and Penny Johnson, "Palestinian Women: Building Barricades and Breaking Barriers" in Lockman and Beinin, eds., *Intifada,* 155–69; Phyllis Bennis, *From Stones to Statehood: The Palestinian Uprising* (New York: Olive Branch Press, 1990), pp. 31–37; Shalev, *The Intifada,* 90–91.

103. See, for example, I. Gad, "From Salon Ladies to Popular Committees: Women in Uprising" in *Readings in Contemporary Palestinian Society,* vol. 2 (Bir Zeit: Bir Zeit University Press, 1989).

104. Rema Hammami, "Women, the Hijab and the Intifada," *MERIP Report* No. 165 (1990): 24–28.

105. Julie Peteet, *Gender in Crisis: Women and the Palestinian Resistance Movement* (New York: Columbia University Press, 1991), p. 209.

106. Sayigh, "Encounters with Palestinian Women under Occupation" in Elizabeth Warnock Femea, ed., *Women and the Family in the Middle East: New Voices of Change* (Austin: University of Texas Press, 1985), p. 206.

107. Quoted in Maya Rosenfeld, "I Don't Want My Body to Be a Bridge for the State," *Challenge* 2 (1991): 25–26.

108. Geoffrey Aronson, *Israel, Palestinians and the Intifada: Creating Facts on the West Bank* (New York: Kegan Paul International, 1987), p. 324.

109. Including Elias Freij, the Christian mayor of Bethlehem; Zakaria al-Agha, chairman of the Arab Medical Association of Gaza; Mustafa Natsche, the dismissed mayor of Hebron; Haidar Abd al-Shafi, a Gazan active in the founding of the PNC and of the Palestinian Red Crescent; and Saeb Erakat, an instructor of political science in the West Bank.

10. The Oslo Process: What Went Right?

1. The PLO representative in London who, immediately following the 1973 War, demanded recognition of Israel on the pages of the London *Times*.

2. An example is Henry Cattan.

3. See for example, Baruch Kimmerling, "Peace for Territories: A Macro-Sociological Analysis of the Concept of Peace in Zionist Ideology," *Journal of Applied Behavioral Sciences* 23 (1987): 13–34.

4. A dunum is a Middle Eastern territorial measure, approximately equivalent to one acre.

5. See Baruch Kimmerling, "The Power-Oriented Settlement: Bargaining between Israelis and Palestinians," in M. Maoz and A. Sela, eds., *The PLO and Israel: From the Road to the Oslo Agreement and Back?* (New York: St. Martin's Press, 1997), pp. 223–51.

6. For an in-depth analysis of the issue of Jerusalem in the current developments of the Israeli-Palestinian conflict and negotiations, see Menachem Klein, *Jerusalem: The Contested City* (New York: New York University Press, 2001).

7. Most of the land plots of the West Bank were never registered by the state but were considered as private or communal property according

to the traditional holding customs. Israel refused to recognize these unofficial titles.

8. At the time, Benvenisti was the head of a project to gather statistics concerning the occupied territories. See, for example, Meron Benvenisti, *Report: Demographic, Economic, Legal, Social and Political Developments in the West Bank* (Jerusalem: Jerusalem Post, 1987). See also Benvenisti, "The Shepherds' War," *Jerusalem Post* (1989).

9. Ilja A. Luciak, *After the Revolution: Gender and Democracy in El Salvador, Nicaragua, and Guatemala* (Baltimore: Johns Hopkins University Press, 2001), p. 95.

10. Etel Solingen, *Regional Orders at Century's Dawn: Global and Domestic Influences on Grand Strategy* (Princeton: Princeton University Press, 1998)

11. Edward Said, "Palestinian Elections Now," *Al-Ahram Weekly*, June 13–19, 2002.

12. The Israeli academics were primarily some junior academics such as Yair Hirshfield and Ron Pundik, later joined by some officials and junior politicians such as Uri Savir and Deputy Foreign Minister Yossi Belin, who continued the negotiations. See Yair Hirshfield, *A Formula for Peace: Negotiations on the Oslo Agreements, the Strategy, and its Implementation* (Tel Aviv: Am Oved, 2000) [Hebrew]. See also Ron Pundik, *From Oslo to Taba: The Disrupted Process* (Jerusalem: The Leonard Davis Institute, 2001) [Hebrew]. Each of the participants in the talks has attempted to make his place in history. A slightly different version is that of Uri Savir. See Uri Savir, *The Process* (New York: Random House, 1998).

13. The Gaza-Jericho Agreement, of May 4, 1994.

14. Israeli-Palestinian Interim Agreement on the West Bank and the Gaza Strip, Washington DC, September 28, 1995.

15. See *The Palestinian-Israeli Peace Agreement: A Documentary Record*, 2nd ed. (Washington: Institute for Palestine Studies, 1994).

16. It is interesting to point out that, at this stage, neither side seriously brought up the refugee problem or the issue of the "right of return." It seems that there was awareness that this subject would break up all other agreements and further incite Palestinian diaspora communities against the agreement. The evacuation of settlements and the nature of arrangements concerning Jerusalem were also not discussed for similar reasons. Essential topics such as the joint water aquifer were also not discussed. See Sari Hanafi, *Here and There: Towards an Analysis of the Relationship Between the Palestinian Diaspora and the Center*

(Jerusalem and Ramallah: Muwatin and the Institute of Jerusalem Studies, 2001). Also see Alwyn R. Rouyer, *Turning Water into Politics: The Water Issue in the Palestinian-Israeli Conflict* (New York: St. Martin's Press, 2000).

17. Gershom Gorenberg, "Barak, Stay Home," *Jerusalem Report,* vol. 13, July 29, 2002, p. 24.

18. Sara Roy, "Palestinian Society and Economy: The Continued Denial of Possibility," *Journal of Palestine Studies* 30 (Summer 2001): 5–6.

19. Khalil Shikaki, "Palestinian Public Opinion about the Peace Process, 1993–1999," Special Report, Center for Policy Analysis on Palestine, *http://www.palestinecenter.org/cpap/pubs/19991026ib.html.*

20. Arafat succeeded to marginalize the most vehement dissidents from PLO and Fatah, but he kept those willing to cooperate with old comrades with whom he had strong personal relations, such as Salim Za'nun, the former chair of the PNC; Abbas Zaki, head of Fatah's operations branch; or Sakr Habash (Abu Nizar), head of the Revolutionary Committee.

21. They called the entity "Bantustan" after the client states that white South Africa created at the height of the apartheid regime to create the appearance of granting freedom to the black population.

22. In the beginning, "return" was perceived as reinstatement in villages, neighborhoods, fields, and houses from which they had been uprooted. Israel claimed that a "population exchange" had been made when it "absorbed" approximately the same number of Jews from Arab countries, who had also been uprooted from their property and places of living. Some Palestinian political thinkers in recent years redefined "the right of return" as return and resettlement of Palestinians from the diaspora within the state of Palestine and not necessarily within the borders of Israel. Yet this definition was not accepted by all streams, especially by the Palestinians in the diaspora and the Islamic movements. It is foreseeable that some Palestinians will be willing to convert their lost assets for fair compensation as part of a final arrangement. When talks between the Palestinians and the Israelis broke down during the second Camp David Conference (July 11–26, 2000), it seemed that the Palestinians had returned to the original version of "the right of return."

23. Naseer Aruri, ed. *Palestinian Refugees: The Right to Return* (London: Pluto Press, 2001).

24. Akiva Eldar, "Arafat to Ha'aretz: I Accept Clinton's Plan; Peace Is Possible," *Ha'aretz,* June 22, 2002.

25. The full text of the accord can be found in Department of State Dispatch Supplement, Volume 4, number 4, September 1993, "Recent Developments in the Middle East Peace Process" published by the Bureau of Public Affairs.

26. Shlomo Avineri, "Political Ideologies: From Consensus to Confrontation," p. 198. A powerful argument about Israel's pre-1967 war boundaries is made by Adriana Kemp, "'Talking Boundaries': The Making of a Political Territory in Israel, 1949–1957" (Ph.D. diss., Tel-Aviv University, 1997) [Hebrew].

27. Joel S. Migdal, *Through the Lens of Israel: Explorations in State and Society* (New York: Cambridge University Press, 2001).

28. The text of the speeches at the signing ceremony can be found in Department of State Dispatch Supplement, Volume 4, number 4, September 1993, "Recent Developments in the Middle East Peace Process" published by the Bureau of Public Affairs.

29. Mohammed Dahlan, "We'll Choose Our Leaders," *The Guardian*, July 2, 2002.

30. Leslie Susser, "The Privatization of Peacemaking," *The Jerusalem Report*, August 26, 2002, p. 14.

31. Mixed into a fascinating account of the official negotiations are all sorts of references to back-channel talks in Menachem Klein, *Shattering a Taboo: The Contacts Toward a Permanent Status Agreement in Jerusalem 1994–2001* (forthcoming).

32. Rashid Khalidi, *Palestinian Identity: The Construction of Modern National Consciousness* (New York: Columbia University Press, 1997), p. 203.

33. This decision is reminiscent both of the Jewish leadership's decision to accept the Partition Plan in 1947 and of the dilemmas it faced during the same period. This decision did not necessarily stand in contrast to their hidden ambition one day to control the entire territory of historic Palestine. In Israel, right-wing circles saw this as the first stage in fulfilling "a program of stages." Yehoshafat Harkabi was warning against a similar plan on the part of the Palestinians when the twelfth PNC (July 1974) adopted the idea of the establishment of "a Palestinian National Authority in all the territory liberated from Israeli control."

34. See Abdul Hamid, *Legal and Political Aspects of Palestinian Elections* (Jerusalem: Israel/Palestine Center for Research and Information, 1995).

35. Jamil Hilal, *The Palestinian Political System after Oslo* (Washington: Institute of Palestine Studies, 1998) [Arabic].

36. Helena Lindholm Schulz, *The Reconstruction of Palestinian Nationalism:*

Between Revolution and Statehood (New York: Manchester University Press, 1999), p. 98.

37. See Khalil Shakaki, *Old Guard and New Guard* (Ramallah: Palestinian Center for Policy and Survey Research, 2001).

38. Glenn E. Robinson, *Building a Palestinian State: The Incomplete Revolution* (Bloomington: Indiana University Press, 1997), p. 178.

39. It is possible that Arafat himself was interested in multiple concentrations of underground armed forces, which would prevent the creation of one, large, united force with the potential of overthrowing his regime. See Jamil Halil, *The Formation of the Palestinian Elite: From the Emergence of the National Movement to the Establishment of the National Authority* (Ramallah and Amman: Muwatin and Al Urdun al Jadid, 2002) [Arabic].

40. The Palestinian community in most dire economic, political, and perhaps even existential distress is the Lebanese community (numbering 300-350,000 people).

41. On the relationship between state image and state practices, see Joel S. Migdal, *State in Society: Studying How States and Societies Transform and Constitute One Another* (New York: Cambridge University Press, 2001).

42. The ministry was originally set up as the Ministry of Education and Higher Education. In 1996, Higher Education received its own ministry.

43. Blair G. Van Dyke and E. Vance Randall, "Educational Reform in Post-Accord Palestine: A Synthesis of Palestinian Perspectives," *Educational Studies* 28 (2002): 18-32.

44. Agustín Vellooso de Santisteban, "Palestinian Education: A National Curriculum against All Odds," *International Journal of Educational Development* 22 (2002): 145-54.

45. Van Dyke and Randall, "Educational Reform," p. 26.

46. *Amnesty International Index,* News Service No. 90,15/089/2002. The approximately 2,000 held in administrative detention during February and March were released, but those detained after March 29 were held for a long time under the most difficult conditions. According to a military order issued on April 5, 2002 (Order 1500), it was permissible to hold someone under administrative detention for eighteen days without a court order and without contact with a lawyer or family member. After that, it was possible to request from the courts an extension to ninety days. By the end of May, fewer than 1,000 men remained in detention, conditions improved, and visits from Red Cross representatives were made possible.

47. Yezid Sayigh, *Strengthening Palestinian Public Institutions* (New York: Council on Foreign Relations, 1999).

11. The Oslo Process: What Went Wrong?

1. Daoud Kuttab, "Danger of Lawlessness in Palestine." This piece appeared in several places, including the *Jerusalem Post*, PNet website, and, on August 16, 2002, in the *Jordan Times* and Lebanon's *Daily Star.*

2. The Palestinians have not posed a military threat to Israel's existence since 1948. The Palestinian guerilla war inside Israel and in the territories against the settlements and settlers is only a tactical threat.

3. B'Tselem, *Land Grab: Israel's Settlement Policy in the West Bank: Comprehensive Report,* May 2002.

4. There were indeed additional reasons that brought about early elections and his defeat—principally his personal leadership and a public affair surrounding it. Yet the main political reason, alongside increasing Islamic terror, was his loss of a parliamentary majority.

5. Glenn E. Robinson, *Building a Palestinian State: The Incomplete Revolution* (Bloomington: Indiana University Press, 1997), pp. 28–33.

6. Ghazzi al-Khalili, writing in *Shu'un Filastiniyya,* quoted in Hillel Frisch, *Countdown to Statehood: Palestinian State Formation in the West Bank and Gaza* (Binghamton: State University of New York Press, 1998), p. 42.

7. Frisch, *Countdown to Statehood,* p. 92.

8. Robinson, *Building a Palestinian State,* pp. 95 and 65.

9. As'ad Ghanem, *The Palestinian Regime: A "Partial Democracy"* (Portland, OR: Sussex Academic Press, 2001), p. 125.

10. Quoted in Robinson, *Building a Palestinian State,* p. 154, based on an interview with the Israeli daily *Ha'aretz.*

11. PASIA, *The Islamic Movement: A Challenge for Palestinian State-Building* (Jerusalem: Palestinian Academic Society for Study of International Affairs, 1999).

12. Quoted in Helena Lindholm Schulz, *The Reconstruction of Palestinian Nationalism: Between Revolution and Statehood* (Manchester: Manchester University Press, 1999), p. 111.

13. Shaul Mishal and Abraham Sela, *The Palestinian Hamas: Vision, Violence and Coexistence* (New York: Columbia University Press, 2000); Khaled Hroub, *Hamas: Political Thought and Practice* (Washington: Institute for Palestine Studies, 2000).

14. An Islamic group sympathizer, quoted in Schulz, *The Reconstruction of Palestinian Nationalism*, p. 113.

15. Amira Hass, "Israel's Closure Policy: An Ineffective Strategy of Containment and Repression, *Journal of Palestine Studies*, 31, 3 (2002): 5–20.

16. Robinson, *Building a Palestinian State*, p. 37.

17. Ghanem, *The Palestinian Regime*, p. 104.

18. Frisch, *Countdown to Statehood*, p. 125.

19. Immediately upon construction of the PA, the issue of human rights became prominent, partially because of the PA's obligation to Israel to wipe out Islamic and other terrorist activities against Israel. Although the PA and its agencies did act on this obligation, they also acted against anyone who seemed subversive to the regime and endanger it. See, B'tselem, *Neither Law Nor Justice: Extra-judicial Punishment, Abduction, Unlawful Arrests and Tortures of Palestinian Residents of the West Bank by the Palestinian Preventive Security Service, 1995.*

20. Schulz, *The Reconstruction of Palestinian Nationalism*, p. 93.

21. Robinson, *Building a Palestinian State*, pp. 181–182.

22. Ian Lustick, *Unsettled States, Disputed Lands: Britain and Ireland, France and Algeria, Israel and the West Bank-Gaza* (Ithaca: Cornell University Press, 1993).

23. 3.5 million is the registered number of those living in refugee camps under the auspices of the United Nations Relief and Works Agency (UNRWA). According to the estimates, there are about another million uprooted Palestinians scattered throughout the world.

24. PSR—Survey Research Unit: Public Opinion Poll #3, 19–24 December 2001, *http://www.pcpsr.org/survey/polls/2001/p3a.html.*

25. *http://www.pcpsr.org/OnlineReports/IsrPalConflict/findings.pdf.*

26. On the PA and the media, see Amal Jamal, "The Palestinian Media: An Obedient Servant or a Vanguard of Democracy?" *Journal of Palestine Studies,* 29 (Spring 2000): 45–59.

27. On the impact of economic well-being on attitudes toward the peace process, see Jodi Nachtwey and Mark Tessler, "The Political Economy of Attitudes toward Peace among Palestinians and Israelis," *Journal of Conflict Resolution,* 46 (April 2002): 260–285.

28. Shimon Peres, *The New Middle East* (New York: H. Holt, 1993).

29. Gershon Shafir and Yoav Peled, eds., *The New Israel: Peacemaking and Liberalization* (Boulder: Westview Press, 2000).

30. Sara Mae Roy, *The Palestinian Autonomy and the Oslo Process* (Abu Dhabi: Emirates Center for Strategic Studies, 1998).

31. Shaul Mishal, *Investment in Pace: Politics of Economic Cooperation Between*

Israel, Jordan and the Palestinian Authority (Brighton: Sussex Academic Press, 2001).

32. If the economic agreement had been put into effect, it would have granted the Palestinians substantial benefits, but would have prevented them from issuing their own money, a symbol of economic sovereignty. Bernard Phillippe and Christopher Pissarides, "Evaluating the Paris Protocol: Economic Relations between Israel and the Palestinian Territories" (Working Paper, 1999).

33. From the beginning, donors showed concern about procedures in the PA. "Donor Concern over Palestinian transparency, accountability, and institution building did lead to the formal Understanding on Revenues, Expenditures and Donor Funding for the Palestinian Authority, signed by donors and the PA at the November 1994 meeting of the AHLC [Ad-Hoc Liaison Committee]." Rex Brynen, *A Very Political Economy: Peacebuilding and Foreign Aid in the West Bank and Gaza* (Washington, D.C.: United States Institute of Peace Press, 2000), pp. 106–7.

34. At the same time, Israel demanded $18 million for telephone services it had provided to the PA. For example, the PA encouraged private investors to establish telephone and telecommunications companies like Paltel, a company independent from Bezek or any other Israeli company. For the same reason of economic and political independence as well as because of issues of "national prestige," the PA tried to speed up establishment of a deep-water port and airport in the Gaza Strip. Israel tried to hold up the construction of both these projects by any means possible, claiming reasons of "security" and environmental damage to Israeli coastlines.

35. Brynen, *A Very Political Economy,* ch. 5.

36. An example of the PA's problematical relations with civil society can be seen in its treatment of the umbrella organization for trade unions, the Palestinian General Federation of Trade Unions. See Nina Sovich, "Palestinian Trade Unions," *Journal of Palestine Studies,* 29 (Summer 2000): 66–79.

37. Thus for example, the Khan Yunis "Association for Culture and Free Thought" (in the Gaza Strip), which ran a children's club (a sort of complementary education program), a teen center, and a cultural center for adults, was funded mostly by the European community and lost 60 percent of its budget in 1995. The Gaza Center for Care of Disabled Children, which cared for 2,500 disabled children all over the strip, ran on annual American funding of $1.5 million. When

most of this funding was transferred to the PA, the center had to let 180 employees go. Most recipients of these welfare services were not awarded alternative assistance through governmentally organized welfare services.

38. Take for example, Abdul Majid Shoman, head of the Arab Bank, Omar al Aqqad, Sabih al Masri, and Said Khoury, who all began investing in development projects in the PA but tried to avoid involvement with the regime. The only large capitalist to both invest and serve as an official was Minister of Industry Maher al Masri, who came from a veteran merchant family in Nablus.

39. See the anthology of articles, Ishac Diwan and Radwan A. Shaban, eds., *Development under Adversity: The Palestinian Economy under Transition* (Washington: Palestine Economic Policy Research Center and the World Bank, 1999).

40. Leila Farsakh, *Palestine Employment in Israeli: 1967–1997* (Jerusalem: Palestinian Economic Policy Research Institute, 1999). Fadle Naquib, *The Palestinian Economy in the West Bank and Gaza Strip* (Washington: Institute for Palestine Studies, 1997).

41. World Bank, "Fifteen Months: Intifada, Closures and Palestinian Economic Crisis." An assessment. *http://www.worldbank.org/html/extdr/regions.html.* March 2002. A general survey of the influences of Palestinian employment in Israel. See also Farssakh, *Palestinian Employment,* and Aamira Hass, "Israel's Closure Policy." The Israeli economy was also severely damaged.

42. Brynen, *A Very Political Economy,* p. 4.

43. Sara Roy, "De-development Revisited: Palestinian Economy and Society since Oslo, *Journal of Palestine Studies,* 28 (Spring 1999): 64–82.

44. Brynen, *A Very Political Economy,* p. 201.

45. See, for example, Menachem Klein, *Shattering a Taboo: The Contacts Toward a Permanent Status Agreement in Jerusalem 1994–2001* (forthcoming).

46. Only later did his previous deeds in Qibiya and Gaza become widely known among Palestinians. Qibiya was a Jordanian village between Latrun and Qalkilliya attacked on October 15, 1953, as a reprisal for the murder of a woman and two children in the Israeli town of Yehud two days before. All 45 houses in the village were blown up with their inhabitants inside. Men, women, and children died. The unit that carried out the attack was led by Major Ariel Sharon. At first, Israel tried to deny that the massacre was carried out by a military unit and claimed that it was carried out by enraged "border-area settlers." Sharon was also appointed as the military commander of the Gaza

Strip in the early 1970s, in the framework of which numerous young Palestinians were executed without trial following a rebellion attempt there.

47. Thus for example, on December 30, 2000, Dr. Thabet Thabet, the Fatah secretary in the West Bank, was "eliminated." On April 4, 2001, Iyyad Hardan, leader of the Islamic Jihad in Jenin was killed, and on August 25, 2001, Ali Mustafa, secretary of the Popular Front, was also killed. From the outbreak of the Intifada until July, the Israelis carried out 77 assassination operations, in which 126 Palestinians were killed. Of the killed, 87 were "targeted" persons, 39 were bystanders, among them, 11 were children (5 of them girls), 8 were women. An additional 125, 17 targeted and 108 bystanders, have been injured in the operations. The figures were provided by the Palestinian Center for Human Rights, Gaza: pchr@pchrgaza.org.

48. The new discourse of transfer was fueled by the internal contradiction of the Israeli right-wing ideology of preserving "Greater Israel" without transforming it into a bi-national entity. An example fueling the heightened fears of the Palestinians could be seen in the ambiguous statement made by Sharon in an interview published in Ha'aretz on April 12, 2001, by Ari Shavit, that Israel has to complete the job that was not finished in 1948: "The War of Independence has not ended. No, 1948 was just one chapter. If you ask me whether the State of Israel is capable of defending itself today, I say yes, absolutely. And if you ask me whether the State of Israel is facing the danger of war, I say no. But are we living here securely? No. And therefore it is impossible to say that we have completed the work and that now we can rest on our laurels."

49. Sharon did express several times (for example, in a speech to the Knesset on May 14, 2002) that a "new authority" should be established. Although he remained loyal to "peacemaking" on a rhetorical level (after achieving security), he never drew clearly the outlines of this peace. This led many Israelis to hope that he would be a sort of Israeli De Gaulle, who would surprise everyone by taking courageous steps in solving the conflict. Aiding the image that he might be such a peacemaker was his determination in forming a "national unity" government including the Labor party and Shimon Peres (Rabin's partner in the Oslo agreements), which collapsed in November 2002.

50. It seems that Sharon had indeed learned from his failure when, in 1982, he tried to force a "new order" onto Lebanon without taking measures to create legitimacy for his moves.

51. Some limited attempts to tackle the problems within the PA were made earlier, including the May 1997 report by a Palestinian parliamentary committee on the misuse of public funds. PA officials quickly responded dismissively to the report to international donors. See Ilan Halevi, "Self-Government, Democracy, and Mismanagement Under the Palestinian Authority," *Journal of Palestine Studies,* 27 (Spring 1998): 35–48.

52. Annabel Ferriman, "Palestinian Territories Face Huge Burden of Disability," *BMJ* 324 (February 9, 2002): 320.

53. Quoted in "Report on the Destruction to Palestinian Governmental Institutions in Ramallah Caused by IDF Forces Between March 29 and April 21, 2002" (mimeo), p. 2.

54. "Report on the Destruction to Palestinian Governmental Institutions in Ramallah Caused by IDF Forces Between March 29 and April 21, 2002" (mimeo), p. 3.

Conclusion

1. The large, wealthy, aristocratic families in the territories were the Shak's, Misris, Tuqans, 'Abd al-Hadis, Nimrs, Qasims, and Jarrars of Mount Nablus. In Jaffa, the center, the main families were the Dajanis, Qasims, Bitars, Bayydas, Abu Khadras, and Tayyans. In Ramle, they were the Tajis and al-Ghusayns. In Gaza, the local branches of the Shawwas and Husaynis possessed estates of orchards, textiles, pottery, and soap industries. The 'Amrs controlled the Hebron area for a century manufacturing glass products and breeding sheep and goats. The Shuqayrs had a base in Acre. Only in Haifa was there a Maronite family—the Bustani—and the Greek-Orthodox Hakim and Nassar families. Some intermarriage *(musahara)* eventually took place among the big clans, such as between the Nashashibis and Jabris or 'Alamis, or between the Khalidis and the wealthy Salam clan of Beirut. For a brilliant and detailed description of the Nablusian families and their role in the economic and social development of the territory, see Bishara Doumani, *Rediscovering Palestine: Merchants and Peasants in Jabal Nablus, 1700–1990* (Berkeley: University of California Press, 1995). He also demonstrated the intensive regional trade networks developed by these families, contrary to the previous image that only the coastal region, urban families were involved in "international trade."

2. Rashid Khalidi, *Palestinian Identity: The Construction of Modern National Consciousness* (New York: Columbia University Press, 1997); Baruch Kimmerling, "Process of Formation of Palestinian Collective Identities: The Ottoman and Colonial Periods," *Middle Eastern Studies*, 36 (2000): 48–81.

3. Quoted in *The New York Times*, September 5, 2002, p. A7.

4. Thus in a proclamation published in December 2001, thirty-two of the most prominent Palestinian intellectuals conditioned the success of the struggle against Israeli occupation and colonization on democratization of the PA.

5. For example, on June 17, 2002, a group of Palestinian leaders and intellectuals announced the launching of a "Palestinian National Initiative" at a press conference in Ramallah, led by Dr. Haidar Abdul Shafi, Dr. Mustafa Barghouthi, and Ibrahim Dakkak. The main objective of the initiative was the realization of Palestinian national rights and a durable, just peace. Both of these objectives, it argued, could best be achieved at this juncture through the establishment of a national emergency leadership, the immediate implementation of democratic elections at all levels of the political system, and the reform of political administrative and other institutional structures in order to meet the needs of the Palestinian people. *Palestinian Monitor,* June 17, 2002.

6. Quoted in *The New York Times*, September 5, 2002, p. A7.

7. Resolution 194, issued on December 11, 1948, states, "Refugees wishing to return to their home and live at peace with their neighbors should be permitted to do so at the earliest practical date, and that compensation should be paid for the property of those choosing not to return and for loss of or damage to property which, under principles of international law or in equity, should be made good by the Governments or authorities responsible."

8. *http://www.ipcri.org/dri.htm*. Also see Elia Zureik, *Palestinian Refugees and the Middle East Peace Process* (Washington, DC: Institute for Palestine Studies, 1996).

9. Rates of support in 2000 for the Islamic movements among the Palestinian population were estimated around 20–25 percent (more in Gaza and less in the West Bank).

10. Nahla Abdo, "Gender and Politics Under the Palestinian Authority," *Journal of Palestine Studies*, 28 (Winter 1999): 38–51.

11. See Frances S. Hasso, "'The Women's Front' Nationalism, Feminism, and Modernity in Palestine," *Gender & Society* 12 (August 1998): 441–

66; and Cheryl Rubenberg, *Palestinian Women: Patriarchy and Resistance in the West Bank* (Boulder: Lynne Rienner, 2001).

12. On February 11, 1985, Arafat and Hussein agreed to form a confederation between Jordan and Palestine, but both the Central Committee of Fatah and the Executive Committee of the PLO refused to authorize it for the reasons mentioned above, as well as because the agreement did not grant equal status to the two sides and did not call for formation of a Palestinian state before establishment of the confederation and setting an agreement based on the "territories for peace" principle. The agreement would probably have made Jordan the central representative of the Palestinians at the Madrid Conference. On July 30, 1988, Hussein announced severance of constitutional relations between the Kingdom and the West Bank and stopped salary payments to veteran Jordanian civil servants in the West Bank. Concerning the confederation agreement, Hussein announced its "suspension." In April 1987, Israeli Foreign Minister Peres outlined an agreement with the King of Jordan for the gradual transfer of control over the West Bank to Jordan. The agreement, however, was not passed by the national unity government in Israel. The PLO saw the agreement as a pact directed against it.

13. In a study conducted in Jordanian refugee camps in 1991, only a third said they would remain in Jordan under any circumstances—that is, even if a Palestinian state were established in the West Bank. Fifty-six percent expressed support for the idea of confederation.

14. Niall O Murchu, "Labor, the State, and Ethnic Conflict: A Comparative Study of British Rule in Palestine (1920–1939) and Northern Ireland (1972–1994)." (Seattle: University of Washington Ph.D. Dissertation, 2001).

INDEX